USEFUL REFERENCE SERIES NO. 46

INDEX TO ONE-ACT PLAYS

SUPPLEMENT

1924–1931

AN INDEX TO
ONE-ACT PLAYS
SUPPLEMENT 1924-1931

COMPILED BY

HANNAH LOGASA, Ph.B.
LIBRARIAN, UNIVERSITY HIGH SCHOOL, THE UNIVERSITY OF CHICAGO

AND

WINIFRED VER NOOY, B.L.S.
REFERENCE LIBRARIAN, THE UNIVERSITY OF CHICAGO LIBRARIES

BOSTON
F. W. FAXON COMPANY
1932

TABLE OF CONTENTS

PREFACE

So prolific are one-act plays that to index them all is impossible. The many forms in which they appear, the numerous sources from which they originate, and the inaccessibility of the material, adds to the difficulty of making an index that will be inclusive.

While this supplement to the "Index to one-act plays" does not claim to be exhaustive, it contains over 500 collections, as well as a large number of separate pamphlets, and also, a body of plays that have appeared in periodicals. In all, over 7000 plays have been included.

During the period covered by this supplement, many one-act plays of literary value have been reprinted in collections. Therefore, this index contains both the older plays, and the new plays that have appeared more recently. It is hoped, therefore, that this supplement will be useful to libraries that do not have the "Index to one-act plays" in their reference collection.

For the many librarians who have found the "Index to one-act plays" a useful reference tool, the supplement offers an extension of service. It will be found an improvement over the earlier work in that page headings will be supplied for the sections,—key, title, author, subject, collections.

The compilation of this supplement was made possible through the kindness of many libraries. Special mention must be made of the wealth of material which the Library of Congress has placed at the services of the compilers. Without that, no index could have been undertaken.

The compilers hope this supplement will serve as a bibliographic guide through the maze of the one-act play. This literary form at present is very popular with the reading and the acting public. To make this body of material immediately available is one of the problems of a library.

HOW TO USE THIS INDEX

The key is the bibliographical identification of a play. Key letters refer to the book in which play may be found, or, if a pamphlet, to the publisher responsible for its publication. Periodical references are given the identification used by the Reader's Guide to Periodical Literature.

The title index contains full information about each individual play, e. g., author, number and kind of characters, setting or background, suitability for elementary or high school pupils, and letters which refer to the Key showing in what book or magazine the play may be found.

Refer to the title index from author, subject and collection indexes.

PERIODICALS INDEXED AND THE ABBREVIATIONS USED

Adelphi	Adelphi. London
Amer Childhood	American Childhood. Springfield, Mass.
Amer Mercury	American Mercury. N. Y.
Atlan	Atlantic Monthly. Boston
Bermondsey	Bermondsey Book. London
Bookm (Lond)	The Bookman. London
Bookm	The Bookman. N. Y.
Calendar	The calendar of modern letters. London
Canad Forum	The Canadian Forum. Toronto
Carolina	The Carolina Play-Book. Chapel Hill
Cath World	The Catholic World. N. Y.
Cent M	Century Magazine. N. Y.
Child Health M	Child Health Magazine. Washington
Child Welf	Child-Welfare Magazine. Washington
Christian Cent	Christian Century. Chicago
Cornhill M	Cornhill Magazine. London
Country Gent	Country Gentleman. Philadelphia
Country Life	Country Life in America. Garden City
Criterion	Criterion. London
Delin	Delineator. N. Y.
Dial	Dial. Chicago
Drama	Drama. N. Y.
Educa	Education. Boston
English J	English Journal. Chicago
Etude	Etude. Philadelphia
Fortn	Fortnightly Review. N. Y.
Forum	Forum. N. Y.
Golden Bk	Golden Book. N. Y.
Harper's B	Harper's Bazar. N. Y.
Harper	Harper's Magazine. N. Y.
Hist Outl	Historical Outlook. Philadelphia
Home Economist	Home Economist. N. Y.
Hygeia	Hygeia. Chicago
Ind Arts M	Industrial Arts Magazine. Milwaukee
Inter-America	Inter-America. N. Y.
Int J Relig Ed	International Journal of Religious Education. Chicago
J Chem Ed	Journal of Chemical Education. Baltimore
Kind and First Grade	Kindergarten and First Grade. Springfield, Mass.
Ladies H J	Ladies Home Journal. Philadelphia
Living Age	Living Age. New York
Lond Mercury	London Mercury. London
Math Teacher	Mathematics Teacher. N. Y.
McNaught's	McNaught's Monthly. N. Y.
Menorah J	Menorah Journal. N. Y.
Mis R	Missionary Review of the World. Harrisburg
Mod Ed	Modern Education. Cleveland
Mod R	Modern Review. Calcutta
Nat Review	National Review. London
New Masses	New Masses. N. Y.
New Repub	New Republic. N. Y.
19th Cent	Nineteenth Century. London

PERIODICALS INDEXED AND ABBREVIATIONS USED

Norm Inst	Normal Instructor and Primary Plans, changed to The Instructor, Danville, N. Y.
Overland	Overland Monthly. San Francisco
Pict R	Pictorial Review. N. Y.
Players Mag	Players Magazine. Racine, Wis.
Playground	Playground. N. Y.
Poet Lore	Poet Lore. Boston
Poetry	Poetry. Chicago
Pop Educ	Popular Educator. Boston
Prac Home Econ	Practical Home Economics. N. Y.
Prim Educ	Primary Education. Boston
Queen's Q	Queen's Quarterly. Kingston (Canada)
Relig Ed	Religious Education. Chicago
St N	St. Nicholas. Pittsburg
Sat Even Post	Saturday Evening Post. Philadelphia
Sat R	Saturday Review. London
Sat R Lit	Saturday Review of Literature. N. Y.
School Arts M	School Arts Magazine. Worcester
Scrib	Scribners. N. Y.
Sierra Ed News	Sierra Educational News. San Francisco
Southw Rev	Southwest Review. Austin, Texas
Sunset	Sunset Magazine. San Francisco
Survey	Survey. N. Y.
Theatre Arts M	Theatre Arts Magazine. N. Y.
Va Q Rev	Virginia Quarterly Review. University, Va.
Volta R	Volta Review. Washington
Wilson Bull.	Wilson Bulletin. N. Y.
Woman's H C	Woman's Home Companion. Springfield, Ohio
Woman's Press	Woman's Press. N. Y.
World R	World Review. Mount Morris, Ill.
Yale R	Yale Review. New Haven

ABBREVIATIONS

C.	suitable for children.
J.	suitable for high schools.
Apr.	April.
Aug.	August.
b.	boy.
c.	children.
char.	characters.
Dec.	December.
Feb.	February.
g.	girl.
il.	illustrated.
Jan.	January.
m.	men.
Mar.	March.
n.d.	no date.
Nov.	November.
Oct.	October.
Sc.	scene.
Sept.	September.
tr.	translated or translator.
w.	women.

AN INDEX TO ONE-ACT PLAYS

KEY

A B	Abel, Barbara. Finance behind footlights. N. Y. Woman's Press, 1930.
A B E	Abercrombie, Lascelles. Interludes and poems. London. John Lane, n.d.
A B I	Abingdon Press. Plays (pamphlets) N. Y.
A D E	Adelphi Co. Plays (pamphlets) N. Y.
A L D	Alehin, A. F. The first sin and other one-act plays. Boston. Expression Co., 1927.
A L E	Alexander, Hartley. Manito masks. N. Y. Dutton, 1925.
A L E X	Alexander, R. C. & Goslin, O. P. Worship through drama. N. Y. Harper, 1930.
A L L	Allendale Press. Plays (pamphlets). Lake Villa, Illinois.
A M	Amberg File & Index Co. Plays (pamphlets) N. Y.
A N D E	Anderson, Lee. Ten one-act plays. N. Y. Walter V. McKee, 1928.
A N D R	Andreas, Eulalie. Four one-act comedies. Hollywood, Cal. The Playworker's studio, 1924.
A P N	Applegate, Margaret T. More missionary plays. N. Y. Doran, 1923.
A P O	Applegate, Margaret T. Short missionary plays. N. Y. Doran, 1923.
A P P L	Appleton, D. & Co. Plays (pamphlets) N. Y. Appleton book of Christmas plays. See Shay, Frank. Appleton book of holiday plays. See Shay, Frank. Appleton book of short plays. See Nicholson, Kenyon. Appleton book of short plays. Second series. See Nicholson, Kenyon.
A S S	Associated Press. Plays (pamphlets) N. Y. Atlantic book of junior plays. See Thomas, C. S.
A U	Auditorium plays and stunts for high school. Franklin, Ohio. Eldridge Entertainment House, 1930.
A V	Avondale Press. Plays (pamphlets) N. Y.

B

B A I	Bailey, Carolyn S. Plays for the children's hour. Springfield, Mass. Milton Bradley Co., 1931.
B A K	Baker, Walter H. Co. Plays (pamphlets) Boston. Bakers' anthology of one-act plays. See Phillips, Le Roy & Johnson, Theodore.
B A L	Balch, Norman. Six plays of business life. Franklin, Ohio. Eldridge Entertainment House, 1930.
B A N N	Banner Play Bureau. Plays (pamphlets) San Francisco, Cal. Banner anthology of one-act plays by American authors. See Carter, L. H. & Gall, Ellen.
B A N S	Banta, N. M. Autumn and winter festivals. Chicago. A. Flanagan Co., 1924.

11

BANT   Banta, N. M. St. Nicholas Christmas book. Chicago. A. Flanagan Co., 1925.

BARN   Barnes, Djuna. A night among horses. N. Y. Horace Liveright, 1929.

BARP   Barr, Carolyn. Six plays for six grades. Philadelphia. Penn Pub. Co., 1930.

BARR   Barrie, J. M. The plays of J. M. Barrie. N. Y. Scribner, 1928.

BARS   Barrie, J. M. Shall we join the ladies? N. Y. Scribner, 1928.

BART   Barrnett, J. H. & others. The green entertainment book. Chicago. A. Flanagan Co., 1930.

BAT   Bates, Katharine L. Little Robin stay-behind and other plays in verse for children. N. Y. Woman's Press, 1923.

BATE   Bates, Katharine L. The pilgrim ship. N. Y. Woman's Press, 1926.

BEA   Beard, Patten. Acting plays for boys and girls. Chicago. Beckly-Cardy Co., 1927.

BEB   Beck, Warren. Imagination and four other one-act plays for boys and girls. Boston. Baker, 1925.

BEC   Beck, Warren. Six Little Theatre plays. Boston. Baker, 1931.

BECK   Beckley-Cardy Co. Plays (pamphlets) Chicago.

BEN   Benton, Rita. The elf of discontent and other plays. N. Y. Doran, 1927.

BER   Berman, Henry. Life demands! and other plays. N. Y. Brentano's, 1931.

BEST   Best, Mrs. A. S. & Patten, Cora M. Dickon goes to the fair and other plays. N. Y. Doran, 1927.

BIN   Binyon, Laurence. Three short plays. London. Sidgwick & Jackson, 1930.

BIS   Bissell, W. L. Plays (pamphlets) Cleveland, Ohio.

BIT   Bitney, Mayme. Pageants and plays for holidays. Dayton, Ohio. Paine Pub. Co., 1926.

BLA   Blackwell, Basil. Pub. Plays (pamphlets) Oxford, England.

BLO   Bloch Pub. Co. Plays (pamphlets) N. Y.

BLP   Block, Etta. One-act plays from the Yiddish. Second series. N. Y. Bloch Pub. Co., 1929.

BOG   Boggs, H. O. Children's comedies and comic recitations. Chicago. Beckley-Cardy, 1929.

BOGG   Boggs, H. O. Comic plays and dialogues. Chicago. Beckley-Cardy, 1926.

BOGH   Boggs, H. O. Funny plays for happy days. Chicago. Beckley-Cardy, 1928.

BOSS   Bosschere, Jean de. The closed door. tr. by F. S. Flint. N. Y. John Lane, 1917.

BOST   Boston Theatre Guild Plays. Boston. Baker, 1924.

BOTS   Bottomley, Gordon. A parting and The return. N. Y. Macmillan, 1928.

BOTT   Bottomley, Gordon. Scenes and plays. N. Y. Macmillan, 1929.

BRAN   Brandane, John. The treasure ship; Rory aforesaid; The happy war. London. Constable, 1928.

BRI 1   Briggs, T. H. & others, ed. Literature for the junior high school. Book 1. Chicago. Rand McNally, 1929.

BRI 3	Briggs, T. H. & others, ed. Literature for the junior high school. Book 3. Chicago. Rand-McNally, 1929.
BRI O	Brighouse, Harold. Open air plays. N. Y. French, 1926.
BRI R	British Drama League Library. Four one-act plays. Oxford, England. Basil Blackwell, 1923.
BRI S	British Drama League Library of modern British Drama. Oxford, England. Basil Blackwell, n.d.
BRI T	British Drama League Library. Three one-act plays. N. Y. French, 1925.
BRO	Brody, Alter. Lamentations. Four folk-plays of the American Jew. N. Y. Coward-McCann, 1928.
BROW	Brown, Abbie F. The lantern and other plays for children. Boston. Houghton Mifflin, 1928.
BROX	Brown, L. F. & LeCompte, Fay P. Script. Richmond, Va. Williams Printing Co., 1930.
BRY	Bryce, Catherine T. Bound or free and The wizard of words. Boston. Atlantic Monthly Press, 1922.
BUF	Bufano, Remo. Pinocchio for the stage in four short plays. N. Y. Knopf, 1929.
BUG	Bugbee, Willis N. Co. Plays (pamphlets) Syracuse, N. Y.
BUGT	Bugbee, W. N. & Irish, Marie. Tip top Christmas book. Syracuse, N. Y. The Willis N. Bugbee Co., 1927.
BUT	Butler, Mildred A. Literature dramatized for classroom use. N. Y. Harcourt. Brace, 1926.

C

CAC	Cactus Club. Plays (pamphlets) Denver, Colorado.
CAL	Caldwell, Sybil & Hendrie, Ernest. Top dog and other sketches. London. French, 1926.
CAME	Cameron, Eleanor. Many-a-way for Christmas day. Boston. Baker, 1929.
CAMP	Campbell, Wayne. Amateur acting and play production. N. Y. Macmillan, 1931.
CANA	Canadian Authors Ass'n. One-act plays by Canadian authors. Montreal Branch Canadian Authors' Ass'n, 1926.
CANB	Canadian plays from Hart House Theatre, ed. by Vincent Massey. Vol. 1. Toronto, Canada. Macmillan, 1926.
CANF	Canfield, Curtis. Plays of the Irish Renaissance. 1880–1930. N. Y. Ives Washburn, 1929.
CANN	Cannan, Gilbert. Seven plays. London. Martin Secker, 1923.
CAR2	Carolina folk-plays. Second series. ed. by F. H. Koch. N. Y. Holt, 1924.
CAR3	Carolina folk-plays. Third series. ed. by F. K. Koch. N. Y. Holt, 1928.
CART	Carter, L. H. & Gall, Ellen M. The banner anthology of one-act plays by American authors. San Francisco, Cal. Banner Play Bureau, 1929.
CAS	Casey, Beatrice M. Good things for Halloween. Chicago. Denison, 1929.
CASE	Casey, Beatrice M. The popular Christmas book. Chicago. Denison, 1927.
CAT1	Catchy plays and recitations. Syracuse, N. Y. The Willis N. Bugbee Co., 1929.

CAT2   Catchy plays and recitations. No. 2. Syracuse, N. Y. The Willis N. Bugbee Co., 1930.

CATH   Catholic Dramatic Movement. Plays (pamphlets) Briggsville, Wisconsin.

CAV   Cavanah, Frances. The knight of the funny bone and other plays for children. Boston. Baker, 1929.

CEN   Century Co. Plays (pamphlets) N. Y.

CG   Chapin, Katherine G. Outside of the world. N. Y. Duffield, 1930.

CHA   Charlton, Basil & others. Green room rags. London. French, 1925.

CHEC   Checkhov, Anton. The plays of Anton Checkhov. First modern library edition. N. Y. Modern Library, 1930.

CHES   Chesterton, Frances. Three plays for children. London. French, 1924.

CHR   Christensen, Mayme. Christmas week in the primary grades. Chicago. Dramatic Pub. Co., 1930.

CJ   Clark, Ada & others. Little plays for Christmas. Chicago. Beckley-Cardy, 1928.

CL   Clark, Barrett H. & Nicholson, Kenyon. The American scene. N. Y. Appleton, 1930.

CLAR   Clark, Sarah G. Ready-made programs for every month. Dayton, Ohio. Paine Pub. Co., 1928.

CLAS   Clarke, Amy K. & others. Three one-act plays. London. French, 1925.

CLP   Clements, Colin C. Plays for pagans. N. Y. Appleton, 1924.

CLS   Clements, Colin C. Sea plays. Boston. Small Maynard, 1923.

COC   Cochran, Eva O. A half hour at the gate. Boston. Badger, 1930.

COF   Coffman, G. R. A book of modern plays. Chicago. Scott Foresman, 1925.

COH   Cohen, Helen L. More one-act plays by modern authors. N. Y. Harcourt Brace, 1927.

COJ   Collins, Lillian F. The Little Theatre in the school. N. Y. Dodd Mead, 1930.

COL4   Columbia University,—University extension. Copy 1924. N. Y. Columbia Uni. Press, 1924.

COL5   Columbia University,—University extension. Copy 1925. N. Y. Appleton, 1925.

COL6   Columbia University,—University extension. Copy 1926. N. Y. Appleton, 1926.

COL7   Columbia University,—University extension. Copy 1927. N. Y. Appleton, 1927.

COM   Conkle, E. P. Crick bottom plays. N. Y. French, 1928.

COMN   Connelly, J. M. Co. pub. Juvenile plays and readings. Hot Springs Nat'l Park, Arkansas. 1929.

CON   Conrad, Joseph. Laughing Ann; One day more. Garden City, N. Y. Doubleday Page, 1925.

CONW   Conway, Olive. Costume plays. London. French, 1926.

COO   Cooper, W. J. & Woolfolk, E. T. Four plays. Blue Pencil Club of Sigma Upsilon. Charlotte, N. C. The Queen City Printing Co., 1923.

COR   Corkery, Daniel. The Yellow bittern and other plays. London. T. Fisher Unwin, 1920.

COW   Cowan, Sada. Pomp and other plays. N. Y. Brentano's, 1926.

COWL	Cowles Press. Plays (pamphlets) St. Johnsbury, Vt.
CRA	Crawshay-Williams, Eliot. Five Grand Guignol plays. London. French, 1924.
CRAA	Crawshay-Williams, Eliot. More Grand Guignol plays. London. French, 1927.
CRE	Creigh-Henry, May. Four mystical plays. London. Society for Promoting Christian Knowledge. 1924.
CRO2	Cross, T. P. & others. Good. readings for high schools. II. Achievement. Boston. Ginn, 1930.
CROA	Cross, T. P. & others. Good reading for high schools. American writers. Boston. Ginn, 1931.
CROE	Cross, T. P. & others. Good reading for high schools. English Writers. Boston. Ginn, 1931.
CROT	Crothers, Rachel. Six one-act plays. Boston. Baker, 1925.
CUD	Cuddy, Lucy & others. Mother Goose plays. Chicago. Rand-McNally, 1925.
CUM1	Cummins, S. L. Plays for children. Book 1. N. Y. Doran, 1923.
CUM2	Cummins, S. L. Plays for children. Volume 2. N. Y. Doran, 1923.
CUM3	Cummins, S. L. Plays for children. Volume 3. N. Y. Doran, 1923.
CUR	Curtis, Agnes. Clever plays for women. Syracuse, N. Y. The Willis N. Bugbee Co., 1929.
CURT	Curtis, Agnes. Holiday plays for young people. Syracuse, N. Y. The Willis N. Bugbee Co., 1929.
CUT	Cutherell, Faith B. Sign posts. Boston. Small Maynard, 1924.

D

DAL	Dall, Ian. Noah's wife. Oxford, England. Basil Blackwell, 1925.
DAN	Dane, Essex. Shadows and lights. Boston. Baker, 1930.
DAQ	Darlington, Anne C. The Lady Joanna and two other plays. N. Y. Woman's Press, 1928.
DAR	Darlington, Anne C. Yelenka the wise. N. Y. Woman's Press, 1926.
DAZ	Dean Alexander. Seven to seventeen. N. Y. French, 1931.
DE	Deane, H. F. W. & Sons. Plays (pamphlets) London, England.
DEH	DeHuff, Elsie. Five religious education plays. Franklin, Ohio. Eldridge Entertainment House, 1927.
DEL	Denison, Merrill. The unheroic north. Toronto, Canada. McClelland & Stewart, 1923.
DENI	Denison, T. S. & Co. Plays (pamphlets) Chicago.
DENT	Denton, Clara J. Denton's best plays and dialogues. Chicago. Albert Whitman Co., 1925.
DENU	Denton, Eleanor. Sing-a-song-o'-sixpence. Oxford, England. Basil Blackwell, 1927.
DES	Deseo, Lydia G. & Phipps, Hulda M. Looking at life through drama. N. Y. Abingdon Press, 1931.
DET	Detroit, Players. The players book of one-act plays. N. Y. Walter V. McKee, 1928.
DIC3	Dickinson, T. H. Chief contemporary dramatist. Third series. Boston. Houghton Mifflin, 1930.
DOL	Dolan, Leonora K. Short plays and pageants for all occasions and grades. Franklin, Ohio. Eldridge Entertainment House, 1930.

DON   Donnelly, G. B. Pease porridge hot. St. Louis, Mo. The Queen's Work Press, 1928.

DOW   Down, Oliphant. Three one-act plays. Boston. L. Phillips, 1923.

DQ   Drama Bureau. Plays (pamphlets) Kansas City, Mo.

DR   Drama League—Longmans Green. Playwriting contest for 1928. N. Y. Longmans Green, 1929.

DRA   Dramatic Pub. Co. Plays (pamphlets) Chicago.

DUA   Dunsany, Lord. Alexander and three small plays. N. Y. Putnam, 1926.

DUS   Dunsany, Lord, Seven modern comedies. N. Y. Putnam, 1928.

E

EAK   Eakman, Florence E. Plays (pamphlets) Long Beach, Cal.

EAS   Eastman, Fred. Modern religious dramas. N. Y. Holt, 1928.

EAT   Eaton, W. P. Twelve one-act plays. N. Y. Longmans Green, 1926.

EDL   Edland, Elisabeth. The children's king and other plays for children. N. Y. Abingdon Press, 1928.

EDLP   Edland, Elisabeth. Plum blossoms and other plays. N. Y. Abingdon Press, 1925.

EDU   Educational Thrift Service. Plays (pamphlets) N. Y.

ELD   Eldridge Entertainment House. Plays (pamphlets) Franklin, Ohio.

ELDR   Eldridge Entertainment House. Church plays and entertainments for young people. Franklin, Ohio, 1924.

EM   Emerson College of Oratory. The Cathedral clock and other one-act plays. Boston. Expression Co., 1927.

ENL   Enloe, Mary A. Year around primary programs. Chicago. A. Flanagan Co., 1928.

ER   Ervine, St. John G. Four one-act plays. London. George Allen & Unwin, 1928.

ES   Esson, Louis. Dead timber and other plays. London, Hendersons, 1920.

F

FARJ   Farjeon, Herbert. Happy New Year, and Your kind indulgence. London. French, 1929.

FARK   Farma, W. J. Prose, poetry and drama for oral interpretation. N. Y. Harper, 1930.

FARQ   Farquhar Play Bureau. Plays (pamphlets) Franklin, Ohio.

FARR   Farrar, John. The magic sea shell and other plays for children. N. Y. Doran, 1923.

FAW   Faxon, Grace B. Many-a-way to closing day. Boston. Baker, 1926.

FAX   Faxon, Grace. Many-a-way for Memorial day. Boston. Baker, 1926.

FED   Federal Council of the Churches of Christ in America. Religious dramas. N. Y. Century, 1924.

FEDE   Federal Council of the Churches of Christ in America. Religious dramas. Volume 2. N. Y. Century, 1926.

FEL   Felton, Mrs. Carl. Plays (pamphlets) Madison, Wisconsin.

FER   Fernand, Weyl. Three gallant plays, tr. by Clarence Stratton. N. Y. William Edwin Rudge, 1929.

FI C	Field, Rachel. The cross-stitch heart and other plays. N. Y. Scribner, 1927.
FI E	Field, Rachel. Patchwork plays. Garden City, N. Y. Doubleday Doran, 1930.
FI F	Field, Rachel. Six plays. N. Y. Scribner, 1924.
FI N	Finney, Stella B. Plays old and new. N. Y. Allyn & Bacon, 1928.
FI R	Firkins, O. W. Two passengers for Chelsea and other plays. N. Y. Longmans Green, 1928.
FI S	Fish, Helen R. Drama and dramatics. N. Y. Macmillan, 1930.
FI T	Fitzgerald Publishing Corporation. Plays (pamphlets) N. Y.
FITZ	Fitzhugh, Carroll. Mon ami Pierrot and other plays. Boston. Houghton Mifflin, 1928.
FI U	Flaurier, Noel. The last day of school in the primary grades. Dayton, Ohio. Paine Pub. Co., 1928.
FI V	Flaurier, Noel. The Thanksgiving treasure book. Dayton, Ohio. Paine Pub. Co., 1928.
F J	Flaurier, Noel & others. Winning plays and dialogues. Chicago. Beckley-Cardy, 1930.
FLA	Flavin, Martin. Brains and other one-act plays. N. Y. French, 1926.
FOL	Folmsbee, Beulah. Guki the moon boys and other plays. N. Y. Harcourt Brace, 1928.
FOR4	47 Workshop plays. Fourth series. N. Y. Brentano's, 1925.
FOS	Foster, Caroline H. W. Little comedies of to-day. Los Angeles, Cal. The Arroyo Press, 1906.
FOU	Four Seas Co. Plays (pamphlets) Boston.
FRA	Francis, Celia. Junior high varieties. Franklin, Ohio. Eldridge Entertainment House, 1930.
FRAZ	Freeman, Carolyn R. & others. The kiddies Christmas book. Syracuse, N. Y. The Willis N. Bugbee Co., 1925.
FRE1	French, Samuel. Pub. One-act plays for stage and study. First series. N. Y. French, 1924.
FRE2	French, Samuel. Pub. One-act plays for stage and study. Second series. N. Y. French, 1925.
FRE3	French, Samuel. Pub. One-act plays for stage and study. Third series. N. Y. French, 1927.
FRE4	French, Samuel. Pub. One-act plays for stage and study. Fourth series. N. Y. French, 1928.
FRE5	French, Samuel. Pub. One-act plays for stage and study. Fifth series. N. Y. French, 1929.
FRE6	French, Samuel. Pub. One-act plays for stage and study. Sixth series. N. Y. French, 1931.
FREL	French, Samuel. Pub. Plays (pamphlets) London, England.
FREN	French, Samuel. Pub. Plays (pamphlets) N. Y.
FREP	French, Samuel. Pub. Play-bits. London. French, 1922.
FREQ	French, Samuel. Pub. Pulling the show together. London. French, 1928.
FRER	French, Samuel. Pub. Quite a nice cat and other sketches. London. French, 1927.
FRET	French, Samuel. Pub. Try one of these! London. French, 1927.
FRI E	Friendship Press. Plays (pamphlets) N. Y.
FYL	Fyleman, Rose. Eight little plays for children. N. Y. Doran, 1925.

G

GAK	Gallup, G. H. Best creative work in American high schools. Iowa City, Ia. The National Honorary Society for High School Journalists, 1927.
GAL	Galsworthy, John. Plays. N. Y. Scribner, 1928.
GAP	Gardner, Flora C. & Gardner, Margaret. Up-to-date Christmas programs. Lebanon, Ohio. March Bros., 1930.
GAQ	Gardner, Flora C. & Gardner, Margaret. Up-to-date community programs. Lebanon, Ohio. March Bros., 1930.
GAR	Garnett, Louise A. Three to make ready. N. Y. Doran, 1923.
GAT	Gates, Barrington. The Mulligatewny medallion. London. Ernest Benn, 1926.
GEQ	Gerstenberg, Alice. Comedies all. N. Y. Longmans Green, 1930.
GER	Gerstenberg, Alice. Four plays for four women. N. Y. Brentano's, 1924.
GIB	Gibson, Emily M. English-class plays for new Americans. N. Y. Woman's Press, 1927.
GIK	Gibson, Wilfred. Kestrel edge and other plays. N. Y. Macmillan, 1924.
GIT	Githens, H. W. Dramatized stories from the Old Testament. Cincinnati, Ohio. The Standard Pub. Co., 1927.
GITH	Githens, H. W. New Testament stories dramatized. Cincinnati, Ohio. The Standard Pub. Co., 1929.
GLA	Glaspell, Susan. Trifles and six other short plays. London. Ernest Benn, 1926.
GOG	Gogol, Nikolay. The government inspector and other plays. N. Y. Knopf, 1927.
GOG6	Gogol, Nikolay. The government inspector and other plays. Vol. VI. The Works of Nikolay Gogol. London. Chatto & Windus, 1926.
GOIN	Going, C. B. Folklore and fairy plays. Boston. Baker, 1927.
GOL	Golden, John. Three John Golden plays. N. Y. French, 1925.
GOLD	Goldstone, G. A. One-act plays. Boston. Allyn & Bacon, 1926.
GOO	Goodman, K. S. & Hecht, Ben. The wonder hat. N. Y. Appleton, 1925.
GRA	Granville, Edward. Tammy and four other plays. London. French, 1929.
GRED	Green, Paul. The House of Connelly and other plays. N. Y. French, 1931.
GREE	Green, Paul. In the valley and other Carolina plays. N. Y. French, 1928.
GREF	Green, Paul. Lonesome road. N. Y. McBride, 1926.
GREL	Green, Paul. The Lord's will and other Carolina plays. N. Y. French, 1928.
GREM	Greenlaw, Edwin & others. Literature and life. Book 2. Special edition. Chicago. Scott Foresman, 1929.
GREN	Greenlaw, Edwin & Miles, Dudley. Literature and life. Book 3. Chicago. Scott Foresman, 1923.
GREO	Greenlaw, Edwin & Miles, Dudley. Literature and life. Book 3. Special edition. Chicago. Scott Foresman, 1929.
GREP	Greenlaw, Edwin & Miles, Dudley. Literature and life. Book 4. Chicago. Scott Foresman, 1924.

GREQ   Gregory, Lady. Three last plays of Lady Gregory. N. Y. Putnam, 1929.

GRI   Griffith, Mary M. Westward the course of empire. Austin, Texas. E. L. Steck Co., 1924.

H

HAG   Haggard, Audrey. Little plays from Greek myths. N. Y. Dutton, 1929.

HAGG   Haggerty, M. E. & Smith, Dora V. Reading and literature. Book 3. Yonkers-on-Hudson, N. Y. World Book Co., 1928.

HAH   Hallock, Grace T. Dramatized child health. N. Y. American Child Health Ass'n, 1925.

HALI   Hamilton, Dorothy T. Primary Christmas programs. Chicago. A. Flanagan Co., 1928.

HAM   Hampden, John. Nine modern plays. London. Thomas Nelson & Sons, 1926.

HAMA   Hampden, John. Ten modern plays. London. Thomas Nelson & Sons, 1928.

HANE   Hanemann, H. W. As is; a book of miscellaneous revelations. N. Y. Harcourt Brace, 1923.

✓HANF   Hanes, Ernest & McCoy, Martha J. Readings in contemporary literature. N. Y. Macmillan, 1928.

HAP   Hartley, R. E. & Power, C. M. Short plays from great stories. N. Y. Macmillan, 1928.

HAQ   Harvard Dramatic Club Miracle plays, ed. by D. F. Robinson. N. Y. French, 1928.
Harvard plays—The 47 Workshop. See 47 Workshop.

HAR   Harwood, H. M. Three one-act plays. London. Ernest Benn, 1926.

HAT   Hatfield, W. W. & Roberts, H. D. The spirit of America in literature. N. Y. Century, 1931.

HAY   Haylofters Co. Plays (pamphlets) Hartford, Conn.

HAZ   Hazard, Lucy L. In search of America. N. Y. Crowell, 1930.

HEL   Hellener, J. R. Plays (pamphlets) Atchison, Kansas.

HERB   Herbert, A. P. & others. Double demon and other one-act plays. N. Y. Appleton, 1924.

HERV   Hervey, W. L. Junior literature. Grade 7A. N. Y. Longmans Green, 1929.

HEY   Heywood, Delia A. & others. The red entertainment book. Chicago. A. Flanagan Co., 1930.

HOB   Hobbs, Mabel & Miles, Helen. Six Bible plays. N. Y. Century, 1924.

HOF   Hofer, Marie R. Festival and civic plays from Greek and Roman tales. Chicago. Beckley-Cardy, 1926.

HOK   Holland, Norah M. When half-gods go and other poems. N. Y. Macmillan, 1924.

HOL   Holloway, Pearl. The paramount missionary book. Chicago. Meyer & Bros., 1926.

HOT   Housman, Laurence. Cornered poets. London. Jonathan Cape, 1929.

HOUF   Housman, Laurence. Followers of St. Francis. Boston. Small Maynard, n.d.

HOUS   Housman, Laurence. Little plays of St. Francis. London. Sidg-
             wick & Jackson. 1927.

HOV   Hoxie, Evelyn. Hints and ha'nts for Hallowe'en. Franklin, Ohio.
             Eldridge Entertainment House, 1931.

HOVA   Hoxie, Evelyn. Patriotic programs for patriotic plays. Boston.
             Baker, 1926.

HOX   Hoxie, Evelyn. Seven snappy entertainments for adults. Boston.
             Baker, 1926.

HUN   Hughes, Glenn. New plays for mummers. Seattle, Washington.
             University of Washington Book Store, 1926.

HUO   Hughes, Glenn. Short plays for modern players. N. Y. Appleton,
             1931.

HUR   Hughes, Richard. A rabbit and a leg. N. Y. Knopf, 1924.

I

I N   Indiana Prize Plays—1922–23. Indianapolis, Indiana. Bobbs-
             Merrill, 1924.

I NG   Inge, Benson & Chupet, Charles. The curtain rises. N. Y. Book
             Mart Pub. Co., 1926.

I NT   Intercollegiate Literary Magazine Conference. Young Pegasus.
             N. Y. Dial Press, 1926.

I Q   Irish, Marie. The grade school play book. Boston. Baker, 1929.

I QA   Irish, Marie. Hallowe'en merrymakers. Syracuse, N. Y. The
             Willis N. Bugbee Co., 1930.

I R   Irish, Marie & others. Sunshine plays and dialogues. Syracuse,
             N. Y. The Willis N. Bugbee Co., 1929.

I RI   Irish, Marie. Tip-top Thanksgiving book. Syracuse, N. Y. The
             Willis N. Bugbee Co., 1930.

I S   Isaacs, Edith J. R. Plays of American life and fantasy. N. Y.
             Coward-McCann, 1929.

I W   Iwaski, Y. T. & Hughes, Glenn. New plays from Japan. N. Y.
             Appleton, 1930.

J

J AC   Jacob, Fred. One-third of a bill. Toronto, Canada. The Macmillan
             Co., 1925.

J AF   Jagendorf, M. Fairyland and footlights. N. Y. Brentano's, 1925.

J AN   Jagendorf. M. Nine short plays written for young people to
             stage. N. Y. Macmillan, 1928.

J AO   Jagendorf, M. One-act plays for young folks. N. Y. Brentano's,
             1924.

J AR   Jasspon, Ethel R. & Becker, Florence. Ritual and dramatized
             folkways. N. Y. Century, 1925.

J AS   Jast, L. S. The lover and the dead woman and five other plays
             in verse. London. George Routledge & Sons, 1923.

J EA   Jeans, Ronald. Bright intervals. London. French, 1927.

J EC   Jeans, Ronald. Charlot revue sketches. London. French, 1925.

J EO   Jeans, Ronald. Odd numbers. London. French, 1927.

J EP   Jeans, Ronald. "One dam' sketch after another." London. French,
             1928.

J ER   Jeans, Ronald. The revue of revues. London. French, 1925.

J ES   Jeans, Ronald. Sundry sketches. London. French, 1924.

J O H	John, Gwen. Plays. London. Duckworth & Co., 1916.
J O H A	John, Gwen. Plays of innocence. London. Ernest Benn, 1925.
J O H B	John o' London's Weekly. Competition for one-act plays. Prize plays. London. Deane & Sons, 1930.
J O H C	Johnson, Ella B. & others. Christmas joy book. Syracuse, N. Y. The Willis N. Bugbee Co., 1930.
J O H D	Johnson, Mamie T. Rural community plays. Lebanon, Ohio. March Bros., 1925.
J O H E	Johnson, Marie M. Plays and pageants for church school. Boston. The Beacon Press, 1929.
J O H F	Johnson, Philip. Four plays. London. Ernest Benn, 1929.
J O H G	Johnson, Theodore. The gingerbread house and eight other plays for children. Boston. Baker, 1928.
J O H M	Johnson, Theodore. Miniature plays for stage and study. Boston. Baker, 1928.
J O H N	Johnson, Theodore. More plays in miniature. Boston. Baker, 1929.
J O H P	Johnson, Theodore. Plays in miniature. Boston. Baker, n.d.
J O N	Jones, J. E. Scenes from Dickens. Toronto, Canada. McClelland & Stewart, 1923.

K

K A M	Kampmeier, Roland. Contemporaries! current forms of composition from L. C. Woodman's Coe College Freshman English classes 1927–28. Vinton, Ia. Kruse Pub. Co., 1928.
K A S	Kaser, A. L. Talking acts for two. Chicago, Denison, 1927.
K A Y	Kaye-Smith, Sheila. Saints in Sussex, N. Y. Dutton, 1927.
K E K	Kelley, Owen. Stunt plays for your club night. N. Y. Town & Country Pub., 1930.
K E L	Kelly, George. The flattering word and other one-act plays. Boston. Little Brown, 1925.
K E M	Kemp, Harry. Boccaccio's untold tales and other plays. N. Y. Brentano's, 1924.
K E N	Kennedy, C. R. A repertory of plays for a company of seven players and two short plays for smaller casts. Chicago. The University of Chicago Press, 1930.
K I M	Kimball, Rosamond. The wooing of Rebekah and other Bible plays. N. Y. Scribner, 1925.
K L	Klein, Yetta & Schwarz, Florine. Our children's stage. Boston. Baker, 1928.
K L E	Klein, Yetta & Schwarz, Florine. Plays for school children. Boston. Baker, 1930.
K M	Knickerbocker, E. Van B. Short plays. N. Y. Holt, 1931.
K N	Knickerbocker, E. Van B. Twelve plays. N. Y. Holt, 1924.
K O V	Koven, Joseph. The miracle of Saint Masha and other plays. N. Y. Lester L. Schick, 1924.
K R	Kreymborg, Alfred. Puppet plays. N. Y. French, 1926.
K R R	Kreymborg, Alfred. Rocking chairs and other comedies. N. Y. French, 1925.
K R S	Krohn, Josephine E. Old King Cole and other Mediaeval plays. N. Y. Doran, 1925.
K U	Kummer, F. A. Phryne. Philadelphia. Dorrance & Co., 1924.

L

LAB   Labour Pub. Company. Plays (pamphlets) London, England.

LAD   Ladies' Home Journal. One-act plays. Garden City, N. Y. Doubleday Page, 1925.

LAN   Lane, Bertha P. Lad and other story-plays for children to read or act. N. Y. Woman's Press, 1926.

LAR   Larrimer, Mary. Plays with a prologue. Boston. Badger, 1925.

LAW   Law, F. H. Modern plays, short and long. N. Y. Century, 1924.

LAWT   Lawton, V. B. Ballads for acting. London. Sheldon Press, 1927.

LEE   Lee, Mackenzie. For chaps and chits. London. French, 1930.

LEO   Leonard, S. A. & Moffett, H. Y. Junior literature. Book 2. N. Y. Macmillan, 1930.

LEU   Levy, S. J. Broken bridges. Brooklyn, N. Y. S. J. Levy, 1924.

LEV   Levinger, Elma E. Jewish festivals in the religious school. Cincinnati, Ohio. Union of American Congregations, 1923.

LEVT   Levinger, Elma E. Through the school year. Boston. Baker, 1925.

LIB   Liberty Press. Plays (pamphlets) Richmond, Va.

LL   Lloyd, Gladys. The complete Christmas book. Lebanon, Ohio. March Bros., 1923.

LLO   Lloyd, Gladys. Thanksgiving school programs. Franklin, Ohio. Eldridge Entertainment House, 1928.

LOC   Locke, Alain & Gregory Montgomery. Plays of negro life. N. Y. Harper, 1927.

LON   Longmans, Green & Co. Plays (pamphlets) N. Y.

LONG   Longmans, Green & Co. Goin' home and other plays of the 1927 contest. N. Y. Longmans, Green, 1928.

LOO   Lord, D. A. Boyland and maidland. St. Louis, Mo. The Queen's Work Press, 1927.

LOP   Lord, D. A. Facts and fairy tales. St. Louis, Mo. The Queen's Work Press, 1930.

LOQ   Lord, D. A. The magic gallery. St. Louis, Mo. The Queen's Work Press, 1927.

LOR   Lord, D. A. Six one-act plays. N. Y. Benzinger Bros., 1925.

LORE   Lorenz Publishing Co. Plays (pamphlets) Dayton, Ohio.

LOU   Louisville (Ky.) Girls' High School Drama class. Tested plays for high schools. Boston. Baker, 1928.

LUT   Lutkenhaus, Anna & Knox, Margaret. New plays for school children. N. Y. Century, 1929.

LY   Lyman, R. L. & Hill, H. C. Literature and living. Book 3. N. Y. Scribner, 1925.

M

MACC   McCollum, Elsie M. Pieces and plays for all ages. Melmar, N. J. E. S. Werner & Co., 1929.

MACG   McGraw, H. W. & Parry, J. N. Prose and poetry for the twelfth year. Syracuse, N. Y. L. W. Singer Co., 1930.

MACH   Mackay, Constance D'A. Youth's highway. N. Y. Holt, 1929.

MACK   Mackaye, Percy. Kentucky Mountain fantasies. N. Y. Longmans, Green, 1924.

MACL   Mackaye, Percy. Kentucky Mountain fantasies. N. Y. Longmans, Green, 1928.

MACM	Mackaye, Percy. Yankee fantasies. New & revised ed. N. Y. French, 1928.
MACS	Mackendrick, Marda. Short plays for adult foreigners. Marda Mackendrick, 1928.
MACT	McMullen, J. C. An evening of plays for men. Boston. Baker, 1930.
MACU	McPharlin, Paul. A repertory of Marionette plays. N .Y. Viking Press, 1929.
MAG	Magnusson, Elva C. Three plays. Lancaster, Pa. Lancaster Press, 1928.
MAI	Major, Clare T. Playing theatre. London. Oxford Uni. Press, 1930.
MAJ	Major, Mabel & Smith, Rebecca. The southwest in literature. N. Y. Macmillan, 1929.
MAN	Manley, W. F. Bible dramas, radio plays adapted for church and social gatherings. N. Y. Revell, 1928.
MANL	Manley, W. F. A second book of Bible dramas. N. Y. Revell, 1930.
MAR1	Marriott, J. W. One-act plays of to-day. Boston. Small Maynard, 1924.
MAR2	Marriott, J. W. One-act plays of to-day. Second series. Boston. Small Maynard, 1926.
MAR3	Marriott, J. W. One-act plays of to-day. Third series. London. George G. Harrap & Co., 1927.
MARC	March Brothers. Plays (pamphlets) Lebanon, Ohio.
MARK	Marks, Jeannette. The merry merry cuckoo and other Welsh plays. N. Y. Appleton, 1927.
MARS	Marsh, Florence, A. Plays for young people. Boston. Allyn & Bacon, 1931.
MASE	Masefield, John. A poem and two plays. London. Heinemann, 1919.
MASF	Masefield, John. Prose plays. N. Y. Macmillan, 1925.
MASG	Masefield, John. Verse plays. N. Y. Macmillan, 1925.
MEA	Means & McLean Co. Plays (pamphlets) Chicago, Illinois.
MEI	Meigs Publishing Co. Plays (pamphlets) Indianapolis, Indiana.
MER	Merrill, John & Fleming, Martha. Play-making and plays. N. Y. Macmillan, 1930.
MIK	Millay, Edna St. V. (Nancy Boyd, pseud.) Distressing dialogues, N. Y. Harper, 1924.
MIL	Millay, Edna St. V. Three plays. N. Y. Harper, 1926.
MILL	Miller, H. A. Adventures in prose and poetry. N. Y. Harcourt Brace, 1929.
MILN	Milne, A. A. First plays. N. Y. Knopf, 1930.
MILO	Milne, A. A. Four plays. London. Chatto & Windus, 1926.
MIN	Minchin, Nydia E. The jester's purse and other plays for boys girls. N. Y. Harcourt Brace, 1926.
MIS	Missionary Education Movement of U. S. & Canada. Plays (pamphlets) N. Y.
MIST	Mitchell Printing Co. Plays (pamphlets) Raleigh, N. C.
MIT	Mitchison, Naomi. Nix-nought-nothing. London. Jonathan Cape, 1928.
MOL	Molnar, Ferenc. The plays of Ferenc Molnar. N. Y. Macy-Masius. The Vangard Press, 1929.

MOO   Moore, F. F. Kitty Clive and other plays in one act. London, A. & C. Black, 1929.

MORK   Morley, Christopher. Off the deep end. Garden City, N. Y. Doubleday, Doran, 1928.

MORL   Morley, Christopher. One-act plays. Garden City, N. Y. Doubleday Page, 1924.

MORR   Morrette, Edgar. Six one-act plays. Boston. Badger, 1924.

MORS   Morse, Katharine D. Goldtree and silvertree fairy plays to read and act. N. Y. Macmillan, 1925.

MOSA   Moses, M. J. Another treasury of plays for children. Boston. Little Brown, 1926.

MOSR   Moses, M. J. Representative British dramas Victorian and modern. Boston. Little Brown, 1918.

MOSS   Moses, M. J. Representative British dramas. New revised ed. Boston. Little Brown, 1931.

N

NAT   National Safety Council. Plays (pamphlets) N. Y.

NIA   Nichols, Adelaide. The haunted circle and other outdoor plays. N. Y. Dutton, 1924.

NICA   Nicholson, Kenyon. The Appleton book of short plays. N. Y. Appleton, 1926.

NICB   Nicholson, Kenyon. The Appleton book of short plays. Second series. N. Y. Appleton, 1927.

NICG   Nicholson, Kenyon. Garden varieties. N. Y. Appleton, 1924.

NICH   Nicholson, Kenyon. Hollywood plays. N. Y. French, 1930.

NICR   Nicholson, Kenyon. Revues. N. Y. Appleton, 1926.

NIE   Niemeier, Minnie A. New plays for every day the schools celebrate. N. Y. Noble & Noble, 1928.

NIEM   Niemeier, Minnie A. New plays for every day the schools celebrate. Enlarged edition. N. Y. Noble & Noble, 1929.

NOR   Northwestern Press. Plays (pamphlets) Minneapolis, Minn.

NORT   Northwestern University and Drama Club of Evanston (Illinois) Playshop plays. N. Y. French (various dates).

O

OAK   Oakden, E. C. & Sturt, Mary. Pattern plays. London. Thomas Nelson & Sons. 1926.

OLC   Olcott, Virginia. Household plays for young people. N. Y. Dodd Mead, 1928.

OLD   Olcott, Virginia. Industrial plays. N. Y. Dodd Mead, 1927.

OLE   Olcott, Virginia. International plays for young people. N. Y. Dodd Mead, 1925.

OLF   Olcott, Virginia. World friendship plays for young people. N. Y. Dodd Mead, 1929.

OLG   Old Tower Press. Plays (pamphlets) Chicago, Illinois.

OLI   Oliver, Margaret S. Tea and little rice cakes. Boston. Badger, 1926.

OLL   Oller, Marie & Dawley, Eloise K. Little plays from Greek myths. N. Y. Century, 1928.

OMI   Oneal, Billie. Prize-winning one-act plays. Book 1. Dallas, Texas. Southwest Press, 1930.

O N	O'Neill, Eugene. The Great God Brown; the fountain; the moon of the Caribbees and other plays. N. Y. Boni & Liveright, 1926.
O R Y	O'Ryan, Frances & O'Ryan, Anna W. Plays from American history adapted for elementary grades by Myrtle G. McGee. N. Y. Hinds, Haydon & Eldridge, 1925.
O S F	Osgood, P. E. Old-time church drama adapted. N. Y. Harper, 1928.
O S G	Osgood, P. E. Pulpit dramas. N. Y. Harper, 1929.
O S G O	Osgood, P. E. The sinner beloved and other religious plays. N. Y. Harper, 1928.
O T	Ould, Hermon. New plays from old stories. London. Oxford University Press, 1924.
O U	Ould, Hermon. Plays of pioneers. London. French, 1925.
O U L	Ould, Hermon. Three comedies. London. French, 1925.
O U L E	Ouless, E. U. Seven Shrovetide plays. London. Deane & Sons, 1930.
O V	Overton, Grace S. Dramatized activities for young people. N. Y. Century, 1927.

P

P A	Pageant Publishing Co. Plays (pamphlets) Los Angeles, Cal.
P A I N	Paine Publishing Co. Plays (pamphlets) Dayton, Ohio.
P A I S	Painton, Edith F. A. U. & others. The blue entertainment book. Chicago. A. Flanagan Co., 1930.
P A I T	Painton, Edith F. A. U. The commencement manual. Chicago. Denison, 1915.
P A R R	Parsons, Margaret G. In the children's play-house. Boston. Baker, 1923.
P A R S	Parsons, Margaret G. Ten stirring Bible plays. Franklin, Ohio. Eldridge Entertainment House, 1927.
P A Z	Peach, L du Garde. Broadcast sketches. London. French, 1927.
P E	Pearson, P. M. The humorous speaker. N. Y. Noble & Noble, 1925.
P E A	Peattie, Elia W. The wander weed and seven other Little Theatre plays. Chicago. C. H. Sergel Co., 1923.
P E N	Pence, R. W. Dramas by present-day writers. N. Y. Scribner, 1927.
P E N N	Penn Publishing Co. Plays (pamphlets) Philadelphia, Pa.
P E R	Pertwee, Guy & Pertwee, Ernest. Scenes from Dickens. London. Routledge, n.d.
P H I	Philippine Islands, Government Bureau of Education, Department of Public Instruction. Philippine prose and poetry. Manila Bureau of Printing, 1927.
P H I J	Phillips, LeRoy & Johnson, Theodore. Baker's anthology of one-act plays. Boston. Baker International Play Bureau, 1925.
P H I L	Phillips, LeRoy & Johnson, Theodore. Types of modern dramatic composition. N. Y. Ginn, 1927.
P I L	Pilgrim Press. Plays (pamphlets) Chicago, Illinois.
P I R	Pirandello, Luigi. The one-act plays of Luigi Pirandello, tr. from Italian. N. Y. Dutton, 1928.
P L A Y	Playground and Recreation Association of America. Community drama. N. Y. Century, 1926.

PO   Pohl, F. J. When things were new. Brooklyn, N. Y. F. J. Pohl, 1925.

POL   Pollock, John. Twelve one-acters. London. The Cayme Press, 1926.

PR   Presbyterian Church in the U. S.—Board of Foreign Missions. Plays (pamphlets) N. Y.

PRE   Preston, Effa. The Christmas gayety book. Dayton, Ohio. Paine Publishing Co., 1924.

PRES   Preston, Effa. Ten clever plays for children. Franklin, Ohio. Eldridge Entertainment House, 1927.

PRI   Price, Olive M. American history in masque and wig. Boston. Baker, 1931.

PRI 1   Price, Olive M. Short plays from American history and literature. N. Y. French, 1925.

PRI 2   Price, Olive M. Short plays from American history and literature. Volume 2. N. Y. French, 1928.

PRI D   Pride, L. B. The shadow of the mine and other plays of the coal fields. N. Y. French, 1928.

PRI E   Priestly, J. B. & others. The second omnibus book. London. Heinemann, 1930.

Q

QU   Queen's Work Press. Plays (pamphlets) St. Louis, Mo.

R

RAI   Raine, J. W. Bible dramatics. N. Y. Century, 1927.

RAW   Rawlings Junior High School (Cleveland, Ohio). One winter's night and other plays for assembly programs. Cleveland, Ohio, 1928.

REE   Reely, Mary K. Three one-act plays. Boston. Baker, 1924.

REI   Reighard, Catherine F. Plays for people and puppets. N. Y. Dutton, 1928.

REZ   Reznikoff, Charles. Nine plays. N. Y. Charles Reznikoff, 1927.

RIC   Rich, Mabel I. Classified types of literature. N. Y. Century, 1926.

RICH   Richardson, Willis. Plays and pageants from the life of the negro. Washington, D. C. The Associated Publishers, 1930.

RID   Ridge, W. P. London please; four Cockney plays. London. French, 1925.

RIL   Riley, Alice C. D. The Mandarin coat and five other one-act plays for Little Theatres. N. Y. Brentano's, 1925.

RIN   Ring, Barbara. Three plays under three flags. Boston. Baker, 1928.

RO 4   Robins, Gertrude. Makeshifts & realities. Fourth edition. London. T. Werner Laurie, n.d.

ROC   Roche, Mazo de la. Low life and other plays. Boston. Little Brown, 1929.

ROH   Rohrbough, Katherine F. Successful stunts. Garden City, N. Y. Doubleday, Doran, 1929.

ROS 7   Ross, J. M. Adventures in literature. Book 7. N. Y. Harcourt Brace, 1927.

ROS 8   Ross, J. M. Adventures in literature. Grade 7B. N. Y. Harcourt Brace, 1928.

R O S 9	Ross, J. M. & Schweikert, H. C. Adventures in literature. Book 9. N. Y. Harcourt Brace, 1928.
R U B	Rubinstein, H. F. What's wrong with the theatre? N. Y. Stokes, n.d.
R U S	Russell, Mary M. Dramatized Bible stories for young people. N. Y. Doran, 1921.
R Y	Ryerson, Florence & Clements, Colin. All on a summer's day and six other short plays. N. Y. French, 1928.

S

S A	Sand, Maurice. Plays for Marionettes, tr. fr. French by Babette & Glenn Hughes. N. Y. French, 1931.
S A A	Sanford, A. P. & Schauffler, R. H. Armistice Day. N. Y. Dodd Mead, 1927.
S A G	Sanford, A. P. George Washington plays. N. Y. Dodd Mead, 1931.
S A L	Sanford, A. P. & Schauffler, R. H. Little plays for little people. N. Y. Dodd Mead, 1929.
S A M	Sanford, A. P. & Schauffler, R. H. The magic of books, an anthology for Book Week. N. Y. Dodd Mead, 1929.
S A O	Sanford, A. P. Out door plays for boys and girls. N. Y. Dodd Mead, 1930.
S A N P	Sanford, A. P. Plays for graduation. N. Y. Dodd Mead, 1930.
S A R B	Sargent, H. C. Bits and pieces. London. French, 1924.
S A R M	Sargent, H. C. Mrs. Hamblett again. London. French, 1930.
S A R P	Sargent, H. C. Pierrotechnics. London. French, 1923.
S C H 1	Schauffler, R. H. & Sanford, A. P. Plays for our American holidays. Volume 1. N. Y. Dodd Mead, 1928.
S C H 2	Schauffler, R. H. & Sanford, A. P. Plays for our American holidays. Volume 2. N. Y. Dodd Mead. 1928.
S C H 3	Schauffler, R. H. & Sanford, A. P. Plays for our American holidays. Volume 3. N. Y. Dodd Mead, 1928.
S C H 4	Schauffler, R. H. & Sanford, A. P. Plays for our American holidays. Volume 4. N. Y. Dodd Mead, 1928.
S C H O	Schofield, Stephan. The marble god and other one-act plays. N. Y. Brentano's, 1927.
S C H P	Scholastic Publishing Co. Saplings. Third ser. Pittsburgh, Pa., 1928.
S C H W	Schweikert, H. C. & others. Adventures in American literature. N. Y. Harcourt Brace, 1930.
S C H Y	Schweikert, H. C. & others. Adventures in English literature. N. Y. Harcourt Brace, 1930.
S C R	Scribner's, Charles & Sons. Plays (pamphlets) N. Y.
S C U	Scudder, Antoinette. The maple's bride and other one-act plays. Boston. Badger, 1930.
S E H	Seiler, Conrad. The husband of Xanthippe and other short plays. Boston. Baker, 1929.
S E I	Seiler, Conrad. Suicide and other one-act comedies. N. Y. French, 1926.
S E X	Sexton, Ethelyn. Mistletoe and holly. Franklin, Ohio. Eldridge Entertainment House, 1927.
S H A	Shay, Frank. The Appleton book of Christmas plays. N. Y. Appleton, 1929.

S HAB   Shay, Frank. The Appleton book of holiday plays. N. Y. Appleton, 1930.

S HAF   Shay, Frank. Fifty more contemporary one-act plays. N. Y. Appleton, 1928.

S HAP   Shay, Frank. Plays for strolling mummers. N. Y. Appleton, 1926.

S HAQ   Shay, Frank. Twenty contemporary one-act plays (American). Cincinnati, Ohio. Stewart Kidd Co., 1922.

S HAT   Shay, Frank. Twenty-five short plays—International. N. Y. Appleton, 1925.

S HER   Sheridan, Don. Impromptu entertainments. Chicago. Dramatic Publishing Co., 1930.

S I D   Sidgwick & Jackson. Plays (pamplets) London, England.

S I MA   Simpson, Harold. Airy nothings. London. French, 1927.

S I MH   Simpson, Harold. Harold Simpson's Revue sketches. London. French, 1924.

S I MM   Simpson, Harold. Nine to eleven. London. French, 1927.

S I MN   Simpson, Harold & Harvey, Morris. The "nine o'clock revue" book. London. French, 1924.

S I MO   Simpson, Harold. Oh—by the way. London. French, 1926.

S I MS   Simpson, Harold. Straws on the wind. London. French, 1925.

S I S   Sisters of Mercy—Grand Rapids, Michigan. Chrysalid; a collection of student writing. Grand Rapids, Mich. Sisters of Mercy, 1929.

S K   Skinner, Ada M. Christmas stories and plays. Chicago. Rand McNally, 1925.

S M   Smith, Evelyn. Form-room plays—Intermediate book. N. Y. Dutton, 1926.

S MF   Smith, Evelyn. Form-room plays—Senior book. N. Y. Dutton, 1921.

S MI   Smith, M. M. Short plays of various types. N. Y. Charles E. Merrill Co., 1924.

S MI T   Smith, W. P. Prose and verse for speaking and reading. N. Y. Harcourt Brace, 1930.

S OR   Sorenson, Grace. Juvenile comedies. Chicago. Denison, 1926.

S OU   South High School—Minneapolis, Minn. Glints in the sand. Minneapolis, Minn., 1928.

S Q   Squires, Edith L. Ten little plays for little tots. Boston. Baker, 1930.

S TAC   Stackhouse, P. J. Bible dramas in the pulpit. Philadelphia. Judson Press, 1926.

S TAL   Stallard, Mrs. Arthur. Small plays of St. Cuthbert. London. Society for Promoting Christian Knowledge, 1930.

S TEE   Steele, W. D. The terrible woman and other one act plays. N. Y. Appleton, 1925.

S TET   Stevens, H. C. G. "To meet the King!" and three other plays. London. Deane, 1930.

S TEU   Stevens, T. W. The nursery-maid of heaven and other plays. N. Y. Appleton, 1926.

S TEV1   Stevenson, Augusta. Children's classics in dramatic form. Book 1. New Edition. Boston. Houghton Mifflin, 1928.

S TEV2   Stevenson, Augusta. Children's classics in dramatic form. Book 2. New Edition. Boston. Houghton Mifflin, 1928.

STEV3   Stevenson, Augusta. Children's classics in dramatic form. Book 3. New Edition. Boston, Houghton Mifflin, 1930.

STEV4   Stevenson, Augusta. Children's classics in dramatic form. Book 4. Boston. Houghton Mifflin, 1928.

STEV5   Stevenson, Augusta. Children's classics in dramatic form. Book 5. Boston. Houghton Mifflin, 1928.

STON   Stone, Mary I. Plays from Bible stories. Kansas City, Mo. Burton Pub. Co., 1927.

STOP   Stopes, Marie & Sakurai, Jogi. Plays of old Japan the 'Nō.' London. The Eclipse Press, 1927.

STRA   Stratford Company. Plays (pamphlets) Boston, Mass.

STRI   Strindberg, August. Easter and other plays. London. Jonathan Cape, 1929.

STRO   Strong, Austin. The drums of Oude and other one-act plays. N. Y. Appleton, 1926.

STRU   Strutton, Rebecca & others. Best primary plays. Chicago. Beckley-Cardy, 1930.

SV   Swartout, Norman Lee, Publisher. Plays (pamphlets) Summit, N. J.

SW   Swinton, Phyllis McN. Plays for classroom and auditorium. Paterson, N. J. The Call Printing & Pub. Co., 1929.

T

TAX   Taylert, Gertrude E. & Rodney, Martina B. Three splendid plays for junior high. Franklin, Ohio. Eldridge Entertainment House, 1927.

TAY   Taylor, Katharine & Greene, H. C. The shady hill play book. N. Y. Macmillan, 1928.

TAYL   Taylor, Rica B. Four Jewish sketches. N. Y. French, 1927.

TAYM   Taylor, Sara V. Word-hoard. Omaha, Nebr. Douglas Printing Co., 1931.

THOM   Thomas, C. S. The Atlantic Book of junior plays. Boston. The Atlantic Monthly Press, 1924.

THON   Thompson, Edward & Thompson, Theodosia. Three eastern plays. London. George Allen & Unwin, 1927.

THOQ   Thornton, E. W. More Christian Endeavor playlets. Cincinnati, Ohio. Standard Pub. Co., 1929.

✓THOR   Thorpe, C. D. & Walter, E. A. University readings. N. Y. Harper, 1931.

TITB   Titheradge, Dion. Behind the curtain. London. French, 1926.

TITF   Titheradge, Dion. From the prompt corner. London. French, 1925.

TITO   Titheradge, Dion. Out of the box. London. French, 1925.

TITU   Titheradge, Dion. Ups and downs from revue. London. French, 1926.

TOT   Totheroh, Dan. One-act plays for everyone. N. Y. French, 1931.

TUC   Tucker, S. M. Twelve one-act plays for study and production. Boston. Ginn, 1929.

TUL   Tuller & Meredith Company. Plays (pamphlets) N. Y.

TURG   Turgenev, I. S. The plays of Ivan S. Turgenev. tr. fr. the Russian by M. S. Mandell. N. Y. Macmillan, 1924.

TURN   Turner, J. H. Rescued from revue. London. French, 1924.

TWO   Two prize health plays. Boston. Baker, 1930.

U

UM   University of Michigan. Plays ed. by K. T. Rowe. Ann Arbor, Mich. Wahr, 1929.

UNM2   University of Michigan. Plays. Book 2. Ann Arbor, Mich. Wahr, 1930.

UNND   University of Notre Dame. Plays (pamphlets) Notre Dame, Ind.

UNU   University of Utah. Plays ed. by B. R. Lewis. Boston. Baker, 1928.

UNW2   University of Washington. Plays ed. by Glenn Hughes. Seattle, Wash. Univ. of Washington Press, 1924.

UNW3   University of Washington. Plays. Third series. N. Y. French, 1927.

V

VAN   Van Derveer, Lettie C. Short plays for just us fellows. Franklin, Ohio. Eldridge Entertainment House, 1930.

W

WA   Wade, Leila A. Plays from Browning. Boston. Cornhill Pub. Co., 1923.

WEB   Webber, J. P. Short plays for junior and senior high schools. Boston. Houghton Mifflin, 1925.

WEBB   Webber, J. P. & Webster, H. H. Typical plays for young people. Boston. Houghton Mifflin, 1929.

WER   Werner, E. S. Company. Plays (pamphlets) N. Y.

WH   White, Kate A. Tested project plays for grade school. Boston. Baker, 1929.

WHG1   Whitney, Margaret A. Plays and pageants for children. Volume 1. Boston. Educational Pub. Co., 1925.

WHH   Whitney, Mary E. Bible plays and how to produce them. N. Y. Revell, 1927.

WHI   Whitney, Mary E. Some little plays and how to act them. Chicago. Beckley-Cardy, 1927.

WIK   Wilde, Percival. The inn of discontent and other fantastic plays. Boston. Little Brown, 1924.

WIL   Wilde, Percival. A question of morality and other plays. Boston. Little Brown, 1922.

WILD   Wilde, Percival. Ten plays for Little Theatres. Boston. Little Brown, 1931.

WILT   Wilde, Percival. Three-minute plays. N. Y. Greenberg, 1927.

WILV   Wilde, Percival. Pub. Plays (pamphlets) N. Y.

WILY   Wilder, Thornton. The long Christmas dinner and other plays in one act. N. Y. Coward-McCann, 1931.

WILZ   Wilder, Thornton. The angel that troubled the waters and other plays. N. Y. Coward-McCann, 1928.

WIM   Williams, E. H. Three fairy plays. London. French, 1925.

WIMA   Williams, Joseph, Publisher. Plays (pamphlets) London, Eng.

WIMS   Willis, Richard. Six playlets. N. Y. Richard Willis, 1928.

WIMT   Wilson, H. W. Company. Plays (pamphlets).

WIN   Wilson, Walter & Company. Plays (pamphlets) Glasgow, Scotland.

WO   W. C. T. U. Publishing House. Plays (pamphlets) Evanston, Ill.

WOM   Woman's Press. Plays (pamphlets) N. Y.

WOR   Wordsworth, Elizabeth. Poems and plays. London. Oxford Uni. Press, 1930.

WOW   Woods, Marjorie. Why we celebrate, holiday plays for young people. N. Y. French, 1927.

Y

YAL   Yale one-act plays. N. Y. French, 1930.

YALP   Yale Playcraftsmen plays. Boston. Baker, 1924.

YATE   Yates, Elizabeth H. Small plays for small casts. Philadelphia, Penn., 1926.

YD   Yeats, W. B. Later poems. N. Y. Macmillan, 1924.

YE   Yeats, W. B. Plays and controversies. N. Y. Macmillan, 1924.

YEA   Yeats, W. B. Plays in prose and verse. N. Y. Macmillan, 1924.

YOU   Youmans, Raymond. Publishing Co. Plays (pamphlets) Kansas City, Missouri.

YOUN   Young, Stark. Sweet times and the blue policeman. N. Y. Holt, 1925.

A

C **Achilles' quarrel with Agamemnon.** M. Oller and E. K. Dawley. 4b., 1g. Sc. Tent. OLL

C **Achilles sulks in his tent.** M. Oller and E. K. Dawley. 5b. Sc. Tent. OLL

Acid test, The. Mrs. C. P. Smith. Comedy. 2w. Sc. Living room in progressive town in the Middle West. BAK

Across the border. C. Clements. 2m., 1w. Sc. Main room of an adobe ranch house. CL, SHAF

Across the Jordan. E. H. Culbertson. 2m., 1w. Sc. Stuffy old-fashioned bedroom in Middle West. Theatre Arts M. 13: 931–9, Dec. 1929.

J **Act foolish and be wise.** E. Hoxie. 2g. Sc. Living room. HOV

Action! H. Hudson. Farce. 2m., 4w. Sc. Roof of an adobe house. APPL

A. D. 2000. E. Preston. Farce. 10m., 5w. Sc. Boxing ring. FREP

Addio. S. Young. 3m., 1w. Sc. Room. CL

C **Adopted by Santa Claus.** F. R. Page. 11 char., chorus. Sc. Santa Claus's workshop. BAK

J **Adopted one, The.** G. Sorenson. Comedy. 2b., 3g. Sc. Living room. SOR

J **Adopted son, An.** H. W. Githens. 3b., 5g. Sc. Any stage. GIT

C **Adoption of Bob.** M. Irish. 4b., 6g. Sc. Interior. BUG

C **Adoption of the Constitution, The.** M. A. Niemeier. 12b., 8g. Sc. Parlor of a Colonial House. NIEM

Adorable woman, The. E. Bourdet. Translated from the French by Arthur Hornblow, Jr. 1m., 1w. Sc. An attractive bedroom. Harper's Bazaar 62: 92–3, May 1927.

Adoration of the three kings, The. P. E. Osgood. 4m., 2w. Sc. Church OSF

Adults, The. E. H. Yates. 4m., 3w. Comedy. Sc. Drug store. PENN

C **Advent of spring, The.** F. I. Hope and M. B. Carpenter. Many c. Sc. Platform with throne. Norm. Inst. 34: 76, Apr. 1925.

Adventure! D. Titheradge. Farce. 3m., 3w. Sc. Doctor's consulting office. TITU

J **Adventure in friendship, An.** B. Abel. 6g., chorus. Sc. Girl's room. WOM

Adventures of Ella Cinders, The. 6 char., 9 episodes. WOM

Adverbs. A. Kreymborg. Fanciful. 9m. Sc. Interior. KRR

Aesthetics; a palaver. L. Mumford. 4m. Sc. Corner of a library in a country house. Amer. Mercury 3: 360–5, Nov. 1924.

Affairs of men, The. W. Beck. 2m. Sc. Waiting room in a railway station in Chicago. BEC

After all these years. W. Beck. 3m., 2w. Sc. Living room. BEC

After glow, The. E. F. Corbett. 2m., 2w. Sc. Main room of kitchenette flat. Poet Lore 36: 311–316, Summer 1925.

After midnight. V. Wyngate. Comedy. 1m., 1w. Sc. Fashionable night club. FREL

After the funeral. I. L. Peretz. 1m., 3w. Sc. Interior. BLP

After the journey's end. E. A. Jelf. 15m. Nat. Review 94: 921–4, Feb. 1930.

After the Reunion dinner. M. Lane-Norcott. Revue. 3m. Sc. Backcloth of the statue of Eros, Piccadilly Circus, London. FRET

After twenty-five years. O. W. Firkins. 3m., 1w. Sc. Sitting room of hotel suite. Drama 15: 99–101, 109, Feb. 1925.

Aftermath, The. H. Glynn-Ward. 2m., 1w. Sc. A backwood's kitchen. Poet Lore 37: 501–11, Winter 1926.

Aftermath. L. B. Pride. 3m., 2w. Sc. Sitting room of farmhouse. PRID

C **Afternoon, An.** M. Buchanan. 2b., 2g., 12c. Sc. living room. Prim. Educ. 32: 46–8, Jan. 1924.

Afternoon. P. Johnson. 1m., 3w. Sc. Drawing room in country house. BLA, FREN

Afternoon orator, The. C. T. Crowell. 6m., 4w. Sc. Parlor in Plushengilt Hotel. New Repub. 39: 72–5, June 11, 1924.

Afterwards. M. Robertson. 3w. Sc. Interior. BAK

Age of accountability, The. M. C. Boatright. Tragedy. 2m., 7w. Sc. Parlor of home in Southwest. Poet Lore 40: 295–302, Summer 1929.

Age of compromise, The. R. Jeans. Farce. 2m., 2w. Sc. Interior. JEP

Age of discretion, The. H. Berman. 4m., 2w. Sc. Library in a home. BER

J **Age-old dream, The.** G. S. Overton. 9g. Sc. Garden. OV

Ahasverus. H. Heijermans. Trans. from the Dutch by Caroline Heijermans-Houwink and Dr. J. J. Houwink. 5m., 3w. Sc. Small dirty room in Russian farmhouse. Drama 19: 145–7, Feb. 1929.

Ahaz casts away the heritage. J. W. Raine. 12m., 2w. Sc. King's palace at Jerusalem. RAI

C **Aided by St. Patrick.** M. Bitney. 3b., 2g. Sc. Stage trimmed with green. BIT

"Ain't no use fer larnin'." B. Inge and C. Chupét. 2m., 3w. Sc. Interior of a crude log cabin in Carolina mountains. ING

C **Air gun, The.** E. Ferris. Many c. Sc. Any stage. Prim. Educ. 32: 267–8, Apr. 1924.

J **Aladdin and his wonderful lamp.** C. T. Major. 9b., 8g. Sc. Before the curtain and on the stage in Arabia. MAI

J **Aladdin and the wonderful lamp.** E. B. Dooley. 5b., 3g., chorus. Sc. Street in Bagdad. FREN

Aladdin's wife. B. Hughes. Romantic comedy. 3m., 1w. Sc. Magnificently furnished oriental room. UNW 3

C **Albert's garden, a thrift play for fourth grade.** W. Dresback. Many c. Sc. Garden. School Arts M. 28: 245–9, Dec. 1928.

C **Alcestis.** M. Oller and E. K. Dawley. 3b., 3g. Sc. Banquet hall of palace. OLL

J **Alchemist, The.** E. Smith. Adapted from Jonson, The Alchemist. 3b., 1g. Sc. Room in London in 17th century. SMF

CJ **Alias Santa Claus.** P. Wilde. 11b., 3g. Sc. Large room decorated for Christmas. SCH1, Pict. R. 28: 16–17, 72, Dec. 1926.

C **Alice in dreamland.** V. Offult, ed. 12c. Sc. A wood. Pop. Educ. 41: 355–7, Feb. 1924.

Alice in Everydayland. E. H. Van Delden. 3m., 5w. Sc. Corner of a tea room in New York. Poet Lore 38: 96–105, Spring 1927.

C **"Alice in Wonderland" Trial scene.** L. Carroll. 27c. Sc. Court. LUT

Alien note, The. J. L. Latham. Comedy. 10w. Sc. Interior. DRA

Alimony Rastus. W. Richardson. Farce. 3m., 1w. Sc. Sitting room in Mandy's home. BUG

All aboard. H. P. Powell. Farce. 8m., 1w. Sc. Waiting room of railway station. PENN

C **All aboard for North Pole land.** F. C. Gardner. 4b. Sc. Interior of gigantic "Zep." GAP

C **All America's children.** Y. Klein and F. Schwarz. 14c. Sc. Any interior. KLE

C **All eyes.** S. Young. Fanciful. 4b., 3g. Sc. Slope of a long hill. YOUN

All for Christ. M. Glassburner. 6w. Sc. Any platform. Mis. R. 54: 447–54, June 1931.

All gummed up. H. W. Gribble. Satirical comedy. 3m., 2w. Sc. Consulting room. SHAQ

All Hallows' Eve. P. B. Perrigard. 5m., 2w. Sc. Drawing room. CANA

C **All in a Christmas garden.** E. D. Yale. 7 char., chorus. Sc. Background of green. ELD

C **All in the lantern's glow.** H. L. Clark. 10b., 6g. Sc. Stage. CLAR

All jam. L. du G. Peach. Farce. 1m., 1w. Sc. Strand, London, on a busy day. PAZ

J **All on a summer's day.** F. Ryerson and C. Clements. 4g. Sc. Interior. RY

All on a summer's day. C. C. Clements. Fanciful. 4w. Sc. Interior. SHAP

C **All on the king's highway, a play for Easter.** M. E. Carpenter. 3b., 3g., chorus. Sc. Front of a cottage on the King's Highway. BAI, Amer. Childhood. 13: 27–30, 64, Apr. 1928.

All or none. F. K. Gifford. 1m., 2w. 12g. Sc. Campfire. Drama 16: 207–9, 237–8, Mar. 1926.

All out of tune. O. Wells. 1m., 2w. Sc. Living room. PAIN

All the world's a links. H. Simpson. Farce. 1m., 1w. Sc. Suburban sitting room. SIMO

Allison's lad. B. M. Dix. 6m. Sc. Chamber in village inn in 1648. HAM, KM

Almighty waiter, The. B. D. Steward. 4m., 2w. Sc. Restaurant. DE

J **Alphabet tree, The.** V. Olcott. 3b., 1g. Sc. A deep green wood in Holland. OLD

"Altogether," The. D. Titheradge. Farce. 2m., 2w. Sc. Studio. TITO

Always polite. H. C. Sargent. Farce. 5m., 2w. Sc. London street. SARB

C **Amateur fireman, The.** E. M. Quackenbush. 8b., 2g. Sc. Living room. ELD

Amateur night. G. Buck. Humorous skit. 7m., 4w. Sc. Drop curtain in N. Y. theatre in 1908. NICR

J **Ambassador in bonds, An.** H. W. Githens. 16b. Sc. Temple in Jerusalem. 5 scenes. GITH

Ambition. K. Kavanaugh. 2m., 3w. Sc. Interior. DRA

Ambitious guest. N. Hawthorne. 4m., 3w. Sc. Living room of a simple inn. HAP

Ambush, The. R. Hughes. 10m. Sc. Tent on battle field in Georgia in 1864. HUO

Ambush. J. H. Whitehouse. Farce comedy. 4m., 2w. Sc. Kitchen. NICB

Amends. E. Crawshay-Williams. 1m., 1w. Sc. Squalid and untidy attic. CRA

C **America, the beautiful, Democracy's goal.** M. Knox and A. M. Lütkenhaus. Many c. Sc. Assembly. LUT

American grandfather, An. M. S. Smith. 4m., 1w., others. Sc. Bare interior of immigration office. Poet Lore 35: 443–455, Autumn 1924.

C **Americanizing the alien.** H. W. Luzadder. 3b., others. Sc. Any class room. Pop. Educ. 42 : 526, May 1925.

C **Americans all, an Americanization pageant.** A. C. Gilmore. Many c. Sc. Stage. Pop. Educ. 41 : 577–78, June 1924.

C **Americans all.** F. B. Linsky. 36c. Sc. Stage. ELD

   America's place in history, an Irish dialogue. J. Murphy, *ed.* 2m., 1w. Forum 83 : 96–100, Feb. 1930.

   Amicable settlement, An. I. S. Turgenev. Comedy. 10m., 1w. Sc. Dining room. TURG

   Among old instruments. I. Dall. Fantasy. Sc. Musicians loft. DAL

C **Among the stars.** B. W. Hanson. 42c. Sc. Classroom. WHG1 Prim. Educ. 33 : 52, 54–58, Jan. 1925.

   Among thieves. W. Gillette. 2m., 1w. Sc. Exterior in Arizona. FRE2

   Amos. University ot Oklahoma. 9m., 2w., chorus. Sc. Outdoors in ancient Palestine. WOM

   Amusements of Khan Kharuda, The. Lord Dunsany. Fanciful. 4m., 2w. Sc. Room in a hotel. DUA

   And he came to his father. E. Kruckemeyer. 4m., 2w., chorus. Sc. Exterior, in ancient Palestine on Easter. DRA, FREN

   And other stories. R. Littell. 2m. Dialog between Ring Lardner and a still small voice. New Rep. 48 : 147–9, Sept. 29, 1926.

   And points west. R. M. Toms. 6m. Sc. Lobby of a small town hotel in Kansas. DET

   And the devil laughs. A. Thurston. 4m., 2w. Sc. A cleared space in the wooded brush grown section of the country. UNU

   And the sea shall give up its dead. T. Wilder. 4m., 2w. Sc. Judgment Day. WILZ

   And the third day. J. G. Rogers for the Cactus Club, Denver, 1923. 8m., Sc. Glade in high altitude forests of the Rocky Mountains. CAC

J **And the tribes shall pass.** C. Myall. 5b., chorus. Sc. A slight depression in a prairie landscape. BRI1

   And there was light. C. C. Kennedy founded on I. S. Cobb's short story. 1m., 3w. Sc. Office of a nerve specialist. FREN, FRE2

   And they met again. F. Jacob. Comedy. 3m., 1w. Sc. Private dining room of a Country Club. JAC

J **Andy sees Lincoln.** P. M. Swinton. 6b., 6g., chorus. Sc. Country town. SW

   Angel on the ship, The. T. Wilder. 2m., 1w. Sc. Foredeck of a ship disabled in midocean. WILZ, Harper 157 : 564–5, Oct. 1928. Bermondsey Book 6 : 10–12, Dec.–Feb. 1928–9.

   Angel that troubled the waters, The. T. Wilder. 3m., 1w. Sc. A pool in a vast gray hall open to the sky. WILZ

C **Angels of prayer.** D. A. Lord. 1b., 12g. Sc. Interior. LOP

C **Angel's song, The.** M. I. Stone. 8b., 4g., chorus. Sc. White back-ground. STON

   Angelus. H. L. Taylor. 2m., 3w. Sc. A dingy parlor. FRE5

J **Animals protest, The.** L. Porter. 3b., 3g. Sc. Emma Willard School Hygeia 8 : 466–8, May 1930.

C J **Animated art room, The.** E. Ernesti. 29c. Sc. Any stage. School Arts M. 25 : 328–331, Feb. 1926.

J **Animated slang.** M. Elliott. Comedy. 6 char. Sc. Interior. ELD

C **Animated toys.** M. Corell and I. Liccione. 13c. Sc. Playroom. STRU

Anniversary, The. A. Chekhov. Trans. from the Russian. 2m., 2w., chorus. Sc. Chairman's office. CHEC

Annunciation, The. P. E. Osgood. 1m., 1w. Sc. Nazareth. OSF

Anonymous letter, The. K. Nicholson. 2m., 1w. Sc. The Swank home. NICG

Another moon. R. Coon. Comedy. 2m., 4w. Sc. Den of country home. KAM

Another pair of spectacles. V. Bridges. Farce. 2m., 1w. Sc. Well furnished dining room in London. FREL

Answer, The. O. W. Firkins. 3m., 1w. Sc. Main room of a small town inn. FIR

C **Ant and the grasshopper, The.** M. E. Whitney. 2b. Sc. 1 A field. Sc. 2 Ant's house. WHI

Anti-gossip club, The. B. E. Palmer. Farce. 10w. Sc. Interior. BAK

Anti-marriage club, The. H. Simpson. Farce. 5m. Sc. A club room. SIMA

Anti-Pashto. H. W. Hanemann. Burlesque. 3m., 1w. Sc. Bench in a public square in Rome. HANE

Antick, The. P. Mackaye. 2m., 3w., chorus. Sc. An old stone wall. MACM

Antiques. E. Russell. Comedy. 3w. Sc. An old-fashioned parlor. BAK

Antoinette comes to town. J. C. McMullen. Farce. 3m. Sc. Dress-making establishment. MACT

Any evening. A. Turner. Comedy. 3m., 2w. Sc. Living room. PENN

Apache. C. Méré and R. Livingston. Trans. from the Hungarian. Melodrama. 3m., 3w. Sc. Dilapidated parlor. LON

Apartments to let. E. Nugent and H. Lindsay. Farce. 1m., 3w. Sc. Living room in apartment. NICA

Appearances. R. Taylor. 2m., 2w. Sc. Living room in brownstone front house. NICB

C **Apple of discord, The.** M. Oller and E. K. Dawley. 3b., 4g. Sc. Banquet hall. OLL

Apple of discord, The. E. Wordsworth. Burlesque. 4m., 5w., chorus. Sc. Before the garden of the Hesperides. WOR

C **April fool.** K. L. Bates. Verse. 5c. Sc. Edge of an enchanted forest. BAT

April fools. W. F. Chapman. Farce. 3m. Sc. Interior. DRA, FIT

Arabesque. L. Anderson. Farce. 2m., 1w. Sc. An island in the southern Pacific. ANDE

Arabian barber shop. W. L. Lamar. 2m. Sc. Any stage. J. Chem. Ed. 6: 2011–18, Nov. 1929.

J **Arachne and Athene.** M. R. Hofer. 3g., 6 chorus groups. Sc. Any stage. HOF

C **Arachne and the spider.** M. Oller and E. K. Dawley. 5g. Sc. Cottage. OLL

C **Arbor Day fantasy, An.** L. Maher. Several c. Sc. Any stage. Prim. Educ. 44: 654, Apr. 1927.

Architect, The. E. DeHuff. 5m., 3w. Sc. Study in a well-to-do home. DEH

Ardvorlich's wife. G. Bottomley. Dramatic poetry. 3m., 8w. Sc. Vacant space. BOTT

Are all men like that? B. Ring. 6m., 2w. Sc. Coat room. RIN

Are we sentimental? N. Chatterton. Comedy. 2m., 2w. Sc. Studio. BAK

Aria da Capo. E. St. V. Millay. Fantasy. 4m., 1w. Sc. Stage set for Harlequinade. APPL, MIL

Arms and the drama. H. F. Rubinstein. 4m. Sc. Military camp in England in 1918. RUB

Arms and the maid or rustic ribaldry. A. Jagger. 6m., 1w. Sc. Village green. FREL

Arnold. J. H. Turner. Farce. 2m., 1w. Sc. Flat. TURN

C   **Around the world.** K. A. White. 5b., 4g. Sc. Living room. WH

C   **Around the world with the children.** H. R. Bailey. 8b., 7g., others. Sc. Living room. Norm. Inst. 39: 47–48, May 1930.

C   **Around the world with the children.** N. Wagner. 8b., 8g. Sc. Any stage. Norm. Inst. 37: 72, 74, Mar. 1928.

Arrested for speeding. E. M. Glenn. 2m., 7w. Sc. Exterior. PAIN

Arrow, The. J. E. Downey. 4m., 3w., others. Sc. The desert. Poet Lore 38: 297–306, Summer 1927.

Arrow by day, The. L. J. Hines and F. King. 2m., 2w. Sc. Cloth merchant's house in Cheapside during the plague. FREL

J   **Arrow maker's daughter.** G. E. Smith and G. Knevels. A campfire play adapted from Hiawatha. 6b., 7g. Sc. Camp fire. FREN

Art and Mrs. Palmer. G. Hughes. Farce-comedy. 3m., 3w. Sc. Living room. FRE5

Art in the home (cacophony in many flats). P. Stevenson. 4m., 3w., 1b. Sc. Living room in typical American home. Southw. Rev. 13: 217–33, Jan. 1928.

Artichokes for dinner. L. Barbee. Comedy. 9w. Sc. Interior. YOU

Artist, The. H. L. Mencken. Satire 8m., 2w., chorus. Sc. Large gloomy hall with many rows of seats. FREN

Artist, The. A. A. Milne. Comedy. 1m., 1w. Sc. Hall of a country cottage. COH

As I remember you. S. Cowan. 2m., 4m. Sc. Before the black velvet curtains. COW

J   **As it was in the beginning.** P. E. Osgood. Morality play. 8 char. Sc. A central throne. OSGO

C   **As Mr. Clean sees it.** N. Flaurier. 2b. Sc. Any stage. Norm. Inst. 34: 73, Sept. 1925.

As others see us. R. Jeans. Farce. 3m., 3w. Sc. Stage. JEP

C   **As the twig is bent, a Children's Day pageant.** P. Noble. 10b., 1g. Sc. In Judea beside the well. Int. J. Rel. Educ. 1: 28–9, June 1925.

C   **Asclepius.** M. Oller and E. K. Dawley. 4b. Sc. Room in Grecian house. OLL

Ashes of romance. P. Wilde. Fantastic. 1m., 2w. Sc. Spotlessly clean room in a western hospital. WIK

Ask me another. H. P. Powell. Farce. 3m., 2w. Sc. Interior. Penn.

At any cost. L. North. 6m. Sc. Interior of a farm kitchen near Ypres. BAK

At stake. B. P. Inge and C. Chupét. 5m., chorus. Sc. Interior of a corner saloon in 1919. ING

J   **At the beautiful gate.** H. W. Githens. 8b., chorus. Sc. Steps of the temple. GITH

At the Brig End. S. Asgold. Romantic. 4m., 2w. Sc. Scotch end of Coldstream Bridge. DE

At the club. A. Gerstenberg. Comedy. 5m., Sc. Lounge of man's club. GEQ

At the Costumier's. G. Grace. Revue. 3m., 1w. Sc. Office of theatrical costumiers. FRET

At the creepy inn. S. S. Tibbals. Burlesque. 2m. Sc. Office of an old inn. FARQ

At the doctor's office. B. Herford. 3w. Ladies Home Journal 44: 263, Apr. 1927.

J   **At the fair.** A. C. Darlington. 3b., 5g., chorus. Sc. Russian fair. DAR

J   **At the feet of the Apostles.** H. W. Githens. 2b., 1g., chorus. Sc. Home of Ananias in Rome. GITH

J   **At the ferry.** 2b., 1g. Sc. A ferry landing. JOHN

J   **At the first tee.** H. Connell. 1b., 1g. Sc. Ridgewood Golf Club. AU

J   **At the fountain.** R. C. Bull and E. G. Steinmetz, Jr. Comedy—farce. 13b., 7g. Sc. Soda fountain of a small town drugstore. DAZ

At the gate. L. Pirandello. Trans. from the Italian. 2m., 1w., 1c. Sc. A gate in a wall outside of a graveyard. PIR

At the gate. S. Richmond. 2m., 2w. Sc. Outside of the gate of a country gaol. DE

At the gate beautiful. H. S. Mason. 5m., 2w., chorus. Sc. Street in Jerusalem in front of the Temple. FEDE, FREN

J   **At the gates.** E. E. Levinger. 5b., 1g. Sc. Interior. BLO

J   **At the gates of La Rabida.** E. E. Levinger. 4b. Sc. Gate of a convent. LEVT

At the hairdresser's. B. Herford. 2w. Ladies Home Journal 43: 147, July 1926.

At the Hawk's well. W. B. Yeats. Mask play. Poetic. 6m. Sc. Bare space before a wall. YE

At the junction. R. Field. Fantasy. 2m., 2w. Sc. Small country station of a New England town. FIC

J   **At the mile-stone.** J. Thorp. Poetic. 14b or g. chorus. Sc. Stage with mile-stone. SANP

J   **At the Misses Brontë's establishment.** 2m., 4w., children. Sc. Large Schoolroom of 1859. Cornhill M. 70: 151–168, Feb. 1931.

J   **At the Mule: a fragment.** D. B. W. Lewis. 7m., 2w. Sc. Tavern in France on Christmas Eve in 1456. SCH4

J   **At the rainbow.** M. A. Butler. Adapted from Eliot. Silas Marner. 8b. Sc. Kitchen of the Rainbow Inn. BUT

At the sign of the Boar's Head. V. R. Sutton. 2m., 9w., chorus. Sc. Old Revolutionary mansion in Virginia. SAG, WOM

At the sign of the Bumblebee, an operetta. B. J. Thompson. Many c. Sc. Mother Nature's workshop. Norm. Inst. 36: 70–2, Apr. 1927.

At the sign of the cleft heart. T. Garrison. Fantasy. 1m., 1w. Sc. Interior. JOHP

At the sign of "The Sturgeon Head." W. J. Cooper and E. T. Woolfolk. 14m., 1w. Sc. Gate keeper's lodge. COO

At the stroke of twelve. A. E. Bishop. Comedy. 1m., 4w. Sc. Living room. BANN

At the telephone. A. de Lorde. Trans. from the French. 5m., 3w., 1c. Sc. 1 Large sitting room. 2 A study. FRE2

At the wakehouse. F. O'Connor. 3m., 3w. Sc. Any. Theatre Arts Mag. 10: 412–14, June 1926.

C   **At the wishing well.** H. Clark. 3b., 6g., chorus. Sc. Interior. BUG

Atlanta in Wimbledon. Lord Dunsany. Fanciful. 5m., 1w. Sc. Room in a villa. DUS, FREN

Awkward maid, The. W. N. Bugbee. 3w. Sc. Sitting room. CAT1

Aye, aye Sir! J. M. Ellicott. 7m. Sc. Covered bridge of a man-of-war. CART

B

Babbitt's boy. G. Hughes. 2m., 4w., 1 bird. Sc. Breakfast room. FRE6

Babe in the bulrushes, The. M. Parsons. 3g. Sc. Either indoors or outdoors. PARS

Babe of Bethlehem, The. J. W. Raine. 14m., 1w. Sc. 1 Field near Bethlehem. 2 Stable in Bethlehem. 3 Interior of house. RAI

Babe of Bethlehem, The. P. J. Stackhouse. 10m., chorus. Sc. On a mountain top. 3 scenes. STAC

Babouscka. E. Van der Veer. 1m., 5w. Sc. Interior of a peasant's home in Russia during the reign of the Czar. FRE5

Bab's book. A. L. Kaser. Farce. 1m., 1w. Sc. Street. KAS

C **Baby New Year.** R. Arkwright. 2b., 1g. Sc. Snowy country. SCH2

C **Baby show, The.** J. A. Baxter. 2b., 6g. Sc. Interior. PAIS

C **Baby show at Pineville, The.** N. H. Pelham. Musical play. 19c. chorus. Sc. Interior. BECK

J **Baby's fortune, The.** M. S. Beagle. 1m., 2w., 1b. Sc. Ferry farm in Virginia in 1732. SAG

Bachelor of Gray Crags, The. B. King. 7w. Sc. Living room. FREN

Bachelor's club, The. E. W. Merriman. Burlesque. 13m. Sc. Interior. BUG

Bachelors forever. L. Crites. Comedy. 7m., 8w. Sc. Interior. BUG

Back of the yards. K. S. Goodman. 3m., 2w. Sc. Kitchen of a small flat "back of the yards" in Chicago. TUC

J **Back to school.** H. M. Paull. Comedy. 7g. BAK

"Back to the woodshed." T. Keenan. Comedy. 2m., 2w. Sc. A plainly furnished room in a farmhouse. NICR

Back to your knitting, a mystery farce. J. E. Goodman. 4m., 5w., 1b. Sc. Lounge in a small summer resort hotel. Country Gentleman 93: 21, 93–98, Dec. 1928.

Backing a winner. H. Simpson. 2m. Sc. Back of a box at Ascot on Cup day. SIMN

Backward child, A. H. C. Pemberton. Comedy. 2g. Sc. Room. DRA

Backway, The. J. L. Hodson. 3m., 2w. Sc. Interior. FREN

J **Backwoods.** M. Holbrook. 4m., chorus. Sc. A camp. SAO

C **Backwoodsman, The.** A. Van Noorden. 13b., 5g. Sc. Interior or exterior. ELD

C **Bad baby molar, The.** L. W. Morrey. Many c. Sc. Mouth. Home Econ. 7: 14+, Jan. 1928.

J **Bad bargain, A.** H. W. Githens. 3b., 1g. Sc. House of Isaac. GIT

C **Bad molar.** L. W. Morrey. 11c. Sc. The mouth. Child Health Mag. 5: 438–40, Oct. 1924.

Bad penny, The. R. Field. 4w. Sc. Parlor of a house on the outskirts of a New England city. FRE6

Badge of honor, The. F. E. Eakman. 13c. and chorus. Sc. Street. EAK

C **Bag of fresh air dreams, The.** H. L. Sorden. 7c. and chorus. Sc. Bedroom. HAH

Baggage, The. B. Moore. Comedy. 1m., 1w. Sc. Interior. JOHP

J **Baking the cake.** C. Francis. 7g. Sc. Kitchen. FRA

Bal masque. O. Down. 1m., 2w. Sc. Balcony that looks on to the river at Chelsea. DOW

Balanced diet. E. L. Green. Comedy. 5m., 3w. Sc. Kitchen of farmhouse in New York State. FREN

Ball and the chain, The. S. Cowan. 4m., 3w. Sc. A gaudy over decorated balcony of a restaurant. COW

Balm. M. Denison. 3w. Sc. Second floor back room in delapidated boarding house. CANB

Balo. J. Toomer. 7m., 2w. chorus of children. Sc. Inside negro farmhouse. LOC

C **Bank of English, The.** M. G. Moore. 4b., 3g. Sc. Any stage. Norm. Inst. 36: 74, Feb. 1927.

Barabbas. D. Leamon. 5m., 1w. Sc. Along road leading from Jerusalem to the tomb of Jesus. FEDE

Barbara. J. K. Jerome. Comedy. 2m., 2w. Sc. Interior. PENN

J **Barbara Frietchie.** M. G. Parsons. 3g. Sc. Parlor. WOM

Barbara's wedding. J. M. Barrie. 4m., 2w. Sc. Sitting room in a country village in England. BARR

Barbarians, The. L. B. Pride. 5m. Sc. Side view of a chamber off sub-entry in a coal mine. CL, PRID

J **Bardell vs Pickwick.** J. W. Bengough. 16b., 3g. Sc. Stage. JON

Bardell vs Pickwick. G. Pertwee and E. Pertwee. 12m., 3w., chorus. Sc. Court of Common Pleas in 1830. PER

Bargain, The. I. Dall. Verse. 2m. Sc. Out of doors. DAL

Bargain day at Bloomstein's. E. Mumford. Farce. 5m., 10w. Sc. Interior of store. PENN

Bargains. K. Kester. 1m., 3w. Sc. Fitting room of a department store basement. JOHM

"Bargains in Cathay." R. Field. Comedy. 4m., 3w. Sc. Book department in a large department store. FIC

J **Barrel of fun, A.** A. W. Norton. 17g. Sc. Sunday School classroom. ELD

Barren. C. Powell-Anderson. Tragedy. 1m., 3w. Sc. Interior. FREN

Barring of the door, The. V. B. Lawton. 3m., 1w. chorus. Sc. Old English interior. LAWT

Basket, The. F. Jacob. 2m., 2w. Sc. Living room of a log-house. JAC

C **Basket of beautiful things, A.** A. W. Norton. 9g. Sc. Stage. FJ

Bathing beauty contest. J. C. Kneas. 2m., 4w. Sc. Public platform. CAT2

Baths of Borcovicus, The. R. Walker. Comedy. 4m., 2w. Sc. Roman camp. DE

C **Battle, The.** D. Schaefer. 21c. Norm. Inst. 37: 64, June 1928.

J **Battle of Cressy, The.** P. J. Barrow. 16g. Sc. Schoolroom. FREL

Battle of San Jacinto. M. M. Griffith. 22m. Sc. Large live oak tree. GRI

C **Battle with the giant, The.** M. Helfen. Comedy. 14b. Sc. An open place in the woods. CATH

C **Baucis and Philemon.** M. E. Carpenter. 3b., 1g., chorus. Sc. The front of a rude cottage. BAI, Amer. Child. 15: 26–28, Nov. 1929.

C **Baucis and Philemon.** M. R. Hofer. 6b., 2g., 2 chorus groups. Sc. Either indoors or outdoors. HOF

C **Baucis and Philemon.** M. Oller and E. K. Dawley. 3m., 1g. Sc. Interior of a lowly cottage. OLL

Be a little Cuckoo! H. Reed. Farce. 2m., 3w. Sc. Platform. DRA

Be careful, doctor. C. Barr. Comedy. 1m., 4w. Sc. Living room of a summer cottage. PENN

Beaded buckle, The. F. Gray. Comedy. 2m., 4w. Sc. Sitting room in a North Carolina home. CAR2

C **Bean boy, The.** T. Adair. Fanciful. 5b., 1g., chorus. Sc. Outside a cottage. JAN

Beating the boss. N. Balch. 4m., 1w. Sc. Modern sales office. BAL

Beau and Belle. C. S. Armfield. 1m., 1w. Sc. Garden. WOM

J **Beau of Bath, The.** C. D. Mackay. 2b., 1g. Sc. Room in Beaus apartment in 1750. GREM, SMIT

Beautiful old things. E. Wilson. 5m., 2w. Sc. Drawing room. New Repub. 63: 313–317, July 30, 1930.

C Beautiful song, The. A. Stevenson. 12c. chorus. Sc. A meadow. STEV1

Beautiful story, The. P. Wilde. 1m., 1w., 1c. Sc. Cheerful fire in an old-fashioned hearth. WIL

J **Beauty and the beast.** E. H. Williams. 4m., 4g. Sc. Cottage. WIM

Beauty secrets. E. R. Bills. Comedy. 5w. Sc. Beauty shop. DRA

Bebele. P. Hirschbein. Idyll. 3m., 4w. Sc. A small white-washed room. BLP

Becky Sharp. O. Conway. Episode from Thackeray's Vanity Fair. 3m., 2w. Sc. Interior. BAK, CONW, MAR1

Bed for three. L. Anderson. 2m., 1w. Sc. Woman's bedroom. ANDE

Bed of roses, A. L. S. Beazley. Comedy. 5m., 3w. Sc. Office of the mayor. PENN

Bedroom suite. C. Morley. 2m., 1w. Sc. Show window of a department store. LON, MORL

Bedside manners. K. Nicholson and S. Behrman. Comedy of convalescence. 2m., 3w. Sc. Interior of a hospital. FREN

Bedtime stories. H. C. Barr. Comedy. 1m., 3w. Sc. Living room. BAK

Bee, The. L. Saunders. 1m., 1w. Sc. Interior of poor apartment. Drama 14: 170-2, Feb. 1924.

Before and after. B. Herford. 1m., 1w. Ladies Home Journal 44: 233, Nov. 1927.

Before Fort Duquesne. A. J. Harnwell. 8m. Sc. Woods on shores of lake in 1755. SAG

J **Beggar and the king, The.** W. Parkhurst. Morality. 3b. Sc. Chamber in the palace. MACG

J **Beggar maid, The.** A. Rowell. Operetta. 4b., 2g., chorus. Sc. In the king's garden. SAO

C **Beginning of the states; an historical playlet for deaf children.** 24b., 6g. Sc. Any stage. Volta R. 33: 53–6, Feb. 1931.

J **Beginning the tale of the Ancient Mariner.** M. A. Butler. 6b. Sc. Roadway. BUT

C **Behind the scenes.** S. Clark. 12c. Sc. House of Santa. PAIN

C **Behind the scenes in Santa Land.** P. Holloway. 2b., 3g., chorus. Sc. Santa's house. BANT

Behold the man. B. Tynan. Based on the story "The unbroken seal" by Francis C. Kelley. 3m., 2w. Sc. Interior. FREN

C **Being a hero.** M. S. Dickson. 4b. Sc. School playground. FAW

C **Being like Washington.** R. L. Jenkins. 12 or more c. Sc. School yard. WHG1

C **"Bell of Atri."** O. J. Roberts. 10b. Prim. Educ. 44: 461–462, Feb. 1927.

C **"Bell of Atri, The."** M. M. Walker. 6b. and others. Sc. Village street. Norm. Inst. 39: 58, Apr. 1930.

Bella Wilfer's return. G. Pertwee and E. Pertwee. Adapted from Dickens. Our mutual friend. 3m., 3w. Sc. Parlor in English home in 1860. PER

C **Belling the cat.** R. Rice. 4c. Sc. Any stage. Amer. Child. 15: 24, 59, Apr. 1930.

J **Beloved, it is morn.** A. C. Rowell. Fantasy. 3b., 2g. Sc. Charming bit of woods. SANP, Poet Lore 36: 101–125, Spring 1925.

Below par. M. Atkins. Farce. 3m., 3w. Sc. Well furnished living room. UNW3

Ben takes a hand. M. E. Roberts. Comedy. 4m., 3w. Sc. Front porch. ELD

Bénéad and the Moor Elves. C. B. Going. 3m., 3w., chorus. Sc. Yard of a peasant cottage in Spain in 16th century. GOIN

Bened: Ktbeuren play, The. D. F. Robinson, adaptor. 16m., 5w. Sc. Stage. HAQ

C **Benjamin and the silver cup.** M. Parsons. 8b., Sc. Room in Jacob's house. PARS

Benjamin Franklin, journeyman. C. D. Mackay. 3m., 2w. Sc. Tavern in Colonial Philadelphia. LAW, WEB

C **Bennie's dream.** C. Barr. 1b., 1g., chorus. Sc. Playroom. BARP

Benny proposes! R. B. Taylor. Comedy. 1m., 3w. Sc. Parlor in small flat. TAYL

C **Ben's box.** M. T. Johnson. 3m., 2g. Sc. Farm living room. Norm. Inst. 34: 68, 70, Jan. 1925.

C **Bernard Palissy, enameller to His Majesty.** A. Stevenson. 10b., 7g., chorus. Sc. Living room in cottage in France in 1533. STEV4

Bernard Shaw reviews his war record, a dialogue between Bernard Shaw and Archibald Henderson. 2m. Sc. Country house in Hertfordshire. Century 109: 291–304, Jan. 1925.

Bernstein tries 'em out. E. Sexton. 9m., 7w. Sc. Manager's office. FREN

Bertha brings home the bacon. H. O. Boggs. 3m., 3w. Sc. Interior. BOGG

C **Best book folks, a play for Children's Book Week, The.** Hackensack, N. J. Eighth grade. Many c. Sc. Any stage. Child Welfare Mag. 21: 77–79, Oct. 1926.

C **Best food for all, The.** Y. Klein and F. Schwarz. Many c. Sc. Any interior. KL

Best hand, The. J. C. Squire. 3m. Sc. Card room of a club. Lond. Mercury 13: 251–4, Jan. 1926.

Best of all ways, The. J. F. Whitely. Romantic adventure. 2m., 2w. Sc. Crossroad in Ireland. NORT

Best policy, The. H. Simpson. Farce. 2m., 3w. Sc. Interior. SIMM

C **Best study, The.** O. V. Roe. 3b., 1g. Sc. School room. FJ

Bet, better, best! F. C. Brunton. 3m., 1w. Sc. Sitting room in a Scottish country town. FREL

Bethlehem. L. Housman. Poetic mystery play. 14m., 1w., chorus. Sc. Interior. BAK, PHIL

Betrayal, The. P. Colum. 3m., 1w. Sc. Inn in an Irish country town in 18th century. FRE3

Betrayal. C. E. Van Norman. 8m., 2w. Sc. Council chamber of chief priests. DR

Betsy Baker. J. M. Morton. Farce. 2m., 2w. Sc. Interior. PENN

Betsy Ross. E. Gibson. 7w. Sc. Workroom in Betsy's shop in Philadelphia. GIB

C **Betsy Ross episode, A.** I. R. Hess. 3b., 3g. Sc. Living room—colonial. Norm. Inst. 39: 48-9, June 1930.

Better man, The. K. Parsons. 3m., 1w. Sc. Sitting room. FIT

J **Better mouse trap, A.** M. Holbrook. 5b., 4g. SANP

Better never than late. L. Diesel. 1m., 3w. Sc. Sitting room. BAK

Better speech fairy, The. O. V. Roe. 4b., 11g. BUG

C **Better speech wins.** K. A. White. 7 char., chorus. Sc. Stage. WH

Betti-attitudes, The. M. B. Miller. 8w. Sc. Interior. ELD

J **Betty, behave!** R. Campion. 3g. Sc. Dormitory room in boarding school. DRA

Betty Blight's style show. W. W. Adair. Burlesque. 9m. Sc. Stage. ELD

C **Betty in bookland.** E. Horner. Any number of c. Sc. Interior. ELD

Betty Jo's want ad. V. B. Edwards. 1m., 2w. Sc. Cabin in mountains of Tennessee. WER

C **Betty Wantitall.** 17 char. Sc. Interior. DRA

Between the devil and the deep she. H. Simpson. Farce. 2m., 2w. Sc. Sitting room. SIMA

Between the soup and the Savoury. G. Jennings. 3w. Sc. Kitchen. MAR3

Between the tides. E. Lewis. 3m., 2w. Sc. Wild part of the British coast in 1918. DE

Between trains. P. Macmanus. 4w. Sc. Waiting room of suburban railway station. DRA

Biddie sweeps out, The. L. F. Thanhouser. Comedy. 2m., 2w. Sc. Dormitory sitting room at a University. YALP

C **Big Claus and little Claus.** A. Stevenson. 9b., 4g., chorus. Sc. Field on the high road. STEV3

Big day in Bulger, A. H. E. McBride. Farce. 3m., 3w. Sc. Interior. PENN

Big depression, A. A. C. Davison. Comedy. 7w. Sc. Dining room. HEL, PENN

Big event, The. A. Cowles. Comedy. 2m., 3w. BAK

Big fleas and little fleas. R. Jeans. 4m., 1w. Sc. Private office. JER

Big house, The. L. Robinson. 8m., 3w. Sc. Drawing room. CANF

Big time at the cross-roads, A. W. Macauley. Comedy. 12m., 9w. Sc. Exterior. PENN

C **Billy's awakening.** M. B. Carpenter. 1b., 3g., 5c. Sc. Sitting room. Norm. Inst. 36: 72-73, Apr. 1927.

Billy's coming. A. L. Kaser. Comedy. 4m., 3w. Sc. Interior. PAIN

Bimbo, the pirate. B. Tarkington. Comedy. 4m., 1w. Sc. Stage with large brass lantern. APPL, LAD, Ladies Home Journal 41: 18-19+, June 1924.

Bina's fortune. E. Hewitt. Comedy. 4w. Sc. Washhouse. WIMA

Bird child, The. L. White. 2m., 3w. Sc. Library in a southern home. LOC

Bird in the hand, A. E. P. Heath. 2m., 2w. Sc. Living room of flat. NICH

Bird strike, a June entertainment, The. Tommy Tiptoe play. H. E. Davis. Many c. Sc. Schoolroom. Delin. 108: 17–18, June 1926.

Birdcatcher, The. S. O'Brien. 4m., 1w. Sc. Interior of cottage in Ireland. SHAF

C **Birds' community sing, The.** J. M. Vandever. 5c. and chorus. Sc. Garden. Norm. Inst. 34: 70, Apr. 1925.

Birds' party, The. D. M. Dore. 11c. Norm. Inst. 33: 64, Apr. 1924.

Birth of God, The. C. Morley. 1m., 1w., 2c. Sc. Interior of stony cave. MORK

J **Birthday ball, The.** M. Woods. 1b., 5g. Sc. Colonial living room. WOW

J **Birthday cake, The.** N. E. Minchin. 32c. Sc. Throne room. MIN

C **Birthday cake, The.** M. G. Parsons. 1b., 2g., 2 chorus groups. Sc. Front parlor. PARR

J **Birthday dance at the red house, The.** M. A. Butler. Adapted from Eliot. Silas Marner. 9b., 5g., chorus. Sc. Parlor. BUT

Birthday gift, The. G. Elton. Farce. 1m., 2w. Sc. Drawing room of a small flat in Mayfair, London. CHA

C **Birthday gift, The.** G. D. Ruthenberg. 4b. Sc. Roof of Royal palace. SAL

J **Birthday of a Prince, The.** E. E. Levinger. 2b., 6g. Sc. Around a Christmas tree. LEVT

C **Birthday of Plum Blossom, The.** M. N. Drake. 3g. Sc. Japanese mats and screens. Norm. Inst. 38: 72, Apr. 1929.

C **Birthday of the Infanta, The.** O. Wilde. 5b., 2g. Sc. Royal balcony overlooking a garden in Spain in 16th century. MOSA, THOM

C **Birthday of the little prince, a Christmas fantasy, The.** P. H. Fowle. 20 or more c. Int. J. of Rel. Educ. 2: 35–37, Nov. 1925.

C **Birthday party, The.** A. P. Sanford. Comedy. 14b., 5g. Sc. Bedroom in a poor little boy's house. SCH4

C **Birthdays come in February.** J. Farrar. 8b., 3g. Sc. High in the mountains. FARR

Bishop's candlesticks, The. N. McKinnel. Adapted from Hugo. Les Miserables. 3m., 2w. Sc. Kitchen of Bishop's cottage in France. HAM, MAR3

Bit o'Dimocrasy, A. B. Ring. 2m., 2w. Sc. A three-cornered kitchen. RIN

Bit o' Laikin', A. D. A. Rowland. Comedy. 2m., 3w. Sc. Kitchen. DE

Bit of brother, A. R. Jeans. Farce. 5m., 2w. Sc. Outside a public house in the East End. JES

Bit of gossip, A. C. Mack. Comedy. 2m., 4w. Sc. Kitchen. DENI

Bit of heather, A. M. L. Davidson. Comedy. 3m., 2w. Sc. Living room. YOU

J **Biter bites and the bitter bits, The.** G. Steuger. 8b. and chorus. Sc. Cave on the Atlantic coast. SAO

Bitter end, The. R. B. Taylor. 2m., 1w. Sc. Country cottage parlor. BAK, PHIJ

Bitter herbs. E. Robbin. 3m., 1w. Sc. Inside of hovel in village in Czechoslovakia. Menorah J. 15: 147–157, Aug. 1928.

Black bottle, The. S. O'Brien. Comedy. 4m., 2w. Sc. Interior of a sailor's house in Ireland. FRE2

C **Black cat entertains, The.** E. E. Preston. Many c. Sc. A moor. Prim. Educ. 45: 112–113+, Oct. 1927.

Black death, The. C. Reznikoff. 12m. Sc. Room in a town in western Europe in the 14th century. REZ, Menorah J. 10: 381–385, Aug.–Sept. 1924.

Black diamonds. C. Anderson and L. Lessig. 3g. Sc. College girl's room. Mis. R. 52: 784–8, Oct. 1929.

J **Black horseman, The.** W. Richardson. 8b., 3g., chorus. Sc. Spacious hall in Castle in East Numidia 204 B. C. RICH

Black Oliver. J. Guiman. 3m. Sc. Room in a lonely farm house. FRE5

J **Black pearl, The.** A. Stevenson. Adapted from Sardou's The Black Pearl. 8b., 2g. Sc. Living room in house in Amsterdam. STEV5

C **Black rose of Halloween.** B. M. Casey. 5b., 4g., chorus. CAS

Black scarab, The. B. Plechner. Comedy. 3m., 1w. Sc. Modern living room. UNW2

Black suitcase, The. A. C. D. Riley. Farce. 7m., 3w. Sc. Suburb of a mid-west American city. RIL

J **Black tents, The.** F. C. Means. 4b., 3g., 3 chorus groups. Sc. Out of doors. FRIE

Black water. L. C. Bailey. Sequel to "Job's kinfolks." 2m., 3w. Sc. Living room of home in mill section in N. Carolina. Carolina Playbook. Mar. 1929.

Blackadder. W. Gibson. Poetic. 3m., 2w. Sc. Horse-coper's camp. GIK

Blackball, The. A. S. Winston. Satire. 7w. Sc. Interior. LON, SV

Blackbeard. P. Greene and E. L. Green. Melodrama. 6m. Sc. Interior in 1718. GREL

Blackbird and the girl, The. J. de Bosschère. Trans. from the French. 3 char. Sc. Out of doors in the early morning. BOSS

C **Blackbird pie.** E. D. Denby. 1b., 6g. Sc. Society for prevention of cruelty to birds. FAW

C **Blackbird pie, The.** C. R. Wise. Any number of char. Sc. Interior. BAK

Blackmailing lady, The. A. Sutro. 3m., 1w. Sc. Interior. FREN

Blarney stone, The. Farce. 1m., 1w. Sc. Out of doors. BAK

Bless our home. O. Kelley. Comedy. 1m., 1w. Sc. Living room in apartment. KEK

C **Blessed bird, The.** S. Young. Fanciful. 1b., 2g. Sc. Nursery. YOUN

Blind. L. Abercrombie. Poetic. 3m., 1w. Sc. Road. ABE

Blind. M. C. Spence. 2m., 1w. Sc. Grove. ELD

Blind, The. E. H. Yates. 1m., 4w. Sc. Eye-clinic of a city-hospital. YATE

J **Blind alley.** M. C. Richmond. 13b. Sc. Courtroom. Ind. Arts Mag. 17: 238–41, July 1928.

J **Blind boy of Bethlehem, The.** K. L. Bates. 1b., 1g., chorus. Sc. Dim curtained alcove. BATE

Blind eyes. L. Housman. 7m., 2w. Sc. Loggia of the market-square of Assisi. HOUS

Blind man, The. M. Flavin. Pantomime. 3m. Sc. Interior. FLA

C **Blind men and the elephant, The.** A. Stevenson. 7b. Sc. In India. STEV2

Blockade. O. H. Dunbar. 3m., 3w. Sc. Rear of a simple frame house in New Hampshire. IS

Blood o' Kings. J. Dransfield. 8m. Sc. Isolated spot near river front. CL, FREN

Blood ties. A. M. Parish. 1m., 3w. Sc. Kitchen. BANN

Blood will tell. S. Kemper. Comedy. 4w. Sc. Drawing room of an old house. FRER

Blood will tell. H. Simpson. Farce. 2m., 1w. Sc. Dining room. SIMO

Bloom on the grape, The. O. W. Firkins. 1m., 2w. Sc. Studio. FIR

Blue and green. A. Kreymborg. Shadow-play. 1m., 1w. Sc. Outdoors with large trees. KR

Blue and green mat of Abdul Hassan; an Arabian adventure, The. C. G. Wilcox. 5m., 2w., chorus. Sc. Interior. APPL

Blue blood. G. D. Johnson. 2m., 3w. Sc. Large kitchen. SHAF

Blue gate, The. J. S. Knapp. 3m., 2w. Sc. A very plain living room. BAK

Blue lupines. L. A. Cuddy. Tragedy. 2m., 1w. Sc. Mountains in California. BANN

Blue moon, The. N. B. Miller. A dream play. 6m., 3w. Sc. Interior. FREN

Blue pitcher, The. T. M. Morrow. 2m., 2w. Sc. Kitchen of an old homestead. CANA

C **Blue policeman, The.** S. Young. Fanciful. 7b., 1g. Sc. Street. YOUN

Blue ribbon hat, The. P. Phelps. 4w. Sc. Interior. FREN

Blue thunder. P. Green. 1m., 3w. Sc. A negro cabin. FRE4

J **Bluebeard.** S. L. Cummins. Burlesque. 3b., 2g. Sc. In the Harem. CUM1

J **Boaster, The.** A. F. Alehin. 3b., 3g. Sc. House. ALD

J **Bob Cratchit's Christmas dinner.** G. Pertwee and E. Pertwee. Adapted from Dickens. Christmas carol. 5b., 3g. PER

J **Bob Sawyer's supper party.** G. Pertwee and E. Pertwee. Adapted from Dickens. Pickwick Papers. 9b., 2g. Sc. English sitting room. PER

Bobbed hair. L. S. Beazley. Comedy. 8w. Sc. School. PENN

C **Bobby meets the good health fairy.** V. R. Lehman. 6b., 1g. Sc. Woods. Prim. Educ. 46: 50+, Sept. 1928.

Boccaccio's untold tale. H. Kemp. 4m., 3w., chorus. Sc. Room in a house in Florence in 1348. KEM

Bogie man, The. Lady Gregory. 2m. Sc. Shed in Ireland. SCH1

Bolt from the blue. H. M. Paull. 2m., 1w. Sc. Comfortable living room in London. 19th Century 94: 843–55, Dec. 1923.

Bombito. C. Stratton. 3m., 2w. Sc. Quarters of matador's family. FREN

C **Bonbon tree, The.** K. L. Bates. Verse. 17c. Sc. North Pole. BAT

C **Book folks' Christmas, The.** S. E. Gosselink. 5b., 6g. Sc. Stage with Christmas tree. BANT

Book of Job, The. J. S. Stevens. 10m., 1w. Sc. In ancient Palestine. BLO

J **Book play for high schools.** M. McAulis, *ed.* 14c. Wilson Bull. 4: 323–7, Mar. 1930.

J **Book revue, The.** M. S. Beagle. Pageant. Any number of c. Sc. School room. SAM, WIMT, World Review 6: 40–41, Feb. 20, 1928.

C **Bookcase, The.** E. I. McClure. 3b., 3g. Sc. Sitting room. Norm. Inst. 38: 76, Nov. 1928.

C **Bookland; an oral language play.** Irving School. St. Paul, Minn. Many c. Sc. Court room. Pop. Educ. 43: 136, Nov. 1925.

C **Books in Sally's cupboard, a play for Good Book Week, The.** M. M. Walker. 13c. Sc. Living room. Prim. Educ. 46: 194–95+, Nov. 1928.

Boomer, The. E. Stoker. 2m., 1w. Sc. At the head of a narrow gorge in Utah. UNU

Boomerang!, The. R. B. Taylor. Comedy. 2m., 3w. Sc. Small sitting room. TAYL

J **Boor, The.** A. Chekhov. Trans. from the Russian. Comedy. 2m., 1w. chorus. Sc. Elegantly furnished drawing room. FARK, GOLD, Golden Book 2: 654–60, Nov. 1925.

Boots. R. Rideout. Tragi-comedy. 4m., 2w. Sc. Kitchen of an inn. APPL

Boots and shoes. J. H. Turner. Farce. 2m., 2w. Sc. Boot and shoe establishment. TURN

Born nurse, A. B. W. Chandler. Farce. 2w. Sc. Interior. BAK

Borrowing trouble. T. S. Denison. Farce. 3m., 5w. Sc. Interior. BUG

Bos'n. D. Kaucher. 3m., 3w. Sc. River bank. Poet Lore 36: 583–99. Winter 1925.

Boss of the King, The. A. L. Rice. Comedy. 4m., 1w. Sc. King's palace. ROH

C J **Boston Tea Party, The.** C. D. Mackay. 9b. Sc. Tavern room in Dec. 1773. WEB

J **Boston Tea Party, The.** F. A. Marsh. 16b., 15g., chorus. Sc. Boston street. MARS

C **Bothersome books.** M. Bitney. 8c. Sc. Schoolroom. BIT

Bottled in bond. G. Hughes. Tragic farce. 2m., 2w. Sc. Interior. APPL

Bound east for Cardiff. E. O'Neill. 11m. Sc. British tramp steamer. CL, ON

Bound for Mexico. B. Hughes. Melodrama. 4m., 1w. Sc. Interior. FREN

C **Bound or free.** C. T. Bryce. 1b., 3g., chorus. Sc. Hall in castle. BRY

C **Box from the attic, The.** F. B. Linsky. 6b., 4g. Sc. Schoolroom during the noon recess. FAX

Box of Myrrh, The. E. Phelps-Jones. 4m., 2w. Sc. In front of the tomb of Jesus. BAK

C **Box of Pandora, The.** J. Merrill and M. Fleming. 5 char. Sc. Room in the home of Epimetheus. MER

Box seats. C. Seiler. 5m., 1w. Sc. Box at the opera. SEH

C **Boy and the echo, The.** M. E. Whitney. Fanciful. 1b., 2g. Sc. Woods. WHI

C **Boy and the nuts, The.** M. E. Whitney. 2b. Sc. The pantry. WHI

Boy bishop, The. P. E. Osgood. 2m., choir. Sc. Inside a church. OSF

Boy comes home, The. A. A. Milne. Comedy. 2m., 3w. Sc. Mid-Victorian room. FREL, MAR1, MILN

C **Boy heroes of the Bible.** M. Parsons. 7b. Sc. Living room. PARS

C **Boy Hiawatha, The.** V. Lehman. 1b., 1g., others. Sc. A wood. Prim. Educ. 33: 470–71, Sept. 1925.

J **Boy in blue, The.** O. Price. 4b., 4g. Sc. Corner of drawing room in a Colonial mansion. BAK, SCH3

C J **Boy on the meadow.** E. Van der Veer. 1b., 4g. Sc. Interior of a peasant's hut in Germany during the Middle Ages. FREN, SCH1, SHA

C **Boy they turned away, The.** M. Pipes. 22c. Sc. Interior. BAK, DRA

J **Boy wanted.** L. C. Van Derveer. 6b. Sc. Store door. VAN

Boy who discovered Easter, The. E. McFadden. 5m., 1w. Sc. Study. FREN

C **Boy who hated trees, The.** M. E. Whitney. 2b., 3g., chorus. 5 scenes. WHI

C **Boy who painted cats, The.** 7b., 1g. Sc. Japanese screens. Prim. Educ. 44: 801–3, June 1927.

C **Boy who was kind.** M. Bitney. 3b., 2g. Sc. Interior. BIT

J **Boy who went, The.** L. Y. Erskine. 16b. Sc. In a cabin. PENN

J **Boy without a flag, The.** A. Curtis. 3b., 2g. Sc. Sitting room. CURT

C **Boyhood Pt. I. Land of desires.** D. A. Lord. 17b. and chorus. Sc. Interior. LOO

C **Boyhood Pt. I. Land of dreads.** D. A. Lord. 11b., chorus. Sc. Courtroom of Judge Examination. LOO

C **Boyhood. Pt. I. Land of dreams.** D. A. Lord. 7b., chorus. LOO

C **Boys who knew Columbus.** M. B. Carpenter. 4b. Sc. Street scene in Spain. Prim. Educ. 45: 558, Mar. 1928.

Brace of sixes, A. J. A. Davitt. 2m., 1w. Sc. Interior. FREN

Brain waves. L. Phillips. Comedy. 1m., 2w. Sc. Small reception room in a large hotel. BAK

Brains. M. Flavin. 3m. Sc. Interior. FLA

J **Brand, The.** F. I. Berkley-Boone. 3b. Sc. Settler's cabin in the Dakotas. DAZ

Brandywine. M. Holbrook. 5m. Sc. Yard of a lonely farmhouse. SAG

Brass bandit, The. P. Dickey. 5m., 1w. Sc. Wells-Fargo express office in Arizona. FREN

Bread. F. Eastman. 2m., 4w. Sc. Living room of a farm home. CL, DES, EAS, FREN, Christian Cent. 45: 633–6, May 17, 1928.

J **Breakfast.** G. W. Cook. Farce. 2b., 4g. Sc. Dining room at breakfast time. DAZ

Breakfast breeze, A. W. Macfarlane. Farce. 1m., 3w. Sc. Around breakfast table. FREP

Breakfast for two. C. Lindsay. Farce. 1m., 1w. Sc. Dining room. PENN

Breakfast in bed. E. St. V. Millay. Satire. 1m., 1w. Sc. A bedroom. MIK

Breaking of the calm, The. D. Totheroh. 5m., 1w. Sc. Deck of a ship. FREN, TOT

C **Bricks.** C. Barr. 23b., 7g., chorus. Sc. A library in a house. BARP

Bride, The. H. Ford. Comedy. 2m., 2w. Sc. Interior. FREN

Bride and gloom. A. A. Hoffman. Farce. 3m., 2w. Sc. Salon of a steamer. BAK

Bride and the burglar, The. F. L. Speare. Comedy. 2m., 1w. Sc. Room in a home in a suburban town. FREN

Bride feast, The. L. Housmann. 8m., 2w. Sc. A broad arched loggia opening on a garden. HOUS

Bride maid, The. S. M. Armstrong. Farce. 3m., 3w. Sc. Living room. HEL

Bridegroom, The. L. Biro. 5m., 6w. Sc. Interior. SHAT

Bridemaide, The. S. M. Armstrong. Farce. 3m., 3w. Sc. Interior. PENN

Bride's orders, The. B. Herford. 2w. Ladies Home Journal 44: 157, July 1927.

Bridge as the ladies play it. W. T. Gregory. Comedy. 6w. Sc. Parlor. FREN

Brief life. L. Housman. 8m., 2w. Sc. Outside the walls of Assisi. HOUS

Brighter Dartmoor. H. C. Sargent. Farce. 5m., 2w. Sc. A large cell. SARB

Bringers of gifts. Pageant. 11 char., chorus. Sc. Manger. WOM

Bringers of gifts, a Christmas pageant. M. L. McMillan. 35m. and others. Pict. R. 30: 18–19, Dec. 1928.

J **Bringing up nine.** M. K. Reely. 3b., 5g. Sc. Pleasant sitting room of home on Wisconsin farm. SAM

Brink of silence, The. E. E. Galbraith. 4m. Sc. Inside a log house on a rocky island in the Antartic. CLS, ROS9, SMI

British Museum's vacation, The. W. R. H. Trowbridge. Many c. Sc. Reading room of British Museum. Cornhill 58: 195–205, Feb. 1925.

C **Broadcast from Bookland.** A. E. Allen. 14 or more char. Sc. Interior with radio. FAW

J **Broadcast KDKA; the book review; University of Pittsburgh studio.** E. Collette. Many c. Eng. J. 19: 313–18, Apr. 1930.

Broke. I. S. Turgenev. Comedy. 10m., 1w. Sc. A well furnished room. TURG

Broken banjo, The. W. Richardson. 4m., 1w. Sc. Dining room in negro tenement. LOC

Broken bridges. S. J. Levy. Farce. 4m., 3w. Sc. Small room adjoining the operating room in hospital. LEU

Broken bridges. H. Wimbury. 4m., 2w. Sc. On the Malayan coast. DE

Broken commandment, The. J. C. McMullen. 4m., 3w. Sc. Interior. BAK

Broken pines. C. Hilton. 5m., 1w. Sc. White-washed kitchen of farmhouse. Poet Lore 40: 461–473, Autumn 1929.

Bronze bride, The. B. Inge and C. Chupét. 2m., 3w., chorus. Sc. Home in a town in Switzerland in 1798. ING

Brooding calves. H. Sachs. A shrovetide play. Trans. from the German by J. Krumpelmann. 2m., 1w. Poet Lore 38: 435–46, Autumn 1927.

Brother Bill. A. Kreymborg. Farce. 1m., 1w. Sc. The sofa of a Harlem parlor. FRE4, IS, Theatre Arts M. 11: 299–306, Apr. 1927.

Brother Elias. L. Housman. 6m. Sc. A room adjoining the refectory. HOUS

Brother Fire. T. Wilder. Poetic. 1m., 2w. Sc. Hut in the mountains of northern Italy. WILZ

Brother India. E. Field. 3m., 1w. Sc. Office of hospital in India. PR

Brother Juniper. L. Housman. 4m., chorus. Sc. In the consistory. HOUS

Brother Musicians. A. P. Sanford. Comedy. 6m., 3 chorus groups. Sc. 1 Street outside an inn. 2 Street outside a police station. SCH4

Brother Sin. L. Housman. 3m. Sc. A large cell in a monastery. HOUS

Brother Sun. L. Housman. 4m. Sc. Camp of the Saracens. HOUS

Brother Wolf. L. Housman. 7m. Sc. Rocky defile. HAMA, HOUS

Brotherhood. W. H. Wells. Dialect. 9m. Sc. Old wooden dock in New York. FOR4

Brothers. W. L. Bissell. 4m., 1w. Sc. Room in a farmhouse. BIS

Brothers. D. G. King. 3m. Sc. Luxuriously furnished room. IN

Brothers. J. C. McMullen. 3m. Sc. Living room. BAK

Brothers. A. Raisen. Comedy. 8m., 1w. Sc. Room off a long corridor. BLP, SHAF

Brothers in arms. M. Denison. 3m., 1w. Sc. Hunting camp in the backwoods. CANB, DEL, SHAT

C **Brownies' colors, The.** E. B. Margerum. Many c. Sc. Dull brown scene with rocks. Norm. Inst. 33 : 56–57, Sept. 1924.

C **Brownie's dream, The.** V. P. Matthias. A play for Girl Scouts. 3b., 19g. Sc. Stage. FREN

Browns' Merry Christmas, The. M. Irish. Comedy. 3m., 5w. Sc. Living room. BECK

C **Bruin's inn.** A. Townsend. 8b., 1g., 2 chorus groups. Sc. Woods. SAL

Bruiser's election, The. S. Schofield. Farce. 5m., 2w. Sc. Living room. LAB

Budapest salesman should not read French illustrated magazines, A. B. Szenes. Comedy. 10m., 3w. Sc. Modest suburban apartment in Budapest. SHAF

Budding star, A. H. Simpson. Farce. 2m., 1w. Sc. Private office of theatrical manager. SIMN

Budget ghost, The. M. L. Carr. 13 char. Sc. Boarding house. WOM

Bug man, The. K. Nicholson. 1m., 2w. Sc. A model kitchen. NICG

Bugginses' picnic. M. Constanduros and M. Hogan. 1m., 2w., 2c. Sc. Out of doors. FREL

Builders, The. L. Housman. 9m., 1w., chorus. Sc. Inner walls of a small ruined chapel. HOUS

C **Building a character.** S. S. Stevens. 15c. Sc. Any home or school. LUT

Bumblepuppy. J. W. Rogers. 3m. Sc. Shade trees near farmhouse. CL, IS, SHAF, Theatre Arts Mag. 10 : 604–12, Sept. 1926.

C **Bumbo and Scumbo and Blinko.** M. Jagendorf. 3b., 1g. Sc. Forest. JAO

Bumbo the clown. L. Gibson. Fantasy. 3m., 1w. Sc. Bedroom. SHAF

Bunney's blunder. H. Collett. Farce. 2m., 3w. Sc. Interior. BAK

J **Bunnie's Easter quiz, The.** F. Cavanah. 7b., 8g. Sc. Bunny Schoolhouse. CAV

Burglar, The. F. C. Gardner. 1m., 1w. Sc. Interior. GAQ

Burglar-proof. M. Wilson. Comedy. 2m., 2w. Sc. Living room. PENN

Burglars. R. Julian. Comedy. 2m., 2w. Sc. Parlor. DRA

Burglars at Mrs. Day's, The. C. J. Denton. Farce. 6w. Sc. Home interior. DENT

Burial of Alleluia, The. P. E. Osgood. 2m., 2 choirs, chorus. Sc. Church inside or outside in 11th century. OSF

Burning her alive. S. Sudzuki. Trans. from the Japanese. 3m., 2w. Sc. Interior of Japanese studio. IW

Bush queer. C. Habberstad. 2m., 1w. Sc. Interior of hut. COL5

Bushido. T. Idzumo. Drama of Japan. 5m., 3w., 1b. 4 chorus groups. Sc. Japanese schoolroom. LAW

Business a la mode. M. A. Chaffee. Comedy. 3m., 8w. Sc. Modern office. BUG

Business in 2030 A. D. N. Balch. Fantasy. 3m., 1w. Sc. Laboratory. BAL

Business is business. E. Carroll. Comedy skit. 5m., 2w. Sc. A bedroom. NICR

Busy bee, The. H. C. Sargent. Farce. 2m., 2w. Sc. English interior. SARB

But is it art? D. Titheradge. Farce. 6m., 1w. Sc. Street. TITU

But this is different. R. Cook. Comedy farce. 3m., 6w. Sc. Interior. FIT

C **Butterfly, The.** P. Beard. 1b., 5g. Sc. Stage with dark green curtain. BEA

Butterfly girl and mirage boy. H. Alexander. Music. 1m., 2w. Sc. Interior or exterior. ALE

C **Butterfly wings.** O. Price. 11 char. Sc. A glade in Fairyland. BAK

Buying a tie. R. Jean. Farce. 2m. Sc. Hosiery shop. JEP

Buying Biddy. A. Bartle. Comedy. 4m., 3w. Sc. Vicar's study. DE

Buying culture. C. A. Wood. Comedy. 1m., 2w. Sc. Cheap, gaudy living room in Iowa. BOST

By judgment of court. L. Pirandello. Trans. from the Italian. 5m., 1w. Sc. Room of a judge in Sicily. PIR

C **By radio.** D. A. Lord. 11b., chorus. Sc. In a frame. LOQ

By the beard of the prophet. J. Koven. 13m. Sc. A Holy City in the Orient. KOV

By the roadside. A. C. Darlington. 5w. Sc. Beside a well in ancient. Palestine. DAQ

By unanimous vote. L. Simpson. 5m., 3w., 4c. Sc. Interior. 2 scenes. ELD

Byzantine afternoon, A. W. Fernand. Trans. by Clarence Stratton. 4m., 3w. Sc. Private room. FER

C

C.C., a tragedy. M. C. Boatright. 7m., 1w., others. Sc. Outdoor scene in southwest. Poet Lore 41: 124–31, Spring 1930.

Cabaret drama, A. R. Jeans. Farce. 2m., 2w. Sc. Library in a home. JES

Cabbages. E. Staadt. Cartoon. 3m., 4w. Sc. Living room. NORT

CJ **Cabbages and kings.** R. Fylerman. 8b., 3g. Sc. Room in a palace. FYL, PHIL

Cackle, cackle, cackle. M. T. Johnson. 2m., 2w. Sc. Chicken yard. JOHD

Cadenza on a popular theme. W. A. Percy. 1m., 1w. Sc. Garden of Portofino, Southwest Review 13: 303–306, Apr. 1928.

Cage, The. P. Johnson. 1m., 3w. Sc. Living room of cottage in slum district of a large industrial town. JOHF

Cain and Abel. W. F. Manley. Radio version. 4m., 1w. Sc. On the mountain. MAN

Cajun, The. A. J. Carver. 4m., 2w. Sc. Front room in Cajun home in swamps of Louisiana. CL, FREN

Calamity howler, The. R. Eskil. Comedy. 3m., 4w. Sc. Public room of tourist shack. DENI

Caleb Stone's death watch. M. Flavin. Satire. 6m., 4w. Sc. Bedroom. FLA, FREN, Drama 14: 143–147, Jan. 1924.

C **Calendar for poets' birthdays, A.** M. A. Niemeier. 10b. or g. Sc. The woods. NIEM

J **Calendar of joyful saints, A.** C. D. Mackay. 37c., chorus. Sc. Narrow strip of stage. MACH

Calf that laid the golden eggs, The. B. Hughes. Farce. 1m., 6w. Sc. Living room. HUO

J **Calico land.** 3m., 1w., 4b., 4g., chorus. Sc. Interior. BAK

Call, The. C. F. Boxer. 4m., 1w. Sc. Kitchen of farmhouse. FREL, FREN

Call, The. Mrs. A. Stallard. 8m., 1w. Sc. Outside the Monastery of old Melrose in 651 A. D. STAL

Call of the campus, The. R. L. Melville. Comedy. 3m., 2w. Sc. Sitting room. BANN

C **Call of the church, The.** S. J. Wilson. 15c. or more. Int. J. of Rel. Educ. 1: 24–25, Sept. 1925.

Call of the ninth wave, The. L. S. Jast. Verse. 1m., 1w. Sc. Shore looking towards the sea. JAS

C **Call of the spring fairies, an Arbor Day play for fourth year children, The.** S. Millimet. Many c. Prim. Educ. 45: 628, 662+, Apr. 1928.

Calvary. W. B. Yeats. Mask play. 9m. Sc. Bare place. YE

Calypso. M. Baring. 3m., 1w. Sc. Grotto in Island of Ogygia. Lond. Mercury 18: 245–48, July 1928.

Calypso. H. Kemp. 2m., 1w. Sc. At the mouth of a Grotto in the Homeric age. KEM

Camberley triangle, The. A. A. Milne. Comedy. 2m., 1w. Sc. Drawing room. FREL, FREN

J **Camillus and the schoolmaster.** M. R. Hofer. 2b., 1g., 3 chorus groups. Sc. Any stage. HOF

Campaigner, The. A. N. Lewis. Comedy. 5w. Sc. Interior. PAIN

Campbell of Kilmhor. J. A. Ferguson. 4m., 2w. Sc. Interior of a lonely cottage after the rising of '45. MAR1

Campden wonder, The. J. Masefield. 4m., 2w. Sc. Kitchen. MASF

J **Campus, The.** C. O. Lyon. 9 char. Sc. A park with flowers. AU

Can prohibition succeed? A Socratic dialogue. H. G. Leach, ed. 6m. Forum 81: 257–262, May 1929.

Can we make our children behave? A Socratic dialogue. John B. Watson vs. Will Durant. H. G. Leach, ed. 5m. Forum 82: 346–350, Dec. 1929.

Canary, The. J. H. Whitehouse. 4m., 1w. Sc. St. Dunstan's Home for the Blind. Poet Lore 37: 589–596, Winter 1926

Candid critics. A. Marshall. 1m., 4w. Sc. Library. Bookman 58: 410–412, Dec. 1923.

Candidate for Trepagny, The. M. Sand. Comedy. 14m., 4w., chorus. Sc. Courtyard of an inn. MACU

Can't you listen a moment? B. E. Palmer. 4m., 3w. Sc. Interior. ELD

C **Canterbury pilgryms: a playlet based on Chaucer's prologue.** High School Juniors of Dubuque, Iowa. Many c. Sc. Tabarde Inne, Southwerk, England. Pop. Educ. 42: 280–8, Jan. 1925.

J **Canticles of Mary, The.** M. D. Cooper. Mystery play. 11b., 2g., chorus. Sc. Room in the house of the Beloved disciple at Jerusalem. CEN

Captain, The. H. C. G. Stevens. 3m., 1w. Sc. Through open French windows, a garden. STET

Captain Cook and the widow. S. Ready. Comedy. 3m., 2w. Sc. Kitchen in English cottage. DE

J **Captain Lincoln's way.** R. Woodman. 6b., chorus. Sc. A military camp in northern Illinois. SAO

Captain Washington. O. W. Garvey. 5m. Sc. Tent on battle field in 1755. SAG

J **Captain's confession, A.** H. W. Githens. 7b., 3g., chorus. Sc. Home in Caesarea. GITH

Captive Israel. C. Reznikoff. 14m., 4w. Sc. Jerusalem 30 B. C. REZ, Menorah J. 10: 38–45, Feb. 1924.

J **Captive maid, A.** H. W. Githens. 6b., 2g. Sc. Naaman's home. GIT

C **Captive princess, The.** A. M. Mitchell. 9 char. Sc. Interior. FIT

C **Capture of Major André, The.** F. O'Ryan and A. W. O'Ryan. 4b. Sc. Open country in 1780. ORY

Car of time, The. R. Tagore. Many char. Sc. Roadside. Modern Review 35: 203–208, Feb. 1924.

J **Caractacus and the Romans.** M. R. Hofer. 10b., 2g., 2 chorus groups. Sc. Simple setting. HOF

Cardinal Mercier's hands, a dialogue in verse. J. W. Lynch. 2m. Sc. Garden behind the Archepiscopal residence. Cath. World 128: 128: 22–26, Oct. 1928.

C **Careful city's plans for safety for all.** J. Keenan. 17b., 12g., others. Sc. Mayor's office. Prim. Educ. 44: 120–123, Oct. 1926.

C **Carelessness.** A. H. Grant. 7b., 1g. Norm. Inst. 35: 84, Oct. 1926.

C **Carelessness.** I. S. Turgenev. Comedy. 5m., 2w. Sc. Street. TURG

Carnival, or Mardi Gras in New Orleans. Comedy. 8w. Sc. Interior. DRA

Carota, La. M. E. Stahl. 3m. Sc. Attic room. JOHM

C **Carrie, the courteous cook.** E. Preston. 20c., chorus. Sc. Yard. PRES

Carrying out a theory. W. Spencer. Farce. 4m., 1w. Sc. Hotel. PENN

C **Cart-load of kettles, A.** V. Olcott. 3b., 2g. Sc. Kitchen in rural England. OLC

Carved woman. H. B. Alexander. Play based on an American Indian myth on the Orpheus and Eurydice theme. Blank verse. 2m., 1w. Sc. Out of doors about the statue of the carved woman. ALE, COH

Case of suspension, A. L. L. Wilson. Comedy. 5m., 5w. Sc. Dormitory room. BUG, ELD

Case of Teresa, The. G. John. 2m., 3w. Sc. Drawing room. JOH

Cash—$2000. N. G. Chatterton. 2m., 2w. Sc. Dining room of cheap flat. Drama 15: 78–80, Jan. 1925.

Casino gardens, The. K. Nicholson. 6m. Sc. Orchestral platform. NICG

Castaway; adapted from the story of that title by W. W. Jacobs. W. W. Jacobs and H. C. Sargent. Farce. 2m., 2w. Sc. Interior. FREN

Casualties. M. Flavin. 2m., 1w. Sc. Interior. FLA

Cat, The. S. Cowan. 3m., 3w. Sc. Interior of a Japanese house. COW

Cat and the moon, a play for dancers, The. W. B. Yeats. 5m. Sc. Any stage. Dial 77: 23–30, July 1924.

C **Cat and the mouse, The.** A. Stevenson. 1b., 2g. Sc. A garret. STEV3

J **Cat at school, A.** H. O. Boggs. 6b., 6g. Sc. Classroom. BOGH

Cat comes back, The. C. Habberstad. Comedy. 3m., 1w. Sc. Kitchen. COL4

Cat fear. M. N. Gleason. 2w., 2m. Comedy. Sc. Garden. WOM

C **Cat that waited, The.** A. Stevenson. 3 char. Sc. A garden. STEV1

Cat-boat, The. P. Mackaye. Fantasy. 2m., 2w. Sc. Workshop. MACM

Cataclysterium's medicine. L. E. Duranty. 3m., 1w. Sc. Bedroom. MACU

Catching the male. R. Jeans. Farce. 1m., 1w. Sc. Front-cloth scene. JEA

Cathedral clock, The. L. J. Smith. 4m., 1w. Sc. Room in house in old Dantzig in the 15th century. EM

Catherine explains. L. Crites. 6w. Sc. Living room. ELD

Catherine Parr or Alexander's horse. M. Baring. Diminutive comedy. 1m., 1w. Sc. Over the breakfast table. JOHP, PRIE

Cathleen ni Houlihan. W. B. Yeats. Symbolic. 3m., 2w. Sc. Interior of cottage in Ireland in 1798. MOSR, MOSS, YEA

Caught in the act. R. Jeans. Farce. 3m., 2w. Sc. Interior. JER

J **Cavalier.** O. M. Price. 4b., 2g., chorus. Sc. Inaugural Ball, N. Y. 1789. PRI

C **Celebrating Christmas in Mother Goose land.** S. B. Carter. 4b., 6g., others. Sc. Christmas tree. Norm. Inst. 33: 58, Dec. 1923.

Centaurs. T. Wilder. 2m., 1w. Sc. In a theatre. WILZ, Bermondsey Book 6: 8–10, Dec.–Feb. 1928-9.

Chair of evil, an experiment in character building, a dialogue. 5m., 1w. Forum 84: 116–121, Aug. 1930.

Chances. W. Lindsay, *pseud.* 5m. Sc. Somewhere in the depths of the Brazilian forest. JOHB

Change of heart, A. N. W. Walter. 5m., 1w. Sc. Modern business office. CAT1

C **Change of heart, A.** K. A. White. 2b. Sc. Interior. WH

C **Change of mind, A.** N. Flaurier. 2b., 2g. Sc. Interior. FIV

Change of mind, A. R. Spiers. 1m., 2w. Sc. Living room. FRE6, Drama 20: 13–14, Oct. 1929.

Change-house, The. J. Brandane (Dr. John MacIntyre). 5m., 2w. Sc. Interior of the change-house. COH

Changing Emma's mind. A. A. Keen. Comedy. 3w. Sc. Living room. FIT

Changing places. I. L. Ehrlich. Comedy. 2m., 2w. Sc. Dining room. FRE3

Chapter, The. L. Housman. 8m., chorus. Sc. Hill slope under the walls of Assisi. HOUS

Charity begins at home. K. Asbrand. 3m., 4w. Sc. Living room. FIT

Charivari. N. B. Stephens. 3m., 2w. Sc. Drawing room in New Orleans in 1804. IS, Theatre Arts Mag. 12: 814–22, Nov. 1928.

Charles! Charles! L. Housman. 8m. Sc. Interior. HOT, 19th Cent. 105: 127–41, Jan. 1929.

Charles, the conqueror. M. Irish. 4m., 4w. Sc. Living room. IR

Charlotte's ruse. L. R. Phillips. Comedy. 2m., 2w. Sc. Interior. BAK

Chased lady, The. R. Welty. Comedy. 1m., 2w. Sc. Sitting room. FREN

Chatterton. C. Reznikoff. 9m., 9w. Sc. Tombs within a church. REZ

J **Cheaters.** H. O. Boggs. 3b. Sc. On floor. BOGG

Chee-Chee. L. Pirandello. Trans. from the Italian. Farce. 3m., 1w. Sc. Room in first class hotel. PIR

J **Chemistry saves the day.** A. Bateman. 3m., 3w. Sc. Shabby dining room. J. Chem. Ed. 7: 164–6, Jan. 1930.

Cherry Blossoms River, The. C. C. Clements, adaptor. 3m., 1w., chorus. Poetic. Sc. A Japanese street at dusk. SHAT

Cherry pie. E. Arnold. 2m., 2w. Sc. Farmhouse. ELD

Cherry reads the message. Mrs. C. F. Johnston. 5w. Sc. Living room in Philadelphia in 1772. ELD

Cherry special. B. H. McNeil. 1m., 6w. Sc. Beauty shop. BAK, Players Mag. 5: 18–21, Nov.–Dec. 1928.

C **Chief Black Hawk.** C. F. Wells. 9b. Sc. Indian camp in the forest. SAO

C **Chief's Thanksgiving invitation, The.** F. M. Nelson. 5b., 4g., chorus. ELD

Child born at the plough. S. Kaye-Smith. 17m., 7w. Sc. Lambing hut. KAY

C **Child Handel, a play written by the art class, The.** *In* E. R. Taylor. Making picture study creative. Amer. Childhood 13: 15–18, Jan. 1928.

Child in Flanders, The. C. Hamilton. Nativity play. 8m., 2w., 1b. Prologue vision has 4m., 1b. Sc. 1 Cottage a few miles behind the trenches. Sc. 2 Christmas Eve during the war. MAR2

Child in the midst, The. M. T. Applegarth. 39 char. Sc. Platform. APN

J **Child of the frontier, A.** E. E. Levinger. 3w. Sc. Room in log dwelling. APPL, SHAB

J **Child who saw Santa Claus, The.** B. White. 4b., 2g. Sc. Interior. BAK, DRA

Childe Roland to the dark tower came. T. Wilder. 1m., 1w. Sc. A great marsh. WILZ

Children, The. G. H. Ruthenburg. 2w., 1m. Sc. Drab sitting room. Drama 15: 131–132, Mar. 1925.

C **Children decide, The.** G. Lloyd. 35c. Sc. Winter in the woods. LL

Children of Eve, The. E. U. Ouless, translator. Trans. from the German. 11m., 1w. Sc. Interior. OULE

C **Children of the Civil War.** W. Rice. 4b., 4g. Sc. Clearing in a wood. SAL

C **Children's bookshelf, The.** P. Beard. 3b., 2g. Sc. Children's playroom. BEA, BECK

J **Children's crusade, The.** F. Chesterton. 14b., 4g. Sc. Castle. CHES

C **Children's king, The.** E. Edland. 5b., 5g., chorus. Sc. Flower garden. EDL

C **Chimney sweeps' holiday.** R. Field. 6b., chorus. Sc. Library of Greenswood Hall. FIE

Chin-Chin Chinaman. P. Walsh. Thriller. 2m., 1w. Sc. Interior. FREL

Chinese clippers, The. O. D. Adams. Comedy. 2m., 1w. Sc. Interior. BANN

Chinese water wheel, The. E. H. Strachan. 3m., 2w. Sc. Combination dining and living room in northern California. FRE6, Drama 21: 15–16+, Oct. 1930.

Chintamani. G. C. Ghose. Trans. by Mukerji. 10m., 4w., 4c. Sc. In front of house in Bengal. SHAT

Chip woman's fortune, The. W. Richardson. 4m., 3w. Sc. Plain dining room of poor colored family. SHAF

Choice, The. J. Emerson. 2m., 2w. Sc. Interior of the Washington home at Pine Grove. SAG

J **Choice of Coriolanus, The.** M. R. Hofer. 2b., 2g., 9 chorus groups. Sc. Set stage. HOF

Choice of Giannetta, The. A. E. Applegate. 4m., 1w., others. Sc. Hallway of Florentine palace. 1500 A.D. Poet Lore 36: 405-414, Autumn 1925.

C **Choosing a doll.** A. W. Norton. 11b., 17g. Sc. Stage. CJ

C **Choosing a statue for Lincoln Park, Chicago.** M. A. Niemeier. 11b., 7g. Sc. Sculptor's studio. NIE, NIEM

J **Choosing the way.** Sister of St. Joseph. 11g. Sc. Stage. ELD

Christ is born in Bethlehem. V. R. Sutton. 16 char. Sc. Stage all dark with blue hangings. WOM

Christian slave, A. H. K. Russell. 4m., 1w. c. Room in the palace of the caliph. COO

J **Christmas angel, The.** M. Woods. 3b., 3g. Sc. Winter forest. WOW

Christmas at Crane's corners. M. Irish. 4m., 3w. Sc. Living room in a farm house. BUG

Christmas at Dinky flats. M. Irish. 4m., 6w. Sc. Interior. BECK

C **Christmas at Finnegan's flat.** S. S. Tibbals. Comedy. Any number of c. Sc. Interior. BECK

Christmas at Gooseberry Glen. S. S. Tibbals. 8m., 8w. Sc. Sitting room. ELD

Christmas at Joyville Junction. M. Irish. 4m., 5w. Sc. Farmhouse. BECK

J **Christmas at McCarthy's.** E. F. Guptill. 11b., 10g. Sc. Interior. PAIN

J **Christmas at mother's.** A. Curtis. 3m., 7w. Sc. Interior. BAK, DRA

C **Christmas at Old Lady's Shoe.** K. R. Coontz. 7b., 4g. Sc. Inside the shoe. ELD

J **Christmas at Piney Ridge.** G. York. 4b., 4g. Sc. Interior. ELD

C **Christmas at Stebbinses'.** M. Irish. Comedy. 5b., 5g. Sc. Farmhouse. BECK

Christmas at the old folks' home. 10w. Sc. Old folks' home. BAK

C **Christmas at Timothy Corners.** W. N. Bugbee and M. Irish. 6b., 6g. Sc. Country schoolroom. BUG, BUGT

C **Christmas ballad to be acted in pantomime, A.** F. S. Page. Several c. Woman's Home Companion 54: 51, Dec. 1927.

C **Christmas book, A.** M. E. Phipps and M. Van Horn. Tableaus with dancing. 17c., chorus. Sc. Living room. WOM

C **Christmas card, The.** V. D. Amico. 2b., 6g. Sc. Stage. BAI, Amer. Childhood 13: 35, 78, 80, Dec. 1927.

J **Christmas carol, A.** C. Dickens. Dramatized by Geo. M. Baker. 6m., 3w. Sc. Interior. BAK

Christmas carol, A. C. Dickens. Dramatized by Frank Shay. 26m., 6w. Sc. Stage. SHA

C **Christmas carol come to life, A.** G. H. Bevans. Many c. Woman's Home ompanion 53: 72, Dec. 1926.

C **Christmas contributions.** B. M. Casey. 10b. Sc. Club room. CASE

Christmas cradle, The. E. W. Bates. 2m., 2w., chorus. Sc. Interior of a peasant's cottage. BAK

J **Christmas dinner, The.** A. Cortes. 4m., 4w. Sc. Interior. BAK

C **Christmas dolls for sale.** B. M. Casey. 2b., 8g. Sc. Office of factory. CASE

C **Christmas dream, A.** M. A. Hayes. 30c., chorus. Sc. Room with fireplace. BAI, Amer. Childhood 14: 24-25, 65-67, Dec. 1928.

Christmas eve. S. O'Brien. 4m., 3w. Sc. Interior of Irish cottage. FRE4, SHA

Christmas eve at the Poor Farm. L. P. Martin. 7w. Sc. Living room. BUG

Christmas eve dream, A. J. Shively. 6m., 2w. Sc. Living room. DRA

C **Christmas eve in a shoe.** E. E. Preston. Any no. of c. Sc. In a shoe. PRE

C **Christmas eve in Fairyland.** L. H. Vanderveer. 25c. Sc. Court of Queen Titania. BUG

C **Christmas eve in Santa's workshop.** F. J. Martin. 14c. Sc. Stage. WHG1

C **Christmas eve in the land of Nod.** E. Spencer. Many c. Sc. Child's bedroom. Norm. Inst. 34: 74, Dec. 1924.

Christmas eve on Pine Knob. M. Irish. 3m., 3w. Sc. Cabin on a mountainside. CAT1

J **Christmas eve on the trolley car.** A. W. Norton. Any no. of c. Sc. A street car. CJ

J **Christmas eve prince, The.** R. Rice. 6b., 1g. Sc. Peasant home in in the middle ages. CJ

C **Christmas eve visitor, A.** E. Spencer. Many c. Sc. Fireplace. Prim. Educ. 33: 704, Dec. 1925.

C **Christmas exiles.** B. M. Casey. 8g. Sc. Room in a boarding school. CASE

C **Christmas flowers, The.** E. W. Bates. Mystery play for children. 20c. Sc. Platform. BAK

J **Christmas ghost, The.** M. Woods. 6g. Sc. Interior. BAK, DRA

C **Christmas gift, The.** F. Chesterton. 5b., 5g. CHES

C **Christmas gifts.** M. Hunter. Many c. Sc. Christmas tree. Norm. Inst. 35: 67–8, Dec. 1925.

Christmas "good turn," The. L. C. Van Derveer. 8b., Sc. Any interior, VAN

CJ **Christmas guest, The.** C. D. Mackay. 6g., 2b. Sc. Interior. DRA, THOM

Christmas highwayman, A. D. Stevens. 3m., 1w., 2b., 4g. Sc. Sitting-room. BAK

C **Christmas idea, The.** 5g. Sc. Interior. DRA

C **Christmas in America.** E. Spencer. Many c. Sc. Living room. Norm. Inst. 37: 56–8, Dec. 1927.

C **Christmas in many lands.** A. M. Skinner. 14c. Sc. Living room of German cottage. SK, WHG1

C **Christmas in many lands.** 1b., 2g., others. Sc. Home in America. Prim. Educ. 32: 674, 676, Dec. 1924.

Christmas in the flop house. J. A. Carter. 5m. Sc. Lobby of lodging house in Philadelphia. DRA

C **Christmas in the mouse-hole.** N. A. Smith. 6c. Sc. A pantry. Amer. Childhood 15: 30–1+, Dec. 1929.

C **Christmas joke, A.** A. Clark. 4b. Sc. Christmas tree. CJ

C **Christmas journey, A.** M. A. Enloe. 3b., 2g. Sc. Street. ENL

C **Christmas language project, A.** A. Morizot. Many c. Sc. Room in home of Santa Claus. Prim. Educ. 44: 320+, Dec. 1926.

C **Christmas lesson, A.** M. E. Whitney. Fairy play. 3b., 4g. Sc. 1 Tom's room. Sc. 2 Tom's schoolroom. Sc. 3 Tom's room. Sc. 4 The Kelly living room. WHI

Christmas magic. A. B. Curtis. Comedy. 3w., 3g. Sc. Living room. BANN

Christmas memories. M. Mackendrick. 8w., 3m. Sc. Classroom. MACS

C **Christmas message, The.** M. G. Parsons. 14c. chorus. Sc. Children's room. PARR

C **Christmas miracle, A.** A. H. Branch. 2b., chorus. Sc. Shoemaker's shop. ADE

J **Christmas mix-up, A.** B. E. Palmer. 6b., 3g. Sc. Interior. ELD

Christmas on a day coach. A. L. Whitson. Comedy. 7m., 1w. Sc. R. R. Coach. ELD

J **Christmas on crutches.** M. Irish. 5b., 5g. Sc. Kitchen. BUG

J **Christmas on Piney Ridge.** G. M. York. 4b., 4g. Sc. Living room on a wheat ranch. ELD

C **Christmas on time.** L. C. Swartz. 9c., chorus. Sc. Interior. DRA

C **Christmas party, The.** C. S. Bailey. 17c., chorus. Sc. Stage. BAI

Christmas party, The. W. N. Bugbee and M. Irish. 7b., 7g. Sc. Living room. BUGT

J **Christmas party, The.** J. L. Latham. Adapted from Zona Gale's Christmas party. Comedy. 2b., 6g. Sc. Dining room. DRA

Christmas party at Sir Rogers, A. M. R. Davidson. 10m., 4w. Sc. English country home in 1710. BAK

Christmas path, The. M. Christensen. 12b., 8g. Sc. Stage. CHR

C **Christmas pitcher, The.** A. Stevenson. 4b., 3g., chorus. Sc. A palace. STEV1

C **Christmas play, A.** M. Trowbridge. 9b., 9g. Sc. Inside hut in devasted France. St. Nich. 51: 194–200, Dec. 1923.

C **Christmas play, A.** G. C. Warner. 2b., 2g. Sc. Stage. WHG1

C **Christmas play written by primary-grade children, edited by M. A. Grimm, A.** Many c. Sc. Living room with Christmas tree. Amer. Childhood 15: 47–8, Dec. 1929.

Christmas playlet for primary grades, A. 3g. Sc. Pioneer home. Sierra Educ. News 25: 15, Dec. 1929.

J **Christmas pull, A.** M. Bonham. 5b., 4g. Sc. Well furnished room decorated for Christmas. BUG

J **Christmas scouts.** L. C. Van Derveer. 10b. Sc. Meeting room of Boy Scouts. VAN

C **Christmas sheep, The.** B. P. Lane. Interlude. 7b., 8g., chorus. LAN

J **Christmas spirit, The.** M. A. Butler. Adapted from Dickens. Christmas carol. 8b., 4g. Sc. Country house. BUT

C **Christmas spirit, The.** S. T. Payson. 10b., 9g. Sc. Interior. BECK

J **Christmas spirit of Swift Deer, The.** 6b., 3g., chorus. Sc. Living room in colonial times. ELD

J **Christmas spirit tarries, The.** L. E. Dew. 8b., 2g., chorus. Sc. A New England family's living room. PAIN

J **Chrstmas star asks a question, a fantasy, The.** H. L. Nugent. Many c. Sc. Living room. Int. J. Rel. Educ. 2: 40+, Dec. 1925.

C **Christmas stocking, The.** P. Beard. 4b., 2g. Sc. Room with a large fireplace. BEA

C **Christmas stocking, The.** A. Curtis. 3b., 5g. Sc. Dining room. CURT

C **Christmas stocking, A.** M. Irish. 4b., 4g. Sc. Stage. HALI

C **Christmas strike, The.** C. R. Freeman. 6c. Sc. Stage. FRAZ

C **Christmas strike, A.** E. E. Preston. Comedy. 5b., 3g., chorus. Sc. Interior. DEN, DRA

Christmas tale, A. H. Harper. 2m., 2w. Sc. Home in Paris in 15th century. SHA

C **Christmas time at Santa's headquarters.** A. W. Norton. 8b., 5g. Sc. Mrs. Santa's home. CJ

Christmas topsy-turkey. K. H. Chapman. Comedy. 1m., 6w. Sc. Interior. DRA, PENN

C **Christmas toy shop, The.** H. Wilbur. Musical. 13b., 12g. Sc. Toy shop. BECK

Christmas tree bluebird, The. M. S. Edgar. 3 char., chorus. Sc. Sitting room with fireplace. WOM

J **Christmas troubles.** M. Bitney. 4b., 2g. Sc. Living room. BIT

Christmas truants. B. E. Palmer. 10w. Sc. Living room. DRA

C **Christmas windows.** M. Christensen and F. M. Frick. DRA

J **Christmas with a bachelor.** 2b., 4g. Sc. Living room. JOHC

C **Christmasse in Merrie England.** M. R. Hofer. Many c. Sc. Any stage. World Review 5: 200–1, Dec. 19, 1927.

C **Christopher Columbus.** A. Stevenson. 14b., 3g., chorus. Sc. Street. STEV3

Chuck. P. MacKaye. Fantasy. 3m., 1w. Sc. Orchard. CL, MACM

C **Chug's challenge.** E. M. Larson. 8b. Sc. Grotto at the North Pole. WOM

Church. F. S. Mead. 2m., 1w., 1b., 1g. Sc. Living room of home in 1929. Christian Cent. 46: 611–12, May 8, 1929.

Churching of Bruddah Harrison, The. W. H. Leach. 8m., Sc. Interior. ELD

J **Cinderella.** C. T. Major. 6b., 5g. Sc. Palace scene. MAI

J **Cinderella married.** R. L. Field. Fanciful. 2b., 4g. Sc. Little morning room. FIF

J **Cinderella of the metals, The.** M. E. Farson. Chemical play. 9 char. Sc. Home of a rich family. J. Chem. Educ. 2: 57–61, Jan. 1925.

C **Cinderella's reception.** M. Bonham. Many c. Sc. Interior. BUG

J **Cinderella's sisters.** P. Beard. 2b., 4g. Sc. Kitchen of Cinderella's home. ELD

C **Circe.** M. Oller and E. K. Dawley. 3b., 2g. Sc. Court of palace. OLL

J **Circumstances alter cases.** R. Giorloff. Comedy. 2m., 3w. Sc. Living room MACG

Circumventin' Saandy. Z. K. MacDonald. 3m., 2w. Sc. Best parlor in Nova Scotia. Drama 16: 291–3, May 1926. Reprinted with corrections: Drama 17: 145–6, 157+, Feb. 1927.

C **Circus comes to town, The.** L. K. Dolan. 18b., 6g. Sc. A big tent. DOL

C **Circus Day.** H. F. Dunlap. 2b., 2g. Sc. Living room. FAW

Citizenship. J. M. Cain. 6m., 1w. Sc. Governor's office. Amer. Mercury 18: 403–8, Dec. 1929.

City, a grotesque adventure, The. D. Novak. 9m., others. Sc. Exaggerated office. Poet Lore 35: 208–21, Summer 1925.

J **City Council wakes up, The.** K. A. White. 5 char. WH

J **City walls and open plains.** P. E. Osgood. 4b., 2g., chorus. Sc. Chancel of church. OSGO

Clackville Choir's Christmas carols. M. Irish. 4m., 4w. Sc. Old-fashioned sitting room. BUG

Clan Falvey. D. Corkery. 7m. Sc. Interior of a peasant's hut. COR

Claribel capers. G. D. Goldenburg. Comedy. 1m., 1w. Sc. Living room. MEA

Classic dancing school, The. W. Duncan. 4w. Sc. Back stage dressing room. Drama 17: 235–42, May 1927.

Classmates, or A brother at large. H. E. Jewett. Farce. 4m., 4w. Sc. Interior. BAK

Claude. H. Ould. 1m., 1w. Sc. Stage of an English provincial theatre. FRE2, OUL

Clean linen. H. Reed. Comedy. 3m., 3w. Sc. Office of hand laundry. BAK, YOU

C   **Clean up!** F. K. Russell. 10b., 2g., chorus, with music. Sc. Interior of dirty, disorderly lunch room. SCH4

Cleansing the stage. H. Simpson. Farce. 3m., 4w. Sc. Drawing room. SIMO

Cleopas. A. L. Barton. 3m., 2w. Sc. Room in house of Cleopas. DR

C   **Clever cock, The.** A. Stevenson. 4b. Sc. In the woods. STEV1

Clever Isabel. A. Robinson. Comedy. 10w., chorus. Sc. Living room. ELD

C   **Clever kid, The.** A. Stevenson. 3b. Sc. A pasture. STEV2

Clever one, The. F. Jacob. Satire. 2m., 4w. Sc. End of a croquet lawn. JAC

Climax, The. M. Gilchrist. Comedy. 2m., 2w. Sc. Interior. BAK

C   **"Climb though the rocks be rugged."** E. F. A. Painton. 9g. Sc. Outdoor scene. PAIT

Clipped. T. M. Hanna. Comedy. 2m., 2w. Sc. Breakfast room. FREN

J   **Clock shop, The.** J. Golden. Fantasy. 5m., 1w. Sc. Clock shop. GOL

J   **Cloelia, the Roman Girl Scout.** M. R. Hofer. 6g., 2b., 4 chorus groups. Sc. Bare stage with tent at side. HOF

C   **Close call, A.** G. A. Muse. 5b. SCH4

Close the book. S. Glaspell. Comedy. 4m., 4w. GLA

Close to the wind. E. A. Barnes. 1w., 2g. Sc. Sitting room of New England farm. COL7, Poet Lore 40: 588–96, Winter 1929.

Closet, The. J. C. Brownell. 2m., 1w. Sc. Living room. DENI

Closet, The. D. F. Halman. Fantasy. 4w. Sc. Upstairs corridor. PHIL

C   **Closing day review, A.** G. Lloyd. Many c. Norm. Inst. 37: 60, 62, May 1928.

Cloudbreak. A. O. Roberts. Tragedy. 3m., 1w. Sc. Lonely cottage in Wales. BRIS, BRIT, CLAS

Clouded mirror, The. E. Thompson and T. Thompson. 6m., 1w., chorus. Sc. Queen's garden. THON

Clown and the undertaker, The. A. L. Preis. 3m., 1w. Sc. Funeral parlor. SCHP

C   **Clown of Doodle Doo, The.** M. Barrows. 6c. Sc. Interior. JAN

Club paper, The. E. O. Cochran. 3m., 3w. Sc. Living room in college town. COC

Club's husband, The. M. C. Johnson. Farce. 3m., 11w. Sc. Banquet table. BAK

J   **Coat of many colors, The.** H. W. Githens. 11b. Sc. Home of Jacob. GIS

Cobbler's den, The. S. O'Brien. 4m., 1w. Sc. Shoemaker's workroom. FRE3

Cobbler's shop. C. Forrest. Comedy. 3m., 2w. Sc. Interior. BAK

Cobra's head. F. J. Pohl. Fanciful. 9m., 1w. Sc. Hamalayan valley. PO

Cobweb kings. M. C. Davies. Fanciful. 9m., 2w. Sc. Gardens of the palace. FRE4

Cocktails. A. L. Weeks. Travesty. 3m. Sc. Apartment. DET

Codfish aristocracy. W. N. Bugbee. 6w. Sc. Living room CAT2

Coffee stall, The. M. E. Forwood. 5m., 2w. Sc. London coffee stall. DE

J **Coiners, The.** E. Hendrie. 10b., 1g., chorus. Sc. Public room of the "Wild Dog" in 1775. FREL

Cold cream. N. E. Minchin. 2m., 1w. Sc. Small room with low ceiling. EM

Collaboration. S. Cowan. 2m., 1w. Sc. A study. COW

Colman and Guaire. Lady Gregory. Verse. 5m., chorus. Sc. Hall in King's house. FRE6

Colombine. R. Arkell. 5m., 1w. Fantasy. Sc. Fairy ring in the South Downes. HAMA

C **Color demonstration.** E. Strong. 9b., 9g., others. School Art M. 26: 54–5, Sept. 1926.

C **Color fairies, a play to teach color.** A. M. Storts. Many c. School Arts M. 27: 98–9, Oct. 1927.

C **Color fantasy.** R. Harwood. 7c. Sc. Color wheel. School Arts M. 27: 77–80, Oct. 1927.

Color line, The. I. T. MacNair. 3m., 3w. Sc. Outer office of college president. EAS

C **Color play.** J. Gaines. 12c. Sc. Color wheel. School Arts M. 30: 513–17, Apr. 1931.

Color play for grade children. L. F. Struble. 4b., 1g. Sc. Stage. School Arts M. 30: 292–4, Jan. 1931.

C J **Color wheel revue, The.** B. E. Anthony. Many c. Sc. Huge color wheel. School Arts M. 24: 353–63, Feb. 1925.

J **Columbine in business.** R. Field. Harlequinade. 3b., 1g. Sc. Before the curtain. FIF

J **Columbine Madonna.** H. Hughes. Harlequinade. 4b., 1g. Sc. Stage of a theatre on Christmas eve. SHAB

C **Columbus and Queen Isabella.** V. Lehman. 8b., 1g. Sc. Court of Queen Isabella. Prim. Educ. 33: 542, Oct. 1925.

C **Columbus and the prior.** M. H. LaRue. 7b. Sc. Courtyard of Spanish convent. Norm. Inst. 37: 76, 78, Oct. 1928.

J **Columbus, the courageous.** P. M. Swinton. 7b., 4g., chorus. Sc. Thorne room of Royal Palace of Spain. SW

J **Come back, Mr. Turkey.** N. Flaurier. 3b., 4g. Sc. Kitchen. FIV

Come-back, The. P. Dickey. 6m., 1w. Sc. Any old University. FREN

Come here. G. Riddle. 2m., 1w. Sc. Office. JOHN

C **Come to my party.** E. L. Squires. 4b., 2g., chorus. Sc. In front of garden gate. SQ

Come true. Mazo de la Roche. 5m., 2w. Sc. Day ward in men's section of an old people's home. CANA, ROC

Come what may, a comedy. A. France. Trans. from the French by

F. Chapman and J. L. May. 3m., 2w. Sc. Drawing room in Paris, 1895. Golden Book 6: 631–41, Nov. 1927.

Comeback, The. W. F. Manley. 2m., 2w. Sc. Prison house in Gaza. MANL

Comedie royall, A. E. G. Sutherland. 4m., 2w. Sc. Audience chamber in Queen Elizabeth's palace about 1580. SMI

Comedy of danger, A. R. Hughes. A play for broadcasting. 2m., 1w., chorus. Sc. Gallery in a Welsh mine. SHAF, Golden Book 14: 82–87, Aug. 1931.

Comedy of death, A. G. E. Harris. 4m., 5w. Sc. Library of New York apartment. Poet Lore 36: 63–75, Spring 1925.

Comforts. H. C. Sargent. Farce. 2m., 2w. Sc. Kitchen. SARB

"Coming." E. Dane. Fantasy. 1m., 1w., 2 voices. Sc. Curtain. DAN

Coming events. R. Jeans. Farce. 2m., 2w. Sc. Bedroom in a flat. JES

Coming of Fair Annie, The. G. Price. 2m., 2w. Sc. Hall in castle. HANF

Coming of spring, The. R. Blackburn. Many c. Norm. Inst. 39: 57, Apr. 1930.

J   **Coming of summer, The.** G. P. Driscoll and C. B. Peterson. 10c. and chorus. Sc. Indian village. MIN

Coming of William Dane, The. M. R. Davidson. Adapted from Eliot. Silas Marner. 4m., 3w., 1g. Sc. Interior of cottage in Raveloe, England in 1825. BAK

C   **Commander in chief.** M. E. Whitney. 7b., 3g., 1 chorus. Sc. 1 Room in Washington's house at Mount Vernon. Sc. 2 Assembly Hall of the Continental Congress. WHI

J   **Commencement dilemma, A.** F. Skinner. Any no. of c. Stage on class day or commencement day. ELD

Common bond, The. E. M. Gibson. 1m., 5w. Sc. Street in front of house. GIB

Common sense. F. C. Brunton. 2m., 3w. Sc. Living room in lonely cottage in the West Highlands. FREL

Community singing at home. R. Jeans. Farce. 3m., 6w. Sc. Boarding house dining room. JEP

Companion-mate Maggie. H. Dortch. Comedy. 3m., 2w. Sc. Farm in eastern North Carolina. Carolina Play Book. Sept. 1929.

Company will recite, The. D. Titheradge. Farce. 2m., 2w. Sc. Stage. TITO

Comparisons are odious. H. Simpson. Farce. 1m., 2w. Sc. Sitting room. SIMM

Compleat lover, The. E. Crawshay-Williams. Comedy. 2m., 6w. Sc. Sitting room of flat. CRAA

Complete success, A. C. H. W. Foster. Comedy. 3m., 3w., 1 dog. Sc. Quaint and cosy morning-room in California. FOS

Comp'ny, 'tention! A. L. Kaser. Travesty. 12m. Sc. In a woods. PAIN

Con amore. P. Wilde. 2m., 1w. Sc. An apartment. WILT

Concerning Coralie. G. Elton. 2m. Farce. Sc. Bedroom in a fashionable London hotel. CHA

Conchita. J. Pollock. 12m., 1w. Sc. Old fortress in Spain. POL

Conclusions. E. E. Olson. Comedy. 2m., 2w. Sc. Apartment living room. BAK

Condemned cell, The. G. Elton. Farce. 8m. Sc. Ante-room. CHA

Confederates, The. H. M. Harwood. Comedy. 2m., 1w. Sc. A room in a house in New York. HAR

Confession. K. Nicholson. 2m., 2w. Sc. Near an American rest camp in 1918. NICG

Confession, The. R. Willis. 2m., 1w. Sc. Living room of a comfortably furnished bachelor's flat. WIMS

Confessional. P. Wilde. 3m., 3w. Sc. Parlor of a trim little cottage. EAS, GOLD, MILL, PEN, TUC, WIL

Confessions. Sir A. Conan Doyle. 1m., 1w., Sc. Interior. JOHP

Conflict, The. C. V. McCauley. 1m., 2w. Sc. Kitchen in farmhouse. SHAQ

Conjurer's stone. J. C. McMullen. Negro farce. 6m. Sc. Living room. MACT

Conn-eda. K. Spencer. 2w. Sc. Wood by moonlight. TAYM

C **Conscience elf, The.** M. Corell and I. Liccione. 1b., 3g. Sc. House. STRU

C **Conscientious turkey, The.** K. L. Bates. 5c. Sc. Henyard. BAT

Conscript fathers!, O. H. W. Henemann. Burlesque. 4m. Sc. House of Misrepresentatives. HANE

C **Conspiracy, The.** K. A. White. 6 char. Sc. Untidy school room. WH

C **Conspiracy of spring, The.** M. S. Edgar. 10b., 4g., chorus. Sc. Out of doors. SCH2, WOM

Conspirators, The. P. Merimee. 9m., 2w. Sc. Dining room of French chateau. Golden Book 1: 537–53, Apr. 1925.

C **Constitutional Convention.** Z. Dalton. Several b. Sc. Any stage. Pop. Educ. 41: 348–52, Feb. 1924.

C **Constitutional Convention, The.** E. Lowry. 11b. and others. Sc. Any stage. Pop. Educ. 43: 108–9, Oct. 1925.

Contrast, The—a home economics play. D. Witt. 2b., 5g. Sc. Dining room. Prac. Home Econ. 7: 213, 217–8, July 1929.

Conversation on drama, A. E. Wilson. A dialog. 2m. Atlantic Mo. 137: 235–42, Feb. 1926.

Conversation on the art of writing plays, A. Henry Arthur Jones with Archibald Henderson. 2m. Sc. Dining room of house in London. Virginia Q. Rev. 1: 323–37, Oct. 1925.

Conversation on the highway, A. I. S. Turgenev. 3m. Sc. Highway. TURG

Conversations: a dialogue playlet in prose and verse. C. Brontë. 2m. Sc. None. Bookman (Lond.) 69: 155–6, Dec. 1925.

Conversion of a dishonest tax-collector, The. P. J. Stackhouse. 4m., 1w. Sc. Room in a house in Jericho. STAC

J **Conversion of Saul, The.** M. E. Whitney. 4b. Sc. Court of the high priest. WHH

Cook. H. Simpson. Farce. 1m., 2w. Sc. Sitting room. SIMA

Cook gets her notice. H. Simpson. 1m., 2w. Farce. Sc. Sitting room. SIMM

"Cooled off!" E. Dane. Fantasy. 4w. Sc. Curtains. DAN

Cophetua. J. Drinkwater. Poetic. 7m., 2w., chorus. Sc. Hall of King's palace. PEN

Copper pot, The. F. Healey. 7m., 5w., chorus. Sc. Village street. WEBB

Copy. K. Banning and H. Kellock. Comedy. 7m. Sc. Office. EAT, LON

Coq brothers, The. L. Mourguet. 5m., 1w. Sc. Public square in Lyons. MACU

Coral. C. Reznikoff. 12m., 1w. Sc. A field at night. REZ

Coral beads. E. H. Yates. Comedy. 1m., 2w. Sc. Public parlor of a Metropolitan hotel. YATE

Corinna. J. Green. 4m., 8w. Sc. Comfortable room in Georgian house in the Midlands. JOH

J **Corn bringers, The.** J. Ross. 12b., 9g. Sc. Mandan camp on the prairie. ELD

J **Cornelia the Mother of the Gracchi.** M. R. Hofer. 3b., 3g., 5 chorus groups. Sc. Two settings. Roman garden and Forum. HOF

Cornelia's jewels. E. Gibson. 3w., 2b. Sc. Drawing room in ancient Rome. GIB

Cornfed babies. A. L. Kaser. Farce. 2m., 3w. Sc. Interior. DEN

Correct attire for business. D. Bartleheim. 2w. Sc. Broker's office. Prac. Home Econ. 7: 280, Sept. 1929.

Corsican Lieutenant, The. R. Housum. 8m., 4w. Sc. Corner of the park of a French residence in 1786. FRE2

Costume de rigeur. P. Wilde. A Shadow play. Farce. 2m., 2w. Sc. Doctor's office. WILT

C **Cotton roses.** E. Edland. Fanciful. 6g. Sc. Around an old high table. EDL

J **Cottons and cookery.** A. C. Herberton. Comedy. 6g. Sc. Interior. FREN

C **Cotton's dresses, The.** L. K. Dolan. 1b., 8g. Sc. Stage. DOL

Cough, The. C. Fitzhugh. 1m., 1w. Sc. Any country club. FITZ

Counsel retained. C. D. Mackay. 2m., 1w., chorus. Sc. Room that gives evidence of extreme poverty. PEN

Countersign, The. M. Lee. Farce. 3m., 2w. Sc. A room. LEE

Country woman, The. I. S. Turgenev. Comedy. 4m., 3w. Sc. Reception-room of a poor official. TURG

Coup-de-Main, A. C. H. W. Foster. 2m., 2w. Sc. Parlor of a California boarding house. FOS

Courage. W. F. Manley. Radio version. 4m., 1w. Sc. Hillside near David's home. MAN

Courageous men. L. S. Beazley. Comedy. 6m., 4w. Sc. Interior. HEH, PENN

Course in piracy, A. P. Russell. Burlesque comedy. 7m. Sc. Cabin of pirate ship. SHAP

J **Courtesy play, A.** Rawlings Junior High School. 3b., 2g., chorus. Sc. Assembly platform. RAW

Courtin' Chrisina. J. J. Bell. Comedy. 2m., 3w. Sc. Interior. BAK

Courtship. F. Eastman. 2m., 3w. Sc. Living room. BAK, YOU

C **Courtship of Miles Standish, The.** L. F. Collins. 14b., 1g., chorus. Sc. In Plymouth in 1621. COJ

Cousin Sarah's quilt. F. Bone. 2m., 6w. Sc. Farmhouse. DE

Cow with wings, The. E. E. Levinger. Comedy. 2m., 5w. CL

Coward. T. Ewen. 5m., 2w. Sc. Interior. FIT

Cowards. R. Willis. 3m. Sc. A library. WIMS

Cowology. A. L. Kaser. Burlesque farce. 2m. Sc. No scenery required. KAS

Cowpunchers. W. B. Hare. Comedy. 5m., 3w. Sc. Interior. BAK

Crabbed youth and age. L. Robinson. Comedy. 3m., 4w. Sc. Comfortably furnished room. FREL, Theatre Arts M. 8: 51–63, Jan. 1924.

Cracked teapot, The. C. C. Dobie. 2m., 1w. Sc. Interior. CART

C **Cracker conspiracy, The.** A. Townsend. 10c. Sc. Street, 3 scenes. SAL

Cranford dames. A. Byington. Adapted from Gaskill's Cranford. 8w. Sc. Interior. FIT

C **Cratchits' Christmas dinner, The.** F. M. Ball-Smith. Adapted from Dickens' Christmas Carol. 5b., 3g. Sc. Kitchen of an English home. JON

Crazy love affair, A. B. Bowers. Comedy. 3m., 4w. Sc. Living room in summer cottage. FIT

Crazy to reduce. D. Sheridan. Comedy. 17w. Sc. Interior. DRA

Creatures of impulse. W. S. Gilbert. Musical comedy. 4m., 3w. Sc. Interior of country inn in England. SHAP

Creeds. F. Healey. 3m., 2w. Sc. Roof-top in an Arab village. SHAF

Crib, The. M. Creagh-Henry. 3m., 3w. Sc. Ante-room of a sculptor's studio. FREL

Crime. C. Seiler. Comedy. 2m. Sc. Secluded place in a public park. SEI

Crime conscious. S. Giffin. 5m. Sc. Library in home. BAK

Criminals. E. Mendez Calzada. 5m., 3w., others. Sc. Doctor's office. Inter-America 7: 115–25, Dec. 1923.

C **Crinkum-Crankums.** K. Dickerson. 3b., 5g., chorus. Sc. Backyard of mission school in China. MARC

J **Cripples, The.** H. O. Boggs. 4b., 1g. Sc. Interior. BOGG

C **Criss Cross ways.** E. L. Squires. 2b., 2g. Sc. Crossroads. SQ

Cristo, El. M. Larkin. 4m., 2w. Sc. Interior. FREN

Critics: a conversation, The. E. Wilson. 4m., 1w. New Repub. 43: 292–3, Aug. 5, 1825.

Cross-stitch heart, The. R. Field. Fanciful. Poetical. 2m., 3w. Sc. Before a curtain. FIC

Crossed wires. E. M. Gall and L. H. Carter. Comedy. 3m., 2w. Sc. Interior. BANN

Crossroads. P. Dickey. 3m., 2w. Sc. Country road. FREN

C **Crow and the fox, The.** A. Stevenson. 1b., 2g. Sc. A high tree in a grove. STEV 3

Crowd, The. H. Gordon. 19 char., chorus. Sc. A central railroad station. WIMA

Crown of St. Felice, The. F. Sladen-Smith. 5m., 3w. Sc. Heaven and Earth. BAK

Crowning glory, The. E. A. Collamore. 1m., 5w. Sc. New England kitchen. BAK

J **Crowning of Peace, The.** N. A. Smith. 2b., 2g., Pageant. Sc. Stage. SAA

J **Crowning of Saul, The.** M. E. Whitney. 6b., 2g. Sc. House of Samuel. WHH

J **Crowning of Solomon, The.** M. E. Whitney. 5b., 1g. Sc. Room in palace of David. WHH

C **Crowning the May Queen.** E. Guptill. 9b., 8g. Sc. Around a Maypole. MARC

Crude and unrefined. M. E. Bowen. 4m., 3w. Sc. Farmhouse in north Texas. OM1

Cruiter. J. Matheus. 2m., 2w. Sc. Farm cottage in lower Georgia. LOC

Crumbs that fall. P. Hubbard. 9m. Sc. Dining room of Straggler's Club, Piccadilly. BAK, PHIL

C **Crystal gazing.** G. Lloyd. 8b., 7g. Norm. Inst. 33: 62, Jan. 1924.

Crystal set, The. J. H. Bone. Comedy. 1m., 2w. Sc. Interior. BAK

Cujun, The. A. J. Carver. 4m., 2w. Sc. Interior. FREN

Cup of coffee, A. D. Reynartz. Comedy. 7w., 2c. Sc. Sitting room. DRA

Cup of life, The. F. Marion. 5m., 2w. Sc. Isolated garden of an insane asylum. NICH

Cup of tea, A. F. Ryerson. Farce. 2m., 2w. Sc. Study. NICB

Cupboard love. E. Crawshay-Williams. Comedy. 1m., 2w. Sc. Bedroom in up-to-date hotel. CRA

C   **Cupboard was bare, The.** C. Brink. 8c. Sc. Interior. ELD

C   **Cupid and Psyche.** M. Oller and E. K. Dawley. 6g. Sc. Room of a palace. OLL

J   **Cupid and the cutlets.** P. Greenbank and P. Barrow. Burlesque operetta. 2b., 3g. Sc. Kitchen of a suburban house. FREL

Cupid in Clapham. E. Baker. Comedy. 2m., 1w., 2c. Sc. Kitchen in small suburban house. FRE 3

Cupid in shirt sleeves. W. A. Scott. Farce. 2m., 3w. Sc. Living room. DRA

Cupid is speedy. A. L. Kaser. Burlesque. Farce. 1m., 1w. Sc. Street in small town. KAS

Cure, The. D. Titheradge. Farce. 2m., 2w. Sc. Sitting room. TITF

Cure for authors, A. L. Sherwin. 2m. Sc. Street near Gramercy Park, N. Y. Amer. Mercury 11: 365–8, July 1927.

J   **Cure for discontent, A.** M. Norton. Farce. 12b., 2g. Sc. An office. BART

Cure of souls. L. Housman. 7m., chorus. Sc. Pope's palace at Perugia in 1216. HOUF

Cure-all, The. J. C. McMullen. Farce. 3m., 3w. Sc. Interior. BAK

Cured. I. L. Ehrlich. Comedy. 3m., 3w. Sc. Living room. FRE4

Cured. M. S. Hurley. Comedy. 6m., 4w. Sc. Living room in home in suburban town. EM

Curing him. H. C. Sargent. Farce. 3m., 3w. Sc. Interior. SARM

Curing of Dad, The. N. S. Russell. Comedy. 3m., 2w. Sc. Living room. ELD

C   **Curing the invalid.** E. Preston. 3b., 2g. Sc. Interior. PRES

Curious herbal, The. C. S. Armfield. Rhymed verse. 2m., 1w. Sc. An old Chelsea garden. WOM

C   **Current events plea, The.** Y. Klein and F. Schwarz. 5c. Sc. Home of one of the children. KLE

Curses what a night! A. L. Kaser. 3m., 2w. Sc. Interior. DEN

Curtain! C. C. Clements. Comedy. 1m., 2w. Sc. Interior. FREN

Curtain, The. H. F. Flanagan. 4m., 2w. Sc. Small room in New York apartment house. RIC

Curtain call, The. G. Grant. 6m., 1w. Sc. Star's dressing room in theatre. LON

Customer is always right, The. R. Jeans. Farce. 4m., 4w. Sc. Manager's office in department store. JEA

Cutty-stool, The. L. Housman. 5m. Sc. Inside Scotch church in 1784. HOT, Cornhill M. 60: 100–10, Jan. 1926.

Cynthia looks ahead. G. R. Bridgham. Comedy. 11w. Sc. Interior. PENN

Cyrano de Bermondsey. H. Simpson. Farce. 2m., 2w. Sc. Bar of the "Three Feathers Inn." SIMM

D

C **Daedelus and Icarus.** M. Oller and E. K. Dawley. 4b. Sc. In a labyrinth. OLL

Dagger of the Goth, The. J. Zorilla. Trans. by W. K. Jones. 4m. Sc. Inside of cabin in desert of Pederneira in Portugal. Poet Lore 40: 426–42, Autumn 1929.

Daggers and diamonds. K. P. Moseley. Satirical travesty. 2m., 2w. Sc. a salon. PHIL

Daily bread. M. K. Reely. 1m., 4w. Sc. Kitchen of tenement. REE, SCH4

Daily bread, a drama of domestic life. J. H. Whitehouse. 1m., 4w. Sc. Living room of middle class home on Long Island. Poet Lore 40: 129–41, Jan. 1929.

Daily doesn't, The. C. Knox. Comedy. 1m., 1w. Sc. Large bedroom. NICR.

Dais, The. E. F. Ibbetson. 4m., 1w. Sc. Studio. DE

Damages for breach. W. P. Ridge. 1m., 3w. Sc. Tea room in Holborn. RID

Damages—two hundred! R. B. Taylor. 2m., 1w. Sc. Shabby little office. TAYL

Damaging evidence. C. Crews. 2m., 2w. Sc. Interior. PAIN

Dame truth. E. U. Ouless, trans. Trans. from the German. 1m., 2w. Sc. Open place near village. OULE

J **Damon and Pythias.** M. R. Hofer. 8b., 2g., 1 chorus. Sc. Street. HOF

Dance below, The. H. Strode and L. Hornthal. 2m., 1w. Sc. Bare looking room in hell. SHAF, Harper's Bazaar 62: 110, Oct. 1927.

C J **Dance of the books.** F. Hornaday. 12b. Sc. Any stage. Wilson Bull. 5: 382, Feb. 1931.

Dance of the red, red rose, The. E. Sexton. 1m., 2w. Sc. Rooms in house in Madrid in ancient times. ELD

Dancing dolls. K. S. Goodman. Fantastic comedy. 4m., 3w. Sc. Interior of a tent. SHAP

Dandy dolls, The. G. Fitzmaurice. Comedy. 6m., 2w., 1c. Sc. Interior of kitchen. CANF

Danger. R. Hughes. (Listening-play.) 2m., 1w. Sc. Gallery in a Welsh coal-mine. HUR

Danger line, The. A. L. Kaser. Farce. 2m. Sc. A meadow. KAS

C **Daniel and the lions.** M. Parsons. 4b., chorus. Sc. Court of the lions. PARS

J **Daniel Boone: patriot.** C. D. Mackay. 9b., 3 chorus groups. Sc. Open woodland in Kentucky 1778. FIN

C **Daniel Boone.** A. Stevenson. 16b., 3 chorus groups. Sc. 1 Camp in 1778. 2 British Fort, Detroit. STEV4

J **Daniel in the lions' den.** M. E. Whitney. 5b. Sc. Small room in palace. WHH

Daniel's loyalty. J. W. Raine. 14m. Sc. 1 Halt in desert. 2 Open court in palace at Babylon. RAI

The danse calinda. R. Torrence. Pantomime. 4m., 1w., chorus. Sc. Mardi Gras in the 19th century. LOC

C **Darby and Joan.** R. Fyleman. 1b., 2g. Sc. Little cardboard houses. FYL

Darinda dares. A. Morris, 2m., 2w. Sc. Drawing room in London home. BOST

Daring daughters. G. Kinyon. 6w. Sc. Living-room. ELD

Dark days ahead. H. G. Leach, *ed.* 4m. A dialogue on the bankruptcy of business leadership. Forum 84: 200–07, Oct. 1930.

Dark of the dawn, The. B. M. Dix. (A martial interlude.) 4m. Sc. Living room of a burgher dwelling. SMI

Dark roses. L. F. Doyle. 7m., 2w., 2c., others. Sc. Porch of a Cobbler's house in Ireland. Cath. World 121: 158–62, May 1925.

Darkey insurance agent, The. W. W. Bugbee. 2m. Sc. Interior. CAT1

Darkness and dawn. F. LeF. Bellamy. 3m., 3w., 10c., chorus. Sc. Hillside near Joseph's garden. WOM

Dave. Lady Gregory. 3m., 2w. Sc. A well furnished room. FRE3, GREQ

J   **David and Goliath.** M. E. Whitney. 8b. Sc. Camp of Saul. WHH

J   **David and Jonathan.** M. Hobbs and H. Miles. 5b., chorus. Sc. In the tent of Saul. HOB

J   **David and Jonathan.** R. Kimball. 16b., chorus. Sc. Curtains or scenes. 4 parts. KIM

C   **David and the Good Health elves.** M. Downes. 18c., chorus. Sc. Child's bedroom. SAL

C   **David anointed king.** M. I. Stone. 15b. Sc. White background, 5 scenes. STON

J   **David at Aunt Betsy's.** A. J. Rostance. Adapted from Dickens. David Copperfield. 2b., 2g. Sc. In front of Betsy Trotwood's house. JON

J   **David Copperfield and his aunt.** G. Pertwee and E. Pertwee. 3b, 3g. Sc. Parlor of Betsy's cottage. PER

C   **David, the shepherd boy.** M. Parsons. 5b. Sc. Outdoors or indoors. PARS

  – **Dawn.** P. Wilde. 2m., 1w., 1c. Sc. Room in rough shack in mining district. PHIL

C   **Dawn of freedom, The.** E. V. Leighton. 9b., 4g., chorus. Sc. Street facing Lexington Common. JOHG

Dawning, The. L. Anderson. 2m., 1w. Sc. Entrance hall of a large house. ANDE

Dawning of the morning, The. E. Rhodé. 3m. Sc. Place Near Medan, Sumatra. ABI

J   **Day at Rawlings, A.** Rawlings junior high school. 7b., 2g., chorus. Sc. Assembly platform. RAW

C   **Day before, The.** N. Flaurier. 2b., 2g. Sc. Sitting room. FIV

C   **Day before the test, The.** K. A. White. 3b., 1g. Sc. Living room. WH

C   **Day dream,** a play for book week, **The.** L. T. O'Niell. 5b., 5g. Primary Educ. 32: 598, 600, Nov. 1924.

Day off at the old ladies' home, A. H. W. Munro. 6w. Sc. Sitting room. ELD

Day that Lincoln died, The. P. Warren and W. Hutchins. 5m., 2w. Sc. Front yard of house in 1865. SCH3

Day light saving. A. S. Macomber. Comedy. 5m., 5w., 3c. Sc. Interior. BUG

Day's end. A. Pieratt. 1m., 3w. Sc. Farmhouse kitchen. CL

Day's work, The. B. Gates. 1m., 2w. Sc. Poverty stricken room. GAT

Day's work, The. E. W. Smith. 3m. Sc. Courtyard of N. Y. City tenement. UNM2

Deacon's hat, The. J. Marks. Comedy. 3m., 3w. Sc. A little shop in north Wales. MARK

Dead expense. M. Bland. 2m., 2w. Sc. Mountain hut. ELD

J **Dead nephew, The.** A. V. Kotzebue. Tr. by B. B. Beebe. Comedy. 5m., 1w. Sc. Interior in German tavern. Poet Lore 38: 160–76, Summer 1927.

Dead past, The. A. E. Wills. 2m., 1w. Sc. Interior in Nevada. FREN

Dead timber. L. Esson. 3m., 2w. Sc. Scene on an English farm in the Bush. Farm Tragedy. ES

Dead woman bites not, A. G. Doane. 4m., 1w. Sc. Room in Queen Elizabeth's palace. CANA

Deadman's pool. V. P. Bridges and T. C. Bridges. 4m. Sc. Valley in the heart of Dartmoor. DE

Dear departed, The. S. Houghton. Comedy. 3m., 2w., 1g. Sc. Sitting room in a lower middle-class district of a provincial town. COH, MAR2

Death. T. Arishima. Tr. from Japanese. 9m., 2w., 3c. Sc. Stage in the Japanese manner. IW

Death dance, The. T. Duncan. 3m., 1w., chorus group. Sc. In a village stockade near an African jungle. LOC

Death in the tree. E. U. Ouless. Tr. from German. 4m. Sc. A wood. OULE

Death of Nero, The. H. Gorman. 4m., 1b., 1g. Sc. A sparsely furnished room in Roman villa. SHAF, Theatre Arts M. 8: 195–204, Mar. 1924.

Death of Pierrot, The. H. Green. 3m., 2w. Sc. Garret. CANA

J **Death of Sohrab, The.** M. A. Butler. 2b. Sc. Sandy plain between two armies. BUT

Death says it isn't so. H. Broun. Satire. 3m., 1w. Sc. Sick room. SHAF

Deathless world, The. J. M. S. Tompkins. 6m., 1w. Sc. Room. EAS, BAK

Deceivers. W. C. DeMille. 2m., 1w. Sc. A comfortably furnished living room. FRE1

Decimal point, The. A. B. Joder. Farce. 3m., 2w. Sc. Law office. Players Mag. 5: 18–20, Mar.–Apr. 1929.

Declaration of Independence, The. Z. Dalton. Many c. Sc. Stage Pop. Educ. 41: 566–67, 594, June 1924.

Declaration of Independence. M. M. Griffith. 15m. Sc. Poor room. GRI

Decorating the interior. H. W. Hanemann. 2m., 1w., Burlesque. Sc. Antique shop. HANE

Defeat. J. Galsworthy. 1m., 1w. Sc. An empty room. GAL

Deirdre. W. B. Yeats. 5m., 1w., chorus. Sc. Guest-house in a wood. YEA

Delaying tactics. D. Titheradge. Farce. 3m., 1w. Sc. Before the curtain. TITU

Delicate child, The. M. Gee and H. McIntyre. 4w. Sc. Cell in city jail. FREN

Delilah. G. Emery. Tragedy. 2m., 2w. Sc. House in ancient Palestine. NICB

Deliverance. K. Nicholson. 2m., 1w. Sc. Room in a hotel in Kansas City. BAK

J **Delivered from bondage.** H. W. Githens. 6b., 1g., chorus. Sc. Pharaoh's courtroom. GIT

J **Delivered from prison.** H. W. Githens. 12b., chorus. Sc. In prison at Jerusalem. GITH

Delivered from the lion's mouth. J. W. Raine. 7m., 3w. Sc. Paul's house in Rome. RAI

Delta wife, The. W. McCellan. 1m., 1w. Sc. Cabin behind the levee in a far southern state. APPL

Demands of society, The. O. E. Hartleben. Tr. from German. Comedy. 1m., 2w. Sc. Boudoir. Place—large German watering place. SHAF

C **Demeter and Triptolemus.** M. Oller and E. K. Dawley. 2b., 3g. Sc. Room in a palace. OLL

Demos and Dionysus E. A. Robinson. 2m. Sc. None. Theatre Arts M. 9: 32–42, Jan. 1925.

Demshur man, A. Nesbitt, C. M. Comedy. 5m., 1w. Sc. Interior of cottage. FREL

Denial. E. G. Hornsey. 7m., 1w. Sc. Interior. BAK

J **Departure, The.** J. Merrill and M. Fleming. Adapted from Thackeray. Vanity Fair. 4g. Sc. Drawing room in Miss Pinkerton's academy in 1812. MER

Deportation dialogue, A. Y.W.C.A. office of Dept. of Immigration. 2w. Woman's Press 25: 546–48, Sept. 1931.

Desert smoke. D. L. Clarke. 3m., 4w. Sc. Blue-black mass of the Sierras. BOST

Deserter, The. A. Kotzebue. Farce. 4m., 1w., soldiers. Sc. Street in a city occupied by enemy troops. Golden Book 7: 193–202, Feb. 1928.

C **Deserting desserts, The.** W. K. Rugg. 9 or more c. Sc. Dining-room decorated with Xmas greens. Child Welfare 19: 177–79, Dec. 1924.

J **Destiny.** P. E. Osgood. 5b. Sc. Screens. OSG

Detour ahead. P. MacManus. 4m., 3w. Sc. Interior. DRA

C **Deus volt: God wills it.** K. Taylor and H. C. Greene. 12b., 3g., chorus. TAY

Devil comes to Alcaraz, a warm weather fantasy, **The.** W. H. Fulham. 5m., 5w. Sc. In town of Alcaraz in New Castile, Spain. Theatre Arts M. 14: 797–803, Sept. 1930.

Devils, The. L. B. Pride. 2m., 1w. Sc. Kitchen of a cottage in mining district. PRID

C **Devil's field, The.** A. Nichols. 6b., 7g. Sc. Hilltop field. NIA

Devil's Lane, a modern morality play. L. S. Perry. 3m., 1w. Sc. Kitchen of a farmhouse. FREN

Devoted Elsie. M. Constanduros. Comedy. 3m., 2w. Sc. Kitchen. FREL

Diabolical circle, The. B. Bomstead. 3m., 1w. Sc. Living room. GOLD

Diadem of snow, A. E. L. Rice. Farce. 2m., 3w. Sc. A room in Tobolsh Siberia in 1917. FRE5

Dialogue of the dead. Lucian. 5m. Golden Book 13: 61–62, Jan. 1931.

Diamond pin, The. R. Holmes. 9m. Sc. A Banquet. ELD

Diana of the Ephesians. W. F. Manley. Radio version. 4m., 1w., chorus. Sc. Home of Demetrius. 5 Sc. MAN

Dick Swiveller and the Marchioness. G. Pertwee and E. Pertwee. Adapted from Dickens. Old Curiosity Shop. 1m., 1w. Sc. Office of Solicitor. PER

Dick Whittington at Strutham. M. Constanduros. Burlesque. 5m., 3w. Sc. Bare, badly-lighted stage. FREL

Dickey Bird, The. H. O'Higgins and H. Ford. 1m., 3w. Sc. Living-room in New York apartment. FREN

J **Dickon goes to the fair.** A. W. Alden. 17b., 8g., chorus. Sc. Outdoors. BEST

C **Did you ever?** E. L. Squires. 1b., 2g. Sc. Sleeping-porch. SQ

Difference, The. M. Boulton. 2m., 1w. Sc. Library. FREL

Difference, The. D. Titheradge. Farce. 1m., 1w. Sc. Drawing room. TITF

Difference, of opinion, A. H. O. Boggs. 3m., 3w. Sc. Interior. BOGG

Dime lunch, The. J. T. McIntyre. 4m., 3w. Sc. Cheap restaurant in the Bowery. PENN

C **Ding-a-Ling.** M. Relonde. Fanciful. 20 either b. or g. Sc. Backdrop with scene to suggest spring. JAN

Dinner bridge. Lardner, R. 8m. Sc. Area under repair on N. Y. Bridge. New Repub. 51: 227–229, July 20, 1927.

Diplomatic Bridget. M. Davis. Comedy. 3m., 3w. Sc. Simple interior. FIT

Disciple of the night, The. J. P. Stackhouse. 6m. Sc. Jerusalem street. STAC

C **Discontented daughter, The.** D. A. Lord. 35c., chorus. Sc. Interior. LOP

Discordia descends. J. Shmutzer. 1m., 2w. Sc. Artistically furnished drawing-room. SCHP

J **Discovery, The;** an episode in the life of Columbus. H. Ould. 7m. Sc. Aboard Columbus's flagship. FREN, OU

Disenchanted, The. Izzet-Melyh. 2m., 2w. Sc. Richly furnished drawing-room. SHAT

Disgrace. C. Campion. Farce. 2m., 1w. Sc. Flat in Mayfair. CHA

Dish of scandal, A. E. M. Wild. Comedy. 6w., Sc. Sitting room. FREL

Dispatch goes home. F. L. Mansur. Satirical comedy. 3m., 1w. Sc. Oriental interior. JOHM

Dispelling of big Jim, The. S. C. Brewer. Farce. 8m. Sc. A negro church. MARC

Divorce specialist, The. E. Andreas. Comedy. 1m., 1w. Sc. Office. ANDR

C **Dixie noon, A.** B. J. Thompson. 4b., 4g. Sc. Cotton field. Norm. Inst. 39: 49, May 1930.

Do I hear twenty thousand? R. Benchley. 8m. Sc. Clubroom. Bookman (N. Y.) 69: 14–17, March 1929.

J **Do you believe in luck?** A. Jenks and T. Jenks. Comedy. 5b., 3g. Sc. Interior. LOU

Do you remember? E. M. Rice. Rhymed comedy. Any number of char. Sc. Living room. BAK

C **Do your Christmas shopping early.** M. Bitney. 2b., 4g. Sc. Living-room. BIT

Doctor. O. Kelly. Comedy. 3m., 1w. Sc. Doctor's Office. KEK

C **Dr. Arithmetic establishes a hospital.** K. A. White. 17c. Sc. Office of hospital. WH

C **Dr. Bluejay's patient.** M. Corell and I. Liccione. 17 or more c. Sc. A garden. STRU

C **Doctor Foster's patients.** L. H. Vanderveer. 11b., 8g. Sc. Interior. BUG

C **Doctor Health.** M. M. Wyckoff. Many c. Sc. Throne room. Prim. Educ. 45: 26, 60, 65, Sept. 1927.

Doctor Snowball. J. Barnes. Farce. 3m. Sc. Plain room. FIT

Doctor's duty, The. L. Pirandello. Tr. from Italian. 5m., 3w. Sc. Room in a house in Southern Italy. PIR

Dodging the cops. E. L. Walton. Comedy. 3m., 2w. Sc. Living room. PENN

Does America discourage art? H. G. Leach, *ed*. Socratic Dialogue. 11m. Forum 81 : 232–237, Apr. 1929.

Does bridge develop the mind? H. G. Leach, *ed*. Socratic Dialogue. 8m. Forum 81 : 16–22, Jan. 1929.

Does the modern world need religion? H. G. Leach, *ed*. Socratic Dialogue. 5m., 2w. Forum 82 : 72–76, Aug. 1929.

C   **Dog in the manger, The.** M. E. Whitney. 2b. dressed as animals. Sc. A stable. WHI

Dog's life, A. D. Titheradge. Farce. 3m., 1w. Sc. Room. TITF

Doll shop, The. E. M. McIlquham. 18c. Sc. Doll shop. Norm. Inst. 37 : 62, June 1928.

C   **Doll shop, The.** R. Strutton. 7b., 7g. Sc. Doll shop. STRU

C   **Dolls.** L. V. V. Armstrong. Nonsense play. 11 char., 3b., 8g. LON, SV

C   **Dolls' first Christmas, The.** S. K. Alden. 1b., 2g., 13c. as dolls. Norm. Inst. 38 : 60–62, 64, Dec. 1928.

C   **Doll's midnight frolic, The.** D. Maltz. 9c. Sc. Toy shop. Grade Teacher 46 : 706–707, May 1929.

C   **Dolls take a hand, The.** C. L. Austin. 1b., 2g., fairies and brownies. Sc. Room in Santa Claus house. Norm. Inst. 34 : 67–69, Dec. 1924.

Dolly's little bills. H. A. Jones. Comedy. 2m., 1w. Sc. Drawing-room. FRE1, Golden Book 8 : 641–649, Nov. 1928.

Domestic bliss. D. Titheradge. Farce. 4m., 1w. Sc. Lounge of the Hydo. TITF

Don Juan in a garden. H. Kemp. Poetic. 1m., 2w. Sc. A Spanish garden near Madrid. KEM

Don Juan's Christmas Eve. H. Kemp. Miracle. 14m., 2w. Sc. Interior of an inn in Spain, 14th century. SHAF

Don Juan's failure. M. Baring. 1m., 2w. Sc. Hall in English house. Golden Book 13 : 69–71, Apr. 1931.

C   **Don Quixota.** A. Stevenson. 3b., 2g. Sc. 1 Living room in Spain 1600. 2 Courtyard of inn. 3 High road. 4 Duke's country Palace. STEV4

Donated by the ladies' aid. V. D. Knauer. Comedy. 11w. Sc. Interior. PAIN

Done on both sides. J. M. Morton. Farce. 3m., 2w. Sc. Interior. DRA

"Don't believe everything you hear!" M. R. Levis. Comedy. 3m., 1w. Sc. Stage. NICR

Don't believe it. C. Andrews. Farce. 3m., 2w. Sc. Reception room in a small hotel. DENI

Don't make me laugh. B. Trivers. Comedy. 5m., 1w. Sc. Stage of the only theatre in town. FREN

Door, The. F. C. Brunton. 2m., 1w. Sc. Living room of a lonely cottage in England. FREL

Door, The. H. C. Crew. 8m., 15w. Sc. Springtime in Judea. DR

Doormat, The. G. E. Lonergan. Fanciful. 10m., 2w. Sc. Palace steps. EM

Door mats. S. D. Whipkey. 2m., 2w. Sc. Neat kitchen of house in small town. Poet Lore 40 : 92–109, Spring 1929.

Door must be either open or shut, A. A. de Musset. Comedy. 1m., 1w. Sc. Living room in Paris. Golden Book 4 : 67–74, July 1926.

C   **Door of success, The.** M. Overholt. 15 char. Sc. Interior. ELD

Door on t'chain, The. F. C. Brunton. 2m., 3w. Sc. Kitchen of a Vicarage in Yorkshire village. DE

C **Dora's kidnapper.** W. Bugbee. 6b., 6g. Sc. Interior. BUG

Dot and go two. H. Simpson. Farce. 2m., 1w., Sc. Sitting-room. SIMM

Dotted line, a peace petition playlet, **The.** B. Abel. 2m., 9w. Sc. Any stage. Woman's Press 25: 540–543, Sept. 1931.

Double demon. A. P. Herbert. An absurdity. 10m. Sc. Jury room. BRIR, HERB

Double dummy. E. S. Hunting. Comedy. 1m., 1w. Sc. Studio. JOHN

Double honeymoon, The. K. Parsons. Comedy. 3m., 3w. Sc. Country hotel lobby. PAIN

C **Double surprise, A.** M. C. Johnson. 6b., 6g. Sc. In front of the school house. STRU

Doughboy Joe. J. H. Connor. 4m. Sc. Somewhere in France in 1918. ELD

Dove, The. D. Barnes. 3w. Sc. Apartment in the heart of the city. BARN

C **Dove and the ant, The.** M. E. Whitney. 3b. Sc. By a pond. WHI

J **Down, Fido.** S. Shute. 8g. Sc. A shooting lodge in the country. BAK

J **Down through the roof.** H. W. Githens. 6b. Sc. A roadway near Capernaum. GITH

C **Downfall of poor speech, The.** K. A. White. 8b., 4g., chorus. Sc. Interior. MARC

C **Dowry of Columbine, The.** B. Goes. Fanciful. 10b., 4g. Sc. Platform. JAN

C **Dragon-fly, insect play in Tommy Tiptoe's theatre** H. E. Davis. 2b., 2g. Sc. Top of a pond with stones and leaves. Delineator 106: 17–18, Apr. 1925.

Dragon's Glory. G. Knevels. Comedy. 6m., 2w. Sc. Chinese interior. APPL

Drama, The. F. Karinthy. 4m. Sc. Office of theatrical manager. LON

Drawback, The. M. Baring. Burlesque. 1m., 1w. Sc. Corner in Kensington Gardens. JOHN

Dream, The. M. W. Brooks. 1m., 2w. Sc. Bedroom. CANA

Dream-child, The. O. Down. 2m., 1w. Sc. Dwelling-room of a small, sparsely furnished cottage. DOW

C **Dream dolls, The.** F. Cavanah. 21 char., chorus. Sc. Packing room in a big store. CAV

C **Dream-maker, The.** E. Preston. Any number of c. Sc. Stage. PRES

Dream of a winter evening, A. J. Pollock. 1m., 1w. Sc. A mean room in a town in Finland in 1920. POL

C **Dream of Christmas, A.** M. A. Stillman. Many c. Sc. Bedroom. Prim. Educ. 33: 708, 712, 715, Dec. 1925.

Dream play, A. A. Strindberg. 8m., 7w., chorus. Sc. 1 Cloud-domes. 2 Forest. STRI

Dreaming of the bones. W. B. Yeats. 5m., 1w. Sc. Any bare place in a room close to wall. YE

Dreamy kid, The. E. O'Neill. 1m., 3w. Sc. Bedroom in a N. Y. tenement. IS, LOC, SHAQ

Drovers, The. L. Esson. 7m. Sc. A droving camp. ES

J **Druid Oak, The.** M. Woods. 4b., 2g. Sc. Great forest. WOW

Drum dance, The. Tsou Ku Chan Mien. Chinese shadow play. 1m., 2w., chorus. Sc. Scene with a throne and a drum. MACU

Drums of Oude, The. A. Strong. 7m., 1w. Sc. Interior of a palace in Northern India. FRE2, STRO, Golden Book 10: 103–110, Oct. 1929.

Dryad of the oak, The. M. J. Trachsel. 11b., 10g. Sc. A grove. Norm. Inst. 36: 76, 78, March 1927.

Duchess, The. A. Curtis. Comedy. Sc. Old ladies home. 6w. CUR

C **Duchess of Trent, The.** M. W. Fox. 8g. Sc. Living room. Hygeia 8: 846–848, Sept. 1930.

Duchess says her prayers, The. M. C. Canfield. 1m., 2w. Sc. Chapel in Milan. SHAF

Duck and drake. R. Jeans. 3m., 1w. Farce. Sc. Sitting room. JEO

Duel about nothing, A. W. S. Ament. 4m., 1w., chorus. Sc. before a house in Russia in 1861. HUO

Duetto. K. S. Burgess. 1m., 1w. Romantic. Sc. Garden of an old French Chateau. FRE3

Duetto. P. Wilde. Farce. 3m. Sc. A concert hall. WILT

Duke, The. J. S. Knapp. Comedy. 4m., 3w. Sc. Drawing room. FREN

Duke and the dices, The. H. Hall. 5m., 1w. Sc. Manager's office in a speak-easy restaurant. LON

Duke of Gordon's daughter, The. V. B. Lawton. 7m., 3w., 2 chorus groups. Sc. Mediaeval interior. LAWT

Dumb and the blind, The. H. Chapin. Cockney comedy. 3m., 2w., 1g. Sc. Top room in a tenement-house. MAR3

Dumb as a door knob. L. Kaser. Comedy. 2w. Sc. Interior. BECK

Duquesne Christmas, The. T. W. Stevens. Mystery play. 13m., 1w., chorus. Sc. Road at the foot of a hill. SHA, STEU

Dust of the road. K. S. Goodman. 3m., 1w. Sc. Living room of Middle western farmer. EAS, FED, GOLD, HANF, LON, SHA, World Review 3: 204–205, Dec. 20, 1926.

C **Dutch doll, The.** M. Carter. 2b., 2g., 28c. Sc. Back parlour of a shop in village in Holland. FREL

C **Dutch garden, A.** H. L. Bowman and B. L. Green. 2b., 1g., others. Sc. Garden in Holland. Prim. Educ. 44: 535, 561, Mar. 1927.

Dutchman in Ireland 3m. Sc. Interior. FIT

Dwellers in the darkness, The. R. Berkeley. 4m., 2w. Sc. Card room of a country house. PHIL, BAK

Dying wife, The. L. Taylor. 1m., 1w. Sc. Charmingly furnished boudoir. FREI

J **Dyspeptic ogre, The.** P. Wilde. 2m., 1w., 74 or more c. Sc. Interior. BAK, THOM

E

E & O. E. E. Crawshay-Williams. Comedy. 3m., 2w. Sc. Bedroom. CRA

C **Each in his own place.** A. Stevenson. 5 char. Sc. In a tiny house. STEV 3

Early closing. W. P. Ridge. 1m., 2w. Sc. Small draper's shop in Kentish town. RID

Early frost. H. B. Stevens. 1m., 2w. Sc. Kitchen. JOHM

C **Early shyness of an orator.** F. O'Ryan and A. W. O'Ryan. 11b. Sc. Classroom Philips Exeter in 1796. ORY

Earth-trapped. H. Alexander. 2m., 1w., music. Sc. Interior, or exterior. ALE

East of Eden. C. Morley. Comedy. 2m., 2w., 1 baby. Sc. Any scene which suggests. LON, MORL, New Rep. 39 : 318–323, Aug. 13, 1924.

C **East wind's revenge, The.** S. Janney. Fantasy. 11c. Sc. Living-room. JAO

C **Easter bonnet, The.** P. Beard. 2b., 4g. Sc. Back yard. BEA

Easter evening. E. Thompson and T. Thompson. 3m.. 3w. Sc. Room in a Syrian town four years after death of Christ. THON

C **Easter lily, The.** A. Curtis. 3g. Sc. Living room. CURT

C **Easter lily, The.** M. G. Parsons. 1b., 2g., chorus. Sc. Out of doors. PARR

C **Easter lily garden, The.** M. Bonham. Any number of c. Sc. Stage. ELD

J **Easter morn.** M. M. Russell. 3b., 3g., chorus. Sc. Stage. RUS

C **Easter mystery play, An.** N. Longenecker. Many c. Sc. Church. Int. J. Relig. Educ. 6 : 28–29, 47, Apr. 1930.

Easter pageant. E. B. Coburn. Many c. Sc. Woods in early spring. Norm. Inst. 38 : 70, Mar. 1929.

C **Easter song bird, The.** B. E. Palmer. 8b., 8g. Sc. Stage. ELD

C **Easter song bird, The.** 8b., 8g. Sc. Exterior. DRA

Easy money. L. Osborn. Farce. 3m. Sc. Living room. PENN

Ebb-tide. R. Lambert. 5m., 3w. Sc. Lounge-cabin of yacht. DE

C **Echo and Narcissus.** M. Oller and E. K. Dawley. 2b., 4g. Sc. Cleared spot in the woods. OLL

Economical boomerang, An. W. H. Neall. Comedy. 3m., 3w. Sc. Interior. PENN

Edge o'dark. G. John. English dialect. 5m., 1w. Sc. Parlour kitchen in two-roomed miner's cottage in England. JOH

Educatin' Mary. N. L. Fischer. 4m., 4w. Sc. Living room. BECK, DEN, DRA

C **Education's Progress.** A. M. Lütkenhans. 4b., 2g., chorus. Sc. Stage. LUT

Edward about to marry F. Sladen-Smith. Farce. 5m., 4w. Sc. Interior. BAK

Ee, Fah, Lahso, Fahso. A. L. Kaser. Farce. Dancing play. Sc. Interior. KAS

C **Efficiency Phillip manages Christmas.** E. E. Preston. Comedy. 8b. Sc. Interior. PAIN

Efficiency test, The. G. Meyrick. Comedy. 3m., 1w. Sc. Business office. PENN

Egging on Egbert. R. Eskil. Comedy. 4m., 4w. Sc. Dining room. DENI

Eighth wonder, The. D. Titheradge. Farce. 2m., 3w. Sc. Rooms. TITF

El Christo. M. Larkin. 4m., 2w. Sc. Interior of a morado in Loas New Mexico. EAS

Eldest, The. E. Ferber. 3m., 4w. Sc. Dining room of a flat in a cheap neighborhood. APPL, CL, NICB

J **Election day tea, An.** K. A. White. 6w. Sc. Interior. WH

Electra. H. Von Hofmannsthal. 7m., 7w. Sc. Inner court of palace. DIC3

Elegy of a country churchyard. L. Housman. 4m., chorus. Sc. Churchyard. HOT

C **Elf and the Christmas candles, The.** M. T. Johnson. 6b., 2g. ELD

C **Elf of discontent, The.** R. Benton. 5b., 13g., 5 chorus groups. Sc. A fairy garden. BEN

C **Elfen Hill.** N. Mitchison. 8b., 3g., chorus. Sc. Stage with green back cloth. MIT

C **Elfin knight of Hallowe'en, The.** M. Parsons. 3b., 3g., chorus. Sc. Outdoors in Scotland. SCH1

Elfin knight of Hallowe'en. Washington School, Mt. Vernon, N. Y. Several c. Sc. Hallowe'en. Pop. Educ. 42 : 108, 110, 112, Oct. 1924.

C **Eli Whitney.** C. Hepler. 5b., 1g., others. Sc. Inventions. Hist. Outlook 17 : 130–131, Mar. 1926.

Eligible Mr. Bangs, The. R. Housum. Comedy. 2m., 2w. Sc. Living room of an apartment. FRE3

Elijah. P. E. Osgood. 6m., 1w., choir chorus. Sc. Church with a chancel. OSF

J **Elijah and Elisha.** R. Kimball. 20 or more b., 2g., chorus. Sc. Curtains or scenes, 3 parts. KIM

Elisha. L. M. Dunning. 2m., 2w., 1b. Sc. Courtyard of the Shunamite dwelling. DR

Eliza gets kissed. D. Stevens. Farce. 4m., 5w. Sc. Living-room. ELD

C **Elizabeth, the quaker maiden,** arranged from Longfellow's Elizabeth. E. J. Fleming. 2b., 2g., 24 others. Pop. Educ. 43 : 12–13, 50, 54, Sept. 1925.

J **Elizabeth refuses.** M. Macnamara. Comedy. Episode from Austin, Pride and Prejudice. 1m., 4w. Sc. An 18th century English house. BAK, HAMA

Ellis Bean (1800–1807). M. M. Griffith. 12m. Sc. Bare Mexican prison. GRI

Elmer. B. H. McNeil. 3m., 6w. Dining room. BAK, Players Mag. 6 : 18–21, 24, Mar. and Apr. 1930.

J **Elmer and Elias.** 2b., 1 dog. Sc. Stage. AU

Elopement, The. R. Jeans. Farce. 5m., 3w. Sc. Stage. JER

Elsie. A. L. Weeks. 2m. Sc. Office. DET

C **Elsie in Bookland.** M. Parsons. 8b., 8g. Sc. Before the curtain. SAL

C **Elsie in Mother Goose land.** C. C. Cooke. 5b., 4g. Sc. One-room country school. FAW

Embarrassing baby, The. F. J. Pohl. Farce. 4m., 2w. Sc. A city park. PO

Emeralds, The. O. W. Firkins. 1m., 3w., 1g. Sc. Living room of flat. FIR

Emergency case, An. M. Flavin. 2m., 2w. Sc. Interior. FLA

Emilia Viviani. Wiegand, C. V. 2m., 2w. Sc. A dressing room in a villa in 1822 in Florence. Poet Lore 36 : 552–568, Winter 1925.

J **Emily's revolt.** B. Akin. Comedy. 3b., 4g. Sc. Clean shabby old fashioned room. BUG

Emperor Jones, The. E. O'Neill. Char. 3m., 1w., chorus. Sc. In the palace. APPL, LOC

J **Emperor's new clothes, The.** E. H. Williams. 6b., 2g. Sc. In a palace. WIM

C **Emperor's test, The.** A. Stevenson. 9b., 3g. Sc. Army camp. STEV3

J **Empty room, The.** D. C. Wilson. 4b., 3g. Sc. Room in the old Khan of Bethlehem. BAK

Empty stockings. M. T. Applegarth. 11 char. Sc. Littered up room in tenement. APN

C **Enchanted book-shelf, The.** J. Thorp. 60c. or more. Pageant. Sc. Stage. SAM

Enchanted Christmas Tree, The. P. Wilde. 3m., 7b., 7g., 2 chorus groups. Sc. Interior. APPL, BAK, SHA, Pict. R. 26 : 14–15, 48+, Dec. 1924.

C   **Enchanted dolls, The.** F. E. Eakman. 13c. Sc. Child's bedroom. EAK

C   **Enchanted garden, The.** S. G. Clark. 7c. Sc. Garden. CLAR

C   **Enchanted garden, The.** League of Red Cross Societies. 26c. Sc. A dimly lighted room. SAO

C   **Enchanted Maypole, The.** M. C. Holbrook. 6b., 5g., chorus. Sc. Greensward. SAL, Amer. Child 14 : 25–27, 63–64, May 1929.

C   **Enchanted summer.** M. C. Blomquist. Masque. 12 char., chorus group. Sc. Rustic throne under a tree. WHG1, Prim. Educ. 33 : 410+, June 1925.

J   **Enchantment of Finn, The.** E. Smith. 9b., 2g. Sc. Beside the grey lake. SM

C   **End of Pinocchio's dream, The.** R. Bufano. 14c., chorus. Sc. Sawdust circular floor of a one ring circus. BUF

End of the dance, The. H. Strode. 2m., 2w. Sc. Interior. FREN

J   **End of the rainbow, The.** Fantasy. 2b., 1g. Sc. Wild wood. WEB

End of the rope, The. L. F. Thanhouser. 2m. Sc. A garret in a deserted house. YALP

End of the row, The. P. Green. 2m., 3w. Sc. Field in eastern North Carolina. GREF, Poet Lore 35 : 58–74, Spring 1924.

End of the trail, The. E. H. Culbertson. 2m., 1w. Sc. Shack in the Cascade mountains. CL, IS, NICA, Theatre Arts M. 8 : 326–340, May 1924.

Endless tale, The. A. Stevenson. 3b., 1g., chorus. Sc. King's palace. STEV2

'Enery Brown. E. Granville. 2w. Sc. Quiet street off Piccadilly Circus. GRA

Engaged for the month. K. Asbrand. Comedy. 2m., 5w. Sc. Living room. PAIN

English as she is spoke. T. Bernard. *tr.* Comedy. 5m., 3w. Sc. Paris hotel lobby. Golden Book 7 : 677–83, May 1928.

Enoch in Arden. C. Thomas. 2m., 2w. Sc. Orchard on a sunny afternoon. DE

Enter Dora—exit Dad. F. Tilden. Comedy. 4m., 1w. Sc. Office. LAD

J   **Enter the champion.** C. M. O'Hara. Comedy. 2b., 4g. Sc. Trophy room in country club. PENN

J   **Enter the hero.** T. Helburn. 1b., 3g. Sc. Upstairs sitting-room. GREM, GREN, KN

J   **Entertaining Aunt Mina.** E. Fleming. Comedy. 5w. Sc. Sitting-room. ELDR

Entremes of the cave of Salamanca, The. M. de Cervantes Saavedra. Tr. by W. K. Jones. 5m., 2w. Sc. Spanish courtyard and street. Poet Lore 39 : 120–131, Spring 1928.

Envy's end. E. Erickson. Tragi-comedy. 2m. Sc. Studio. KAM

Episode. J. S. McManus. 3m. Sc. Abandoned dugout. BAK

Episode. H. Ould. Comedy. 1m., 1w. Sc. Tastefully furnished bachelor apartment. OUL

J   **Eppie's choice.** M. A. Butler. Adapted from Eliot, Silas Marner. 2b., 2g. Sc. Cottage. BUT

Equals. A. Strindberg. 2m. Sc. Simple room in country. Golden Book 7 : 85–91, Jan. 1928.

Ermine cloak, The. H. Simpson. Farce. 2m., 2w. Sc. Private office of a turf commission agency. SIMO

Escape, An. L. Abercrombie. Poetic. 2m. Sc. Among mountains. ABE

Escape. T. Pratt. 6m., 1w., 1b., 1g. Sc. Living and business establishment in one. SHAF

J **Escape from Lochleven, The.** E. Smith. Adapted from Scott's The Abbott. Sc. Courtyard of mansion. SM

C **Escape of the Germs, The.** K. A. White. 27c. Dim forest of long ago. WH

Essential to the action. D. Titheradge. Farce. 2m. Sc. Dramatist's study. TITO

J **Estabrook nieces, The.** W. Beck. 4b., 4g. Sc. Living room of a typical American home. BEB

J **Esther.** M. Hobbs and H. Miles. 6b., 6g., chorus. Sc. Chamber of the Queen. HOB

C **Esther.** M. I. Stone. 5b., 2g., chorus group. Sc. Purple back-drop. STON

J **Esther.** M. E. Whitney. 13b., 3g. Sc. Room in the palace Shushan. WHH

J **Eternal quest, The.** G. S. Overton. 28c. Sc. Stage. OV

Eternal question, The. A. Macbeth and A. Stephenson. 1m., 1w. Sc. Dressing room. FREQ

J **Ethel makes cocoa.** C. Francis. 3b., 2g. Sc. Dining-room. FRA

Ethel's queer complex. R. V. H. Dale. Comedy. 5w. Sc. Woman's tea room. ELD

Ethiopia at the bar of justice. E. J. McCoo. 15m., 14w. Sc. Throne room. RICH

Etiquette. P. Halvey. Comedy. 1m., 1w. Sc. A quiet end of the board-walk. Atlantic City. NICR

Etiquette. C. Morley. Comedy. 2m., 6w. Sc. Shore of tropical island. Sat. R. Lit. 5: 142–143, Sept. 22, 1928.

C **Etta Ket and the goops.** L. H. Vanderveer. 16c. Sc. Home of Old woman in the shoe. BAK, BUG

Euclid was right. A. Stephenson. 2m., 2w. Sc. Mid-victorian room. FREQ

Evangels of the new day. C. C. Chayer. Pageant. Many c. Sc. Church school. Int. J. Relig. Ed. 2: 28–30, 1925.

Evarannie. H. A. Vachell. 1m., 2w. Sc. Interior. BAK, PHIJ

Eve in Evelyn, The. G. Hughes. Comedy. 3m., 2w. Sc. A rustic inn. SHAF

C **Evelyn dreams of Purim.** J. Leiser. 4b., 5g., chorus. Sc. Outdoor sleeping porch. 3 Sc. BLO

C **Evelyn's Christmas lesson.** R. Rice. 4b., 4g. Sc. Nursery. CJ

Evening dress indispensable, an utterly nonsensical playlet. R. Pertwee. 2m., 3w. Sc. Interior. FREN, LAD, Ladies Home Journal 41: 10–11, 123+, Nov. 1924.

Evening in Sorrento, An. I. S. Turgenev. Comedy. 3m., 2w. Sc. Hotel on the shore. TURG

C **Evening in the Studio.** S. P. 1w., 5g. Sc. Studio. Etude 47: 317–318, Apr. 1929.

Evening of bridge, An. O. Kelly. Comedy. 1m., 1w. Sc. Living room. KEK

Evening on Dartmoor, An. N. Munro. 2m., 2w. Sc. Comfortably furnished room. JOHB

C **Evening with the Colonial maids, An.** A. N. Lewis. 8g. Sc. Colonial room. Norm. Inst. 39: 64–65, Jan. 1930.

Evening with the older set. K. Roberts. 5m., 6w. Sc. Rather rich dining room in home. Sat. Eve. Post 199: 10+, May 28, 1927.

Evening's entertainment, An. M. Mackendrick. Comedy. 11 char. Sc. Cross section of a moving picture theatre. MACS

Ever Upwards! P. Wilde. Farce. 2m., 2w. Sc. A Street. WILT

Ever young. A. Gerstenberg. 4w. Sc. Comfortable room. GER

C **Everlasting Christmas tree, The.** E. L. Austin. Pageant. Many c. Sc. Untrimmed Christmas tree. Sierra Ed. News 25: 13–15, Dec. 1929.

C **Every Child's lesson.** M. K. Mason. Health play for deaf children. 15c. Sc. Woods. Volta R. 31: 27–31, Jan. 1929.

Every couple is not a pair. O. G. Roark. Comedy. 2m., 4w. Sc. Kitchen. HEL, PENN

Every dog has his day. M. Dondo. Farce. 2m., 2w. Sc. French provincial kitchen. MACU

Γ **Every student.** E. Everett. 17 char. Sc. Student's room. HEY

Everybody calls me Gene. M. J. Goelitz. Comedy. 2m., 3w. Sc. Front parlor. DENI

Everybody happy? H. Kerr. Comedy. 4m., 5w. Sc. Modern living-room. ELD

J **Everybody Thankful.** M. Irish. 4b., 4g. Sc. Street. IRI

Everybody's husband. G. Cannan. 1m., 5w. Sc. Girl's bed-chamber. CANN

C **Everychild's Christmas.** B. P. Lane. 9c. Sc. Interior. LAN

C **Everyday courtesies.** L. K. Dolan. 7c. Sc. Stage. DOL

Everyman and Mr. Page. M. Lee. Farce. 3m., 4w. Sc. Interior. LEE

J **Everyman of Everystreet.** M. D. Stocks. 15b., 2g., chorus. Sc. On the road to Bethlehem. SID

Everything comes to her who waits. K. Parsons. Comedy. 2m., 3w. Sc. Living room. ELD

C **"Everywhere, everywhere, Christmas tonight!"** E. A. Collamore. Many c. Sc. Living room. Norm. Inst. 36: 72, 74, Dec. 1926.

J **Everyyouth.** W. L. Bissell. Morality play. 23 char. Sc. The well at the crossroads. BIS

J **Evil kettle, The.** Lord Dunsany. 2m., 1w. Sc. Room in cottage. DUA, MOSA, SCH4

Evolution of style, The. B. de Meyer. 1m., 1w. Sc. French living room. Harper's Bazaar 65: 49+, Jan. 1930.

Exchange, The. A. Thurston. 4m., 1w. Sc. Office. UNU

J **Excuse me.** M. Irish. Comedy. 3b., 4g. Sc. Living room. IQ

Executioner, The. A. DeSoto. 2m., 2w. Sc. Interior Parisian inn in 1793. UNW3, Players Mag. 2: 17–20, Nov. 1925.

Exile. A. Doyle. 3m., 1w. Sc. Lonely farm in N. Y. State. APPL, SHA

Exit Miss Lizzie Cox. A. M. Boyd. 3m., 6w. Sc. Interior of the Nuttville Bibliopathic Sanitarium. WIMT

Exit Mrs. McLeerie. J. J. Bell. Farce. 3m., 3w. Sc. Photographer's studio. BAK

Exit the Grand Duchess. C. M. O'Hara. Comedy. 7w. Sc. Drawing room. PENN

Eye for an eye, An. C. Seiler. Melodrama. 3m., 1w. Sc. Cabin in the Northwest. SEI

Eyes. M. Block. Tragedy. 3m., 3w. Sc. Room in tenement house in N. Y. City. FREN

Eyes. C. Seiler. 5m. Sc. Second-story apartment in inn. SEH

Eyes that cannot see. A. Gnudtzmann. tr. from Dutch. 2m., 3w. Sc. Interior. APPL, SHAT

Eyes that see, The. F. Kerigan. 2m., 5w. Sc. Rose garden by moonlight. PENN

F

Face to face with the mike. D. Sheridan. Farce. 6m., 6w. Sc. Broadcasting studio. SHER

Facing fact. A. Gerstenberg. Comedy. 1m., 2w. Sc. Living room. GEQ

Facts, The. P. Wilde. 1m., 1w. Sc. A camp in a Canadian wilderness. WILT

Facts are stubborn things. P. J. Stackhouse. 6m., 1w. Sc. At one of the gates of the temple. STAC

J   **Fads and frills.** M. C. Richmond. 4b., 1g. Sc. Living room. Ind. Arts Mag. 19: 91–93, Mar. 1930.

Faint heart. E. O. Jones. Farce. 2m., 3w. Sc. Boudoir. FREN

Fair award, The. W. Whitman. 4m. Sc. Space between heaven and earth. McNaught's Monthly 1: 157–158, Mar. 1924.

Fair enough. R. Connell. Comedy. 17w., 1m. Sc. A courtroom. NICR

Fair exchange. H. Sander. Farce. 6m. Sc. Exterior and interior. FIT

C   **Fair play.** M. J. Maroney. 12b. Sc. Outdoors. FJ

J   **Fairies and a Christmas tree, The.** A. W. Norton. Acrostic. 1b., 11g. Sc. Barely furnished room. CJ

C   **Fairies' Christmas party, The.** R. Rice. 5b., 11g. Sc. Stage. CJ

C   **Fairies' May fete, The.** G. E. Miller. Many c. Sc. Rose garden. Prim. Educ. 33: 336, May 1925.

C   **Fairy and the cat, The.** A. Stevenson. 5b., 3g. Sc. A Palace. STEV1

C   **Fairy and the doll, The.** R. Fyleman. 2g. Sc. Garden. FYL

C   **Fairy cakes, The.** A. E. Allen. 30 or more c. Sc. Stage. WHG1

C   **Fairy dust.** F. Cavanah. 2b., 3g., chorus. Sc. Nursery at bedtime. CAV

J   **Fairy facts.** L. McDonald. Fantasy. 1b., 1g., 2 chorus groups. Sc. Mountain grove. SIS

C   **Fairy garden, A.** L. Arbogast and M. Morgan. Many c. Sc. Fairy garden. Norm. Inst. 36: 62, 64, May 1927.

C   **Fairy gifts.** S. S. Stevens. 9c., chorus group. Sc. School-room. LUT

C   **Fairy grasshopper, The.** A. Halsey. 10c., chorus. Sc. Woodland effect. FREL

C   **Fairy riddle, The.** R. Fyleman. 3g. Sc. A glade. FYL

C   **Fairy ring, The.** M. Anderson. Pageant. 40b. or g., chorus. Sc. In the open. JAN

C   **Fairy ring, The.** B. P. Lane. Fantasy. 43c. Sc. In the woods. LAN

J   **Faith and what it does.** M. M. Browne. 3m., 2w. Sc. Living room. THOQ

Faith of their fathers, The. F. K. Frank. 2m., 2w. Sc. Living room of modern house. Menorah J. 11: 377–81, Aug. 1925.

Faithful admirer. E. Baker. Comedy. 2m., 1w. Sc. Dressing room in theatre. SHAF

J **Faithful daughter, A.** H. W. Githens. 1b., 3g. Sc. Home in Bethlehem. GIT

Faithful servant, The. W. F. Manley. 3m., 3w. Sc. Village in the west. 5 Sc. MANL

Falcon, The. A. L. Tennyson. Poetic. 2m., 2w. Sc. Italian cottage. SMI

Falcon and the lady, The. M. Penney. Comedy. 2m., 3w. Sc. Courtyard of Italian villa. BAK

C **Fall day, A.** N. Flaurier. 11c. Sc. Stage. FJ, STRU

Fall of the Alamo. M. M. Griffith. 9m., 1w., 1c. Sc. Cubicle of Church. GRI

J **Falling in love with plain geometry.** C. Hatton and D. H. Smith. 16c. Sc. Living room. Math. Teacher 20: 389–402, Nov. 1927.

C **Falling Leaf.** E. Edland. 7b., chorus. Sc. Open space of the forest. EDL

Falling out of Mrs. Gamp and Mrs. Prig, The. G. Pertwee and E. Pertwee. Adapted from Dickens. Martin Chuzzlewit. 2w. Sc. Small English apartment. PER

False colors. C. M. Lindsay. 1m., 2w. Sc. Interior. PENN

J **False pretenses.** W. Beck. 6b., 5g. Sc. Library room of an ordinary public school. BEB

Fame and the poet. Lord Dunsany. 2m., 1w. Sc. Poet's room in London. Golden Book 12: 87–89, Nov. 1930.

Family budget, The. M. Hurst. 3m., 3w. Sc. Living room. BUG

Family comedy, A. (1840). M. Bowers. Comedy. 2m., 4w. Sc. Parlour. FREL

Family failing, The. K. Haviland-Taylor. Melodrama. 4m., 4w. Sc. Living room of farmhouse. Country Gent. 95: 21–22, 96+, Nov. 1930.

Family group, The. M. Constanduros. Comedy. 3m., 3w. Sc. Photographer's studio. FREL

Family in the upper flat, The. W. N. Bugbee. 2m., 2w. Sc. Living room. CAT2

Family reunion. E. W. Peattie. 2m., 3w. Sc. Pleasant interior. PEA

Family round-up, The. A. L. Kaser. 2m., 1w., children (any no.). Sc. Interior. DRA, ELD

Famous Bugle diamond, The. H. Melvill. Mystery. 2m., 4w. Sc. Library. FREQ

Fan and two candlesticks, A. M. MacMillan. 2m., 1w. Sc. A room at the end of a great hallway in a fine Georgian mansion. APPL

Fan Tan. J. Finn, Jr. 3m., 1w. Sc. Chinese home. CART

Fanatic, The. R. W. Tucker. 2m., 1w. Sc. Interior of shanty. MEA

Fannie and the ghost. D. Halman. Fantasy. 3m. Sc. Little old house falling to decay. JOHN

Fanny Otcott. T. Wilder. 2m., 1w. Sc. Lawn before a cottage. WILZ

Fantasia. C. Seiler. Fanciful. 3m., 1w. Sc. Garden in the land of nowhere. SEI

Far-away princess, The. H. Sudermann. Tr. by G. Frank. Comedy. 2m., 6w. Sc. Veranda of an inn in watering place in Germany. Golden Book 5: 625–633, May 1927.

J **Farce of the Worthy Master Pierre Patelin, the lawyer, The.** Tr. by M. Jagendorf. 4m., 1w. Sc. Street scene in little town of France about 1400. APPL, FIN

C **Farmer Brown's Christmas.** E. Macbeth. 2b., 3g., 6c. Sc. Living room. Norm. Inst. 39: 78, 80, Nov. 1929.

C **Farmer's helpers, The.** M. F. Fox. 10b., 16g. Sc. Rural setting. Pop. Educ. 42: 46, 48, Sept. 1924.

    Fascinating Mr. Denby, The. S. Sage and H. M. Jones. Feminine comedy. 4w. Sc. Smart restaurant. Drama 14: 175–7, 187, Feb. 1924.

    Fashion show, The. M. P. Johnson. 1m., 10w., chorus. Sc. Ante room of large hotel ball room in N. Y. City. FREN

J **Fat and happy.** M. C. Minard. 1b., 1g. Sc. Interior. CAT2

    Fat kine and the lean, The. G. Cannan. 7m., 2w. Sc. At the gate of heaven. CANN

    Fata Deorum. C. W. Guske. Poetic. 6m. Sc. Room in the home of Marius in Rome 15 A. D. SHAQ

    Fatal quest, The. Burlesque. 5b., 2g. Sc. Throne room. DAZ

    Father and sons. B. F. Smith. 2m., 1w., 2b. Sc. Living room. ELD

C **Father Christmas.** R. Fyleman. 2b., 1g. Sc. A night nursery. FYL

J **Father of nations, The.** H. W. Githens. 7b., 1g. Sc. Abraham's camp. GIT

    Father of Texas is no more, The. M. M. Griffith. 4m. Sc. Unfinished clapboard room. GRI

C **Father-of-a-Hump and old cobble shoes.** V. Olcott. 4b., chorus. Sc. Among the Lebanon hills. OLF

    Father Time's Workshop. L. Mitchell. 8c. Sc. Workshop. Norm. Inst. 33: 61, Jan. 1924.

    Father's day on; or Mother's day off. M. Murphy. 1m., 5w., 2b. Sc. Interior. BUG, FIT

    Faustus. C. Norman. Poetic. 2m. Theatre Arts Mag. 14: 309–312, Apr. 1930.

    Favours of my Lady Leone, The. M. Elliot. 4m., 1w., chorus. Sc. Castle in the 17th century. CANA

    Feast, The. Mrs. A. Stallard. 4m., 4w., chorus. Sc. Inside cottage. STAL

C **Feast of adventure.** F. Cavanah. 11c. Sc. Room in a summer cabin. CAV

    Feast of Belshazzar, The. H. Borsook. Many char. Sc. Chief chamber of palace of Belshazzar. Canad. Forum 9: 400–403, Aug. 1929.

    Feast of faith, The. B. M. Russell. 5m., 4w. Sc. Home of Mary in Jerusalem. BAK

    Feast of the Holy Innocents, The. S. M. Ilsley. 5w. Sc. A little old-fashioned parlor. CL, FREN

C **February's birthday party.** M. E. Carpenter. 8b., 7g. Sc. Any stage. American Child 13: 23–25, Feb. 1928.

C **February's famous birthdays.** Texas teacher. 3b., 4g. Prim. Educ. 34: 128, Feb. 1926.

    Fellow-Prisoners. L. Housman. 7m. Sc. Prison in Perugia. HOUS

    Felton mystery, The. 6m., 6w. Sc. Interior. MARC

C **Fern Dust.** E. L. Squires. 4b., 2g. Sc. Kitchen. SQ

    Fernseed in the shoe. E. Van der Veer. Comedy. 7m., 2w. Sc. A glen in the forest. FREN

    Festival of Bacchus, The. A. Schnitzler. Tr. from German. Comedy. 4m., 2w., chorus. Sc. Railway station. SHAT

C **Festival of feasts, A.** R. E. Levy. Fantasy. 5b., 7g. Sc. Interior. BLO

C **Festival of the Harvest Moon.** S. A. Wilson. 15b., 2g., 21 chorus groups. SCH2

J **Fiery furnace, The.** H. W. Githens. 9b., chorus groups. Sc. Throne-room in the palace in Babylon. GIT

Fifi's fortune. J. H. Cook. Comedy. 3m., 2w. Sc. Living room. PENN

J **Fifteenth candle, The.** R. L. Field. 2b., 3g. Sc. Small dark room in the basement of a city block. THOM

Fifth commandment, The. W. Steell. 3m., 1w. Sc. Drawing room. JOHM

C **Fight for good English, The.** Wild Rose School, Monrovia, California. 4b., 2g., others. Sc. Garden. Sierra Ed. News 25 : 24–5, June, 1929.

C **Fight for health, The.** Mrs. B. H. Blalock. 6b., 9g. Sc. Mass meeting of citizens. Norm. Inst. 34 : 72, Sept. 1925.

Fighting it out at the Cheer club. B. E. Palmer. Burlesque. 12w. Sc. Interior. ELD

Figureheads. L. Saunders. Romantic fantasy. 3m., 2w. Sc. Interior. GOLD

Figures don't lie. M. Johnson. 4m., 1w. Sc. Farmhouse interior. JOHD

Final refuge, The. K. Tomita. 3m., 3w. Sc. Japanese interior. BAK, JOHM

Finders-Keepers. G. Kelly. 1m., 2w. Sc. Living room. APPL, NICA, SHAQ

Fine feathers. E. O. Jones. Comedy. 2m., °2w. Sc. Library in home. FREN

Fine frenzy. W. Beck. 5m., 2w. Sc. An inn yard. BEC

Finer clay. F. A. Kummer. 2m., chorus. Sc. Deck of a life raft in South Africa. 5 Sc. KU

Finest flower of the age, The. R. Littell. 2m. Sc. Automobile show. New Rep. 49 : 109–110, Dec. 15, 1926.

Fingerbowls and Araminta. H. Hamilton. Comedy. 5w. Sc. Interior. LON, SV

Finishing touch, The. H. Simpson. Farce. 1m., 3w. Sc. Dining room. SIMS

Fire affair, A. L. duG. Peach. Farce. 1m., 2w. Sc. Hotel bedroom. PAZ

Fire-lighters, The. L. Housman. 2m., 2w. Sc. A low square parlour. HOT, Lond. Mercury 19 : 263–277, Jan. 1929.

J **Fire of icicles, The.** V. Olcott. 2b., 2g. Sc. Toy-maker's home in Nuremburg. OLD

C **Fire spirits.** Sierra Vista, California, upper grades. 5b., 6g., chorus. Sc. Pilgrim kitchen. WHG1

C **Firefly night.** M. Jagendorf. 17c., chorus groups. Sc. Clearing. JAF

Fireworks. G. E. Jennings. Comedy. 2m., 3w. Sc. Smoking room of country home. FREL

First aid. F. A. Hyde. Comedy. 2m., 3w. Sc. Small living room of cottage. DE

C **First aid for Kitty.** S. Henderson. 1b., 1g., 1 cat. Sc. Stage. MARC

First and the last, The. J. Galsworthy. 2m., 1w. Sc. Study. GAL

First Christmas, The. M. Marquis. 17m., 1w., 5c., others. Sc. 1 Hilltop in Judea. 2 Interior of a stable. Ladies Home Journal 47 : 14–15, 51, 53, Dec. 1930.

J **First Christmas, The.** M. M. Russell. 4b., 2g. Sc. Stable. RUS

C **First Christmas carol, The.** F. C. Gardner. 7 char. Sc. A dark cold exterior. GAP

  First client, The. P. Wilde. Farce. 2m., 1w. Sc. Office. WILT

J **First day of the week, The.** P. E. Osgood. 3g. Sc. Wall of upper room. OSG

  First dress-suit, The. R. Medcraft. 2m., 2w. Sc. Living room. FRE5

C **First Easter bunny, The.** G. Colby. 2b., 6g. Sc. Field near a church in Europe many years ago. SCH1

  First gift, The. W. F. Manley. 2m., 1w. Sc. Inn at Bethlehem. MANL

J **First martyr, The.** H. W. Githens. 9b., 1g., chorus. Sc. House in Jerusalem. GITH

C **First Memorial Day, The.** M. B. Carpenter. 2g. Sc. Street in Columbus, Mississippi. Norm. Inst. 38 : 64, May, 1929.

J **First mirror, The.** E. Wood. 2b., 2g. Sc. Cave in pre-historic ages. AU

J **First Noël, The.** C. D. Mackay. 16c., chorus groups. Sc. An inn. MACH, St. Nicholas 56 : 108–109, 154, Dec. 1928.

J **First Nowell, The.** C. E. Clement. Nativity. 25 char. Sc. Mediaeval Inn. WOM, Woman's Press 20 : 843–846, Dec. 1926.

  First of May, The. O. Kelley. Comedy. 1m., 1w. Sc. Library of home. KEK

C **First public appearance of a noted character.** F. O'Ryan and A. W. O'Ryan. 7b. Sc. The fields, N. Y. City 1774. ORY

C **First rehearsal, The.** R. Strutton. 9g. Sc. Room in home. STRU

J **First sin, The.** A. F. Alehin. 1w., 3b., 1g. Sc. General living room. ALD

  First Thanksgiving, The. T. Carter. 4m., 9w., 1b., 1g. Sc. Plymouth. Hist. Outlook 20 : 343–5, Nov. 1929.

C **First Thanksgiving, The.** A. D. White. Many children. Sc. Interior of cabin. School Arts M. 24 : 167–173, Nov. 1924.

C **First Thanksgiving, The.** K. A. White. 4b. Sc. Edge af Plymouth. WH

C **First Thanksgiving council, The.** M. Liles. 8b. Sc. Gov. Bradford's Office. Norm. Inst. 36 : 72, 74, Nov. 1926.

  First three hundred. M. M. Griffith. 8m., 2w. Sc. Double log cabin. GRI

J **Fish story, A.** H. W. Githens. 4b., chorus. Sc. Jonah's quarters in Zebulum. GIT

J **Fisherman, The.** H. W. Githens. 3b., 2g. Sc. Courtyard in the house of Simon. GITH

C **Fishing on dry land.** A Stevenson. 4b., 2g., chorus. Sc. Before the King's palace. STEV2

C **Five Ghosts.** R. Wright. 5c. Sc. Haunted house. JAO

C **Five hours to go.** N. Flaurier. Comedy. 4b., 4g. Sc. Interior. BECK, PAIN

  Five minutes from the station. E. S. Carrington. Comedy. 2m., 1w. Sc. Interior. HUO

  Five poor travellers. E. U. Ouless. Tr. from German Morality. 6m. Sc. Interior of inn. OULE

C **Five prim little patriots.** H. O. Boggs. Comedy. 5g. Sc. Front porch or lawn. BOG

  Fixed canon, The. W. Beck. 9m., 3w. Sc. A night court in an American city. BEC

  Fixer, The. E. Nichols. 2m., 3w. Sc. Sanitarium. ELD

Fixin's. E. Green and P. Green. Tragedy. 2m., 1w. Sc. Kitchen of a North Carolina farmhouse. CAR2, SCH4

J **Flag makers, The.** M. B. Rodney and G. E. Taylert. Fantasy. 15 char., chorus group. Sc. A street. TAX

Flageolet, The. M. Sand. Tr. from French by B. Hughes and G. Hughes. Comedy. 5m., 1w. Sc. An inn court. SA

C **Flags at war, The.** H. F. Dunlap. 2b., 4g. Sc. Interior or out of doors. FAX

J **Flambo, the Clown.** E. J. Tunnell. 7b., 3g. Sc. Small side tent of a circus. ELD

Flame leaps up, The. D. A. Lord. 6m., 1w. Sc. Spacious library. LOR

C **Flamingo feather, The.** K. Lounberg. Fantasy. 16c. Sc. Playroom. SOU

Flapper and her friends, The. R. Cramb. Comedy. 4w. Sc. Living room of an old mansion in Washington. BAK

Flash, The. J. C. McMullen. 3m. Sc. Doctor's office. BAK

Flash-back. A. B. Joder. From the short story of A. B. Holland. 1m., 2w. Sc. Alcove off ballroom in home near Washington. Players Mag. 8: 20–21, Sept.–Oct. 1931.

Flattering word, The. G. Kelly. Satire. 2m., 3w. Sc. Room in a parsonage. KEL

C **Flavor lasts, The.** G. B. Donnelly. 4b. Sc. Curtains or drapes. DON

Fleurette and Company. E. Dane. 2w. Sc. Interior. JOHP

J **Flight, The.** O. M. Price. 7b., 3g., chorus. Sc. Le Bourget field near Paris May 21, 1927. PRI

Flight. A. Scudder. 1m., 5w., chorus. Sc. A convent in western France in 6th century. SCU

Flight into Egypt, The. T. Wilder. 2m., 1w. Sc. A revolving cyclorama of the Holy Land and Egypt. WILZ

Flight of the herons, The. M. C. Kennard. 3m., 2w. Sc. Prison cell. Drama 14: 97, 98, 107, Dec. 1923.

Flight of the natives, The. W. Richardson. 6m., 2w. Sc. Interior of crude slave hut in South Carolina in 1860. LOC

C **Flippety-flop.** S. Henderson. 3b., 6g. Sc. Interior. MARC

Flirtation, The. F. Forrester. Pantomime comedy. 2m., 2w. Sc. Small retreat in a public park. SHAP

Flittermouse. M. K. Reely. Comedy. 1m., 3w. Sc. Cottage. ELD, Drama 14: 104–107, Dec. 1923.

Fliver family, The. C. Hicks. Comedy. 2m., 2w. Sc. Exterior. ELD

Flop goes the flapper. A. Patterson. Comedy. 1m., 2w. Sc. Interior. PAIN

Florist shop. W. Hawkridge. Comedy. 3m., 2w. Sc. Impressionistic setting or florist shop. BAK, KM

Florist's daughter, The. H. W. Hanemann. Burlesque. 2m., 2w. Sc. In front of a florist shop. HANE

Flossie for short. H. Brighouse. Comedy. 4m., 3w. Sc. Private room in majestic hotel. FREL

C **Flower garden.** 7c. Sc. Flower garden. Hygeia 7: 728, July 1929.

C **Flower of cheer, The.** A. E. Allen. 20 or more c. Sc. Stage. WHG1

Flower of Yeddo, A. V. Mapes. Comedy. 2m., 2w. Sc. Room in Japanese house. FRE1

C **Flower tree, The.** S. Young. Fanciful. 6b., 2g. Sc. Garden. YOUN

Flowers for Flossie. S. Henderson. Comedy. 3m., 3w. Sc. Very disordered bedroom. MARC

C **Flowers, music and sunbeams.** M. S. Bariteau. Many c. Sc. Woods. Etude 48: 397–8, June 1930.

C **Flowers' sacrifice, The.** E. F. Clarridge. Many c. Sc. A garden. Grade Teacher 46: 704, 730, May 1929.

Flyin'. E. W. Hart. Comedy. 3m., 2w. Sc. Home laundry. BANN

Flying doctor, The. J. B. P. Molière. Farce. 5m., 2w. Golden Book 1: 672–677, May 1925.

Flying prince, The. P. Wood and E. Wood. Comedy. 3m., 3w. Sc. Exterior. APPL

Fog. J. H. Neebe. Melodrama. 3m. Sc. Living room of summer cottage. DET

J **Folk in our neighborhood.** 18g. Sc. Dining room. WOM

Follow suit! L. Phillips. Comedy. 2m., 2w. Sc. Interior. BAK

Followers. H. Brighouse. Adapted from Gaskill's Cranford. 1m., 3w. Sc. Parlour at Cranford in 1859. MAR1

C **Food fairies, The.** M. Irish. 6c. Sc. Interior. IQ

C **Food for thought.** Miss Willson's Book Club at the Sophie Mee School. 2g. Sc. Any schoolroom. Prim. Educ. 46: 192, Nov. 1928.

CJ **Food revue.** M. E. Kern. 20c. Prac. Home Econ. 8: 156–7, May 1930.

Fool of a man, A. E. Finnegan. Comedy. 2m., 1w. Sc. Interior. BAK, PHIL

J **Fool of Dunvegan, The.** E. Smith. 4b. Sc. Castle in Scotland in 18th century. SM

Foolin' 'em. R. E. Hurd. 5m., 2w. Sc. In a children's hospital. LON

Fools adventure, The. L. Abercrombie. Poetic. 2m. Sc. Hermits cave. ABE

Fools and angels. M. L. Carr. 3m., 2w. Sc. Living room. ELD

Fool's errand, The. L. Housman. 2m. Sc. Community house at Perugia in 1243. HOUF

Fools errand. E. Spence. 4m., 4w., chorus. Sc. Living room in Negro cabin. FREN

Fools of April fool, The. H. O. Boggs. 6m. Sc. Street. BOGH

C **Fool's story, The.** E. Edland. 2b., 4g. Sc. Cozy corner of sitting room of Princess. EDLP

Football club supper, The. M. Clifton. 2m., 1b., chorus. Sc. Supper at the "Fitzwoolly Arms." FREL

For distinguished service. F. C. Knox. 3w. Sc. Boudoir. JOHM, LON

For England. D. Titheradge. Farce. 4m., 2w. Sc. Stage. TITB

J **For God and for Spain.** D. Willson. 6b., 1g. Sc. On a private ship. SHAB

C **For his Country.** R. Woodman. 4b., chorus. Sc. Washington's headquarters. SAO

For his name's sake. H. L. Todd. 1m., 2w. Sc. Upper room of an Oriental dwelling. DR

For Russia. J. Pollack. 5m. Sc. Tent in the camp of the Russian army near Moscow in 1812. POL

For the Empire. G. Doane. 2m., 2w. Sc. Apartment of Napoleon I. CANA

For the love of Kitty. A. Patterson. Comedy. 1m., 3w. Sc. Interior. PAIN

J **For the love of Pete.** H. F. Cattell. 3w. Sc. Interior. LON

For their sakes. E. DeHuff. 9 or more w. Sc. Woman's Church society meeting. DEH

J **For thirty pieces of silver.** H. W. Githens. 7b., chorus. Sc. In council chamber. GITH

J **For what shall I be thankful?** A. Curtis. 1b., 4g. Sc. Sitting room. CURT

For Winter, for summer. E. St. V. Millay. Satire. 1m., 1w. Sc. Screened-in porch. MIK

Forbidden fruit. L. Larrimore. Comedy. 1m., 2w. Sc. Garden. PENN

Forbidden fruit. G. J. Smith. Comedy. 3m., 2w. Sc. Large living room. SHAQ

Foreigner, The. J. W. Fitzpatrick. 5m., 2w. Sc. A street in N. Y. City. ELD

C **Forest of the blue fairy, The.** R. Bufano. 10c., chorus. Sc. Road. BUF

J **Forever and —.** F. E. Freehof. 2b., 3g. Sc. Small room in the Ghetto of the city. BLO

Forfeit, The. C. C. Howell. 4m., 1w. 2 neighbors. Sc. Bedroom in a southern cottage. Poet Lore 36: 136–141, Spring 1925.

Forfeit, The. T. B. Rogers. 3m., 2w. Sc. Manager's office of merchant. KN

J **Forks of the Dilemma, The.** P. Flowers. Comedy. 5b., 2g. Sc. Tower room in Kenilworth Castle. DAZ

Fortinbras in plain clothes. G. S. Brooks. Farce. 7m., 2w. Sc. A room in a palace. FRE4

J **Fortune teller, The.** O. Steiner. 4g. Sc. Stage. DRA

J **Fortune telling.** E. Hoxie. 3g. Sc. Outdoors or stage representing out door scene. HOV

Fortune's hired man. L. B. Pride. 3m., 2w. Sc. Back porch of a farmhouse. PRID

C **Forty-'leven Bunnies.** S. G. Clark. 4b., 1g., chorus. Sc. Briar patch. Norm. Inst. 37: 66, 68, Apr. 1928.

Forty miles an hour. C. D. Gilpatric. 4m., 3w. Sc. Living room. BAK, BUG

Four in a box. E. L. Squires. 4m., 4w. Sc. House on Long Island. MARC

Four to six-thirty. R. Jeans. Farce. 2m., 2w. Sc. Room in a flat. JEO

Four who were blind. C. C. Clements. 5m. Sc. Interior of a coffee house in Jerusalem. CLP

Four's Company. H. C. G. Stevens. Revue. 2m., 2w. Sc. Boudoir. FRET

Foursquare. L. B. Pride. 5m. Sc. Carpenter's workshop in a mining village. PRID

Fourteenth guest, The. C. Barrett. Comedy. 16w. Sc. Sitting room. FREN

C **Fourteenth veteran, The.** H. W. Munro. 3b., 2g. Sc. Lodge hall. BAK

Fourth degree, The. M. Lee. Farce. 5m. Sc. Interior. LEE

Fourth Mrs. Phillips, The. C. Glick. 3m., 4w. Sc. Theatre dressing-room FRE4

C **Fox and his tail, The.** R. Rice. 5c. Sc. Any. Amer. Child 15: 24, Apr. 1930.

Fragment, A. N. Gogol Tr. from Russian. 3m., 1w. Sc. Room in Russian house. GOG, GOG6

Fragments of a play. K. D. Wiggin. 1m., 3w. Sc. Living room. Poet Lore 40: 281–287, Summer 1929.

Frail Ferdinand. K. C. Kelly. 2m., 3w., 2b. Sc. Lawn garden. ELD

France. L. F. Doyle. 6m., 1w. Sc. Interior of a Chalet. Cath. World 124: 788–97, Mar. 1927.

Frances and Francis. J. P. Webber. 1m., 1w., 1g. Sc. Back stage. BAK, WEBB

Frank Glynn's wife. Comedy. 2m., 5w. Sc. Parlor. DRA

J **Frank goes on a diet.** K. A. White. 3b., 3g. Sc. Living room. WH

C **Franklin's forebodings.** F. O'Ryan and A. W. O'Ryan. 8b., chorus. Sc. Simple room in 1755. ORY

C **Frank's Valentine.** M. Bitney. 3b., 4g. Sc. Stage. BIT

Fraternity initiation, The. W. L. Lamar. Burlesque. 8m., Sc. Initiation room of a fraternity. J. Chem. Ed. 6: 2254–9, Dec. 1929.

Fred joins the firm. N. Balch. 3m., 1w. Sc. Sales office of a wholesale builders' supplies. BAL

Fredonian rebellion. M. M. Griffith. 8m. Sc. Old stone fort. GRI

Free-for-all discussion, A. 10m. Sc. Parlors of Y.M.C.A. Missionary Review 52: 384–388, May 1929.

Freedom or the good sports. M. Mackendrick. 3m., 4w. Sc. Living-dining room combined. MACS

Freeing of grandpa, The. M. Neff and Mrs. C. Johnstone. 3m., 1w. Sc. Interior. ELD

J **Friar Tuck and the Black Knight.** A. E. Thompson. Adapted from Scott's Ivanhoe. 6b. Sc. In a monk's cell. SAO

C **Friday afternoon.** O. V. Roe. 5g. Sc. Sitting room. FJ

Friday for luck. G. F. Mountford. Comedy. 3m., 1w. Sc. Interior. DEN

C **Friend Lincoln.** M. Bitney. 3b., 3g. Sc. Living room. BIT

Friend Mary. T. W. Stevens. 2m., 2w. Sc. Living room on Apr. 15, 1865. STEU

Friend of all men, The. A. B. Ferris. 14m., 7w., 4c. Sc. Mountain pass. FED

Friend of his youth, A. E. See. Tr. by M. E. Brandon. 4m., 1w. Sc. Apartment of assistant secretary of State in France. Poet Lore 36: 159–187, Summer 1925.

Friend of Potiphar's wife, The. C. A. Rollins. 5m., 2w. Sc. Inner room of Potiphar's dwelling in Memphis on the Nile. DR

Friendly advice. M. Irish. 2m., 3w. Sc. Kitchen. IR

C **Friendly brushes, The.** H. Wedgwood. 11c. Sc. Any stage. Hygeia 2: 262–263, Apr. 1924.

C **Friendly dark, The.** A. P. Hooe. Many c. Sc. Nursery. Prim. Educ. 45: 288–289, 300, 309, Dec. 1927.

C **Friendly neighbors.** J. A. Stewart. 7c. Sc. Disarmament. Norm. Inst. 33: 72, May 1924.

C **Friendly Valentines.** M. Bitney. 6c. Sc. Interior. BIT

Friends. H. Farjeon. Comedy. 3m., chorus. Sc. Roadside. MAR3

Friends indeed. F. C. Gardner. 1m., 4w., 1g. Sc. Street. GAQ

Friends invited. R. L. Jackson. Comedy. 2m., 3w. Sc. Living room. FREN

Frock for Francie, A. L. Larrimore. Comedy. 3m., 3w. Sc. Drawing room of train. PENN

C **From danger valley to safety hill.** L. J. Roberts. 1b., 1g., 25 others. Sc. 1 Palace of King of good health. 2 Mary's home in danger valley. Hygeia 2: 36–44, Jan. 1924.

From darkness to dawn. D. C. Wilson. Easter. 6m., 4w. Sc. Room in Jerusalem home. Int. J. of Rel. Ed. 5: 24–26, 36, Feb. 1929.

J **From palace to prairie.** H. W. Githens. 5b., 5g., chorus. Sc. A brick-yard. GIT

From small beginnings. P. Holloway. 8w. Sc. Living room. HOL

From their own place. M. Denison. 5m., 1w. Sc. Living room of a cottage of a small backwoods village. DEL

Frontispiece. J. Harewood. 17m. Sc. Front line trenches. Bermondsey Book 7: 62–65, Dec.–Jan.–Feb. 1929–30.

J **Fun at camp.** J. Bennett. 10g. Sc. Interior of summer cottage on shore of lake. PAIN

Fun for old and young. E. Wilson. Expressionist play. 6m., 1w. New Rep. 46: 20, Feb. 24, 1926.

Fun in a school room. H. E. Shelland. 4m. Sc. Interior. FIT

Funeralizing of Crickneck, The. P. Mackaye. 3m., 1w., chorus. Sc. Interior of log cabin in Kentucky mountains. MACK, MACL

Fur and warmer. V. Melick. Comedy. 4m., 3w. Sc. Interior. PENN

Fur coat, The. J. H. Turner. Farce. 6m., 2w. Sc. 1 Office. 2 Restaurant. TURN

Furnished apartments. Farce. 5m. Sc. Interior. FIT

C **Future democracy of America as our young folks see it, The.** M. Knox and A. M. Lütkenhaus. Pageant. 10b., 6g., chorus groups. Sc. Stage. LUT

Future of marriage, The. H. G. Leach, *ed.* Socratic dialogue. 4w. Sc. Home of H. G. Leach. Forum 86: 74–78, Aug. 1931.

G

J **Gabbatha.** P. E. Osgood. 1b., 1g. Sc. Tall screen. OSG

Gabriel's horn. H. O. Boggs. 5m., 2w. Sc. Out of doors. BOGG

Gadgets. P. Wilde. Tragi-comedy. 5m., 4w., chorus. Sc. Outside a fashionable shop. WILD

Gaff, which expresses an impression. H. K. Carmichael. 3m., Sc. Office. Player's Mag. 7: 22–25, Nov.–Dec. 1930.

C **Gaining a member.** A. L. Whitson. 3b., 3g. Sc. Platform. ELDR

Gaius and Gaius Jr. L. M. Cobb. Comedy. 5m., 1w. Sc. Plantation before the civil war. CAR2

Gala night at Galashiels, A. R. Jeans. Farce. 6m., 8w. Sc. Interior. JEO

Galatea takes a lease of life. M. T. Applegarth. 27 char. Sc. Stage with statue on it. APN

J **Gallant pilgrim, The.** E. G. Hornsey. 12b., 5g. Sc. Transept of church in 1212. BAK

Gamblers, The. N. Gogol. Tr. from Russian. 9m. Sc. Room in provincial inn. GOG, GOG6

Game, The. L. F. Thanhouser. 3m. Sc. Parlor. BAK

Game called kiss, The. H. Kemp. Fanciful. 3m., 3w. Sc. Valley in Arcadia. KEM

Game of adverbs, The. F. Anstey. Comedy. 4m., 7w., 1b. Sc. Drawing room of English manor. Golden Book 10: 99–102, Dec. 1929.

Game of chess, The. K. S. Goodman. 4m. Sc. A wainscoted room in a Russian home. KM, KN

Game to the end. R. Jeans. Farce. 2m., 2w. Sc. Interior. JER

C **Garden drama, A.** F. Shaw. Fanciful. 21g. Sc. Garden. DRA

Garden in Mitylene, A. F. B. Cuthrell. 7 char. Sc. Garden. CUT

C **Garden of the zoo, The.** J. Farrar. 14c. Sc. The zoo. JAO

Garden play for jolly juniors, A. B. Creighton. 10g. Sc. Garden with picket fence. Woman's Home Companion 58: 54, June 1931.

Gardener, The. V. I. Arlett. 5b. Sc. Garden in 303 A. D. in Sinope. Poet Lore 41: 305–313, Summer 1930.

C **Gardener's cap, The.** A. Nichols. 3b., 2g., chorus. Sc. Before a prim old-fashioned house. NIA

Garrick revised. D. Titheradge. Farce. 5m., 4w. Sc. Stage. TITB

Gas. F. J. Pohl. 5m., 2w. Sc. Private dining room in a N. Y. City hotel. PO

Gas, Air and Earl. B. Bloch. Comedy. Sc. Sitting room in huge hotel on Maine coast. NICB

Gate, The. M. O'Connor. 4m., 2w. Sc. Reception room of an up-to-date newspaper office. UNW2

Gate of heaven, The. Mrs. A. Stallard. 5m., chorus. Sc. On Farne Island 687. STAL

Gate of Montsalvat, The. M. McKittrick. 4m., 1w. Sc. Dark mountain top. WOM

J **Gate of the west, The.** E. R. Jasspon and B. Becker. 5b., 1g. Sc. Screen or back-drop. JAR

Gate of vision, The. M. Creagh-Henry. 14 char. Sc. Dark curtains. CRE

Gauge of youth, The. K. B. Rigby. 14w. Sc. Stage. BAK

Geisha's wedding, The. L. S. Jast. 2m., 5w. Sc. Room in house in old Japan. JAS

General George Washington. P. B. Corneau. 11m., chorus. Sc. Interior of a tent at Washington's headquarters. SAG

J **General goes home, The.** L. Barton. 11g. Sc. Drawing-room of a house in New York in 1783. SAG, Playground 20: 568–571, Jan. 1927.

Genesis. C. Reznikoff. 6m., 1w. Sc. At night upon a roof in Haran. REZ

C **Genevieve's health dream.** H. Hannemann. Many c. Sc. Nursery. Grade Teacher 47: 46, 48, 67, Sept. 1929.

Gentle-man, The. H. Simpson. Farce. 2m., 1w. Sc. Sitting room. SIMH

Gentlemen of the road. C. McEvoy. Farce. 5m., 3w. Sc. Exterior. BAK

Gentlemen prefer bonds. C. Orwig. Comedy. 2w. Sc. Living room. PENN

Genuine antique. C. Roberts. 3m., 2w. Sc. An inn parlour in Cumberland. FREL

Geoffrey's wife. O. W. Firkins. 3m., 1w. Sc. Manor-hall in a dreary district of England in the reign of Queen Elizabeth. FIR

J **Geometry humanized.** E. Scott. Many c. Sc. Stage. Math. Teacher 21: 92–101, Feb. 1928.

George—and the Dragon. F. L. Mansur. 2m., 1w. Sc. Kitchen. BAK

George Bernard Shaw self-revealed. A. Henderson. 2m. Sc. Living room of Shaw's apartment. Fortn. 125: 433-443, Apr. 1926; 610-618, May, 1926.

George Moore and John Freeman. G. Moore. 2m. Dial 75: 341-362, Oct. 1923.

George Washington. B. W. Gue. 14m. Sc. Library of Washington's home in Mt. Vernon. FOU

George Washington (the spirit of Americanization). P. Marschall. Pageant. Many char. Sc. Stage. SAG

George Washington and the hatchet. H. O. Boggs. 2m., 1b. Sc. Washington's garden. BOGH

George Washington at the Delaware. P. MacKaye. 4m., voices. Sc. By the Delaware River in 1776. NICA, SCH3

C   **George Washington at the Helm of State.** M. A. Niemeier. 6b., 1g. Sc. Washington's home. NIE

J   **George Washington, midshipman.** A. E. Thompson. 1m., 3b., 1w., 3g. Sc. Washington's home near Fredericksburg. SAG

George Washington's birthday. E. Gibson. 3w. GIB

George Washington's wedding. W. Archer. 10m., 5w., 2 chorus groups. Sc. Spacious room in Virginia in 1759. SCH3

Georgie plays his hand. N. Balch. Comedy. 2m., 2w. Sc. Office of Real Estate firm. BUG, ELD

C   **Georgie's piece.** M. Bitney. 1b., 1g. Sc. Interior. BIT

Germs. H. S. Sharp. Fantasy. 3m., 3w. Sc. Interior of a man's body. Drama 16: 167-8, 170, Feb. 1926.

Gertrude Mason M.D. L. M. C. Armstrong. Farce. 7w. Sc. Plain room. FIT

Get in the talkies. D. Sheridan. Musical farce. 8m., 5w. Sc. Office. SHER

Getting a marriage license. A. James. Comedy. 2m., 1w. Sc. Interior. PAIN

Getting a permanent wave. A. Steward. Comedy. 2w. Sc. Beauty parlor. PAIN

J   **Getting by.** M. Barrymore. 2b. 1g. Sc. Recitation room in school. ELD

J   **Getting into step.** M. Irish. 2b., 3g. Sc. Living room. IRI

Getting Los Angeles. E. O. Jones. Comedy. 2m., 2w. Sc. Interior. FREN

Gettysburg. P. Mackaye. 1m., 1w. Sc. Woodshed. MACM

Geysers, Ltd. H. C. Sargent. Farce. 4m., 3w. Sc. Private office. SARB

Ghost, The. H. E. Davis. Hallowe'en. Any no. c. Sc. Living room. Delineator 109: 33-34, Oct. 1926.

Ghost, The. C. P. Romulo. 4m., 2w. Sc. Typical Filipino Salr. PHI

Ghost hunters, The. L. W. Watkins. Comedy. 4m., 2w. Sc. Sitting room. BAK

J   **Ghost in the boarding school, The.** O. Steiner. Comedy. 5w. Sc. Interior. DRA

Ghost of Jerry Bundler, The. W. W. Jacobs and C. Rich. Comedy. 7m. Sc. Commercial room in an old-fashioned hotel. FRE1

Ghost of the past, A. W. Richardson. Comedy. 3m., 1w. Sc. Sitting room. PAIN

Ghost Sonata, The. A. Strindberg. 8m., 5w. Sc. Ground floor of a modern house. STRI

J   **Ghost story.** B. Tarkington. Comedy. 5m., 5w. Sc. Pleasant living room. APPL, CRO2, ELD, NICA

Girl who slipped, The. L. Campbell. 5m., 1w. Sc. A rich drawing room of a N. Y. house in December. Drama 17: 203–5, Apr. 1927.

C **Girl who trod on the loaf, The.** A. Stevenson. 11 char. Sc. Interior. STEV3

Give the audience a chance. L. Anderson. Comedy. 6m., 6w. Sc. Block of seats in the body of a theatre. ANDE

Giving not getting. J. E. Douglass. 1b., 3g. Sc. Living room. Pop. Educ. 42: 232, Dec. 1924.

C **Giving thanks today.** E. E. Olson. 6b., 5g. Sc. Parlor. BAK, ELD

J **Glad Tidings to all people.** E. G. Wallace and A. B. Mead. 6b., 3g. Sc. Court of house in Antioch. BUG

Glimpses of great people. G. Bradford. 5m., 3w. Sc. In the Tuileries garden in 1811. Forum 73: 545–551, Apr. 1925.

Gloom. E. Preston. Comedy. 4m., 3w. Sc. Room in a Russian house. FREP

Gloria Mundi. P. Brown. Irony. 2m., 4w. Sc. Interior. FREN

Glorious martyr, A. C. S. Pike. 4m. Sc. Around a table in Italy. DET

J **Glorious wish, The.** F. Cavanah. 5b., 3g., chorus. Sc. Upholstery shop of Betsy Ross, July 4, 1776. CAV

Glove of gold, The. S. Young. Fanciful. 5b., chorus. Sc. Opening in the heart of a wood. YOUN

J **Glutton, The.** A. F. Alehin. 1b., 3g. Sc. Room. ALD

Goal, The. H. A. Jones. 4m., 2w. Sc. Parents and children. PEN

Goat Alley. E. H. Culbertson. 3m., 5w. Sc. Sitting room of a negro's squalid dwelling in Washington D. C. SHAQ

C **Goblin and the Hackster's Jam, The.** A. Stevenson. 5b., 1g., chorus group. Sc. 1 The Hackster's shop. 2 Students' garret. STEV4

Goblins, The. P. Beard. 5b., 2g. Sc. A cornfield. BEA

God of Quiet, The. J. Drinkwater. Symbolic. 8m. Sc. Road at summit of hill. GOLD

J **God of the Mountains, The.** O. M. Price. 7b., 1g. Sc. Homestead in Vermont in 1923. PRI

C **God Pan forgotten.** J. Farrar. Myth. 4b., 4g. Sc. Forest. FARR

God save the heir. J. Koven. 7m., 1w., chorus. Sc. A palatial chamber. KOV

God winks. K. S. Burgess. 2m., 2w. Sc. Living room. EAT, LON, SCH3

Godfather's Christmas. E. Wilbur. 2m., 1w., 2b., 2g. Sc. Living room. BANN

C **God's adopted son.** D. Lord. 29 or more b. Sc. Interior. LOP

Gods churn the sea, The. P. Claudel. Fantasy. 8 char. Sc. Forum 82: 95–97, Aug. 1929.

God's move. B. Payne. 3m., 1w. Sc. Room at All Saints' mission. BANN

Gods of the Mountain, The. Lord Dunsany. Romantic. 10m., 5w. Sc. Outside a city wall. MOSR

Godstow nunnery, The. L. Binyon. Verse. 7w. Sc. The cloister. BIN

J **Gohalt of Weirhawk.** E. S. Lyon. 10b. Sc. Clearing in front of woods. SAO

"Going." E. Dane. Fantasy. 2m., 3w., 2 voices. Sc. Curtain. DAN

C **Going to the party.** M. Irish. 6b., 5g. Sc. Stage. IQA

Gold altar, The. L. V. V. Armstrong. Comedy. 12m. Sc. Monastary of the Spanish friars in The Amicas in 1700. FREN

Gold machine, The. E. Selnick. 3m., 1w. Sc. Interior small negro farm house. Drama 20 : 173–175, 190, Mar. 1930.

Gold of the Sun God. F. J. Pohl. 10m. Sc. A small plateau in Peru in 1536. PO

C Golden bracelet, The. V. Olcott. 3b., 3g., chorus. Sc. Court of a rich home in Cairo. OLF

C Golden bucket, The. A. Stevenson. 2b., 1g. Sc. The woods. STEV1

J Golden calf, The. H. W. Githens. 2b., 3 chorus groups. Sc. Plain in the wilderness. GIT

C Golden Cornstalk goes home. F. C. Comfort. Fanciful. 5b., 2 chorus groups. Sc. Corn field with scare crow. JAN

J Golden doom, The. Lord Dunsany. Poetic. 10b., 1g., chorus. Sc. Outside the King's great door. FIN, MAR3

Golden eagle child, The. J. E. Lobner. 8m., 3w. Sc. Out of doors. CART

J Golden Easter egg, The. G. Sorenson. Comedy. 3b., 5g. Sc. Corner of lawn. SOR

C Golden goose, The. E. P. Guptill. 6b., 7g. Sc. Mother Goose's home. BECK

C Golden goose, The. K. D. Morse. 11b., 6g. Sc. Highway with trees at the back. MORS

Golden rule in courtship, The. R. C. Cook. 1m., 2w. Sc. Comfortable living room. EAS

C Golden touch, The. M. Oller and E. K. Dawley. 3b., 1g. Sc. Throne room. OLL

Goldenrod Lode, The. J. G. Rogers. 8m. Sc. Spruce forest in Rocky mountains. CAC

C Goldilocks and the three bears. S. L. Cummins. Burlesque. 2b., 2g. Sc. Cottage. CUM3

C Goldilocks finds a new play-house. 2b., 2g. Sc. Home of three bears. Prim. Educ. 44 : 375–377, Jan. 1927.

C Goldtree and silvertree. K. D. Morse. 4b., 7g. Sc. Queen's bower. MORS

Goliad massacre. M. M. Griffith. 11m., 1w. Sc. Before Mexican hut. GRI

C Good American, The. P. G. Staats. 2b., 2g., others. Sc. Living room. Norm. Inst. 37 : 76, 78, Sept. 1928.

Good and the bad, The. P. Johnson. 4m., 1w., chorus. Sc. Living room of cottage. JOHF

J Good appearance in school, A. V. Sramek. 5g. Sc. Classroom. Prac. Home Econ. 7 : 278, 280, Sept. 1929.

Good biders. P. Wood. 3m., 2w. Sc. Living room of cottage. DE

C Good book fairy, The. M. M. Walker. 10c. Sc. Schoolroom. Norm. Inst. 34 : 72–73, Nov. 1924.

J Good English comes to town. L. Hunt. 10 char. Sc. Interior. ELD

Good fishing. F. Ferguson. Comedy. 2m., 1w. Sc. A bit of woods. FREN

Good Friday. J. Masefield. 1m., 1w., chorus. Sc. Pavement outside the Roman Citadel in Jerusalem. MASG

C Good George Washington. M. Bitney. 5b., 6g., Sc. Interior. BIT

C Good health. B. N. Hanson. Many c. Sc. Classroom. Prim. Educ. 44 : 812, 814, 816, June 1927.

C Good Health fairies. E. Williams. 30c. Sc. Interior. BUG

C **Good health in the land of Mother Goose.** F. C. Gardner. 25c. Sc. Interior. ELD

C **Good health play, A.** E. Stone. Several c. Sc. Stage. Pop. Educ. 42: 114, Oct. 1924.

C **Good health prepares for good citizenship.** G. A. Kennard. Many c. Prim. Educ. 33: 402, 416, June 1925.

C **Good Health Way and Queen of May.** F. W. Blose and J. M. Blose. 30c. Sc. Interior. Comedy. ELD

C **Good King Arthur.** G. Lloyd. 35c. Sc. Kitchen of King Arthur's Castle LL

Good medicine. J. Arnold and E. Burke. 1m., 2w. Sc. Living room and office of doctor. EAT, LON

Good morning, Teacher. F. G. Johnson. 8m., 3w. Sc. Schoolroom. BECK

Good Night. M. S. Smith. 1m., 1w. Sc. Front porch. Drama 16: 174, 199, Feb. 1926.

J **"Good Night, Babette!"** A. Dobson. Fanciful. 1b., 1g. Sc. A small room. WEB

Good old days, The. A. C. Thompson. Comedy. 11w. Sc. Interior. PENN

J **Good old times, The.** D. A. Heywood. 4b., 1g. Sc. In the forest. HEY

Good old Uncle Amos. S. Schofield. 4m., 3w. Sc. Library in home. FREL

Good provider, A. E. S. Carrington. 3m., 3w. Sc. Interior. APPL

C **Good resolutions.** K. L. Bates. 14c. Sc. Solar system. BAT

Good roads. L. V. V. Armstrong. 6m., 1w. Sc. Kitchen farmhouse. FREN

Good Sainte Anne, The. H. Gilbert. 1b., 3w. Sc. French Canadian kitchen. Poet Lore 35: 576–586, Winter 1924.

Good Samaritan, The. A. Ferris. 11b. Sc. Road. FED

Good theatre. C. Morley. Comedy. 4m., 1w., chorus. Sc. Lobby of a New York theatre. COH, LON, Sat. R. Lit. 2: 695–7, Apr. 10, 1926.

Good vintage. D. Totheroh. 2m., 6w. Sc. Bedroom in ranch house in Sonoma county. CL, TOT

Goodbye, The. P. Green. 2m., 1w. Sc. Room. GREE

Good-for-nothing, The. K. Parsons. Comedy. 3m., 3w. Sc. Living room. MARC

Gooseberries in Piccadilly. D. Titheradge. Farce. 3m., 2w. Sc. Living room. TITB

Gooseberry Mandarin, The. G. D. Ruthenburg. Poetic. 3m., 1w. Sc. At the wall of a garden. IS, Theatre Arts Mag. 12: 501–504, July 1928.

J **Goose-girl, The.** E. Smith. 5b., 5g. Sc. Room in palace. SM

C **Goosey-goosey-gander.** E. Denton. 10c. Sc. A green. DENU

Gospel according to the telephone, The. M. T. Applegarth. 4 char. Sc. Platform. APO

Gown and out. R. Jeans. Farce. 3m., 2w. Sc. Bedroom. JEA

Grace. M. Lee. Farce. 3m., 2w. Sc. Lounge hall of a superior dwelling house. LEE

J **Graduate, The.** F. J. Passmore. Burlesque. 4b., 3g. Sc. Stage. AU

C **Graduation gifts.** M. Parsons. 11b., 12g., chorus. Sc. Large frame on a stage. SANP

Grain of truth, A. H. C. Sargent. Farce. 3m., 2w. Sc. Dining room. SARB

C **Grammar fairies.** K. Chalmers. Many c. Sc. Living room. Prim. Educ. 45: 197, 217, 221, Nov. 1927.

Grand Cham's diamond, The. A. Monkhouse. Mystery. 3m., 2w. Sc. Interior. BAK, CRO2, MAR1, TUC

Grand evening, A. J. C. McMullen. 3m., 2w. Sc. Interior. FREN

Grand Guignol. R. Jeans. Farce. 3m., 1w., chorus. Sc. Stage in semi-darkness. JEO

Grand Guignol. H. F. Rubinstein. 2m. Sc. Uninteresting interior. RUB

Grand march, The. H. Reed. Comedy. 3m., 3w. Sc. Ante-room of dance palace. BAK, YOU

Grandfather's chair. W. P. Eaton. Comedy. 4m., 4w. Sc. Interior. FREN

Grandma Gay slips into high. R. B. Putnam. 2m., 4w. 1 dog. Comedy. Sc. Living room. BANN

C **Grandma Green's Thanksgiving.** M. Bitney. 3b., 3g. Sc. Kitchen. BIT

—**Grandma pulls the string.** E. B. Delano and D. Carb. 1m., 5w. Sc. Interior. BAK, PHIL

Grandma Shaw's visit. J. A. Baxter. 1m., 5w. Sc. Interior. PAIS

Grandma's Christmas guest. R. Farquhar. 4m., 5w. Sc. Living room. DRA, ELD

C **Grandmother dozes.** J. Farrar. 1w., 1b., 1g., chorus. Sc. End of a library. FARR

Grandmother man, The. L. Larrimore. Comedy. 2m., 3w. Sc. Studio. PENN

C **Grandmother's recollections of Thanksgiving.** O. J. Roberts. 1b., 2g., others. Sc. Living room in Puritan home. Prim. Educ. 44: 228–229, 237, Nov. 1926.

Granny Maumee. R. Torrence. 3w. Sc. Living room in an old cabin. LOC

Grapes hang high, The. Mrs. C. P. Smith. Comedy. 4w. Sc. Interior. FREN

Grass grows red, The. E. A. Wright. 2m., 2w. Sc. Interior. CART

Grasshopper and the ant, The. R. Rice. 5c. Sc. Any stage. Amer. Childhood 15: 23–24, Apr. 1930.

Grasshopper at the home of the ants, The. Trans. from French by A. L. Barney. Comedy. 2m., 2w. Sc. Living room in Paris. BANN

Grave, The. R. Speirs. 3m. Sc. Graveyard in Scotland. Poet Lore 40: 113–118, Spring 1929.

Grave v. Gay. H. Simpson. Farce. 1m., 1w. Sc. A poorly furnished garret. SIMN

Grave woman, The. E. C. Koenig. 2w. Sc. Inside gate-house of cemetery. Poetry 32: 206–209, July 1928.

J **Graven images.** M. Miller. 5b., 2g., chorus. Sc. Arena before the tabernacle in Egypt 1490 B. C. RICH

Gray Switch, The. S. Keener. 1m., 2w. Sc. Combination sitting room and dining room. UNU

Greasy luck. R. Field. 3m., 1w. Sc. Parlor. CL, FIC

Great arrival. G. W. H. Griffin. Farce. 3m. Sc. No scenery needed. FIT

C **Great bell of Peking, The.** L. F. Collins. 7b., 2g., chorus. Sc. On the Road to Peking many many years ago. COJ

J **Great Caesar.** W. Beck. 5b., 2g. Sc. Roomy barn loft. BEB

Great Cham, The. C. E. Lawrence. 4m., 5w. Sc. Dr. Johnson's room in Fleet St. in 1766. Cornhill M. 71: 271–283, Sept. 1931.

Great dark, The. D. Totheroh. 6w. Sc. At edge of mine shaft. TOT, Drama 21: 19–20, 22, Feb. 1931.

C   **Great decision, The.** A. L. Whitson. 3b., 2g. Sc. Stage. ELDR

Great delusion, The. E. W. Peattie. 3m., 3w., chorus. Sc. A dignified apartment. PEA

Great expectations. R. Jeans. Farce. 3m., 3w. Sc. Private office. JEC

Great God O'Neill, The. W. Katzin. 3m. Sc. Private library. Bookman (N. Y.) 68: 61–66, Sept. 1928.

C   **Great gold penny, The.** C. Pierce. 2b., 4g. Sc. Living room. MARC

C   **Great Grandmother's attic.** E. L. Squires. 2b., 2g. Sc. Attic. SQ

J   **Great Lexicographer, The.** W. L. Bissell. 4m., 1w. Sc. Room in Johnson's House. BIS

Great minds. W. A. Kimball. Farce. 2m., 5w. Sc. Living room. UNW3

Great moments. R. Moore. Comedy. 2m., 2w. Sc. Gardens of a summer hotel. SHAP

Great Pearl mystery, The. L. Phillips. Comedy. 1m., 2w. Sc. Living room. BAK

C   **Great quest for character, A.** E. A. Thomey. 14c. Sc. Stage. LUT

Great snakes. H. C. Sargeant. Burlesque. 4m., 3w. Sc. Deck of ship. SARP

J   **Great Thanksgivings in American history.** Rawlings Junior High School. Any no. char. Sc. Assembly platform. RAW

Great war and the aftermath, The. A dialogue between Bernard Shaw and A. Henderson. 2m. Sc. Country house in Hertfordshire. Fortn. 123: 1–12, Jan. 1925, 145–152, Feb. 1925.

Greater law, The. L. C. White. Comedy. 7m., 4w. Sc. Interior. BAK

"Greater love hath no man." M. Creagh-Henry. 4m., 3w. Sc. Room adjoining the upper room. CRE

C   **Greatest dreamer of the world, The.** Y. Klein and F. Schwarz. 14b., 1g. Sc. Any interior. KL

Greatest force, The. Mrs. G. S. Squires. Pageant for parent-teachers associations. Many c. Prim. Educ. 45: 278, 299, Dec. 1927.

Greek as she is taught. R. Jeans. 2m. Sc. School room. JER

J   **Greek games, and festivals.** M. R. Hofer. 15b., 1g., 9 chorus groups. Sc. Indoor or outdoor. HOF

Greek vase, The. M. Baring. Satire. 2m. Sc. No scenery. JOHM

Green Chartreuse. C. D. Heywood. Comedy. 3m., 1w. Sc. Bachelor's apartment in London. NICR

Green cuckatoo, The. A. Schnitzler. 20m., 2w. others. Sc. Cellar room in Paris. Golden Book 4: 637–653, Nov. 1926.

Green field, The. T. Kelly. Comedy. 4m., 1w. Sc. Irish cottage kitchen. DE

Green helmet, The. W. B. Yeats. Heroic farce. 6m., 1w., chorus. Sc. House made of logs. YEA

Green monkey, The. V. Bridges. Comedy. 3m., 3w. Sc. Sitting room. DE

Green paint. D. P. Ricks. Comedy 5m., 1w. Sc. North Carolina cotton mill village store. PENN

C   **Green Rowan.** A. H. Branch. 9 char. Sc. Outside the house. HAH

J   **Green shadows.** L. Marshall. Comedy. 3b., 3g. Sc. Interior. BANN

C **Greene and Morgan on the Yadkin.** F. O'Ryan and A. W. O'Ryan. 5b., 1g. Sc. Country road 1781. ORY

Greene Christmas, A. E. E. Preston. 8m., 8w. Sc. Living room. DRA

Green-eyed monster, The. D. Titheradge. Farce. 3m., 1w. Sc. Study. TITF

Grensal green. E. Crawshay-Williams. Comedy. 2m., 1w. Sc. Sitting room of flat. CRAA

Grief (La pena). Serafin and Joaquin Quintero. 1m., 1w. Sc. Dining room. Poet Lore 41: 391–402, Autumn 1930.

Grill, The. G. W. Johnston. 2m., 2w. Sc. Library of district Attorney's office. EAT, MACG

J **Griselda married, being the further adventure of "The Dutch Doll."** M. Carter. 2b., 2g. Sc. A garden outside a windmill house. FREL

Grotesquerie. I. Urquhart. Mystic. 5m. Sc. A grave-yard. UNW3

Grown-up Children. M. F. Simmonds. 2m., 4w. Sc. Cheery modern living room. Poet Lore 36: 434–440, Autumn 1925.

C **Grown-up folks.** H. C. Eldridge. 6b., 5g. Sc. Tea party. ELD

C **Grumps meet the grouches.** M. Irish. 5b., 5g. Sc. Living room. IQ

C **Guarding angels, The.** H. F. Dunlap. 4c. Sc. Cemetery. FAX

J **Gudrun.** E. Smith. 3b., 4g., chorus. Sc. Hall of King of Normandy in in the 9th century. SM

Guiding light, The. I. Bolton. 20m., 2w. Sc. A hill. WOM

C **Guki the moon boy.** B. Folmsbee. Fanciful. 6b., 2g. Sc. Room in attic. FOL

Gull of unrest, The. M. Larrimer. Allegory. 1m., 1w. Sc. Winding path. LAR

C **Gumps in Grammar Land, The.** E. Preston. 42c. Sc. Stage. ELD

Gundy Shop, The. A. P. Wilson. 6w. Sc. Shop in Scotland. WIN

Guts. J. H. Neebe. Melodrama. 3m., 1w. Sc. Shack on river front. DET

Guy upstairs, The. E. H. VanDelden. 5m. Sc. Two prison cells. Poet Lore 40: 251–263, Summer 1929.

J **Gym and Jerry.** B. Abel. 9g., chorus. Sc. Girl's room. WOM

Gypsy's prophecy, The. E. R. Noyes. 5w., 2c. Sc. Stuffy crowded mid-Victorian parlor. FREL

J **Gypsy's secret, The.** N. Z. Wagner. 2b., 3g., chorus. Sc. Gypsy camp. ELD

H

C **Hades and Persephone.** M. Oller and E. K. Dawley. 3b., 2g. Sc. Throne room of Hades. OLL

Haiduc, The. C. C. Clements. 7m., 4w., chorus. Sc. Large set. CLP

Half an hour. J. M. Barrie. 5m., 3w. Sc. Interior. BARR, BARS

Half Back's interference. M. S. Beebe. Farce. 10m. Sc. Interior. BUG

Half brother, a modern morality play. D. L. W. Worcester. 1m., 1w., 1b. Sc. Probation office in San Diego in 1929. Survey 64: 82–5, Apr. 15, 1930.

Half hour at the gate, A. E. O. Cochran. Symbolic. 4m., 4w., chorus. Sc. Out of doors before a gate. COC

Half of my goods, an Easter play, The. R. P. Clagget. 4m., 3w. Sc. Home in Jerusalem. Int. J. Rel. Educ. 6: 27–30, 52, Mar. 1930.

C **Half-past thirteen.** M. Carter. 3b., 3g. Sc. A nursery with a large grandfather's clock in the hall. FREL

Halfway, a harlequinade. M. E. Plummer. 1m., 2w. Sc. About a fireplace. Player's Mag. 3: 17–19, Nov.–Dec. 1926.

Hall-marked. J. Galsworthy. Satire. 6m., 4w. Sc. Sitting room and veranda of bungalow. GAL

Hallie in high. M. S. Oliver. Comedy. 1m., 1w. Sc. Living room. OLI

C **Hallowe'en.** M. E. Enloe. 18c. Sc. A wood. ENL

C **Hallowe'en adventure, A.** E. L. Koogle. 8b., 8g. Sc. Sleepy hollow. MARC

C **Hallowe'en guest.** B. M. Casey. 2b., 3g. Sc. Poorly furnished living room. CAS

C **Hallowe'en hold-up, A.** M. Irish. 4b., 4g. Sc. An old cabin. IQA

C **Hallowe'en in the garden.** L. Tuers. 10c. Sc. Garden fence, scarecrow in garden. ELD

C **Hallowe'en Merrymakers.** M. Bitney. 10 or more c. Sc. Interior. BIT

C **Hallowe'en nutting party, A.** M. Corell and I. Liccione. 14c. Sc. The woods. STRU

J **Hallowe'en on Baldy.** M. Bitney. 4b., 4g. Sc. Old cabin. BIT

C **Hallowe'en party, A.** M. R. Hoge. Many c. Sc. Home. Prim. Educ. 33: 551, 567, Oct. 1925.

C **Hallowe'en party, The.** E. E. Olson. 4b., 5g. Sc. Interior. BAK, ELD

C **Hallowe'en party, A.** C. Swaney. 4b., 4g. Sc. Living room. Norm. Inst. 36: 78, Oct. 1927.

Hallowe'en porch party. G. Sorenson. Comedy. 5b., 3g. Sc. Front of house. SOR

C **Hallowe'en pumpkins.** J. Ross. 6b., 5g. Sc. Interior. ELD

C **Hallowe'en surprise, A.** Mrs. M. T. Johnson. 5b., 3g. Sc. Dimly lighted street. Prim. Educ. 46: 130, 132, 136, Oct. 1928.

J **Hallowe'en wish, The.** A. Curtis. 3b., 6g. Sc. Sitting room in city apartment. CURT

Halt on the trail, A. C. H. W. Foster. Comedy. 3m., 2w. Sc. Narrow trail in the Sierra Madre mountains. FOS

Haman of today. A. Burnstein and J. Bacher. 4m., 2w. Sc. Living room. BLO

Haman pops the question. A. L. Kaser. Comedy. 2m., 3w. Sc. Kitchen in shack. PAIN

Hamburger King, The. M. S. Smith. 5m., 3w., 1c. Sc. Exterior of hamburger stand. Drama 15: 125–27, 136, Mar. 1925.

Hand of Siva, The. K. S. Goodman and B. Hecht. 5m. Sc. Room in small French hotel in 1914. GOO

Hands up! M. T. Applegarth. 10 char. Sc. Wild rocky place. APO

Hands up. E. B. Longnecker. 2m., 1w. Sc. Living room in country house. PENN

J **Handwriting on the wall, The.** H. W. Githens. 3b., 1g., chorus. Sc. Banquet hall in Babylon. GIT

C **Handy Andy Irons.** E. L. Squires. 3b., 8g. Sc. Fireplace in living room. SQ

"Hang It!" H. C. Sargent. Farce. 3m., 2w. Sc. Dining room. FREP

Hanger back, The. E. F. Corbett. 2m., 1w. Sc. Living room in cottage in the woods. Poet Lore 41: 91–104, Spring 1930.

Hanging and wiving. J. H. Manners. 1m., 3w. Sc. Sitting room of a furnished flat in London. FRE1

Hans Bulow's last puppet. G. D. Ruthenburg. 2m., 2w. Sc. Shop of puppet maker. YAL

C **Hans the shepherd boy.** M. E. Whitney. 3b. Sc. A field. WHI

Hans von smash. T. S. Denison. Farce. 4m., 3w. Sc. Interior. BUG

C **Hans who made the princess laugh.** M. E. Carpenter. 10b., 2g., chorus. Sc. Out of doors or indoors. BAI, Amer. Childhood 12 : 21–22, 64, May 1927.

C **Hansel and Gretel.** M. Parsons. 2b., 3g. Sc. Witch's house. SCH1

Ha'nts. F. C. Gardner. 5m., 3w., 1b. Sc. Porch. GAQ

Happiest place, The. M. S. Threlfell. Phantasy. 3m. Sc. Grassy meadow. CANA

Happy hoboes, The. H. Ford and A. S. Tucker. Comedy. 1m., 11g. Sc. In girl's summer camp. FREN

Happy journey to Trenton and Camden, The. T. Wilder. 3m., 3w. No scenery necessary. WILY

Happy man, The. M. E. F. Irwin. Fantastic comedy. 9m., 6w. Sc. Exterior. BAK

Happy New Year. H. Farjeon. 3m., 1w. Sc. Bedroom. FARJ

C **Happy prince, The.** R. Benton. From Oscar Wilde. 5b., 7g. Sc. Marketplace. BEN

C **Happy prince, The.** E. R. Jasspon and B. Becker. 18b., 5g., chorus. Sc. Outdoors. JAR

Happy returns. W. P. Ridge. 2m., 2w. Sc. Shop parlour. RID

C **Happy summer time.** K. M. Coventry. Pageant. Many c. Int. J. Rel. Educ. 2 : 44, July–Aug. 1926.

Happy war, The. J. Brandane. 5m. Sc. Room in a deserted monastery in France. 1917. BRAN

Harbour. L. S. Jast. Verse. 2m., chorus. Sc. Blue curtains. JAS

Hardhead, The. N. Rankin. 2m., 1w. Sc. Interior of a kitchen. CANA

Hardscrabble town meeting, The. G. B. Sampson. Burlesque. 12m., 6w., chorus. Sc. Country town hall. ELD

C **Hare and the hedgehog, The.** A. Stevenson. 2b., 1g. Sc. Cabbage field. STEV2

C **Hare and the tortoise, The.** A. Stevenson. 3c., chorus. Sc. A meadow. STEV1

C **Hare and the tortoise, The.** M. E. Whitney. 3b. Sc. A road. WHI

Harlequin. C. C. Clements. 3m., 1w. Sc. Garden. CLP

Harlequinade in green and orange. G. Hughes. Fantasy. 3m., 3w. Sc. Interior. FREN

J **Haroun el Rashid.** S. L. Cummins. Burlesque. 8b., 4g. Sc. On bridge. CUM1

C **Harvest blessings.** L. H. Campbell. 2b., 3g., chorus. Sc. Stage. WHG1

C **Harvest feast.** J. Merrill and M. Fleming. 5b., 4g. Sc. Interior of barn. MER

Harvest storm, The. C. H. Hazelwood. 10m. Sc. Landscape. FIT

C **Harvest Thanksgiving, The.** D. M. Moore. Many c. Sc. Harvest time. Norm. Inst. 38 : 74, 76, Oct. 1929.

Hast thou considered my servant Job? T. Wilder. 2m. Sc. Heaven. WILZ

Hat shoppe, The. E. C. Magnusson. 8w. Sc. Corner of hat shop. MAG

Hat trick. L. duG. Peach. Farce. 2m., 1w. Sc. Street. PAZ

C **Haunted circle, The.** A. Nichols. 16c., chorus. Sc. Village green. NIA

Haunted coal mine, The. L. B. Pride. 6m. Sc. Miner's room. FRE5

J **Haunted cottage.** B. M. Casey. 4b., 8g. Sc. Interior of haunted house. CAS

Haunted hotel, The. J. L. Patterson. Farce. 5m. Sc. Office of cheap hotel. FIT

Have a pill. A. L. Kaser. 1m., 1w. Sc. Interior. DEN

Have it out. H. Simpson. Farce. 1m., 2w. Sc. A typical Dentist's waiting room. SIMH

Have you anything to declare? G. E. Jennings. Farce. 4m., 6w. Sc. Customs House at a Channel Port in England. FREL

J **Havelok the Dane.** E. Smith. 6b., 1g., chorus. Sc. Hut. SM

Haven, The. F. Rickaby. 3m., 2w. Sc. Living room. BAK

He came seeing. M. P. Hamlin. 3m., 2w. Sc. Room in a small store house in Jerusalem. ALEX, FREN

He failed but succeeded. N. Balch. Comedy. 3m., 1w. Sc. Outside office of general contractors. ELD

He lives. G. R. Gowdey. 4m., 6w. Sc. Housetop in Jerusalem. BAK

He loved Kipling. L. C. Vanderveer. Comedy. 3m., 4w. Sc. Living room of summer home. BAK

He, on whom a sandel fell. M. S. Oliver. 9m., 2w. Sc. Courtyard of the royal palace at Memphis. OLI

J **Healing of Naaman, The.** M. Hobbs and H. Miles. 8b., 2g., chorus. Sc. Court of house. HOB

C **Health fairies at school.** B. Alston. Many c. Prim. Educ. 45: 198–199, 232, Nov. 1927.

C **Health party, The.** I. T. Gaily. Many c. Sc. Schoolroom. Prim. Educ. 45: 390, 392, Jan. 1928.

C **Health Play, A.** M. Gilchrist. 19c. Sc. Stage. Prim. Educ. 32: 606, 608, Nov. 1924.

Heart of Frances, The. C. G. Wilcox. 11 char. Sc. Dressing room of Frances. APPL

J C **Heart of Oak, a play of long ago.** R. N. Kerr. 9b., 2g. Sc. Before an immense oak tree. School Arts M. 27: 587–593, June 1928.

Heart of old Kentucky, The. G. Hughes. Burlesque. 5m., 3w. Sc. Interior. HUN

Heart too soon made glad, A. W. Beck. 3m., 3w. Sc. Reception parlor in a girls' dormitory at a mid-western college. BEC

Hearts enduring. J. Erskine. 1m., 1w. Sc. Interior of a hut. COH

Hearts to mend. H. A. Overstreet. Fantasy. 2m., 1w. Sc. Living-room and kitchen combined. APPL

J **Heaven on Friday.** V. Motter. 6 char., chorus. Sc. Interior. LON

Heir at large, An. M. Aldis. 8m., 6w., chorus. Sc. Basement room. OLG

Heir of Linne, The. V. B. Lawton. 4m., 3w., chorus. Sc. Mediaeval interior. LAWT

C **Help us to live.** L. K. Dolan. 12c. Sc. Stage. DOL

Help yourself. W. de Leon. Comedy. 3m.. 2w. Sc. Living room. FREN, Country Gent. 95: 23, 120–122, Jan. 1930.

Helping hands, The. G. E. Jennings. Farce. 1m., 6w. Sc. Office of the helping hands. FREL

Helping hands. M. Mackendrick. 2m., 2w. Sc. Family living room. MACS

C **Helping Mildred.** E. M. Bertie. Many c. Norm. Inst. 36: 70, 72, Sept. 1927.

Helpless Herberts. A. Kreymbory. Mask comedy. 1m., 1w. Sc. Man's study. KRR, Theatre Arts M. 8: 119–132, Feb. 1924.

Hemp. J. M. Cain. 3m. Sc. Sheriff's office in a county jail. Amer. Mercury 10: 404–409, Apr. 1927.

Henpeck Holler gossip. O. L. Smith. Comedy. 10w. Sc. Interior. BUG, DENI

J **Henri makes a sale.** K. A. White. 1b., 2g., chorus. Sc. Style shop. WH

C **Henry Hudson.** A. Stevenson. 14b., 5g., 2 chorus groups. Sc. 1 Office of Dutch East India Co. 2 Forest of the Hudson 3 On board The Discoverer. STEV4

C **Henry W. writes a poem.** P. Ring. 4b., 1g. Sc. Home of chief Justice in Portland in 1820. Prim. Educ. 45: 451, 482, Feb. 1928.

Henry's mail-order wife. F. A. Bundy. Comedy. 4m., 2w. Sc. Rancher's rough cabin. ELD

Henry's "Tux." N. M. Linn. 2m., 2w. Sc. Living room. ELD

Her country. E. V. R. Wyatt. Tragedy. 2m., 1w. Sc. Cottage near the English coast. COL4, LON

Her husband's watch. B. King. 7w. Mystery. FIT

Her social aspirations. F. C. Gardner. 3w. Sc. Lodge hall. GAQ

J **Herald of the cross, A.** H. W. Githens. 10b., 2g., chorus. Sc. Street in Philippi. GITH

Here comes the bride. H. Connell. Comedy. 4m., 3w. Sc. Country railroad station. PAIN

J **Here, there, and everywhere.** C. L. Sehon. 15g. Sc. Interior. WOM

J **Here we are!** B. Abel. 5b., 3g. Sc. A corridor. WOM

C **Here we come!** R. E. Henderson. 25c., chorus. Sc. A roomy lawn. SAO

Heritage, The. J. S. Knapp. 3m., 2w. Sc. Interior. FREN

C **Heritage, The.** N. Purdy. 16c. Sc. Lawn. JAO

Hermit, The. Mrs. A. Stallard. 8m., 2w. Sc. Outside a hermit cell in 684. STAL

Hero, The. J. M. Cain. 3m. Sc. Office of town commissioners. Amer. Mercury 6: 52–57, Sept. 1925.

J **Hero, The.** E. E. Levinger. 3b., 5g. Sc. Room in a kitchen in Illinois at the close of the Civil War. LEVT

Hero of Santa Maria, The. K. S. Goodman and B. Hecht. Farce. 6m., 1w. Sc. Living room. GOO, SHAQ

Hero-worship. F. Hargis. 2m., 2w. Sc. Sitting room in a small town in Georgia. FREN

C **Hero worshipers.** H. O. Boggs. Comedy. 3b. Sc. Reading room of a public library. BOG

Herod play, The. P. E. Osgood. 7m. Sc. Herod's court. OSF

C **Heroes of the haunted house, The.** H. O. Boggs. 8b. Sc. Attic of an old house. BOG

He's a lunatic. F. Dale. Farce. 3m., 2w. Sc. Interior. DRA

Hessian Christmas play, The. D. F. Robinson. 21m., 3w., chorus. Sc. Stage. HAQ

Hiartville Shakespeare club. B. M. Locke. Farce. Sc. Interior. PENN

C **Hiawatha.** O. M. Price. From Longfellow's poem. 12c., chorus. Sc. In the woods. PRI1

C **Hiawatha's childhood.** E. K. Jelliffe. 5b., 3g. Norm. Inst. 34: 70, Oct. 1925.

C **Hiawatha's friends.** E. K. Jelliffe. 10b., 5g. Norm. Inst. 36: 72–74, Oct. 1927.

C **Hiawatha's wedding feast.** E. K. Jelliffe. 7c., others. Norm. Inst. 35: 74, 76, Oct. 1926.

Hicksville community club, The. W. N. Bugbee. 8m., 6w. Sc. Interior. BUG

C **Hiding of the Charter, The.** F. O'Ryan and A. W. O'Ryan. 8b., chorus. Sc. Platform. ORY

High Hattie. C. B. Orwig. Comedy. 6w. Sc. Insurance office. PENN

High heart, The. A. C. Rowell. 7m., 2w. Sc. Living room in old southern mansion in Tenn. in 1863. SCH3, Drama 17: 173–176, 190–91, Mar. 1927.

J **High lights in American history.** Wesleyan College-Junior class 1926. 15c., chorus. Sc. Any stage. AU

High prices and danger. M. Mackendrick. 6w. Sc. Living room. MACS

High-low-brow, The. L. Mack. Farce. 2m., 3w., chorus. Sc. Reception room. FARQ

Hightones buy a car, The. P. Holloway. Farce. 8w. Sc. "Overdone" living room. ELD

C **Highway of Brotherly Love, The.** Y. Klein and F. Schwarz. 14c. Sc. Schoolroom. KLE

Highways cross. T. W. Stevens. 6m., 2w. Sc. Inn at Oxford, 1611. STEU

Hildegard's elopement. E. Hoxie. Comedy. 3m., 3w. Sc. Living room. HOX

C **Hill, The.** M. E. Whitney. Fanciful. 1b., 1g. Sc. The shore. WHI

J **Hilltop.** L. A. Garrett. Poetic. 7b., 2g. Sc. Clearing with thatched cottage in foreground. GAR

Hiring a new teacher. K. A. White. 3b. Sc. Schoolroom. WH

Hiring a servant. J. A. Baxter. 3m., 3w. Sc. Intelligence office. PAIS

His and hers. A. R. Kidder. 1m., 2w. Sc. Interior. FREN

J **His best seller.** Farce. 1b., 2g. Sc. Interior. LOU

His blue serge suit. B. M. Ritchey. Comedy. 4m., 1w. Sc. Interior. LON

His children. R. Learsi. 4m., 1w. Sc. Interior. BLO

His chorus girl. H. H. Haslett. 3m., 3w. Sc. Theatrical booking office. BANN

C **His Christmas tree.** L. Murray and H. Willet. 1b., 2g., many others. Sc. Living room meagerly furnished. Norm. Inst. 33: 62, 64, Dec. 1923.

His clever scheme. C. M. Adams. Comedy. 1m., 4w. Sc. Real estate office. BUG

His Come-Uppance. M. DeMott. Comedy. 2m., 5w. Sc. Interior. FREN

His day off. G. N. Roberts. Comedy. 1m., 3w. Sc. Living room. BAK

C **His first book of poetry (Whittier).** P. F. Ring. Prim. Educ. 45: 556, 562, Mar. 1928.

His first case. O. Kelley. 1m., 2w. Sc. Law office. KEK

His neighbor. W. Hill. 3m., 1w. Sc. Living room in bungalow in England. DE

His only way. E. Dane. 3m. Sc. Luxurious bedroom. JOHN

His sainted grandmother. Lord Dunsany. 1m., 3w. Sc. Old room with a four-poster in the middle. DUS, FREN

His Son. T. D. Mygatt. 2m., 4w. Sc. Delightful Philadelphia living room. Poet Lore 39 : 605–631, Winter 1928.

J   **His sweet bouquet.** J. A. Baxter. 3b., 4g. Sc. Interior. PAIS

His-voice-is-a-whisper. H. Alexander. 3m., 1w., music. Sc. Interior or exterior. ALE

His widow's husband. J. Benavente. Tr. by J. G. Underhill. 2m., 5w. Sc. Living room. Golden Book 3 : 342–354, Mar. 1926.

His wife's first husband. E. J. Sharpsteen. Comedy. 2m., 2w. Sc. Living room. DENI

Hist! she's a man! G. York. Comedy. 4m., 3w. Sc. Living room. DENI

C   **Historical coincidence, An.** F. O'Ryan and A. W. O'Ryan. 5b., chorus. Sc. Wharf in 1732. ORY

C   **History review at Petersville School.** 5b., 5g. Sc. Interior. BUG

C   **History slightly mixed.** E. Hoxie. 1b., 2g. Sc. Living room. HOVA

Hitting on all six. H. P. Powell. Comedy. 5m., 2w. Sc. Showrooms of Motor Co. PENN

C   **Hobyah! Hobyah!** N. Mitchison. 10b., 4g., chorus. Sc. The forest. MIT

Hogan's Successor. R. Speirs. 3m., 1w. Sc. Present day poor apartment. Drama 19 : 233–234, May 1929.

Hold-up, The. A. G. Higgins and H. Ford. 8m., 5w. Sc. Juvenile court room. FREN

Hole in one. J. P. Heald. Mock trial. 14m., 2w. Sc. District court. BAK

C   **Hole in the dike, The.** A. Stevenson. 3b., 3g., chorus. Sc. Holland. STEV2

C   **Holiday clock, The.** L. C. Swartz. 10b., 4g. Sc. Comfortable and cheerful rooms in Father Time's house. DRA, ELD

C   **Holiday in Haverhill, A.** P. F. Ring. 3b., 2g. Sc. Front yard of Whittier home. Prim. Educ. 45 : 556, Mar. 1928.

C   **Holland project.** A. LeFond. Many c. Sc. Market scene. Prim. Educ. 33 : 162–165, 202, 211, Mar. 1925.

C   **Hollanders, The.** U. V. Roe. Any number of b. and g. Sc. School room. FJ

J   **Holly-tree Inn, The.** G. Pertwee and E. Pertwee. Adapted from Dickens, Boots at the Holly-tree Inn. 3b., 2g. Sc. Coffee room in inn in 1820. PER

Holy terror, A. O. Wenlanot. Farce. 4m. Sc. Plain room. FIT

Home at last. R. Jeans. Farce. 1m., 3w. Sc. Daintily furnished dining room. JES

Home coming, The. E. O. Cochran. 3m., 3w. Sc. Living room of a prosperous farmhouse. COC

C   **Home-coming, The.** W. E. Howe and C. S. Bailey. 10c., chorus. Sc. Large forbidding door is painted in the center of a drop curtain. BAI

Home cured. L. Crites. Farce. 3m., 1w. Sc. Interior. ELD

C J   **Home economics play.** L. Dunlap. 2b., 5g. Sc. Living room. Prac. Home Econ. 7 : 301, Oct. 1929.

Home for the friendly, The. F. K. Frank. Comedy. 4m., 3w. Sc. Large old-fashioned sitting room. SHAF

Home for the holidays. A. W. Norton. 8m., 15w., 6c. Sc. Waiting room of a small-town railroad station. PENN

Home Sweet Home. P. Phelps. Comedy. 5w. Sc. Room in old ladies home. FREN

C **Honest critic, An.** A. Stevenson. 7b., 1 chorus group. Sc. A throne room in the palace of the tyrant Dionysius. STEV4

C **Honest woodman, The.** A. Stevenson. 2b., 1g. Sc. A river bank. STEV1

Honeymoon Hall. H. Simpson. Farce. 2m., 3w. Sc. Sitting room in a seaside boarding house. SIMO

Honeymoon specialist, The. R. G. Carter. Comedy. 1m., 3w. Sc. Tourist agency. ELD

C **Honor of a scout, The.** J. C. McMullen. 11b. Sc. Boy Scout camp in the mountains. BAK

J **Honorable guest, The.** F. Cavanah. 9g., chorus. Sc. Japanese room. FRIE

C **Honorable Madame.** M. Bitney. 2b., 4g. Sc. Interior. BIT

Honour among thieves. H. Simpson. Farce. 2m., 3w. Sc. London flat. SIMS

Honour thy father. H. M. Harwood. 2m., 4w. Sc. Cheaply furnished but cleanly kept room in Bruges. HAR

Honours list, The. J. H. Turner. Farce. 4m., 2w. Sc. Library. TURN

C **Hope.** C. V. Coyle. 10 char. Sc. In front of a wood-chopper's cottage. JOHE

Hope of the Spingarns, The. L. Stitely. 2m., 3w., 1b. Comedy. Sc. Pleasant living room. BAK

Hopeless passion of Mr. Bunyon, The. Lord Dunsany. 2m., 1w. Sc. Interior of shop. DUS, FREN

Horatius at the Bridge. H. Singley. 7b., others. Sc. Street near the Tiber. Hist. Outlook 17: 130, Mar. 1926.

J **Horror walks, The.** J. S. Knapp. 8b., 1g. Sc. Dirty dark room in a deserted house. BAK

Horse thief, The. Trans. from German by E. U. Ouless. Farce. 4m. Sc. Open place near village. OULE

Hospitality. F. Downey. 2m. Sc. Room in a palace. Ladies Home Journal 41: 144, Aug. 1924.

Host, The. F. C. Molnar. Trans. from the Hungarian. 6m., 4w., chorus. Sc. Dining room. FRE2, Golden Book 7: 781–6, June 1928.

Hot air. M. M. Parker. Burlesque. 5m., 2w., chorus. Sc. Receiving set. DRA

Hot iron, The. P. Green. 2m., 3w. Sc. Negro cabin. GREF, Poet Lore 35: 48–57, Spring 1924.

Hot lemonade. F. Ryerson and C. Clements. 3m., 1w. Sc. Sitting room on a Pacific mail steamer. FRE5

Hot stuff. A. L. Kaser. Farce. 2m. KAS

Hot waffles. D. DeJagers. Comedy. 2m., 1w. Sc. Interior. FREN

Hot water. E. Gibson. 4m., 5w. Sc. Hall of a tenement house. GIB

Hour-glass, The. W. B. Yeats. Morality. 3m., 2w., 2c. Sc. A large room. YEA, Golden Book 3: 641–646, May 1926.

House agent, The. G. Grace. Revue. 2m., 1w. Sc. Real estate office. FRET

House beautiful, The. T. M. Hanna. 2m., 1w. Sc. Attractive living room in modern bungalow. FREN, Drama 15: 112–114, Feb. 1925.

House by the side of the road, The. A. von Kotzebue. Trans. by B. B. Beebe. 2m., 1w. Sc. A highway in the country. Golden Book 10; 89–93, July 1929.

How she managed it. A. Humbolt. Comedy. 1m., 1w. Sc. Parlor. MARC

C **How spring came to Fern Dale.** E. Preston. 12c., chorus. Sc. Out of doors. PRES

C **How Succoth came to Chayim.** E. E. Levinger. 5b., 3g. Sc. A kitchen. LEV

How the bag was mended. C. J. Denton. Farce. 2m., 1w. Sc. Comfortable interior. DENT

C **How Thanksgiving came to November.** G. V. R. Wolf. 3b., 5g. Sc. Any room with table. Norm. Inst. 34: 78, Nov. 1924.

C **How the fairies play.** M. A. Enloe. 1b., 4g. Sc. Plain stage. ENL

J **How the great guest came.** L. Adams. Fantasy. 6b., 2g. Sc. Cobbler's shop on the Danube in 1825. FREN

How the Princess Capricious became Empress of Tiny Isle. J. Russell. 10m., 4w., chorus. Sc. Throne room. Satire. FREN

How the Sukkoth came to Chayim. E. E. Levinger. 5m., 3w. Sc. Interior. BLO

C **How the turtles went to war.** F. Densmore. 16c. Sc. Indian village. WOM

How the weather is made. H. Brighouse. 4m., 13w. Sc. Open space. BRIO, MAR3

How they practiced their trio. C. H. W. Foster. Comedy. 3w. Sc. Practice-room of a Young Ladies' College Music Club. FOS

C **How they saved the Fort.** A. Stevenson. 11b., 10g. Sc. A Kentucky fort in 1782. STEV4

Human pillar, The. K. Okamoto. Trans. from the Japanese. 8m., 4w. Sc. Bank of river in the province of Sehsu. FREN

Hundredth trick, The. B. M. Dix. 4m. Sc. Dim. wainscoated parlor. TUC

Hunger. E. M. Moses. 5m., 3w. Sc. Interior. PENN

Hunt the tiger. H. A. Hering. 2m., 1w. Sc. Salon in Paris in 1781. FREN, LON

C **Hunting for spring.** O. V. Roe. 5g. Sc. Any platform. FJ

Hurricane. N. G. Lawrence. 3m., 4w., chorus. Sc. Farmer's curb market in Miami, Florida. BAK

Husband of Xanthippe, The. C. Seiler. 4m., 1w. Sc. Garden of Socrates' house. SEH

Husband wanted. E. O. Jones. 1m., 1w. Farce. Sc. Living room. DENI

Hush money. P. Wilde. Farce. 2m., 1w. Sc. Room in hotel. WILT

Hyacinth Halvey. Lady Gregory. Comedy. 4m., 2w. Sc. Outside the post-office. CANF

Hyacinths. T. M. Hanna. 3w. Sc. Living room. RIC

I

I am come. E. G. Rockwell. 5m., 2w. Sc. Outer court in the home of Peter. BAK

I did but jest. G. P. Schmidt, Jr. 2m., 1w. Sc. Funeral chamber of a castle around 1400. Poet Lore 35: 130–139, Spring 1924.

I do. E. T. Woolfolk. 3m., 2w. Sc. Living room. COO

I do! I do! I do! D. Sheridan. Farce. 3m., 2w. Sc. Living room. SHER

C **I don't want to.** E. W. Arnold. 4b., 1g. Sc. Interior. ELD

C **I never thought of that.** H. E. Davis. 2b., 2g. Sc. Study table of American Child. Delineator 104: 17–18, Feb. 1924.

Ibsenism, a dialogue. P. McBrien. 2m. Catholic World 118: 192–196, Nov. 1923.

C **Ichabod Crane.** K. A. Jensen. Many c. Sc. Stage. Pop. Educ. 42: 164, 166, Nov. 1924.

Ici on parle Français. T. J. Williams. Farce. 3m., 4w. Sc. Interior. PENN

Idealist, The. O. Down. 2m., 2w. Sc. Drawing room. FRE2

J **Idlings of the king, The.** E. Remington. Burlesque. 5b., 1g. Sc. Room in the palace of King Arthur. LON

Idyll. M. Grahn. 2w., 7m., others. Sc. Rustic garden. Drama 16: 255–6, Apr. 1926.

Idyll. M. Sierra. Trans. by C. M. Lorenz. 5m., 3w. Sc. Spanish exterior on December 31. Poet Lore 37: 63–72, Spring 1926.

J **Idyll of the New Year, An.** C. Frances. Fantasy. 21 char. Sc. Living room. FRA

Idyll of the shops, An. K. S. Goodman and B. Hecht. 3m., 3w. Sc. Loft in Chicago. GOO

C **If,** a play showing the importance of mathematics. R. L. Snyder. Several c. Sc. Study table. Math. Teacher 22: 482–6, Dec. 1929.

C **If Lincoln were with us today.** Y. Klein and F. Schwarz. 6c. Sc. Any interior. KLE

If men played cards as women do. G. S. Kaufman. Satire. 4m. Sc. Interior. FREN

C **If the children of Europe could speak to us.** Y. Klein and F. Schwarz. 8c. Sc. Any interior. KLE

C **If we only had "Time."** F. F. Palmer. 2b., 6g. Sc. Studio. Etude 48: 149, Feb. 1930.

C **If wishes came true.** E. W. Trout. Morality. 11c. Sc. Old-fashioned kitchen. PAIN

Ile. E. O'Neill. 5m., 1w. Sc. Cabin on board of steam whaling ship. GOLD, HAT, ON, PEN, THOR

I'll tell you exactly what to do. F. C. Gardner. 5m., 1w. Sc. Interior. GAQ

Illumination. M. Lee. Farce. 8m., 4w. Sc. Interior. LEE

Imaginary conversation of P. Rosenfeld and M. Josephson, An. E. Wilson. 2m. New Rep. 38: 179–182, Apr. 9, 1924.

Imaginary Conversation of Van Wyck Brooks and Scott Fitzgerald. New Rep. 38: 249–54, Apr. 30, 1924.

C **Imagination.** W. Beck. Satire. 3b., 2g. Sc. Darkened stage. BAK, BEB

Imbecile, The. L. Pirandello. 8m., 1w. Sc. Very plain study. PIR

Immersion. M. Humphrey. 2m., 2w. Sc. Main room of a small frame house in a middle western village in 1850. YAL

Immortal beloved, The. M. Leonard. 1m., 1w. Sc. Interior. FREN

Immortality, a present day fantasy. C. P. MacInnis. 4m., 2w. Sc. Garden. Drama 16: 258–260, Apr. 1926.

Immortals, The. C. C. Dobie. Fantasy. 3m., 2w. Sc. Indoors or outdoors. CART, Overland 84: 74–76, 94, Mar. 1926.

Immovable movie, The. H. P. Powell. Farce. 4m. Sc. Office of Platinum Pictures. PENN

Implacable Aphrodite, The. N. Boyd and E. St. V. Millay. Satire. 1m., 1w. Sc. Studio. MIK

Importance of being a woman, The. R. Crothers. 1m., 3w. Sc. Drawing room. CROT

Importance of being clothed, The. R. Crothers. 5w. Sc. Sitting room. CROT

Importance of being married, The. R. Crothers. 4m., 5w. Sc. Dressing room at theatre. CROT

Importance of being nice, The. R. Crothers. 2m., 5w. Sc. The "Ritz" at lunch time. CROT

Importance of Mary, The. B. King. 2m., 6w. Sc. Garden. PENN

Imprisonment of Peter and John, The. M. E. Whitney. 14b., 2g. Sc. Portico of Peter's house in Jerusalem. WHH

In a subway station. K. Parson. 4m., 3w. Sc. Subway station in N. Y. PENN

In a window. C. Seiler. Romance. 3m., 1w. Sc. Street in small town near London. SEH

In Abraham's bosom. P. Green. 6m., 1w. Sc. Woods in North Carolina. GREF, LOC

In an aeroplane, an imaginary conversation. G. Seldes. 4m. New Repub. 44: 35–36, Sept. 2, 1925.

In an airplane passenger station. A. L'R. Kaser. Comedy. 7m., 5w. Sc. Airplane station. PAIN

C **In an old diary.** N. Flaurier. 3g. Sc. Storehouse where discarded articles are put away. FIV

C **In Arcady.** R. Fyleman. 2b., 1g. Sc. Glade. FYL

In Arden forest. J. A. Holmes. 8m., 2w. Sc. Woodland not far from Stratford village near Avon in 1582. BAK

In Aunt Mahaly's cabin. P. Green. Melodrama. 10 char. Sc. Negro cabin in swamp in North Carolina. GREE, GREE

C **In bad company.** A. Stevenson. 5b., 2g., chorus. Sc. A corn field. STEV1

In broad daylight. L. Blanning. Comedy. 6w. Sc. Living room. ELD

In chambers. E. O. Jones. 2m., 2w. Sc. Private office of Delinquency court. FREN

In confidence. A. Prydz. Trans. from Norwegian. Satire. 2w. Sc. Interior. APPL, SHAT

In Dixon's kitchen. W. Stout and E. Lay. Comedy. 4m., 2w. Sc. Kitchen. CAR3

In 1864. V. R. Sutton. 9w. Sc. Sitting room of a New England home. WOM

C **In Father World's garden.** Y. Klein and F. Schwarz. 8c. Sc. Garden. KLE

J **In Herod's dungeon.** P. E. Osgood. 2b. Sc. Crude iron gate or door. OSG

In Holy Russia. Lord Dunsany. 5m., 2w. Sc. Outside a Russian cottage. DUS, FREN

In honor bound. S. Grundy. 2m., 2w. Sc. Interior. PENN

C **In Jack-o'-Lantern row.** N. Flaurier. Any number c. Sc. Before curtains. STRU

C **In King Lugdub's forest.** M. Jagendorf. 20c. Sc. Clearing in the King's park. JAF

In May. E. Szep. Trans. from Hungarian by J. Szebenyei. Satire. 3m., 1w. FREN

In the morgue. S. Cowan. 4m. Sc. In the morgue of a foreign city. COW

C **In the palace garden.** Y. Klein and F. Schwarz. 17c. Sc. In the palace garden. KL

In the park. G. Cannan. 2m., 1w. Sc. A park in a modern city. CANN

C **In the path of the children.** V. Olcott. 2b., 2g., chorus. Sc. Village near Cologne in Germany. OLF

In the rector's study. G. John. In English dialect. 4m., 6w. Sc. Study of English rector. JOH

In the secret places. E. B. Nessenson. 4m., 4w. Sc. Living room of Baronical castle in 19th century. Drama 17: 43–45, 62, 63, Nov. 1926.

In the small hours. O. W. Firkins. 2m. Sc. Bridge over a large river in a great city. FIR

In the swath. E. Morrette. 8m., 3w., chorus. Sc. Living room in house in a Belgian village near the German frontier in 1914. MORR

J **In the Terem.** A. C. Darlington. 7g., chorus. Sc. Woman's quarters in a Russian palace. DAR

In the thousands of years to come. L. Anderson. Farce. 5m., 3w. Sc. Study of professor's home. ANDE

In the tunnel. R. Jordan. 4m., 4w. Sc. First class coach on the London-Paris-Marsailles express. DE

In the valley. P. Green. 11m., 2w., chorus. Sc. At the edge of a college town in North Carolina. GREE

In the wall papers. B. Herford. 2m., 1w. Ladies Home Journal 43: 263, Apr. 1926.

C **In the white house attic.** M. B. Carpenter. 7b., 2g., others. Sc. Attic of white house 1861. Norm. Inst. 39: 65, 81, Jan. 1930.

In the zone. E. O'Neill. 9m. Sc. Seaman's forecastle on British tramp steamer. ON

Inasmuch, a medical playlet. A. B. Grey. 9w. Sc. Dispensary of mission doctor. Mis. Review 52: 50–4, Jan. 1929.

Incentive. M. Irish. 4m., 3w. Sc. Living room. IR

Incorrigible. A. J. Talbot. 10m. Sc. Garret. SCHO

Incredible happenings. R. Jeans. Farce. 20 char. Sc. Interior. JES

C **Indian boy's pet, An.** A. Stevenson. 10b., 1g., chorus. Sc. Indian camp. STEV1

Indian Summer. J. H. Whitehouse. Comedy. 1m., 3w. Sc. Small town well-furnished drawing room. Poet Lore 39: 455–466, Autumn 1928.

C **Indians' Thanksgiving, The.** H. and M. Hastings. 8b., 5g. Sc. Wigwam. Norm. Inst. 38: 74, Nov. 1928.

Indicator, The. D. Titheradge. Farce. 2m., 1w. Sc. Study. TITO

In'ependence. E. M. Alger. 4m., 4w., 6c. Sc. Living room colonial home in the North. Poet Lore 41: 140–149, Spring 1930.

J **Injured, The.** V. Methley. 4g. Sc. Schoolroom. FREL

In-laws. H. Ford. Comedy. 4m., 3w. Sc. Dining room in N. Y. apartment. FRE4

J **Inn of Discontent, The.** P. Wilde. 5b., 3g. Sc. 1 A great portal at night. 2 Inner side of portal in morning. SANP, WIK

Inside information. M. T. Johnson. 4m., 1w. Sc. Farmhouse living room. ELD

Inside stuff. T. Pratt. Fantasy. 10m. or women, or mixed. Sc. Interior. SHAP

Insomnia. H. T. Rubinstein. Morality. 8 char., chorus. Sc. Interior. PHIJ

Inspiration, The. B. Oneal. 4w. Sc. Studio of a small N. Y. apartment. OMI

Interior. M. Maeterlinck. 3m., 2w., chorus. Sc. An old garden planted with willows. SHAT

Interpolated. K. B. Brookman. 11m., 2w. Sc. Tomb of Tut-Ankh-Amen A. D. 1923. Poet Lore 35: 78–88, Spring 1924.

J **Interpretative reading.** C. Francis. Farce. 7g., chorus. Sc. An English classroom. FRA

J **Interrupted coronation, An.** H. W. Githens. 6b., 2g. Sc. Market place at Lystra. GITH

C **Interrupted wedding, The.** A. Steward. 12c. Sc. Toy shop. PAIN

Interview, The. O. Kelley. Comedy. 2m. Sc. Office. KEK

J **Into Galilee.** L. Bayard. 6m., 2w. Sc. Lake shore at Capernaum. PA

Into the Everywhere. E. Heal. 2m., 2w., 1g. Sc. English parlor. Poet Lore 38: 466–472, Autumn 1927.

Into the light. G. B. Fife. 2m., 2w. Sc. Living room country house. Harper's Bazaar 63: 88–89, 112+, June 1928.

Intolerance. R. Jeans. Farce. 2m., 1w. Sc. Dining room. JER

J **Introducing Scrooge.** E. Sexton. Adapted from Dickens. Christmas carol. 6b. Sc. Scrooge's office. SEX

Invention of Dr. Metzler, The. J. Pollock. 3m., 2w. Sc. Salon of a country house in Hungary 1849. POL

Invisible Duke, The. F. Sladen-Smith. Farce. 5m., 1w. Sc. Room of astrologer. BAK

Invitation. E. J. Basshe. 2m. Sc. Combined study and library. FRE4

Irish alibi, An. J. Branen. 1m., 2w. Sc. Interior. BUG

C **Irish riddles.** B. Creighton. 6b., 6g. Sc. Any stage. Woman's Home Companion 56: 97, Mar. 1929.

Irish, Too. A. L. Kaser. Farce. 2m. Sc. No scenery required. KAS

Is man a machine? A Socratic dialogue. J. B. Watson vs. Will Durant. H. G. Leach, ed. 3m. Forum 82: 264–270, Nov. 1929.

Is peculiar. L. Anderson. 4m. Sc. Interior of a lob cabin in Canada. DET

Is religion necessary for progress? A Socratic dialogue. H. G. Leach, ed. 6m., 2w. Sc. Home. Forum 82: 8–13, July 1929.

C **Is Santa coming?** M. Kibbe. 3b., 4g. Sc. Interior. CJ

Ishmael. W. F. Manley. 4m., 2w. Sc. Tent of Abraham. MAN

Isle of smiles, The. L. Osborn. Farce. 2m., 2w. Sc. "Sunrise Key" not far from Miami, Florida. PENN

Isn't it exciting? R. F. Jones. Farce. 4m., 1w. Sc. Interior. BAK

C **Israel's arrow.** E. E. Levinger. Fantasy. 6b., 1g. Sc. Out of doors. BLO

It can't be done. B. E. Palmer. Comedy. Sc. Living room. FIT

J **It happened at Christmas.** F. G. Bundy. 14 char. Sc. Interior. ELD

It happens every day. O. Kelley. Comedy. 1m., 2w. Sc. City park. KEK

It is so simple. B. Charlton. Farce. 2m., 1w. Sc. Office. CHA

It isn't being done. A. V. Harp. Comedy. 2m., 3w. Sc. Living room. BANN

It isn't done. C. Glick. 3m. Sc. Outdoor at night. FREN

C **It isn't my dolly.** M. Bitney. 2g. Sc. Interior. BIT

"It isn't what you say but how you say it." B. Block. Comedy. 4m., 1w. Sc. Living room. NICR

It must be love. R. W. Tucker. Comedy. 3m., 2w. Sc. Living room of bachelor apartment. PENN

It sometimes happens. Comedy. 1m., 1w. Sc. Interior. JOHP

C **It was a surprise.** N. Flaurier. 2b., 2g. Sc. Sitting room. FIV

It will be all right on the night. J. Knox. Comedy. 9m. Sc. Stage. FREN

It's all a matter of dress. J. M. Hammond. Comedy. 2m., 3w. Sc. Interior of a town shop. CART

It's all over town. E. Hoxie. Farce. 1m., 9w. Sc. Kitchen. BAK, YOU

It's an ill wind. M. Baumer. 2m., 3w. Sc. Interior of a photographer's shop in a small town. FRE5

It's no use to argue. W. Beck. 2m., 2w. Sc. Living room in 1950. BEC

It's the poor that 'elps the poor. H. Chapin. 7m., 6w. Sc. Living sleeping room. MAR2

It's time something happened. A. Doyle. 6m., 2w. Sc. Stage. APPL

C **Ivan the Fool.** R. Benton. From Tolstoi. 19b., 4g., chorus. Sc. 1 Home. 2 Palace. BEN

J

C **Jack and Jill.** L. Cuddy. 2b., 3g. Sc. Remote corner of Mother Goose land. CUD

Jack and Jill and a friend. C. Hamilton. Comedy. 3m., 1w. Sc. Studio. SHAF

C **Jack and the Beanstalk.** C. F. Reighard. 5b., 2g. Sc. Farmyard. REI

C **Jack smuggles in a guest.** N. Flaurier. 2b., 1g. Sc. Dining room. FIV

J **Jack the giant-killer.** M. T. Applegarth. 4 char. Sc. Lawn. APN

C **Jack-in-the-box.** Someple, *pseud.* of G. Lloyd. 1b., 1g. Sc. Interior. MARC

C **Jack-in-the-pulpit is preaching today.** M. A. Niemeier. 11c. Sc. The woods. NIEM

Jack's House. A. Kreymborg. Cubic-play. 1m., 1w. Sc. Small room. KR

J **Jacob's journey.** R. Kimball. 6b., 4g. Sc. Curtain or screens. KIM

C **Jacquenetta and the Queen's gown.** B. Folmsbee. Fanciful. 5b., 6g. Sc. Interior. FOL

C **Jamboree.** N. Kruger. 4b., 2g. Blackface play. Sc. No scenery necessary. PENN

James and John. G. Cannan. 3m., 1w. Sc. Interior. BAK

C **James learns about Arbor Day.** R. Thompson. 9b., 7g. Sc. Edge of a forest. Norm. Inst. 37: 68, 70, Mar. 1928.

James of Galilee. W. F. Manley. 2m., 1w. Sc. House of James on the shore of the lake of Galilee. MAN

Jane, Jean and John. A. Kreymborg. Whimsical. poetic. 3m., 1w. Sc. Stage. FRE3

Jane wins by a hobby. R. S. Barclay. 3m., 5w., chorus. Sc. Parlor. ELD

J **Janitor's life, A.** W. W. Heintz. 1m., 1w. Sc. Any stage. J. Chem. Educ. 6: 1793–6, Oct. 1929.

Janitor's new broom, The. C. J. Hicks. Comedy. 5m., 1w. Sc. Deacon's room in church. ELD

CJ **Japanese Madonna, A.** L. C. Deseo. Many c. Sc. College girl's room. Int. J. of Rel. Educ. 5: 24–26, 35, Nov. 1928.

C **Japanese pageant for beginners.** K. M. Coventry. Pageant. Many c. Int. J. of Rel. Educ. 2: 44–45, May 1926.

C **Japanese play.** M. Lear, *ed.* Many c. Sc. Stage. Pop. Educ. 41: 514–18+, May 1924.

Jar, The. L. Pirandello. Trans. from Italian. Comedy. 9m., 3w. Sc. Grass-grown yard before Italian farmhouse. PIR

Jasmine and the Poet. C. V. Wiegand. 3m., 1w. Sc. An exquisite living room. Poet Lore 37: 418–431, Fall 1926.

J **Jason and the Golden Fleece.** M. R. Hofer. 22b., 2g., chorus. Sc. A stage scene arranged in three sections. HOF

Jasper Henry Clay Applesauce. A. L. Kaser. Farce. 1m., 1w. Sc. Back yard. KAS

Jazz and minuet. R. Giorloff. Comedy. 2m., 3w. Sc. Living room of apartment. EAT, LON, SCH1

Jazz health play. Skidmore College Students. 3m., 1w., 1c. Child Welfare M. 20: 552–53, May 1926.

Jealous husband. G. Kobbe. 2m., 2w. Sc. Interior. FIT

Jed's love affairs. A. G. Evans. Comedy. 1m., 5w. Sc. Living room. DENI

J **Jelly fish, The.** G. James. 5m., 2w. Sc. Dragonland. FREL

J **Jephthah's daughter.** E. E. Levinger. Tragedy. 6b., 5g., 2 chorus groups. Sc. Before a house in ancient Palestine. FIN, THOM

Jeremiad. J. H. Whitehouse. 2m., 4w. Sc. Servant's dining room. FREN

Jerry. C. E. Shute. Comedy. 2m., 2w. Sc. Interior. BAK, BUG

Jessamy bride, The. F. F. Moore. 4m., 2w. Sc. Goldsmith's lodgings in Islington. MOO

Jest of Hahalaba, The. Lord Dunsany. 4m. Sc. Smoking Room in London house. DUS, FREN, Atlantic M. 139: 58, 62, Jan. 1927; World Review 4: 252–253, May 30, 1927.

C **Jester's intrigue, The.** H. Trébor. Fantasy. 3b., 1g. Sc. Throne room of the King's palace. FREL

J **Jester's purse, The.** N. E. Minchin. 9b., 6g., chorus. Sc. Highway. MIN

J **Jewel boy of Florence, The.** V. Olcott. 4b., 2g., chorus. Sc. Shop of the goldsmith. OLD

Jewel merchants, The. J. B. Cabell. 2m., 1w. Sc. Garden in Tuscany in 1533. Golden Book 12: 88–96, Sept. 1930.

Jewels of Isabella, The. A. P. Sanford, *tr.* 4m., 3w. Sc. 1 Small room in the Alhambra. 2 Walled garden of the Alhambra in 1492. SCH4

Jezebel. D. Stockbridge. 4m., 2w. Sc. Room in Royal palace. SHAQ

Jilted. F. Ryerson and C. Clement. 2m., 2w. Sc. Living room. YOU

Jimmie. G. N. Madison. 2m., 2w. Sc. Living room. BAK

C **Jimmie goes back to school.** A. H. Grant. 6c. Prim. Educ. 46: 12, 75, Sept. 1928.

J **Jimmie or Ned.** C. Barr. Comedy. 5w. Sc. Room in dormitory of a small mid-west college. PENN

C **Jimmie's magic whistle.** R. Smyth. 4b., 1g., chorus. Sc. Stage. LORC

C **Jimmy Jenkins' hallowe'en.** M. Sharpe. 11c. Sc. Jimmy's bedroom. BAK

J **Jimmy's little sister.** I. M. Gray. Farce. 8b. Sc. Living room in a college dormitory. BAK

J   **Jingle's wooing of the spinster aunt.** G. Pertwee and E. Pertwee. Adapted from Dickens' Pickwick Papers. 6b., 2g. Sc. Sitting room. PER

Joan the maid. H. Ould. 3m., 3w. Sc. French interior in 1429. FREN, OU

Joanna the wife of Chuza. K. L. Bates. 1m., 1w. Sc. Open court in house near Herod's palace. BATE

Job's kinfolks. L. C. Bailey. 1m., 4w. Sc. Living room. CAR3, Carolina Play Book 1: 24–38, June 1928.

Job's tears. E. W. Peattie. 4m., 7w. Sc. Poor cottage in the outskirts of a North Carolina village. PEA

Joe. J. Dransfield. Dialect play. 4m., 3w. Sc. Cottage in a lonely spot. FREN, SHAT

John Borden's daughter. C. W. Russell. 3m., 1w. Sc. Interior. FIT

John Citizen's dream. H. Simpson. Farce. 1m., 1w. Sc. Office of inspector of taxes. SIMM

C   **John Hancock.** S. F. Thomas, *ed.* 1b., 1g. Sc. Living room of Hancock Home. Norm. Inst. 38: 53–54, June 1929.

J   **John Silver off duty.** R. L. Stevenson. Adapted from Stevenson's Treasure Island. 3b. Sc. Rather plain interior. WEB

John Smith. W. Hancock. Farce. 5m., 3w. Sc. Interior. FIT

C   **Johnny has a design dream, an art play.** R. C. Merry. 9b., 3g. Sc. Johnny's bedroom. School Arts M. 26: 301, Jan. 1927.

C   **Johnny on colonial history.** E. Hoxie. 2b., 2g. Sc. Living room. HOVA

J   **John's gang.** M. Johnson. 6b., 2g. Sc. Living room. JOHD

Joiners, The. A. M. Hinkley. Satirical comedy. Sc. Backroom in plumbing company. UM

Joint owners in Spain. A. Brown. Comedy. 4w. Sc. Chamber in old ladies home. BAK, FRER

C   **Joke on Santa Claus, The.** E. E. Preston. 10b., 1g., chorus. Sc. Santa's living room. PRE

C   **Jolly health clown and his helpers, The.** M. Simpson. Many c. Norm. Inst. 39: 49–50, May 1930.

C   **Jolly smiles crew, The.** W. B. Longacre. 10b., 2g. Sc. Captain's cabin of pirate ship. Hygeia 8: 1050–1052, Nov. 1930.

Jon. D. O. Savage. 3m., 3w., chorus. Sc. Fisherman's hut. PHIJ

Jonathan and the lovely lie. E. Hartzell. 4m., 5w., 1b., 1g. Sc. Well furnished hall of boarding house. Players Mag. 2: 18–20, Mar.–Apr. 1926.

Jones family, The. T. A. Funk. 3m., 3w. Sc. Living room. BART

C   **Jongleur de Dieu (the clown of God), Le.** K. Gibson. Many c. Sc. In front of chapel. Indiv. Inst. 1: 24–31, Dec. 1928.

J   **Joseph and his brethren.** M. Hobbs and H. Miles. 5b., chorus. Sc. On a hill outside the city of Dothan. HOB

Joseph, the dreamer. P. J. Stackhouse. 9m., 1w., chorus. Sc. Land of Canaan. STAC

C   **Joseph, the dreamer of dreams.** M. Parsons. 6b. Sc. Either outdoors or indoors. PARS

Joseph, the interpreter of dreams. P. J. Stackhouse. 6m., chorus. Sc. Prison in Memphis. STAC

Josephine. B. Crocker. 3m., 1w., chorus. Sc. Palace of the Tuileries in 1813. FRE6

Joseph's dreams come true. P. J. Stackhouse. 9m., 1w. Sc. Room in palace. STAC

Joshua's decision. J. W. Raine. 11m. Sc. A rock before a small tent. RAI

C **Journey of life, The.** E. M. Bacon. Morality. 32 char. Sc. Outdoor. FIT

Journey of the soul, The. Lord Dunsany. 6m., 1w. Sc. Lord Chamberlain's theatre. DUS, FREN

J **Journeyman, The.** C. D'A. Mackay. 3m., 2w. Sc. Room in Philadelphia tavern 1723. World Review 5: 232–233, Jan. 16, 1928.

Joy lady, a Chinese playlet, The. J. W. Hall. 5m., 2w. Sc. Chinese private courtyard of 18th century. Drama 18: 250–252, 268–269, May 1928.

C **Joys of the New Year, The.** M. A. Niemeier. 26c. Sc. Hall of time. NIEM, NIE

Jubilee. H. Heijermans. 7m., 2w. Sc. Office of prison. SHAT

Judaism and paganism, an imaginary conversation with Norman Douglas. L. Golding. Sc. Terrace of island of Capri. Menorah J. 10: 327–332, Aug.–Sept. 1924.

Judas Iscariot. W. F. Manley. 6m. Sc. Room of High priest. MANL

Judas Maccabaeus. P. E. Osgood. 3m., 1w., chorus. Sc. Church or platform. OSF

J **Judas of Kerioth drives a bargain.** P. E. Osgood. 3b. Sc. Rich curtain. OSG

J **Judge and the speeder, The.** N. Flaurier, 3b., 1g. Sc. Street. FIU

Judge Lynch. J. W. Rogers. 2m., 2w. Sc. Back porch of Southern farmhouse. FRE1, FREN, LOC, MAJ, Southw. R. 10: 3–23, Oct. 1924.

Judith. H. Kemp. 3m., 2w., chorus. Sc. Encampment of the Assyrian army during the reign of Nebuchadnezzar. KEM

Judith. W. F. Manley. 5m., 1w. Sc. Home in Bethulia. MAN

Juliet and Romeo. H. W. Githens. Romance. 3m., 2w. Sc. Stage where Romeo and Juliet is being played. SHAF

Jumbo Jum. Farce. 4m., 3w. Sc. Interior. FIT

Jumpin' the broom. C. M. Green. 4m., 2w. Sc. Sitting room of a tenant farmhouse in North Carolina. FRE5

Junkdump Fair. J. W. von Goethe. 13m., 4w., chorus. Sc. A German market place. MACU

Jupiter Jones, detective. H. P. Powell. Comedy. 3m., 1w. Sc. Country newspaper office. PENN

C **Jus' 'fore Christmas.** W. N. Bugbee and M. Irish. 4b., 4g. Sc. Living room. BUGT

J **Just a family affair.** R. E. Faulds. 1b., 2g. Sc. Living room. TWO

Just a love nest. A. L. Kaser. Farce. 2m., 1w. Sc. Living room. BAK

Just across the road. L. A. Fowler. 2m., 2w. Sc. Cabin on the edge of the Colorado desert. ELD

Just advertise. Mrs. G. C. Cobb. Comedy. 2m., 1w. Sc. Living room. JOHN

C **Just after the Civil War.** D. A. Lord. 3g., chorus. Sc. In a frame. LOQ

C **"Just as I please."** O. V. Roe. 1b., 2g. Sc. Anywhere. FJ

Just before midnight. M. Irish. 2m., 2w. Sc. Scantily furnished. IR

Just before the wedding. K. H. Patton. Comedy. 2m., 4w. Sc. Living room. HEL, PENN

Just bluff. C. R. Averell. 3m., 4w. Sc. An elaborately furnished living room. FIT

Just carrying on. B. E. Palmer. 14w. Sc. Living room. ELD

Just mere women. M. Hutton. 4w. Sc. Living room. KAM

Just neighborly. A. Dean. 2m., 2w. Sc. Kitchen. FREN, LAW, RIC

C **Just one Christmas.** M. Bitney. 8c. Sc. Interior. BIT

Just out of the hospital. K. Parsons. Comedy. 1m., 2w. Sc. Living room. MARC

Just suppose. M. T. Applegarth. 10 char. Sc. Platform. APO

Just two men. E. Pilot. 2m. Sc. Bow of a coast wise freighter. CLS

J **Justinian code, The.** M. R. Hofer. 11b., 4 chorus groups. Sc. Roman interior. HOF

K

Kalim's messenger. E. Granville. 3m., 2w. Sc. Exploration party's rest house in the Arabian desert. GRA

J **Katherine decides.** C. Barr. Comedy. 4g. Sc. Room in a dormitory of a small mid-western college. PENN

J **Katy-did.** M. T. Applegarth. 12 char. Sc. Front porch. APN

C **Katy did, Katy didn't.** H. E. Davis. 3b., 2g. Sc. Giant blades of grass. Delineator 105: 17–18, Oct. 1924.

J **Keener's Christmas gifts.** F. C. Vice. 2m., 3w. Sc. Living room with Christmas tree. CAT1

C **Keeping faith.** B. Vollmer. Many c. Norm. Inst. 35: 70, 72, Nov. 1925.

Keeping him home. K. Haviland-Taylor. Tragic comedy. 2m., 4w. Sc. Entrance hall. FREN, Country Gentleman 92: 24, 27+, Nov. 1927.

Keeping up appearances. D. A. Heywood. 2m., 2w. Sc. Kitchen. HEY

Kelly Kid, The. K. Norris and D. Totheroh. Comedy. 3m., 4w. Sc. Kitchen on hot afternoon. PHIL

C **Kellys' friendship Thanksgiving dinner.** 4b., 4g. BUG

Kelly's friendship Thanksgiving dinner, The. M. C. Minard. 3m., 2w. 4c. Sc. Front room. CAT2

Kestrel Edge. W. Gibson. Poetic. 2m., 1w. Sc. Parlour of farmstead. GIK

Kettle singing, The. M. Paxton. 1m., 3w. Sc. Kitchen of a farmhouse in Missouri. BAK

C **Key to health, The.** S. B. McCready. 14c. Sc. Temple of health. Hygeia 5: 528–530, Oct. 1927.

C **Key to true happiness.** E. Ginsberg. 2b., 3g. Sc. Gate of land of true happiness. Sierra Ed. News 25: 41, Nov. 1929.

C **Keys of Calais, The.** A. Stevenson. 7b., 7g., 4 chorus groups. Sc. Sea shore near English camp not far from the walls of Calais, France in 1347. STEV4

Kid, The. R. Moore. Comedy. 1m., 2w. Sc. Living room. KAM

Kidnapping Betty. E. Hafer. Comedy. 3m., 4w. Sc. In the country. ELD

J **Kill or cure.** E. M. Cullis. 7b. Sc. Living room. BAK

Killarney. M. Radke. 1m., 4w. Sc. Interior. ELD

Killer, The. A. Cowles. Comedy. 3m., 1w. Sc. Interior. BAK, PHIL

Killing of Aaron Kale, The. G. Hughes. Burlesque. 4m., 3w. Sc. Exterior. HUN

Kill-joy. A. Patterson. Comedy. 2m., 5w. Sc. Interior. PAIN

Kills-with-her-man. H. Alexander. 2m., 1w. Sc. A grove in the Blackfoot Country. IS, Theatre Arts M. 12: 439–446, June 1928.

Kimono. M. T. Applegarth. 10 char. Sc. Platform. APO

C   **Kind enemy.** V. Olcott. 4b., 3g. Sc. A peasant home. OLF

King, The. P. B. Perrigard. 5m., 2w. Sc. Poor peasant's cottage. CANA

King Alfred and the neat herd. M. Baring. Burlesque. 2m., 1w. Sc. Interior of hut. PRIE

King and hermit. D. Corkery. 6m. Sc. A forest glade. COR

C   **King and the cakes, The.** M. Carter. 3b., 2g. Sc. Interior. FREL

C   **King Arthur, posture play.** 7b. Sc. King Arthur's court. Hygeia. 7: 826–827, Aug. 1929.

King dreams, The. W. F. Manley. 6m., 2w. Sc. Palace of King Nebuchadnezzar. MANL

J   **King forgets, The.** J. W. Raine. 8b., 4g. Sc. Court of the temple adjoining the King's palace in Jerusalem. RAI

C   **King Groog and his grouch.** M. Jagendorf. 5b., 4g. Sc. Early morning in the woods. JAF

King in England, A. J. Pollock. 25m., 1w. Sc. Room on the ground floor of the University Schools in 1681. POL

C   **King Lazybones.** A. B. Bacon. 2b., 3g. Sc. A breakfast room. Hygeia 7: 171–174, Feb. 1929.

King of Barvender, The. A. Monkhouse. Melodrama. 5m., 1w. Sc. Royal palace. BAK

C   **King of the bookcase.** F. Cavanah. 7b., 7g. Sc. Living room or nursery. JOHG

C   **King of the Golden River, adapted from Ruskin's "King of the Golden River," The.** C. F. Reighard. 9b. Sc. Kitchen. REI

C   **King orders the drums to be beaten, The.** E. R. Jasspon and B. Becker. 3b., 2g., chorus. Sc. The court. JAR

J   **King Quarrel and the beggar.** E. W. Arnold. 5b., 3g., chorus. Sc. Throne room of King Quarrel. ELD

C   **King Richard calls for ale.** G. B. Donnelly. 8b., 4g., chorus. Sc. Green drapes representing a glen in Sherwood forest. DON

J   **King Tarquin and the Sibyl.** M. R. Hofer. 2b., 1g., 2 chorus groups. Sc. Roman interior. HOF

C   **King winter.** O. F. W. Burt. Many c. Sc. Woodland. Pop. Educ. 42: 228–31, Dec. 1924.

C   **King with the iron heart, The.** S. Young. 7b., 3g. Sc. A great chamber in the Palace of the King. MOSA, YOUN

Kingdom of books, The. W. L. Bissell. 26 char. Pageant. Sc. A pathway in front of curtains. BIS

C   **Kingdom of the Rose Queens, The.** J. Farrar. 4b., 29g. Sc. Garden in light of the forest. FARR

J   **King's choice, The.** A. W. Arnett. Any number c. Sc. Stage. CJ

C   **King's cobbler, The.** B. Folmsbee. 4b., 2g. Sc. Rough peasant interior. FOL

J   **King's dilemma, The.** W. Richardson. 5b., 1g., chorus. Sc. High-ceilinged hall. RICH

King's English, The. H. Bates. 12m., 1w. Sc. Tropical island in the South Seas. GOLD

King's fool, The. D. Clark. Fantasy. 3m., 2w. Sc. Poorly furnished garret. COWL

C **King's good friend, The.** A. Stevenson. 3b. Sc. In the woods. STEV1

J **King's great-aunt sits on the floor, The.** S. Walker. Fantasy. 10b., 5g. Sc. Interior. APPL

King's hard bargain, A. W. P. Drury. 5m., 1w. Sc. Garden of the "Coach and Horses." MAR3

Kings in Nomania. P. Wilde. 4m., 1w., 3 adult chorus groups. 11b. Sc. 1 Street in Nomania. 2 House of the miser. 3 A jail. 4 Palace of the king. 5 Street in Nomania. APPL, BAK, Pict. R. 27: 6–7, 34+, Dec. 1925.

King's son, The. E. O. Cochran. 2m., 3w. Sc. Elegant apartment on Riverside Drive, N. Y. COC

King's son, The. M. S. Oliver. 8m., 4w. Sc. Narrow strip of stage which must suggest a woodland. OLI, Drama 16: 297–8, May, 1926.

King's threshold, The. W. B. Yeats. Poetic. 12m., 3w., chorus. Sc. Steps before the palace of a king. YEA

King's waistcoat, The. O. Conway. 5m., 2w. Sc. Room of a manor-house. CONW, FREL, MAR2

Kiss in the dark, A. Farce. 2m., 3w. Sc. Interior. DRA, FIT

Kissing goes by favor. L. N. Brown. 1m., 1w. Sc. A study of a college professor. Drama 16: 14–15, 33, Oct. 1925.

Kissing the wrong girl. W. C. Parker. Farce. 1m., 2w. Sc. Interior. FIT

C **Kit cat and cross patch.** K. D. Morse. 9c. Sc. Room in a cottage. MORS

Kit Marlowe. A. Melford. 7m. Sc. Room in Blackfriars Tavern. FREL

C **Kitchen convention, The.** H. O. Boggs. 3b., 8g. Sc. Kitchen. BOGG

J **Kitchen knight, The.** E. Smith. Adapted from Malory's Morte d'Arthur. 10b., 3g., chorus. Sc. Hall of Arthur's castle. SM

Kitchen mechanics. W. Butterfield. Farce. 1m., 2w. Sc. Interior. PENN

Kite, The. H. Hudson. Poetic. 7m., 1w., chorus. Sc. Chinese interior in T'ang Dynasty. FRE3

Kitty Clive. F. F. Moore. Comedy. 2m., 1w. Sc. Parlour of Inn. MOO

Kitty on the keys. H. Simpson. Farce. 1m., 2w. Sc. Sitting room. SIMS

Klubwoman, The. E. Hamilton. Comedy. 2m., 6w. Sc. Club house. PENN

Knave of hearts, The. L. Saunders. 8m., 2w., chorus. Fanciful. Sc. Stage. FIS, LEO, LON, SV

Knife, The. W. Aukes. 4b., others. Sc. Headquarters at Valley Forge. World R. 8: 40–41, Feb. 18, 1929.

Knife, The. A. J. Harnwell and I. J. Meaker. 3m., 3w. Sc. Interior of cottage in small Belgian village in 1915. SCH3

Knife, The. H. A. Jones. 3m., 2w. Sc. Ante room outside an operating room. FRE2

J **Knight and the banner, The.** M. A. Butler, Adapted from Scott's The Talisman. 8b., 4g. Sc. Mound in center of stage. BUT

J **Knight of the funny bone, The.** F. Cavanah. 4b., 1g., chorus. Sc. Throne room in the Land of Hearts. CAV

J **Knight of the piney woods, A.** A. MacLean. 4b., 1g. Sc. Woods. APPL

Knight's mare, The. B. King. 4w. Sc. Interior. BAK

Knights of the silver shield. E. McFadden. 8m., chorus. Sc. Interior of chapel in the castle of Godfrey of Gaunt. FREN

Knives from Syria. L. Riggs. 2m., 2w. Sc. Oklahoma farm living room. FREN, FRE3

Knock out, The. A. D. Patterson. Comedy. 1m., 2w. Sc. Interior. PAIN

Knockout, The. J. P. Heald. Farce. 4m. Sc. Exterior or country lane. BAK

Kogekiyo. Motokiyo. 2m., 1w., chorus. Sc. Mountain side in Japan. STOP

L

"L." L.L. Atlas. 7m., 3w., chorus. Sc. Street over which an elevated line runs. YAL

J **Labor riot, A.** H. W. Githens. 6b., chorus. Sc. In front of the Idol shop of Demetrius. GITH

J **Labors of Heracles, The.** M. R. Hofer. Comedy. 3b., 3g., 5 chorus groups. Sc. Stage with two curtains. HOF

C **Lad or the gift of time.** B. P. Lane. 22c. Sc. Indoors or outdoors. LAN

Ladies' League trims the tree, The. 8w. Sc. Club room. ELD

Lady and the law, A. G. W. Cronyn. 2m., 1w. Sc. Interior of adobe house. SHAF

Lady fingers. G. Hughes. Comedy. 4w. Sc. Interior. FREN

Lady from Philadelphia, The. H. S. Griffith. Farce. 3m., 5w. Sc. Kitchen. PENN

Lady in the sack, The. C. Seiler. Extravaganza. 16m., 4w., chorus. Sc. Chinese interior. SEH

Lady Joanna, The. A. C. Darlington. 1m., 3w. Sc. Walled courtyard in ancient Palestine. DAQ

Lady of destiny, The. P. Hoffman. Comedy. 8w. Sc. Interior. FREN

Lady of dreams. P. Wilde. Fantastic comedy. 2m., 2w. Sc. Secret chamber of Mary's heart. WIK

Lady of pain. E. B. Delano and D. Carb. Comedy. 3m., 6w. Sc. Living room. Country Gentleman 90: 9–10, 62+, Dec. 1925.

Lady of the inn, The. K. G. Chapin. Verse. 2w. Sc. Room at the Inn at Bethlehem. CG, Country Life 55: 33–34, Dec. 1928.

Lady of the lake, The. R. Jeans. Farce. 2m. Sc. Before a curtain. JEO

Lady older than time, The. G. P. Wertenbaker. 3m., 1w., chorus. Sc. Palace of Neldazen. BROX

Lady or the tiger, The. E. L. Gamble. Burlesque. 7m. Sc. Interior. BANN

C **Lady White and Lady Yellow.** V. Olcott. 3b., 7g., chorus. Sc. A deserted garden in Japan. OLE

Lady with a load of hay fever, The. H. Simpson. Farce. 3m., 3w. Sc. Room in an inn. SIMA

Ladybug, ladybug, the first dance-play in Tommy Tiptoe's insect theatre. H. E. Davis. 2b., 2g. Sc. A rose bush. Delineator 104: 17–18, May 1924.

C **Lafayette's toast.** A. Stevenson. 11b., 1 chorus. Sc. Banquet hall in 1777. STEV4

Lafitte (1820). M. M. Griffith. 15m. Sc. Red house. GRI

Laird's lucky number, The. J. J. Bell. Farce. 3m., 1w. Sc. Interior. BAK

Lake, The. L. Barton. 4g., chorus. Sc. Wooded place by lake. SAO

Lamp and the bell, The. E. St. V. Millay. Blank verse. 5m., 6w., chorus. Sc. Interior. APPL

Land ho! E. H. Lamb. 1m., 3w. Sc. Typical New England living room. Drama 21: 13–14, 30, June 1931.

C **Land o' the slowpokes, The,** a folk play of Dixie. P. Poe. 3b., 4g. Sc. Land o' the slowpokes. PAIN

C **Land of books, The.** Y. Klein and F. Schwarz. 27c. Sc. Any interior. KLE

C **Land of color for junior grades, The.** G. L. Wilson. 10c., chorus. Sc. Blackboard in background. School Arts M. 27: 83–86, Oct. 1927.

Land of heart's desire. W. B. Yeats. Poetic. 2m., 3w., 1c. Sc. Room with a hearth. YE

Land of no fences, The. M. Shacklett. 9 char., chorus. Sc. Outdoors. ELD

C **Land of play, The.** M. Sharpe. 14c. Sc. The forest of story books. BAI, Kind. and First Grade 11: 21–24, Mar. 1925.

C **Land of right side out, The.** J. Thorp. 21c. Sc. A terrace. WOM

Land of the outstretched hand. Mrs. F. I. Johnson, *ed.* 2m., 1w. Sc. Mud plastered room in India. Mis. R. 53: 530–4, July 1930.

Lardy cake. I. Gandy. 1m., 3w. Sc. Cottage interior. DE

C **Lark's nest, The.** A. Stevenson. 1b., 3g., chorus. Sc. A garden. STEV1

Larola. H. L. Willcox. 4m., 4w. Sc. Living room of mission bungalow in India. FED

La Salle (1685). M. M. Griffith. 8m., 2w., chorus. Sc. Outside the entrance to a frontier blockhouse. GRI

Lassitude. H. D. Skidmore. 2m., 4w. Sc. Kitchen-living room. UNM2

Last cache, The. I. E. Mackay. 8m., 1w. Sc. Road house near a lumber camp. FREN

Last day for grouse. O. Mack. 2m., 1w. Sc. Log cabin in Colorado. CL, UNW2

C **Last day of school, The.** E. Preston. 4b., 4g. Sc. School room. PRES

Last Disciple, The. L. Housman. 2m., 2w. Sc. Interior of a half-ruined hut in Italy in 1270. HOUF

Last Frontier, The. A. C. Rowell. 6w. Sc. Dressing room of house. Drama 15: 157–160, 163, Apr. 1925.

J **Last journey, The.** H. W. Githens. 14b., chorus. Sc. On ship bound for Rome. GITH

Last man in, The. V. I. Arlett. 2m., 3w. Sc. Outside the gate of heaven. Poet Lore 41: 410–418, Autumn 1930.

Last meeting, The. O. W. Firkins. 2m., 1w. Sc. Section of a ward in a military hospital in France in 1917. FIR

Last of the Joneses, The. L. W. Watkins. Comedy. 1m., 3w. Sc. Librarian's office of Genealogical library. BAK

Last of the Lowries, The. P. Green. 1m., 3w. Sc. Kitchen in rough cabin. COH, HAZ

Last rising, The. S. A. Macphail. Melodrama. 2m., 1w., 1b., 1g. Sc. Tea table outside home in Canada. Queen's Q. 37: 246–258, Spring 1930.

Last straw, The. B. Crocker. 4m., 1w. Sc. Kitchen of flat. CL

Last tag! L. Larrimore. 3m., 2w. Sc. Living room. PENN

Latchkeys. A. Gerstenberg. Comedy. 7m., 5w. Sc. Stair case. GEQ

Late Captain Crow, The. L. V. Armstrong. Comic tragedy. 8m. Sc. Cabin of a ship at anchor. FRE5

Late Mrs. Laite, The. E. O. Jones. Farce. 8w. Sc. Interior. DENI

Latest style, The, a play for vocational students. M. C. Richmond. 7b. Sc. Showroom of a tailoring establishment. Ind. Arts M. 17: 85–6, Mar. 1928.

Latest Victor record, The. M. T. Applegarth. 17 char. Sc. Palms and ferns in front of a tent. APO

Laugh and grow wise. F. J. Pohl. Fanciful. 8m., 2w. Sc. King's court. PO

Laughing child, The. E. H. Yates. Parable. 1m., 1w., 3c. Sc. A roadside near Gethsemane. YATE

C **Laughing doors, The.** S. Young. Fanciful. 7b., 1g. Sc. A great hall. YOUN

Laughing mind, The. H. Brighouse. 5m., 7w. Sc. Lawn. BRIO

Laurel wreath, The. M. Williams and E. Recht. 6m., 4w. Sc. Drawing room of artist's studio. Player's M. 6: 18, 19, Jan. and Feb. 1930.

Lavender bags. R. Jeans. Farce. 5m., 1w. Sc. Smoking room of a golf club. JEC

Law of compensation, The. H. Berman. 5m., 1w. Sc. Luxurious sun parlor. BER

Law takes its toll. R. Blake. 6m., others. Sc. Inside of prison showing cells. Amer. Mercury 17: 263–270, July 1929.

Lawsuit, A. N. Gogol trans. from Russian. 3m. Sc. Study. GOG, GOG6

Layout, The. P. Dickey. 4m., 1w. Sc. Living room. FREN

J **Lazarus tells of his death.** P. E. Osgood. 2b., 2g. Sc. Hill wall of a garden. OSG

C **Lazy Kate.** A. Stevenson. 3g., chorus. Sc. 1 Bedroom. 2 Schoolroom. STEV2

—**Lean years, The.** M. K. Reely. 2m., 2w. Sc. Front porch of a prosperous farmhouse. PHIL, REE

Leap-year bride, A. L. M. Hickson. Comedy. 2m., 1w. Sc. Outer office of automobile company. SHAF

Learning to memorize. F. Corder. 1m., 1g. Sc. Dialogue between teacher and pupil. Etude 42: 519, Aug. 1924.

Least of these, The. E. Wilson and A. W. Field. From Tolstoi. Where love is, God is. 3m., 3w., 5c. Sc. A bare room. WOM

Leave it to Phyllis. E. MacKenzie. 5m., 3w. Comedy. Sc. Interior. PAIN

'Lection. E. P. Conkle. 6m. Sc. Outside school house. COM, FREN

J **Lee the Virginian.** F. Sterling. 6m., 4w., chorus. Sc. Reception room in the Lee home, Arlington Heights, Va. SHAB

Left in charge. B. Bayless. Farce. 4m., 4w. Sc. Interior. PENN

J **Left-over boy, The.** G. Sorenson. Comedy. 1b., 3g. Sc. Attic. SOR

C **Left-over toys, The.** O. W. Burt. 15c. Sc. Interior. DRA, ELD

Legend. P. Johnson. 2m., 2w. Sc. Living room of cottage on the east coast. BLA, FREN

Legend of London, A. M. Arlen. 3m., 1w. Sc. A drawing room. Harper's Bazaar 61: 87–89, 206, Apr. 1926.

Legend of Luz, The. H. Sackler. 8m., 1w., others. Sc. Gate of city wall. Menorah J. 10: 258–266, June–July 1924.

J **Legend of Saint Dorothy, The.** G. G. King. 4b., 1g. Sc. Public place. WEB

J **Legend of the Graal, A.** D. Horton. 6 char. Sc. Chapel of the Graal in the deep greenwood. PIL

J **Legend of the laurel, The.** E. B. Brownell. 8 char. Sc. Exterior. WOM

Leisure. E. Granville. 1m., 1w. Sc. Sitting room. GRA

C **Lemuel wouldn't lie.** H. O. Boggs. 2b., 2g. Sc. Living room of modern home. BOG

Lend me five shillings. J. M. Morton. Farce. 5m., 2w. Sc. Interior. FREN, PENN

Lenna looks down. D. F. Halman. 5m., 1w. Sc. A bare small office. FRE4

Lepers, The. L. Housman. 9m. Sc. Den-like enclosure. HOUS

C **Lesson from an humble source.** H. O. Boggs. Comedy. 3b. Sc. In front of Monticello. BOG

Lesson in dramatics, A. E. G. Sutherland. 2m. Sc. Bachelor. SMIT

Lesson in elegance. B. Herbert. Comedy. 4w. Sc. Parlor. FIT

C **Lesson in geography, A.** M. E. Whitney. 4b., 4g. Sc. 1 Play room. 2 Drawing room. WHI

C **Lesson in thrift, A.** M. DeJong. 16c. Sc. Any. School Arts M. 28: 299–300, Jan. 1929.

Lesson in thrift, A. K. A. White. 4b., 5g. Sc. Living room. Pop. Educ. 41: 462, Apr. 1924.

Lessons in love making. M. Irish. 1m., 3w. Sc. Room. CAT2

Let it go at that. E. Dane. Comedy. 7w. Sc. A den. BAK

Let Mary do it. M. C. Allyn. 12w. Sc. Attractive living room. BAK

Letters. F. Ryerson and C. Clements. 3w. Sc. Office. RY, Drama 16: 253–4, Apr. 1926.

Letters, The. F. G. Tompkins. Satire. 5m. Sc. Interior. APPL, SHAF

Letters and comment, fragment of a Greek tragedy. A. E. Housman. 2m., chorus. Tragedy. Sc. Any stage. Yale R. 17: 414–416, Jan. 1928.

Leviathan. T. Wilder. 2m., 1w. Sc. A wrecked ship in ancient Venice. WILZ

Liar and the unicorn, The. B. Hughes. Comedy. 2m., 1w. Sc. Spacious room in men's club in London. SHAF

"Liars!" F. Bimko. Comedy. 2m. Sc. On board the train enroute to Kalomai. BLP

Liars. S. Aleichem. Comedy. 2m. Sc. (On board a train in Russia). SHAF

C **Liberty Bell, The.** R. Benton. 15b., 3g., chorus. Sc. A small tenement room. BEN

Library and the Joneses, The. C. M. Baker. 2w., 7c. Sc. Living room. WIMT

Library for the first grade, A. G. H. Crocker. Several c. Sc. Library. Norm. Inst. 39: 25–26, June 1930.

Lie, The. W. O'Connell. 6m., 1w. Sc. Home in North Carolina. The Carolina Play book, June 1928.

Lies. M. Larriner. Tragedy. 1m., 2w. Sc. Comfortable living room. LAR

Lies, a comedy of the eternal feminine. F. C. Molnar. Comedy. 2m., 2w. Sc. A park in Budapest. Golden Book 11: 101–102, Feb. 1930.

J **Life in a Succah.** A. Burnstein. Comedy. 6b. Sc. Interior of a small Succah. BLO

Life is like that. B. Abel. Comedy. 1m., 1w. Sc. Library of home. AB

J **Life more abundant.** E. Edland. Many c. Sc. Church platform. Int. J. of Rel. Educ. 1: 52–54, Apr. 1925.

Life on the Steppes. G. Hughes. Burlesque. 4m., 3w. Sc. Russian interior. HUN

Lifting Jimmy's junk. E. J. Sharpsteen. Comedy. 2m., 1w. Sc. Office of Oil Co. in Oklahoma. DENI

C **Light, The.** K. Bryan. 18c., chorus. Sc. Stage. WOM

J **Light in the window, The.** R. Rice. 2b., 4g. Sc. Cottage home. CJ

J **Light of the cross, The.** S. E. Gosselink. 3b., 6g. Sc. Home of Mary Magdalene. ELD

Light that failed, The. C. Bell. Comedy. 11m. Sc. Back room of police station. DRA

Lighted candles, a tragedy of the Carolina highlands. M. Bland and L. Duls. Tragedy. 2m., 3w. Sc. Mountain cabin. CAR3, Carolina Play-Book 1: 17–26, Sept. 1928.

J **Lighting the way.** E. E. Olson. 4b., 3g. Sc. Very humble room. BAK

'Lijah. E. V. Smith. 4m., 1w. Sc. Living room in Southern Colonial home. BAK, CL, PHIL

Lily among thorns; A. G. Sierra and M. M. Sierra. Comedy. 6m., 7w. Sc. House in a Spanish town. DIC3

C **Lily Ling's first Christmas.** H. Sander. 2g., chorus. Sc. Living room. ELD

Lima beans. A. Kreymborg. Fantasy. 2m., 1w. Sc. Interior. FREN, KR

'Limination. J. H. Newett. Comedy. 3m., 2w. Sc. One-room shack of negro tenant. OMI

Limping along. A. Kreymborg. 2m. Sc. Room in a Harlem lodging house. FRE5

C **Lincoln as a young clerk.** F. O'Ryan and A. W. O'Ryan. 8b., 2g., chorus. Sc. Grocery store, New Salem, Illinois in 1832. ORY

C **Lincoln dramatizations.** E. E. Preston. 21c. Norm. Inst. 37: 78, 80, Feb. 1928.

Lincoln highwayman, The. P. Dickey. 4m., 1w., 1 dog. Sc. Garage somewhere between California and Nevada. FREN

Lincoln League. B. C. Rawley. Farce. 13m. Sc. Interior. FIT

C **Lincoln Memorial, Washington D. C., The.** Y. Klein and F. Schwarz. 5c. Sc. Any interior. KLE

Lineman, The. S. Henderson. Farce. 2m., 1w. Sc. Interior. MARC

Lingerie shop, The. E. B. Longnecker. Comedy. 2m., 3w. Sc. Lingerie shop. PENN

Lion and the fox, The. M. E. Whitney. 4b. Sc. In front of the Lion's den. WHI

Lion and the unicorn, The. E. Denton. 7b., 2g., chorus. Sc. Street outside King's palace. DENU

Lion tamer!, The. D. Titheradge. Farce. 2m., 1w. Sc. County fair and menagerie. TITU

Lion's mouth, The. H. L. Kennedy. 1m., 3w., 3b. Sc. Log cabin with bench outside. APPL

J **Lion's whelp, The.** G. R. Leighton. Sc. Room in a Monastery in 1209. 6b. WEB

Lipstick. H. Simpson. Farce. 4m., 2w. Sc. Sitting room. SIMM

Literature and Science, a dialogue between B. Shaw and A. Henderson. 2m. Sc. Dining room of Bernard Shaw. Fortn. R. 122: 504–523, Oct. 1924.

Lithuania. R. Brooke. 5m., 2w. Sc. Peasant hut. APPL

Little bluffer, The. A. N. Dowling. Farce. 2m., 3w. Sc. Lawn near the hotel. BAK

J   **Little boy out of the wood, The.** K. C. Greene. Fanciful. 1b., 1g. Sc. The outskirts of a small wood near Epping forest. WEB

Little brother Sherlock. L. L. Turner. Comedy. Sc. Living room of summer cottage. DENI

Little brown jug. A. L. Weeks. 4m. Sc. Lawyer's office in a small town. DET

C   **Little city of friendly hearts, The.** G. S. Eickmann. Fantasy. 4c. Many chorus groups. Sc. City park. ELD

Little company, A. H. W. C. Foster. Comedy. 4m., 3w. Sc. Hall with stairs. FOS

J   **Little cousin, The.** G. Sorenson. Comedy. 7g. Sc. Living room in bungalow. SOR

Little father of the wilderness, The. A. Strong and L. Osboune. 6m., 1w. Sc. Ante chamber in the palace of Versailles. COH, FRE1, FREN, STRO

C   **Little fir tree, The.** A. C. Rowell. 20c. Sc. Clearing in the forest. SAL

Little fish. H. V. Gamble. 2m., 2w. Sc. Kitchen. Drama 14: 185–187, Feb. 1924.

C   **Little fish, The.** A. Stevenson. 2b. Sc. A river shore. STEV1

Little fool, The. A. E. Meyer. Comedy. 3m., 1w. Mob. Sc. A tailor's shop long ago. Drama 17: 13–14, 29–30, Oct. 1926.

J   **Little general, The.** M. Holbrook. 4b., 3g., chorus. Sc. A clearing. SAO

C   **Little George Washington.** P. Beard. 5b., 3g. Sc. A garden. BEA

Little George Washington's valentine. P. Beard. 1m., 1w., 4b., 2g. Sc. A garden Valentine's Day. SAG

C   **Little girl confessions.** O. V. Roe. 7g. Sc. Any stage. FJ

Little glimpses of great people. G. Bradford. 5m., 1w. Southwest Rev. 10: 40–48, Oct. 1924.

Little good people, The. B. M. Casey. 3b., 3g. Sc. Interior. BAK

C   **Little gray lady, The.** 15 char. Sc. Interior. BAK

C   **Little invisible guest, The.** V. Olcott. 3g., chorus. Sc. Dining room. OLE

C   **Little jackal and the camel, The.** A. Stevenson. 3b., chorus. Sc. Bank of the river. STEV2

Little John and the miller join Robin Hood's band. P. B. Corneau. 8b., chorus. Sc. Edge of Sherwood forest. SAO

C   **Little journey to the land of mathematics, A.** A. E. Crawford. Many c. Sc. Study room. Math. Teacher. 17: 336–342, Oct. 1924.

Little king, The. W. Bynner. 2m., 1w., 2c. Sc. Room in the Temple in Paris 1793. WEB

Little ladies' style show, The. W. N. Bugbee. 4m. Any number of w. Sc. Stage. CAT1

C   **Little lady Dresden.** O. M. Price. 4b., 5g. Sc. Mount Vernon shortly after the close of the American Revolution. PRIC, PRI1

Little learning now and then, A. E. G. Utterback. 7w., 2c. Sc. Modern schoolroom. ELD

Little liberty, The. H. Brighouse. Comedy. 2m., 3w. Sc. Room in a nicely furnished Mayfair flat. FREL, FREN

C Little lost aster. V. Olcott. 2b., 2g., chorus. Sc. Pumpkin field. NAT, SAL

Little man, The. J. Galsworthy. Farce. 9m., 3w. Sc. Platform of an Austrian railway. GAL, HAM, MAR1

C Little man in the moon, The. M. Jacob. Comedy. 15 char. Sc. Room decorated for a Christmas. WOM

C Little Miss Muffett. L. Cuddy. 10c. Sc. Just-as-you-see-it place. CUD

C Little Nellie's Christmas dream. M. Helfen. Operetta. 18c. Sc. A child's play room. CATH

Little old gent, The. R. Willis. 3m., 3w. Sc. Interior of an abandoned summer cottage. WIMS

C Little pageant of story books, The. Any number of c. Sc. Interior. ELD

Little patriot, The. M. G. Parsons. 4m., 1g. Sc. Dining room of a colonial house. WOM

J Little princess who traveled far to worship the king, The. D. R. Schenck. 6b., 2g. Sc. A sheepfold near Bethlehem. WOM

C Little prophet, Samuel, The. M. Parsons. 5b., 1g. Sc. Room in Temple. PARS

Little red shoes. H. Brighouse. Comedy. 3m., 2w. Sc. Interior. BAK, PHIJ

C Little Robin stay-behind. K. L. Bates. Verse. 8c. Sc. Woods of late autumn. BAT

C Little scar-face. A. Stevenson. 2b., 5g. Sc. Indian village. STEV2

C Little Scarface. A. H. Walker. 2b., 4g. Sc. By a wigwam. SAO

C Little shadows, The. A. F. Brown. 2b., 3g. Sc. In the children's bedroom. BROW

J Little sheperdess, The. A. Rivoire. Trans. from French. 1b., 2g. Sc. A little wood. RIC

C "Little Square-toes." R. Field. 5g. Sc. Clearing near a village in colonial America. FIE

Little stone house, The. G. Calderon. 5m., 2w. Sc. Russian interior. BAK

C Little Sun's birthday. E. L. Squires. 5b., 4g. Sc. Platform. SQ

C Little vegetable men, The. E. G. Griffith. 10c. Sc. Garden. HAH

J Little women. M. A. Butler. 5g. Sc. Living room. BUT

C Little Yashmak, The. V. Olcott. 2b., 3g. Sc. Before the dropped curtain. OLF

C Littlest pumpkin's Thanksgiving, The. Mrs. M. Jones, Jr. 8c. Sc. Pumpkin patch. Norm. Inst. 38: 78, 80, Oct. 1929.

C Littlest shepherd, The. F. Ryerson and C. Clements. 12c. Sc. Stage. SAL, SHA

Live and grow wise. F. J. Pohl. Fanciful. 7m., 1w. Sc. Emperor's court. PO

J Living Christ, The. G. S. Overton. 25c., chorus. Sc. Platform. OV, Int. J. of Rel. Educ. 2: 28–31, Feb. 1926.

C Living pictures. M. I. Stone. 10b., 17g., chorus. Sc. Interior. STON

Living solid face. H. Alexander. Music. 2m. Sc. Interior, or exterior. ALE

Lo, the poor suitcase. B. O. Edey. 21g. Sc. Bedroom. FREN

Locked chest, The. J. Masefield. 3m., 1w., chorus. Sc. A room with a chest. MASE, MASF

Lofty motives. A. Weinberg. 2m., 1w. Sc. Interior of heroine's home. Poet Lore 38 : 603–606, Winter 1927.

Lolotte. J. Pollock. 4m., 2w. Sc. London drawing room. POL

"Londonderry Air, The." R. Field. 2m., 2w. Sc. Kitchen of a remote New England farmhouse. FIC, FRE3

Lone Worlds! P. Hirschbein. 3m., 3w. Sc. A deep cellar dwelling. BLP

Lonely hearts. E. G. Hall. 3m., 4w., chorus. Sc. Interior decorated for Christmas. TUL

C **Lonely little fir tree, The.** R. Rice. Many c. Sc. In a forest. Prim. Educ. 46 : 327, 332, Dec. 1928.

C **Lonely little tree, The.** Y. Klein and F. Schwarz. 7c. Sc. Out of doors. KL

Lonesome-like. H. Brighouse. 2m., 2w. Sc. Room in a Lancashire cottage. FRE1, MAR2

Long ago in Judea. V. Sanderson. 16m., 1w. Sc. Audience chamber of Herod. FREN

Long box, The. S. K. MacDonald. 2m., 2w., others. Sc. Interior of mountain lodge. Drama 14 : 180–182, 200, Feb. 1924.

Long Christmas dinner, The. T. Wilder. 4m., 5w., chorus. Sc. Dining room of home. WILY

J **Long courtship, A.** H. W. Githens. 4b., 2g., chorus. Sc. Desert. GIT

Long distance. H. Upson. 3 char. Sc. Interior. LON

Long voyage home, A. E. O'Neill. 8m., 3w. Sc. Bar of a low dive on the London water-front. ON

Longfellow and the gun. P. E. Ring. 2b., 3g. Sc. Back porch of Wadsworth-Longfellow home in Portland in 1814. Prim. Educ. 45 : 450–451, Feb. 1928.

Long's fort. M. M. Griffith. 2m., 3w. Sc. Inside of Fort. GRI

Look out for the Constables. W. N. Bugbee. 6m., 1w. Sc. Office. CAT1

Look to the End. J. Marks. 3m., 3w. Sc. A flagstoned areaway outside a thatched cottage. MARK

Looking-glass, The. O. W. Firkins. 3m., 2w. Sc. Section of the deck of an ocean liner. FIR, Drama 16 : 171–173, Feb. 1926.

Loose. E. M. T. Shaler. Comedy. 3w. Sc. The salon of a ship. NICR

Lord Bateman. V. B. Lawton. 3m., 3w., 4 chorus groups. Sc. On shore of ocean. LAWT

Lord Byron. E. Ferber. 8m., 9w. Sc. Overlooking park in London. APPL

Lord's prayer, The. F. Coppee trans. by M. Aldis. 3m., 3w. Sc. Paris at the time of the French Commune. ALEX, HANF

Lord's will, The. P. Green. Tragedy. 1m., 2w. Sc. Interior. GREL

Losing side, The. D. Hewlett. 4m., 1w. Sc. Kitchen-living room in London. FREL

Lost—a sale. N. Balch. 5m., 1w. Sc. Purchasing office. BAL

C **Lost aster, The.** V. Olcott. 7c. Sc. In the pumpkin field. SAL

C **Lost camping place, The.** M. Foote. 5b., 5g. Sc. Pretty green plot. NAT

Lost child, The. M. S. Oliver. 4m. Sc. Around a camp fire. OLI

Lost coin, The. L. W. Wood and L. P. Martin. 3m., 5w. Sc. Oriental home in ancient times. ELD

Lost collar button, The. G. Cameron. Comedy. 2m., 2w. Sc. Interior. FREN

Lost elevator, The. P. Wilde. Comedy. 6m., 5w. Sc. In an elevator. WILD

C **Lost firewood, The.** 20c. Sc. Interior. BAK

Lost Lenore, The. B. R. Tucker. 2m., 1w. Sc. Living room in Richmond, Virginia in 1835. LIB

C **Lost penny, The.** H. E. Davis. Several c. Sc. A candy counter. Delineator. 109: 33–34, Dec. 1926.

J **Lost princess, The.** D. Totheroh. 14 char., chorus. Sc. Stage with curtains. FRE6, TOT, Drama 19: 107–109, 112, Jan. 1929.

C **Lost Proserpine, The.** 16 or more c. Prim. Educ. 44: 731, 746, May 1927.

J **Lost purse, The.** A. Curtis. 3b., 5g. Sc. Sitting room. CURT

Lost saint, The. D. Hyde. 3 adults, 1 group of c. Sc. In the schoolroom. JOHM

Lost silk hat, The. Lord Dunsany. 5m. Sc. Fashionable street in London. CROE, GOLD, MILL, Golden Book 10: 89–91, Aug. 1929.

C **Lost son, The.** J. W. Raine. 5b. Sc. Corner of house with vine above door. RAI

Lost souls. R. Jeans. Farce. 3m., 3w. Sc. Apartment in Paris. JEP

C **Lost violin, The.** E. R. Worrell. 7b. Sc. Interior. ELD

Lot's wife. P. Wilde. Burlesque. 1m., 3w. Sc. Hilly spot on the road beyond Sodom. WILD

Lotus flowers. J. C. McMullen. 2m., 4w. Sc. Interior. BAK

Love and grow wise. F. J. Pohl. Fanciful. 8m., 2w., chorus. Sc. King's court. PO

Love and how to cure it. T. Wilder. 2m., 2w. Sc. Stage of Tivoli Place, London, 1895. WILY

Love and insurance. W. Fitzpatrick. 4m., 1w. Sc. Interior. ELD

Love and lather. K. Kester. Farce. 2m., 1w. Sc. Barber shop. JOHM

Love at first sound. I. Cordy. Farce. 2m., 2w. Sc. Private room in Lakeside Hospital. ELD

Love in a cupboard. D. Heyward. Comedy. 2m., 2w. Sc. Interior. FREN

Love in a French kitchen. C. Clements and J. M. Saunders. Trans. from French. 1m., 2w. Sc. Kitchen. FRE4

Love in an attic. C. Divine. 1m., 1w. Sc. An attic room. FREN

Love in the desert. L. Binyon. Verse. 2w. Sc. Tent in the desert. BIN

Love, incorporated. J. S. McCabe, Jr. Comedy. 2m., 2w. Sc. Interior. BAK

Love is blind. P. Wilde. Farce. 3m., 1w. Sc. A hotel. WILT

Love is like that. F. Ryerson and C. Clements. Comedy. 3w. Sc. Interior. FREN, RY

Love letters. J. Marks. Comedy. 2m., 3w. Sc. Pastor's study. MARK

Love passage, A. W. W. Jacobs. Comedy. 3m., 1w. Sc. Saloon of tramp steamer. PEN

Love of Mrs. Pleasance, The. J. Pollock. 2m., 2w. Sc. Gym-room in a Cambridge College. POL

Love of one's neighbour. L. Andreyev. Comedy. 13m. 3w. 1b., 1g. Sc. Wild place in mountains. Golden Book 4: 181–190, Aug. 1926.

Love or lucre. L. duG. Peach. Farce. 2m., 1w. Sc. Ancient castle hall. PAZ

J   **Loveliest thing, The.** R. Pertwee. Fanciful. 3m., 4w., chorus. Sc. Comfortable room on Christmas morning. LAD

Lovely miracle, The. P. Johnson. 1m., 3w. Sc. Living room of humble cottage. JOHF

Lover and the dead woman, The. L. S. Jast. Verse. 1m., 1w. Sc. Beside a grave. JAS

Lover of Killcairne, The. J. E. Connor. 3m., 1w. Sc. A smithy in an Irish village in 1916. EM

Lovers meeting. L. Housman. 8m. Sc. Exterior of Community house of the Friars Minor in Perugia in 1240. HOUF

Loves of Lionel, The. R. Welty. Comedy. 1m., 4w. Sc. Interior. DRA

Loves of the elements, The. L. S. Jast. 16 char. Sc. An arid and rocky landscape. JAS

Low-boy wins, The. M. S. Smith. Comedy. 5m., 3w., chorus. Sc. Antique shop. FARQ

Low life. M. Roche. 2m., 1w. Sc. Poor room of a lodging house in Canada. CANA, ROC

Lower road, The. C. C. Mather. 2m., 1w. Sc. Living room. Player's M. 1: 18–20, June 1925.

Lowing in the night. A. Brody. 1m., 1w. Sc. Bedroom back of a candy store in the Bronx. BRO

C   **Lu Li learns about Lincoln.** S. G. Clark. 1b., 8g. Sc. Living room. Norm. Inst. 36: 70–71, Feb. 1927.

Lucindy captures the minister. W. N. Bugbee. 2w. Sc. Sitting room. CAT1

Luck king, The. J. Pollock. 4m., 1w. Sc. American consulate in a new republic on the confines of Persia. POL

Luck o'Land. A. N. Dowling. 3m., 1w. Sc. Combination living and dining room of a homestead. EM

C   **Luck of Santa Claus, The.** B. C. Porter. 11b. Sc. Interior. DRA

Luck of war. G. John. 3m., 3w. Sc. Kitchen living room in the Northern Midlands. JOHA

Luck-piece, The. P. Wilde. Fantastic comedy. 5m., 2w. Sc. Saloon in a small American seaport. WIK

Lucky fool, The. H. Burnham. Comedy. 2m., 3w. Sc. Living room of a bachelor apartment. PAIN

C   **Lucky Hallowe'en, A.** M. Irish. 3b., 4g. Sc. Living room. IQA

Lucky Jim. H. Simpson. Farce. 1m., 1w. Sc. Sitting room. SIMO

C   **Lucky moon.** M. Murphy. 5c., chorus. Sc. Moonland. ELD

Lucullus's dinner party. M. Baring. 2m., 4w. Sc. Room in Lucullus's house. Golden Book 5: 778–780, June 1927.

C   **Lucy chooses.** G. Henderson. 3b., 5g. Sc. Indoor or outdoor setting. FJ

Lucy the farmer's daughter. G. Hughes. Burlesque. 4m., 2w. Sc. Interior. HUN

J   **Lunch hour, The.** 2b., 2g. Sc. Gymnasium or study hall. AU

C   **Lunch hour at the Greenwood cafteria.** M. Davis and M. T. Lofgren. 8c. Sc. Cafeteria. Prim. Educ. 45: 124–125, Oct. 1927.

Lunch party, The. B. Herford. 4w. Ladies Home Journal 44: 255, May 1927.

Lure of the stage, The. E. Andreas. Comedy. 2m., 2w. Sc. Living room. ANDR

J   **Lycurgus the law maker.** M. R. Hofer. 5b., 5 chorus groups. Sc. Market place in Sparta. HOF

Lydia. R. P. Kimball. 8m., 2w. Sc. Street in Philippi. BAK

M

Maastricht play, The. 16m., 4w., chorus. Sc. Stage. HAQ, Theatre Arts M. 11: 947–952, Dec., 1927.

J   **Mabel's aunt.** M. B. Carpenter and F. I. Hope. 5g. Sc. College girl's room. BUG

Machine age, The. E. Kelley. 2m., 4w., 1b. Sc. Living room-kitchen of pioneer's cabin in 1870. LONG

Mad breakfast, A. I. M. Gray. Farce. 4m., 6w. Sc. Breakfast room of a modest boarding house. BAK

J   **Mad tea-party, The.** M. A. Butler. Adapted from Carroll. Alice in Wonderland. 3b., 1g. Sc. Garden with a table under a tree. BUT

Madame Delphine. G. W. Cable. 3m., 2w. Sc. Parlor. HAP

C   **Madame Summertime's guest.** M. Bitney. 6c. Sc. Hotel lobby. BIT

Mademoiselle Diana. J. Pollock. 5m., 2w. Sc. Behind the scenes of a traveling circus at Sheffield. POL

Mademoiselle Tania. O. Kelley. Comedy. 2m., 1w. Sc. Circus tent. KEK

Mademoiselle, Vivine. M. R. R. Hatch. 4m., 2w. Sc. Stage. FOU

Madonna of the Golden Hart, The. R. Newton. 7m., 4w. Sc. Public bar of the Golden Hart. DE

J   **Madonna's picture, The.** E. Edland. 6b. Sc. Reception room of Japanese Prince in 1549. EDLP

Maganimous lover, The. S. G. Ervine. 3m., 2w. Sc. Kitchen in cottage in North Irish village. ER

Magda. E. G. Rockwell. 4m., 2w., chorus. Sc. Interior. BAK

C   **Magic basket, The.** American Red Cross. 17c. Sc. Fairy forest. SAO

C   **Magic bell, The.** W. Pailler. 9b., 8g., chorus. Sc. In an ancient house. DRA

C   **Magic Cargoes.** V. Olcott. 8b., 1g. Sc. A room in a working home in London. OLC

C   **Magic Christmas tree, The.** R. E. Chew. 17c. Sc. Kitchen in crude cabin. ELD

C   **Magic fishbone, The.** L. F. Collins. Adapted from Dickens. 12b., 8g. Sc. Living room in a palace. COJ

C   **Magic fluid, The.** H. C. Phibbs. 6b., 2g., others. Sc. Great hall of a palace. Hygeia. 4: 275–278, May 1926.

C   **Magic gift, The.** Z. M. Walters. 2b., 5g. Sc. Interior Christmas. BUG

Magic hour, The. F. S. Rutherford. Fantasy. 18m., chorus. Sc. Camp of Voyageurs in 1680. CAC

C   **Magic in the house.** D. F. Pierson. Fanciful. 12b., 16g., chorus. Sc. Girl's playroom. FREN

C   **Magic jack-o'-lantern, The.** K. A. White. 13c. Sc. Glen in a forest. Grade Teacher 47: 121+, Oct. 1929.

C   **Magic May basket.** Oregon Tuberculosis Association. Many c. Child Welf. 21: 335, Mar. 1927.

C   **Magic oat field, The.** E. G. Griffith. 12c. Sc. Fairy garden. HAH

C   **Magic sea, The.** S. Young. Fanciful. 1b., 2g., chorus. YOUN

J **Magic sea shell, The.** J. Farrar. 3m., 2w., 2 chorus groups. Sc. Dock at the edge of a pool, lake or the seashore. CLS, FARR

C **Magic Thanksgiving pie, The.** B. Casey. 9b., 9g. Sc. Sitting room. ELD

C **Magic thrift lamp, The.** R. P. Bramwell. 7c. Sc. Living room. Norm. Inst. 35 : 59, Jan. 1926.

J **Magic touch, The.** H. W. Githens. 2b., 2g., chorus. Sc. House in Jerusalem. GITH

C **Magic whistle, The.** G. A. Mahoney. Many c. Sc. Woods. Norm. Inst. 39 : 50–51, Apr. 1930.

C **Magic windows.** M. Barrows. 5b., 4g. Sc. Interior with library table. SAL

C **Magic word, The.** E. F. Guptill. Any number of c. Sc. Interior. ELD

   Magnolia's man. G. W. Coffin. Comedy. 2m., 2w. Sc. Village in North Carolina in 1834. Carolina Play Book, Dec. 1929.

   Mah-Jongg. A. Gerstenberg. 4w. Sc. Interior. GER

   Maid, The. S. Armour. 4m., 1w. Sc. Dugout in the British lines in France. CANA

   Maid of France. H. Brighouse. 3b., 2g. Sc. Side of a square in a French town. SCH1

J **Maid of the Nile, The.** C. T. Major. 10b., 5g. Sc. Room in ancient Egypt. MAI

   Maiden in distress, A. O. Kelley. Comedy. 5m. Sc. Railway car. KEK

J **Maiden vain of dress, The.** E. I. Mackenzie. 14g. Sc. Dressing table. PAIN

   Maiden's tomb, The. Kiyotsugu. 1m., 4w., chorus. Sc. Field in Japan. STOP

C **Maidland Pt. II, the land of desires.** D. A. Lord. 3g., chorus. Sc. Interior. LOO

C **Maidland Pt. II, the land of dreads.** D. A. Lord. 3g., chorus. Sc. Interior. LOO

C **Maidland Pt. II, the land of dreams.** D. A. Lord. 2g., chorus. Sc. Stage. LOO

   Maizie. R. Giorloff. 1m., 3w. Sc. Furnished room in a cheap east-side rooming house. FRE5

   Major Kelly's cork leg. O. E. Young. Farce. 5m., 3w. Sc. Interior. FIT

   Make your choice. M. Irish. 8 char. Sc. Living room. IR

J **Maker of dreams, The.** O. Down. 2b., 1g. Fantasy. Sc. Room in an old cottage. HANF, MAR1, SMI

C **Makers of the world, The.** V. Olcott. 7b., chorus. Sc. On the shores of the Atlantic Ocean. OLF

   Makeshifts. G. Robins. Comedy. 2m., 2w. Sc. Sitting room in English lower-middle class home. RO4

C **Making Molly merry.** M. Bitney. 3b., 3g. Sc. Living room. BIT

C **Making of a flag, The.** P. Beard. 2b., 4g. Many chorus groups. Sc. A small garden in 1776. BEA

C **Making of a nation, The,** a play for Lee-Jackson days. The K. L. Perry. 1b., 2g., chorus. Sc. Living room with fireplace. Norm. Inst. 36 : 59, Jan. 1927.

C **Making of an art scrapbook, The.** Y. Klein and F. Schwarz. 12c. Sc. Any interior. KLE

C **Making of the flag, The.** R. Kimball. 10b., 4g. Sc. Interior of shop in Philadelphia in 1716. SAL

Man with the flower in his mouth, The. L. Pirandello. Trans. from Italian. 2m. Sc. An avenue. PIR, Dial 75: 313–22, Oct. 1923.

Man with the iron jaw, The. C. O. Kennedy. Comedy. 3m., 3w. Sc. Dressing tent of a small town circus. HUO

Man without a head, The. L. F. Thanhouser and T. J. Foster, Jr. 3m. Sc. A dilapidated chamber in a Chateau. YALP

Managers, The. a comedy of Cape Cod. J. C. Lincoln. Comedy. 2m., 1w. Sc. Interior. APPL, NICA

Manager's trials, A. A. L. Fisher. Farce. 9m. Sc. Stage. FIT

Mandarin coat, The. A. C. D. Riley. Comedy. 2m., 3w. Sc. Drawing room in a California city. RIL

C **Manger in Bethlehem, The.** F. C. Gardner. 8b., 4g. Sc. Interior in Bethlehem. GAP

Manhood. L. Anderson. Comedy. 7m., 1w. Sc. Warden's office. ANDE

J **Manikin and Minikin.** A. Kreymborg. Comedy. 2b., 1g. Sc. Parlor. FIN, KR

Manners and manors. G. Hughes. Burlesque. Sc. Interior. HUN

Man's world. F. Jacob. Comedy. 4m., 3w. Sc. Inner office of printing. JAC

Mansions. H. Flanner. 1m., 2w. Sc. Living room. APPL

"Many Happy returns!" R. Wetzel. 3m., 3w. Sc. Living room: UNM2

Many happy returns of the day. F. C. Knox. 6w. Sc. Interior. LON

Maple's bride, The. A. Scudder. 2m., 2w., chorus. Sc. Room in Japanese house. SCU

C **Marathon.** M. H. Lawson. Many c. Sc. Any stage. Hist. Outlook 18: 83–87, Feb. 1927.

Marble arch. E. Rose and A. J. Garriway. Comedy. 2m., 2w. Sc. Interior. FIT

Marble god, The. S. Schofield. 2m., 2w. Sc. Interior of a house in a Cornish village. SCHO

C **March interrogation point, The.** Many c. Prim. Educ. 45: 535, 574+, Mar. 1928.

C **Marching Home!** M. Barrows. 1b., 3g., chorus. Sc. Old fashioned living room. SAL

Marching men. J. H. O'Brien. 7m., 1w. Sc. Section of Chateau-Thierry. FREN

C **March of the mile stones, The; or, The story of Fifth Avenue and the growth of New York.** F. Schwarz. 6c. Many chorus groups. KLE

C **March wind, The.** M. Corell and I. Liccione. 8 or more c. Sc. School yard. STRU

J **Marchioness, The.** E. Smith. Adapted from Dickens. Old Curiosity Shop. 5b., 3g. Sc. Office. SM

Margaret in Natos. C. Fitzhugh. 1m., 2w. Sc. Salon in a small Swiss hotel. FITZ

C **Marian's wish.** E. W. Merriman. 2b., 3g. Sc. Interior. DRA

Marie misses marriage. H. O. Boggs. 2m., 2w. Sc. Living room of farm. BOGH

J **Maripoza Bung, or, The pirate's daughter.** 4b., 1g. Sc. Cabin of ship. FREL, FREN

Marital mishap. A. L. Kaser. Burlesque. 1m., 1w. Sc. Bedroom. KAS

Marketing. B. Herford. 1m., 2w., 1g. Sc. A market. Ladies Home Journal 41: 211, Sept. 1924.

J **Marks of a good citizen.** E. C. Averill. 3g. Sc. Schoolroom. THOQ

C **Marpessa.** M. Oller and E. K. Dawley. 2b., 2g. Sc. Humble room in a deserted hut. OLL

Marriage, The. D. Hyde. Trans. from the Gaelic by Lady Gregory. 2m., 1w., chorus. Sc. Cottage kitchen. SHAT, Golden Book 6: 327–332, Sept. 1927.

Marriage cake, The. E. Wilbur. Comedy. 1m., 2w. Sc. Neat corner of a kitchen. BANN

J **Marriage contract, The.** M. A. Butler. Adapted from Longfellow's Evangeline. 4b., 1g. Sc. Living room. BUT

Marriage gown, The. J. K. Sollenberger. Tragedy. 2m., 3w. Sc. Combined kitchen and dining room in a cottage on the coast of Maine. IN

Marriage has been arranged, A. A. Sutro. Comedy. 1m., 1w. Sc. Conservatory. MAR2, PEN, Golden Book 12: 98–101, July 1930.

Marriage is so difficult. L. Harris. Farce. 2m., 2w. Sc. Living room of studio apartment. Poet Lore 38: 452–463, Autumn 1927.

Marriage morning, The. H. Simpson. Farce. 2m., 1w. Sc. Room in a lodging house. SIMA

Marriage of Dotty, The. C. Thornton. Comedy. 2w. Sc. Drawing room. JOHN

Marriage of little Eve, The. K. Nicholson. 3m., 3w. Sc. Star dressing room of opera house in Indiana. NICG, SHAF

J **Marriage proposal, A.** A. Tchekoff. Comedy. 2m., 1w. Sc. Reception room in Russian house. KN, RIC, THOM

Marriages are made in heaven and elsewhere. G. Price. Comedy. 2m., 2w. Sc. Interior. BAK

Marrying off brother. M. E. Roberts. Comedy. 3m., 5w. Sc. Living room. ELD

Marrying off father. Z. Hartman. Comedy. 3m., 3w. Sc. Interior. BECK, DEN

Marse Covington. G. Ade. 5m. Sc. At the steel door of a gambling house. FREN

Marshall. F. Molnar. 5m., 1w. Sc. Hunting lodge. MOL

Martha Jeffries' mother. R. B. Parrish. 3m., 2w. Sc. Kitchen of a farmhouse in West Virginia. UNND

Marthe. N. Armstrong. 4m., 2w. Sc. Room in eastern farmhouse, psychological study. SHAF

J **Martyrdom of Stephan, The.** M. E. Whitney. 4b. Sc. Council room. WHH

Marvelous romance of Wem Chun-Chin, The. 6m., 3w., assistants. Sc. Chinese stage. Poet Lore 35: 298–313, Summer 1924.

Mary Ann's truce. R. P. Bramwell. 2m., 2w. Sc. Dining room of farmhouse. ELD

Mary Brice. T. F. Murphy. 6m., 2w. Sc. Office interior. DET

Mary comes home from college. L. Crites. 3m., 2w. Sc. Comfortable living room. ELD, MARC

Mary Jane and the census man. W. N. Bugbee. 1m., 2w. Sc. Kitchen. CAT1

Mary means what she says. J. W. Rogers. 3m., 2w., 2c. Sc. A farmhouse in the South. FRE3, FREN

Mary Muldoon's morning. A. J. Walker. 1m., 4w. Sc. Pleasant kitchen in N. Y. tenement. BAK

C **Mary Rich's Christmas party.** 4c., chorus. Sc. Living room. Volta R. 31: 775–777, Dec. 1929.

C **Mary's garden.** P. McGinley. Verse. 6 char., chorus. Sc. Garden. EDU

Mary's lamb. H. Osborne. 5m., 3w. Sc. Corner in a Broadway cabaret. HAY

Ma's new boarders. W. C. Parker. 4m., 4w. Sc. Boarding house. FIT

Mask, The. H. M. Harwood. 2m., 1w. Sc. Kitchen in house in Cornish village. HAR

Masks. P. B. Corneau. 1m., 1w. Sc. Pleasantly furnished room. LAW

C **Masque of old loves, A.** F. V. Vilas. 5g., 4b., c. Sc. Any audience hall. Child Wel. M. 20: 341–344, Feb. 1926.

Masquerading Santa, A. C. B. Margach. 3m., 4w. Sc. Living room. DRA

Master of the house, The. S. Houghton. Comedy. 4m., 2w. Sc. Parlour. MAR3

Master Patelin, the lawyer, the most famous medieval French farce brought up to date. M. Jagendors. 4m., 1w. Sc. Street scene. Golden Bk. 13: 74–79. Mar. 1931.

Master salesman, The. W. H. Upson. 2m., 1w. Sc. Salesroom. EAT, FREN

Master wayfarer. J. E. H. Terry. 3m., 1w. Sc. Parlour of "The Pigeon Pie." MAR3

Match maker, The. R. Jeans. Farce. 2m., 2w. Sc. Sitting room. JEP

Matchmakers, The. M. C. Russell. 2m., 3w. Sc. Kitchen of a farm-house. DE

J **Mateo Falcone.** P. Merimée. 6m., 1w. Sc. A little clearing before a rough hut. HAP

J **Mathematical night mare, A.** J. Skerrett. 8b., 2g. Sc. Living room. Math. Teacher 22: 413–17, Nov. 1929.

J **Mathesis.** E. Brownell. 14 or more c. Sc. Underground studio. Math. Teacher 20: 459–465, Dec. 1927.

Matinate. L. Langner. 2m., 1w. Sc. Small room in a large city. SHAQ

Matrimony. C. Seiler. 3m., 2w. Sc. Moving street car. SEH

Matrimony up to date. C. D. Tucker. Comedy. 3m., 3w. Sc. Interior. CART

Matter of choice, A. W. J. Farma. 3m., 4w., 2c. Sc. Living room. FARK, FREN

Matter of choice, A. W. J. Tannewitz. 2m., 5w. Sc. Living room of well-to-do home in small city. Player's M. 1: 15–19, Nov. 1924.

J **Matter of diplomacy, A.** O. M. Price. 4b., 2g., chorus. Sc. Secluded corner just off the ballroom at the Embassy, 1906. PRI

Matter of policy, A. G. Phillips. Revue. 2m., 2w. Sc. Breakfast room. FRET

Mattie discovers a Merry Christmas. M. Irish. 4m., 4w. Sc. Living room in boarding house. BUG

J **Matzoth Shalet, The.** E. G. Gerson. 4b., 2g. Sc. Interior. BLO

Maundy Thursday. E. K. Doten. Miracle play. 3m., 1w. Sc. Interior of a poor family's kitchen in the reign of James I of England. DR

J **Maurice's own idea, a dream play.** M. Malleson. Comedy. 14b., 1g. Sc. Night nursery. PHIL

May and December. C. Fitzhugh. 2m., 2w. Sc. Living room. FITZ

May basket magic. B. Creighton. 12g. Sc. Maypole. Woman's Home Companion 57: 64, May 1930.

C **May day, old and new.** M. MacLennan. Many c. Hygeia 8: 375–377, Apr. 1930.

J **May madness.** B. Gilbert. Fantasy. 1b., 5g., chorus. Sc. Part of school campus. SANP

May night. P. Flowers. 2m., 4w. Sc. A boudoir hung in rose taffeta. Poet Lore 36: 551–564, Winter 1927.

C **May pageant.** M. Cutler. Many c. Sc. Garden. Prim. Educ. 45: 706, 737, May 1928.

C **May Queen, The.** F. I. Hope and M. B. Carpenter. 2b., 11g. Sc. Any stage with throne. Norm. Inst. 34: 70, May 1925.

J **May treasure.** F. Cavanah. 7b., 7g. Sc. Cozy nook in the valley of spring. CAV

J **Mayflower compact, The.** O. M. Price. 6b., 2g., chorus. Sc. Cabin of the Mayflower, 1620. PRI

Mayor and the manicure, The. G. Ade. Comedy. 2m., 2w. Sc. Office FRE1, FREN

C **Maypole, The.** C. S. Bailey. 5b., 3g., 3 chorus groups. Sc. Out of doors. BAI, Amer. Childhood 13: 25–26, 61–62, May 1928.

Maypole morning. H. Brighouse. 5m., 4w., chorus. Sc. Village green in England in 1665. BRIO

Maze. A. C. White. 3m., 2w., 1g. Sc. Farm kitchen, very clean. Poet Lore 36: 147–153, Spring 1925.

C **Meaning of America, The.** I. M. Aitken. 10c. Sc. Interior. LUT

C **Mechanical dolls.** S. T. Payson. 15c. Sc. Home of Santa. BECK

Meddlesome Mrs. Mars, The. B. E. Palmer. 9w. Sc. Living room. ELD

Meddlin'. E. E. Olson. Comedy. 1m., 3w. Sc. Kitchen. BAK, YOU

Medica. W. K. Engle. Farce. 7m. Sc. Doctor's office. FIT

Medicine show, The. S. Walker. 3m. Sc. On the south bank of the Ohio River. CL

C **Mee-Mee and But-Zee.** M. Jagendorf. 2b., 3g., chorus. Sc. Home of Chinese boy. JAF

"Meet the family." J. W. Fitzpatrick. Comedy. 4m., 4w. Sc. General utility room in apartment. ELD

Meet the husband. L. Merrin. Comedy. 2m., 2w. Sc. Living room. PAIN

Meet the Missus! K. Nicholson. 1m., 2w. Sc. Room in a New York hotel. FRE2

Meeting at the well, a Chinese folk-drama. K. Chen *tr.* 1m., 1w. Sc. No scenery. Theatre Arts M. 14: 971–975. Nov. 1930.

C **Meeting of the hearts.** M. Irish. 7c. Sc. School room. IQ

Meeting of the three kings, The. P. E. Osgood. 3m. Sc. Road to Jerusalem. OSF

C **Meeting of "The Young Citizens' League of America,"** A. Y. Klein and F. Schwarz. 12c. Sc. Any interior. KL

Meeting of the Young Ladies' Club. E. Latour. Comedy. 8w. Sc. Interior. DRA

Melancholy Dame, The. O. R. Cohen. Comedy. 3m., 2w., chorus. Sc. Cheap cabaret. NICB

Melchizedek, Abraham and Isaac. P. E. Osgood. 6m., chorus. Sc. Church OSF

Mellissa makes good. A. Patterson. Comedy. 1m., 1w. Sc. Interior. PAIN

Memmon. L. Binyon. Verse. 1m., 3w. Sc. Temple in Ethiopia. BIN

C **Memorial day.** Y. Klein and F. Schwarz. Any number of girls. Sc. A flower garden. KL

C **Memorial day fantasy, A.** F. B. Linsky. Fantasy. 18c. Sc. Stage. FAX

C **Memorial day pageant, A.** D. B. Smith. Pageant. Many c. Sc. Forest scene. Norm. Inst. 33 : 70, May 1924.

C **Memorial day parade, A.** M. E. Whitney. 3b., 3g. Sc. A street corner. WHI

C **Memories.** O. M. Price. 13c. Sc. Living room. PRI1

C **Memories of Christmas.** E. Cameron. Pantomime. 24c. Sc. Stage. CAME

Men Folk. F. Ryerson and C. Clements. Tragedy. 3w. Sc. Interior with rough board walls and unfinished timber ceiling. RY

Men, women and goats. C. O. Kennedy. 3m., 2w. Sc. Office of warden of State's Prison in Mass. FRE6

Mended day, A. M. Irish. 3m., 2w. Sc. Kitchen. IR

C **Mender man, The.** J. L. Vandevere. 9b., 9g. Sc. Interior. BUG

Menu, The. A. Gerstenberg. Comedy. 5m., 1w. Sc. Interior of a fashionable restaurant. GEQ

Mercurial youth. M. Larrimer. Comedy. 1m., 2w. Sc. Artistic apartment in New York. LAR

Mere man. A. Gerstenberg. Comedy. 5w. Sc. Apartment. GEQ

Mereden's right hand. A. H. Gibbs. Farce. 2m., 2w. Sc. Morning room of a London flat. PHIL

J **Meriwether fortune, The.** G. Sorenson Comedy. 2b., 4g. Sc. Lawn of home in summer. SOR

Meriwether Lewis. C. Reznikoff. 8m. Sc. Around the fires of a Sioux encampment. REZ

Merlin's grave. G. Bottomley. Dramatic poetry. 3m., 2w. Sc. Vacant space. BOTT

J **Merman's pipe, The.** Mrs. J. R. Commons. 3b., 4g., chorus. Sc. Wooded spot near a lake. BEST

J **Merry Christmas, A.** L. S. Beazley. 4m., 15w. Sc. Interior. PENN

Merry Christmas in the old home town. A. Curtis. 5m., 7w. Sc. Living room. DRA

Merry merry cuckoo, The. J. Marks. 4m., 1w. Sc. A garden. MARK

C **Merry Tyll.** M. Jagendorf. Fanciful. 9b., 4g., chorus. Sc. Market scene in Bruges. JAN

Merry widow welcome. E. Percy. Comedy. 3m., 5w. Sc. Room in Mid-Victorian cottage. FREL

Mess of pottage, The. W. F. Manley. 2m., 2w. Sc. The hut of Esau. MAN

Message, The. H. W. Gribble. 2m., 2w. Sc. Before the grave of the unknown dead. SCH3

Message and Jehanne, The. T. Wilder. 2m., 1w. Sc. Interior of a goldsmith's shop in the Paris of the Renaissance. WILZ

Message from heaven, A. S. J. Levy. 4m., 1w. Sc. Court in heaven. LEU

Message from Sinai, The. W. F. Manley. 5m., crowd. Sc. Ten commandments. MAN

C **Message of Easter, The.** M. A. Niemeier. 42c. Sc. Outdoors. NIEM

Messenger, The. J. W. Fitzpatrick. 3m., 4w., 1b. Sc. Sunday school room. ELD

Messengers, The. L. Housman. 4m., 2w. Sc. Window of low cottage-chamber of William Blake. HOT, 19th Century 150: 269–285, Feb. 1929.

Messiah, The. a Christmas play. T. J. McKeon. 6m. Sc. Camp fire. Cath. World 120: 321–334, Dec. 1924.

Meticulous customer, The. P. Wilde. Farce. 3m. Sc. A bake shop. WILT

J **Micawbers dine with David, The.** G. Pertwee and E. Pertwee. Adapted from Dickens. David Copperfield. 4b., 3g. PER

C **Mice will play, The.** E. L. Squires. 7c. Sc. Kitchen. SQ

Miching Malecho. I. Dall. 3 char. Sc. Marsh near corner of a wood. DAL

J **Michio.** C. T. Major. Fanciful. 6b., 7g. Sc. In a Japanese orchard. MAI

J **Midas.** A. Haggard. 5b., 4g. Sc. Outdoor scene. HAG

Midnight excursion, A. H. O. Boggs. 7m. Sc. Farm. BOGG

C **Midnight in the toy shop.** K. Dickerson. Musical. 15c., chorus. Sc. Toy shop. MARC

Midnight murder. A. Ashdown. 3m. Sc. Library of "The Towers." FREQ

Midnight of Monsieur St. Jean, The. L. G. Barnard. 3m. Sc. Bed-room of Monsieur Riviere. CANA

C **Midshipmen, The.** L. K. Dolan. 1b., 5g. Sc. Stage arranged to resemble the deck of a ship Naval Academy at Annapolis. DOL

J **Midsummer eve.** C. D. Mackay. 25 char. Fanciful. Sc. Forest. FREN

J **Midsummer night.** O. F. W. Burt. 8c., 2 chorus groups. Sc. Sky on mid-summer night. BEST

C **Midwinter's night dream.** M. Irish. 3b., 6g. Sc. Interior. IQ

Might-have-beens. R. Sneddon. Fantasy. 2m., 2w. Sc. Interior. FREN

Miguel. G. Hughes. 1m., 2w. Sc. Patio of ranch house in California. Player's M. 1: 16–19, Feb. 1925.

Milk. M. H. Bro. 4m., 3w. Sc. Farmhouse dining room. FREN

C **Mill that ground hot porridge, The.** A. Stevenson. 14c., chorus. Sc. Elf land. STEV1

Millennium morning. E. H. Yates. Farce. 3m., 1w. Sc. Room in a natural history museum. YATE

C **Miller, his son, and their donkey, The.** A. Stevenson. 6b., 6g. Sc. A bridge near a town and not far from a fair. STEV3

Mimi. O. Conway. Comedy. 3m., 3w. Sc. Room in the Latin quarter. MAR3, CONW

Mimi lights the candle. E. I. Coulter. 1m., 8w. Sc. Interior. FREN

C **"Mind your mother" club, The.** O. V. Koe. 7g. Sc. Ordinary sitting room. FJ

J **Mine eyes have seen the glory.** A. Curtis. 2b., 3g. Sc. Sitting room. CURT

Mine Gracious! A. L. Kaser. Burlesque. 2m. Sc. A street. KAS

Minister comes to tea, The. S. Shute. Comedy. 10w. Sc. Cozy living room. BAK

Ministering angel, The. R. Jeans. Farce. 2m., 3w. Sc. Bedroom. JEC

Minnie Field. E. P. Conkle. 5m. Sc. Kitchen of a small farmhouse. CL, COM, YAL

J **Minuet, The.** J. S. Knapp. 9b, 4g. Sc. Drawing rooms in 1775. BAK

J **Minuet, A.** L. N. Parker. 2m., 1w. Sc. Living room in Gaoler's quarters. FRE1, THOM, TUC

C **Minuet, The.** G. Stenger. 2b., 2g. Sc. Room in a city tenement. SAL

Miracle, The. H. Simpson. Farce. 2m., 2w. Sc. A ward in a nursing home. SIMO

Miracle, The. Mrs. A. Stallard. 2m., 3w. Sc. Bit of wild country in Ireland. STAL

Miracle of Saint Martin, The. M. Dondo. 4m., 1w., chorus. Sc. Before a walled town in old France of the 14th century. FRE4

Miracle of Saint Masha, The. J. Kovers. 5m., 2w. Sc. Interior of a peasant's home in Russia. KOV

C **Miracle of Saint Nicholas, The.** C. D. Mackay. Many c. Sc. Forest. Woman's Home Companion 55: 28–29, 136, 138, Dec. 1928.

C **Miracle of Theophile, The.** K. Taylor and H. C. Greene. 5b., 1g. TAY

Mirage. G. M. P. Baird. 2m., 4w. Sc. Roof of adobe house. APPL, SHAQ

Mirror, The. A. Curtis. 5w. Sc. Before a dressing table. CUR

Mirror, The. K. M. Roof. 2m., 1w. Sc. Interior. FREN

C **Mirthful Marionettes.** D. Totheroh. 4b., 5g. Sc. Marionette Stage. TOT, Drama 21: 19–20+, Apr. 1931.

C **Miss Ant, Miss Grasshopper, and Mr. Cricket.** 1b., 2g. Sc. A quaint little cottage (may be played out doors). FIE

Miss Baxter. M. Fulton. 3m., 2w. Sc. Ordinary living room. NICH

Miss Bennett's house party. G. Sorenson. Comedy. 5g. Sc. Corner of of a lawn. SOR

J **Miss Burney at court.** M. M. Frank. 3b., 3g. Sc. Interior of palace. WEB

Miss Hope Hall's sale. B. E. Palmer. 12w. Sc. Interior. ELD

C **Miss Iva Newway's school.** J. Ross. Pantomime. 8c. Sc. A school room. MARC

Miss Manda. G. B. Taber. 3m. 4w. Sc. Interior of country store. Poet Lore 38: 412–321, Autumn 1927.

Miss Mary Smith. I. Metcalfe. Comedy. 2m., 4w. Sc. Interior. DRA

Miss Milly wins. M. Bonham. 4m., 2w. Sc. Kitchen. ELD

J **Miss Miranda.** M. Irish. Comedy. 3b., 4g. Sc. Living room. IQ

Miss Nonchalance. O. Steiner. Comedy. 7w. Sc. Interior. DRA

Miss Tabitha's garden. M. M. Seavey. 3m., 5w., 2c. Sc. Old fashioned garden. FREN

Miss Tom Boy. N. Dunne. Comedy. 3w. Sc. Interior. DRA

C **Miss Usa's peach party.** F. Wells. 18 char. Sc. Japanese interior. ELD

Missing links. R. Jeans. Farce. 2m., 4w. Sc. Room in a flat. JEA

Mission barrel, The. M. C. Allyn. 11w. Sc. Living room. MEI

C **Mission days.** R. Keeney. Many c. Sc. Platform. Sierra Ed. News 26: 45–6, Sept. 1930.

J **Mission of Midas, The.** Mrs. Eva Baird. 4m., 3w. Sc. Living room with fireplace. IR

Missionary box, The. L. Larrimore. Comedy. Sc. Parlor. PENN

C **Missionary Christmas play, A.** M. M. Walters. 14w., 1b. Sc. Living room. Mis. R. 52: 862–8, Nov. 1929.

J **Missionary clinic, A.** E. Fleming. 9 char. Sc. Doctor's reception room. ELDR

J **Mistake, The.** G. Sorenson. Comedy. 3g. Sc. Well furnished living room. SOR

J **Mistake at the manor,** M. M. Frank. 4m., 2w. Sc. Dining hall at Manor. WEBB

C **Mistake they left behind them, The.** N. Flaurier. 8c. Sc. School room. FIU

J **Mister Punch.** C. Clements. Tragedy. 13b., 3g. Sc. Curtains drawn part way. SANP

C **Mister Tree.** A. B. Bacon. Many c. Sc. School yard. Norm. Inst. 39: 56, Mar. 1930.

Mistletoe and moonlight. E. Wilbur. Comedy. 5m., 3w. Sc. Interior. CART

Mistress, The. M. Gnesin. 4m. Sc. Log-hut in mining section of N. Y. YAL

Mistress Castlemaine's Christmas dinner. D. A. Lord. 4m., chorus. Sc. With drawing room in a stately mansion in North Carolina. LOR

C **Mistress Mary's garden.** L. E. Morgan. Many c. Sc. Garden scene. Norm. Inst. 37: 62, 64, Apr. 1928.

C **Mistress Spring's surprise party.** A. H. Grant. Many c. Norm. Inst. 38: 72, 74, Apr. 1929.

C **Mite-box demonstration, A.** 5c. Mis. R. 52: 468–471, June 1929.

Mix well and stir. K. Haviland-Taylor. Comedy. 6m., 5w. Sc. Living room in a small town. FREN, Country Gent. 94: 24–26, 51+, Nov. 1929.

Mixed methods. R. Jeans. Farce. 3m., 3w. Sc. Drawing room. JEC

Mixed wave lengths. R. Farquhar. Radio burlesque. 2m. Sc. Stage with receiving set. FARQ

C **Modern Alice, A.** Public School 15 Manhattan. 10c. Sc. Anywhere. LUT

Modern David Garrick, A. E. Andreas. Comedy. 2m., 2w. Sc. Living room in a hotel suite. ANDR

Modern ideas. R. Cramb. Comedy. 1m., 1w. Sc. Tastefully furnished living room. BAK

C **Modern knight—Theodore Roosevelt, A.** A. M. Lutkenhaus. 6b., chorus. Sc. Interior. LUT

Modern Magi. C. S. Brown. 5m., 1w. Sc. Interior of prairie farmhouse. EAS

J **Modern pirates, The.** M. Irish. 7b. Sc. Stage. CAT1

Modern Viking, A. F. Sterling. 13m., chorus. Sc. Forecastle of ship. SHA

Mollie and the milliner. M. Stayton. Farce. 1m., 3w. Sc. Hatshop. FREL

C **Mollie teaches the code of the flag.** E. Hoxie. 3b., 3g. Sc. Stage. HOVA

C **Molly's Merry Christmas.** W. N. Bugbee and M. Irish. 3b., 4g. Sc. Stage. BUGT

Mon Ami Pierrot. C. Fitzhugh. 2m., 4w. Sc. Upstairs sitting room at the Tuckers'. FITZ

Money. M. Gold. 6m. Sc. Gloomy east side cellar. CL, FREN

Monkey's paw, The. W. W. Jacobs. 4m., 1w. Sc. Living room of an old fashioned cottage. MAR2, Golden Book 5: 511–519, Apr. 1927.

Monsieur Tytgat. B. Ring. Comedy. 1m., 2w. Sc. A workshop. RIN

Monster, The. T. G. Schwartz. 2m., 2w. Sc. Living room. Poet Lore 37: 597–606, Winter 1926.

C **Month of birthdays, The.** A. C. Gilmore. 8b., 8g., others. Norm. Inst. 38: 88, 90, Feb. 1929.

C **Months, The.** a pageant. M. Buchanan. 6b., 6g. Sc. Room in a cottage. Prim. Educ. 32: 48–50, 61, Jan. 1924.

C **Monument's message, The.** Y. Klein and F. Schwarz. 6c. Sc. Any interior. KLE

C **Moods of spring, The.** L. K. Dolan. 12b., 21g. Sc. Stage decorated with foliage. DOL

Moon and the moonstruck, The. P. Phelps. Whimsical. 3m., 2w. Sc. Interior. FREN

J **Moon for a Prince, The.** G. Ruthenberg. Fantasy. 4b. Sc. Roof of royal palace. DAZ

J **Moon magic.** E. E. Perkins. 18 or more char., chorus. Sc. Court of warrior. DAZ

Moon of the Caribbees, The. E. O'Neill. 17m., 4w. Sc. Deck of a British tramp steamer. ON, SHAF

C **Moonbeams.** E. Granville. Fantasy. 17 char. Sc. Fairy isle. FREL, FREN

C **Moon's silver cloak, The.** A. Stevenson. 8 char., chorus. Sc. The sky. STEV1

Moonshine. A. Hopkins. 2m. Sc. Hut in mountain wilds of North Carolina. FRE1, HAMA, HAT, IS, MACG, TUC, Golden Book 10: 102–105, Nov. 1929.

Moonshine. L. Osborn. Farce. 4m., 6w. Sc. Study. PENN

Moral Courage. F. Salten. 3m., 1w. Sc. Sitting room in country house. SHAF

Morality for the leisure class, A. J. L. Balderston. Satire. 2m. Sc. Heaven. APPL, SHAF, Golden Book 10: 87–90, Sept. 1929.

More about apples. A. H. Phipps. 1m., 1w. Sc. An apple orchard. Poet Lore 40: 144–149, Spring 1929.

More ado about nothing. S. J. Hankin. 3m., 1w. Sc. Garden of house in Padua. Golden Book 11: 99–101, June 1930.

More blunders than one. T. G. Rodewell. Farce. 4m., 3w. Sc. Interior. DRA, FIT

Morning in a Superintendent's office, A. B. Mitchell. Comedy. 2m., 6w. Sc. Office. PENN

Mortuary, The. L. Housman. 2m., 1w. Sc. Outside Deanery of St. Paul's. HOT

Mose Johnson's new job. M. Hurst. 5m., 1w. Sc. Lodge rooms of Ethiopian Scientific Club. ELD

J **Moses.** M. Hobbs and H. Miles. 9g. Sc. By the river's bank. HOB

J **Moses in the bulrushes.** R. Kimball. 3g., chorus. Sc. River bank. KIM

J **Most beautiful Valentine, The.** G. Sorenson. Comedy. 6b., 1g. Sc. St. Valentine's workshop. SOR

Most foolish virgin, The. H. G. Gaskill. 2m., 10w. Sc. Stage with arrangement of dark curtain to represent King's court. EAT

J **Mother Blessing's job.** C. Lorenz. 9 char. Sc. Pretty garden. ELD

J **Mother dear.** E. R. Baird. 5b., 11g. Sc. Business office. ELD

C **Mother forest at Witching Hollow.** A. E. Toepp. 7b., 3g. Sc. Interior of Witch's hut. BANN

J **Mother's gift, A.** H. W. Githens. 4b., 2g., chorus. Sc. Temple at Shiloh. GIT

Mother's influence, A. K. Haviland-Taylor. Comedy. 4m., 3w. Sc. Living room in small town. FREN, Country Gent. 93: 27–28, 107+, Oct. 1928.

Mothers of men. P. Wilde. 2w. Sc. Sumptuously furnished drawing room. SCH4

Mother's old home. O. F. Cornelius. 1m., 6w. Sc. Interior. BECK, DENI

C **Mothers they forgot, The.** M. Parsons. 12g., chorus. Sc. Interior. SCH4

Mountain laurel. C. Cooksey. Comedy. 2m., 1w. Sc. Room in a log house on the mountains. SHAF

Mountain wedding, A. P. Franklin. 3m., 2w. Sc. Interior. FREN

Mountains of Bether, The. C. Fitzhugh. 3m., 4w. Sc. Living room. FITZ

J **Mounting Mount Sinai.** A. Burstein. Comedy. 4b., 2g. Sc. Living room. BLO

Mourner, The. J. Mahoney. 7m., 3w. Sc. Stage. FOR4

Mouse, The. L. V. V. Armstrong. 4m., 1w. Sc. Deserted hut in a lonely place on the outskirts of English sea-farming town. LON

Movieless movies. E. Breitenfeld and B. Ireland. 2m. Sc. Bare stage. WILT

Moving day. C. D. Gilpatric. Comedy. 2m., 3w. Sc. Disordered living room. BAK

Moving finger, The. P. Wilde. 7m., 1w. Sc. Top room of an inn. FRE6

Mozart and the gray steward. T. Wilder. 2m., 1w. Sc. Mean room in a Vienna house. WILZ, Harper 157: 565–7, Oct. 1928.

Mr. Bumble's proposal. G. R. Hatton and Mrs. G. R. Hatton. Adapted from Dickens. Oliver Twist. 2m., 1w. Sc. English interior. JON

C **Mr. Bunny's prize.** F. Cavanah. 4b., 5g. Sc. Nook in a forest. JAO

Mr. Editor. W. Macauley. Comedy. 7m., 2w. Sc. Editorial office. PENN

Mr. Enright entertains. A. Abbott. 5m., 4w. Sc. Dining room. DRA

C **Mr. February Thaw.** 10 char. Sc. Interior. BAK

Mr. Friendly's philosophy, a one-act drama of community life. O. Ryan. 3b., 6g. Sc. Any stage. Pop. Educ. 43: 255–6, 279, Jan. 1926.

Mr. Gardner forges ahead. F. N. Weaver. 3m., 3w. Sc. Living room. BAK

Mr. Goodman and Mrs. Gracious. L. De Neuville. 1m., 1w. Sc. A drawing room. MACU

Mr. Jardyne. G. John. 5m., 2w. Sc. Manager's room of a theatre. FREN

Mr. John. S. Caldwell and E. Hendrie. 7w. Sc. Sitting room. CAL

Mr. Jonas Chuzzlewit proposes marriage. G. Pertwee and E. Pertwee. Adapted from Dickens. Martin Chuzzlewit. 2m., 2w. Sc. Parlour. PER

Mr. Massy makes a fourth at bridge. G. Lloyd. Farce. 1m., 3w. Sc. Interior. MARC

Mr. Moore and Mr. Chew. S. C. Chew. 2m., 1w. Sc. Dining room in London home. Amer. Mercury 1: 39–47, Jan. 1924.

J **Mr. Richey changes his mind.** 4m., 4w. Sc. Interior. DRA

C **Mr. Santa Claus.** M. Stedman. 1b., 1g. Sc. Bedroom. BANN

Mr. Smallworth's mistakes. S. Emery. Satire. 4m., 3w. Sc. Interior. FIT

Mr. Smith, an Anglo-American sketch. E. W. Fordham. 2w. Sc. Open car in London. Nat. Review 95: 811–814, Oct. 1930.

Mr. Susan Peters. H. Ford. Comedy. 4m., 2w. Sc. Comfortable room with book-lined walls. FREN

Mr. Utley's etiquette. C. Divine. Comedy. 3m., 4w. Sc. Library in house. FREN

Mr. Weatherman, a health play. M. A. Grimm, *ed.* 4b., 5g. Sc. Any stage. Amer. Child. 15: 44–45, Feb. 1930.

Mr. X. S. Rosenfeld. Farce. 3m., 3w. Sc. Interior. DRA

Mrs. Adis. S. Kaye-Smith and J. Hampden. 5m., 1w. Sc. Kitchen. FRE5, HAMA

Mrs. Bright's visitor. M. R. P. Hatch. Comedy. 2m., 1w. Sc. Dining room. FOU

Mrs. Brown's Thanksgiving turkey. K. L. Carver. 10c. Prim. Educ. 32: 610, Nov. 1924.

Mrs. Corney's tea party for two. G. Pertwee and E. Pertwee. Adapted from Dickens. Oliver Twist. 1m., 2w. Sc. Sitting room in the workhouse. PER

Mrs. Gray of Lonesome mountain. F. Packard. 2m., 7w. Sc. Cabin. ELD

Mrs. Greevy's boarders. W. Macauley. Comedy. 6m., 5w. Sc. Dinner scene in a boarding house. PENN

Mrs. Hamblett insures against fire. H. C. Sargent. Farce. 1m., 2w. Sc. Sitting room. SARM

Mrs. Hamblett records her vote. H. C. Sargent. Farce. 2m., 2w. Sc. Polling booth. SARP

Mrs. Harrison. J. Masefield. 3m., 1w. Sc. Room. MASF

Mrs. Jarley's Wax-works. M. T. Applegarth. 18 char. Sc. Stage. APN

J **Mrs. Magician's mistake.** V. Dixon. 3b., 2g., chorus. Sc. Room in the house of magician. DAZ

Mrs. Markham continues on hotels. H. Belloc. 1w., 1b., 1g. Sat. R. 143: 592–93, Apr. 16, 1927.

Mrs. Markham on elephants. H. Belloc. 1w., 1b., 1g. Sat. R. 145: 315–316, Mar. 17, 1928.

Mrs. Markham on hotels. H. Belloc. 1w., 1b., 1g. Sat. R. 143: 513–514, Apr. 2, 1927.

Mrs. Markham on poetry. H. Belloc. 1m., 1b., 1g. Sat. R. 145: 91–92, Jan. 28, 1928.

Mrs. Mulcahy. M. Hageman. Comedy. 5m., 9w. Sc. Interior. DRA

J **Mrs. Newlywed attends school.** K. A. White. 1b., 2g. Sc. Dining room. WH

Mrs. Nickleby and the gentlemen next door. G. Pertwee and E. Pertwee. Adapted from Dickens. Nicholas Nickleby. 2m., 2w. Sc. Garden of English cottage in 1836. PER

Mrs. Pat and the law. M. Aldis. 3m., 2w. Sc. Small poor room in a tenement flat. SCH1

Mrs. Peabody's boarder. D. A. Heywood. 5w. Sc. Boarding house. HEY

Mrs. Plodding's nieces. N. Dunne. 9w. Sc. Interior. DRA

Mrs. Rushington's rest cure. H. N. Connell. Comedy. 9w. Sc. Living room. PAIN

Mrs. Ryan's boarders. A. Curtis. Comedy. 8w. Sc. Dining room. CUR

J **Mrs. Santa Claus.** W. N. Bugbee. 6g. Sc. Living room. JOHC

C **Mrs. Santa to the rescue.** G. P. Williams. 1b., 2g., chorus. Sc. Santa's home at the North Pole. MARC

Mrs. Toorich comes to college. L. A. Miller. Burlesque. 1m., 3w., chorus. Sc. Study No. 23, a girl's room at college. ELD

Mrs. Willis's will. E. Souvestre. Comedy. 5w. Sc. Interior. DRA, FIT

Mrs. Wright gets in wrong. L. X. Perience. Burlesque. 4m., 2w. Sc. Private office. AM

Much ado about ducats. B. Abel. Burlesque. 6w. Sc. Around banquet table. AB

J **Muffins.** L. A. Garnett. Poetic. 23c. Sc. Stage. GAR

Mug, The. H. C. Sargent. Farce. 3m. Sc. Cozily furnished room. SARP

Mulligatawny medallion, The. B. Gates. 3m., 1w. Sc. Breakfast room. GAT

C **Mung T'eo,** a play for grammar grades who are studying China. M. Wentworth. 5b., 3g. Prim. Educ. 44: 525, 527, 573. Mar. 1927.

Municipal davenport, The. J. Wren. Farce. One-word play. 1m., 1w. Sc. City park. BAK

Murder at the Bugginses. M. Constanduros and M. Hogan. Farce. 3m., 6w. Sc. Living room. FREL

Murder most-polite. H. C. G. Stevens. 3m., 1w. Sc. Boudoir. FRET

Murder! Murder! Murder! B. Hughes. 2m., 2w. Sc. Interior of a small tea room. FRE6

Murder of Marat, The. P. Kearney. Farce. 4m., 2w., soldiers and others. Sc. Seven o'clock P. M. in poor French Inn, July 13, 1793. Drama 18: 208–210, Apr. 1928.

Murder will out. L. M. Elwyn. Farce. 6w. Sc. Interior. FIT

Murder will out. C. C. Winningham. 2m., 1w. Sc. Babbitt living room in a small Iowa town. DET

"Murera Baranda," an African demonstration. Mrs. Donald Fraser. 2m., 4w., others. Sc. Native village in Africa. Mis. R. 52: 209–12, Mar. 1929.

C **Music fairy's story, The.** P. Sherman. 1b., 2g. Sc. Music room. Etude 47: 777, Oct. 1929.

Mustard. B. Charlton. Farce. 3m., 2w. Sc. Kitchen. CHA

Mutiny. L. Anderson. 6m. Sc. Cheerful sitting room in cottage. DET

J **My ain sel'.** N. Mitchison. 2b., 5g. Sc. Open place in the lowlands. MIT

My Aunt's heiress. Comedy. 9w., 2c. Sc. Interior. DRA, FIT

"My Dear!" P. O'Connor. 3m., 4w., 1b. Sc. Patio and garden. Drama 14: 188–9, Feb. 1924.

J **My double and how he undid me.** E. E. Hale. 4m., 2w., chorus. Sc. Meeting hall in church basement. HAP

My lady's rose. E. Knoblock. 1m., 3w. Sc. A dingy dark room in the East End. FIS

My last Duchess. L. A. Wade. From Browning's My last duchess. 2m., 1w. Sc. Garden near the castle of the Duke of Este in Italy. WA

My man. J. F. McCarthy. 3m., 2w. Sc. Cheap restaurant. UM

"My neighbor." E. Dane. Fantasy. 1m., 2w. Sc. Curtains. DAN

My own impressions of London. B. deMeyer. Harper's Bazaar 65: 55–60, 158, Feb. 1930.

My tailor. A. Capus. Comedy. 1m., 2w. Sc. Small drawing-room in Paris apartment. SHAP

My turn next. T. J. Williams. 4m., 3w. Sc. Interior. DRA, FIT

J **Mysterious Thanksgiving guest.** B. Brown. 4b., 3g. Sc. Interior. BUG

J **Mysterious valentine, The.** M. W. Lippencott. 4b., 4g. Sc. Interior. MARC

Mystery man, The. E. J. True. Comedy. 1m., 7w. Sc. Studio. BAK

J **Mystery of the buried box, The.** G. Sorenson. Comedy. 1b., 3g. Sc. Living room. SOR

J **Mystery play for Christmas, A.** M. M. Bradley. 24b. Sc. Stage. ALL

J **Mystic numbers.** E. Cameron. Pageant. 27 char. Many chorus groups. Sc. Open space. BAK

C **Mystic pipes.** H. Clark. 12c., chorus. Sc. Outdoors. ELD

C **Mvthland of nature, The.** L. K. Dolan. 23c. Sc. Stage. DOL

N

J **Naaman the leper.** M. E. Whitney. 5b., 3g. Sc. Apartment in house. WHH

C **Naaman, the Syrian leper.** M. I. Stone. 8b., 2g., chorus. Sc. Purple back-ground. STON

Naaman's cloak. W. F. Manley. 3m., 1w. Sc. Stage. MANL

Naboth's vineyard. W. F. Manley. 6m., 1w. Sc. Garden of King Ahab. MANL

Naboth's vineyard. J. W. Raine. 5m. Sc. Room in King's palace. RAI

Naked evil. P. E. Osgood. Sc. Ante room outside the Sanhedrin Council Hall. OSG

J **Nancy and George listen in.** M. Ainsworth. 2b., 2g., chorus. Sc. Interior. ELD

Napoleon crossing the Rockies. P. Mackaye. 3m., 1w. Sc. Cabin in Kentucky mountains. FRE3, MACK, MACL, Century 107 : 867–882, Apr. 1924.

Napoleon's barber. A. Caeser. 3m., 1w. Sc. 18th century barber shop in French village. SHAQ

Narcissus, The. Notre Dame Academy, Omaha, Neb. 1m., 3w. Sc. Interior. MARC

Nascuntur Poetae. T. Wilder. Poetic. 1m., 2w. Sc. Before a painting by Piero di Cosimo. WILZ

Nathan Hale. E. Brown. 5b., 1w. Sc. Living room 1776. Pop. Educ. 41 : 340, 345, Feb. 1924.

Nathan Hale (Act three). C. Fitch. 2m., 4w., chorus. Sc. Long Island in 1776. SAG

Nathanael's quest. O. G. Herbrecht. 9m., 2w. Sc. Oriental garden. Int. J. of Rel. Educ. 5 : 27–28, July 1929.

National anthem, The. P. Wilde. Farce. 5m., 2 chorus groups. Sc. A Swiss summer resort. WILT

Nativity, The. R. C. Burrell. 9m., 1w. Golden Book 12 : 77–80, Dec. 1930.

J **Nativity, The.** R. Kimball. 10b., 2g. Sc. Curtains. KIM

Nativity, The. P. E. Osgood. 1m., 1w. Sc. Bethlehem. OSF

Nativity (the Chantilly play), The. E. Sanchez. D. F. Robinson trans. 18m., 1w. Sc. Stage. HAQ

Nativity of our Lord Jesus Christ. 4m., 1w. Sc. Manger. Drama 21: 20–22, Dec. 1930.

C **Nature's thrifty workers.** L. K. Dolan. 10c. Sc. Stage. DOL

C **Naughty duck, The.** S. Young. Fanciful. 1b., 1g. Sc. A garden with a wall and a gate. YOUN

C **Nausicaa.** M. Oller and E. K. Dawley. 3b., 2g. Sc. Inner court of palace. OLL

J **Nausicaa and her maidens.** A. E. Thompson. 1b., 4g., chorus. Sc. Out of doors in ancient Greece. SAO

Near tragedy, A. F. B. Miller. Many c. Sc. Throne of Father Mathematics. Math. Teacher 22: 472–81, Dec. 1929.

Necessary evil, The. C. R. Kennedy. 2m., 2w. Sc. Living room. KEN

Necklace, The. G. Maupassant. 1m., 2w. Sc. Attic room. HAP

Necktie hero, The. B. E. Palmer. 2m., 5w. Sc. Living room. ELD

Needles. A. L. Kaser. Farce. 1m., 1w. Sc. Village street. KAS

J **Neighbor and his work, The.** M. M. Russell. 6b. Sc. Road. RUS

Neighborly neighbors. M. L. Farnham and O. V. Roe. Farce. 1m., 12w. Sc. Interior. BUG

Neighborly neighbors. O. V. Roe. 1b., 13g. Sc. Farmhouse kitchen. FJ

Neighbourly love. F. A. Carter. Comedy. 3m., 2w. Sc. Living room of cottage. DE

Neighbours, The. Z. Gale. 2m., 6w. Sc. Kitchen. CROA, EAS

Nelagony, or Good Water. A. Pemberton. 8b. Sc. Forest. SCH4

Nell of the Golden West. G. Hughes. Burlesque. 3m., 2w. Sc. Interior. HUN

Nephew in the house, A. B. King. 1m., 3w. Sc. Living rooms. BAK

Neptune's theatre. M. Lescarbot. Trans. from French. 15m. Sc. Seashore with a blue expanse of water. FREN

Nerves. J. Farrar. 9m. Sc. Mess hall of a flying squadron in France. FREN, THOM

Net, The. C. M. Nesbitt. 1m., 1w. Sc. Interior. SCHO

Nettie. G. Ade. Comedy. 5m. Sc. Interior. FREN

Never again. G. L. Clements. Comedy. 2m., 2w. Sc. Doctor's office. PENN

Never ending wrong, The. A. Scudder. 2m., 2w. Sc. Interior of the Emperor's pavilion. SCU

Never reckon your chickens. W. Reeve. Farce. 3m., 4w. Sc. Interior. DRA

Never the twain. L. G. Deseo. 3m., 3w. Sc. Living room mountain cabin. Poet Lore 41: 272–292, Summer 1930.

Nevertheless. S. Walker. 1m., 1w., 1b. Sc. Interior. APPL

J **New assistant, a metric play, The.** A. L. Hall. Many c. J. Chem. Educ. 2: 600–604, July 1925.

J **New boy, The.** H. O. Boggs. 4b., 2g. Sc. Schoolroom. BOGG

New cook, The. M. Helfen. 6w. Sc. Living room. CATH

New faith emerges, The. R. C. Alexander and O. P. Goslin. 5m., 1w. Sc. Humble home of-a village priest. ALEX

New fur coat, The. A. G. Evans. Comedy. 1m., 1w. Sc. Living room. DENI

New God, The. L. Abercrombie. Poetic. 2m., 1w. Sc. Extreme coast of the world. ABE

New god, The. F. J. Pohl. Fanciful. 8m., 1w., chorus. Sc. Inner court of the temple of Bhool. PO

New hangman, The. L. Housman. Satire. 6m. Sc. Office of prison. FREN

New holiday, The. M. Parsons. 11c. Sc. Stage. SAL

New moon, The. A. C. D. Riley. 10m., 2w., chorus. Fantasy. Sc. Chinese stage. FREN

C **New Mother Goose, The.** E. R. Baird. Many c. Sc. Home of Mother Goose. Prim. Educ. 45: 366, 402+, Jan. 1928.

C **New Year's party for primary grades, A.** E. Burrowes. Many c. Sc. Drawing room. Prim. Educ. 45: 376, 404, Jan. 1928.

New Portia, The. D. Titheradge. Farce. 1m., 1w. Sc. Study. TITO

J **New scholar, The.** J. A. Baxter. 6g. Sc. School room. PAIS

J **New teacher, The.** G. Sorenson. Comedy. 5b., 7g. Sc. Interior of a small country school house. SOR

New trails. C. A. Berry. 5w. Sc. Interior. BAK

New wing at Elsinore, The. S. J. Hankin. 6m. Sc. Platform before old part of Castle. HAMA

New word, The. J. M. Barrie. 2m., 2w. Sc. Dining room. BARR

J **New worlds.** E. Gibson. 1b., 3g. Sc. Street in Genoa. GIB

J **New Year's gift, A.** M. Woods. 3b., 4g. Sc. Sacred grove. WOW

Newcomer, The. S. Armour. 3m. Sc. A costly furnished bed-sitting room. CANA

J **New-fangled Thanksgiving, A.** M. Bitney. 2b., 4g. Sc. Living room. BIT

C **News of the adoption of the constitution.** M. A. Niemeier. 12b., 8g. Sc. Parlor of colonial home. NIE

Next-of-kin. S. Caldwell and E. Hendrie. 5w. Sc. Room in an English home. CAL

Nicked. J. C. McMullen. 2m. Sc. Living room of well-to-do home. MACT

C **Nicodemus, a ruler of the Jews.** M. I. Stone. 7b., 5g., chorus. Sc. White background. STON

Night and morning. M. L. Conger. 6m., 4w., chorus. Sc. Room in Pilate's home. WOM

Night at an inn, A. Lord Dunsany. Melodrama. 8m. Sc. Room of an inn. FIS, HANF, MAR1, PEN, SMI, TUC, Golden Book 4: 377–381, Sept. 1926.

C **Night before Christmas, The.** A. E. Allen. 7b., 7g. Sc. Interior. MARC

C **Night before Christmas, The.** P. Beard. 3b., 1g. Sc. Santa Claus workshop. BEA

J **Night in alchemy, A.** R. D. Billinger. Pageant. 3b. Sc. Alchemist's laboratory. J. Chem. Ed. 5: 715–724, June 1928.

Night of "Mr. H.," The. H. Brighouse. 5m., 4w. Sc. Charles Lamb's rooms, inner temple, 1806. COH, FREL

Night porter, The. H. Wall. 3m., 1w. Sc. Interior. FREN

Night watches. A. Monkhouse. Comedy. 2m., 1w. Sc. Interior. BAK MAR2

Nightcap of the prophet Elias, The. A. Kotzebue. Trans. from German by B. B. Beebe. Farce. 7m., 1w. Sc. Estate with linden trees. Poet Lore 40: 391–406, Autumn 1929.

Nightingale, an Arabian night's fantasy. A. H. Ernest. 9m., 2w. Sc. Square in merchant's section of Bagdad. Poet Lore 37: 293–314, Summer 1926.

Nightingale, The. an operetta after Hans Christian Anderson. A. L. Feiner. Many c. Sc. Chinese garden. Prim. Educ. 34: 260–261, Apr. 1926.

C **Nightingale and the rose, The.** L. F. Collins. 11 char. Sc. Campus garden of a University in England in the early 19th century. COJ

Night's work, A. K. Nicholson and S. Behrman. Comedy. 2m., 1w. Sc. Private office in a down town. FREN

Nightshade. R. Giorloff. 3m., 2w. Sc. A secluded corner in any public park. COL6

Night-watchman, The. H. Rees. Comedy. 8m., 3w. Sc. A road. WIMA

Nine, The. A. C. Darlington. 12m., 3w., chorus. Sc. Open space before a walled village in Galilee. DAQ

Nine and twenty candles. O. Kelley. Comedy. 1m., 1w. Sc. Living room. KEK

Nine days' queen, The. R. Field. 5m., 2w. Sc. Room in the tower of London. FIC

Nine-ten express, The. E. Morrette. Farce. 6m., 2w., chorus. Sc. Interior of typical American suburban railway. MORR

J **'Nitiated, The.** E. P. Conkle. 6b. Sc. Grove at night. DAZ

J **Nix-nought-nothing.** N. Mitchison. 5b., 3g. Sc. A desert. MIT

No bigger than a man's hand. E. St. V. Millay. Satire. 1m., 1w. Sc. Breakfast table. MIK

No cause for complaint. G. S. Brooks. 5m., 2w. Sc Office of police headquarters. CL

No change. R. Jeans. Farce. 7m., 1w. Sc. Street in London. JES

No children. B. Puddicombe. 1m., 1w. Sc. Interior. BANN

No 'count boy, The. P. Green. 2m., 2w. Sc. Small yard immediately before a Negro cabin. CL, GREE, GREL, IS, LOC, Theatre Arts M. 8: 773–784, Nov. 1924.

No cure, no pay. Farce. 1w., 3m. Sc. Interior. FIT

No jazz to-night. D. Titheradge. Farce. 4m., 3w. Sc. The ledge under a gabled roof. TITB

No more Americans. B. Hughes. Comedy. 6m., 2w. Sc. In a Paris Café, FRE5

No one knows what a woman will do. Mrs. A. L. McMahan. Comedy. 2m., 2w. Sc. Living room. ELD

C **No room at the inn.** L. W. Clarke. Any number of c. Sc. Stage or room. BUG, FIT

C **No room at the inn.** E. E. Olson. 3b., 1g. Sc. Lowly hut. BAK

J **No room at the inn.** 2b., 2g. Sc. Exterior in Palestine. DRA

No Sabe. E. Cook. 4m., 1w. Sc. Interior. DRA

No tips acepted. A. L. Huntington. Comedy. 3m., 5w. Sc. Interior of tea-room. ELD

C **Noah's Ark,** a play for toys. M. A. Seiffert. 4b., 1g. Sc. Child's playroom. Poetry 32: 1–14, Apr. 1928.

Noah's wife. I. Dall. Verse. 1m., 1w., chorus. Sc. General living compartment below deck on the ark. DAL

Noble lord, The. P. Wilde. 2m., 1w. Sc. Secluded spot in the Maine woods. KM, SCH2

Noctes Ambrosiae. K. L. Roberts. 5m., 2w. Sc. A studio. Sat. Eve. Post. 201: 33–6, Aug. 11, 1928.

Nocturne. H. L. Earnest. Fanciful. Sc. Imaginary garden on some far-off imaginary planet. IN

Nocturne. S. Sackett. 1m., 2w. Sc. Study of Madame Sand's home in Paris. NORT

Nocturne. P. Wilde. Fantastic. 3m. Sc. An old wooden bridge. WIK

Noël. M. Bouchor. Mystery. 8m., 2w. Sc. Near Bethlehem. MACU

Noël. D. Lewis and B. Wyndham. 7m., 2w. Sc. A poor tavern in Paris on Xmas Eve in 1456. Sat. R. 142: 671–3, Dec. 4, 1926.

C **Noël's Christmas celebration.** B. M. Casey. 3b., 4g. Sc. Living room. CASE

C **Non Palma since Labore.** E. F. A. U. Painton. 7g. Sc. Interior. PAIT

J **Non-step flight, The.** L. C. VanDerveer. Comedy. 15b. Sc. Woodsy spot. VAN

J **None too good for Dodo.** G. Hughes. Comedy. 4m., 3w. Sc. Interior. APPL

Noose, The. T. D. Mygatt. 4m., 2w. Sc. In home of Georgia family. Drama 20: 42–48, Nov. 1929.

Nora's cape. A. E. Bishop. Farce. 2m., 3w. Sc. Living room in apartment. BANN

C **Nora's elves.** S. G. Clark. 3b., 3g., chorus. Sc. Nora's cabin. CLAR

Noreen. H. Simpson. Farce. 3m. Sc. Interior of a typical cottage in Ireland. SIMM

North wind blowing, The. C. B. Going. 4m., 4w. Sc. Work room in Spain 1550. GOIN

Northeast corner, The. B. Tynan. 5m., 1w. Sc. Irish interior. FREN

Not according to schedule. R. P. Bramwell. Comedy. 2m., 4w. Sc. Living room. ELD

Not lost. R. Jeans. Farce. 3m. Sc. Hospital ward. JEC

J **Not quite such a goose.** E. Gale. Comedy. 2m., 3w. Sc. Interior. BAK, ELD, PHIJ, ROS9

Not smart. W. D. Steele. Comedy. 2m., 3w. Sc. Living room of typical village. STEE

Not too far from angels. A. Kreymborg. Farce. 3m., 5w. Sc. A beach in California. KRR

Not worth mentioning. H. W. Caroline. Comedy. Sc. Parlor of hotel in southern California. FOS

C **Noughts and crosses.** R. Fyleman. 2b., 1g. Sc. Room. FYL

Now take it from me. M. Irish. 5m. Sc. Clubroom. CAT2

Now the servant's name was Malchus. T. Wilder. 3m. Sc. Skies. WILZ

Now Trixie. E. M. Gall and L. H. Carter. Comedy. 6w. Sc. Interior. BANN

Number one on the docket. W. F. Manley. 4m., 2w. Sc. Stage. MANL

Number thirteen. H. Simpson. Farce. 5m., 2w. Sc. Lounge of an hotel. SIMA

Nursery-maid of heaven, The. T. W. Stevens. Fanciful. 3m., 7w., 2 chorus groups. Sc. Chapter room in convent. STEU

Nutcracker suite, The. W. E. Crawshay. 3m., 2w. Sc. Boudoir sitting room. CRA

O

C **O come, let us adore him,** a Christmas service. E. M. Baxter. Many c. Sc. Church. Int. J. of Rel. Educ. 6 : 26–27, 45, Dec. 1929.

O conscript fathers! H. W. Hanemann. Burlesque. 4m. Sc. House of Misrepresentatives. HANE

O Death, where is thy sting? A. Monkhouse. 2m., 2w. Sc. Interior. BAK

Oak, a character sketch. H. Troyer. 4m., 1w. Sc. Living room of old colonial farm house. Player's M. 6 : 18–20, May–June 1930.

Obedient Princess, The. A. Penland. Comedy. 2m., 2w. Sc. In a palace. ROH

Object lesson, An. C. Owen. Comedy. 1m., 2w. Sc. Luxurious drawing room in a London flat. DE

Obstinate family, The. Farce. 3m., 3w. Sc. Interior. DRA, FIT

C **October days.** I. R. Hess. 5b., 3g. Sc. Living room. Norm. Inst. 37 : 82, Oct. 1928.

C **October gave a party.** E. E. Olson. Any number of c. Sc. A bit of the out of doors. JOHG

Odd entanglement, An. O. W. Firkins. 2m., 2w. Sc. 1 Dining room 2 Parlor. FIR

Oddervise und so on. A. L. Kaser. Farce. 2m. Sc. No scenery required. KAS

Odour of sanctity, The. L. Housman. 4m. Sc. Corner of a wall with scaffolding. Sat. R. 142 : 372–374, Oct. 2, 1926.

C **Odysseus at Ogygia.** M. Oller and E. K. Dawley. 2b., 3g. Sc. Interior of grotto. OLL

C **Odysseus returns home.** M. Oller and E. K. Dawley. 4b., 2g. Sc. Small banquet hall. OLL

J **Oececea.** P. McManus. 5g. Sc. A rough cabin. DRA

Of an early morning. I. L. Pertez. 2m., 2w., 1 baby. Sc. A very poor room. BLP

Off Nags Head. D. MacMillan. Tragedy. 2m., 3w. Sc. Fisherman's hut. LAW

Off the lines. R. Jeans and H. C. G. Stevens. Farce. 1m., 1w. Sc. Breakfast room. JEA

Off the main road. C. R. Averrell. Comedy. 3m., 6w. Sc. Interior. FIT

Off the road. P. R. Young. 1m., 1w. Sc. Ranch house kitchen. Poet Lore 36 : 300–305, Summer 1925.

J **Off with his head!** K. Hatch. 31 char. Sc. Clearing in the woods. BAK

Offering of Plebs, The. J. deBosschère. Trans. from French. 3 char. Sc. Exterior. BOSS

Official bondage. M. Larrimer. 2m., 1w. Sc. Quaint sitting room. LAR

Official's morning, An. N. Gogol. Trans. from Russian. 5m., 1w. Sc. An office in Russia. GOG, GOG6

Oft in the stilly night. M. S. Smith. 1m., 1w. Sc. Dark. Drama 15 : 75, Jan. 1925.

Oh, Auntie! A. I. Tooke. Comedy. 2m., 2w. Sc. Bachelor bed-sitting room. PENN

Oh, papa! D. de Jagers. Comedy. 2m., 1w. Sc. Interior. FREN

Oh! teacher. A. L. Kaser. Comedy. 5m., 5w. Sc. School. PAIN

Oh, these authors. G. E. Jennings. 3m., 8w. Sc. Pit of theatre. FREL

C   **Oh, you mathematics.** E. Vokes. Any number of c. Sc. Interior. ELD

J   **Old boyhood.** H. F. Rubinstein. Comedy. 4m. Sc. Interior. BAK

Old bull, The. B. Gilbert. 4m., 1w. Sc. Kitchen in small village in England. HAM

Old Chester secret, An. S. Kemper. 3m., 2w. Sc. Library of home. BOST

Old country store, The. E. W. Bradley and J. R. Reeves. Farce. 14m., 1w. Sc. Old country store. FREN

Old friends. J. M. Barrie. Tragedy. 2m., 2w. Sc. Interior on a winter evening. BARR, BARS

C   **Old friends are best.** E. Preston. 15c. Sc. Stage. PRES

Old game, The. Trans. from German by E. U. Ouless. 3m., 2w., chorus. Sc. Kitchen. OULE

C   **Old gentleman gay.** R. Benton. 5b., 5g. Sc. Road. BEN

Old grouch, The. R. Willis. 3m., 1w. Sc. A London park. WIMS

J   **Old ironsides.** P. M. Swinton. 9b., 5g., chorus. Sc. Street scene near Charleston navy yard in Boston. SW

Old king's tale, The. Lord Dunsany. Fanciful. 3m., 1w. Sc. Out of doors. DUA

Old lady Kendell. A. Curtis. Comedy. 7w. Sc. Dining room. CUR

Old lady shows her medals, The. J. M. Barrie. 3m., 4w. Sc. A poorly furnished room in a basement flat. BARR

Old lady shows her muddles, The. R. Jeans. Farce. 2m., 2w. Sc. Interior suggesting country vicarage. JEC

Old love affair, The. A. V. Kotzebue. Trans. by B. B. Beebe. Comedy. 1m., 2w. Sc. A park on an estate. Poet Lore 38 : 220–239, Summer 1927.

C   **Old man and his grandson, The.** A. Stevenson. 3b., 1g. Sc. House. STEV3

Old man of the sea, The. S. Ready. Comedy. 4m., 1w. Sc. Saloon bar of the Mariner's Arms. DE

C   **Old man Rabbit's Thanksgiving.** R. L. Milam. 19c. Sc. Old man Rabbit's house. WHG1

C   **Old mathematics.** B. L. Gordan. 1b., 8c. Norm. Inst. 34 : 74, May 1925.

C   **Old mother Hubbard.** E. Denton. 4c. Sc. Cottage kitchen. DENU

Old nurse, The. E. Hayes. Comedy. 6w. Sc. Old nursery. FREL

Old, old, story, The. H. Holland. Farce. 1m., 1w. Sc. Stage. FREP

C   **Old pipes and the dryad.** B. Barnes. 7b., 4g., others. Sc. Hillside. Prim. Educ. 33 : 476–478, 489, Sept. 1925.

C   **Old Santa Claus remembers.** E. W. Trout. 5b., 4g., chorus. Sc. Santa Claus' workshop. BAK

J   **Old Sleuth, The.** W. Beck. 5b., 5g. Sc. Physiology class. BEB

Old timers' bureau, The. J. H. Munson. 6m., 4w. Sc. Farm kitchen. FREN

J   **Old walnut.** A. Harris. Comedy. 2m., 2w. Sc. Old fashioned attic. LON, SV

Old Wash Lucas. P. Green. Tragedy. 3m., 1w. Sc. Farmhouse. GREL, Poet Lore 35 : 254–270, Summer 1924.

C   **Old witch carelessness.** L. McIlhargey. Many c. Sc. Bedroom. Norm. Inst. 34 : 76, 78, Feb. 1925.

Ole George comes to tea. S. G. Ervine. 2m., 1w. Sc. Living room of a workman's house in London. ER

'Ole in the road, The. A. J. Small. 2m. Sc. A Street. FREL

Oliver Twist in Fagen's den. G. Pertwee and E. Pertwee. 5m., 1w. Sc. Black, dirty hole. PER

Olives, The. L. de Rueda. Trans. by W. K. Jones. 1m., 3w. Sc. Entrance to house in Spain. Poet Lore 39: 310–313, Summer 1928.

On and off. Jeans. Farce. 2m., 2w. Sc. Theatre dressing room. JEC

On Baile's strand. W. B. Yeats. 5m., chorus. Sc. Great hall at Dundealgan. CANF, YEA

On Bayou La Batre. B. C. Moore. 1m., 2w. Sc. Interior of fisherman's cottage. Poet Lore 37: 576–583, Winter 1926.

C **On being a goop.** A. M. Wofford. 4b., 1g. Wilson Bull. 5: 635, June 1931.

C **On board the S. S. health.** L. Sissman. 4b., many others. Sc. Deck of a ship. Hygeia 5: 151–154, Mar. 1927.

C **On Christmas eve.** C. D. Mackay. Fantasy. 11 char. Sc. Interior. FREN, SK

On second thought. B. B. Willis. 6w. Sc. Interior of Beauty shop. CAMP

On self-government, a dialogue in Limbo. G. Santayana. 2m. Dial 78: 181–192, Mar. 1925, 302–312, Apr. 1925.

On the frontier. J. Pollock. 6m. Sc. On the Austrian frontier in 1910. POL

On the high road. A. Chekhov. Trans. from Russian. 8m., 3w., chorus. Sc. Room in Inn. CHEC

On the highway. A. Checkhov. 7m., 2w., chorus. Sc. Russian tavern. SHAT

On the journey. H. Simpson. Farce. 2m., 1w. Sc. Table in a restaurant car. SIMO

On the lot. F. Ryerson and C. Clements. Comedy. 2m., 1w. Sc. Old fashioned garden. RY, SCH1, Drama 19: 46–47, Nov. 1928.

On the moor. S. Schofield. 3m., 3w. Sc. Sitting room in a Dartmoor cottage. FREL

On the P.D.Q. A. L. Kaser. Farce. 2m. Sc. A rural waiting room. KAS

On the park bench. E. Dane. Comedy. 3m., 3w. Sc. Interior. BAK, PHIJ

On the racecourse. Lady A. Gregory. 2m., 1w., chorus. Sc. Stage of a field. FRE2, Golden Book 8: 364–368, Sept. 1928.

On the razor edge. R. Hughes. 2m., 2w. Sc. Moonlit piazza of a hotel. NICH

On the road. G. John. 2m., 1w., 1c. Sc. A workman's coffee-house in Sheffeld. JOHA

J **On the road of yester year.** A. L. Melville and D. M. Vance. 3m., 1w. Sc. Country roadside in England. BANN

J **On the road to Bethlehem.** G. Stenger. 6b., 1g., chorus. Sc. Hillside overlooking the town of Bethlehem. ELD

On the road to Cork. N. Robinson and W. G. Fay. Comedy. 2m., 3w. Sc. Public house on the road to Cork. FREL

On the road to Egypt. M. R. Davidson. 3m., 1w. Sc. A cave near Beersheba. BAK

J **On the shelf.** C. Morley. Comedy. 4m., 4w. Sc. Section of book shelf. LON, MACG, MORL, SCH4

On the way home. E. E. Olson. Comedy. 1m., 1w. Sc. Exterior. JOHP

On the way home. L. B. Pride. 11m., 1w., chorus. Sc. Interior of half-way house. PRID

C **On the way to school.** K. A. White. 4b. Sc. Highway leading to the school house. WH

On to San Antonio. M. M. Griffith. 6m., 1w., 1b., chorus. Sc. Blacksmith shop of logs. GRI

On vengeance height. A. Davis. Melodrama. 2m., 2w. Sc. Cabin in Tennessee mountains. KM, KN

On with the dance. S. M. Hugo. Farce. 3m., 5w. Sc. Reception room of college for girls. FREN

On with the old. R. Jeans. Farce. 1m., 2w. Sc. Private office. JEC

C **Once in a hundred years.** M. Jagendorf. 6b., 1g. Sc. Japanese interior. JAO

C **One country, one flag, one language.** M. A. Niemeier. 21b. or g. Sc. A class room. NIE, NIEM

One day more. J. Conrad. 4m., 1w. Sc. Near a sea wall. CON

One egg. B. Hughes. 2m., 1w. Sc. Small restaurant in N. Y. NICA

J **One gift above another.** D. Sherrill. 5m., 10w. Sc. Interior. BAK, LOU

One hundred dollars. I. L. Ehrlich. Comedy. 1m., 4w. Sc. Interior. FREN

One madding day and knight. A. G. Lloyd. Comedy. 4m., 4w. Sc. Interior. MARC

One of those days. M. Cameron. Comedy. 8w. Sc. Living room. FREN

One of those things. G. Kelly. 3m., 2w. Sc. Office. FRE3

One-sided affair, A. R. Jeans. Farce. 11m., 11w. Sc. Stage. JEP

One sunset. I. Dall. 2 animals. Sc. Lonely corner of a hill. DAL

One thing needful, The. A. A. Wilson. 3w. Sc. Home in ancient Judea. CAMP

One touch of nature. H. Simpson. Farce. 2m., 2w., chorus. Sc. Sitting room. SIMN

C **One true gift of Christmas, The.** M. R. Merriman. 3b., 4g. Sc. Modern living room. Norm. Inst. 36: 65–66, Dec. 1926.

J **One winter's night.** Rawlings Junior High School. 25c. RAW

One woman in the world, The. R. Jeans. Farce. 2m., 2w. Sc. In curtains. JEO

One word play. F. Egan. Comedy. 1m., 1w. Sc. Garden. LON

C **Onesimus, the runaway slave.** M. I. Stone. 5b., 3g. Sc. White background. STON

C **Only an only child.** H. O. Boggs. 2b., 1g. Sc. Breakfast room. BOG

J **Only day I have, The.** E. DeHuff. 4b., 4g. Sc. Living room. ELD

C **Only good children, The.** S. E. Hall. 3b., 10g. Sc. Grove near Plymouth. Norm. Inst. 34: 70, 72, Nov. 1924.

Only jealousy of Emer, The. W. B. Yeats. 5m., 1w. Sc. Curtains. CANF, YE

Only thing to do, The. M Lee. Farce. 3m., 1w. Sc. A street. LEE

Open door, The. E. Rohde'. 1m., 5w. Sc. Chinese home in Malaya. ABI

Open highway, The. E. R. Jasspon and B. Becker. 22 char. WOM

Open windows. N. E. Gammill. 3w. Sc. Sitting room. BANN

J **Opened eyes.** H. W. Githens. 9b., 1g., chorus. Sc. Street in Jerusalem. GITH

Opening the gate. E. Gibson. 2w. Sc. Two adjoining backyards in a city. GIB

Opera matinée, The. A. Gerstenberg. Comedy. 14w. Sc. Opera house. GEQ, LON, SV

'Op-o'-Me-Thumb. F. Fenn and R. Pryce. 1m., 5w. Sc. Working room in a laundry. FRE1, MAR2

Or what have you? B. Abel. Burlesque. 1m., 1w. Sc. Interior. AB

Orange colored necktie, The. A. B. Curtis. Farce. 3m., 4w. Sc. Interior. BANN

Order of release, The, a little play of Saint Francis. L. Housman. 2m., 2w. Sc. Wall of convent of St. Damien. Fortn. R. 126: 289–97, Sept. 1926.

Organ, The. G. E. Pendray and K. Nicholson. 9m., 3w., chorus. Sc. Front yard of homestead. CL, FREN

Oriental bazaar, The. B. Katibah. 1m., 1w., 1b. Woman's Press 21: 779, Nov. 1927.

Orlando Furioso. R. Bufano. Marionette. 7m., 1w. Sc. A vast amount of space—Forest of Ron Cevalle. SHAF

C **Orpheus and Eurydice.** M. Oller and E. K. Dawley. 4b., 2g. Sc. Throne room at the entrance to Hades. OLL

Other people's husbands. M. Penney. Comedy. 4m., 6w. Sc. Interior. BAK

Other room, The. F. Witherspoon. 3m., 2w. Sc. Living room. Poet Lore 38: 269–290, Summer 1927.

Other side of the door, The. E. Dane. 2w. Sc. Old country house. BAK

Other side of the door, The. R. E. Hartley. 3m., 1w. Sc. Kitchen of country boarding house. Poet Lore 41: 223–238, Summer 1930.

C **Other side of very bad luck, The.** C. Humphries. Many c. Sc. Public square. Prim. Educ. 45: 802, 805, 815, June 1928.

Other voice, The. S. K. Fairbanks. 3 voices. Sc. A river flowing. JOHN

Other wise man, The. R. C. Alexander and O. P. Goslin. 11m., 1w. Sc. Home among the mountains of Persia. ALEX

Our American language. M. Marks. Comedy. 1m., 2w. Sc. Stage. NICR

C **Our country and its flag.** I. M. Aitken. 14c. Sc. Interior. LUT

Our Frank. A. V. Kotzebue. Trans. by B. B. Beebe. 2m., 2w., 1b. Sc. Rural scene near village. Poet Lore 38: 206–219, Summer 1927.

C **Our friends the trees.** M. Irish. 11c., chorus. Sc. Stage with vines and green branches. IQ

C **Our health play.** Many c. Sc. Breakfast table. Prim. Educ. 44: 576, 583, Mar. 1927.

Our John. Z. K. MacDonald. 8m., 3w. Sc. Kitchen in a village in Nova Scotia. COL5

Our lady of poverty. L. Housman. Poetic. 7m., 3w. Sc. Formal garden. HOUS

C **Our lady tumbler.** K. Taylor and H. C. Greene. 4b., 3g., chorus. Sc. Chapel. TAY

C **Our library,** a Dewey Decimal play. A. F. Gilmore. Many c. Wilson Bull. 5: 186–91, Nov. 1930.

Our lord of the ship. L. Pirandello. Tr. from Italian. 7m., 2w., chorus. Sc. Section of the open space in front of a little rural church. PIR

C **Our manners and our morals,** a playlet for Education Week. C. Wilson. 1b., 1g. Sc. Table. Prim. Educ. 46: 182+, Nov. 1928.

Our Mothers. 9w. Sc. Interior. BUG

C **Out of the book.** M. E. Steele. Many. Sc. Outdoor scene. Norm. Inst. 39: 47–48, June 1930.

Out of the dark. H. Berman. 3m., 1w. Sc. Living room. BER

Out of the dark. D. C. Guinn. Pageant. 7m., 6w., chorus. Sc. Interior or exterior. WOM

Out of the darkness. R. E. Farndon. 3m., 1w. Sc. A desolate field just outside Jerusalem, A. D. 30. LON

Out of the midst of hatred. A. R. Troubetzkoy. 2m., 1w., others. Sc. Bourgeois room. Va. Q. Rev. 2: 226–237, Apr. 1926.

Out of the mouths of . . . P. Wilde. Semi comedy. 1m., 1w. Sc. Interior with a parrot in its cage. WILD, WILT

Out of the night. J. Smith. 5m., 2w. Sc. Dining room. FREN

Out of the river. J. G. Jay. 4m., 1w. Sc. Polish settlement. UNND

J **Out to win.** M. Irish. 6b., 4g. Sc. School. PAIN

J **Outcast.** P. E. Osgood. 5b., chorus. Sc. Archway in a house-wall. OSG

Outcasts. M. Creagh-Henry. 9 char. Sc. In a churchyard outside a Chelsea church. CRE

Outcasts. E. R. Sammis. 1m., 1w. Sc. Outdoors. Poet Lore 36: 306–310, Summer 1925.

Outcasts of Poker Flat, The. B. Harte. 3m., 2w. Sc. Log cabin in mountains of California, HAP

Outclassed. C. Glick. Melodrama. 2m., 2b. Sc. Interior of barn. FREN

J **Outcome of a secret, The.** M. M. Russell. 2b., chorus. Sc. Village street. RUS

Outlaws. G. John. English dialect. 3m., 1w. Sc. Back of an English cottage. JOH

Outside, The. S. Glaspell. 3m., 2w. Sc. Room in a house once a life saving station. CLS, GLA

Outside this room. D. L. Ackerman. 1m., 5w. Sc. Living room in an apartment in Zurich. UM

Outsider. H. D. Saddler. 5m., 3w. Sc. Interior. FREN

Outwitted. H. L. Newton. 1m., 1w. Sc. Interior. JOHP

Outwitting Lucy Lee. M. Bonham. Comedy. 2w. Sc. Kitchen. PAIN

Over the garden wall. J. Hampden. Adapted from Dickens. Nicholas Nickleby. Farce. 3m., 2w. Sc. Garden, FREN

Over the hills. J. Palmer. Comedy. 2m., 2w. Sc. Interior. BAK, KN

Overheard. W. J. Farma. 3m., 3w. Sc. Reception room in apartment. Player's M. 3: 16–22, Jan.–Feb. 1927.

Overheard in Seville during the processions on Maundy, Thursday. G. Santayana. Several. Sc. The street. Dial 82: 282–286, Apr. 1927.

P

Pact, The. C. Campion. Farce. 1m., 1w. Sc. Room in a flat. CHA

Paddly pools. M. Malleson. 10 char., chorus. Sc. Out of doors. BAK

C **Pageant of play.** M. P. Harris. 4g., 1b., 5 chorus groups. Sc. Setting out of doors. PLAY

J **Pageant of sunshine and shadow, The.** 28c., chorus. Sc. Garden. MACH

C **Pageant of the flag, The.** Y. Klein and F. Schwarz. 20 or more c. Sc. Any interior. KLE

Pageant of the Shearmen and the tailors, The. J. M. Brown. 11m., 1w. Sc. Stage. HAQ, Theatre Arts M. 9: 824–835, Dec. 1925.

C **Pageant of time, A.** A. G. Robeson. 26c. Sc. Any interior. BAI

Pageant of women, A. L. Driscoll. 2w. Drama 14: 263–265, May–June 1924.

Paging John Harvard. E. Kelley. 1m., 1w. Sc. A table for two. Bookman (N. Y.) 65: 163–166, Apr. 1927.

Paid on both sides, a charade. W. H. Auden. Many char. Sc. Any stage. Criterion 10: 268–290, Jan. 1930.

Paid to worry. N. Balch. 2m., 2w. Sc. Office. ELD

Pain of it, The. B. Abel. Burlesque. 1m., 1w. Sc. Bare room. AB

J **The palace of Knosses.** E. McFadden. 3b., 2g., chorus. Sc. Throne of palace about 1450 B. C. DAZ

Palaver—That's all. A. L. Kaser. Farce. 1m., 1w. Sc. No scenery required. KAS

Pan in Pimlico. H. Simpson. Fantasy. 3m., 1w. Sc. Street in London. BRIR, HERB, SHAT

Pan or Pierrot. M. MacMillan. Masque. 5m., 3w., chorus. Sc. Open space sloping to a little lake. APPL

J **Pandora.** B. P. Lane. 10b., 5g. LAN

C **Pandora.** M. Oller and E. K. Dawley. 6b., 2g. Sc. In a cave. OLL

J **Pan's secret.** M. Barrows. 23c., chorus. Sc. At the edge of a forest. SAO

Pantaloon. J. M. Barrie. Fanciful. 3m., 1w. Sc. Private room. BARR

Papa's daughter. M. A. James. Burlesque. 4m., 2w. Sc. Interior. ELD

C **Paper angel, The.** H. E. Davis. Several c. Sc. Christmas Tree. Delineator 105: 17–18, Dec. 1924.

C **Paper dolls.** E. L. Squires. 7g. Sc. Playroom. SQ

Papers. C. Kummer. Comedy. 3m., 3w. Sc. Living room in a suburb of New York. FRE3

J **Parable of the Good Samaritan, The.** M. E. Whitney, 5b. By the roadside. WHH

J **Parable of the great supper, The.** M. E. Whitney. 5b. Sc. Threshold of banquet hall. WHH

J **Parable of the prodigal son, The.** M. E. Whitney. 6b., 1g. Sc. Room in the home of Urbane. WHH

J **Parable of the rich fool, The.** M. E. Whitney. 2b. Sc. Before the house of Nicholas. WHH

J **Parable of the talents, The.** M. E. Whitney. 5b. Sc. Counting room. WHH

J **Parable of the tares, The.** M. E. Whitney. 4b. Sc. Before the door of Nicanor's house. WHH

J **Parable of the wicked servant, The.** M. E. Whitney. 5b. Sc. Hall of judgment. WHH

Parable of the wise and foolish virgins. M. Lacey-Baker. 12 char., chorus. Sc. Interior. WOM

Paradise. S. Shute. 3m., 1w. Sc. Small station in a country town in New Hampshire. BAK

Parcel for King Solomon, A. E. P. Russell. 5m., 3w. Sc. Throne room in Solomon's palace. New Masses 5: 10–12, May 1930.

Paris labels. L. Larrimore. Comedy. 9w. Sc. Shop of exclusive modiste. PENN

Parlor tricks. E. E. Olson. 5w. Sc. Parlor. BAK

Parson of Pine Mountain, The. W. A. Lathrop. 3m., 1w. Sc. Cabin interior. FREN

Part-time job. L. Hornickel. Comedy. 1m., 4w. Sc. Modern interior. FREN

Parting, A. G. Bottomley. Poetic. 2 char. Sc. Interior. BOTS, BOTT

Parting, The. R. Jeans. Farce. 1m., 1w. Sc. Interior. JEC

C **Partisans of precaution.** V. R. Grundy. Many c. Sc. Schoolroom. Prim. Educ. 45: 350, 412, Jan. 1928.

J **Party, The.** Rawlings Junior High School. 14g. Sc. Assembly platform. RAW

C **Party from Bookland, A.** M. H. Swindells. Many c. Sc. Living room. Norm. Inst. 37: 66, 68, Jan. 1928.

Party of the third part, The. C. Stow. Comedy. 1m., 2w. Sc. City square. Drama 15: 110–111, Feb. 1925.

Pa's income tax. W. N. Bugbee. 3m., 3w. Sc. Sitting room. CAT1

Passers by, The. P. Dickerson. 12 char. Sc. Simple wayside. DRA

Passing of chow-chow, The. E. L. Rice. Comedy. 3m., 1w. Sc. Office. FRE2

Passing of Mr. Peal, The. E. B. Longnecker. Comedy. 2m., 4w. Sc. Library in home. PENN

C **Passing of the year.** E. J. Leonard. 14 char. Sc. Cosy living room, large clock on the mantel set to strike 12. IR

Passion's progress. R. L. Askren. 3m., 1w. Sc. Living in apartment. UM

Passover rehearsal, The. A. Burstein. Comedy. 7b. Sc. Interior. BLO

C **Password, The.** H. C. Crew. 6b., 3g., chorus. Sc. Professor's study. JAO

Past pluperfect, The. P. Wilde. Farce. 2m., 1w. Sc. An apartment. WILT

Pat entertains. A. Cripps. Farce. 3m. Sc. Interior. ELD

Pat Hooligan's bet. W. N. Bugbee. 2m., 1w. Sc. Tailor shop. CAT1

Patch between, The. H. G. McCabe. 4w. Sc. Living room. CART

Patchwork. T. J. Brandon and F. W. Barrett. 3m., 2w. Sc. Village post office. FREL

J **Patchwork quilt, The.** R. Field. Fantasy. Sc. Upstairs bedroom and sitting room combined. FIE, MACG

C **Path of roses.** E. VanderVeer. 5b., 5g., chorus. Sc. Ante room in the palace. SAL

J **Pathfinder, The.** H. Ould. 5b. Sc. Native hut in central Africa in 1871. OU

C **Patience's dream.** M. B. Moore. 3g. Sc. Street in Holland town. Prim. Educ. 33: 616, Nov. 1925.

Patria Potestas. M. R. Hofer. 9b., 4 chorus groups. Sc. Roman interior. HOF

J **Patriotic assembly, A.** Rawlings Junior High School. 6b., 6g. Sc. Assembly program. RAW

J **Patriotic pepper.** M. Woods. 6g. Sc. Living room. DRA

Patriots. W. Wellock. 6m., 3w. Sc. Workman's cottage. Mod. Rev. 36: 531–537, Nov. 1924.

Patron of art, A. D. A. Shoemaker. 7w. Sc. Interior. PENN

Pat's dilemma. Comedy. 4m., 3w. Sc. Interior. FIT

Patsy Dugan's Christmas. M. Irish. 5m., 5w. Sc. Interior. BUG

J **Paul and Silas at Philippi.** M. E. Whitney. 7b., 1g. Sc. A street in Philippi. WHH

Paul robs Peter! R. B. Taylor. Comedy. 2m., 1w. Sc. Little office. TAYL

J **Pauper becomes a prince, The.** M. A. Butler. Adapted from Mark Twain's Prince and the Pauper. 6b., 2g., chorus. Sc. Sumptuous apartment in the Prince's suite. BUT

Pay as you go. O. G. Roark. Comedy. 4m., 4w. Sc. Living room in city home. FIT

Pea-green cats. N. S. Snell. Comedy. 2m., 3w. Sc. Sitting room. PENN

Peace and comfort. T. H. Stafford. Farce. 4m., 2w. Sc. Living room in English farmhouse. FREL

Peace and quiet. R. Jeans. Farce. 3m., 3w. Sc. Doctor's consulting room. JES

C **Peace fairies win, The,** a pageant for Good Will Day. V. M. Lyle. 22c. Sc. Platform with throne. Norm. Inst. 36: 64, 66, May 1927.

Peace manoeuvres. R. H. Davis. 3m., 1w. Sc. A country road. FRE1

Peakland wakes, A. G. John. 2m., 5w., 1g. Sc. An open space in the street. JOHA

Peanuts. E. O. Jones. Farce. 2m., 3w. Sc. Living room. FREN

Pearl of dawn. H. Hudson. Fantasy. 7m., 3w., chorus. Sc. A street. SHAQ

Pearl thief, The. G. H. Phelps and M. I. Pitkin. 5m. Sc. 1 Bench in central park N. Y. 2 Sc. Raja's study. DET

Pearls. D. Totheroh. Comedy. 2m., 2w. Sc. Living room in flat in large city. COH, TOT

Pearls before swine. J. Meadon. 2m. Sc. Irish farmyard. DET

Pease and beans. P. Phelps. Satirical farce. 1m., 3w. Sc. 1 Living room. 2 Sc. same. FREN

Peculiar old duffer, A. J. C. McMullen. 4m. Living room. MACT

Pedlar, The. F. G. Lanham. Sc. Drawing room. OMI

C **Pedlar man.** E. L. Squires. 2b., 3g. Sc. Village green. SQ

Peg O'Nell's night. Z. F. Radford. 1m., 2w. Sc. Interior of an Irish farmhouse. UNW2

Peggy. R. Crothers. 3m., 4w. Sc. Room in an old house. CROT, PHIL, Scrib. M. 76: 175–83, Aug. 1924.

Peggy. H. Williamson. 4m., 1w., 1b. Sc. Tenant farm in North Carolina. HANF

C **Pen and the inkstand, The.** A. Stevenson. 8b., 1 chorus. Sc. A poet's room. STEV4

C **Pennies nickels and dimes.** F. W. Skinner. Any number of c. Sc. Interior. ELD

Penningtons, too. J. C. Bardin. 2m., 3w. Sc. Old-fashioned southern kitchen. BAK

Penny a flower. K. Kester. Fantasy. 7m., 2w., 1g., 1b. Sc. Market place. Drama 15: 59–63, Dec. 1924.

C **Penny sense.** F. E. Eakman. 19c. Sc. Front of a bank. EAK

Penny that beauty spent, The. T. Wilder. 2m., 1w. Sc. Jeweler's shop in Paris. WILZ

C **Pentecost of youth, The,** a pageant of religious education. D. C. Wilson.

Many c. Sc. Any stage. Int. J. of Rel. Educ. 6 : 25–27, 36, 44, Sept. 1930.

People, The. S. Glaspell. 10m., 2w. Sc. Office of "The people." GLA

People who die. A. Kreymborg. Echo play. 1m., 1w. Sc. Bench in front of closed curtain. KR

J **Pepita's adventure in friendship.** F. C. Means. 20c. Sc. Interior of a New Mexican home. ELD

Peregrinus. L. Abercrombie. Poetic. 2m., chorus. Sc. On the road. ABE

Perfect fool, A. E. Percy. Comedy. 2m., 1w. Sc. Room in a country house. FREL

Perfect housekeeper, The. G. Price. Comedy. 1m., 3w. Sc. Interior. BAK

Perfect partnership, The. C. M. Balm. 3m., 1w. Sc. Living room. Int. J. of Rel. Educ. 6 : 37, Oct. 1929.

Perfect service. K. Norris. Farce. 2m., 1w. Sc. Hotel sitting room. Harper's B. 65 : 82–83, 150, Sept. 1930.

Perfumes. M. Lee. Farce. 2m., 2w. Sc. Stage. LEE

J **Pericles and the builders of Athens.** M. R. Hofer. 20b., 9 chorus groups. Sc. An Athenian street scene. HOF

Peril of the moon, The. H. Kemp. 3m., 3w. Sc. Rose-bower in the King's palace gardens. KEM

Permanent wave, The. D. Titheradge. Farce. 2m., 2w. Sc. Living room. TITB

Perplexing Pirandello, The. C. L. Palm. Satire. 2m., 1w., 1g. Sc. Library of wealth. Drama 15 : 102–104, Feb. 1925.

Persecuted Dutchman. J. Barry. 6m., 3w. Sc. Interior. FIT

Persecuted prophet, A. H. W. Githens. 11b., chorus. Sc. Palace garden in Babylon. GIT

Persephone. A. K. Clarke. Masque. 2m., 5w. Sc. 1 Open glade. 2 Sc. Another part of wood. 3 Sc. Same a year later. BRIS, BRIT, CLAS

C **Persephone.** A. Stevenson. 3b., 3g., 3 chorus groups. Sc. 1 Barron hilltop. 2 Sc. Pluto's realm. STEV4

Persian poppy, The. G. Emery. Comedy. 1w. Sc. Scenery used or imagined. LON

Persians of Aeschylus, The. P. Long. Burlesque. 8m., 1w. Sc. Outside palace at Susa 48 B. c. BAK

Persimmon Thief, The. K. Nakazawa. 3m. Sc. Japanese garden. Drama 16 : 97–8, Dec. 1925.

Personally or by letter. I. Hay. Comedy. Sc. Dining room. FREL

Perverted history. J. H. Turner. Farce. 4m., 1w. Sc. Open fireplace. TURN

J **Peter, a great Evangelist.** M. M. Browne. 3b., 3g. Sc. Living room. THOQ

Peter Gink. A. H. Nethercot. 5m., 3w., others. Sc. Interior of a pickled Herring club in a stable. Poet Lore 35 : 118–126, Spring 1924.

J **Peter Pain and the good health kids.** E. Fraser. Any number of char. Sc. Interior. ELD

C **Peter Pan.** A. L. Feiner. Operetta. 4b., 2g., chorus. Sc. Out of doors. WHG1

C **Peter Rabbit helps the children.** E. Williams. 20c. Sc. Out of doors. MARC

C **Peter the Great's school.** A. Stevenson. 11b., 1g., chorus groups. Sc. 1 Room in Royal Palace. 2 Sc. In Russia in 1688. STEV4

C **Peter, the pied piper.** H. Ould. 20 char. Sc. Exterior. BAK, OT

Peter's night out. B. R. More. Farce. 4m., 4w. Sc. Interior. FREN

Petrarch d'Annunzio. R. Nichols. 2m. The Calendar 1: 451–460, Aug. 1925.

Petroushka. E. Y. Mitcoff. Puppet. 4m., 1w. Sc. A street in a Russian village. MACU

Petticoat politics. H. N. Connell. Comedy. 12w. Sc. Interior. PAIN

C **Phaethon and the sun chariot.** M. Oller and E. K. Dawley. 3b., 3g. Sc. Throne room in palace. OLL

Pharaoh's daughter. A. V. Kotzebue. Tr. from German. 4m., 1w. Sc. A street. WEBB, Golden Book 8: 53–59, July 1928.

Pharisees K. L. Bates. 4m., 1w. Sc. In Jerusalem. BATE

Phases of the moon. W. B. Yeats. 2m. Sc. Out of doors. YD

Phial, The. P. Wilde. Farce. 2m., 1w. Sc. Living room. WILT

J **Philemon and Baucis.** A. Haggard. 5b., 1g. Sc. Cottage in Greece. HAG

Philippa comes back. J. Gabbot. Comedy. 2m., 1w. Sc. Library in small home. FREL

J **Philosopher of Butterbiggins, The.** H. Chapin. 3b., 1g. Sc. Tenement. FIN, HAM, Golden Book 9: 87–90, Jan. 1929.

Philosophy of the tooth brush, The. A. and A. Weinberg. 1m., 1w. Sc. Bedroom. Poet Lore 36: 615–623, Winter 1925.

Phipps. S. Houghton. 2m., 1w. Sc. Library of London house. FRE1

Phoebe revels. S. Caldwell and E. Hendrie. 5w. Sc. Sitting room in a small country house in Wales. CAL

C **Phoebe's Christmas Eve.** E. A. Zeller. 14c. Sc. Humble room. BAK

Phonetics. H. Simpson. Farce. 1m., 1w. Sc. Interior. SIMA

Photographing the family. F. C. Gardner. 14m., 12w. Sc. Exterior. GAQ

Phryne. F. A. Kummer. 9m., 1w. Sc. Studio. KU

Pianissimo. A. Kreymborg. 2m. Sc. Park bench. KR

Pickles and tickles. T. Barnes. Farce. 6m. Sc. Interior. FIT

Picnic, The. P. Green. 4m., 4w., chorus. Sc. Woods in eastern North Carolina. GREE

C **Pictures from Bookland.** G. H. Leach. 13c. Sc. Stage. MARC

Pictures out of the past. L. Witt. 2m., 4w. Sc. Interior. BLO

Pie and the tart, The. M. Dondo. Farce. 3m., 1w. Sc. French interior in 15th century. APPL, SHAB

J **Pie and the tart, The.** M. Jagendorf. 3m., 1w. Sc. A market square. FRE6

Pie in the oven, The. J. J. Bell. Comedy. 2m., 2w. Sc. Interior. BAK

C **Pie, pickle and ham.** F. W. Skinner. Any number of char. Sc. Interior. ELD

C **Piece of cheese, A.** Stevenson. 3b. Sc. Kitchen. STEV1

Pierre. D. C. Scott. 2m., 3w. Sc. Little village in province of Quebec. CANB

Pierre Patelin. M. Jagendorf. Farce. 4m., 1w. Sc. Street. SHAT

Pierre Patelin. C. F. Reighard. Farce. 5m., 1w., chorus. Sc. Village market place. REI

Pierrette's heart. E. Shephard. 2m., 1w. Sc. A garden. FREN

Pierrot before the seven doors. A. Cantillon. Morality. 6m., 1w. Sc. A bare stage. BAK, PHIL

Pierrot——his play. T. Schwartz. Fanciful. 1m., 2w. Sc. A room barely furnished. DRA

Pierrot in hospital. G. Cannan. 4m., 2w. Sc. Hospital in a modern city. CANN

Pierrot's mother. G. Hughes. 1m., 2w. Sc. Interior. APPL, NICA

Pietro the foolish. L. K. Deighton. Comedy. 3m., 2w. Sc. Interior. LON

Pigs ears and purses. R. L. Melville. Satire. 4m., 2w. Sc. Library of apartment. CART

C **Pilgrim, The.** E. E. Levinger. 3c., chorus. Sc. Stage. LEVT

Pilgrim and the book, The. P. Mackaye. 13m., 7 chorus groups. Sc. Any large stage or space. FED

C **Pilgrim ladies plan for the first Thanksgiving, The.** M. Liles. 14w. Sc. Sitting room. Prim. Educ. 46: 208–209, 229, 246, Nov. 1928.

C **Pilgrim maiden's dream, The.** M. T. Johnson. 12b., 10g. Sc. Bit of autumn woodland. ELD

Pilgrim mother, A. H. M. Crockett. 6m., 3w. Sc. Home in Plymouth in 1621. PIL

J **Pilgrim thankfulness.** P. M. Swinton. 4b., 3g., chorus. Sc. Large log cabin which serves as a fort. SW

Pilgrims of the way. D. C. Wilson. 4m., 2w. Sc. In a garden. BAK

Pin money. R. Wheeler. Comedy. 2m., 2w. Sc. Living room. BAK

J **Pine-tree shillings, The.** J. Merrill and M. Fleming. 8b., 1g. Sc. Stage. MER

J **Pine tree's blossoming, The.** F. Cavanah. 4b., 5g. Sc. A lone pine tree on a wind-swept plain. BANN

Pinin' f'r the skipper. J. M. Ellicott. 8m., 2w. Sc. Captain's cabin on the S.S. Hawaii. BANN

Pink and patches. M. Bland. Comedy. 1m., 3w. Sc. Interior. FREN

C **Pinocchio runs away.** R. Bufano. 10b., 2g., chorus. Sc. Before the curtain. BUF

C **Pinocchio turns donkey.** R. Bufano. 12c., chorus. Sc. Street on the waterfront. BUF

Pipe in the fields, The. T. C. Murray. Poetic. 3m., 2w., chorus. Sc. Living room in a farmhouse. FRE4

Pipe of peace, A. M. Cameron. 1m., 2w. Sc. Dining-room. KN

Piper of Salem, The. R. S. Holland. 4m., 5w., 2b. Sc. Sitting room in Salem, Mass. 1692. PENN

J **Pirate gold.** O. M. Price. 3b., 2g., chorus. Sc. Cabin og U.S. frigate "Philadelphia." PRI

C **Pirate Percy and the slovenly sloop.** H. N. Calver. 4b., chorus. Sc. Cabin of a ship. SAL

C **Pirates bold, The.** D. A. Lord. 2b., chorus. Sc. In a frame. LOQ

J **Pirate's life's the life for me, The.** E. S. Lyon. 11c. Sc. Small level clearing. SAO

Pirtle drums it in. C. Divine. Comedy. 5m., 5w. Sc. Business office. APPL

Pity. E. W. Peattie. 1m., 2w. Sc. Interior. PEA

Pity the city guy. H. P. Powell. Farce. 3m., 1w. Sc. Lunch room. PENN

Place Aux Dames. M. Porter. Burlesque. 4w. Sc. Interior. DRA, FIT

J **Plan to set free runaway nigger Jim, The.** M. A. Butler. Adapted from Mark Twain's Adventure of Huckleberry Finn. 4b. Sc. Open space in front of a small cabin. BUT

Planning the husband's banquet. A. L. Heath. Comedy. 6w. Sc. Sitting room. ELD

J **Planter of friends, The.** E. E. Levinger. 3b., 1g. Sc. Out of doors in Ohio in 1804. LEVT

C **Play for carolers, A.** S. C. Clapp. 1b., 4g. Sc. Home bedroom. Amer. Child 13 : 34, 77, Dec. 1927.

C **Play for good book week, A.** R. Carter. 3b., 3g. Sc. Library table. Prim. Educ. 44 : 230, 235, Nov. 1926.

J **Play of the luck of Troy, The.** E. C. Oakden and M. Sturt. 5b., 1g. Sc. Hut of Diomede. OAK

J **Play of Mediaeval magic, The.** E. C. Oakden and M. Sturt. 4b., 1g. Sc. Room in palace. OAK

J **Play of Pastorella, The.** E. C. Oakden and M. Sturt. Adapted from Spenser. Fairy Queen. 6b., 3g., chorus. Sc. An open flowery field. OAK

J **Play of Saint George, The.** J. M. C. Crum. Farce. 11b., 9g. Sc. Needs no scenery. THOM

Play of Saint George, The. T. Hardy. Old English Mummers play. 9m., 3w. Sc. English interior. FREN

J **Play of the Pied Piper, The.** E. C. Oakden and M. Sturt. 4b., chorus. Sc. The council hall. OAK

C **Play of the travelling musicians, The.** E. C. Oakden and M. Sturt. 8b. Sc. Near a milestone on the road. OAK

J **Play of twice is too much, The.** E. C. Oakden and M. Sturt. Comedy. 7b., 3g., chorus. Sc. House in Arabia poorly furnished. OAK

Played before the Emperor. O. J. Fitch. 10m., 1w., others. Sc. Stage setting plain. Player's M. 6 : 18–19, Nov.–Dec. 1929.

Player Queen, The. W. B. Yeats. 6m., 3w., chorus. Sc. Open space. YEA

Playgoers. A. W. Pinero. 2m., 6w. Sc. Morning-room in a home in London. FARK

Playing for health. E. Cole. Hygeia 4 : 646–47, Nov. 1926.

C **Playing Pilgrim.** H. and M. Hastings. 3b., 5g. Sc. Outdoors. Prim. Educ. 46 : 214, Nov. 1928.

Playing square. J. Wilder. 3m., 1w. Sc. Interior. PENN

Playing with fire. P. Wilde. 1m., 2w. Sc. Kitchen. KN

Play's the thing, The. H. Simpson. Farce. 4m., 5w. Sc. Sitting room. SIMN

Pleasant disappointment, A. I. Roberts. 2m., 3w. Sc. Den. FIT

Please stand by. C. D. Gilpatric. 16 char. Sc. Sitting room. BAK

Plenty of time. M. MacMillan. Comedy. 9m., 9w. Sc. Rural district of America. APPL

J **Plowshare or the sword, The.** E. E. Levinger. Pageant. 7b. Sc. Out of doors. LEVT

J **Plum blossoms.** E. Edland. 6g., 1b. Sc. Open door with plum trees in bloom just outside. EDLP

Plumbers, The. H. Grattan. Farce. 2m., 2w. Sc. Breakfast room. FREL

Plumes. G. D. Johnson. Folk play. 1m., 3w. Sc. Kitchen. FREN, LOC

J **Plymouth's first Thanksgiving.** M. Irish. 5b., 5g. Sc. Stage. BAK

Poacher, The. J. O. Francis. 3m., 1w. Sc. Living room of Welsh cottage. Theatre Arts M. 9: 327–337, May 1925.

C **Pocahontas and Captain Smith.** A. Stevenson. 5b., 2g., chorus. Sc. Forest. STEV2

C **Pocahontas saves Jamestown.** A. Stevenson. 5b., 1g., chorus. Sc. Indian camp. STEV2

C **Pocahontas, the Indian maiden.** A. R. Parr. 2b., 3g. Sc. Forest near Jamestown. Pop. Educ. 42: 44, 46, Sept. 1924.

Poet passes, A. P. T. Gantt. 2m., 1w. Sc. Living room. PENN

Poetasters of Ispahan, The. C. Bax. Comedy. 6m., 1w. Sc. Interior. BAK, HAM

Poetry and plaster. R. Medcraft. 2m., 2w. Sc. Drawing room. FRE6

Poets all. C. Seiler. Comedy. 4m. Sc. Editorial room. SEI

C **Poets cornered, The.** H. O. Boggs. 4g. Sc. Interior. BOGG

Poet's paradise, The. E. Sammis. 4m., 1w. Sc. Ornate and artificial paradise built in hell. Poet Lore 36: 569–576, Winter 1925.

Point of view, The. M. Osborne. 3m., 1w. Sc. Fashionable drawing room in London. CANB

Polar post, The. M. Pakington. 3m. Sc. In the arctic region. FREN

Police matron, The. C. Glick and M. Hight. Melodrama. 3m., 1w. Sc. Office of police matron, in a Chicago station. BAK

Polite art of conversation, The. G. Cannan. 3m., 4w. Sc. Dining room of a London house. CANN

C **Polite Priscilla and Gertie the Goop.** E. A. Preston. 4b., 6g. Sc. Playground. PAIN

C **Polly's Christmas eve.** J. L. Richardson. Many c. Norm. Inst. 39: 76, 78, Nov. 1929.

C **Polly Patchwork.** R. Field. 3b., 5g., chorus. Sc. Interior of a cottage. FIE

C **Pollyanna's guest of honor.** S. G. Clark. 6b., 3g. Sc. Parlor. CLAR

J **Polly's hero.** 6b., 5g. Sc. Interior. LOU

J **Polly's troubles.** E. Tielkemeier. 4b., 8g. Sc. Stage. BUG

J **Polonaise.** A. C. Darlington. 8b., 7g., chorus. Sc. Inside a Polish cottage. DAR

J **Pomona.** A. Haggard. Pastoral. 1b., 2g., chorus. Sc. Orchard. HAG

J **Pomona and Vertumnus.** M. R. Hofer. 14g., 1 chorus. Sc. Indoors or outdoors. HOF

Pomp. S. Cowan. 4m., 2w. Sc. Poorly and scantily furnished room. COW

Pompons. N. L. Strobach. Fantasy. 2m., 1w. Sc. Interior with fireplace. UNW2

Poor actress, A. F. F. Moore. Comedy. 3m., 1w. Sc. Library in house of Peg Woffington. MOO

Poor Aubrey. G. Kelly. Comedy. 1m., 3w. Sc. Sitting room. KEL

Poor Columbine. A. R. Russell. 4m., 1w. Sc. Interior. FREN

Poor dear mamma. R. Kipling. From his Story of the Gadsbys. Comedy. 2w. Sc. Interior of bedroom at Simla, India. PE

Poor house, The. L. Driscoll. 2m., 2w. Sc. Kitchen. COH

Poor Izzy! A. L. Kaser. Burlesque. 2m. Sc. No scenery required. KAS

Poor Judas. C. E. Lawrence. 4m. Sc. Plain room in Jerusalem. Cornhill 66: 503–510, Apr. 1929.

C **Poor little Turkey maiden, The.** M. E. Carpenter. Many c. Amer. Child. 13: 27–30, 62, Nov. 1927.

Poor Maddalena. L. Saunders. 2m., 1w. Sc. Land of fantasy. KM, KN

C **Poor Richard says.** L. K. Dolan. 12c. Sc. Living room. DOL

J **Poor Richard's dream.** C. A. Hubbard. 13b., 1g. Sc. Parlor of Franklin's home. Norm. Inst. 39: 61–63, Jan. 1930.

J **Poor teacher.** H. O. Boggs. 6b., 6g. Sc. School room. BOGG

Poppet, The. A. Scudder. 3m., 3w., chorus. Sc. Interior of English cottage in 1692. SCU

Porch climber, The. K. Kavanaugh. 2m., 1w. Sc. Interior. DRA

Porphyria's lover. L. A. Wade. From Browning's poem. 1m., 1w. Sc. Room with fireplace. WA

Portia pulls a pinch play. R. Farquhar. Burlesque. 6m., 2w. Sc. Dark blue or black setting. FARQ

J **Portrait of a gentleman in slippers.** A. A. Milne. 3b., 1g. Sc. Room in King's palace. FREL, MILO

Portrait of Tiero, The. Z. Akins. 3m., 2w., 2 chorus groups. Sc. A room in an Italian Villa in the 16th century. IS

Post Mortems. C. Divine. Comedy. 3m., 1w. Sc. Interior. APPL, MACG, NICB

Post-scripts. E. Augier. Comedy. 1m., 2w. Sc. Well-furnished room in Paris. RIC

C **Posture through the ages.** Several c. Hygeia 7: 728–729, July 1929.

Pot boiler, The. A. Gerstenberg. Farce. 5m., 2w. Sc. Stage half set for rehearsal. KN

Pot of broth, The. W. B. Yeats. Comedy. Sc. Cottage kitchen. MAR3, YEA

C **Pot of gold, The.** A. Stevenson. 5b. Sc. Vineyard. STEV2

Potter Pancake Co., The. N. Balch. Comedy. 2m., 2w. Sc. Outer office. BAL

C **Potter's dream, The.** D. A. Fraser. 10c. Sc. Potter's studio. ELD

Potter's field. P. Green. 13m., 3w., chorus. Sc. Negro settlement in valley close by white folks. GRED

Pottery. H. Hudson. 8m., 1w., chorus. Sc. Wing of the Metropolitan Museum. SHAF

Pound of flesh, A. T. J. Geraghty. 6m., 1w. Sc. Office of manager of Globe hotel. NICH

Poverty. H. Alin. 2m., 2w. Sc. Small gloomy dark room. SHAT

Powder, rouge and lipstick. E. S. Millay. Satire. 1m., 1w. Sc. Dressing table. MIK

Prairie doll, The. E. C. Carpenter. 2m., 1w. Sc. A camp. FRE2

Prairie dread. L. Maloney. 4m. Sc. Inside a prairie shack. UNND

Prayer meeting, The. P. Green. 5m., 7w. Sc. Interior of negro home in North Carolina. GREF, Poet Lore 35: 232–253, Summer 1924.

C **Precarious situation in Boston's history, A.** F. O'Ryan and A. W. O'Ryan. 12b. Sc. Washington's headquarters, 1775. ORY

Precedence, a near tragedy. K. L. Roberts. 7m., 3w. Sc. High ceilinged airy office. Sat. Eve. Post 202: 14–15, July 20, 1929.

Precious art of dressing, The. B. Meyer. 2w. Sc. Restaurant of the Ritz at noon. Harper's Bazaar 62: 63–66, 126, Jan. 1927.

Present-day courtship. R. Bottomley. 1m., 1w. Sc. Exterior. FREN

J **Present for Mr. Lincoln, A.** E. E. Levinger. 4b., 1g. Sc. Parlour in a home in a village in Illinois at the close of the Civil War. LEVT

J **Press gang, The.** W. J. Minnion. 5b., 2g. Sc. Room in seaport town looking out upon harbour. FREL

Pretty farmer's daughter, The. A. E. Robinson. 3m., 2w. Sc. Front parlor of farmhouse. FARQ, PAIN

Pretty little Plum-pit. G. Hughes. Burlesque. 4m., 2w. Sc. Interior. HUN

Pretty piece of business. T. Morton. Comedy. 2m., 3w. Sc. Parlor. FIT

C **Prevention goes marching on.** G. Lloyd. 1b., 1g., others. Sc. Autumn woods. Norm. Inst. 39: 36, Oct. 1930.

Price, The. R. Jeans. Farce. 3m., 1w. Sc. Sitting room. JEO

Price of coal, The. H. Brighouse. 1m., 3w. Sc. Lancashire colliery village. HAM

Price of love, The. A. Rouveyrol. 2m., 1w. Sc. Living room in apartment hotel. Drama 16: 219–220, 238–239, Mar. 1926.

C **Primary book pageant, A.** Mrs. R. E. Crump. 33c. Sc. Child's playroom. WHG1

Prince Gabby. J. Murfin. Comedy. 3m., 1w. Sc. Dark stage. NICB

C **Prince Goldenrod.** K. L. Bates. 9c., chorus. Sc. Yellow throne-room of Prince. BAT

C **Prince in the moon, The.** S. Young. Fanciful. 1b., 4g. Sc. Low level plain. YOUN

Prince of court painters, The. C. D. Mackay. 1m., 1w., 1c. Sc. Living room of a peasant like cottage. WEBB

C **Prince of Ko-Am, The.** H. F. Dunlap. 7b., 4g. Sc. Stage. FAW

J **Prince of Stamboul, The.** Lord Dunsany. Fanciful. 4b., 2g. Sc. Room in a cottage. WEB

Prince Pentaur. A. Scudder. 4m. Sc. Long room with walls decorated with Egyptian paintings. SCU

Prince who was a piper, The. H. Brighouse. 5m., 8w., chorus. Sc. Palace garden. BRIO

Princely fortune, A Chinese folk-drama. K. Chen, *tr.* 1m., 1w. Sc. No scenery. Theatre Arts M. 14: 967–971, Nov. 1930.

J **Prince's secret, The.** C. T. Major and K. Hincks. Fanciful. 10b., 8g. Sc. Private room of the prince. MAI

C **Princess and the crystal pipe, The.** B. Folmsbee. 5b., 8g. Sc. Garden. FOL

C **Princess and the pea, The.** C. C. Cooke. 2b., 2g. Sc. Hall. FAW, WHG1

Princess Annabel and the Christmas elves, The. M. S. Millard. WOM

C **Princess in the sleeping wood, The.** H. Ould. 8b., 12g., chorus. BAK, OT

C **Princess Mirabelle and the swineherd.** H. Ould. 11b., 6g. Sc. Garden. FREL, FREN

C **Princess of Moonbeams castle, The.** E. M. Bacon. Fanciful. 22c., chorus. Sc. Interior of castle. FIT

J **Princess on the road, The.** K. C. Greene. Fanciful. 1b., 1g., 3 chorus groups. Sc. Street of a country village. WEB

C **Princess rosy cheeks.** E. S. Balph. Any number of c. Sc. Interior. ELD

C **Princess who could not dance, The.** M. Bland. 9b., 4g. Sc. Garden. ELD

J **Prisoner promoted, A.** H. W. Githens. 13b. Sc. Pharaoh's courtroom. GIT

Private Jones. E. R. Schayer. 9m. Sc. Cave-like dugout. NICH

Prize winner, The. M. Denison. Comedy. 9m., 2w. Sc. Tent show dressing room. APPL

Prodigal, The. W. F. Manley. 8m., 2w., chorus. Sc. Room. MANL

Prodigal comes home, The. M. S. Hitchcock. 12m., 11w., chorus. Sc. Interior DEN

J **Prodigal comes home, The.** M. M. Parker. 5b., 3g. Sc. House in a city of ancient Palestine. DRA

Prodigal son, The. R. C. Alexander and O. P. Goslin. 4m., 3 chorus groups. Sc. Porch of a rich Hebrew dwelling. ALEX

J **Prodigal son, The.** R. Kimball. 3b., chorus. Sc. In a field. KIM

C **Professor makes a mistake, The.** K. A. White. 9b., 2g. Sc. Office of a publishing company. WH

Profits and depressions. G. Soule. 2m. New Rep. 52: 91–93, Sept. 14, 1927.

Progress. S. G. Ervine. 1m., 2w. Sc. Study in a remote village in the North of England. ER

Project club, The. W. N. Bugbee. 4m., 4w. Sc. School yard on Saturday morning. CAT1

C **Prologue.** D. A. Lord. 2b., 1g. Sc. Before the front curtain. LOO, LOP, LOQ

Prologue to balloon. P. Colum. Comedy. 6m., 2w., others. Sc. A square in Megalapolis. Dial 85: 490–500, Dec. 1928.

Prologue to King Lear, A. F. Molnar. 10m., 1w. Sc. Stage before the performance of Shakespeare's King Lear. MOL

Prometheus bound, The. Aeschylus. Trans. by E. Hamilton. 7 char., chorus. Theatre Arts M. 11: 545–562, July 1927.

J **Prometheus the friend of man.** M. R. Hofer. 3b., 4 chorus groups. Sc. One stage setting. HOF

Prominent author, The. I. P. Richardson. Comedy. 8w. Sc. Living room. ELD

Promise of peace, The. E. W. Bates. Nativity. 7m., 2w., chorus. Sc. Chancel of a church or platform. BAK

Promised land, The. H. Robinson. 7m., 5w. Sc. Settler's home. CAMP

Proof, The. J. L. Hodson. 5m., 2w. Sc. Interior. FREN

J **Prophecy, The.** M. G. Parsons. 10b. Sc. Camp in the western part of Virginia. PARR, SAG

C **Prophets, The.** K. Taylor and H. C. Greene. 18b., 3g. Sc. Stage. TAY

Proposal, The. A. Chekov. Farce. 2m., 1w. Sc. Drawing room. FIS, Golden Bk. 13: 70–75, Feb. 1931.

Proposal, The. O. Kelley. Comedy. 1m., 1w. Sc. Living room. KEK

Props. D. Titheradge. Farce. 6m., 1w. Sc. A moving picture studio. TITF

Proserpina and the devil. T. Wilder. 3m. Sc. Puppet-show in Venice in 1640. WILZ

Protectors of the poor. a drama in the manner of the Moscow Art Theater. K. L. Roberts. 6m. Sc. Parlor of luxurious hotel suite in Washington, D. C. Sat. Eve. Post 202: 44–7, Sept. 21, 1929.

C **Proud princess, The.** K. D. Morse. 14b., 7g. Sc. King's court. MORS

C **Proud ring-finger, The.** A. Stevenson. 10 char. Sc. Bedroom. STEV2

Provençal play, The. D. F. Robinson. 11m., 3w., chorus. Sc. Stage. HAQ

Proverbs. H. Simpson. Farce. 3m., 2w. Sc. Sitting room. SIMN

Proxy bridegroom, The. K. Parsons. Comedy. 1m., 3w. Sc. Living room. MARC

Prudence corner. O. Conway. 6m., 4w. Sc. Garden of an old farmhouse. CONW

Psychotherapist, A. C. B. Going. 14m. Sc. Court of king. GOIN

Publicity. L. Harris. 4m., 2w. Sc. Lavishly furnished bungalow. Poet Lore 38 : 590–602, Winter 1927.

C **Puck in exile.** G. Richardson. 1b., 3g. Sc. Sitting room. JOHG

C **Pudding pan, The.** K. D. Morse. 7b., 1g. Sc. A room in a cottage. MORS

Pulling the show together. A. Stephenson. 3m. Sc. Office. FREQ

Pullman Car Hiawatha. T. Wilder. 7m., 5w. Sc. Stage. WILY

Pulse of passion, The. R. Jeans. Farce. 4m., 2w. Sc. Interior. JES

Pumpkin, The. Lord Dunsany. 4m., 1w. Sc. A roadside in Kent, England. London Mercury 24 : 122–129, June 1931.

C **Pumpkin pie, The.** T. C. Cressey. 7b., many g. Sc. Any stage. Pop. Educ. 43 : 154–5, Nov. 1925.

C **Pumpkin pie Peter.** M. Irish. 6b., 5g. Sc. Interior. PAIN

Punch and go. J. Galsworthy. Comedy. 8m., 2w. Sc. Stage of theatre. GAL

J **Pun'kin-headed servant, The.** M. Irish. 5b. Sc. Plain room. IQA

Punter's friend, The. H. Simpson. Farce. 3m. S. Office. SIMM

Puppet. H. E. Adler. Allegory. 4m., 1w. Sc. Before curtains. UM

Puppeteer, The. A. Gerstenberg. Comedy. 1m., 1w. Sc. Decorative staircase. GEQ

J **Purim on trial.** J. A. Kates. 21b. Sc. Courtroom. BLO

J **Purloined letter, The.** E. A. Poe. 3m. Sc. Study in Paris during the restoration. HAP

Purple at the window, orange at the window. M. Hodenfield. Fantastic comedy. 2m., 2w. Sc. A street. BAK

J **Purple iris, The.** A. Withington. 2m., 5g. Sc. Garden of the emperor. WOM

Purple pig, The. B. King. Comedy. 5m., 5w. Sc. Tea room. MARC

C **Put on your thinking cap.** L. Allen. Nonsense play. 5b., 4g. Sc. Roadside. PAIN

Pyentsa. J. Smith, *tr.* Fanciful. 6m., 11w., chorus. Sc. Exterior. SHAT

C **Pygnalion and Triptolemus.** M. Oller and E. K. Dawley. 3b., 1g. Sc. Large room. OLL

Pyjamas. V. Wyngate. Comedy. 1m., 1w. Sc. Nurses' study in nursing home. FREL

C **Pyramus and Thisbe.** M. Oller and E. K. Dawley. 3b., 2g. Sc. Tomb of Ninus. OLL

J **Pyramus and Thisbe.** W. Shakespeare. 6b. Sc. Quince's house. HAGG, KM, SMI, WEB

Q

Quack Doctor. J. W. Smith. Farce. 4m., 1w. Sc. Interior. FIT

Quakers, The. A. V. Kotzebue. Trans. by B. B. Beebe. 5m., 1w. Sc. Army headquarters. Poet Lore 38 : 177–191, Summer 1927.

Quality of mercy, The. B. Mansfield. 3m., 1w. Sc. Interior. FREN

Quare medicine. P. Green. Comedy. 3m., 1w. Sc. Sitting room of farmhouse. CAR3, GREE, SHAF

C **Quarrel, The.** K. A. White. 2b., 1g. Sc. Interior. WH

C **Quarrel of the seasons, The.** M. A. Niemeier. 4b., 4g. Sc. The home of winter. NIEM

Quarry, The. J. A. Clark. 5m., 1w. Sc. County jail. CL

C **Queen Christmas.** C. Wells. 14c. Sc. Interior. DRA, PENN

Queen comes to pray, The. J. F. McDermott, Jr. 5m., 1w. Sc. The temple of Koh. Poet Lore 36 : 450–456, Autumn 1925.

C **Queen cross-patch and the scullery wench.** R. Benton. 7b., 7g. Sc. Queen's boudoir. BEN

Queen Jezebel. E. L. Squires. 8m., 3w. Sc. Marble palace in Jezreel, Canaan in 800 B. C. Poet Lore 40 : 615–626, Winter 1929.

C **Queen of Roseland, The.** R. Strutton. 14 or more b. and g. Sc. Out door effect. STRU

Queen ruin, The. E. Thompson and T. Thompson. 5m., 2w. Sc. The great hall of the Rana's palace. THON

Queen of Sheba, The. S. Young. Fanciful. 3m., 2w. Sc. 1 Gothic Chamber. IS

C **Queen of the garden.** G. Hopler. Many c. Sc. Flower garden. Prim. Educ. 45 : 691, 737, May 1928.

C **Queen of the May, The.** K. L. Bates. 13c. Sc. Out of doors in Sherwood forest. BAT

C **Queen of the May, The.** N. Wagner. Many c. Sc. Woodland scene. Norm. Inst. 37 : 62, 64, May 1928.

C **Queen of the year.** M. C. Blomquist. Masque. Many c. Sc. Wood. Norm. Inst. 35 : 66–67, June 1926.

C **Queen Sabath.** N. Abraham. 15c. Sc. Interior. BLO

Queen who saved a nation from death, A. P. J. Stackhouse. 3m., 2w. Sc. House of Haman. STAC

Queen's enemies, The. Lord Dunsany. 9m.. 2w., slaves. Sc. Underground temple in Egypt. Golden Book 6 : 258–263, Aug. 1927.

C **Queens examine Alice, The.** M. L. Gill. Adapted from Carroll. Through the Looking Glass. 3g. Norm. Inst. 34 : 78, Sept. 1925.

C **Queen's message, The,** a Columbus Day play. M. G. Lawlor. 6b., 1g. Sc. Country inn in 1492 in Spain. Norm. Inst. 39 : 56, 81, 83, Oct. 1930.

Queens of France. T. Wilder. 2m., 4w. Sc. Lawyer's office in New Orleans 1869. WILY, Yale Review 21 : 72–85, Sept. 1931.

Queen's shift, The. J. H. Ingersoll. Satirical comedy. 2m., 2w. Sc. Queen Elizabeth's boudoir. CART, BANN

Queer duck, The. K. Asbrand. Comedy. 6m., 3w. Sc. Interior. PAIN

Queer people, The. C. J. Denton. 2m., 2w. Sc. Comfortable living room. DENT

Quem Quaeritis. P. E. Osgood. 5w., 5m. Sc. Inside church. OSF

J **Quest of Perseus, The.** M. R. Hofer. 6b., 11g., chorus groups. HOF

Question of morality, A. P. Wilde. Comedy. 3m., 1w. Sc. Interior. WIL

Question of principle, A. M. Flavin. Satire. 6m., 1w. Sc. Interior. FLA, FRE2

Quiet family. W. E. Suter. Farce. 4m., 4w. Sc. Plain room. FIT

Quiet game, A. E. O. Jones. 2m., 2w. Sc. Living room. FREN

Quiet rubber, A. H. Simpson. Farce. 2m., 2w. Sc. London interior. SIMH

Quite a nice cat. E. Hendrie and S. Caldwell. 7w. Sc. Boarding house. FRER

C **Quiz, The.** H. O. Boggs. Comedy. 2b., 2g. Sc. Living room. BOG

R

C **Rabbit who wanted red wings, The.** C. S. Bailey. 7c., others. Sc. Stage. BAI, Amer. Child. 12: 35–38, Apr. 1927.

Rabbits, The. L. G. Peach. Farce. 2m., 2w. Sc. Tennis court. PAZ

C **Race of the ants, The.** F. Densmore. 9b., 5g., chorus. Sc. A field. WOM

Rackey. E. H. Culbertson. 3m., 1w. Sc. Sitting room of cottage. LOC

Radio. A. C. D. Riley. 2m., 1w. Sc. New farm on the plains of western Kansas. RIL

J **Radio Christmas, A.** M. C. Wick. 6g. Sc. Room. DRA

J **Radio for the family.** P. V. Wilcox. 8b., 1g. Sc. Living room. Ind. Arts M. 17: 202–204, June 1928.

C **Radio playlet, A.** M. Nerison. Many c. Sc. Living room with radio. Grade Teacher 46: 782, June 1929.

Radio widow, The. E. P. Milbank. Comedy. 3m., 2w. Sc. Living room. PAIN

Raffle, The. Lord Dunsany. 4m., 1w. Sc. Smoking room in house in country. DUS, FREN

C **Rag doll's Christmas eve, The.** N. Wagner. 15 to 30 c. Sc. A nursery. DRA, ELD

Ragged edge, The. F. Eastman. Comedy. 9m., 2w. Sc. A city park. ASS

C **Raggedy-girl's dream, The.** B. Williams. 3b., 3g. Sc. Bedroom. JOHG

Rain. D. Burnett. 6m., 1w. Sc. Interior. BAK, Drama 14: 20–23, Oct. 1923.

J **Rainbow gold.** A. L. Barney and H. Kotsch. Fantasy. 10 char., chorus. Sc. A grassy glade. BANN

Rainbow gold. D. A. Lord. Fanciful. 7 char. Sc. Land of Rainbow's end. LOR

C **Rainbow robe, The.** V. Olcott. 3b., 8g., chorus. Sc. A forest cottage hundreds of years ago. OLC

C **Rainbow's end.** F. M. Nelson. 30c. Sc. Woods. ELD, MARC

Raising the devil. E. E. Gardner. 4m., 2w. Sc. Interior of a log hut in the Catskill Mountains. Poet Lore 39: 134–153, Spring 1928.

Raising the wind. H. C. Sargent. Farce. 4m., 1w. Sc. Stage. SARB

Ramadan. L. Smith. 3m. Sc. Interior of a mud-plastered hut. TAYM

Rameses dreams. M. N. Gleason. 4 char., chorus. Sc. Interior of tomb of Rameses. WOM

Rapunzel. A. Brody. 1m., 2w. Sc. Kitchen of a Harlem flat. IS, Theatre Arts M. 9: 257–266, Apr. 1925.

J **Rash vow, A.** H. W. Githens. 4b., 1g., chorus. Sc. Camp in Mizpah. GIT

Rashi. C. Reznikoff. 5m. Sc. Interior. REZ

Rat poison. H. Simpson. Farce. 1m., 2w. Sc. Poorly furnished room in Whitechapel. SIMH

Rational princess, The. H. Brighouse. 4m., 4w. Sc. Palace garden. BRIO

Rats. M. J. Fruchter. 2m., 2w. Sc. Small dimly lit room. Poet Lore 37: 154–157, Spring 1926.

Rats! G. Henderson. 13c. Sc. Anywhere. FJ

Rats! G. F. Mountford. Farce. 2m., 2w. Sc. Interior. DEN

Raw men. N. Houston. 4m. Sc. Log cabin in Alaska. CAMP

J **Rawlings Record Assembly.** Rawlings Junior High School. 9 char. Sc. Assembly platform. RAW

Razor, The. K. Nakamura. Japanese play. 5m., 1w. Sc. Interior of village barber shop. SHAF

J **Reaching for the moon.** M. C. Richmond. 7b., others. Ind. Arts M. 18: 210–14, June 1929.

C **Reading wins his case.** K. A. White. 5 char. WH

Real antiques. E. O. Jones. Comedy. 3m., 2w. Sc. Second hand store. FREN

C **Real Christmas, A.** G. Scherr. Many c. Sc. Christmas tree. Prim. Educ. 45: 271, 314, Dec. 1927.

C **Real Santa, The.** M. N. Drake. 6b., 6g. Sc. Christmas tree. Norm. Inst. 39: 80, Nov. 1929.

C **Real Santa Claus, The.** M. A. Enloe. 10c. Sc. Santa Claus house. ENL

C **Real Santa Claus, The.** L. R. Smith. 10c. Sc. Santa Claus' House. HALI

C **Real Thanksgiving, A.** N. M. Banta. 4b., 3g. Sc. Old fashioned room with fire place. BANS

C **Real Valentines.** G. V. R. Wolf. 5c. Norm. Inst. 33: 63, Feb. 1924.

Realities. G. Robins. Comedy. 2m., 2w. Sc. Parlour in the suburbs. RO4

Really—Mr. Jenkins! R. D. Skinner. 3m., 1w. Sc. Study in a New York apartment. FREN

Really, my dear . . . C. Morley. Fantastic comedy. 1m., 5w., 4c. Sc. Pleasingly furnished conventional home. HUO, MORK, Forum 79: 723–35, May 1928.

Realm of Thanatos, The. M. Northey. 6m. Sc. Lighthouse. KAM

J **Rebellion in the Milton family.** S. A. Wallace. 2m., 4w. Sc. Milton's study. Educ. 50: 400–406, Mar. 1930.

Recess for memorials. A. Brody. 1m., 2w. Sc. Women's gallery of a synagogue on the day of Atonement. BRO

Reckless. L. Riggs. 4m., 1w. Sc. Side of a road through the woods. CL, FRE4

Reckoning, The. J. E. Brereton. Comedy. 3m., 3w., 1c. Sc. Interior. BAK, WIMA

Reckoning, The. C. E. Lawrence. 5m., 1w. Sc. Shabby room in an Inn. Cornhill 69: 10–28, July 1930.

Reckoning, The. H. H. Snyder. 4w., 2m. Sc. Living room in a small town. DQ

Rector, The. R. Crothers. Comedy. 1m., 6w. Sc. Study in a country parsonage. FRE1

Red carnations. G. Hughes. Comedy. 2m., 1w. Sc. A secluded corner in a city park. FRE2

C **Red dusk.** O. M. Price. 5b., 2 chorus groups. Sc. Mt. Hope on Narragansett Bay in 1676, PRI2

Red feathers, The. A. A. Milne. Operetta. 2m., 3w. Sc. Living room of a country house. MILN

Red mill, The. M. A. Buell. 2m., 3w. Sc. Coney Island. INT

Red owl, The. W. Gillette. Melodrama. 3m., 1w. Sc. Hall of house. FRE1

Red Rowan. W. Gibson. Poetic. 4m., 3w. Sc. Horse copper's camp. GIK

J **Resurrection, The.** R. Kimball. 12b., 4g. Sc. Curtains. KIM

Resurrection, The. W. B. Yeats. 4m., 3 musicians. Sc. An upper chamber in Jerusalem. Adelphi 4: 714–729, June 1927.

Reticent convict, The. O. W. Firkins. 3m., 1w. Sc. Governor's private office in State Capitol. Drama 18: 141–143, 160, Feb. 1928.

Return, The. G. Bottomley. Poetic. 1m., 1w. Sc. In elfland. BOTS, BOTT

Return, The. H. W. Clark. Comedy. 2m., 1w. Sc. Living room in a small apartment. NICR

Return of Bob Gregory, The. C. Seaver. 2m., 2w. Sc. Interior. ELD

Return of Buck Gavin, The. T. C. Wolfe. Tragedy. 2m., 1w. Sc. Cabin in a remote cave of the Carolina Mountains. CAR2

Return of Davy Jones, The. A. Lang. Farce. 2m., 2w. Sc. Sitting room in Mariner's home on Cape Cod. BAK

Return of Eurylochus, The. R. Budwin. Verse. Tragedy. 5m., 3w., chorus. Sc. Before a palace in Ithaca. STRA

Return of King Christmas, The. 15 char. Sc. Interior. BUG

Return of Letty, The. A. C. Thompson. Comedy. 6w. Sc. Interior. PENN

J **Return of Rip Van Winkle, The.** M. A. Butler. 4b., 2g., chorus. Sc. Yard before the tavern of a little village in the Kaatskills. BUT

J **Return of spring, The.** E. E. Levinger. 2b., 3g., chorus. Sc. Vale of Enna. LEVT

C **Return of spring, The.** A. Stevenson. From Browning's Pied Piper. 12 char., chorus. Sc. A town on a river. STEV1

J **Return of the Christmas Special, The.** H. W. Munro. 3b., 2g., chorus. Sc. Poor home in a mine town. ELD

Return of the emigrant, The. M. Roche. 3w. Sc. Peasant's cabin in Ireland. ROC

J **Return of the Prodigal, The.** E. E. Levinger. 5b.. 1g., chorus. Sc. Open place in the days where the temple stood. PIL

J **Reuben springs a surprise.** W. N. Bugbee. 2b., 2g. Sc. Living room. JOHC

J **Reunion, The.** J. D. Ross. 5b., 2g. Sc. Dilapidated tenement in N. Y. slums. DAZ

J **Reunion at Pine Knot Ranch, The.** M. Irish. 5b., 6g. Sc. Ranch house. PAIN

Revelation, The. C. J. Denton. 1m., 1w. Sc. Interior. DENT

Revellers, The. L. Housman. 7m., 1w. Sc. Small square with its stone fountain in Perugia. HOUS

Revenge. J. V. H. Andrews. 4m., 4w. Sc. A tiny hall bedroom in N. Y. MIST

J **Reverie.** P. Wilde. 9b., 6g. Sc. Living room in New England country homestead. BAK, Pict. Review 25: 12–13, 54+, Dec. 1923.

Reversed triangle, A. H. Simpson. Farce. 2m., 3w. Sc. Sitting room. SIMS

C **Revising a geography.** F. E. More. As few or as many children as available. Sc. School room. BAK

C **Revivified lily, The.** B. E. Palmer. 2b.. 10g. Sc. Garden. ELDR

C **Rhoecus.** A. F. Brown. Masque. 3b., 1g. Sc. Glade in the wood. BROW

Rhymes and reactions. G. Sterling. 1m., 2w. Sc. Glade in a forest. Overland M. 84: 293–294, Sept. 1926.

Rhythm. A. Gerstenberg. Comedy. 2m., 1w. Sc. Before the fireplace in the living room. GEQ

Rich man, poor man. B. Y. Burrill. Farce. 9w., 3m. Sc. Rummage sale. NORT

Rich man—poor man. H. P. Powell. Farce. 2m. Sc. Office. PENN

Rich young lady, A. E. H. Yates. Satire. 3m., 1w. Sc. Veranda-café of a transatlantic liner. YATE

Rich young ruler, The. P. J. Stackhouse. 4m., 2w. Sc. In a small village on the Mount of Olives. STAC

Riches. G. Emery. 2m., 2w. Sc. Interior. APPL

Rider of dreams, The. R. Torrence. 3m., 1w. Sc. Interior of a one room cottage in the south. LOC

Riders to the sea. J. M. Synge. Tragedy. 1m., 3w., chorus. Sc. An island off the west of Ireland. CANF, COF, HAM, MOSR, MOSS, SCHY, Golden Bk. 13: 80–84, June 1931.

J   **Riding the goat.** M. Miller. 2m., 2w. Sc. Stuffy sitting room. RICH

Right about—face. M. Mackendrick. 2m., 1w. Sc. Dining room. MACS

Right answer, The. L. K. Brown. Comedy. 1m., 9w. Sc. Interior. BUG, DRA

Right around the corner. E. E. Olson. Comedy. 3m., 2w. Sc. Living room. BAK

C   **Right of boyhood, The.** H. O. Boggs. Comedy. 7b. Sc. Room. BOG

Rim of the desert, The. O. W. Firkins. 4m., 1w. Sc. Level sandy open space around a French fort or the margin of the Sahara. FIR

Ring in the new. R. Jeans. Farce. 1m., 3w. Sc. A drawing room. JEA

J   **Ring leader.** J. W. Rogers. 6b. Sc. House master's bedroom in school for boys. DAZ

C   **Ring of salt, The.** G. Richardson. 2b., 4g. Sc. Nursery. JOHG

Ringing the changes. B. Moore. Comedy. 1m., 1w. Sc. Interior. PE

J   **Rip Van Winkle.** W. Irving. 8b., 2g., chorus. HAP

J   **Rip Van Winkle.** F. A. Marsh. 29c., chorus. Sc. Indoors or out. MARS

C   **Rip Van Winkle.** H. Ould. 29c. Sc. Outside Inn. OT

J   **Rise of Marion Allen, The.** A. Schmotzer. 3g. Prac. Home Econ. 7: 280–81, Sept. 1929.

Rising of the moon, The. Lady Gregory. 4m. Sc. Side of a quay in a seaport town. MAR2, RIC, SMI

J   **Rival peach-trees, The.** A. C. D. Riley. Fantasy. 9b., 3g., chorus. Sc. Court of white Oleanders. DAZ

Road of poplars, The. V. Sylvaine. 6m., 1w. Sc. Parlour of an estaminet on the Merim Road. Yyres in 1922. JOHB

Road to Agincourt, The. E. A. Zeller. 4m., 2w. Sc. Room in chateau near Calais. BAK

C   **Road to Bethlehem, The.** E. Bain. 9b., 6g., chorus. Sc. Any stage. AV

Road to Connaught, The. D. A. Lord. 2m., 1w. Sc. Living room of a small house in the Protestant plantation of Lenister. LOR

Roads. A. E. Peterson. Comedy. 1m., 2w. Sc. Kitchen of a farmhouse in the middle west. LONG

Robber, The. N. Allport. 2m., 1w. Sc. Interior of a lonely cottage. FREL

Robbery, The. C. Kummer. 3m., 2w. Sc. Sitting room. FRE1

J   **Robe of wood, The.** J. Golden. Fantasy. 4m., 1w. Sc. Study in rich Chinese Mandarin home. GOL

Robert Burns. P. Wilde. Farce. 2m., 1w. Sc. Office of insurance company. WILT

C **Robert Morris.** P. Coggin. 11b. Sc. Any stage. Hist. Outlook 17: 131–132, Mar. 1926.

Robert of Sicily. R. C. Alexander and O. P. Goslin. 5m. Sc. Kings Chapel. ALEX

J **Robin Hood.** C. T. Major. 18b., 1g., chorus. Sc. Theatre. MAI

J **Robin Hood in Sherwood.** A. Noyes. 9b., 3g., 2 chorus groups. Sc. Sherwood forest. FIN

Rocking chair row. E. M. Stevens. Comedy. 6w. Sc. Pleasant Pines, a mountain resort. BAK

Rocking chairs. A. Kreymborg. Comedy. 3w., chorus. Sc. Drawing room. KRR

J **Roderick Dhu's proposal.** M. A. Butler. Adapted from Scott's Lady of the Lake. 3b., 3g. Sc. Interior of the hut on Ellen's Isle. BUT

C **Roger Sherman at his last and at his best.** F. O'Ryan and A. W. O'Ryan. 11b. Sc. Cobbler's shop in 1750. ORY

C **Roland.** K. Taylor and H. C. Greene. 13b., 1g., chorus. Sc. Garden. TAY

Rolls and salt. E. S. Millay. Satire. 1m., 1w. Sc. Dining room of a fashionable hotel. MIK

C **Romance of the willow pattern plate, The.** B. S. Provost. 4b., 2g. Sc. The willow pattern. School Arts M. 27: 616–620, June 1928.

Romance of the willow pattern. E. B. VanderVeer. 4m., 1w. Sc. Play presented in Chinese manner. EAT, FREN

Romancers, The. E. Rostand. Satire. 3m., 2w., chorus. Sc. Stage divided by old wall. GOLD, SMI

Romantic interval, A. F. Ryerson and C. Clements. Comedy. 1m., 1w. Sc. Interior. FREN, RY

Romantic Melisande. B. King. Comedy. 2m., 3w. Sc. Private sitting room. PENN

J **La Ronda.** A. C. Darlington. 1b., 2g. Sc. Night in a corner of an old garden. DAR

Rondo. L. Anderson. 4m., 2w. Sc. Personal sitting room in a modern apartment. ANDE

Rondo. B. Ochsner. 2m., 1w. Sc. Studio apartment. Player's M. 1: 16–19, Apr. 1925.

Rondo Capriccioso. K. Kester. 1m., 2w. Sc. Under a rose framed window. Poet Lore 37: 458–467, Autumn 1926.

Room for argument. A. D. Patterson. 1m., 1w. Sc. Interior. PAIN

Room to rent; lit and het. I. M. Barnes. 2m., 4w. Sc. Living room in typical college town. ELD

Room 226. M. Fagin. 1m., 8w. Sc. Bare room on Ellis Island, N. Y. Harbor. Poet Lore 36: 610–614, Winter 1925.

Room with the black door, The. H. Stiles. 1m., 2w., 3g. Sc. A tenement kitchen. Poet Lore 39: 101–116, Spring 1928.

Rope, The. E. O'Neill. 3m., 2w. Sc. Interior of an old barn. ON

Ropes. W. D. Steele. Tragedy. 2m., 1w., 1g. Sc. Living room in light house. STEE

Rory aforesaid. J. Brandane. 5m., 1w. Sc. Sheriff-court. BRAN, MAR3, PHIJ

Rosalind. J. M. Barrie. 1m., 2w. Sc. Parlor of a cottage by the sea. BARR

Rosamond. J. Pollock. 2m., 2w. Sc. A chamber in the palace of the King of the Lombards. POL

Rosamund at the tracks. A. Ryttenberg and A. Weinberg. Melodrama. 2m., 1w. Sc. A clearing in woods near railroad track. Poet Lore 39: 436–448, Autumn 1928.

Rosberry Shrub Sec. F. C. Drake. 3w. Sc. Country sitting room. FREN

Rose, The. R. Jeans. Farce. 3m., 3w. Sc. Interior. JER

Rose lamp shade, The. M. T. Harding. Farce. 2m., 1w. Sc. Interior. ELD

J **Rose of Ann Rutledge, The.** O. M. Price. 2b., 2g. Sc. Studio in Washington. PRI

Rose of the Alhambra, The. W. Irving. 6m., 3w., chorus. Sc. Tower of the Princess in the Alhambra. HAP

Rose-queen of Viremollet, The. M. Sand. Trans. from French. B. Hughes and G. Hughes. 10m., 14w. Sc. Interior of inn. SA

Rose-shaded lamp, The. M. T. Harding. 2m., 1w. Sc. Living room. ELD

Rose windows. S. Young. 2m., 2w. Sc. Interior. IS, Theatre Arts M. 9: 682–693, Oct. 1925.

Rosebud's first ball. F. Boldt. 2g. Sc. Garden. Sierra Ed. News 25: 45, June 1929.

C **Roses.** K. L. Bates. 7c. Sc. Out of doors near a rose garden. BAT

C **Rosetta runs away.** E. E. Preston. 3b., 1g., chorus. Sc. Santa's store room. PRE

Rough diamond, The. J. B. Blackstone. Farce. 4m., 3w. Sc. English interior. PENN

Rough diamond. J. B. Buckston. Farce. 4m., 3w. Sc. Parlor. FIT

J **Rough riders, The.** H. F. Dunlap. 4b. Sc. Crest of San Juan Hill. FAX

Rounding the triangle. W. E. Crawshay. Comedy. 1m., 2w. Sc. Bachelor's flat. CRA

Royal complex, A. E. C. Magnusson. 3m., 7w. Sc. Music room. MAG

C **Royal gift, The.** N. Flaurier. Any number of c. Sc. Court of health. FJ

Royal order of ham and eggs, The. A. L. Kaser. 10m. Sc. Lodge room. DRA

Ruby red. C. Stratton. 2m., 2w. Sc. Room in hotel in Biskra on the edge of desert. BAK

Rufus Learsi. 4m., 3w. Sc. Parlor. Drama 14: 26–28, Oct. 1923.

Ruling class, The. M. Winter. 1m., 3w. Sc. Interior of a one room apartment. Drama 15: 150–152, Apr. 1925.

Rummage sale, The. M. Parsons and M. Pool. 14w., 1b., Sc. Interior. DRA

Rumor. R. C. Knudten. 4m., 8w. Sc. Front porch. BAK

C **Rumplestiltskin.** C. F. Reighard. 4b., 1g. Sc. Room in a mill. REI

C **Runaway clowns.** B. Creighton. 1b., 1g., chorus. Sc. Clearing in a wood. BAI, Amer. Child. 14: 19–22, Mar. 1929.

C **Runaway posies.** S. G. Clark. 1b., 7g. Sc. Outdoor scene. Norm. Inst. 35: 70, June 1926.

J **Runaway Robots.** E. Lowell. 6b., 1g. Sc. Street. BAK

Runaways. L. D. Hollister. 2w. Sc. Railway station. DEN

J **Runaways, The.** G. Sorenson Comedy. 3b., 2g. Sc. An attractive place in the woods. SOR

Rural belle, A. E. J. Sharpsteen. Comedy. 1m., 1w. Sc. Living room. DENI

C **Rustling leaves,** a play for Arbor Day. E. Kunz. Many c. Sc. Forest. Pop. Educ. 42: 462–464, 466, Apr. 1925.

Rusty door, The. H. Southgate. 7m., chorus. Sc. On board of a trawler off Newfoundland. CLS

J **Ruth.** R. Kimball. 12b., 5g., chorus. Sc. Draperies. KIM

J **Ruth.** E. E. Levinger. 3g. Sc. Lonely road. BLO

Ruth. W. F. Manley. 2m., 2w. Sc. On the road to Bethlehem. MAN

C **Ruth.** M. Parsons. 1b., 4g., chorus. Sc. Out of doors in the land of Canaan. PARS

J **Ruth.** M. E. Whitney. 1b., 5g. Sc. On the road to the land of Judah. WHH

J **Ruth and Naomi.** M. Hobbs and H. Miles. 3m., 2w., chorus. Sc. On the road near Bethlehem. HOB, SAO

J **Ruth of Moab.** E. E. Levinger. 3b., 2g., chorus. Sc. A road. LEV

S

C **Sacajawea,** an Indian play. L. Schmidli. 6g. Sc. Wigwam. Norm. Inst. 37: 74, 76, Sept. 1928.

Sacred cat, The. F. Sladen-Smith. 2m., 1w. Sc. On the way to the Temple of Thebes. BAK

Sacred place, The. L. Esson. 6m. Sc. Indian Hawker's room. ES

J **Sacrifice.** T. M. Duncan. 2b., 2g. Sc. Living room of kitchenette apartment. RICH

Sacrifice. M. Larrimer. Miracle. 1m., 2w. Sc. Living room in home in Maine lumber camp. LAR

Sacrifice. W. F. Manley. 2m., 1w. Sc. In the tent of Abraham. MAN

J **Sad jester, The.** E. Levinger. Fanciful. 6b., chorus. Sc. A palace garden. LEVT

Sad shepherd, The. W. B. Yeats. 2m. Sc. Out of doors. YD

C **Sad tale of the tarts of the terrible Queen of Hearts, The.** M. Jagendorf. 14c. Sc. Clearing in the woods. JAF

Safe bet, A. H. Simpson. Farce. 2m., 1w. Sc. Sitting room. SIMH

C **Safety dialogue, A.** A. B. Fikenscher. 6b., others. Sc. Street corner. Norm. Inst. 33: 58, Sept. 1924.

C **Safety first.** M. Corell and I. Liccione. 21c. Sc. Interior. STRU

C **Safety first.** E. Ward. 12c., others. Norm. Inst. 38: 64, 66, Jan. 1929.

C **Safety law court, The.** Many c. Sc. Courtroom. Grade Teacher 47: 50, 78, Sept. 1929.

C **Safety on the streets.** Y. Klein and F. Schwarz. 10c. Sc. In the classroom. KL

C **Safety playlet, A.** A. M. Keedy. 5b., 2g. Prim. Educ. 45: 12–13, 70, Sept. 1927.

C **Safety Sam.** E. Preston. 11c. Sc. Interior. PRES

C **Safety's victory.** E. A. Bear. 12c. Sc. Platform. Norm. Inst. 35: 66, Apr. 1926.

Sahdja, an African Ballet. R. Bruce. 7m., 2w., chorus. Sc. An open clearing. LOC

J **Sail right in.** E. I. Winter. 3b., 2g., Comedy. Sc. Living room in summer home. BANN

J   **Sailing of the Mayflower, The.** E. E. Levinger. 4b., 1g. Sc. Interior of a house in Plymouth in 1621. LEVT

Saint and the fairies, The. J. Ross. 5m., 1w., chorus. ELD

Saint Cyprian and the devil. E. VanderVeer. 3m., 2w. Sc. Laboratory of Magician in Antioch. FREG

Saint Denis (1716). M. M. Griffith. 6m., 1w. Sc. Inside Presidio. GRI

C   **St. Francis and the wolf.** A. H. Branch. 2b., 1g., chorus. Sc. Outdoors. SCH4

Saint Francis of Assisi. M. L. Conger. 33 char. Sc. Winter wood. WOM

J   **St. George and the dragon.** S. L. Cummins. Burlesque. 7b., 4g. Sc. Room in palace. CUM2

Saint George and the dragon. L. B. Goodrich. 10m. Player's M. 7: 22–23, Jan.–Feb. 1931.

C   **St. Patrick's day in the land of the west.** M. A. Niemeier. 10b., 10g. Sc. Stage. NIEM

St. Simeon Stylites. F. Sladen-Smith. 6m., 2w. Sc. Top of a Column. BRIR, FREN, HERB

C   **Saint Valentine.** R. Keeney. 1b., 2g., others. Sc. A country lane. Norm. Inst. 38 : 84, 86, Feb. 1929.

C   **Saint Valentine entertains.** K. L. Bates. Verse. 9c. Sc. Bare trees and patches of snow. BAT

C   **St. Valentine's day with Mother Goose.** M. A. Enloe. 2b., 2g., chorus. Sc. Interior. ENL

C   **St. Valentine's eve.** M. W. Reeve. 6g. Sc. Any stage. Child Welfare 19 : 294–296, Feb. 1925.

Saint's comedy, The. F. Sladen-Smith. 6m., 2w. Sc. A bridge. SID

Sal Volatile. L. Housman. 2m., 2w. Sc. Square chamber in France. HOT

Sale by auction. L. duG. Peach. Comedy. 1m., 2w. Sc. Interior. BAK

Sally of the music store. G. B. Sampson. Any number of char. Sc. Music store. ELD

Salome. O. Wilde. 11m., 2w., others. Sc. Terrace in palace of Herod. Golden Book 1 : 207–220, Feb. 1925.

Salt water. B. W. Newman. 2m., 1w. Sc. A cabin at sea. Poet Lore 35 : 232–243, Summer 1925.

Salted almonds; or, Playing the game by "F. Anstey" (Anstey Guthrie). 1m., 2w. Sc. At the dinner table. Golden Book 14: 372–375, Nov. 1931.

Salvage. D. K. Thompson and J. Assur. 4m., 2w. Sc. Interior miner's cabin in Tennessee. Drama 21 : 17–18, 20, 39, May 1931.

Salvation am free. H. O. Boggs. 5m., 1w., chorus. Sc. Rude negro church. BOGH

Sam Average. P. Mackaye. 3m., 1w. Sc. An entrenchment near Niagara Falls in 1814. MACM

Sam Weller and the Bath footmen. G. Pertwee and E. Pertwee. Adapted from Dickens. Pickwick Papers. 7m. Sc. Small parlour behind green grocer's shop. PER

J   **Sam Weller visits his mother-in-law.** J. H. Stamford. Adapted from Dickens. Pickwick Papers. Comedy. 3m., 1w. Sc. English interior. JON

Sam Weller's walentine. J. E. Jones. Adapted from Dickens. Pickwick Papers. 2m. Sc. English interior. JON

Samantha changes her mind. W. N. Bugbee. 3w. Sc. Sitting room. CAT1

C **Sambo, Lil Sal, and the pancake party.** P. Poe. 3b., 3g., chorus. Sc. Interior. PAIN

Same boat, The. E. S. Millay. 1m., 1w. Satire. Sc. Deck of steamer. MIK

Same old thing, The. R. C. Megrue. 3m., 2w. Sc. Boudoir. FRE2

Same story, The. G. Cannan. 3m. Sc. Lawyer's office. CANN

Samson a la Mode. D. Carb. Comedy. 3m., 5w. Sc. Dining-living room in apartment. NICB

Samson and Delilah. W. F. Manley. 3m., 2w., chorus. Sc. Council chamber of the Philistines. MAN

J **Samuel in the House of the Lord.** R. Kimball. 6b., 1g. KIM

San Jacinto ball. M. M. Griffith. 13m., 2w., chorus. Sc. New building. GRI

San Jose (1721). M. M. Griffith. 8m., 2w., 2c., chorus. Sc. Open space. GRI

San Jose (1794). M. M. Griffith. 4m., chorus. Sc. Mission. GRI

J **Sanctuary knocker, The.** A. J. Walker. 10b., 1g. Sc. 1 Little clearing in the forest. 2 Sc. Church yard. SANP

C **Sandalwood box, The.** A. Stevenson. Adapted from Irving. The Moor's Legacy. 9b., 1g., chorus. Sc. 1 Hovel in Granada. 2 Sc. Same. 3 Sc. Alhambra tower. STEV4

C **Sandman's brother, The.** T. C. O'Donnell. 4b., 1g., 2 chorus groups. Sc. Front of house. JAO

C **Sandman's pack o' dreams, The.** O. M. Price. 14b., 4g., chorus. Sc. Corner of the living room with open fireplace. BAK

Sandwich glass. S. Brown. 4m., 3w. Sc. Kitchen in isolated Cape Cod fishing village. BAK

C **Santa Claus' busy day.** Z. Hartman. 13b., 11g. Sc. Interior. DRA, FIT

C **Santa Claus gets his wish.** B. P. Fisher. 8c. Sc. Interior of Santa's home on Christmas eve. BAK

J **Santa Claus in the White House.** E. Sexton. 17b., 2g. Sc. Cabinet room of the White House. SEX

Santa Claus' Joke. B. R. Beck. 5 char. Sc. Living room. MARC

J **Santa Claus on the air.** E. E. Preston. Comedy. 5b., 6g. Sc. Living room. DRA

C **Santa Claus package, The.** A. G. Lloyd. 5b., 3g. Sc. A country road. MARC

C **Santa Claus starts on his journey.** C. Barr. 15c., chorus. Sc. Santa Claus' toy shop. BARP

C **Santa Claus's workshop.** D. A. Lord. 30 or more c. Sc. Interior of Santa Claus's workshop. QU

C **Santa gets the blues.** E. Sexton. 3b., 2g. Sc. Interior of Santa's home. SEX

C **Santa's dolls.** M. E. Kolz. 1b., 1g., 6c. as dolls. Norm. Inst. 35: 68, Dec. 1925.

C **Santas gifts plus his surprise.** L. Crites, 3b., 2g. Sc. Room with fireplace. FRAZ

C **Santa's helpers.** E. Cameron. 31 or more c. Sc. Stage. CAME

J **Santa's little king.** F. H. Schoberg. 6b., 3g. Sc. Stage. QU

C **Santa's living toys.** H. Armstrong. 2b., others. Sc. Room decorated for Christmas. Norm. Inst. 33: 66–67, Dec. 1923.

C **Santa's plight.** I. Connor. 8c., or more. Sc. Toy shop. Prim. Educ. 45: 274, 327, Dec. 1927.

C **Santa's shop.** E. M. Bronson. 5b., 5g. Sc. Santa's office. Norm. Inst. 39: 57, Dec. 1929.

C **Santa's surprise.** E. E. Preston. 4b., 2g., chorus. Sc. Santa's den. PRE

J **Santa's ups and downs.** E. E. Preston. 5b., 5g. Sc. Santa's combination office and study. DRA

C **Santa's workshop.** M. L. Manchester. Many c. Norm. Inst. 35: 69–70, Dec. 1925.

C **Santa's worries.** 4b., 1g. Sc. Living room. JOHC

   Sara. O. F. Woolley. 2m., 4w. Sc. Small garden adjoining ancient Israelite house. UNU

   Sardines. C. D. Gilpatric. 5w. Sc. Interior of a cottage in Maine. BAK

   Sasovino. D. Ewens. 6m., 1w. Sc. Italian home. FREN

   Saturday night. P. Green. 5m., 2w. Sc. A farmhouse in eartesn North Carolina. GREE

   Saturday night. P. Johnson. 2m., 2w. Sc. Room in cottage in poor quarter of city. FREL

C **Saturday's lamb.** T. W. Sealock. 12b., 4g. Sc. Interior. DRA, ELD

   Saucy goose. R. Medcraft. Comedy. 1m., 1w. Sc. Living room. FREN

   Saul of Tarsus. W. F. Manley. 5m., 1w. Sc. Street in Jerusalem. MAN

   Saul's awakening. J. W. Raine. 5m., 1w. Sc. Outside of Samuel's house at Ramah. RAI

J **Sausage.** R. Gow. 3b. Sc. Interior. FREN

J **Save the surface and you save all.** E. Wood. Burlesque. 4b., 4g. Sc. Living room. AU

C **Save the wild flowers.** F. Duncan and E. D. Yale. Many c. Woman's Home Companion 54: 49, May 1927.

   Saved. J W. Rogers, Jr. 7w. Sc. Sitting room in a small town in the old south. FRE2, FREN

   Saved! D. Titheradge. Farce. 2m., 1w. Sc. Room. TITU

J **Saved to serve.** H. W. Githens. 20b. Sc. Pharaoh's throne room. GIT

   Saving Dad. M. C. Allyn. 2m., 3w. Sc. Office. BAK

   Saving her face. M. Constanduros and M. Hogan. 1m., 1w. Sc. Kitchen. FREL

   Saving Lady Jane. S. Schofield. 4m., 2w. Sc. Cottage room. FREL

   Saving the situation. R. S. Harris. Comedy. 2m., 3w. Sc. Interior. BAK

   Say it with flowers. A. K. Runner. Comedy. 9w. Sc. Interior French. FREN

   Scalp, The. H. Alexander. 2m., 1w. Sc. Interior or exterior. ALE

   Scandal, The. O. Kelley. Comedy. 5w. Sc. Meeting of Ladies Aid. KEK

   Scene from Shanghraun, A. D. Boncicault. 1m., 2w. Sc. Kitchen. PE

J **Scenes from Oliver Twist.** S. A. Wallace. 18 or more m. 4w. Sc. Any stage. Educ. 50: 499–506, Apr. 1930.

C **Scenes from the childhood of Franz Schubert.** J. F. Cooke. 5m., 1w., 1b., 1g., others. Sc. Room in home of Schubert. Etude 46: 589, 631, 632, Aug. 1928.

J **Scenes from The Old Curiosity Shop.** F. M. Bell-Smith. 4b., 2g. Sc. Law office. JON

J **Scenes in the "Life of Robert Burns."** S. A. Wallace. 4m., 2w., 5c. Sc. Any stage. Educ. 50: 565–7, May 1930.

Scheme that failed, A. A. L. Tubbs. 2m., 4w. Sc. Interior. PENN

Scheming mothers. A. G. Evans. Comedy. 2m., 4w. Sc. Living room. DENI

Scheming six, The. H. Bagg. Comedy. 10w. Sc. School. PENN

Scherzo in two flats, A. E. Morrette. Farce. 3m., 3w. Sc. Living rooms of two adjacent typical N. Y. apartments. MORR

Schnitzleresque. C. L. Palm. Satire. 1m., 4w. Sc. Boudoir. Drama 14: 210–212, 238, Mar.–Apr. 1924.

School. Tom Fool. Interlude. 4b. Sc. Schoolroom near London. MACU

C **School at Padding Lane.** M. Sharpe. 23 char. Sc. School room. MARC

C **School clown, The.** G. Sorenson. Comedy. 4b., 6g. Sc. Schoolroom. SOR

J **School days.** A. E. Allen. 14g. Sc. Classroom or stage. FAW

C **School entertainment.** E. W. Merriman. 2b., 8g. Sc. Schoolroom. DRA

C **School lunch room, The,** a health play. A. M. Stevenson. *ed.* Many c. Sc. School lunch room. Hygeia. 7: 922–924, Sept. 1929.

C **Schoolroom imps, The,** a Hallowe'en play. E. B. Jenkins. 18c. Sc. Back yard. Hygeia 5: 597–600, Oct. 1926.

J **School spirit.** E. Sexton. 3g. Sc. College room in girls dormitory. ELD

C **School-time.** M. A. Enloe. 21c. Sc. Schoolroom. ENL

Science and God. J. Murphy, *ed.* Forum 83: 373–379, June 1930.

Scottsboro, Ltd. L. Hughes. 17m., 2w. Sc. Platform. New Masses 7: 18–21, Nov. 1931.

Scourge of Gulph, The. J. B. Yeats. 3m., 1w., chorus. Sc. Deck of a ship. MACU

Scrambled eggs. L. Mackall and F. R. Bellamy. 2m., 3w., chorus. Sc. Barnyard. APPL

Scraps. G. E. Jennings. Comedy. 1m., 6w. Sc. Servants' sitting room in a house in Eaton Square. FREL

Scrubwoman, The. E. Gibson. 2w., 3c. Sc. Kitchen of a poor Syrian home in an American city. GIB

Scuffletown outlaws, The. W. N. Cox. Tragedy. 6m., 1w. Sc. Cabin in swamp. CAR3, Southwest Review 11: 179–204, Apr. 1926.

Sealing the compact. G. John. 3m., 2w., 2c. Sc. Kitchen in miner's cottage in England. JOH

Séance, The. L. duG. Peach. Farce. 1m., 1w. Sc. Fortune telling room. PAZ

J **Search for a wife, A.** M. M. Russell. 5b., 1g. Sc. Tent. RUS

C **Search for Santa Claus, The.** C. S. Bailey. 5b., 4g., chorus. BAI, Amer. Child 12: 26–28, 61, 62, Dec. 1926

Search for the Christ child, The. F Bedwell. 9 char., chorus. Sc. A deserted street of a city. MEI

J **Searching for a wife.** H. W. Githens. 7b., 6g. Sc. In front of Abraham's tent. GIT

Seaweed. A. Gerstenberg. 4w. Sc. Beach. GER

Second best. W. Gaston. 5m., 3w. Sc. Stern of a ship. CLS

Second honeymoon, The. P. R. Eaton. 1m., 1w. Sc. Dining room. DENI

Second lesson in acting, A. R. Boleslavsky. 1m., 1w. Sc. No scenery. Theatre Arts M. 13: 498–505, July 1929.

Second lie, The. I. E. MacKay. 3m., 2w. Sc. Room comfortably furnished. CANB

Second Samuel. J. C. Bardin. 3m., 2w. Sc. Morning room in Virginia in 1771. BAK

J **Secret, The.** A. F. Alehin. Comedy. 1b., 4g. Sc. Interior. ALD

C **Secret, lovely garden, The.** D. A. Lord. 10g., chorus. Sc. Cold and uninviting looking kitchen. LOQ

Secret of good health, The. R. Jeans. Farce. 1m., 5w. Sc. Boudoir. JEP

C **Secret of happiness, The.** Many c. Sc. A garden. Prim. Educ. 45: 542+, Mar. 1928.

J **Secret of success, The.** M. M. Russell. 4b., 1g., chorus. Sc. Room in palace. RUS

J **Secrets of long ago.** B. Cowden. Fantastic. 5b., 5g. Sc. Stage. ELD

Secrets of the heart. A. Dobson. 1m., 1w. Sc. A Chalet covered with honeysuckle. JOHN

Seeing Nellie home. L. C. Vanderveer. Comedy. 5m., 7w. Sc. Parlor. PENN

Seeing New York. H. W. Gribble. Comedy. 2m., 1w. Sc. Interior. NICR

Seeing stars. M. Lee. Farce. 7m. Sc. Country road. LEE

Seeing things right. Mrs. C. Felton. Comedy. 2m., 5w. Sc. Living room of old homestead in Wisconsin. FEL

Sekala Ka'ajma, an interpretive dance-drama of the Southwest. M. Austin. 3m., many others. Sc. Desert south of Gila River. Theatre Arts M. 13: 267–278, Apr. 1929.

Self-respect. C. Healy. 1m., 4w., others. Sc. Fisherman's cottage in North Ireland. Cath. World 128: 43–51, Oct. 1928.

C **Selfish woman, The.** A. Stevenson. 2g. Sc. Village. STEV2

Selling of Joseph, The. J. W. Raine. 10m. Sc. Paine of Dothan. RAI

Semper Fidelis. A. A. Cohn. 2m., 1w. Sc. Library. NICH

Sending Grandpa to heaven. T. R. Arkell. 1m., 1w., 1b. Sc. Sitting room. FREN

Sense of humour, A. D. Titheradge. Farce. 4m., 1w. Sc. Room TITO

Sentence of death, The. T. F. Issasi. 4m. Sc. A cell with stone walls. SHAT

Sentence of death. G. St. John-Loe. 7m. Sc. Bachelor flat. FREL

C **Sentimental scarecrow, The.** R. Field. 3b., 4g. Sc. Open field. FIE

Seraphic vision, The. L. Housman. 3m., chorus. Sc. Cell on a plateau or rock. HOUS, MAR1

Servant's hall, The. N. Gogol, *Tr.* 6m., 3w. Sc. A hall of a flat in Russia. GOG, GOG6

Servants of the people. J. M. Cain. 4m. Sc. Office of county commissioners. Amer. Mercury 4: 393–398, Apr. 1925.

C **Service the fairies did, The.** H. L. Newman. 50 or more c. Sc. Little home schoolroom. WHG1

C **Set-the-table lady, The.** F. B. Linsky. 2b., 2g. Sc. Dining room. FAW

Setback, The. A. Gerstenberg. Comedy. 1m., 3w. Sc. Roof garden. GEQ

Settin' up with Wilhelmina. H. W. Munro. Comedy. 3m., 2w. Sc. Porch of a dutch house. YOU

Setting the nation right. B. E. Palmer. Comedy. 12w. Sc. No special scenery. ELD

C **Setting the world's Christmas table.** F. A. Gardner. 10 either b. or g. Sc. Platform or stage. GAP

Seven against one. M. Finsterwald. 23m. Sc. Stage. FREN

Seven gifts, The. S. Walker. Pantomime. 5m., 3w., chorus. Sc. Interior. SHA

Seven keys to Mr. Bald Pate. M. T. Applegarth. 8 char. Sc. Platform. APO

C **Seven kings of Atherry, The.** L. G. Gosser. 8b., 1g. Sc. Back yard of palace. SAL

Seven women. J. M. Barrie. 2m., 2w. Sc. Drawing room. BARR, BARS

Seventeen fourteen. E. Granville. 9m., 4w. Sc. London house in 1714. GRA

Severed cord, The. M. Finsterwald. 2m., 1w. Sc. Kitchen. FREN

Shade, The. E. C. Koenig. 1m., 1w. Sc. Room. Poetry 35 : 87–88, Nov. 1929.

J **Shades' Hallowe'en convention.** B. M. Casey. 12b. Sc. Hall. CAS

Shades of Shakespeare. R. Jeans. Farce. 7m., 4w. Sc. Banquet hall. JEA

Shadow, The. N. G. Glover. Fantasy. 6m., 2w. Sc. Interior. FREN

Shadow and substance. M. S. Oliver. 2m., 2w. Sc. A living room. OLI

Shadow of the mine, The. L. B. Pride. 2w. Sc. Sitting room of miner's cottage. PRID

Shadowy waters, The. W. B. Yeats. 4m., 2w. Sc. Mast and a great sail, a large tiller rising several feet above the stage. YEA

Shakespeare smiles. L. Campbell. Comedy. 6m., 2w. Sc. Bypath that leads to the wall in central park. APPL

J **Shakespeare, the playmaker.** University of North Dakota. Masque. 65b., 9g., many chorus groups. Sc. Stage. SANP

Shall we join the gentlemen? H. Simpson. Farce. 4w. Sc. Dining room. SIMA

Shall we join the Ladies? J. M. Barrie. 7m., 8w. Sc. Around dinner table at house party. BARR, BARS, SCR

C **Shall yes stay?** E. A. Smedley. 2b., 5g., others. Norm. Inst. 38 : 86, Feb. 1929.

J **Sham.** F. G. Tompkins. Satire. 3m., 1w. Sc. A darkened room. APPL, GOLD, GREM, GREN, HAT

Sham doctor. C. White. Farce. 4m., 2w. Sc. Interior. FIT

Shame the devil. K. Nicholson and A. DeSola. 3m., 2w. Sc. Hall living room in country house on Long Island. APPL

Shamrock, The. E. S. Lyon. 3b., 2g. Sc. Hill country of Ireland. SCH1

Shattered nerves. H. L. C. Pemberton. Comedy. 2w. Sc. Doctor's office. DRA

She couldn't stay a minute. A. L. James. Comedy. 2w. Sc. Interior. PAIN

She made a "Punkin" pie. N. D. Dunlea. 1m., 5w. Sc. Kitchen. ELD

She, 'n her daughter 'n her daughter. P. Rayburn. Comedy. 2m., 2w. Sc. Kitchen of a country farmhouse. ELD

She was no lady. S. G. Ervine. 2m., 2w. Sc. Study. ER, Golden Book 13 : 81–85, July 1931.

She who will not when she may. A. J. Harnwell. 2m., 4w. Sc. Small room off large hall in 1758. SAG

C **Shepherd boy who called wolf, The.** 6b., chorus. Sc. Hillside near the village. STEV2

Shepherd in the distance, The. H. Hudson. Pantomime. 10 char. APPL

J **Shepherd king, The.** H. W. Githens. 15b., 2g., chorus. Sc. Temple in Bethlehem. GIT

Shepherd lad's gift, The. 6b. Sc. Near Bethlehem. Int. J. of Rel. Educ. 2: 15–17, Dec. 1925.

C **Shepherd of Bethlehem, The.** J. Knox. Nativity. 8b., 8g. Sc. In ancient Jerusalem. BAK, BUG, DRA

Shepherd of Lattenden, The. S. Kaye-Smith. 16m., 7w., chorus. Sc. Street in Rye. KAY

J **Shepherd who stayed behind, The.** G. W. McGavran. 10b., 1g., chorus. Sc. A rocky hillside. BAK

J **Shepherdess and the chimney-sweeper, The.** E. Smith. 5b., 2g., chorus. Sc. Simple sitting room. SM

Shepherds, The. M. N. Goold. 6m., 2w. Sc. On the plains north of Bethlehem. FEDE

C **Shepherds, The.** K. Taylor and H. C. Greene. 5b., 2g. Sc. Before a stable in Bethlehem. TAY

Shepherds all? P. E. Osgood. 14m., 2w. Sc. In a church or hall. OSGO

C **Shepherd's dream, The.** S. Young. Fanciful. 2b., 1g. Sc. Hill at dusk. YOUN

C **Shepherd's pipe, The.** A. Nichols. 6b., 5g., chorus. Sc. Open square before Cathedral. NIA

Shepherds' play, The. P. E. Osgood. 3m. Sc. Fields near Bethlehem. OSF

C **Shining goddess, The.** C. E. Sackett. 44g. Sc. Elevated throne. WOM

Ship comes in, The. H. B. Fuller. 5m., 3w., chorus. Sc. A neglected terrace in front of a dilapidated chateau. CLS

Ship comes in, The. F. A. Hyde. Comedy. 2m., 3w. Sc. Kitchen of farm in England. DE

Shipping Mother east. E. Van der Veer. Satirical comedy. 1m., 5w. Sc. Living room in small house. FREN, SCH4

J **Shipwreck of Paul, The.** M. E. Whitney. 7b. Sc. Cabin of ship. WHH

J **Shoe on the other foot, The.** B. Adam. 3b., 2g. Sc. Living room of bungalow in a California city. BANN

Short cut, The. E. Morrette. 3m., 2w. Sc. Room in a shady N. Y. boarding house. MORR

Short cut, A. P. Wilde. 2m. Sc. Curtain rises on darkness. WILD

Short way with authors, A. G. Cannan. Burlesque. 6m., 2w. Sc. Interior. BAK

Shortest play in the world, The. J. C. Squire. 2m. Sc. Palace of Nero. London Mercury 13: 250, Jan. 1926.

Shot, The. A. Pushkin. 3m., 1w. Sc. Drawing-room in country home in Russia. HAP

Shotgun splicin', A. G. W. Coffin. Comedy. 3m., 3w. Sc. Roadway. CAR3

Should adults play golf? H. G. Leach, *ed.* 9m. Forum 82: 202–206, Oct. 1929.

Should he obey the prohibition laws? H. G. Leach, *ed.* 10m. Forum 81: 328–334, June 1929.

C **Should we be more thankful than the Pilgrims?** M. E. Whitney. 2b., 2g., 1 chorus group. Sc. Drawing room on Thanksgiving Day. WHI

Show must go on, The. R. Willis. 3m. Sc. A tent interior. WIMS

C **Show them the cup, Floyd.** M. Johnson. 6b., 6g. JOHD

Shunamite, The. Yehoash. 3m., 1w. Sc. Interior of king's palace. SHAT

J **Shutting o' the door, The.** W. G. Dickson. 4m., 1w. Sc. Interior. BAK, WEB

Shylock's choice. J. Cournos. 2m. Sc. Venetian country room. Fortn. R. 124: 728–732, Nov. 1925.

Sicilian limes. L. Pirandello, *tr.* 2m., 3w., chorus. Sc. Room in hotel. PIR

C **Sick deer, The.** A. Stevenson. 4b. Sc. A meadow. STEV1

C **Sick doll, The.** E. W. Merriman. 3g. Sc. Interior. DRA

C J **Sick Purim, A.** E. E. Levinger. Comedy. 3b., 5g. Sc. Hospital maid. BLO, LEV

Siege, The. C. C. Clements. 1m., 2w. Sc. Room in an Oriental house. COH

Siege of Berlin, The. A. Daudet. 2m., 2w. Sc. Sitting room of apartment. HAP

J **Siege of Ping, The.** E. Smith. 5b., 1g., chorus. Sc. Within Chinese city about 26 B. C. SM

Sight of the blind, The. D. A. Lord. Poetic. 1m., 3w. Sc. Quiet garden of an Irish convent. LOR

Signals. R. E. Hurd. Comedy. 6m., 1w. Sc. Living room. FREN

C **Sigurd the Volsung.** K. Taylor and H. C. Greene 2b, 1g., chorus. TAY

Silent customer, The. G. Norwood. Farce. 5m. Sc. Dirty barber shop. Canadian Forum 9: 44–51, Nov. 1928.

Silent woman, A. T. H. Lacy. Farce. 2m., 1w. Sc. Interior. DRA

C **Silly goose girls, The.** D. A. Lord 12c., chorus. Sc. Plain interior. LOP

Sillyville school, The. E. Bretherton. Burlesque. 11m., 12w. Sc. New England schoolroom. FREN

J **Silver cup, The.** E. E. Levinger. 4m., 1w. Sc. Interior. BLO, LEV

J **Silver lining, The.** C. D. Mackay. 2b, 1g. Sc. A pleasant room. BRI3 HAGG, SMI

C **Simple Simon.** E. Denton. 4b., 1g., chorus. Sc. Village green. DENU

C **Simple Simon.** E. R. Jasspon and B. Becker. 7b., 5g., chorus. Sc. A country road. JAR

Simple soul, The. L. Anderson. 2m., 2w. Sc. Sitting room. ANDE

Simple soul, A. V. Smith. 3m., 1w. Sc. Living room. NICH

Simultaneous sketches. H. Simpson. Farce. 4m., 3w. Sc. Interior. SIMS

Sinbad the Seller. I. Brown. Pantomime. 4m., others. Sc. A corridor in front of Castle Bunkum. Sat. R. 140: 763–4, Dec. 26, 1925.

C **Sing-a-song man, The.** F. C. Comfort. 5b., 3g. Sc. Office. JAO

C **Sing-a-song-o'-sixpence.** E. Denton. 3b., 2g. Sc. Counting house. DENU

C **Sing a song of sixpence.** J. E. Krohn. 28c. Sc. King's kitchen. KRS

Singapore spider, The. E. Finnegan. Thriller. 3m., 2w. Sc. Interior. JOHM

Singer, The. P. Pearse. 5m., 2w. Sc. Wide clean kitchen of a country house. CANF

C **Singing pipes.** V. Olcott. 4b., 2g., chorus. Sc. Judean hills near Jerusalem. OLF

Singing sands, The. G. Bottomley. 4m., 1w. Sc. Vacant space. BOTT

J **Singing-school teacher, The.** H. O. Boggs. 3g. Sc. Rude schoolroom. BOGG

Sinking. E. Hendrie and S. Caldwell. 5w. Sc. Dancing academy. FRER

Sinner beloved, A. P. E. Osgood. 8b., 1g., chorus. Sc. Market place. FED, OSGO

Sintram of Skaggerak. S. Cowan. 1m., 1w. Sc. A high bare cliff on the edge of the shore. CLS, COW

J **Sir Cleges.** F. Chesterton. 12b., 6g. Sc. Hall of ancient English castle. CHES

J **Sir David wears a crown.** S. Walker. Fantasy. 10b., 5b. Sc. Gateway to King's castle. APPL, SHAQ

Sir Folly. D. A. Lord. 3m., 2w., chorus. Sc. Outward gate of the courtyard of a ducal palace. LOR

Sir Ronald Neville, Bart. R. L. Melville. Comedy. 4m., 2w. Sc. Sitting room in a New York hotel. BANN

C **Sir safety scout.** F. E. Peterson. Many c. Sc. Throne room. Norm. Inst. 36 : 80, Oct. 1927.

Sire de Malétroit's door, The. R. L. Stevenson. 4m., 1w. Sc. Outer hall of mansion. HAP

Sister Clare. L. Housman. 6m., 1w. Sc. Bare stable-like interior. HOUS

Sister Death. L. Housman. 10m., chorus. Sc. 1 Outside the cell of St. Francis. 2 Sc. Inside. HOUS

Sister Gold. L. Housman. 7m. Sc. A hillside road leading up into forest. HOUS

Sister of Pierrot, The. B. J. Thompson. 2m., 4w. Sc. Woods. Player's M. 2 : 17–20, Jan.–Feb. 1926.

Sister who walked in silence, The. P. Johnson. 2m., 2w. Sc. Room in lonely cottage on the marsh. FREL

J **Sisterly scheme, A.** H. C. Bunner. 2b., 3g. Sc. Porch of a large summer hotel in Maine. HAP

Sisters, The. G. Bottomley. 3w. Sc. A bedroom. BOTT

Sisters, The. I. L. Peretz. Comedy. 3m., 4w. Sc. A remote corner of a city square. BLP

Sisters' tragedy, The. R. Hughes. 2m., 3w. Sc. Hall in house in the country used as living room. HUR

Sisters under their skin. J. H. Turner. Farce. 2m., 2w. Sc. Boudoir. TURN

J **Six.** T. Schwartz. 18b. Sc. Courtroom. DAZ

Six hundred chicks! J. Gibson. Comedy. 1m., 3w. Sc. Sitting room of farm in Scotland. WIN

C **Six little mice and yellow pussy.** 8c. Sc. Cellar on the road to the coal bin. CUD

C **Six S's admit Ferdie, The.** H. O. Boggs. 7b. Sc. Hayloft of barn. BOG

C **Six S's hold a session, The.** H. O. Boggs. 6b. Sc. Hayloft. BOG

C **Six S's in action, The.** H. O. Boggs. 6b., 4g. Sc. Classroom. BOG

C **Six S's organize, The.** H. O. Boggs. 6b. Sc. Barn loft. BOG

J **Six who pass while the lentils boil.** S. Walker. 10b., 5g. Sc. Kitchen. APPL

16,000 years ago. Farce. 3m. Sc. Interior. FIT

Sixth hat, The. L. P. Martin. Farce. 6m., 4w. Sc. Living room. ELD

Sixty days or else. W. Richardson Comedy. 6m., 2w. Sc. Living room of summer home. PAIN

Skeletons and dynamite. A. L. Kaser. Farce. 2m. Sc. Street. KAS

J **Sketch for home mechanics.** P. V. Wilcox. 3b. Ind. Arts M. 17 : 202, June 1928.

Skim milk. A. C. D. Riley. 3m., 2w. Sc. Living room of a comfortable bungalow in California during the world war. RIL

Slave, The. E. Yates. 2m., 2w. Sc. Living room. DES, YATE

Slave from Egypt, The. J. Ish-Kishor. 8 char. Sc. Palestinian interior. FREN

Slave with two faces, The. M. C. Davies. Fanciful. 3m., 4w., chorus. Sc. A wood through which runs a path. PEN

C **Sled for Christmas, A.** M. Christensen. 3b., 3g. Sc. Billy's home. CHR

C **Sleeping beauty, The.** M. E. Clifford. 8b., 8g. Sc. Playroom of the Princess' suite. LON

J **Sleeping beauty.** S. L. Cummins. Burlesque. 3b., 2g. Sc. A forest at morning. CUM2, SCH2

C **Sleeping beauty dines with the Prince.** M. Davis and M. T. Lofgren. 1b., 10g. Sc. Palace of a prince. Prim. Educ. 45 : 125, 135, Oct. 1927.

Sleeping-car, The. W. D. Howells. Farce. 1m., 2w. Sc. One side of a sleeping car. HAT

Sleeping out. D. Titheradge. Farce. 4m. Sc. Bench on the embankment. TITO

Slim Jim and the hoodoo. T. Barnes. Farce. 5m. Sc. Grocery store. FIT

Slippers of Aphrodite, The. W. Fernand. Fantasy. 4m., 4w., chorus. Sc. Forest beside the sea. FER

C **Slippers of Cinderella, The.** G. Robertson. 1b., 8g. Sc. Very shabby parlour. MOSA

Slippers that broke of themselves, The. M. Drennan. 5m., 3w. Sc. Cinderella's apartment in royal palace. Poet Lore 37 : 258–273, Summer 1926.

Slippin'. E. Finnegan. 1m., 1w. Sc. Living room. DENI

Slow but sure. M. S. Smith. 2m., 2w. Sc. A very comfortable living room. Drama 17 : 138–140, Feb. 1927.

Slow train to Wolverhampton, The. R. Jeans. Farce. 3m., 1w. Sc. Entrance hall of an hotel. JEA

Slump, The. F. L. Day. 2m., 1w. Sc. Dingy room. FOR4

Small down payment, A. G. Savage. Farce. 5m., 2w. Sc. Interior of a smart and newly furnished apartment. HUO

Small hour, A. B. Gates. Comedy. 2m., 2w. Sc. Library in London house. GAT

Smart set, The. R. Jeans. Farce. 4m., 5w. Sc. Chambers in the Albany. JEP

Smarty's party. G. Kelly. 1m., 3w. Sc. Drawing room of Park Avenue apartment in N. Y. KEL

Smile, please. H. C. Sargent. Farce. 2m., 1w. Sc. Photographic Studio. SARM

Smith family, The. T. A. Funk. 3m., 2w. Sc. Kitchen. BART

Smith mystery, The. L. L. Wilson. 3w. Comedy. Sc. Interior. DRA

Smithfield preserv'd or the divill a vegetarian. I. Brown. Comedy. 6m., 3w. Sc. A public place. London Mercury 12 : 477–491, Sept. 1925.

Smouldering fires. I. J. Crandell. 1m., 2w. Sc. Living room. BAK

Snake, The. C. Fitzhugh. 2m., 2w. Sc. Living room. FITZ

Snake charmer, The. A. Bennett. 2m., 1w. Sc. A richly furnished living room. FRE6

Snake eater, The. K. Nicholson. Comedy. 2m., 1w. Sc. Carnival grounds. FRE4

J **Sneakin's.** L. C. VanDerveer. 9b. Sc. Group of scout tents. VAN

J **Snip the tailor.** V. Bedford. 5b. Sc. Living room. FREL

Snobs. E. T. Thurston. Comedy. 4m., 1w. Sc. Living room. FREL

Snobson's stag-party. L. C. Tises. Farce. 12m. Sc. Parlor. FIT

Snow queen, The. H. E. Davis. 1g., 3b. Sc. Throne of snow queen. Delineator 109: 17–18, Aug. 1926.

J **Snow witch, The.** C. D. Mackay. 2b., 4g., chorus. Sc. Home in Russia. HERV, ROS7, ROS8

C **Snowbound for Christmas.** E. I. Mackenzie. 4b., 4g. Sc. Interior. PAIN

C **Snowflakes and the fairies, The.** C. J. Denton. 25g. Sc. Stage. HALI

C **Snow-man, The.** M. Corell and I. Liccione. 5b., 1g. Sc. A street. STRU

Snowy night, A. R. Bracco. 1m., 2w. Sc. Room in a ground floor tenement. SHAT

So good. C. Roberts. Comedy. 2m., 2w. Sc. Living room in House at Peaceholm. FREL, FREN

So that's that. J. V. A. Weaver. 2m., 2w. Sc. Small flat in N. Y. city. APPL

So this is Paris green! K. Nicholson. 2m., 1w. Sc. Miserable garret in Paris. NICG

C **So this is school.** M. Irish. Sc. Any number of c. Sc. School room. IQ

So you're going to Paris. W. Meredith. Comedy. 3m., 6w. Sc. Living room. DRA, ELD

Sob sister, The. P. Dickey and B. Dickey. 3m., 1w. Sc. A room over the curio shop of Wong Lee in San Francisco. FREN

Social aspirations. H. S. Griffith. Comedy. 5w. Sc. Bedroom. FIT

Social balance. S. Fayden. Satirical comedy. 2m., 2w. Sc. Dandy sitting room in city mansion. NICA

Social inconvenience, A. D. Titheradge. Farce. 2m., 1w. Sc. Sitting room. TITU

Society notes. D. R. West. Comedy. 3m., 3w. Sc. Handsome morning room. APPL, NICA

Socks and social engagements. F. C. Gardner. 1m., 1w. Sc. Interior. GAQ

J **Socrates the philospher.** M. R. Hofer. 9b., 1g., chorus. Sc. Garden. HOF

Socrates up to date. I. H. Myers. 2m. Atlantic M. 143: 78–83, Jan. 1929; 250–253, Feb. 1929.

Soft shoulders. F. L. Mitchell. 2m., 3w. Sc. Living room. ELD

Soil. M. Portner. 4m., 1w. Sc. Mountain resort in New York State. FREN

C **Sojourners.** I. J. Meaker and A. J. Harnwell. 5b., 2g. Sc. Leyden 1620. SCH2, World Review 5: 152–153, Nov. 21, 1927.

Solemn pride. G. R. Leighton. 9w. Sc. Sitting room in New England village, 1865. BAK

Solomon. G. H. Ruthenburg. 6m., 1w., others. Sc. Paved court in Jerusalem. Poet Lore 36: 600–609, Winter 1925.

Solomon sings. M. T. Johnson. 2m., 5w., chorus. Sc. Interior of country schoolhouse. JOHD

Solomon's song. H. Kemp. 3m., 1w. Sc. Throne room of Solomon's palace about 1000 B. C. KEM, SHAQ

J **Solon the legislator.** M. R. Hofer. 2b., 5 chorus groups. Sc. Rocky height. HOF

J **Some good summer reading.** E. R. Baird. 5 char., chorus. Sc. Out of doors. THOQ

J **Some little mother.** H. Bacon. 1b., 11g., chorus. Sc. Living room. ELD

Some party. K. L. Roberts. 4m., 4w. Sc. Country club dining room. Sat. Eve Post 199 : 32–3, 52 + , Apr. 23, 1927.

Some showers. W. P. Ridge. 2m., 1w. Sc. Tree in Regent's Park London. RID

J **Some there are who remember.** F. Shay. 2m., 1w. Sc. Land of the living dead. SHAB

Somebody. R. L. Melville. Tragedy. 3m., 1w. Sc. Sitting room of cottage within prison grounds. BANN

C **Somebody's boy.** E. M. McCollum. 2b., 1g. Sc. Just outside the railroad station. MACC

Someone to whisper to. G. Cannan. 1m., 3w. Sc. Dining room of a London flat. CANN

Something beautiful. A. M. Harvey. Romance. 4m., 3w. Sc. Interior London slum. DE

Something different. P. Black. 3w. Sc. In a Jewish home. BLO

J **Something wrong somewhere.** L. J. Lugsdin. Adapted from Dickens. Little Dorrit. 2b., 2g. Sc. Living apartment on the Grand Canal, Venice. JON

J **Song in the heart, The.** M. B. Rodney and G. E. Taylert. 16 char. Sc. A kitchen. TAX

C **Song in the heart, The.** A. Stevenson. 1b., 6g. Sc. House. STEV3

C **Song of the ripening grave, The.** L. K. Dolan. Dancing. 6b., 8g. Sc. Out of doors. DOL

C **Sonny Santa Claus.** G. Richardson. 4b., 6g. Sc. Interior. BAK

Son's wife, The. J. S. Knapp. 3m., 4w. Sc. Home on the farm. BAK

Sordid world, This. C. H. W. Foster. Comedy. 5m., 3w. Sc. Room with glowing fire. FOS

So's your old antique! C. Kummer. Comedy. 4m., 2w. Sc. Antique shop. FRE4

Soul made clean, A. D. T. George. Comedy. 1m., 2w. Sc. Bedroom. UNW3

C **Soul of the flag, The.** L. K. Dolan. 36c., chorus. DOL

Sounding brass. E. H. Bierstadt. Tragedy. 3m., 1w. Sc. Warden's room of a prison. APPL

Sounds that pass in the night. L. A. Ward. Farce. 4m., 5w. Sc. Living room. HEL, PENN

Soup stone, The. W. A. Stigler. 4m., 6w. Sc. Green before an Irish farm village. Poet Lore 35 : 91–99, Spring 1924.

Southern tonic, A. M. H. Hickman. Comedy. 1m., 6w. Sc. Poorly furnished cabin in the mountains. MARC

Spadassin. M. Major. Fantastic tragedy. 2m., 1w. Sc. Unkept den. Poet Lore 36 : 265–279. Summer 1925.

C **Spare the trees!** M. Corell and I. Liccione. 1b., 2g. Sc. Woods. STRU

Spark, The. E. Pailleron. Comedy. 1m., 2w. Sc. A French garden. Poet Lore 38 : 373–400, Autumn 1927.

J **Spark plugs.** E. E. Olson. Comedy. 2b., 1g. Sc. Parlor. BAK

Sparkin'. E. P. Conkle. 1m., 3w. Sc. Kitchen in farmhouse. COM

Sparkling Lucia. I. J. Crandall. 4w. Sc. Sitting room. BAK

Sparks—an in between. F. W. Erdman. 1m., 8w. Sc. Old Ladies Home. FREN

C **Sparrows in the hat, The.** A. Stevenson. 6b., 5g., chorus. Sc. Near the school house. STEV1

Spatial episode, A. M. Hyman. 5m. Sc. Bookshop. Bermondsey Book 2 : 81–85, Mar. 1925.

C **"Speak to the earth and it shall teach thee."** M. W. Fenner. 14c. Sc. Out of doors. JOHE

J **Speaking of exercise.** R. Whitbeck. 2b., 6g. Sc. Silver Anchor tea room. TWO

Speaking terms. R. Pertwee. 3m., 2w. Sc. Living room. FRE6

Speaking to father. G. Ade. Comedy. 3m., 2w. Sc. Interior. FREN

Specimen, A. H. F. Rubinstein. 1m., 1w. Sc. In the flower walk. RUB

C **Spelling match, The.** J. A. Baxter. 8c. Sc. School room. PAIS

Spiced wine. W. K. Jones. 1m., 2w. Sc. Small dark heavily curtained room in Peru in 16th century. Poet Lore 36 : 84–95, Spring 1925.

C **Spick and span.** G. B. Donnelly. 3g., chorus. Sc. Curtains or scenes. DON

C **Spider and the fly, The.** K. L. Carver. 3c. Prim. Educ. 32 : 381, 389, 397, June 1924.

Spinister from choice, A. P. Phelps. Comedy. 2m., 2w. Sc. In Connecticut in 1750. FREN

Spirals. M. L. Nelson. 3m., 2w. Sc. Exterior. NORT

C **Spirit of beauty, The.** Y. Klein and F. Schwarz. 7c. Sc. Any interior. KLE

Spirit of Christmas, The. G. E. Craig. 9 adults, 7c. Sc. Any room or hall with curtained stage. WOM

C **Spirit of Christmas via Santa Claus, The.** F. A. Gardner. 2 adults, 4c. Sc. Interior. GAP

J **Spirit of Hadassah, The.** M. Wolfson. 19 char. Sc. Living room. BLO

C **Spirit of Independence, The.** Y. Klein and F. Schwarz. 6c., many chorus groups. Sc. Any interior. KLE

Spirit of labor, The. M. Dreier. 11 char. Sc. Interior. WOM

Spirit of Lincoln, The. E. Gibson. 5w. Sc. Dining room in house in 1864. GIB

J **Spirit of the American Constitution, The.** G. L. Ermatinger and A. K. Donaldson. 19b. Sc. Meeting room of constitutional convention. Norm. Inst. 34 : 74, 76, Sept. 1925.

J **Spirit of the Christ, The.** a Christmas Eve story. A. L. Powell. 14b., 7g., or more. Sc. Living room. Int. J. of Rel. Educ. 1 : 40–43, Nov. 1924.

C **Spirit of the Red Cross, The.** Y. Klein and F. Schwarz. 10c. Sc. Any interior. KLE

C **Spirit of the tree, The.** A. Curtis. 4b., 5g. Sc. In the meadow. CURT

Spirit rappers, The. M. Sand. Tr. by B. Hughes and G. Hughes. 5m., 1w. Sc. A hotel. SA

C **Spirits of Autumn.** R. Strutton. 3g. Sc. Outdoor. STRU

C **Spirits of Spring.** R. Strutton. 3g. Sc. Garden scene. STRU

C **Spirits of Summer.** R. Strutton. Any number of c. Sc. Outdoors. STRU

C **Spirits of the day.** L. K. Dolan. With song and dance. 12b., 24g. Sc. Stage. DOL

C **Spirits of winter.** R. Strutton. Any number of c. Sc. Indoor Christmas setting. STRU

Splendid offer, A. G. E. King. Comedy. 5w. Sc. Sitting room, mid-victorian. Drama 16: 213-215, 235, 237, Mar. 1926.

Sponge, The. A. C. D. Riley. Comedy. 2m., 3w. Sc. Room in a furnished studio apartment. RIL

J **Spooky Hallowe'en, The.** G. Sorenson. Comedy. 3b., 3g. Sc. Living room of a haunted house. SOR

Spot. G. E. Jennings. Comedy. 1m., 1w. Sc. Attic. FREL

Spot Cash. E. H. Yates. 2m., 1w. Sc. Corner of a metropolitan cafeteria. YATE

C **Spreading Christmas cheer.** 4b., 4g. Sc. Stage. JOHC

J **Spreading Christmas cheer.** P. M. Swinton. 2b., 3g. Sc. Interior, rich. SW

J **Spreading the news.** Lady Gregory. 7b., 3g. Sc. Outskirts of a fair. BRI3, FIN, FRE1; GREP, PEN, Golden Book 2: 355-362, Sept. 1925.

Sprightly widow Bartlett, The. P. Phelps. 3m., 2w. Sc. Colonial home. FREN

Spring! C. C. Clements. 2m., 1w. Sc. A bench in a park. CLP, JOHN

C **Spring.** M. E. Marcy. 3b., 5g. Sc. Dwarf land, among spring flowers. Norm. Inst. 34: 70-71, Mar. 1925.

Spring cleaning. E. W. Peattie. 1m., 1w. Sc. Abundantly stored attic of a fine old house. PEA

J **Spring dreams.** M. A. Chaffe. Fantasy. 2b., 1g. Sc. A bit of the out of doors. BAK

C **Spring fantasy, A.** M. E. Steele. Many c. Sc. Garden. Norm. Inst. 38: 60, 62, June 1929.

Spring harvest. I. W. Wade. 1m., 2w. Sc. Squatter's hut. Southw. Review 10: 73-77, July 1925.

Spring in Bloomsbury. H. Brighouse. Comedy. 3m., 2w. Sc. Interior. BAK

C **Spring pageant, A.** J. L. Carter. Many c. Sc. Any platform. Int. J. of Rel. Educ. 2: 60-61, May 1926.

Spring sluicing. A. H. Ernst. 4m. Sc. Yukon valley in the early 90's. IS, LONG, Theatre Arts M. 12: 125-138, Feb. 1928.

C **Spring's awakening.** M. S. Butler. 8g., chorus. Sc. Out of doors. WHG1, Prim. Educ. 33: 332-333, May 1925.

C **Spring's flower garden.** V. R. Lehman. 22c. Sc. Garden. Prim. Educ. 45: 624-25, 639, 655, Apr. 1928.

J **Spring's heyday.** M. W. Sanders. 14 char. Sc. Hole of the Easter rabbit. ELD

C **S'prise party, The.** M. C. Johnson. 3g. Sc. Nursery. STRU

C **Spy, The.** A. Stevenson. Based on Cooper. The Spy. 7b. Sc. 1 Around a table in General Washington's headquarters. 2 Sc. Interior of colonial home. 3 Sc. Farm house. STEV4

J **Square pegs.** C. Bax. Fantasy satire. 2w. Sc. Exterior. JOHP, MACG

Square triangle, A. H. Simpson. Farce. 3m., 1w. Sc. Breakfast table. SIMN

Squaring it with the boss. J. C. McMullen. Comedy. 3m., 3w. Sc. Interior. MARC

C   **Stage and the fawn, The.** A. Stevenson. 3b. Sc. Forest. STEV2

Stalemate. H. Simpson. Farce. 3m., 1w. Sc. Corner of a dining-room in in an hotel. SIMN

Standish pride. P. Wilde. Fantasy. 2m., 1w. Sc. Kennel quarters attached to country residence. WILD

Stanley takes the business. E. B. Hauch. 4m., 13w. Sc. Office. ELD

Star, The. The Bilsen miracle play. 20m., 3w. Sc. Stage. HAQ

J   **Star, The.** M. Creagh-Henry. 9 char. Sc. A tavern. CRE

C   **Star, The.** B. P. Lane. 4b., 3g. Sc. Outer court of an Assyrian palace. LAN

J   **Star dust.** A. Gerstenberg. 3b., 3g. Sc. Side veranda of a summer hotel. DAZ

C   **Star in the East, The.** A. L. Skinner. 10b., 1g. Sc. Hills outside Jerusalem. SK

C   **Star of Bethlehem, The.** R. A. Letchworth. Any number of c. Sc. Out of doors. JOHE

J   **Star of the east, The.** H. W. Githens. 9b., 1g. Sc. On the desert. GITH

J   **Stars, The.** A. C. Darlington. 5g. Sc. Room in a rich peasant's house. DAR

Stars and groceries, The. U. Cooke. 3m., 1w. Sc. Interior. FREN

J   **Starter, The.** E. Cornell. 3b., 2g. Sc. Interior. BAK

Starter, The. E. Spence. Comedy. 1m., 3w. Sc. Out of doors. LOC

State forbids, The. S. Cowan. 2m., 3w. Sc. One room dwelling. COW

Station X-M-A-S. R. Adkinson. 6w. Sc. Interior. DRA, ELD

Station Y.Y.Y.Y. B. Tarington. Farce. 3m., 3w. Sc. Interior. APPL, Ladies Home Journal 43 : 6–7, 200 + , May 1926.

J   **Steed in the senate, A.** L. Andreev. Many c. Sc. Roman senate. Living Age 322 : 498–507, Sept. 6, 1924.

C   **Stephen the first Christian martyr.** M. I. Stone. 4b., 4g., chorus. Sc. White back-ground. STON

Stepmother, The. A. Bennett. Farce. 2m., 2w. Sc. Interior. BAK, KM, KN, MAR1

Steppin' westward. J. Marks. 7m., 5w. Sc. A village square in North Wales. MARK

Stepping mother, The. L. K. Devendorf. Farce. 1m., 2w. Sc. Living-room. PENN

C   **"Stick to your bush,"** a Lincoln's Birthday playlet. O. J. Roberts. 7b. Prim. Educ. 34 : 110–111, Feb. 1926.

Stick-up, The. P. Loving. Fantastic. 3m. Sc. Interior. APPL

Still alarm, The. G. S. Kaufman. 5m. Sc. Hotel bedroom. FRE6

Still life. F. Molnar. 1m., 2w. Sc. Actress' apartment. MOL

Stockin' money. E. E. Dean. 2m., 2w. Sc. Kitchen. LON

Stoic, The. D. Titheradge. Farce. 2m., 2w. Sc. Room. TITF

Stoker, The. H. Brighouse. 4m., 2w. Sc. Captain's room on bridge of a vessel. FRE5

J   **Stolen prince, The.** D. Totheroh. Fanciful. 8b., 3g., chorus. Sc. Chinese fashion. TOT, WEB, Delineator 116 : 13, 71 + , June 1930; Drama 15 : 30–33, Nov. 1924.

Stone rolled away, The. J. W. Raine. 10m., 3w. Sc. Narrow low doorway of a tomb. RAI

Stork, The. P. Wilde. Farce. 3m., 1w. Sc. The next room. WILT

Storm. F. Ryerson. C. Clements. Tragedy. 2m., 1w. Sc. Combined living room and kitchen in shack. RY

Storm in a breakfast cup, A. E. Crawshay-Williams. Comedy. 2m., 1w. CRAA

J   **Storming of Torquilstone, The.** M. A. Butler. Adapted from Scott's Ivanhoe. 17b., 2g. Sc. Hall of castle. BUT

C   **Story-book ball, The.** L. K. Dolan. 11b., 13g. Sc. Ballroom of a castle. DOL

C   **Storybook frolics.** N. Flaurier. 7c. Sc. Schoolroom. FIU

C   **Story book pals.** L. Allen. 16b., 9g. Sc. Indoors or out. PAIN

C   **Storybook frolics.** N. Flaurier. 7c. Sc. Schoolroom. FIU

Story books before the judge, The. J. Willets. Many c. Wilson Bull 6 : 127–130, Oct. 1931.

Story of a story, The. P. E. Osgood. 10 char. Sc. Screens. OSGO

C   **Story of Ali Cogia, The.** A. Stevenson. 10 char., chorus. Sc. House of a merchant in Bagdad. STEV3

C   **Story of clothing, The.** J. Welling and M. Hutchings. Many c. Sc. Modern living room. School Arts M. 23 : 342–252, Feb. 1924.

J   **Story of Joseph, The.** R. Kimball. 25b. Sc. Soft curtains or screens. KIM

J   **Story of old Bethlehem, A.** N. K. Brown. 10b., 3g. Sc. Place of Presentation only light enough for easy seating. ABI

C   **Story of silk, The.** L. K. Dolan. 15c. Sc. Plain stage setting. DOL

C   **Story Terrace.** F. E. Atchinson. 6b., 6g. Sc. Dimly lighted stage. SAL, WIMT

J   **Strange lands.** F. Gardner. 1m., 2b. Sc. Interior. GAQ

C   **Stranger, The.** F. E. Eakman. 10c. Sc. A public library. EAK

Stranger, The. I. Gandy. Comedy. 3m., 2w. Sc. Village grocery shop. DE

Stranger, The. A. E. Wills. 2m., 1w. Sc. Interior of cottage in the mountains in North Dakota. FREN

C   **Stranger child, The.** F. Clemans. 3b., 2g., others. Sc. Peasant home. Norm. Inst. 39 : 60, 62, Dec. 1929.

Strategy. L. Anderson. 4m. Sc. Living room of a large country place. DET

C   **Straw stack, The.** S. G. Clark. 3b., 2g. Sc. Hay stack. Norm. Inst. 39 : 42, 78, Oct. 1930.

Stray sheep. M. Creach-Henry. 2m., 2w. Sc. Interior. FREN

C   **Street fair, The.** N. Flaurier. Any number of c. Sc. Stage. FJ

C   **Street of hearts, The.** D. M. Davis. Fantasy. 8b., 7g. Sc. Street. OZ

Street singer, The. J. Echegaray. 1m., 3w., chorus. Sc. Street. SHAT, Golden Book 5 : 192–196, Feb. 1927.

J   **Stricken traveler, A.** H. W. Githens. 8b., 1g. Sc. In the house of Annas in Jerusalem. GITH

Strictly private. M. T. Applegarth. 11 char. Sc. Living room. APN

C   **Striking in the New Year.** N. Flaurier. 4c. Sc. Stage. Norm. Inst. 34 : 67, Jan. 1925.

String of pearls, A. C. S. Pike. 2m., 1w. Sc. Living room in N. Y. city apartment. DET

Stringing beads. L. S. Pelee. 3m., 1w. Sc. Interior of bead shop in Italy. Poet Lore 39 : 295–305, Summer 1928.

Strings. R. Knight. Comedy. 2m., 2w. Sc. Stage of a theatre. LONG

Stroke of mine, The. E. O. Jones. Burlesque. 6m., 1w. Sc. Living room. FREN

Strong situation, A. H. C. Sargent. Farce. 1m., 2w. Sc. Cosily furnished drawing room. SARP

J **Strong tower, The.** A. C. Darlington. 2b., 2g. Sc. Inside a tower room. DAR

Stronger force, The. E. W. Trout. 2m., 2w., chorus. Sc. Library of the house of Governor Livingston. CAT2

Strongest man, The. E. H. Sullivan. 4m., 8w. Sc. Parlor. FOR4

C **Struggle between the Plebians and the Patricians in the Roman senate, The.** S. I. Shearer. Many c. Sc. Roman forum. Pop. Educ. 42 : 404, 413–415, Mar. 1925.

Strutham amateurs present, The. M. Constanduros. 3m., 4w. Sc. Drawing room in town hall. FREL

J **Student Council play.** Rawlings Junior High School. 8 char. Sc. In the corridor. RAW

J **Stupid Christmas, The.** G. Sorenson. Comedy. 2b., 2g. Sc. Beautifully furnished living-room. SOR

Sub Rosa. E. W. Sandford. Burlesque. 2m., 2w. Sc. Shop of old Toyman. FREN

Subscription clinic, The. M. T. Applegarth. 14 char. Sc. Doctor's office. APN

J **Substitute, The.** F. Coppée. 4m. Sc. Small attic room. HAP

Suburbanism. R. Parish. Comedy. 3m., 4w. Sc. Interior. APPL

Successful dentist, A. S. J. Levy. Comedy. 5m., 2w. Sc. Dental office. LEU

J **Successful evangelism in mission fields.** M. M. Browne. 9 char. Sc. Campfire. THOQ

Such a charming young man. Z. Akins. Comedy. 6m., 3w. Sc. Restaurant. FRE1

Such a little Swede. S. C. McMahon. 2m., 1w. Sc. Dining room. ELD

Such a quiet evening. E. L. Walton. Comedy. 1m., 3w. Sc. Living room. PENN

Such a surprise. L. A. Ward. Comedy. 3m., 3w. Sc. Cluttered up living room. HEL

Such as we can't use. B. E. Palmer. 12w. Sc. Cheery living room. ELD

Such is love. L. Anderson. 3m., 1w. Sc. Porch. ANDE

Such things happen in books. T. Wilder. 3m., 1w. Sc. Old house in a New Hampshire village. WILY

Sugar cane. F. H. Wilson. 3m., 2w., 1c. Sc. Small room in an old-fashioned frame house. LOC

Sugar Daddy. R. L. Melville and L. Ryan. 2m., 1w. Sc. Sitting room. BANN

Sugar for tea. K. Dickerson. Comedy. 15 char. Sc. Japanese home. MARC

Suicide. C. Seiler. Farce. 2m., 1w. Sc. Boardwalk. SEI

Sumida river, The. Motomasa. 2m., 2w., chorus. Sc. Banks of the Sumida River in Japan. STOP

C **Summer day dream, A.** E. E. Olson. 15b., 15g. Sc. Lawn. JOHG

C **Summer is calling.** N. A. Smith. Many c. Sc. Any schoolroom. Amer. Child 14: 22–25, June 1929.

Summer morning in June, A. E. Vermazen. 3m. Sc. Empty room. KAM

Summoning of Everyman. P. E. Osgood. 20 char. Sc. Church or pulpit platform. OSF

Sun, The. J. Galsworthy. 2m., 1w. Sc. On a stile close to a river. GAL

Sun-cold. C. Glick. 2m., 4w. Sc. Living room of a farmhouse in Iowa. FREN, Poet Lore 36: 280–293, Summer 1925.

Sun is coming out, The. N. S. Russell. 3m., 3w. Sc. Kitchen of a farm home in the middle west. FARQ

Sun machine. C. Morley. 1m., 2w. Sc. Living room. Sat. R. Lit. 5: 461, Dec. 8, 1928.

C **Sunday at grandmother Field's.** P. F. Ring. 2b., 3g. Sc. Parlor of home in 1860. Prim. Educ. 45: 654, Apr. 1928.

Sundial, The. E. Pillot. Poetic. 4m., 4w., 2c., chorus. Sc. An old garden. FRE3

Sunny morning, A. S. Quintero and J. Alvarez. Comedy. 2m., 2w. Sc. Corner of path in Madrid. Golden Book 12: 106–109, Aug. 1930.

Sunrise. E. W. Peattie. 3m., 2w. Sc. Mountain top. PEA

Sunset. J. K. Jerome. Comedy. 3m., 3w. Sc. Interior. DRA, FIT, PENN

Supper for the dead. P. Green. 1m., 4w. Sc. Swamp in eastern North Carolina. GREE

Suppressed desires. S. Glaspell and G. C. Cook. 1m., 2w. Sc. A Studio apartment. GLA

Surprise for Helen, A. C. W. Crouch. 2m., 1w. Sc. Living room in apartment. UNW2

C **Surprise for Santa, A.** M. Kibbe. 4b., 3g. Sc. Interior. CJ

Surprise package, The. M. Crouch. 4m., 4w. Sc. Living room. BUG

Surprised. C. J. Denton. Comedy. 8w. Sc. Interior. PENN

Surprising bride, The. N. S. Russell. 2m., 2w. Sc. Living room. ELD

Suspended animation. C. Willis. Farce. 4m., 3w. Sc. Doctor's office. BUG

Suspicious drummer, The. G. Hughes. Burlesque. 2m., 3w. Sc. Interior. HUN

J **Suzanne skids.** C. Barr. Comedy. 12w. Sc. Corner alcove of house. LON

Swamp, The. R. K. Mackaye. 2m., 1w. Sc. Shack near New York. Drama 21: 19–20, 22, Mar. 1931.

C **Swat that fly!** P. M. Yates. Comedy. 14c., 6 dolls, chorus. Sc. Clean neat room. COMN

Sweeps of ninety-eight, The. J. Masefield. 7m., 1w. Sc. Inn. MASE, MASF

Sweet and twenty. F. Dell. Comedy. 3m., 1w. Sc. A cherry orchard. APPL, SHAQ

J **Sweet girl graduate, The.** 9b., 14g. Sc. Interior. DRA

C **Sweet times.** S. Young. Fanciful. 4b., 1g. Sc. Garden terrace. YOUN

Sweetheart! E. Dane. Fantasy. 4 voices. Sc. Curtains. DAN

Sweeties. M. Lee. Farce. 6m., 6w. LEE

Swift and Stella. C. E. Lawrence. 2m., 1w. Sc. Library of the Deanery of St. Patrick's in Dublin. Cornhill 60: 672–681, June 1926.

Switch on the moonlight. W. L. Bissell. Farce. 4m., 4w. Sc. Town hall at Plentonville. BIS

Switched. L. G. Peach. Farce. 1m., 2w. Sc. Flat in darkness. PAZ

Swollen angels. I. Brown. Revue. 2m., 3w. Sc. Flat. FRET

J   **Sword in the stone, The.** M. A. Butler. Adapted from Malory's Le Morte d'Arthur. 4b., chorus. Sc. Open space in the courtyard outside the greatest church in London. BUT

Sword of Damocles, The. F. F. Moore. 3m., 1w. Sc. Studio. MOO

Sword of the Samuri, The. T. D. Mygatt. 5m., 4w. Sc. Living room in the Saito home, Tokyo. FEDE

C   **Syncopated health trial, A.** H. M. Bowman. 8g. Hygeia 8: 944–946, Oct. 1930; Tex. Outlook 14: 37–8, Nov. 1930.

C   **Synthetic santa.** E. S. Lyon. 5b., 2g. Sc. Stage. SCH1

T

C   **Tabby's Thanksgiving doll.** R. Rice. 3b., 4w. Sc. A Colonial kitchen. BAI

Table set for himself, The. E. Wilbur. 4m., 5w. Sc. Small cottage on coast of Ireland. LON

Tables and chairs. M. C. Davies. 2m., 1w., chorus. Sc. A window looking into a garden. FRE5

Tables turned. J. Dawson. 1m., 2w. Sc. Interior. CART

C   **Tadpole school, The.** 15b. Sc. On the bank of a stream. BAK

Tai Chen. L. A. Cuddy. Tragedy. 4m., 2w. Sc. Little pavilion within royal gardens of Emperor's palace. BANN

C   **Taking the picnic to the shut-in.** American Junior Red Cross. 10g. Sc. Sick room. SCH4

C   **Tale from India, A.** F. B. Moore. Masque. 6b., 6g., chorus. Sc. Throne room. JAN

Tale of a mule's tail, The. L. Crites. Farce. 3m., 4w. Sc. Living room. ELD

Tale of a royal vest, The. F. Roskruge. Burlesque. 4m., 3w. Sc. Curtains or stage. DE

Tale of a shirt, The. R. T. Innes. Comedy. 3m., 2w. Sc. Living room. BANN

Tale of an embryo, The. M. Mannes. 3m., 1w. Sc. Stage of a theatre. Theatre Arts M. 11: 204–208, Mar. 1927.

Tale of the five mystic colors, A. E. Farmer. 13c. School Arts M. 30: 501–505, Apr. 1931.

Tale that is told, A. G. John. 2m., 2w. Sc. A cottage kitchen in a Derbyshire village. JOHA

C   **Tale the fire told, The.** N. Flaurier. Any number of c. Sc. Improvised fireplace. STRU

Talisman, The. A. W. Brotherton. 1m., 1w. Sc. In front of John Shakespeare's house. Poet Lore 40: 153–157, Spring 1929.

C   **Talking hour, The.** M. L. Conger. Many c. Sc. Park at night. Prim. Educ. 33: 714, 716, Dec. 1925.

Talks with Thomas Hardy. V. H. Collins. 2m., 1w. Sc. Drawing room. Bookman N. Y. 67: 1–6, Mar. 1928.

Tammy. E. Granville. Farce. 3m. Sc. Office. GRA

Tamura. 2m., chorus. Sc. Temple ground in Japan. STOP

Taps. L. G. Peach. Farce. 3m., 3w. Sc. Quiet country road. PAZ

J **Tara finds the door to happiness.** F. C. Means. 3b., 9g. Sc. Village street in India. FRIE

C **Tardy town.** E. Preston. 10c. Sc. Interior. PRES

C **Tattered Tillie of Toy Town.** P. Dickerson. 12c. Sc. Any little girl's playroom. MARC

Tatters. R. Burton. 4m. Sc. Lawyer's chambers in a typical American city. RIC

Tatyana Riepin. A. Tchekhov. Trans. by S. S. Koteliansky. 14m., 6w. Sc. Cathedral church. London Mercury 12 : 579–97, Oct. 1925.

Taxi. A. C. D. Riley. Comedy. 1m., 1w. Sc. Playshop. NORT, Drama 16 : 177–178, Feb. 1926.

J **Taxi.** L. C. Van Derveer. 7b. Sc. Out of doors. VAN

Tea. W. G. Carson. Comedy. 1m., 4w. Sc. Interior. BAK, PHIJ

Tea and gingerbread. M. S. Beagle. 2m., 2w. Sc. Living room at Mary Washington's Home at Fredericksburg in 1793. SAG

Tea and rice cakes. M. S. Oliver. 7m., 1w. Sc. A shallow stage. OLI

Tea fingers of François, The, a Christmas play of Old Provence. D. H. Oglesbee. 2m., 1w., 2b., 3g., 1c., others. Sc. Farmhouse kitchen. Drama 14 : 65–69, Nov. 1923.

Tea for six. W. Butterfield. 3m., 4w. Sc. Drawing room. Drama 16 : 134–6, 155–159, Jan. 1926.

Tea for the nurse. E. S. Millay. Satire. 1m., 2w. Sc. A very crowded room MIK

Tea for three. H. Simpson. Farce. 2m., 2w. Sc. Interior. SIMO

Tea leaves. E. A. Wright. Comedy. 2m., 3w. Sc At the tea table. BANN

C **Tea party in Bookland, A.** Y. Klein and F. Schwarz. 9c. Sc. Any interior. KLE

Tea-shop tattle. D. Titheradge. Farce. 2m., 2w. Sc. Any tea shop. TITO

Tea-time tempest. A. Halsey. Comedy. 7w. Sc. Drawing room. FREL

Teacher, kin I go home? H. L. Newton. 7m., 3w. Sc. Country school. BECK

Teaching Teresa. E. Crawshay-Williams. Comedy. 3m., 1w. Sc. Studio. CRAA

J **Teasing the teacher.** H. O. Boggs. 4b. School room. BOGH

C **Teddy had a toothache.** M. Christensen. 26c. Sc. Interior. DRA

Teja. H. Sudermann. Trans. by Archibald Alexander. 9m., 2w. Sc. King's tent in Italy. Golden Book 6 : 493–503, Oct. 1927.

Telegram, The. E. M. Cullis. 2m., 3w. Sc. Living room. BAK

Telegram, The. B. Herford. 2w. Sc. Telephone. Ladies Home Journal 42 : 205, Feb. 1925.

Telephone episode, A. M. Lane-Norcott. Revue. 2m. Sc. Street pavement. FRET

Telephone tattle! D. Titheradge. Farce. 2m., 3w. Sc. Hallway of an apartment house. TITU

Telephone tragedy, A. H. Simpson. Farce. 2m., 2w. Sc. Telephone booths. SIMS

Tell it to Venus. B. Abel. Comedy. 16 char., chorus. Sc. interior. WOM

Temptation, The. F. A. Kummer. 3m. Sc. Lonely mountains top east of Sea of Galilee. KU

Ten days later. C. Glick. Comedy. 5m., 1w., chorus. Sc. Small town not far from Jerusalem in 1 A. D. FREN

C **Ten fingers of François, The.** D. H. Oglesbee. 5b., 4g., chorus. Sc. 1 Kitchen. 2 Ravine in forest. SCH1

J **Ten good English commandments, The.** F. Rayfeld. Any number of c. Sc. Room. ELD

Ten righteous. E. DeHuff. 6m., 4w. Sc. Living room. DEH

Tender passion, The. V. Douglass. 4m., 1w. Sc. Thames embankment at night. FREN

Tenor, The. F. Wedekind. Trans. by André Tridon. Comedy. 5m., 3w. Sc. Large hotel room in city in Austria. Golden Book 5: 65–73, Jan. 1927.

Tenth man, The. E. E. Levinger. 10m., 1w. Sc. Shabby interior of small Jewish Synogogue. Drama 19: 204–206, 220–221, Apr. 1929.

Terrible meek, The. C. R. Kennedy. 2m., 1w. Sc. Darkness. KEN

Terrible woman, The. W. D. Steele. Comedy. 1m., 2w., 1b. Sc. Living room. STEE, Pict. R. 26: 6–7, 46+, Nov. 1924.

J **Tessa's tongue.** A. C. Darlington. 1b., 7g., chorus. Sc. Inside an Italian shop. DAR

Test, The. P. C. Marivaux. Trans. by W. K. Jones. 3m., 3w. Sc. French country home. Poet Lore 35: 531–561, Winter 1924.

Thank you, doctor. G. Emery. 3m., 2w. Sc. Doctor's reception room. EAT, LON

J **Thankful at last.** B. A. Call. 5g. Sc. Living room. ELD

C **Thankful lives up to her name.** E. E. Preston. Many c. Sc. Living room. Prim. Educ. 45: 204, 242, Nov. 1927.

Thanks, Awfully! J. L. Latham. Comedy. 1m., 15w. Several c. Sc. Living room of apartment. DRA

C **Thanksgiving after-dinner playlet, A.** E. D. Yale. Several c. Woman's Home Companion 54: 43, Nov. 1927.

J **Thanksgiving as usual.** M. Irish. 5b., 3g. Sc. Living room. IRI

C **Thanksgiving day movie, A.** E. M. Hermes. Pageant. 4b., 4g. Sc. Puritan interior. BECK

Thanksgiving dinner dance, The. M. G. Parsons. 6 char. Sc. Playroom. PARR

C **Thanksgiving in a cabin.** M. Bitney. 3b., 2g. Sc. Cabin. BIT

C **Thanksgiving in the barnyard.** M. Corell and I. Liccione. 10c. Sc. Barnyard. STRU

J **Thanksgiving on Hickory slope.** M. Irish. 3b., 3g. Sc. Living room. BAK

C **Thanksgiving play.** M. S. Blaisdell. Many c. Sc. Any stage. World R. 3: 152–153, 157, Nov. 22, 1926.

C **Thanksgiving play, A.** H. and M. Hastings. 5b., 6g. Sc. Outdoors. Prim. Educ. 46: 213, Nov. 1928.

Thanksgiving pumpkin, The. M. G. Parsons. 4c. Sc. Stage. PARR

J **Thanksgiving service, A.** M. M. Russell. 1b., 1g., chorus. Sc. In the wilderness. RUS

J **Thanksgiving turkey, The.** A. Curtis. 3b., 2g. Sc. General store. CURT

C **Thanksgiving with Mother Goose.** G. Lloyd. 45c. LLO

C **Thanksgiving wonders.** F. Cavanah. 11 char. Sc. Workshop of old doll maker. ELD

J **That awful letter.** E. I. Mackenzie. Comedy. 5g. Sc. Interior. PAIN

C **That calf.** M. T. Johnson. 4b., 1g. Sc. Simple farm kitchen. Norm. Inst. 33: 68, June 1924.

That 'ere line fence. M. Irish. 2m. Sc. Out of doors. CAT2

That upper forty. M. Herrick and H. H. Hudson. 4m., 2w. FREN

"That's my hat!" D. Hobart. Farce. 7m. Sc. Banquet. FREL

That's what they all say. I. P. Richardson. Comedy. 3m., 5w. Sc. Living room. ELD

Theatre, The. H. F. Rubinstein. 2m., 12w., chorus. Sc. Back of Dress circle of a London theatre. RUB

Theatre of the soul, The. N. N. Yevreinov. 5m., 4w. Sc. Any interior. DIC3

Theatre ticket agency, The. M. Lee. Farce. 5m., 2w. Sc. Street with counter for the sale of theatre tickets. LEE

Their anniversary. A. C. D. Riley. Comedy. 2m., 3w. Sc. Garden side of house in a suburb of a big city. RIL

Their appointed rounds. R. G. Yerkes. 4m. Sc. Interior of air mail office. DET

C **Their choice.** O. V. Roe. 3b., 2g. Sc. Any platform. FJ

Their day. H. Kemp. 8m., 1w. Sc. Huge cave. KEM

C **Their first meeting.** R. Woodman. 5b., 1g. Sc. Wood near Jamestown in 1609. Norm. Inst. 39: 42, 76–77, Sept. 1930.

Their husband. A. Gerstenberg. 4w. Sc. Interior. GER

Their own people. I. Landman. 6m., 3w. Sc. Interior. BLO

Them buns. E. Roskruge. 5w. Sc. Curtain settings—cottage kitchen. DE

C **Theodore Roosevelt.** Y. Klein and F. Schwarz. 7c. Sc. Any interior. KLE

C **Theodore Roosevelt—a great soldier.** A. M. Lütkenhans. 20c., 2 chorus groups. Sc. Interior. LUT

Theological interlude. J. M. Cain. 2m., 1w. Sc. Porch of summer resort boarding house. Amer. Mercury 14: 325–331, July 1928.

J **Theories and thumbs.** R. Field. 6g. Fantasy. Sc. Corner of Egyptian room in a city museum. FIF

"There is room," a Christmas play. C. C. Noble. 1m., 2w. Sc. Office of a hospital. Christian Cent. 47: 1525–1526, Dec. 10, 1930.

These women! these women! L. A. Biggers. Comedy. 6w. Sc. Interior. FREN

C **Theseus.** M. Oller and E. K. Dawley. 7b., 2g., chorus. Sc. Banquet hall. OLL

J **Theseus and the minotaur.** M. R. Hofer. 7b., 6g., 2 chorus groups. Sc. Stage with curtain drop. HOF

They called him a fool, a Columbus Day playlet. R. Rice. 9c. Sc. Wharf. Grade Teacher 47: 122, 140, 153, Oct. 1929.

They just won't talk. M. K. Reely. 2m., 3w., 1b. Sc. Interior. SAA

They say ——. E. E. Olson. 5w. Sc. Kitchen. BAK

They teach English. D. M. Macdonald. 1m., 7w. Sc. Interior of office of superintendent of schools. ELD

They that sit in darkness, a Christmas play. D. C. Wilson. 10b., 8b. Int. J. of Rel. Educ. 6: 25–26, 46–48, Nov. 1929.

They too. R. L. Askren. 3m., 3w. Sc. Interior. UNM2

They wanted publicity. L. M. Waldo. Comedy. Sc. Church parlor. ELD

J **They went to the game.** L. Crites. Comedy. 2b., 2g. Sc. Living room. AU

They were deceivers ever. R. L. Melville. Comedy. 9w. Sc. Interior. BANN

They who vote should read. E. G. Utterback. 4w., 3m., chorus. Sc. Schoolroom. ELDR

Thing, The. P. Wilde. 2m. Sc. A strange chemical laboratory. WILD

Things is that-a-way. E. P. Conkle. 2m. Sc. Country churchyard. COM, FRE4

Things of beauty. L. S. Beazley. 1m., 3w. Sc. Living room. PENN

Things that we can do, The. P. Holloway. 1m., 5w. Sc. Interior. HOL

Think before you speak. R. Jeans. Farce. 2m., 3w. Sc. Breakfast dining-living room. JES

Third angle, The. F. Ryerson. Comedy. 1m., 2w. Sc. Studio. SHAF

Third Shepherd's play, The. R. Mansel. 6m. Sc. Shepherd's house on the hills above Bethlehem. DR

Third soldier, The. W. F. Manley. 6m., 1w. Sc. Plain room. MANL

"Thirst." J. J. Bell. 3m. Sc. Dungeon in castle. PHIJ

Thirteenth trump, The. O. Kelley. Comedy. 2m., 1w. Sc. Detective bureau. KEK

Thirty minutes in a street. B. Mayor. 11m., 10w. Sc. Street. BRIR, HAMA, HERB

This love business. W. E. Wright. Comedy. 4m., 3w. Sc. Any fair-sized growing city. ELD

J **This-a-way and that-a-way.** G. Stenger. 6g. Sc. A dark wood. SAO

J **Thomas Olifant.** S. L. Cummins. Burlesque. 2b., 3g. Sc. Play room in castle. CUM3

Thomas the Rhymer. A. Scudder. 2m., 5w. Sc. Large high ceilinged room. SCU

Thomas, the twin. P. J. Stackhouse. 5m., 2w. Sc. House of John in Jerusalem. STAC

Thompson's luck. H. G. Glover. Tragedy. 3m., 1w. Sc. Farmhouse kitchen. APPL, SHAQ

C **Thor and his hammer.** M. A. Enloe. 2b., 1g. Sc. In the far north. ENL

Thornless crown, The. B. M. Russell. 7m., 1w., chorus. Sc. Throne room in Pilate's palace. BAK

Those absurd missionaries. I. M. R. Logie. 7m., 5w. Sc. Deck of a transpacific steamer. Int. J. of Rel. Educ. 6: 30–31, Feb. 1930.

Those Christmas gifts. L. Crites. 5w. Sc. Interior. BAK, BUG, ELD

Those class distinctions. J. J. Bell. Farce. 3m., 2w. Sc. Interior. BAK

Those terrible talkies. J. P. Heald. Farce. 1m., 2w. Sc. Wood drop or country lane. BAK

C **Those tricky words.** N. Flaurier. 4c. Sc. Sitting room. FIU

Those who saw him living. F. G. Joplin. Many char. Sc. Church. Int. J. of Rel. Educ. 2: 49–51, Mar. 1926.

Thou faithful servant. W. F. Manley. 3m., 3w. Sc. Village in the west. MANL

Thoughtless giving. L. P. Martin. Comedy. 9w. Sc. Sitting room. BUG

Thousand dollar reward, The. W. Darrow. Comedy. 3m., 3w. Sc. Railroad station. PENN

Thread of scarlet. J. J. Bell. 6m. Sc. Interior. BAK, MAR1

Three-a-day. H. S. Skidmore. 3m., 2w. Sc. Cheap theatrical hotel. UNM2

C **Three bears, The.** M. A. Enloe. 4b., 3g. Sc. Stage. ENL

Three black "Smiths." Farce. 3m. Sc. Interior. FIT

Three brass Bedouins. H. W. Hanemann. Burlesque. 3m., 1w. Sc. A garden in the wilderness. HANE

Three cans of beans. L. Y. Erskine. 9m. Sc. Room in hunting lodge. HUO

C **Three dwarf brothers, The.** P. Beard. 4b. Sc. Living room of a tumble-down house. BEA

C **Three foolish bears.** K. L. Carver. 5b., 1g. Sc. Out of doors. WHG1

Three friends. G. H. Faulkner. Melodrama. 3m. Sc. A poorly furnished room in White Chapel. LON

Three friends. C. Morley. Comedy. Sc. Interior. MORK

C **Three friends, The.** F. M. Morton. Pageant. Several c. Sc. Any platform. St. Nicholas 51 : 530–533, Mar. 1924.

Three from the earth. D. Barnes. 3m., 1w. Sc. Boudoir. BARN

Three gifts, The. F. Converse. 1m., 3w. Sc. Room in a tenement house. BOST

C **Three little runaway trees.** M. T. Cornish. Any number of b. and g. Sc. Outdoors. BECK

C **Three of a different kind.** E. Welff. 9b., 1g. Sc. In a big city. JAN

J **Three pills in a bottle.** R. L. Field. Fantasy. 3b., 2g. Sc. Room in a house. FIF

Three players, a fop and a Duchess. M. Hughes. 3m., 2w. Sc. Greenroom of the Theatre Royal in Drury Lane in 1743. FRE4

C **Three princesses, The.** E. R. Jasspon and B. Becker. 2b., 3g. Sc. Open green. JAR

Three souls in search of a dramatist. E. D. Schwartz. 1m., 4w. Sc. Study. Drama 16 : 247–8, 260, Apr. 1926.

Three strangers, The. T. Hardy. 9m., 4w. Sc. Living room in English cottage. HAP

Three strikes and out. L. Mack. Farce. 1m., 1w. Sc. Steps in grand stand. FRAQ

C **Three thanksgivings, The.** F. V. V. Vilas. 18b., 12g., chorus. Sc. Home. SCH2

C **Three trees, The.** G. Maynard. 9c. Sc. Forest. BAI, Kind. and First Grade 11 : 11–12, Dec. 1925.

Three visitors, The. M. Irwin. 4m., 4w. Sc. Bedroom of Madame de Montespan. Bermondsey Book 3 : 81–93, Sept. 1926.

C **Three wishes, The.** B. P. Lane. Fantasy. 6b., 3g. Sc. Not far from the seashore on a grassy space. LAN

J **Three wishes, The.** C. D. Mackay. 2b., 1g. Sc. Breton kitchen. ROS7

Three wishes. T. W. Stevens. Comedy. 5m. Sc. Hut on the firing line somewhere in France. STEU

Threshold, The. C. V. McCauley. 2m., 2w. Sc. Living room. SHAF

Thrice promised bride, The. C. Hsuing. 8m., 1w. Sc. Chinese stage. GOLD, SHAT, WEBB, Carolina Play Book 1 : 16–28, Des. 1928 ; Golden Book 2 : 230–236, Aug. 1925.

C **Thrift.** K. G. Christy. 4b., 10g. Norm. Inst. 38 : 62, Jan. 1929.

C **Thrift and spendthrift.** H. L. Wheeler. Many c. Prim. Educ. 46 : 362–63, 404, Jan. 1929.

C **Thrift fairie's bank, The.** L. H. VanDerveer. Any number of char. Sc. Home of Mother Goose. BAK

C **Through the calendar to Mount Vernon.** K. A. White. 5b., 4g. Prim. Educ. 33 : 122, 138–142, Feb. 1925.

C **To the rescue of Good English.** J. M. Burdine. 16c. Sc. Schoolroom. Norm. Inst. 37: 82, 84, Feb. 1928.

J **To whom Christ came.** M. B. Jone. Nativity. 23b., 9g., chorus. Sc. Screens. WOM

J **Toast and tea.** A. Dean. 9b., chorus. Sc. Stern deck of ship lying alongside Griffin's Wharf, Boston, in 1773. DAZ

Toast and tea. L. Larrimore. 8w. Sc. Interior of tea shop. BAK

Toast that we can drink, A. S. McCune. 4w. Sc. Cottage room in a French village 1793. BAK, YOU

Today is Monday. T. A. Brown. Satire. 6m., 10w. Sc. Schoolroom. ELD

J **Told in a Chinese garden.** C. Wilcox. 6b., 3g., 3 chorus groups. Sc. Chinese garden. FIN

Tom Taylor's troubles. H. O. Boggs. 3m., 3w. Sc. A schoolroom before books. BOGH

Tombs. M. R. Strong. 2m., 2w., 1c. Sc. Country graveyard in a coal mining town. OMI

Tombstone or washing machine. A. E. Vinje. Comedy. 2m., 4w. Sc. Electrical shop. ELD

Tommy-by-the-way. O. Down. 1m., 1w. Sc. A sunken road behind the forward trenches. DOW

Tommy meets his excuses. F. L. Mitchell. 4b., 2g. Grade Teacher 47: 119, 148, 149, Oct. 1929.

C **Tommy's dream of Christmas night.** A. M. Lütkenhans. 1b., 5g., chorus. Sc. Living room. LUT

C **Tommy's Thanksgiving dinner.** M. T. Cornish. Comedy. 6b., 12g. Sc. Interior. BECK

Tom's arrival. 3w. Interior. FIT

C **Tongue-cut sparrow, The.** J. Keenan. 2b., 3g., others. Prim. Educ. 44: 736+, May 1927.

C **Tongue-twisters tryst, The.** E. M. McCollum. 6b., 6g. Sc. Classroom. MACC

Tonic. M. Stedman. Farce. 1m., 1w. Sc. Living room in a poorly furnished flat. BANN

C **Tony, the color bearer.** E. G. Wallace. 5b., 10g., chorus. Sc. Interior. ELD

Tony Weller's beneficence. J. E. Jones. Adapted from Dickens. Pickwick Papers. 3m., 1w. Sc. English tavern. JON

Too busy. B. E. Wallace. 6w., several c. Sc. Old fashioned sitting room. FREN

C **Too fast for Pharaoh.** D. A. Lord. 14b. Sc. In a frame. LOQ

Too much Christmas. G. York. 4m., 4w. Farce. Sc. Living room. PAIN

Too much crime. R. Willis. 2m., 1w. Sc. Library. WIMS

J **Too much noise.** A. Burnstein. 10b. Sc. Living room. BLO

Too much of a good thing. T. S. Denison. Comedy. 3m., 6w. Sc. A parlor. BECK, PAIN

Too much trouble. A. Curtis. 6w. Sc. Sitting room. CUR

Too perfect husband, The. E. H. Cheever. Comedy. 3m., 2w. Sc. Drawing room in apartment. HEL, PENN

C **Tooth fairy, The.** E. Arnold. Fanciful. Any number of c. Sc. Interior. ELD

Top dog. S. Caldwell and E. Hendrie. 4w., 1 dog. Sc. Morning room. CAL

Topics for topers. R. Littell. 2m. New Rep. 46: 303–304, Apr. 28, 1926.

J **Topsy-turvy patriot, A.** B. A. Budell. 3b., 2g., chorus. Sc. Living room. ELD

J **Torch of Hellas, The.** A. C. Darlington. 21c., chorus. Sc. A grove. DAR

Torches. K. Raisbeck. 2m., 2w., 2b. Sc. Upper terrace walled on two sides by a low parapet. KM

C **Torn dresses, The.** A. Stevenson. 4b., 3g., chorus. Sc. A forest on a river. STEV1

J **Torquil MacFerron.** S. L. Cummins. Melodrama. 2b., 2g. Sc. Room in cottage. CUM3

J **Touchstone, The.** C. Clements. 5b. Sc. Garden of a little house by the side of a road. SAO

Towers. L. Mumford. 2m. Sc. Studio at twilight. Amer. Mercury 4: 193–196, Feb. 1925.

Towie castle. G. Bottomley. 4m., 2w. Sc. A vacant space. BOTT

Town. M. Baumer. 4m., 3w. Sc. Soft drink parlor in small army post. CL

Town hall—tonight. H. Reed. Satire. 3m., 3w. Sc. Town hall in a mid-western village. LON

J **Town mouse and the country mouse, The.** E. Smith. 4b. Sc. Stage. SM

C **Town that Santa forgot, The.** Mrs. J. B. Shacklett. 7b., 4g. Sc. Santa's workshop. ELD

J **Towne hall.** O. M. Price. 3b., 4g., chorus. Sc. Towne hall in Dorchester, Mass. 1652. PRI

Towneley play, The. R. C. Burrell. 10m., 2w. Sc. Stage. HAQ

Toy heart, The. P. Macmanus. 4w. Sc. Reception room of Cho Cho San. DRA

C **Toy inspection.** A. G. Lloyd. Many c. Sc. Santa's toyshop. Norm. Inst. 37: 60, Dec. 1927.

J **Toy shop, The.** P. Wilde. 3m., 1w. 9c. Sc. Interior of toy shop. BAK, SAL, WEB

C **Toy shop mix-up, The.** A. N. Norton. 4b., 3g. Sc. Toy shop workroom. CJ

J **Toy tragedy.** E. Dane. 3b., 5g. Sc. The dolls' house. BAK

C **Toys' Christmas frolic.** J. M. Besio. 15c. Sc. Workshop of Santa. WER

C **Tracks to the den, The.** A. Stevenson. 7b. Sc. A forest. STEV1

Traffic cop, The. E. Mumford. Farce. 7m., 9w. Sc. Exterior. PENN

Traffic signals. A. M. Drummond. About one hundred char. Sc. Busy street corner. FRE6

Tragedy in the upper Wallop, The. M. Constanduros. 9w. Sc. Little general shop. FREL

Tragedy of Jones, The. M. Lane-Norcott. 1m., 1w. Sc. Before the curtain. FRET

J **Tragedy rehearsed, A.** E. Smith. Parody of Sheridan. The Critic. 16b., 5g., chorus. Sc. Drury Lane Theatre. SMF

Train to Manro. S. A. Frost. 2m., 1w., 1b. Sc. Waiting room of railroad station. FIT

Trained nurse, The. H. H. Haslett. 1m., 2w. Sc. Hospital room. BANN

C **Training for the Presidency.** M. E. Whitney. 3b., 3g. Sc. 1 Interior of house. 2 Sc. Woods. WHI

Training Mary. M. S. Page. 2m., 4w. Sc. Interior. ELD

Trains. E. E. Mellon. 1m., 2w. Sc. Room in wooden shack in western mining town. Poet Lore 4: 424–432, Autumn 1930.

Traitor, The. L. G. Barnard. 3m., 2w. Sc. Corner of Library. CANA

J **Trajan and the children of Rome.** M. R. Hofer. 9b., 2g., 1 chorus. Sc. Streets of Rome. HOF

C **Transformation of Mary Lou, The.** B. M. Casey. 1b., 5g. Sc. Living room. CASE

Translated. G. Wilcox. 2m., 3w. Sc. Terraced garden, California. Poet Lore 41: 251–260, Summer 1930.

Trap, The. A. Gerstenberg. Comedy. 2m., 2w. Sc. Half kitchenette and half dinette. EAT

Trap doors. A. Kreymborg. Farce. 7m., 1w. Sc. Village street. IS, KRR, Theatre Arts 9: 742–751, Nov. 1925.

Trapped. L. F. Thanhouser. 5m. Sc. Living room. BAK

Trapped. O. Wells. 4m., 2w. Sc. Living room in homesteader's home. PAIN

Trash. L. F. Thanhouser. Comedy. 3m. Sc. Riverside Drive, N. Y. YALP

Travel is so broadening. K. L. Roberts. Mystery. Sc. Lobby of a French hotel in 1927. Sat. Eve. Post 200: 20–1, 38+, Aug. 6, 1927.

J **Travelers, The.** A. S. Howard. Allegorical. 6b., 1g., chorus. Sc. Stopping place in the road. MARC

Travelers, The. B. Tarkington. 6m., 4w. Sc. Sicilian hotel. APPL, Ladies Home Journal 43: 16–17, 168+, Mar. 1926.

Traveling man, The. Lady Gregory. Mystery. 1b., 2g. Sc. Cottage kitchen. LY, WEB, Golden Book 14: 274–9, Oct. 1931.

C **Travelers and the hatchet, The.** A. Stevenson. 3b. Sc. A high road. STEV3

C **Traveling to a Hallowe'en party.** E. Hoxie. 4b., 3g. Sc. Waiting room in railway station. HOV

Tread the green grass. P. Green. 9m., 2w., a large number of chorus groups. Sc. A countryside. GRED

Treason. M. C. Tull. 6m., 3w. Sc. No man's land in France 1918. IN

Treasure. I. E. Mackay. 4m., 2w., 1c. Sc. Living room of an old fashioned cottage. FREN

C **Treasure chest, The.** J. Thorp. 3b., 3g., 9 chorus groups. Sc. Forest. SCH2

J **Treasure hunt, The.** M. A. Butler. 7b. Adapted from Stevenson's Treasure Island. Sc. On treasure island, a clearing surrounded by trees. BUT

J **Treasure hunt, The.** A. Toepp. 6b., 4g. Sc. Interior. ELD

Treasure trove. J. H. Beith. Fantasy. 2m., 2w. Sc. English interior. FREL

J **Tree of golden fruit, The.** B. E. Palmer. 4b., 7b. Sc. Living room. ELD

C **Tree of life, The.** E. W. Bates. Pageant. 5g., 3b., chorus. SCH1

Tree of memory. G. C. Moses. 3b. or g. Pageant. Sc. Platform. SCH3

Tress of hair, A. J. Marks. 2m., 2w. Sc. Living room a cottage in North Wales. MARK

Trial. P. A. Williams. 3m., 2w. Sc. Combined kitchen and dining room of a poor shack. GAK

Trial by breakfast. W. Mead. 4m., 2w. Sc. Dining room. ELD

Troubled by ghosts. L. Vane. Farce. 4m. Sc. Interior. BECK

Troubles of a hotel clerk. E. O. Jones. Farce. 5m. Sc. Lobby of a cheap hotel. DRA

Troubles of an editor. D. Sheridan. Farce. 4m., 5w. Sc. In the editor's office. SHER

Troubles of Mose, The. H. W. Hamilton. 2m. Sc. Interior. CAT2

J   **Troublesome Christmas tree, A.** L. C. VanDerveer. 7b. Sc. Headquarters of Scout troop. VAN

Troupers. P. G. Ingersoll. 1m., 2w. Sc. Shabby cheap little apartment. NICH

C   **Truant leaves, The.** N. Flaurier. 8c. Sc. Outdoors. FIU

C   **True spirit of Christmas, The.** E. E. McNallan. 4b., 7g. Prim. Educ. 45: 265, 323, Dec. 1927.

Trump, The. H. K. Gordon. 4w. Sc. Living room. BANN

Trump, The. C. E. Lawrence. 2m., 1w. Sc. Outer wall of a country churchyard. Cornhill 68: 42–50, Jan. 1930.

C   **Truth always, The.** C. Childs. 3b., 2g. Sc. Dining room of Washington home. Norm. Inst. 39: 74, 76, Feb. 1930.

J   **Truth for a day, The.** H. T. Darby. Comedy. 6g. Sc. Interior. BUG, DRA

Truth party, The. B. E. Palmer. 13w. Sc. Interior. BAK

Truth, the mischief. A. Thompson. 6w. Sc. Interior. DRA

Truthful husbands. B. E. Palmer. 9m., 7w. Sc. Office. ELD

Trysting place, The. B. Tarkington. Comedy. 4m., 3w. Sc. Room just off the lounge in a fine hotel in the country. APPL, CL, SCHW, TUC

Tugging. N. B. Cox. 3w. Sc. Living room of tenement. Drama 15: 107–109, Feb. 1925.

Tulip and Camellia. O. W. Firkins. 3m., 1w. Sc. Apartment in Paris in 1850. Cornhill 68: 233–254, Feb. 1930.

Tumbler, The. E. Glass. 11m. Sc. 1 Outside of a monastery. 2 Sc. Inside the chapel. Poet Lore 37: 516–536. Winter 1926.

Tune of a tune, A. D. Totheroh. Poetic. 2m., 2w. Sc. Front parlor of a house in England. FRE4, TOT

Turkey girl, The. S. M. Williams. 2m., 1w., 2 chorus groups. Sc. Arid mesas of the southwestern part of the U. S. UNU

Turkey red. M. Woods. 6w. Sc. Living room. DRA

Turkish ambassador, The. A. V. Kotzebue. Trans. by B. B. Beebe. 3m., 4w. Sc. Large lecture room in girls' boarding school. Poet Lore 38: 192–205, Summer 1927.

Turn him out. T. J. Williams. Farce. 3m., 2w. Sc. Interior. DRA, FIT

Turn of a hair, The. P. Hoffman. Farce. 4w. Sc. Hair dressing parlor. Drama 15: 85–7, Jan. 1925.

Turn of the road, The. E. J. Church. 3m., 1w. Sc. Private office of a lawyer. CANA

Turn of the road, The. A. A. Wilson. Melodrama. 8m., 4w. Sc. Interior of a farmhouse in N. Y. CAMP

C   **Turning the tables.** N. Flaurier. 5g. Sc. Room with Hallowe'en decorations. Norm. Inst. 33: 72, Oct. 1924.

Turtle dove, The. M. S. Oliver. 6 char., chorus. Sc. Chinese interior. BAK, SMI

'Twas well done and quickly. J. F. McDermott. 7m., 1w., 1b. Sc. An inn. Poet Lore 39: 415–430, Autumn 1928.

'Twas ever thus. I. L. Ehrlich. Farce. 2m., 2w. Sc. Interior. NICB

'Twas the night before. P. Wilde. Farce. 2m., 1w., chorus. Sc. Living room. WILT

C 'Twas the night before Christmas. A. Curtis. 5b., 5g. Sc. Living room. CURT

C Tweedle-dum and tweedle-dee. G. Lloyd. 2b. Sc. Stage. LLO

J Tweedledum and tweedledee. E. Smith. Adapted from Carroll. Through the Looking Glass. 7b., 1g. Sc. Forest. SM

Twelfth initial, The. 1m., 2w. Sc. Old fashioned kitchen. Player's M. 7: 24–25, May–June 1931.

C Twelfth night festivities. E. L. Knox. 10b., 2g., chorus. Sc. Large stage. SCH2

Twelve before three. T. J. Ahearn. 4m. Sc. Shack. NICH

C Twelve dancing princesses, The. A. Stevenson. 15b., 14g. Sc. King's palace. STEV1

C Twelve o'clock one Christmas even. E. Hains. 2b., 6g. TUL

Twelve-pound look, The. J. M. Barrie. 1m., 2w. Sc. Room in home. BARR

Twilight of the moon. C. B. Going. 3m., 2w. Sc. Room in semi-darkness. GOIN

Twilight saint, The. S. Young. 2m., 2w. Sc. Rather poorly furnished room in Italian home in 13th century. FIS, FREN

"Twinkle, twinkle, little star!" G. Elton. Farce. 3m. Sc. A "star" dressing room at the Metropolis theatre. CHA

C Twins' birthday party, The. B. B. Tatman. 1b., 2g. Sc. Living room. Prim. Educ. 45: 800, 809, June 1928.

C Twins' Christmas, The. A. Clark. 7b., 3g. Sc. Twins' bedroom. CJ

Twisting of the rope, The. D. Hyde. Comedy. 2m., 3w., chorus. Sc. Farmer's house in Munster a hundred years ago. CANF

Two against one less. A. L. Kaser. Farce. 2m. Sc. A street. KAS

Two black sheep. A. C. White. Satire. 1m., 2w. Sc. Kitchen Poet Lore 35: 464–470; Autumn 1924.

J Two blind men and a donkey. M. Dondo. Comedy. 6m., 1 donkey. Sc. Interior of house in medieval France. APPL, SHAB

C Two brothers, The. M. Yelton. Many c. Sc. Living room. Norm. Inst. 34: 74, Jan. 1925.

Two Christmas boxes. 11w. Sc. Interior. BAK

Two crooks and a lady. E. Pillot. 4m., 1w. Sc. Library in an old Fifth Ave. mansion. KM

Two dollars, please! M. Stevenson. Comedy. 5m., 3w. Sc. Matrimonial parlors of the Marryin' Squire. IN

Two Elizabeths. N. Syrett. Comedy. 4m., 4w. Sc. Interior. BAK

C Two flags, The. 6b., 13g., others. Sc. Barracks. Prim. Educ. 32: 87–124, Feb. 1924.

Two flats and one key. H. Simpson. Farce. 2m., 2w. Sc. Sitting room. SIMH

Two gentlemen of Soho. A. P. Herbert. 5m., 3w. FREL, Atlan. 139: 577–92, May 1927; London Mercury 16: 490–503, Sept. 1927.

Two Goyim. S. S. Grossman. Comedy. 4m., 3w. Sc. Interior. BLO

C Two holes, The. A. Stevenson. 2g. Sc. House. STEV1

Two lamps, The. K. S. Goodman and B. Hecht. 7m., 2w. Sc. Room in German house in 1914. GOO

C **Two little trunks.** M. A. Enloe. 7b., 1g., chorus. Sc. Interior of railway. ENL

C **Two millers, The.** A. Stevenson. 3b., 1g. Sc. Mill. STEV2

Two of them. J. M. Barrie. 1m., 1w. Sc. Lawyer's office. HAP

Two on an old pathway. E. C. Koenig. 1m., 1w. Sc. A luxurious living room. Poetry 35: 88–91, Nov. 1929.

Two passengers for Chelsea. O. W. Firkins. 8m., 2w. Sc. Morning room in 1847. FIR, SHAF, Cornhill 60: 163–84, Feb. 1926; Golden Book 11: 95–103, Jan. 1930.

J **Two plum puddings.** C. Clements. Pantomime. 4b., 1g. Sc. Sitting room and kitchen combined in a cobble-stoned house. SHAB

Two plus two. M. Aldis. 2m., 2w. Sc. Interior. DRA

Two quacks and a duck. F. P. Spofford. For deaf children. 2m., 1w. Sc. Doctor's office. Volta R. 31: 484–487, Sept. 1929.

C **Two questions, The.** A. Stevenson. 4b., chorus. Sc. Palace. STEV2

Two sides of the door. M. Cropper. 4m., 4w., chorus. FEDE

C **Two sisters, The.** 4g. Sc. Interior. DRA

Two slaps in the face. F. Molnar. 2m. Sc. A street in Budapest. Golden Book 2: 65–67, July 1925.

Two slatterns and a King. E. St. V. Millay. 2m., 2w. Sc. Before a stage curtain. APPL, MIL, SHAQ

Two souls with but a single thought. E. St. V. Millay. Satire. 1m., 1w. MIK

Two tables of bridge. L. K. Brown. Comedy. 9w. Sc. Cheerful living room in a suburban bungalow. DRA

Two thieves, The. E. W. Bates. 3m., chorus. Sc. Rocky desolate place somewhere between this world and the next. BAK, FEDE

$2000 cash. N. Chatterton. Comedy. 2m., 2w. Sc. Dining room. BAK, YOU

Two Valentines. K. A. White. 5m., 5w. Sc. Corner of 8th grade room. IR

J **Two weeks with pay.** B. Abel. 30g. Sc. Barren roadside. WOM

Two's company. R. Jeans. Farce. 2m., 1w. Sc. Interior. JEA

Two's enough. E. E. Olson. 6w. Sc. Parlor. BAK

J **Tyranny.** S. L. Cummins. Burlesque. 5b., 2g. Sc. Palace. CUM3

Tyranny and tea-cakes. O. M. Popplewell. Comedy. 5w. Sc. Living room of a little house on the outskirts of a Yorkshire town. DE

Tyranny of conscience, The. R. Kelley. 2m. Sc. Small farm in a rural district in Michigan. KAM

U

Ugly duckling, The. F. L. Mansor. Comedy. 1m., 4w. Sc. Living room. BAK

C **Ugly duckling, The.** A. Stevenson. 20 char. Sc. Farmyard. STEV3

Ulysses. S. Phillips. 7m., 6w., chorus. Sc. Seashore of Ithaca. KM

Umbrella duologue, The. E. D. Battiscombe. 2w. Sc. Interior. JOHP

Umbrian play, The. 11m., 1w., chorus. Sc. Stage. HAQ

Unaccepted apology, The. P. Wilde. Farce. 2m., 1w. Sc. An apartment. WILT

Unbidden guest, The. O. W. Firkins. 6m., 1w. Sc. Three parts; house, background, veranda. FIR, Poet Lore 35: 276–297, Summer 1924.

C **Uncle Armory's helpers.** M. E. Wells. 12c. Sc. Home. Prim. Educ. 45: 722, 724, 733, May 1928.

Uncle Bob chooses books. E. Harrington. 1m., 3w. Sc. A bookstore shortly before Christmas. English J. 17: 836–841, Dec. 1928.

Uncle Caleb's quiet Christmas. M. Irish. Comedy. 4m., 4w. Sc. Living room. BECK

Uncle Dick's mistake. E. C. Whelan. Farce. 3m., 2w. Sc. Interior. BUG

Uncle Jack. S. N. Cook. 3m., 4w., 2c. Sc. Interior. FIT

Uncle Jimmy. Z. Gale. 4m., 4w. Sc. Back doorway in a little middle-west town. HUO, PHIL

Uncle Mel's Merry Christmas. M. Irish. 3m., 4w. Sc. Living room. BUG

J **Uncle Ole's uncle.** M. Irish. Comedy. 4b., 4g. Sc. Living room. IQ

C **Uncle Sam P.M.** M. Race. 1b., 9g., chorus. Sc. Interior. BECK

C **Uncle Sam's house party.** M. E. Bugg. 24c. Grade Teacher 46: 628–629, 659, Apr. 1929.

C **Uncle Sam's pantry.** I. F. Lindsay. Many c. Sc. Stage. Sierra Ed. News 25: 46–9, Nov. 1929.

C **Uncle Sam's Thanksgiving reception for the States.** M. L. Hutchinson. As many or as few char. as desired. Sc. Room in White House. ELDR

Uncle Tommy's harem. W. F. Gallaway. 4m. Sc. Study of the typical college professor. COO

Uncle's will. S. T. Smith. Comedy. 2m., 1w. Sc. Interior. FIT

Unconquered, The. W. F. Manley. 3m., 2w. Sc. Room in Jerusalem. MANL

Undaunted female, The. V. B. Lawton. 6m., 1w. Sc. Medieval interior. LAWT

J **Under authority.** P. E. Osgood. 6b. Sc. Portion of white-washed house wall. OSG

C **Under sealed orders.** F. A. U. E. Painton. 8g. Sc. Woodland. PAIT

C **Under the big tent.** G. B. Donnelly. Any number of b. Sc. Drapes. DON

Under the law. J. Wilder. 3m., 1w. Sc. Bank. ELD

Under the oak. D. Wight. Adapted from Chaucer. Canterbury Tales. 6m. Sc. A tavern courtyard in Medieval England. HUO

J **Under the skull and bones.** R. Gow. Burlesque. 10b., chorus. Sc. Pirate ship. BAK

C **Under the snow.** K. L. Bates. 7c. Sc. Out of doors. BAT

Undercurrent, The. F. Ehlert. 2m., 1w. Sc. Interior. FREN, Drama 18: 111–114, Jan. 1928.

Underdog, The. R. Middlemass. 3m., 2w. Sc. City tenement house. LON

Underground. B. W. Newman. 3m., 1b. Sc. Underground absolute blackness. Poet Lore 38: 571–578, Winter 1927.

C **Underground railroad, The.** W. Rice. 4b., 4g. Sc. Clearing in a wood. SAL

Undertones. P. Holffman. Comedy. 4m. Sc. Interior. FREN

Undying prince, The. O. W. Firkins. 10m. Sc. Private dining room in an ancient London inn. FIR, Cornhill 64: 231–254, Feb. 1928.

C **Unexpected guest, The.** S. G. Clark. 3b., 5g., chorus. Sc. Interior of a very crude hut. CLAR

J **Unexpected guest, An.** H. W. Githens. 4b., 2g., chorus. Sc. Home in Jericho. GITH

J **Unexpected guest, The.** E. I. Mackenzie. 6w. Sc. Interior. PAIN

Unforgivable, The. A. Macbeth. 3m., 1w. Sc. Study. FREQ

C **Uninvited guest, The.** F. E. Eakman. 11c. Sc. Turkey's nest. EAK

Uninvited guests. S. M. Armstrong. Comedy. 6m., 2w. Sc. City apartment house. ELD

C **Unknown soldier, The.** Y. Klein and F. Schwarz. 9c. Sc. Any interior. KL

Unlighted Menorah, The. E. E. Levinger. 3m., 1w. Sc. 18th century. BLO, LEV

Unruly member, The. C. Heath. Farce. 3m., 2w. Sc. Living room in a house in Dublin. SHAF

Unseen, The. A. Gerstenberg. 1m., 2w. Sc. Dining room. GOLD

Unseen host, The. P. Wilde. 3m. Sc. American hospital in Paris. SAA

"Unto one of the least of these." P. Holloway. 2m., 5w. Sc. Living room. HOL

Unto such glory. P. Green. 4m., 1w. Sc. North Carolina interior. FRE3, GREE

Unto the least of these, a miracle play. A. C. Rowell. 4m., 6w., 1b. Sc. Big cheery kitchen on Christmas eve in middle ages in home of craftsman. Drama 18: 43–46, 59–62, Nov. 1927.

Unwritten law, The. D. Titheradge. Farce. 3m. Sc. A restaurant. TITO

Up in the air. E. E. Olson. 5w. Sc. Kitchen of farmhouse. BAK

Upon the waters. T. M. Hanna. 2m., 4w. Sc. Sitting room. Drama 14: 58–62, 69, Nov. 1923.

Upstage. A. Gerstenberg. Comedy. 2m., 3w. Sc. Stage of little theatre. GEQ

Uriel Acosta. C. Reznikoff. Sm. Sc. House of the Acosta in Portugal at the close of the 16th century. REZ, Menorah J. 11: 35–42, Feb. 1925.

Us Browns. D. Titheradge. Farce. 3m., 2w. Sc. Sitting room. TITU

V

C **Vacation.** A. G. Lloyd. Any number of c. Sc. Interior. MARC

C **Vacation days.** E. Preston. Any number of c. Sc. Interior. ELD

C **Vain Jackdaw, The.** A. Stevenson. 5 char., chorus. Sc. A public park. STEV2

C **Valentine hearts.** J. Ross. 15c. Sc. Interior. BECK

C **Valentine scraps.** 2b., 1g. Sc. Living room. Norm. Inst. 33: 63, Feb. 1924.

C **Valentine shop, The.** S. E. Gosselink. 4b., 10g. Sc. Booth decorated with hearts. Norm. Inst. 39: 78, 80, Feb. 1930.

Valentines. A. C. D. Riley. 3m., 2w. Sc. Curtain. FREN, NORT

Valiant, The. H. Hall and R. Middlemass. 5m., 2w. Sc. Warden's office in State's prison. EAS, EAT, KM, LON, THOR

Valley Forge. M. S. Beagle. 6m., 2 chorus groups. Sc. A woods near Valley Forge in 1777. SAG

Valley of lost men, The. A. H. Ernst. 5m. Sc. Inside of miner's cabin, Yukon Valley in 1900. Theatre Arts M. 14: 430–440, May 1930.

J **Value of preparation, The.** M. M. Russell. 1b., 10g., chorus. Sc. Stage. RUS

J **Van Dorn's Merry Christmas, The.** M. Irish. 4b., 6g. Sc. Interior. BUG

Van Tromps listen in, The. K. Nicholson. Comedy. 1m., 3w. Sc. Grave yard of Trinity Church in N. Y. BAK

Vanishing princess, The. J. Golden. Fantasy. 2m., -2w. Sc. Musty magic shop. GOL, SHAF

Varnish. E. Lowell. 1m., 5w. Sc. Living room. BAK

Varnishing day. F. J. Pohl. 3m., 4w. Sc. An art exhibit. Poet Lore 38: 128–140, Spring 1927.

C **Vegetable brownies, The.** 10c. Sc. Indoors or outdoors. DRA

Veil, The. G. Rodenbach. Trans. from French. 2m., 2w. Sc. Vast dining room with high ceiling. SHAF

Veil lifts, The. E. Dane. 1m., 4w. Sc. A charming old room in an early Colonial house. BAK

Vengeance of Hello-Hello, The. G. Hughes. Burlesque. 5m., 2w. Sc. Interior or exterior. HUN

Venus and the shepherdess. L. S. Jast. Fantasy. 1m., 2w. Sc. Curtained recess. JAS

C **Verdict for the wishbone, A.** G. Lloyd. 20c. Sc. Kitchen. LLO

Very crude oil. S. D. Whipkey. 3m., 2w. Sc. Dingy room of farmhouse. Drama 20: 236–239, May 1930.

Very devil, The. D. Titheradge. Farce. 3m., 4w. Sc. A Mayfair house. TITB

C **Very first arbor day, The.** Y. Klein and F. Schwarz. 14c. Sc. In a clearing in 1872. KL

C **Very sad unicorn, The.** G. W. Cook and V. Dixon. Fanciful. 9b., 2g. Sc. Throne room. DAZ

Very social service. V. Church. 3m., 2w. Sc. Library of a home. Drama 15: 54–56, 70, Dec. 1924.

Vespers. J. Meadow. Morality. 4m., 2w. Sc. Vestry of church. DET

Vestiges. H. Berman. 1m., 3w. Sc. Bedroom. BER

C **Veteran's story, The.** M. A. Niemeier. 12b., 10g. Sc. Country cemetery. NIE, NIEM

Vicious circle, A. Mrs. Barry Pain. 1m., 1w. Sc. Out of doors with a rustic seat. JOHN

Victims of the plague. K. L. Roberts. 5m., 3w. Sc. An antique shop. Sat. Eve. Post 200: 10–11, July 21, 1928.

C **Victor's tournament, The.** E. F. A. U. Painton. 10b., 9g. Sc. A street. PAIT

J **Victory and thanksgiving.** M. Irish. 3b., 3g. Sc. Colonial house in 1758. IRI

Vigilant Santa Claus, A. A. Curtis. Comedy. 4m., 5w. Sc. Living room. DRA

Vignette. P. Wilde. Comedy. 2m., 1w. Sc. Compartment in a Pullman Car. WILD, WILT, WILV

Village industries. C. Roberts. 6m., 3w. Sc. Bar parlour of "The Hop Pole." FREL

Villain and victim. W. R. Walkes. 1m., 1w. Sc. Interior. DRA

Villain in the piece, The. P. Wilde. Comedy. 2m., 1w. Sc. Just outside of the ballroom. WIL

Violet, The. F. Molnar. 3m., 5w. Sc. Office of producer-manager. MOL

Violin, The. D. Titheradge. Farce. 2m., 1w. Sc. A cheap living room. TITB

J **Violin-maker of Cremona, The.** F. Coppee. 3b., 1g., 3 chorus groups. Sc. In the violin-maker's shop in Cremona in 1750. THOM

Virginia Mummy. C. White. Farce. 6m. Sc. Interior. FIT

C **Virgin's tree, The.** A. R. Kennedy. 8b., 2g. Sc. Oasis in Egyptian desert. SAL

Virtue its own reward. H. Simpson. Farce. 3m., 1w. Sc. Bar parlour in the inn "Three Peckers." SIMS

Vise, The. L. Pirandello. Trans. from Italian. 2m., 2w. Sc. Room in a house in a small country town in Italy. PIR

J **Visit from George Washington, A.** C. H. Gilliland. 2b. Sc. Living room of a modern home. AU

C **Visit from Mr. and Mrs. Santa Claus.** M. A. Niemeier. 5b., 4g. Sc. Comfortable living room. NIE, NIEN

C **Visit from Santa Claus, via radio, A.** F. C. Gardner. 2b., 1g. Sc. Stage with radio. GAP

C **Visit from the white rabbit, A.** M. Reed. 8g. Sc. Living room. Norm. Inst. 39 : 32, Sept. 1930.

C **Visit of the raindrops, The.** N. Flaurier. 13c. Sc. Interior. FJ, STRU

C **Visit to Fairyland, A.** R. Strutton. Any number of c. Sc. Outdoor effect. STRU

J **Visit to London, A.** E. Smith. 5b., 3g. Sc. Room in London in 1815. SM

C **Visit to Santa, A.** A. C. Barrows. 1b., 3g., others. Sc. Workroom in Santa's palace. Norm. Inst. 33 : 57–58, Dec. 1923.

C **Visit to toyland, A.** L. M. Degnan. Many c. Prim. Educ. 44 : 322, 333, Dec. 1926.

C **Visit to Washington's home, A.** M. Cutler. Many c. Prim. Educ. 45 : 443, 491, Feb. 1928.

J **Visiting the gypsy-camp.** E. M. McCullum. 2b., 3g. Sc. Country road. MACC

Vite-em-in, the garden of health. F. C. Gardner. 2w. Sc. Living room. GAQ

C **Vocations for girls.** C. E. White. 14c. Sc. Living room. Prim. Educ. 45 : 521, 564, Mar. 1928.

Voice from the air, The. N. Flaurier. 3b. Sc. Interior. FIU

Voice of the snake, The. D. F. Halman. 4m., 1w. Sc. Cart on wheels during middle ages. FRE3

Voice said "Good night," A. R. Pertwee. 4m. Sc. Study. FREL, FREN

Voices. M. W. Brook. 4m., 5w. Sc. Sitting room. CANA

C **Voices of June.** L. K. Dolan. 17c. Sc. Out of doors setting on stage, or out-of-doors. DOL

W

Wagging tongues. M. C. Allyn. Comedy. 7w. Sc. Living room. DENI

Wagon-Lits. C. Morley. Comedy. 6m., 1w. Sc. A very tiny compartment in a French sleeping car. MORK

Waif, The. E. Grimball. 3m., 5w., chorus. Sc. A narrow street. WOM

Waif, The. E. Morrette. 3m., 2w. Sc. Garret room in Paris in 1794. MORR

Wait a minute. M. T. Applegarth. 17 char. Sc. Interior. APN

Waitin' fer sun-up. E. G. Lawrence. 3m., 5w. Sc. Mountain hut. ELD

Waiting. D. Titheradge. Farce. 3m., 1w. Sc. Doctor's waiting room. TITF

Waiting for Dorothea. E. R. Worrell. 1m., 2w., 3b. Sc. Interior. FREN

Waiting for the 2:40 train. J. A. Baxter. Farce. 2m., 3w., several small c. Sc. Waiting room of station. PAIS

Waiting room, The. G. M. Baird. 6m., 4w., 1g., 1b. Sc. Interior railway waiting room. Drama 15: 6–9, Oct. 1924.

C **Wake! Princess!** S. G. Clark. 19c., chorus. Sc. Stage. CLAR

C **Waking the Christmas spirit.** E. I. Mackenzie. 5g. Sc. Interior. PAIN

Walled-up window, The. A. V. Kotzezue. Trans. by B. B. Beebe. Comedy. 4m., 1w. Sc. Interior of invalid's room. Poet Lore 38: 246–263, Summer 1927.

Walt. C. Morley. 5m., 1w. Comedy. Sc. Sitting room of cottage. MORL, Bookm. 59: 646–62, Aug. 1924.

Wander weed, The. E. W. Peattie. 1m., 3w. Sc. Interior of a well-built log house in the Blue Ridge mountains. PEA

J **Wanderer, The.** H. W. Githens. 8b., chorus. Sc. Border of a field. GITH

Wandering child, The. M. R. Davidson. 2m., 1w., 2c. Sc. Nursery. FREN

Wandering Christmas cakes, The. M. Helfen. Comedy. 6w. Sc. Interior. CATH

Wandering scholar, The. *Tr.* E. U. Ouless. 3m., 1w., chorus. Sc. Open place near village. OULE

Wanderlust. P. Halvey. 3m., 2w. Sc. Living room of flat. CL

Wanderlust. K. Nicholson. 4m., 2w. Sc. Living room of flat in the Bronx. BAK, PHIL

Waning moon, The. L. V. V. Armstrong. 6m., 1b. Sc. Interior in Jamaica in the 17th century. FREN

Wanted: a confidential clerk. W. F. Chapman. Farce. 6m. Sc. Interior. DRA, FIT

Wanted—a detour. C. N. Holmes. Farce. 1m., 1w. Sc. Turnpike. ELD

Wanted, a Mahatma. G. V. May. 4m. Sc. Interior. FIT

Wanted, a nurse. G. Kobbe. 2m., 3w. Sc. Interior. FIT

C **Wanted—a Santa Claus.** B. I. Tobin. 8b., 12g. Sc. Poorly furnished room. ELD

Wanted, a valet. B. L. C. Griffith. 4m. Sc. Interior. PENN

Wanted: an office boy. K. A. White. 4b. Sc. Private office of the editor of the "Times." WH

Wanted—money. H. Ford and A. S. Tucker. Comedy. 5w. Sc. Apartments in N. Y. FREN

War brides. M. C. Wentworth. 3m., 4w., chorus. Sc. Room in peasant's cottage. YALP

War woman, The. C. C. Lovell. 19m., 2w. Sc. A log cabin in north Georgia. RIC

J **Wardle's Christmas party.** A. J. Rostance. Adapted from Dickens. Pickwick Papers. 12b., 4g. Sc. English interior. JON

Wares never did so, The. E. Wilbur. Comedy. 2m., 3w. Sc. Village in Vermont. BANN

Warrior's husband, The. J. F. Thompson. Farce. 4m., 3w. Sc. Tent. NICB

Warter-wucks. E. P. Conkle. 5m., Sc. Back of blacksmith. COM

J **Washington and Betsy Ross.** P. Mackaye. 5b., 2g. Sc. At old south theatre, Phil. in 1778. FREN, SHAB, SCH3

Washington as president. M. S. Beagle. 2m., chorus. Sc. A street in N. Y. in 1789. SAG

C **Washington at the helm of state.** M. A. Niemeier. 6b., 1g. Sc. Washington's home. NIEM

J **Washington at Valley Forge.** E. W. Bates. 8b., 1g. Sc. Snow covered landscape in 1778. BAK

C **Washington at Valley Forge.** M. Bitney, 6b., 2g. Sc. Poorly-furnished room. BIT

Washington the lover. M. S. Beagle. 3m., 3w., chorus. Sc. A Colonial garden. SAG

Washington's first defeat. Comedy. 1m., 2w. Sc. Interior. DRA

J **Washington's life story.** P. M. Swinton. 8b., 3g., chorus. Sc. Various scenes on one stage. SW

C **Washington's teachers.** A. S. Tavender. 7c. Sc. Schoolroom. Pop. Educ. 43: 328, 345, Feb. 1925.

Wasted tip, The. N. Beach. Comedy. 3m. Sc. Pullman train. ROH

J **Watch and the almond tart, The.** A. V. Kotzebue. Trans. by B. B. Beebe. 1b., 1g., 1w. Sc. Poor living room. Poet Lore 38: 240–245, Summer 1927.

C **Watch me change!** E. Fowles. 6b., 2g. Sc. Dining room. Sierra Ed. News 26: 30–1, Nov. 1930.

J **Water in a sieve.** M. Allingham. Fantasy. 5g. Sc. Street. FREL

Waterloo. A. C. Doyle. 3m., 1w. Sc. Front room in English home. MAR2

Way of a maid, The. C. Gray. 2m., 1w. Sc. Interior. FREN

Way of a man, The. L. S. Beazley. Comedy. 1m., 6w. Sc. Comfortable living room. PENN

Way out, A. R. Frost. 2m., 1 voice. Sc. Bachelor's kitchen-bedroom in a farmhouse. THOR, COH

Way to a man's heart, The. L. P. Martin. 3m., 5w. Sc. Sun porch. ELD

C **Way to the wishing gate, The.** E. E. Preston. 20c. Sc. Out of doors. MARC

We aim to please. E. Sexton. 1m., 6w., chorus. Sc. Exclusive shop on Fifth ave., N. Y. ELD

We are three. E. H. Fife. 2m., 1w. Sc. Living room of an artist. Drama 16: 17–18, 36, Oct. 1925.

C **We believe in fairies.** P. Beard. Pageant. 4b., 8g., chorus. Sc. A fairy ring. BEA

We few, we happy few. C. J. Denton. 21w. Sc. 16th century interior. DENT

C **We plant a tree!** E. D. Yale. Many c. Norm. Inst. 36: 78, Mar. 1927.

Weak spot, The. G. Kelly. 1m., 2w. Sc. Dining room in house. KEL

Wealth and wisdom. O. Down. Comedy. 1m., 1w. Sc. Room in small house. FRE1

Weather breeder, The. M. Denison. 4m., 1w. Sc. Back country shack. CANB, DEL, FIS, SHAF

C **Weather clerk, The.** R. Fyleman. 4b., 1g. Sc. Office. FYL

Weathervane elopes, The. A. C. D. Riley. 3m., 1w. Sc. Real garden. FRE3

Wedding, The. A. Chekhov. Farce. 7m., 3w., chorus. Sc. Brilliantly lighted room. CHEC

Wedding, A. J. Kirkpatrick. 4m., 3w. Sc. Tastefully and simply furnished room. FRE4, KM

Wedding, The. L. G. Peach. Farce. 2m., 1w. Sc. Cottage on the cliffs. PAZ

Wedding anniversary, The. M. S. Smith. 1m., 1w. Sc. Living room with open fire. Drama 17: 206–7, Apr. 1927.

Wedding at Mount Vernon, A. M. S. Beagle. 3m., 1w. Sc. Drawing room at Mount Vernon in 1799. SAG

Wedding clothes. G. Kiner. 1m., 2w. Sc. Kitchen in farmhouse. FREN

Wedding dress, The. P. Hoffman. 4m., 4w. Sc. 1 Lumber room of large old-fashioned house. 2 Drawing room. NICA

Wedding list, The. B. Herford. 1m., 2w., 1g. Ladies Home Journal 42: 207, June 1925.

C **Wedding of the flowers, The.** L. K. Doland. 14c., chorus. Sc. Stage or out of doors. DOL

Wedding presests, The. B. Herford. 1m., 3w. Sc. A fashionable jeweler's. Ladies Home Journal 41: 209, June 1924.

Wedding presents. J. W. Rogers. 2m., 3w. Sc. Comfortable back-parlor. Country Gent. 90: 30–44+, Oct. 1925.

Wedding rehearsal, The. J. Farrar. Farce. 5m., 8w., 1b. Sc. Living room. FRE5

Wednesday club entertains, The. M. Carpenter. 7w. Sc. Club room. BUG

J **Wee Macgreegor's party.** J. J. Bell. Burlesque. 5b., 5g., chorus. Sc. Interior. BAK

Wee Willie Winkie. R. Kipling. 3m., 1w., 1b. Sc. Bare plain. HAP

C **Week family, The.** R. Strutton. 8g. Sc. Indoors. STRU

Week of weeks, The. E. C. Magnusson. 2m., 2w. Sc. Living room in apartment. MAG

Weeper, The. H. Alexander. 4m., 1w. Sc. Interior, or exterior. ALE

J **Welcome Miss McGregor.** N. Flaurier. 5b., 6g. Sc. Interior. PAIN

Well, I declare! W. J. Mitchell. 6m. Sc. Interior. BAK

Well-remembered voice, A. J. M. Barrie. 4m., 2w. Sc. In a dark room that later becomes an artist's studio. BARR

Welsh honeymoon. J. Marks. 4m., 2w. Sc. Kitchen in cottage in North Wales. MARK

C **West o' the Alleghenies.** O. M. Price. 8b., 3g., chorus. Sc. In Boonesboro one of the first settlements in Kentucky in 1775. PRI2

Whar's mah pants? V. Clifford. Farce. 3m., 3w. Sc. In negro home. DRA

C **What ailed Maudie.** E. W. Merriman. 3b., 2g. Sc. Interior. DRA

What ails Maria? A. D. Patterson. 3w. Sc. Interior. PAIN

C **What did the sandman bring?** M. F. Kidd. 9b., 1g. Sc. Any platform. Norm. Inst. 33: 70, 72, Feb. 1924.

What do you say? S. G. Clark. 4b., 2g. Sc. Old time sitting room. CLAR

What every smart French woman knows. B. D. Meyer. 4w. Sc. Fitting room of a great dressmaker of Paris. Harper's Bazaar 59: 55–56, 142 + , June 1924.

What happened on Chanuka. G. Lipkind. 6m., 5w. Sc. Living room. BLO

What happened to Brown. M. Irish. 4m., 5w. Sc. Living room. IR

What happened to Jack. C. L. Dalrymple. Farce. 2m., 2w. Sc. Interior. FIT

C **What I would like to be.** C. Wassung. Any number of boys. Sc. Stage. LUT

What if they could? M. C. Wentworth. Whimsical. 2m., 2w. Sc. Interior. BANN

What imagination will do. H. Ford. Comedy. 3m., 3w. Sc. Dining room in N. Y. FREN

"What is truth?" asked Pilate. F. Tilden. 6m. Ladies Home Journal 43: 263, Oct. 1926.

What it may come to. H. Simpson. Farce. 2m., 3w. Sc. House in Mayfair. SIMS

What love can do. R. Frampton. Farce. 4m., 5w. Sc. Living room. FARQ

What makes the man. Man-about-town. 1m., 1w. Harper's B. 61: 114, 158, Sept. 1926.

C **What men live by.** R. Benton. 7b., 8g. Sc. 1 Shop. 2 Sc. Snowy road. 3 Sc. Cobbler's home. BEN

J **What men live by.** V. Church. 7m., 3d., 2c. Sc. Russian interior. EAS

J **What men live by.** L. Tolstoi. 7m., 3w., 2c. Sc. Cobbler shop below the level of the street. HAGG, LAW, THOM

What never dies. P. Wilde. 1m., 3w. Sc. Stock brokerage office. HUO, WILD, Drama 21: 21–24, 26, Jan. 1931.

J **What price flies?** a health play. Girls' high school, Atlanta, Georgia. 8c., 3b., 3g., others. Hygeia 4: 647–650, Nov. 1926.

What price presidency. M. C. Johnson. Farce. 1m., 4w. Sc. Living room. BAK

C **What our flag means to the children of other countries.** Y. Klein and F. Schwarz. 5c. Sc. Any interior. KL

C **What our flag stands for.** H. P. Ryan. 12c. Sc. Any interior or exterior. LUT

C **What Thanksgiving means.** M. Bitney. 6c. Sc. Interior. BIT

C **What the goodman does is always right.** A. Stevenson. 6b., 1g. Sc. A very old farmhouse. STEV3

What they think. R. Crothers. 2m., 2w. Sc. Living room. CROT

What will she be? M. Jones. 23w. Sc. Stage. ELD

What would you do? Mrs. C. P. Smith. Comedy. 1m., 1w. Sc. Living room in a thriving town on the Dixie highway. FREN

J **What's a fixer for?** H. C. Potter. 4b., 2g. Sc. A corner of a midway on a State fair grounds. Tent office of company. DAZ

What's in a name! B. King. 2m., 2w. Sc. Studio. MARC

What's keeping Laura? J. Ridge. Comedy. 4w. Sc. Interior. PAIN

When a clown laughs. G. Harrison. Tragedy. 3m., 1w. Sc. Just outside of the tent during a circus performance. LON

When a man wanders. H. H. Harris. 6w. Sc. Living room of cottage in small town. Poet Lore 40: 602–609, Winter 1929.

C   **When Betty Ann helped Santa Claus.** E. Sexton. 1b., 8g. Sc. Living room. SEX

C   **When day ran away.** L. W. Clarke. 6b., 6g. Fantasy. Sc. Simple scene. FIT

When de clock strikes twelve. G. York. Farce. 1m., 4w. Sc. Old mission at San Diego, California. BUG

When did they meet again? H. Brighouse. 1m., 4w. Sc. Apartment in Paris. FRE3, FREL

C   **When fairies come.** J. Thorp. 7b., 9g., chorus. Sc. Garden. SAL

When father was left to himself. C. J. Denton. 2m., 2w., 1b. Sc. Lawn in front of California bungalow. DENT

When half-gods go. N. M. Holland. 15 or more char. Sc. A glade in Olympus. HOK

When Harold met his mother-in-law. E. Hoxie. Comedy. 1m., 3w. Sc. Living room. HOX

J   **When heroes come.** J. M. Martin. 5b., 3g. Sc. Interior just after the Revolutionary war. ELD

When it's spring. P. Hoffman. Comedy. 2m., 1w. Sc. Interior. BAK

When love dies. J. A. Ramos. Comedy. 4m., 5w. Sc. Small salon, richly furnished. SHAT

When love flies in at the back door. J. H. Turner. Farce. 2m., 1w. Sc. Flat. TURN

When love is young. M. B. Cooke. Comedy. 1m., 3w. Sc. Interior. DRA

J   **When our new was new.** R. S. Hicks. 4g. or more. Sc. Girl's bedroom. Prac. Home Econ. 7: 335, 344, Nov. 1929.

J   **When pictures come to life.** Y. Klein. 10g. or more. School Arts M. 25: 484–86, Apr. 1926.

J   **When romance lived.** M. B. Brown. Adapted from Longfellow's Courtship of Miles Standish. Fantasy. 1b., 5g. Sc. Well furnished living room. FREN

C   **When St. Nicholas comes.** H. E. Davis. Many c. Sc. Schoolroom. Delineator 108: 17–18, Jan. 1926.

C   **When Santa came to the orphanage.** G. P. Williams. 9b., 4g. Sc. Dormitory room of orphanage. MARC

When something turned up. A. Halliday. Adapted from Dickens. David Copperfield. 4m., 1w., 4c. Sc. Living room of the Micawber home. SMIT

C   **When the beanstalk grew again.** P. Beard. 3b., 3g., chorus. Sc. Living room in a fine house. BEA

C   **When the Christmas tree talked.** E. Sexton. 4c. Sc. Sitting room. SEX

When the clock strikes. J. Parrish. Burlesque. 5m., 2w. Sc. Fashionable parlor in oriental style. NICA

When the Darbys dieted. F. L. Mitchell. 3m., 4w. Sc. Interior. ELD

When the horns blow. E. Vander Veer. Comedy. 1m., 6w. Sc. Studio. LON, SCH2

When the moon's three quarters full. O. Lesh. 1m., 3w. Sc. Interior. BAK

When the ship goes down. H. McGuire. 10m. Sc. Seamen's gallery of an American tramp steamer. FREN, Drama 18: 82–84, 94, Dec. 1927.

When the silver bell tree blooms. E. W. Peattie. 1m., 2w. Sc. Lofty, beamed room. PEA

C **When the turkeys turned the tables.** M. T. Cornish. 6 char., chorus. Sc. Any type of room. COMN

When west meets east. E. DeHuff. 4m., 2c. Sc. Room in India. DEH

When the willow nods. A. Kreymborg. 3m., 1w. Sc. Dense wood. KR

C **Where are the flowers and birds?** O. V. Roe. 1b., 1g. Sc. School room. FJ

J **Where but in America.** O. M. Wolff. 1m., 2w. Sc. Dining room. GREO, KN, SMI

Where do we go from here? W. O. Bates. 4m., 5w., chorus. Farce. Sc. Well furnished parlor. IN

Where it is thin, there it breaks. I. S. Turgenev. Comedy. 6m., 4w. Sc. Sitting room. TURG

J **Where lies the child.** D. C. Allan. 3b., 3g., chorus. Sc. Scene with drop curtains. BAK

Where love is. I. Payne. Parable. Adapted from Tolstoi. Where love is there, God is also. 4m., 2w. Sc. Cellar. BAK, Poet Lore 37: 475–485, Winter 1926.

Where the cross is made. E. O'Neill. 6m., 1w. Sc. Cabin erected as a lookout post on top of house on California coast. COF, COH, GREO, KM, ON, SCHW, TUC

J **Where the trails cross.** A. C. Darlington. 3g., 2b. Sc. Interior of a Hogan. MIS

Where there's a will. H. Simpson. Farce. 4m., 4w. Sc. Sitting room. SIMA

Where there's a will. G. M. York. 4m., 6w. Sc. Farm living room in Maine. ELD

Where there's a will, there's a way. M. G. Metcalfe. Comedy. 2m., 3w. Sc. Room in a small farmhouse village. DE

C **Where's my toothbrush?** S. Henderson. 3b., 7g. Sc. Interior. MARC

C **Where's your mother?** E. E. Levinger. 5c., chorus. Sc. Stage. LEVT

Which? F. F. Williams. 6m., 3w. Sc. Living room. CANA

Which is which? H. T. Smith. Comedy. 3m., 3w. Sc. Studio. FIT, PENN

C **Which is witch?** A. Rostetter. Fanciful. 3b., 3g. Sc. Garden. JAO

Which taken at the flood. H. Simpson. Farce. 2m., 2w. Sc. Interior. SIMS

J **Which, three R's or three R's plus industrial arts and domestic science.** A. Feuerstein. 8b., 5g. Sc. Living room. Ind. Arts M. 19: 254–256, July, 1930.

Which way out? F. Wells. 7m., 3w. Sc. Prosperous Chinese home. WOM

While the mushrooms bubble. D. Totheroh. Fanciful Pierrot play. 1m., 2w. Sc. Before the curtains. TOT

While you wait. L. G. Peach. Farce. 3m. Sc. Auto repair shop. PAZ

C **Whim-Wham.** F. Cavanah. 3b., 3g., chorus. Sc. Throne room of Queen's palace. CAV

C **White canoe, The.** A. Stevenson. 9b., 11g., 3 chorus groups. Sc. 1 Forest ibordering Niagara. 2 Sc. Wigwam. STEV4

White cloud, The. F. C. Molnar. 13m., 1w., chorus. Sc. Dugouts and huts of reserve force. MOL

White dresses. P. Green. 2m., 2w. Sc. A negro cabin. GREF, LOC

White elephants. K. Nicholson. 2m., 2w. Sc. Living room. NICG

White hands. E. P. Morrow. 3m., 2w. Sc. Kitchen bedroom of a mountain cabin. COL6

White hawk, The. H. Kemp. From Boccaccio's Decameron. 5m., 1w. Sc. Interior of farm cottage just outside Florence in 13th century. GOLD, KEM

J **White lie.** E. Keatinge. Comedy. 7g. Sc. A library. DRA

C **White Owl's feather.** E. Preston. 1b., 1g., chorus. Sc. Attic. PRES

C **White thorn at Yule.** M. Holbrook. 2m., 1w. Sc. Dwelling in England in 10th century. Child Welfare M. 24: 184–186, Dec. 1929.

Whither. A. M. Griffith. 1m., 2w. Sc. Library-living room of modern home. Poet Lore 35: 140–147, Spring 1924.

Whither goest thou? C. H. Currie. 6m., 1w. Sc. Just outside city of Rome on the Appian way. FEDE, FREL, FREN

Whittle. G. Hughes. Burlesque. 3m., 2w. Sc. Interior. HUN

Who is who? T. J. Williams. Farce. 3m., 2w. Sc. Parlor. FIT

C **Who left the cupboard bare?** E. H. Hanley. 30c. Sc. Interior. DRA

Who said justice? H. P. Powell. Comedy. 15m., 7w. Sc. Street. PENN

Who said pie? E. L. Squires. Comedy. 4m., 3w. Sc. Interior. MARC

Who shall we sue? C. Parker. Farce. 3m. Sc. Office. ELD

C **Who takes the cake?** M. T. Johnson. 8b., 4g. Sc. Room in farmer's hall. Norm. Inst. 35: 68–69, Sept. 1926.

J **Whom seek ye?** L. H. DeWolf. Mystery. 16b., 2g. Sc. Garden of Joseph of Arimathea. BAK

Who's on the line? G. York. Comedy. 2m., 7w. Sc. Old fashioned living room. DENI

Who's the lucky man? G. York. Comedy. 2m., 6w. Sc. Living room. DENI

Who's to inherit? 9w. Sc. Sitting room. FIT

Who's to win him? T. J. Williams. Comedy. 3m., 5w. Sc. Garden. DRA

Who's who? T. J. Williams. Farce. 3m., 2w. Sc. In a fog. PENN

J **Who's who: George Washington.** C. Francis. Farce. 6b., 3g. Sc. Classroom. FRA

C **Who's who in February.** E. Till. 1b., 2g., 11c. Norm. Inst. 37: 76, 78, Feb. 1928.

Who's who in the home. A. L. Kaser. Farce. 2m., 2w. Sc. Interior. DENI

"Whose husband are you?" H. Simpson. Farce. 4m., 2w. Sc. Inner office of lawyer. SIMH

J **Whose money?** Comedy. 3b., 3g. Sc. Interior. LOU

Whose money? L. Dickson and L. M. Hickson. Farce. 2m., 1w. Sc. Living room. SHAF

C **Why cherry trees sing.** J. A. Mills. 7c., and others. Sc. Cherry orchard. Prim. Educ. 32: 86–87, Feb. 1924.

Why girls stay home. M. Humphrey. Satire. 2m., 4w. Sc. Interior. APPL

C **Why! It is spring.** A. Norris-Lewis. 1b., 4g., others. Norm. Inst. 34: 78, Apr. 1925.

C **Why Jack-o'Lantern keeps Hallowe'en.** C. S. Bailey. 6c., chorus. Sc. A farm gate and fence. BAI, Amer. Child 13: 34–35, 61–63, Oct. 1927.

C **Why Johnnie changed his mind.** E. E. Preston. Any number of c.
Sc. Sitting room. PRE

Why lie about it? G. H. Abel. Comedy. 1m., 3w. Sc. Living room.
DENI

Why not Texas? O. G. Roark. Farce. 2m., 3w. Sc. Living room in N. Y.
FIT

Why photographers go mad. E. G. Wallace and A. B. Mead. 3m., 4w.
Any number of c. Sc. Photographer's gallery. BUG

J **Why pray for others?** D. M. Moore. 7 char. Sc. Interior. THOQ

C J **Why the Chimes rang.** E. A. McFadden. 1m., 1w., 2b., chorus. Sc. Interior of a wood chopper's hut. BAK, DRA, ELD, FREN

Why Santa quit. F. Tilden. Tragedy. 7m., 1w. Sc. Private office of
Santa Claus. Ladies Home Journal 42: 191, Dec. 1925.

C **Wicked witch, The.** F. Ryerson and C. Clements. 6b., 3g. Sc. Forest.
SAL

Wickedest woman, The. J. H. Turner. Farce. 4m., 2w. Sc. Drawing
room. TURN

Widdy's mite, The. D. Totheroh. 2m., 2w. Sc. Living room. FRE5, RIC,
TOT

Widow, The. G. Bottomley. Poetic. 1m., 1w. Sc. Low dias with screens.
BOTT

Widow of Wasdale Head. A. Pinero. Fantasy. 5m., 1w. Sc. Room in
inn in reign of George III. FRE1

C **Widow's cruse, The.** M. Parsons. 2b., 1g. Sc. Place near a house in
Zarephath. PARS

Widows' eyes. S. Quintero and A. Joaquim. Comedy. 1m., 2w. Sc. Country landscape of Spain. Poet Lore 40: 552–556, Winter 1929.

Wild boar, The. S. O'Brien. 3w., 6m., soldiers and attendants. Sc.
Interior medieval castle. Poet Lore 38: 536–550, Winter 1927.

C **Wild flowers.** R. Strutton. 3b., 9g. Sc. Out door, woodsy effect. STRU

C **Wild manners.** S. Young. Fanciful. 2b., 3g. Sc. In the heart of a wood
at twilight. YOUN

C **Wild swans, The.** A. Stevenson. 19b., 4g., chorus. Sc. On the seashore.
STEV3

Will, The. J. M. Barrie. 6m., 1w. Sc. Lawyer's office. BARR

Will it come to this? H. Simpson. Farce. 3m., 1w. Sc. Railway station. SIMA

Will-o'-the-wisp. D. F. Halman. 4w. Sc. Interior of a farmhouse. CLS

Will of the people, The. J. M. Cain. 3m. Sc. Committee room in State
capitol. Amer. Mercury 16: 394–398, Apr. 1929.

C **Will went and got lost.** H. O. Boggs. Comedy. 3b., 2g. Sc. Living room.
BOG

C **William and the Sandman.** M. Corell and I. Liccione. 16c. Sc. Interior. STRU

J **William Tell.** J. S. Knowles. 4b., chorus. Sc. Governor's Hall. LY

C **William Tell.** A. Stevenson. 13b., 1g., 2 chorus groups. Sc. Home in
the Swiss mountains. STEV4

C **Willie's success.** O. V. Roe. 5b. Sc. Schoolroom. FJ

C **Willie wouldn't.** A. C. Dion. 1b., 1g. Sc. Dining room table. Prim. Educ.
44: 479, 498, Feb. 1927.

Willing performer, The. G. Ade. 2m., 3w., others. Sc. Living room.
Country Gent. 93: 12–13, 97–100, Feb. 1928.

J **Willow plate, The.** F. Ryerson and C. Clements. 8b., 2g. Sc. Stage with black curtains. FRE6, SANP

Wily one, The. A. Monkhouse. 3m., 1w. Sc. Sitting room. FRE4

Wind, The. A. E. Peterson. 2m., 1w. Sc. Desert cabin. Drama 15: 174–177, 184, May 1925.

C **Wind and the sun, The.** M. E. Whitney. 3b. Sc. A park. WHI

Wind o' the Moors. L. G. Peach. 2m., 1w. Sc. A small room barely furnished. BRIS, BRIT, CLAS, SHAF

Wind-swept hill. G. Petersen. 1m., 1w., 1b. Sc. Living room. KAM

Windblown. E. M. Harris. Fantasy. Sc. Sitting room of a farmhouse. Poet Lore 38: 426–434, Autumn 1927.

Window to the south, A. M. K. Reely. 5m., 3w. Sc. A farm kitchen. REE

C **Wings of Daedalus, The.** V. Olcott. 2b., 7g., chorus. Sc. Near Aegean sea. OLE

Winner, The. H. C. Sargent. 3m., 1w. Farce. Sc. Sitting room. SARB

Winners all. I. L. Ehrlick. Farce. 2m., 2w. Sc. Interior. SHAF

Winter sunshine. L. Marshall. 3m., 4w. Sc. Interior. CART

Winter's night. N. Boyce. Tragedy. 1m., 2w. Sc. Room in farmhouse. SHAF

Winter's Stob. W. Gibson. Poetic. 3m. Sc. Open field. GIK

J **Wisdom teeth.** R. Field. Comedy. 1b., 3g. Sc. Waiting room of a dentist's office. FIF

C **Wise and foolish virgins, The.** E. Edland. 11g., chorus. Sc. Plain background. EDLP

C **Wise crow, The.** A. Stevenson. 2b. Sc. A meadow. STEV2

C **Wise gifts, The.** O. F. W. Burt. 1b., 3g. Sc. Room with fireplace. FRAZ

J **Wise king, A.** H. W. Githens. 9b., 8g. Sc. Temple in Jerusalem GIT

C **Wise men of Gotham, The.** K. D. Morse. 13b. Sc. Street in Gotham. MORS

C **Wise men of Gotham, The.** A. Stevenson. 7b., 1g., chorus. Sc. High-road. STEV2

J **Wise men seek Jesus, The.** F. A. Gardner and M. Gardner. 3b. Sc. Exterior. GAP

C **Wise owl's school, The.** M. G. Merrill. 16c. Sc. In wood. SAO

C **Wise turkey, The.** M. L. Hinman. 4b., 1g. Sc. Farmyard of a Pilgrim farm. WHG1

Wisemen, The. Miracle play. D. F. Robinson. 10m., 3w., chorus. HAQ

C **Wisest wish, The.** A. W. Norton. Fairy play. 3b., 4g. Sc. Stage. FJ

C **Wish-bird, The.** A. Stevenson. 2b., 1g. Sc. Palace gardens. STEV2

C **Wish garden, The.** Morality. 3b., 3g. Sc. Indoors or outdoors. ELD

Wishing gate, The. H. D'Asalena. Fantasy. 5m., 1w. Sc. Curtain. BAK

J **Wishing hut, The.** F. Cavanah. 3b., 5g., chorus. Sc. Shady nook in the woods. CAV

C **Wishing moon, The.** A. F. Brown. 19c. Sc. In a green glade. BROW

Wistful waiting. L. E. Joseph. Comedy. 7w. Sc. Interior. FREN

J **Wistful witch, The.** M. Barrows. 2b., 4g. Sc. Field at harvest time. SAO

Witch, The. F. Molnar. 3w. Sc. Sitting room of apartment. MOL

Witch of Endor, The. J. W. Raine. 7m., 1w. Sc. Sunset on Mount Gilboa. RAI

Witch-wife. M. Hogan and M. Constanduros. 2m., 2w. Sc. Kitchen of farm. FREL

J **Witches Hallowe'en tea party.** B. M. Casey. 1b., 11g. Sc. Garden of a large estate at midnight. CAS

Witch's daughter, The. H. Brighouse. 6m., 1w. Sc. A glade in an English forest in 1450. FRE4

J **With charity toward all.** A. Curtis. 2b., 5g. Sc. Street in the shopping district of a small town. CURT

C **With the watermelon seeds.** E. Edland. 6g. Sc. Chinese interior. EDL

Within the four seas. J. G. Paxton. 12 char. Sc. Interior. WOM

J **"Without a city wall."** P. E. Osgood. 3b. Sc. Striped Bedouin-like tent. OSG

Witness, The. J. Vrchlicky. 4m., 2w. Sc. Dining room in apartment. Blackmail play. SHAT

Wives-in-law. E. W. Smith. 2m., 2w. Sc. Living room. UNM2

C **Wizard of words, The.** C. T. Bryce. 2b. Sc. Room of a wizard. BRY

C **"Wohelo," or a day in every girl's life.** L. Dickinson. 20c. Sc. City yard in front of red brick house. St. Nicholas 51 : 730–734, May 1924.

C **Wolf and the horse, The.** A. Stevenson. 4b., 1g., chorus. Sc. A field of oats. STEV2

C **Wolf and the lamb, The.** A. Stevenson. 2b. Sc. A pasture. STEV2

Wolf at the door, The. D. E. Hanlon. 2m., 1w. Sc. Poorly furnished room. FRE6

Wolf of Zoty. B. Inge and C. Chupet. 2m., 3w. Sc. Indoors of a crude cabin in a village on the Austrian border. ING

Wolves. J. J. Bell. 3m. Sc. Hut in the far north. BAK

Wolves. A. Davis. 6m., 4w. Sc. Home in a village in the Ukraine. FREN

Woman forgives, The. K. Nicholson. Comedy. 2m., 1w. Sc. Living room. BAK

Woman from Nod, The. E. F. Taylor. 3m., 4w. Sc. Rough stone hut. DR

Woman of character, A. E. A. Brown. 9m. Sc. Living room of a middle class American home. EAT, LON

Woman of it, The. E. Andreas. Comedy. 3m., 1w. Sc. Office on Broadway. ANDR

J **Woman of judgment, A.** L. M. Pearson. 5g. Sc. Office. DAZ

Woman-song, a Chinese folk-play. K. Chen. 1m., 1w. No scenery. Theatre Arts M. 14 : 976–978. Nov. 1930.

Woman tamer, The. L. Esson. 4m., 1w. Sc. Front room of cottage. ES

Woman, the silent sufferer. S. Henderson. Satire. 1m., 14w. Sc. Club room. MARC

J **Woman who dared, A.** H. W. Githens. 5b., 2g., chorus. Sc. Gate of the palace in Shushan. GIT

J **Woman who dared, A.** M. M. Russell. 3b., 1g., chorus. Sc. Courtyard. RUS

Woman who understood man, The. J. Kirkpatrick. 2m., 3w. Sc. Living room. FRE6

Womanless divorce case, The. W. D. Padgitt. Farce. 6m., 1w. Sc. Court room. FREN

Woman's honor. S. Glaspell. Comedy. 9 char. Sc. Room in the sheriff's house. GLA

Woman's strategem, A. K. Kavanaugh. 3m., 2w. Sc. Interior. DRA

Woman's verdict, The. E. Morrette. 2m., 1w. Sc. Laboratory of a pathologist. MORR

Woman's wager, A. W. A. Tremagne. Comedy. 2m., 1w. Sc. Den in flat. PENN

Woman's way. A. L. Rice. Comedy. 3m., 2w. Sc. Anywhere in America. ROH

Women-folks, The. J. Kirkpatrick. Comedy. 1m., 6w. Sc. Interior. FREN

Women folks. J. W. Rogers. Comedy. 2m., 3w. Sc. Living room in Tennessee farmhouse. FREN, Country Gent. 91: 29–30, 109+, Nov. 1926.

Wonder hat, The. K. S. Goodman and B. Hecht. Fanciful. 3m., 2w. Sc. A park by moonlight. GOO

Wonderful Mr. Vanderhoof, The. D. A. Heywood. 2m., 5w. Sc. Interior. HEY

Wonderful radio, The. F. Tilden. 3m., 1w. Ladies Home Journal 44: 213, Feb. 1927.

Wonderful son, The. B. Gates. 1m., 2w. Sc. Living room of a small house in a main street in London. GAT

Wondership, The. L. Cunningham. 3m., 2w. Sc. Lonely isle in the deep blue sea. CLS

J **Wooden bowl, The.** E. H. Williams. 2b., 3g. Sc. Interior of cottage. WIM

Wooden leg, The. E. Dane. 1m., 1w. Sc. Public sitting room in an hotel at Nice. JOHN

Woodpile, The. M. Mix. 2m., 1w. Sc. A farmhouse kitchen. FREN

C **Woof! Woof!** E. P. Merryman. Comedy. 11c. Sc. Interior. DRA

Wooing, A. C. B. Going. Fanciful. 5m., 1w., 2 chorus groups. Sc. Late mediaeval interior. GOIN

Wooing Jane. A. Humboldt. Comedy. 2m., 2w. Sc. Interior. MARC

J **Wooing of Rebekah, The.** R. Kimball. 7b., 2g., chorus. Sc. Screens or draperies. KIM

Words and music. K. Nicholson. Comedy. 1m., 1w. Sc. Narrow passage leading off from the large basement furnace room. FRE5

Words and thoughts. D. Marquis. 1m., 2w. Sc. Two drawing rooms exact duplicates. APPL

C **Workers, The.** N. Flaurier. 4b., 1g. Sc. Stage. FJ, STRU

Workhouse ward, The. Lady Gregory. 2m., 1w. Sc. Ward in workhouse. COF, GOLD, MOSR, MOSS, TUC, Golden Book 9: 100–103, June 1929.

World without men. P. Johnson. Comedy. 7w. Sc. Morning room. FREL

C **World's Christmas tree, The.** F. Cavanah. 11c. or more. Sc. Any stage. Woman's Press 22: 836–837, Dec. 1928.

Worm turns, The. F. P. Hill. 2m., 2w. Sc. Kitchen. NOR

C **Worship the nativity.** J. Farrar. 10b., 13g., 13 chorus groups. Sc. A conventional grove. FARR

Would-be gentleman, The. Lady Gregory. 10m., 3w. Sc. A large hall. GREQ

"Wow Wow!" B. Charlton. Farce. 3m. Sc. Restaurant. CHA

J **Wraggle-taggle gypsies, The.** Boys of the Perse school. Fanciful. 5b., 2g. Sc. Open air play. WEB

J **Wrath of Israel, The.** H. W. Githens. 11b., 3g. Sc. Street in Jerusalem. GITH

Wreckage. M. H. Vorse and C. C. Clements. 3m., 3w. Sc. Sitting room in house in small New England village. APPL

Wrong numbers. E. Dane. 3w. Sc. Interior. JOHP

Wrong twin, The. A. C. Davison. Comedy. 2m., 2w. Sc. Living room. HEL, PENN

Wurzel—Flummery. A. A. Milne. Comedy. 3m., 2w. Sc. Morning room. MILN

X

X=O: A night of the Trojan war. J. Drinkwater. 6m. Sc. Grecian tent on the plain before Troy. DES, HAMA

Xanthippe and Socrates. M. Baring. Burlesque. 1m., 1w. Sc. Room in Socrates' house. JOHN, Golden Book 5: 347–349, Mar. 1927.

X-ray dialogue, An. R. Jeans. Farce. 2m., 6w. Sc. Studio. JER

Y

C **Yankee Doodle to the rescue.** F. R. Buchanan. 2b., 2g., many others. Sc. Platform. Norm. Inst. 34: 66–67, June 1925.

Yankee peddler. M. Barnett. 7m., 3w. Sc. Virginia plantation before the war. FIT

Yashmak! P. Wilde. Farce. 3m., 1w. Sc. A park bench. WILT

Yat Pak or the hundredth notch. E. T. H. Bunje. Tragedy. 4m., chorus. Sc. A square in Canton, China. CART

Ye who sit by the fire. F. Bedwell. 10 char. Sc. Living room. MEI

C **Year of holidays, A.** L. K. Dolan. 20c. Sc. Plain stage. DOL

J **Yelenka the wise.** A. C. Darlington. 3b., 4g., chorus. Sc. Before Russian house. DAR

Yella. H. McGuire. Melodrama. 3m., 1w. Sc. Forecastle of an Amer. tramp steamer. YAL

Yellow bittern, The. D. Corkery. 4m., 2w. Sc. Interior of a peasant's hut in Ulster. COR

Yellow peril, The. P. G. Smith. Comedy. 3m., 2w. Sc. Interior. NICR

Yellow roses. A. L. Mathews. 2m., 2w. Sc. Living room COL7

Yellow triangle, The. G. W. Sutton. 6m., 1w. Sc. Interior FREN

J **Yeo ho! Yeo ho!** C. Frances. Any number of b. Sc. Deck of ship belonging to a pirate crew. FRA

Yes and no. N. Balch. 3m., 1w. Sc. Office of furniture co. ELD

Yes and no. A. Bates. 1m., 1w. Sc. Living room. JOHN

Yes and no. H. Simpson. Farce. 2m., 2w. Sc. A sitting room. SIMA

Yes but-ers, The. M. T. Applegarth. 17 char. Sc. Living room. APN

Yes, Lucy. D. H. Harker. Comedy. 3m., 2w. Sc. Old fashioned parlor. DENI

Yes, we have no baking powder. L. Crites. 2m., 2w. Sc. Kitchen. ELD

Yesterday. C. C. Clements. Comedy. 1m., 1w. Sc. A secluded nook off the ballroom of a London house. CLP

Yesterday, to-day, and to-morrow. R. Jeans. Farce. 2m., 3w. Sc. Interior. JER

Yniard. J. Martin. Fantasy. 6m., 2w. Sc. Interior. APPL

You. C. C. Clements. Fantasy. 2m., 1w. Sc. Exterior. FREN

You can't joke with a woman. H. H. Torrence. Satire. 1m., 2w. Sc. Living room DRA

You can't please everyone. M. Mackendrick. 3m., 6w. Sc. Living room of a furnished apartment. MACS

You can't stop cupid. G. F. Mountford. 4m., 3w. Sc. Interior. DEN

You may stay after school. D. Sheridan. Burlesque. 6m., 9w. Sc. School room. SHER

You tell 'em. H. B. Splane. Comedy. 2m., 2w. Sc. Private office. PAIN

J **You tell 'er.** L. C. VanDerveer. 8b. Sc. Doorway. VAN

Young America. F. Ballard and P. Franklin. 4m., 1w. Sc. The office of a judge service. FRE2

J **Young defender, The.** E. E. Levinger. 4b., chorus. Sc. In ancient Jerusalem. BLO

J **Young folk's clubs at the county fair, The.** H. Bailey. 6b., 10g. Sc. Dobbins' home. ELD

J **Young general, The.** M. S. Beagle. 1m., 3b., chorus. Sc. A school yard. SAG

Young glory. M. Mackendrick. 5m., 4w. Sc. Sidewalk or market. MACS

Young love. C. Roberts. 2m., 2w. Sc. Morning room. FREL

Young man with the cream tarts, The. R. L. Stevenson. 5m., chorus. Sc. Meeting room of the suicide club. HAP

Young priest rebels, The. R. C. Alexander and O. P. Goslin. 3m. Sc. Rome in the 11th century. ALEX

J **Young Washington at Mt. Vernon.** P. Mackaye. 14m., 5w., 2c., chorus. Sc. Washington's home. SAG, SHAB

Your fiery furnace. P. Green. 2m., 2w. Sc. Negro cabin. GREF

Your kind indulgence. H. Farjeon. 2m., 2w. Sc. Sitting in a flat. FARJ

J **Your opportunity, an industrial play.** G. L. Parsons. 10b. Sc. Employment office. Ind. Arts M. 18: 51–4, Feb. 1929.

Yours at hand. R. Jeans. Farce. 3m., 2w. Sc. Small drawing room. JEO

Youth goes west. R. Knister. 3m., 2w. Sc. Farmhouse kitchen in Ontario. Poet Lore 39: 582–595, Winter 1928.

Youth must be served. H. Ford. 3m., 2w. Sc. Living room in a farmhouse in Connecticut. FRE3

Youth prays. K. I. Brown. 4m., 7w., 2c. Sc. Any stage. Christian Cent. 46: 681–684, May 22, 1929.

J **Youth's highway.** C. D. Mackay. 8b. Sc. Silver shop in Renaissance Italy. MACH

J **Youth's prophetic vision.** G. S. Overton. 27b. Sc. Outside the city of Jerusalem. OV

Z

Zara the Great. D. Titheradge. Farce. 1m., 3w. Sc. A curtained room. TITB

Zombi. N. V. Scott. 2m., 2w., 2 chorus groups. Sc. Front room of a small house on the edge of swamps near New Orleans. IS, Theatre Arts M. 13: 53–61, Jan. 1929.

Zoological. H. Simpson. Farce. 3m., 2w. Sc. London interior. SIMA

A

Abbott, A.
Mr. Enright entertains

Abel, B.
Adventure in friendship, An
Dotted line, The.
Gym and Jerry
Here we are!
Life is like that
Much ado about Ducats
Or, What have you?
Pain of it, The
Tell it to Venus
Triangle Tess, A
Two weeks with pay

Abel, G. H.
Why lie about it?

Abercrombie, L.
Blind
Escape, An
Fool's adventure, The
New God, The
Peregrinus

Abraham, N.
Queen Sabath

Ackerman, D. L.
Outside this room

Adair, T.
Bean boy, The

Adair, W. W.
Betty Blight's style show

Adam, B.
Shoe on the other foot, The

Adams, C. M.
His clever scheme

Adams, L.
How the great guest came

Adams, O. D.
Chinese slippers, The

Ade, G.
Mayor and the manicure, The
Marse Covington
Nettie
Speaking to father
Willing performer, The

Adkinson, R.
Station X-M-A-S

Adler, H. E.
Puppet

Aeschylus
Prometheus bound

Ahearn, T. J.
Twelve before three

Ainsworth, M.
Nancy and George listen in

Aitken, I. M.
Meaning of America, The
Our country and its flag

Akin, B.
Emily's revolt

Akins, M.
Below par

Akins, Z.
Portrait of Tiero, The
Such a charming young man

Alden, A. W.
Dickon goes to the fair
House in the wood, The

Alden, K. S.
Doll's first Christmas, The

Aldis, M.
Heir at large, An
Lord's prayer, The
Mrs. Pat and the law
Two plus two

Alehin, A. F.
Boaster, The
First sin, The
Glutton, The
Secret, The

Aleichem, S.
Liars

Alexander, A.
Teja

Alexander, H.
Butterfly girl and mirage boy
Carved woman
Earth-trapped
His-voice-is-a-whisper
How death came into the world
Kills-with-her-man
Living solid face
Man who married the Thunder's
daughter, The

Arlett, V. I.
　　Gardener, The
　　Last man in, The
Armfield, C. S.
　　Beau and Belle
　　Curious herbal, The
　　Gilded wreath, The
Armour, S.
　　Maid, The
　　Newcomer, The
Armstrong, H.
　　Santa's living toys
Armstrong, L. M. C.
　　Gertrude Mason, M.D.
Armstrong, L. V. V.
　　Dolls
　　Gold altar, The
　　Good roads
　　Late Captain Crow, The
　　Mouse, The
　　Waning moon, The
Armstrong, N.
　　Marthe
Armstrong, S. M.
　　Bride maid, The
　　Uninvited guests
Arnett, A. W.
　　King's choice, The
Arnold, E. W.
　　Cherry pie
　　I don't want to
　　King Quarrel and the beggar
　　Tooth fairy, The
Arnold, J.
　　Good medicine
Asalena, H. d'
　　Wishing gate, The
Asbrand, K.
　　Charity begins at home
　　Engaged for the month
　　Queer duck, The
Asgold, S.
　　At the brig end
Ashdown, A.
　　Midnight murder
Askren, R. L.
　　Passion's progress
　　They too
Assur, J.
　　Salvage
Atchinson, F. E.
　　Story terrace
Atlas, L. L.
　　✗ "L"

Auden, W. H.
　　Paid on both sides
Augier, E.
　　Post-scripts
Aukes, W.
　　Knife, The
Austin, C. L.
　　Dolls take a hand, The
Austin, E. L.
　　Everlasting Christmas tree, The
Austin, M.
　　Sekala ka'ajma
Averell, C. R.
　　Just bluff
Averill, Esther C.
　　Marks of a good citizen
　　Off the main road

B

Bacher, J.
　　Haman of today
Bacon, A. B.
　　King Lazybones
　　Mister Tree
Bacon, Eva M.
　　Journey of life, The
　　Princess of Moonbeam Castle,
　　　The
Bacon, Hazel
　　Some little mother
Bagg, H.
　　Scheming six, The
Bailey, C. S.
　　Christmas party, The
　　Home-coming, The
　　Maypole, The
　　Rabbit who wanted wings, The
　　Search for Santa Claus, The
　　Why Jack-o'-Lantern keep Hal-
　　　lowe'en
　　Young folk's clubs at the county
　　　fair, The
Bailey, H. R.
　　Around the world with the chil-
　　　dren
Bailey, L. C.
　　Black water
　　Job's kinfolks
Bain, E.
　　Road to Bethlehem, The
Baird, Mrs. Eva R.
　　Mission of Midas, The
　　Mother dear

Biggers, L. A.
These women! these women!
Billinger, R. D.
Night in alchemy, A
Bills, E. R.
Beauty secrets
Bimko, F.
Liars!
Binyon, L.
Godstow nunnery, The
Love in the desert
Memnon
Biro, L.
Bridegroom, The
Bishop, A. E.
At the stroke of twelve
Nora's cape
Bissell, W. L.
Brothers
Everyyouth
Great lexicographer, The
Kingdom of books, The
Switch on the moonlight
Bitney, M.
Aided by St. Patrick
Bothersome books
Boy who was kind
Christmas troubles
Do your Christmas Shopping early
Frank's Valentine
Friend Lincoln
Friendly Valentines
Grandmother Green's Thanksgiving
Georgie's piece
Good George Washington
Halloween Merrymakers
Halloween on Baldy
Honorable Madame
It isn't my dolly
Just one Christmas
Madame Summertime's guest
Making Molly merry
New-fangled Thanksgiving, A
Thanksgiving in a cabin
Washington at Valley Forge
What Thanksgiving means
Black, P.
Something different
Blackburn, R.
Coming of spring, The
Blackmore, M.
To die with a smile
Blackstone, J. B.
Rough diamond, The

Blaisdell, M. S.
Thanksgiving
Blake, R.
Law takes its toll, The
Bland, M.
Dead expense
Lighted candles
Pink and patches
Princess who could not dance, The
Blanning, L.
In broad daylight
Bloch, B.
Gas, Air and Earl
It isn't what you say, but how you say it
Block, M.
Eyes
Blomquist, M. C.
Enchanted summer
Queen of the year
Blose, R. W.
Good Health Way and Queen of the May
Boatright, M. C.
Age of accountability, The
C. C.
Boggs, H. O.
Abe Lincoln's kindness
Bertha brings home the bacon
Cat at school, A
Cheaters
Cripples, The
Difference of opinion, A
Five prim little patriots
Fools of April fool, The
Gabriel's horn
George Washington and the hatchet
Hero worshipers
Heroes of the haunted house, The
Kitchen convention, The
Lemuel wouldn't lie
Lesson from an humble source, A
Marie misses marriage
Midnight excursion, A
New boy, The
Only an only child
Poets cornered, The
Poor teacher
Quiz, The
Right of boyhood, The
Salvation am free
Singing-school teacher, The
Six S's admit Ferdie, The
Six S's hold a session, The
Six S's in action, The
Six S's organize, The

Bridges, V.
  Another pair of spectacles
  Deadman's pool
  Green monkey, The
Bridgham, G. R.
  Cynthia looks ahead
Brighouse, H.
  Flossie for short
  Followers
  Ghosts of Windsor Park, The
  How the weather is made
  Laughing mind, The
  Little liberty, The
  Little red shoes
  Lonesome-like
  Maid of France
  Night of "Mr. H.," The
  Price of coal, The
  Prince who was a piper, The
  Rational Princess, The
  Spring in Bloomsbury
  Stoker, The
  When did they meet again?
  Witch's daughter, The
Brink, C.
  Cupboard was bare, The
Bro, M. H.
  Milk
Brody, A.
  House of mourning, The
  Lowing in the night
  Rapunzel
  Recess for memorials
Bronson, E. M.
  Santa's shop
Brontë, C.
  Conversations
Brook, M. W.
  Voices
Brooke, R.
  Lithuania
Brookman, K. B.
  Interpolated
Brooks, G. S.
  Fortinbras in plain clothes
  No cause for complaint
Brooks, M. W.
  Dream, The
Brooks, V. W.
  Imaginary conversations
Brotherton, A. W.
  Talisman, The
Broun, H.
  Death says it isn't so
Brown, A. F.
  Little shadows, The

Rhoecus
Wishing moon, The
Brown, Alice
  Joint owners in Spain
Brown, B.
  Mysterious Thanksgiving guest
Brown, C. S.
  Modern magi
Brown, E.
  Nathan Hale
Brown, E. A.
  Woman of character, A
Brown, I.
  Sinbad the seller
  Smithfield preserv'd
  Swollen angels
Brown, J. M.
  Pageant of the shearman and
    tailors, The
Brown, K. I.
  Youth prays
Brown, L. K.
  Remnant day
  Right answer, The
  Two tables of bridge
Brown, L. N.
  Kissing goes by favor
Brown, M. B.
  When romance lived
Brown, N. K.
  Story of old Bethlehem, A
Brown, P.
  Gloria Mundi
Brown, S.
  Sandwich glass
Brown, T. A.
  Today is Monday
Browne, M. M.
  Faith and what it does
  Peter, a great Evangelist
  Successful evangelism in mission
    fields
Brownell, E.
  Mathesis
Brownell, E. B.
  Legend of the laurel, The
Brownell, J. C.
  Closet, The
Bruce, R.
  Sahdja
Brunton, F. C.
  Bet, better, best!
  Common sense
  Door, The
  Door on t'chain, The

Storming of Torquilstone, The
Sword in the stone, The
Trail of the bow, The
Treasure hunt, The

Butler, M. S.
Spring's awakening

Butterfield, W.
Kitchen mechanics
Tea for six

Byington, A.
Cranford dames

Bynner, W.
Little king, The

C

Cabell, J. B.
Jewel merchants, The

Cable, G. W.
Madame Delphine

Caesar, A.
Mother Goose thrift play
Napoleon's barber

Cain, J. M.
Citizenship
Hemp
Hero, The
Red, white and blue
Servants of the people
Theological interlude
Trial by jury
Will of the people, The

Calderon, G.
Little stone house, The

Caldwell, A. B.
Attendance play

Caldwell, S.
Mr. John
Next-of-kin
Phoebe Revels
Quite a nice cat
Sinking
Top dog

Call, B. A.
Thankful at last

Calver, H. N.
Pirate Percy and the Slovenly
Sloop

Cameron, E.
Memories of Christmas
Mystic numbers
Santa's helpers

Cameron, G.
Lost collar button, The

Cameron, M.
One of those days
Pipe of peace, A

Campbell, L.
Girl who slipped, The
Shakespeare smiles

Campbell, L. H.
Harvest blessings

Campion, C.
Disgrace
Pact, The

Campion, R.
Betty, behave!

Canfield, M. C.
Duchess says her prayers, The

Cannan, G.
Everybody's husband
Fat kine and the lean, The
In the park
James and John
Pierrot in hospital
Polite art of conversation, The
Same story, The
Short way with authors, A
Someone to whisper to

Cantillon, A.
Pierrot before the seven doors

Capus, A.
My tailor

Carb, D.
Grandma pulls the string
Lady of pain
Samson à la Mode

Carmichael, H. K.
Gaff

Caroline, H. W.
Not worth mentioning

Carpenter, E. C.
Prairie doll, The

Carpenter, M. B.
Advent of spring, The
Girl from Weepah, The
May queen, The

Carpenter, Mary E.
All on the king's highway
Baucis and Philemon
February's birthday party
Hans who made the princess
laugh
Poor little turkey maiden, The

Carpenter, Myrtle B.
Billy's awakening
Boys who knew Columbus, The
First Memorial Day, The
In the days of Franklin
In the days of Washington

Wanted, a confidential clerk

Charlton, B.
It is so simple
Mustard
"Wow, wow!"

Chatterton, N.
Are we sentimental?
Cash—$2000
$2000 cash

Chayer, C. C.
Evangels of the new day

Cheever, E. H.
Too perfect husband, The

Chekhov, A.
Anniversary, The
Boor, The
Marriage proposal, A
On the high road
On the highway
Proposal, The
Tatyana Riepin
Wedding, The

Chen, Kwei
Meeting at the well
Princely fortune
Woman—song

Chesterton, F.
Children's crusade, The
Christmas gift, The
Sir Cleges

Chew, R. E.
Magic Christmas tree, The

Chew, S. C.
Mr. Moore and Mr. Chew

Childs, C.
Truth always, The

Christensen, M.
Christmas path, The
Christmas windows
Sled for Christmas, A
Teddy had a toothache

Christy, K. G.
Thrift

Chupét, C.
Wolf of Zoty

Church, E. J.
Turn of the road, The

Church, L. L.
Beginning of the states

Church, V.
Very social service
What men live by

Claggett, R. P.
Half of my goods, The

Clapp, S. C.
Play for carolers, A

Clark, A.
Christmas joke, A
Mother's day in the primary
Twins' Christmas, The

Clark, D.
King's fool, The

Clark, H. W.
Return, The

Clark, Helen
At the wishing well
Mystic pipes

Clark, Helen L.
All in the lantern's glow

Clark, J. A.
Quarry, The

Clark, Sarah
Behind the scenes
Enchanted garden, The
Forty-'leven bunnies
Lu Li learns about Lincoln
Nora's elves
Pollyanna's guest of honor
Runaway posies
Straw stack, The
Unexpected guest, The
Wake, Princess!
What do you say?

Clarke, A.
Persephone

Clarke, D. L.
Desert smoke

Clarke, L. W.
No room in the inn
When day ran away

Clarridge, E. F.
Flowers' sacrifice, The

Claudel, P.
Gods churn the sea, The

Clemans, F.
Stranger child, The

Clement, C. E.
First Nowell, The
Troubadour's dream, A

Clements, C.
Across the border
All on a summer's day
Cherry Blossom River, The
Curtain!
Four who were blind
Haiduc, The
Harlequin
Hot lemonade
Jilted
Letters

Strutham amateurs present, The
Tragedy in the Upper Wallop, The
Witch-wife

Converse, F.
Three gifts, The

Conway, O.
At the sign of "The Sturgeon
    Head"
Becky Sharp
King's waistcoat, The
Mimi
Prudence corner

Cook, C. R.
Golden rule in courtship, The

Cook, E.
No sabe

Cook, G. C.
Suppressed desires
Tickless time

Cook, G. W.
Breakfast
Very sad unicorn, The

Cook, J. D.
Man of temperament, A

Cook, J. H.
Fifi's fortune

Cook, R.
But this is different

Cook, S. N.
Uncle Jack

Cooke, C. C.
Elsie in Mother Gooseland
In the days of Robin Hood
Princess and the pea, The

Cooke, J. F.
Scenes from the childhood of
    Franz Schubert

Cooke, M. B.
In the good greenwood
When love is young

Cooke, U.
Stars and grocerie

Cooksey, C.
Mountain laurel

Coon, R.
Another moon

Coontz, K. R.
Christmas at Old Lady's shoe

Cooper, M. D.
Canticles of Mary, The

Coppée, F.
Lord's prayer, The
Substitute, The
Violin maker of Cremona, The

Corbett, E. F.
After glow, The
Hanger back, The

Corder, F.
Learning to memorize

Cordy, I.
Love at first sound

Corell, M.
Animated toys
Conscience elf, The
Dr. Bluejay's patient
Hallowe'en nutting party, A
March wind, The
Safety first
Snow man, The
Spare the trees!
Thanksgiving in the barnyard
William and the sandman

Corkery, D.
Clan Falvey
King and hermit
Resurrection
Yellow bittern, The

Corneau, P. B.
General George Washington
Little John and the Miller join
    Robin Hood's band
Masks

Cornelius, O. F.
Mother's old home
Tie that binds, The

Cornell, E.
Starter, The

Cornish, M. T.
Three little runaway trees
Tommy's Thanksgiving dinner
When the turkeys turned the
    tables

Coulter, E. I.
Mimi lights the candle

Cournos, J.
Shylock's choice

Coventry, K. M.
Happy summer time
Japanese pageant

Cowan, S.
As I remember you
Ball and the chain, The
Cat, The
Collaboration
In the morgue
Pomp
Sintram of Skaggerak
State forbids, The

Cowden, B.
Secrets of long ago

Cummins, S. L.
Bluebeard
Goldilocks and the three bears
Haroun el Rashid
St. George and the dragon
Sleeping beauty, The
Thomas Olifant
Torquil MacFerron
Tyranny

Cunningham, L.
Wondership, The

Currie, C. H.
Whither goest thou?

Curtis, A.
Boy without a flag, The
Christmas at Mother's
Christmas dinner, The
Christmas magic
Christmas stocking
Duchess, The
Easter lily, The
For what shall I be thankful?
Hallowe'en wish, The
Lost purse, The
Merry Christmas in the old home
town
Mine eyes have seen the glory
Mirror, The
Mrs. Ryan's boarders
Old lady Kendall
Orange colored necktie, The
Spirit of the tree, The
Thanksgiving turkey, The
Too much trouble
Trials of a dressmaker, The
'Twas the night before Christmas
Vigilant Santa Claus, A
With charity toward all

Cuthrell, F. B.
Garden in Mitylene, A

Cutler, M.
May pageant
Visit to Washington's home, A

D

Dale, F.
He's a lunatic

Dale, R. V. H.
Ethel's queer complex

Dall, I.
Among old instruments
Bargain, The
In the barnyard
Miching Malecho
Noah's wife
One sunset

Dalrymple, C. L.
What happened to Jack

Dalton, Z.
Constitutional Convention
Declaration of Independence, The

Dane, Essex
Coming
Cooled off
Fleurette and Company
Going
His only way
Let it go at that
My neighbor
On the park bench
Other side of the door, The
Red sunset
Sweetheart
Toy tragedy
Veil lifts, The
Wooden leg, The
Wrong numbers

Darby, H. T.
Truth for a day, The

Darlington, A. C.
At the fair
By the roadside
In the Terem
Lady Joanna, The
Nine, The
Polonaise
La Ronda
Stars, The
Strong tower, The
Tessa's tongue
Through the dark
Torch of Hellas, The
Where the trails cross
Yelenka the wise

Darrow, W.
Thousand dollar reward, The

Daudet, A.
Siege of Berlin, The

Davidson, M. L.
Bit of heather, A

Davidson, M. R.
Christmas party at Sir Rogers, A
Coming of Williams Dane, The
On the road to Egypt
Wandering child, The

Davies, M. C.
Cobweb kings
Slave with two faces, The
Tables and chairs

Davis, A.
On vengeance height
Wolves

Davis, D. M.
Man in the moon, The
Street of hearts, The

Davis, H. E.
Bird strike, The
Dragon-fly
Ghost, The
I never thought of that
Katy did, Katy didn't
Ladybug, ladybug
Lost penny, The
Paper angel, The
Snow queen, The
When St. Nicholas comes

Davis, Martha
Lunch hour at the Greenwood
cafeteria
Sleeping beauty dines with the
Prince

Davis, Mary
Diplomatic Bridget

Davis, R. H.
Peace manoeuvres

Davison, A. C.
Big depression, A
Wrong twin, The

Davitt, J. A.
Brace of sixes, A

Dawley, Eloise K., *see* **Oller,
Marie**

Dawson, J.
Tables turned

Day, F. L.
Slump, The

Dean, A.
Just neighborly
Toast and tea

Dean, E. E.
Stockin' money

Degnan, L. M.
Visit to Toyland, A

De Huff, E.
Architect, The
For their sakes
Only day I have, The
Ten righteous
When West meets East

Deighton, L. K.
Pietro the foolish

De Jagers, Dorothy
Hot waffles

DeJong, M.
Lesson in thrift, A

Delano, E. B.
Grandma pulls the string

Lady of pain

Dell, F.
Sweet and twenty

DeMille, W. C.
Deceivers

DeMott, M.
His come-uppance

Denby, E. D.
Blackbird pie

DeNeauville, L.
Mr. Goodman and Mr. Gracious

Denison, M.
Balm
Brother in arms
From their own place
Prize winner, The
Weather breeder, The

Denison, T. S.
Borrowing trouble
Hans von smash
Too much of a good thing

Densmore, F.
How the turtles went to war
Race of the ants, The

Denton, C. J.
Burglars at Mrs. Day's, The
How the bag was mended
Queer people, The
Revelation, The
Snowflakes and the fairies, The
Surprised
We few, we happy few
When father was left to himself

Denton, E.
Goosey-goosey-gander
Lion and the unicorn, The
Old Mother Hubbard
Simple Simon
Sing-a-song-o'-sixpence

Deseo, L. G.
Japanese madonna, A
Never the twain

DeSola, A.
Shame the devil

DeSoto, A.
Executioner, The

Devendorf, L. K.
Stepping mother, The

Dew, L. E.
Christmas spirit tarries, The

DeWolf, L. H.
Whom seek ye?

Dickens, C.
Christmas carol, A

Ragged edge, The
Triumph of the defeated, The

Eaton, P. R.
Second honeymoon, The

Eaton, W. P.
Grandfather's chair

Echegaray, J.
Street singer, The

Edey, B. O.
Lo, the poor suitcase

Edgar, M. S.
Christmas tree bluebird, The
Conspiracy of spring, The

Edland, E.
Children's king, The
Cotton roses
Falling leaf
Fool's story, The
Life more abundant
Madonna's picture, The
Plum blossoms
Red-top
Wise and foolish virgins, The
With the watermelon seeds

Edwards, V. B.
Betty Jo's want ad

Egan, F.
One word play

Ehlert, F.
Undercurrent, The

Ehrlich, I. L.
Changing places
Cured
One hundred dollars
'Twas ever thus
Winners all

Eickman, G. S.
Little city of friendly hearts, The

Eldridge, H. C.
Grown-up folks

Ellicott, J. M.
Aye, aye, sir!
Pinin' f'r the skipper

Elliott, Margaret
Favours of my Lady Leon, The

Elliott, Mary
Animated slang

Ellsworth, E. E.
Trial of Johnny Jones, The

Elton, G.
Birthday gift, The
Concerning Coralie
Condemned cell, The
Twinkle, twinkle, little star

Elwyn, L. M.
Murder will out

Emerson, J.
Choice, The

Emery, G.
Delilah
Persian poppy, The
Riches
Thank you, doctor

Emery, S.
Mr. Smallworth's mistakes

Engle, W. K.
Medica

Enloe, M. A.
Christmas journey, A
Hallowe'en
How the fairies play
Real Santa Claus, The
St. Valentine's day with Mother
Goose
School time
Three bears, The
Thor and his hammer
Two little trunks

Erdman, F. W.
Sparks—an inbetween

Erickson, E.
Envy's end

Ermatinger, G. L.
Spirit of the American constitution, The

Ernst, A. H.
Nightingale
Spring sluicing
Valley of lost men, The

Ernesti, E.
Animated art room, The

Erskine, J.
Hearts enduring

Erskine, L. Y.
Boy who went, Th
Three cans of beans

Ervine, St. J. G.
Magnanimous lover, The
Ole George comes to tea
Progress
She was no lady

Eskil, R.
Calamity howler, The
Egging on Egbert

Esson, L.
Dead timber
Drovers, The
Sacred place, The
Woman tamer, The

Fife, G. B.
  Into the light
Fikenscher, A. B.
  Safety dialogue
Finn, John Jr.
  Fan Tan
Finnegan, E.
  —Fool of a man, A
  Singapore spider, The
  Slippin'
Finsterwald, M.
  Seven against one
  Severed cord, The
Firkins, O. W.
  After twenty-five years
  Answer, The
  Bloom on the grape, The
  Emeralds, The
  Geoffrey's wife
  In the small hours
  Last meeting, The
  Looking-glass, The
  Odd entanglement, An
  Reference, The
  Reticent convict
  Ruin of the desert, The
  Tulip and Camellia
  Two passengers for Chelsea
  Unbidden guest, The
  Undying prince, The
Fischer, N. L.
  Educatin' Mary
Fisher, A. L.
  Manager's trials, A
Fisher, B. P.
  Santa Claus gets his wish
Fitch, C.
  Nathan Hale
Fitch, O. J.
  Played before the Emperor
Fitzgerald, S.
  Imaginary conversations
Fitzhugh, C.
  Cough, The
  Margaret in Natos
  May and December
  Mon ami Pierrot
  Mountains of Bether, The
  Snake, The
Fitzmaurice, G.
  Dandy dolls, The
Fitzpatrick, J. W.
  Foreigner, The
  "Meet the family"
  Messenger, The

Fitzpatrick, W.
  Love and insurance
Flanagan, H. F.
  Curtain, The
Flanner, H.
  Mansions
Flaurier, N.
  As Mr. Clean sees it
  Change of mind, A
  Come back, Mr. Turkey
  Day before, The
  Fall day, A
  Five hours to go
  In an old diary
  In Jack-o'-lantern Row
  It was a surprise
  Jack smuggles in a guest
  Judge and the speeder, The
  Mistakes they left behind them,
    The
  Royal gift, The
  Story book frolics
  Street fair, The
  Striking in the New Year
  Tale the fire told, The
  Those tricky words
  Truant leaves, The
  Turning the tables
  Visit of the raindrops, The
  Voice from the air, The
  Welcome Miss McGregor
  Workers, The
Flavin, M.
  Blind man, The
  Brains
  Caleb Stone's death watch
  Casualties
  Emergency case, An
  Question of principle, A
Fleming, E. J.
  Elizabeth, the Quaker maiden
Fleming, Ethel
  Entertaining Aunt Mina
  Missionary clinic, A
Fleming, M.
  Box of Pandora, The
  Departure, The
  Harvest feast
  Pine-tree, The
Flowers, P.
  Forks of the dilemma, The
  May night
Folmsbee, B.
  Gift of love, The
  Guki the moon boy
  Jacquenetta and the Queen's
    gown

Star dust
Their husband
Trap, The
Unseen, The
Upstage, The

Ghose, G. C.
Chintamani

Gibbs, A. H.
Mereden's right hand

Gibson, E.
Betsy Ross
Common bond, The
Cornelia's jewels
George Washington's birthday
Hot water
Mother tongue, The
New worlds
Opening the gate
Scrubwoman, The
Spirit of Lincoln, The

Gibson, J.
Six hundred chicks!

Gibson, K.
Le jongleur de Dieu

Gibson, L.
Bumbo the clown

Gibson, W.
Blackadder
Kestral edge
Red Rowan
Winter's stob

Giffin, S.
Crime conscious

Gifford, F. K.
All or none

Gilbert, Bernard
Old bull, The

Gilbert, Bonnie
May madness

Gilbert, H.
Good Sainte Anne, The

Gilbert, W. S.
Creatures of impulse
Trail by jury

Gilchrist, Mary
Health play, A

Gilchrist, Murray
Climax, The

Gill, M. L.
Queens examine Alice, The

Gillette, W.
Among thieves
Red owl, The

Gilliland, C. H.
Visit from George Washington, A

Gilmore, A. C.
Americans all
Month of birthdays, The

Gilmore, A. F.
Our library

Gilpatric, C. D.
Forty miles an hour
Moving day
Please stand by
Sardines

Ginsberg, E.
Key to true happiness

Giorloff, R.
Circumstances alter cases
Jazz and minuet
Maizie
Nightshade

Githens, H. W.
Adopted son, An
Ambassador in bonds, An
At the beautiful gate
At the feet of the Apostles
Bad bargain, A
Captain's confession, A
Captive maid, A
Coat of many colors, The
Delivered from bondage
Delivered from prison
Down through the roof
Faithful daughter, A
Father of nations, The
Fiery furnace, The
First martyr, The
Fish story, A
Fisherman, The
For thirty pieces of silver
From palace to prairie
Giant story, A
Golden calf, The
Handwriting on the wall, The
Herald of the cross, A
Interrupted coronation, An
Labor riot, A
Last journey, The
Long courtship, A
Magic touch, The
Mother's gift, A
Opened eyes
Persecuted prophet, A
Prisoner promoted, A
Rash vow, A
Saved to serve
Searching for a wife
Shepherd king, The
Star of the east, The
Stricken traveler, A
Unexpected guest, An
Wanderer, The
Wise king, A

Woman who dared, A
Wrath of Israel, The
Glaspell, S.
Close the book
Outside, The
People, The
Suppressed desires
Tickless time
Trifles
Woman's honor
Glass, E.
Tumbler, The
Glassburner, M.
All for Christ
Gleason, M. N.
Cat fear
Rameses dreams
Glenn, E. M.
Arrested for speeding
Glick, C.
Fourth Mrs. Phillips, The
It isn't done
Outclassed
Police matron, The
Sun-cold
Ten days later
Glover, H. G.
Thompson's luck
Glover, N. G.
Shadow, The
Glynn-Ward, H.
Aftermath, The
Gnesin, M.
Mistress, The
Gnudtzmann, A.
Eyes that cannot see
Goelitz, M. J.
Everybody calls me Gene
Goes, B.
Dowry of Columbine, The
Goethe, J. W. von
Junkdump Fair
Gogol, N.
Fragment, A
Gamblers, The
Lawsuit, A
Official's morning, An
Servant's hall, The
Going, C. B.
Bénéad and the moor elves
North wind blowing, The
Psychotherapist, A
Twilight of the moon
Wooing, A
Gold, M.
Money

Golden, J.
Clock shop, The
Robe of wood, The
Vanishing princess, The
Goldenburg, G. D.
Claribel capers
Golding, L.
Judaism and paganism
Goodman, J. E.
Back to your knitting
Goodman, K. S.
Back of the yards
Dancing dolls
Dust of the road
Game of chess, The
Hand of Siva, The
Hero of Santa Maria, The
Idyll of the shops, An
Two lamps, The
Wonder hat, The
Goodrich, L. B.
Saint George and the dragon
Goold, M. N.
Shepherds, The
Gordan, B. L.
Old mathematics
Gordon, H.
Crowd, The
Gordon, H. K.
In the fog
Trump, The
Gorman, H.
Death of Nero, The
Goslin, O. P. *see* **Alexander, R. C.**
Gosselink, S. E.
Bookfolks' Christmas, The
Light of the cross, The
Making the flag
Valentine shop, The
Gosser, L. G.
Seven kings of Atherry, The
Gow, R.
Sausage, The
Under the skull and bones
Gowdey, G. R.
He lives
Grace, G.
At the costumier's
House agent, The
Grahn, M.
Idyll
Grant, A. H.
Carelessness
Jimmie goes back to school
Mistress spring's surprise party
Mother Goose's children

San Jacinto ball
San Jose
Whither

Grimball, E.
Waif, The

Grimm, M. A.
Christmas play, A
Mr. Weatherman

Grossman, S. S.
Two Goyim

Grundy, S.
In honor bound

Grundy, V. R.
Partisans of precaution

Gue, B. W.
George Washington

Guiman, J.
Black Oliver

Guinn, D. C.
Out of the dark

Guptill, E. F.
Christmas at McCarthy's
Crowning the May Queen
Golden goose, The
Magic word, The
Trip to Storyland, A

Guske, C. W.
Fata Deorum

H

Habberstad, C.
Bush queer
Cat comes back, The

Hafer, E.
Kidnapping Betty

Hageman, M.
Mrs. Mulcahy

Haggard, A.
Aurora and Tithonus
Midas
Philemon and Baucis
Romona

Hains, E.
Twelve o'clock on Christmas even

Hale, E. E.
My double and how he undid me

Hall, A. L.
New assistant, The

Hall, E. G.
Lonely hearts

Hall, H.
Duke and the dices, The
Valiant, The

Hall, J. W.
Joy lady, The

Hall, S. E.
Only good children, The

Halliday, A.
When something turned up

Halman, D. F.
Closet, The
Fannie and the ghost
Lenna looks down
Voice of the snake, The
Will-o'-the-wisp

Halsey, A.
Fairy grasshopper, The
Tea-time tempest

Halvey, P.
Etiquette
Wanderlust

Hamilton, C.
Child in Flanders, The
Jack and Jill and a friend

Hamilton, E.
Klubwoman, The
Prometheus bound, The
Mother Library's tea party

Hamilton, H. L.
Fingerbowls and Arminta

Hamilton, H. W.
Troubles of Mose, The

Hamlin, M. P.
He came seeing

Hammond, J. M.
It's all a matter of dress

Hampden, J.
Mrs. Adis
Over the garden wall

Hancock, W.
John Smith

Hankin, St. J.
More ado about nothing
New wing at Elsinore, The

Hanley, E. H.
Who left the cupboard bare?

Hanlon, D. E.
Wolf at the door, The

Hanna, T. M.
Clipped
House beautiful, The
Hyacinths
Upon the waters

Hannemann, H.
Anti-pashto
Decorating the interior
Florist's daughter, The
Genevieve's health dream

Hazelwood, C. H.
Harvest storm, The
Heal, E.
Into the Everywhere
Heald, J. P.
Hole in one
Knockout, The
Those terrible talkies
Healey, F.
Abu Achmet and the eggs
Copper pot, The
Creeds
Healy, C.
Self-respect
Heath, A. L.
Planning the husband's banquet
Heath, C.
Unruly member, The
Heath, E. P.
Bird in the hand, A
Hecht, B.
Hand of Siva, The
Hero of Santa Maria, The
Idyll of the shops, An
Two lamps, The
Wonder hat, The
Heijermans, H.
Ahasverus
Jubilee
Heintz, W. W.
Janitor's life, A
Helfen, M.
Battle with the giant, The
Little Nellie's Christmas dream
New cook, The
Wandering Christmas cakes, The
Henderson, A.
Conversation, A
George Bernard Shaw
Great war, The
Literature and science
Henderson, G.
A. B. C. fairies, The
Lucy chooses
Rats!
Henderson, R. E.
Here we come!
Henderson, S.
First aid for Kitty
Flippety-flop
Flowers for Flossie
Lineman, The
Where's my toothbrush?
Woman, the silent sufferer
Hendrie, E.
Coiners, The

Quite a nice cat
Sinking
See also plays by Sybil Caldwell
Helper, C.
Eli Whitney
Herbert, A. P.
Double demon
Two gentlemen from Soho
Herbert, B.
Lesson in elegance
Herberton, A. C.
Cottons and cookery
Herbrecht, O. G.
Nathanael's quest
Herford, B.
At the doctor's office
At the hairdresser's
Before and after
Bride's orders, The
In the flower shop
In the hat shop
In the wall papers
Lunch party, The
Marketing
Telegram, The
Wedding list, The
Wedding presents, The
Hering, H. A.
Hunt the tiger
Hermes, E. M.
Thanksgiving day movie, A
Herrick, M.
That upper forty
Hess, I. R.
Betsy Ross episode, A
October days
Hewitt, E.
'Bina's fortune
Hewlett, D.
Losing side, The
Heyward, D.
Love in a cupboard
Heywood, C. D.
Green Chartreuse
Heywood, D.
Good old times, The
Keeping up appearances
Mrs. Peabody's boarder
Trials of a country editor
Wonderful Mr. Vanderhoof, The
Hickman, M. H.
Southern tonic, A
Hicks, C.
Fliver family, The

From small beginnings
Hightones buy a car, The
Things that we can do, The
"Unto one of the least of these"

Holmes, C. N.
Wanted—a detour

Holmes, J. A.
In Arden forest

Holmes, R.
Diamond pin, The

Honors, M. O.
Mother Nature's carnival

Hooe, A. P.
Friendly dark, The

Hope, F. I.
Advent of spring, The
Mabel's aunt
May Queen, The

Hopkins, A.
Moonshine

Hopler, G.
Queen of the garden

Hornaday, T.
Dance of the books

Horner, E.
Betty in bookland

Hornickel, L.
Part-time job

Hornsey, E. G.
Denial
Gallant pilgrim, The

Hornthal, L.
Dance below

Horton, D.
Legend of the Graal, A

Houghton, S.
Dear departed, The
King's waistcoat, The
Master of the house, The
Phipps

Housman, A. E.
Letters and comment

Housman, L.
Bethlehem
Blind eyes
Bride feast, The
Brief life
Brother Elias
Brother Juniper
Brother Sin
Brother Wolf
Builders, The
Chapter, The
Charles! Charles!
Cure of souls

Cutty stool, The
Elegy of a country churchyard
Fellow prisoners
Fire-lighters, The
Fool's errand, The
Last disciple, The
Lepers, The
Lovers meeting
Messengers, The
Mortuary, The
New hangman, The
Odour of sanctity, The
Order of release, The
Our lady of poverty
Revellers, The
Sal Volatile
Seraphic vision, The
Sister Clare
Sister Death
Sister Gold

Houston, N.
Raw men

Housum, R.
Corsican lieutenant, The
Eligible Mr. Bangs, The

Houwink, J. J.
Ahasverus

Howard, A. S.
Travelers, The

Howard, Mrs. Hilda (Glynn) *see*
Glynn-Ward, H.

Howard, K.
Trial of Jimmy Germ, The

Howe, W. E.
Home coming, The

Howell, C. C.
Forfeit, The

Howells, W. D.
Sleeping car, The

Hoxie, E.
Act foolish and be wise
Fortune telling
Hildegard's elopement
History slightly mixed
It's all over town
Johnny on Colonial history
Mollie teaches the code of the
flag
When Harold met his mother-in-
law

Hsiung, C. C.
Marvelous romance of Wen Chun-
Chin, The
Thrice promised bride, The

Hubbard, C. A.
Poor Richard's dream

Bronze bride, The
Wolf of Zoty

Ingersoll, J. H.
Queen's shift, The

Ingersoll, P. G.
Troupers

Innes, T. R.
Tale of a shirt, The

Ireland, Baron
Movieless movies

Irish, M.
Abel Adams happy Christmas
Adoption of Bob
Aunty's Christmas basket
Aw, Gee
Awakening, The
Brown's Merry Christmas, The
Charles, the Conqueror
Christmas at Crane's corners
Christmas at Dinky flats
Christmas at Joyville Junction
Christmas at Stebbinses'
Christmas at Timothy Corners
Christmas eve on Pine Knob
Christmas on crutches
Christmas party, The
Christmas stocking, A
Clackville choir's Christmas carols
Everybody Thankful
Excuse me
Friendly advice
Getting into step
Going to the party
Good fairies, The
Grumps meet the grouches
Hallowe'en hold-up, A
How Grandma caught the Christmas spirit
Incentive
Jus' 'fore Christmas
Just before midnight
Lessons in love making
Lucky Hallowe'en, A
Make your choice
Mattie discovers a Merry Christmas
Meeting of the hearts
Mended day, A
Midwinter's night dream
Miss Miranda
Modern pirates, The
Molly's Merry Christmas
Now take it from me
Our friends the trees,
Out to win
Patsy Dugan's Christmas
Plymouth's first Thanksgiving
Pumpkin pie Peter
Pun'kin-headed servant

Reunion at Pine Knot Ranch
So this is school
Thanksgiving as usual
Thanksgiving on Hickory Slope
That 'ere line fence
Uncle Caleb's quiet Christmas
Uncle Mel's Merry Christmas
Uncle Ole's uncle
Van Dorn's Merry Christmas, The
Victory and Thanksgiving
What happened to Brown

Irving, W.
Rip Van Winkle
Rose of the Alhambra, The

Irwin, M.
Three visitors, The

Irwin, M. E. F.
Happy man, The

Ish-Kishor, J.
Slave from Egypt, The

Issasi, T. F.
Sentence of death, The

Izzet-Melyh
Disenchanted, The

J

Jackson, C.
Mother's day

Jackson, R. L.
Friends invited

Jacob, F.
And they met again
Autumn blooming
Basket, The
Clever one, The
Man's world

Jacob, M.
Little man in the moon, The

Jacobs, W. W.
Castaway, The
Ghost of Jerry Bundler, The
Love passage, A
Monkey's paw, The

Jagendorf, M.
Bumbo and Scumbo and Blinko
Farce of the worthy Master Pierre Patelin
Firefly night
In King Lugdub's forest
King Groog and his grouch
Master Patelin
Mee-Mee and But-Zee
Merry Tyll
Once in a hundred years

K

Judith
Peril of the moon, The
Solomon's song
Their day
White hawk, The

Kemper, S.
Blood will tell
Old Chester secret, An

Kennard, G. A.
Good health

Kennard, M. C.
Flight of the herons, The

Kennedy, A. R.
Virgin's tree, The

Kennedy, C. O.
And there was light
Man with the iron jaw, The
Men, women and goats

Kennedy, C. R.
Necessary evil, The
Terrible meek, The

Kennedy, H. L.
Lion's mouth, The

Kerigan, F.
Eyes that see, The

Kern, M. E.
Food revue

Kerr, H.
Everybody happy?

Kerr, R. N.
Heart of oak

Kester, K.
Bargains
Love and lather
Penny a flower
Rondo Capriccioso

Kibbe, M.
Is Santa coming?
Surprise for Santa, A

Kidd, M. F.
What did the sandman bring?

Kidder, A. R.
His and hers

Kimball, R.
Abraham Lincoln
David and Jonathan
Elijah and Elisha
Great minds
Jacob's journey
Making of the flag, The
Moses in the bulrushes
Nativity, The
Prodigal son, The
Resurrection, The
Ruth

Samuel in the House of the Lord
Story of Joseph, The
Wooing of Rebekah, The

Kimball, R. P.
Lydia

Kiner, G.
Wedding clothes

King, B.
Bachelor of Gray Crags, The
Her husband's watch
Importance of Mary, The
Knight's mare, The
Nephew in the house, A
Purple pig, The
Romantic Melisande
What's in a name!

King, D. G.
Brothers

King, F.
Arrow by day, The

King, G. G.
Legend of St. Dorothy, The

King, Grace, E.
Splendid offer, A

Kinyon, G.
Daring daughters

Kipling, R.
Poor dear Mamma
Wee Willie Winkie

Kirkpatrick, J.
Wedding, A
Woman who understood men, The
Women-folks, The

Kiyotsugu
Maiden's tomb, The

Klein, Y.
All America's children
Best food for all, The
Current events plea, The
Gift of the fairies, The
Greatest dreamer of the world, The
Highway of Brotherly Love, The
If Lincoln were with us today
If the children of Europe could speak to us
In Father World's garden
In the land of books
In the land of clean children
In the palace garden
Lincoln Memorial, Washington, D. C., The
Lonely little tree, The
Making of an Art, The
March of the milestones, The
Meeting of "The Young Citizens' League of America," A

Pilgrim ladies, The

Lincoln, J. C.
Managers, The

Lindsay, C.
Breakfast for two
False colors

Lindsay, H.
Apartments to let

Lindsay, I. F.
Uncle Sam's pantry

Lindsay, W.
Chances

Linn, N. M.
Henry's "Tux"

Linsky, F. B.
Americans all
Box from the attic, The
Memorial day fantasy, A
Set-the-table lady, The

Lipkind, G.
What happened on Chanuka

Lippincott, M. W.
Mysterious Valentine, The

Littell, R.
And other stories
Finest flower of the age, The
Topics for topers

Livingston, R.
Apache

Lloyd, G.
Children decide, The
Closing day review, A
Crystal gazing
Good King Arthur
House that Jack built, The
Jack-in-the-box
Mr. Massy makes a fourth at bridge
One madding day and knight
Prevention goes marching on
Santa Claus package, The
Thanksgiving with Mother Goose
Toy inspection
Tweedle-dum and Tweedle-dee
Vacations
Verdict for the wishbone, A

Lobner, J. E.
Golden eagle child, The

Locke, B. M.
Hiartville Shakespeare Club

Lofgren, M. T.
Lunch hour at the Greenwood cafeteria
Sleeping beauty dines with the Prince

Logie, I. M. R.
Those absurd missionaries

Lonergan, G. E.
Doormat, The

Long, P.
Persians of Aeschylus, The

Longacre, W. B.
Jolly animals crew, The

Longenecker, N.
Easter mystery play, An

Longnecker, E. B.
Hands up
Lingerie shop, The
Passing of Mr. Peal, The

Loomis, R. S.
Play of St. George, The

Lord, D. A.
Aboard the Santa Maria
Angels of prayer
Boyhood Pt. I Land of desires
Boyhood Pt. I Land of dreads
Boyhood Pt. I Land of dreams
By radio
Discontented daughter, The
Flame leaps up, The
Giant and Jack, The
Giant temper, The
God's adopted son
Just after the Civil War
Maidland Pt. II The land of desires
Maidland Pt. II The land of dreads
Maidland Pt. II The land of dreams
Making of the flag, The
Mistress Castlemaine's Christmas dinner
Pirates bold, The
Prologue
Rainbow gold
Road to Connaught, The
Santa Claus's workshop
Secret, lovely garden, The
Sight of the blind, The
Silly goosegirls, The
Sir Folly
Too fast for Pharaoh

Lorde, A. de
At the telephone

Lorenz, C.
Mother Blessing's job

Lorenz, C. M.
Idyll

Lounberg, K.
Flamingo feather, The

McGinley, P.
  Mary's garden
McGuire, H.
  When the ship goes down
  Yella
McIlhargey, L.
  Old witch carelessness
McIlquham, E. M.
  Doll shop, The
MacInnis, C. P.
  Immortality
McIntyre, H.
  Delicate child, The
McIntyre, Dr. John, *see* **Brandane, John**
McIntyre, J. T.
  Dime lunch, The
Mack, C.
  Bit of gossip, A
Mack, L.
  High-low-brow, The
  Three strikes and out
Mack, O.
  Last day for grouse
Mackall, L.
  Scrambled eggs
Mackay, C. d'A
  Abraham Lincoln
  Beau of Bath, The
  Benjamin Franklin
  Boston Tea party, The
  Calendar of joyful saints, A
  Christmas guest, The
  Counsel retained
  Daniel Boone
  First Noël, The
  In the days of Piers Ploughman
  Journeyman, The
  Midsummer Eve
  Miracle of St. Nicholas, The
  On Christmas eve
  Prince of Court Painters, The
  Silver lining, The
  Snow witch, The
  Three wishes, The
  Youth's highway
Mackay, I. E.
  Last cache, The
  Second lie, The
  Treasure
Mackaye, P.
  Antick, The
  Cat-boat, The
  Chuck
  Funeralizing of Crickneck, The

George Washington at the Deleware
808.82 Gettyburg
C6780 Napoleon crossing the Rockies
  Pilgrim and the book, The
  Sam Average
  Timber
  Washington and Betsy Ross
  Young Washington at Mt. Vernon
MacKaye, R. K.
  Swamp, The
Mackendrick, M.
  Christmas memories
  Evening's entertainment, An
  Freedom
  Gift box, The
  Helping hands
  High prices and danger
  How many, Madame?
  Right about—face
  You can't please everyone
  Young glory
Mackenzie, E. I.
  How Bobby put it over
  Leave it to Phyllis
  Maiden vain of dress, The
  Snowbound for Christmas
  That awful letter
  Unexpected guest, The
  Waking the Christmas spirit
McKeon, T. J.
  Messiah, The
McKinnel, N.
  Bishop's candlesticks, The
McKittrick, M.
  Gate of Montsalvat, The
MacLean, A.
  Knight of the piney woods, A
MacLennan, M.
  May day
McMahan, Mrs. A. L.
  No one knows what a woman
    will do
McMahon, S. C.
  Such a little Swede
  Twelfth initial, The
McManus, J. S.
  Episode
Macmanus, P.
  Between trains
  Detour ahead
  Oececea
  Toy heart, The
Macmillan, D.
  Off Nags Head

Marivaux, P. C. de
Test, The

Marks, J.
Deacon's hat, The
Look to the end
Love letters
808.82 L4226 Merry, merry cuckoo, The
Steppin' westward
Tress of hair, A
808.82 C6280 Welsh honeymoon

Marks, M.
Our American language

Maroney, M. J.
Fair play

Marquis, D.
Words and thoughts

Marquis, M.
First Christmas, The

Marschall, P.
George Washington

Marsh, A. M.
Reformation of Bobby

Marsh, F. A.
Boston tea party, The
Rip Van Winkle

Marshall, A.
Accomplice, The
Candid critics

Marshall, L.
Green shadows
Winter sunshine

Martin, F. J.
Christmas eve in Santa's workshop

Martin, J.
Yniard

Martin, J. M.
When heroes come

Martin, L. P.
Aunt Sophy takes charge
Christmas eve at the poor farm
Lost coin, The
Sixth hat, The
Thoughtless giving
Way to a man's heart, The

Masefield, J.
Campden wonder, The
Good Friday
Locked chest, The
Mrs. Harrison
Sweeps of ninety-eight, The

Mason, H. S.
At the gate beautiful

Mason, M. K.
Every child's lesson

Mather, C. C.
Lower road, The

Mathews, A. L.
Yellow roses

Mathews, J.
Cruiter
Ti Yette

Matthias, V. P.
Brownie's dream, The

Maupassant, G. de
Necklace, The

May, G. V.
Wanted, a Mahatma

May, J. L.
Come what may

Maynard, G.
Three trees, The

Mayor, B.
Thirty minutes in a street

Mead, A. B.
Glad tidings to all people
Why photographers go mad

Mead, F. S.
Church

Mead, W.
Trial by breakfast

Meadow, J.
Pearls before swine
Vespers

Meaker, I. J.
Knife, The
Sojourners

Means, F. C.
Black tents, The
Pepita's adventure in friendship
Tara finds the door to happiness

Medcraft, R.
First dress-suit, The
808.82 O580 Poetry and plaster
Saucy goose

Megrue, R. C.
Same old thing, The

Melford, A.
Kit Marlowe

Melick, V.
Fur and warmer

Mellon, E. E.
Trains

Melvill, H.
Famous Bugle diamond mystery, The

Melville, R. L.
Call of the campus, The
On the road of yesteryear

Portrait of a gentleman in slippers

809.82
C618o Red feathers, The

Wurzel-Flummery

Minard, M. C.
Fat and happy
Kellys' friendship, The

Minchin, N. E.
Birthday cake, The
Cold cream
Jester's purse, The

Minnion, W. J.
Pressgang, The

Mitchell, A. M.
Captive princess, The

Mitchell, B.
Morning in a superintendent's office, A

Mitchell, F. L.
Soft shoulders
Tommy meets his excuses
When the Darbys dieted

Mitchell, L.
Father Time's workshop

Mitchell, W. J.
Well, I declare!

Mitchison, N.
Elfen Hill
Hobyah! Hobyah!
My ain sel'
Nix-nought-nothing

Mitcoff, E. Y.
Petroushka

Mix, Morton
Woodpile, The

Molière, J. B. P.
Flying doctor, The

Molnar, F.
Host, The
Lies
Marshall
Prologue to "King Lear," A
Still life
Two slaps in the face
Violet, The
White cloud, The
Witch, The

Monkhouse, A.
Grand Cham's diamond, The
King of Barvender, The
Night watches
O Death where is thy sting?
Wily one, The

Montague, C. M.
Tropics

Moore, B.
Baggage, The
Ringing the changes

Moore, B. C.
On Bayou La Batre

Moore, D. M.
Harvest Thanksgiving, The
How can nations practice the Golden Rule?
Why pray for others?

Moore, F. F.
Jessamy bride, The
Kitty Clive
Poor actress, A
Sword of Damocles, The

Moore, Florence B.
Tale from India, A

Moore, G.
George Moore and John Freeman

Moore, Mildred G.
Bank of English, The

Moore, Minet B.
Patience's dream

Moore, Ralph
Kid, The

Moore, Raymond
Great moments

More, B. R.
Peter's night out

More, F. E.
Revising a geography

Morgan, L. E.
Mistress Mary's garden

Morgan, M.
Fairy garden, A

Morizot, A.
Christmas language project, A

Morley, C.
Abandoned husbands
Bedroom suite
Birth of God, The
East of Eden
Etiquette
Good theatre
In modern dress
On the shelf
Really, my dear
Rehearsal
Sun machine
Three friends
Thursday evening
Wagon-Lits
Walt

Morrette, E.
In the swath
Nine-ten express, The

Nelson, M. L.
Spirals

Nerison, M.
Radio playet, A

Nesbitt, C. M.
Demshur man, A
Net, The

Nesseman, E. B.
In the secret places

Nethercot, A. H.
Peter Gink

Newett, J. H.
'Limination

Newman, B. W.
Salt water
Underground

Newman, H. L.
Service the fairies did, The

Newsome, O. E.
In the art gallery

Newton, H. L.
Outwitted
Teacher, kin I go home?

Newton, R.
Madonna of the Golden Hart, The

Nichols, A.
Devil's field, The
Gardener's cap, The
Haunted circle, The
Shepherd's pipe, The

Nichols, E.
Fixer, The

Nichols, R.
Petrarch, d'Annunzio

Nicholson, K.
Anonymous letter, The
Bedside manners
Bug man, The
Casino gardens, The
Confession
Deliverance
Man pays, The
Marriage of little Eva, The
Meet the Missus!
Night's work, A
Organ, The
Shame the devil
Snake eater, The
So this is Paris Green!
Van Tromps listen in, The
Wanderlust
White elephants
Woman forgives, The
Words and music

Niemeier, M. A.
Adoption of the Constitution, The

Calendar for poets' birthdays, A
Choosing a statue for Lincoln
Park
George Washington at the helm
of state
Jack-in-the-pulpit is preaching to-
day
Joys of the New Year, The
Message of Easter, The
News of the adoption of the Con-
stitution
One country, one flag, one lan-
guage
Quarrel of the seasons, The
St. Patrick's day
Veteran's story, The
Visit from Mr. and Mrs. Santa
Claus, A
Washington at the helm of state

Noble, C. C.
There is room

Noble, P.
As the twig is bent

Noorden, A. van
Backwoodsman, The

Norcott, M. Lane, *see* **Lane-Norcott, M.**

Norman, C.
Faustus

Norris, K.
Kelly kid, The
Perfect service

Norris-Lewis, A.
Why! It is spring

North, L.
At any cost

Northey, M.
Realm of Thanatos, The

Norton, A. W.
Barrel of fun, A
Basket of beautiful things, A
Choosing a doll
Christmas eve on the trolley car
Christmas time at Santa's head-
quarters
Fairies and a Christmas tree, The
Home for the holidays
Toy shop mix-up, The
Wisest wish, The

Norton, M.
Cure for discontent, A

Noorwood, G.
Silent customer, The

Novak, D.
City, The

Pyramus and Thisbe
Theseus

Olson, E. E.
Conclusions
Giving thanks today
Hallowee'n party, The
Lighting the way
Meddlin'
No room at the inn
October gave a party
On the way home
Parlor tricks
Red shoes at Plymouth
Right around the corner
Spark plugs
Summer day dream, A
They say—
Two's enough
Up in the air

Oneal, B.
Inspiration, The

O'Neill, E.
Bound East for Cardiff
Dreamy kid, The
Emperor Jones, The
Ile
In the zone
Long voyage home, A
Moon of the Caribbees, The
Rope, The
Where the cross is made

O'Niell, L. T.
Day dream, The

Ordway, P.
Shepherd lad's gift, The

Orwig, C.
Gentlemen prefer bonds
High Hattie

O'Ryan, A. W., *see* **O'Ryan, F.**

O'Ryan, F.
Capture of Major André, The
Early shyness of an orator
First public appearance of a noted
character
Franklin's forebodings
Greene and Morgan on the Yadkin
Hiding of the charter, The
On historical coincidence
Lincoln as a young clerk
Precarious situation in Boston's
history, A
Roger Sherman at his last

Osborn, L.
Easy money
Isle of smiles, The
Moonshine

Osborne, H.
Mary's lamb

Osborne, M.
Point of view, The

Osbourne, L.
Little Father of the Wilderness,
The

Osgood, P. E.
Adoration of the three kings, The
Annunciation, The
As it was in the beginning
Boy bishop, The
Burial of Alleluia, The
City walls and open plains
Destiny
Elijah
First day of the week, The
Gabbatha
Gift of self, The
Herod play, The
In Herod's dungeon
Judas Maccabaeus
Judas of Kerioth drives a bar-
gain
Lazarus tells of his death
Meeting of the three kings, The
Melchizedek, Abraham and Isaac
Naked evil
Nativity, The
Outcast
"Quem quaeritis"
Shepherds all?
Shepherds' play, The
Sinner beloved, A
Story of a story, The
Summoning of Everyman, The
Under authority
Without a city wall

Ould, H.
Claude
Discovery, The
Episode
Joan the maid
Pathfinder, The
Peter the Pied Piper
Princess in the sleeping wood
Princes Mirabelle and the swine-
herd
Rip van Winkle
Thy father and thy mother

Ouless, E. U.
Children of Eve, The
Dame truth
Death in the tree
Five poor travellers
Horse thief, The
Old game, The
Wandering scholar, The

Schaefer, D.
Battle, The

Schayer, E. R.
Private Jones

Schenck, D. R.
Little Princess who traveled far
to worship the King, A

Scherr, G.
Real Christmas, A

Schmidli, L.
Sacajawea

Schmidt, G. P.
I did but jest

Schmotzer, A.
Rise of Marion Allen, The

Schnitzler, A.
Festival of Bacchus, The
Green cuckatoo, The

Schonberg, F. H.
Santa's little king

Schofield, S.
Bruser's election, The
Good old Uncle Amos
Marble god, The
On the moor
Saving Lady Jane

Schwartz, E. D.
Three souls in search of a dramatist

Schwarz, Florine, *see* **Klein,
Yetta**

Schwartz, T.
Pierrot—his play
Six

Schwartz, T. G.
Monster, The

Scott, D. C.
Pierre

Scott, E.
Geometry humanized

Scott, Mrs. J. E.
Gifts of autumn, The

Scott, N. V.
Zombi

Scott, W. A.
Cupid in shirt sleeves

Scudder, A.
Flight
Maple's bride, The
Never ending wrong, The
Poppet, The
Prince Pentaur
Thomas the Rhymer

Sealock, T.
Saturday's lamb

Seaver, C.
The return of Bob Gregory

Seavey, M. M.
Miss Tabitha's garden

See, E.
A friend of his youth

Sehon, C. L.
Here, there, and everywhere

Seiffert, M. A.
Noah's ark

Seiler, C.
Box seats
Crime
An eye for an eye
Eyes
Fantasia
The husband of Xanthippe
In a window
The lady in the sack
Matrimony
Poets all
Suicide
Time will tell

Seldes, G.
In an airplane

Selnick, E.
The gold machine

Sexton, E.
Bernstein tries 'em out
The dance of the red, red rose
Introducing Scrooge
Santa gets the blues
Santa Claus in the White House
School spirit
We aim to please
When Betty Ann helped Santa
Claus
When the Christmas tree talked

Shacklett, Mrs. J. B.
Town that Santa forgot, The

Shacklett, M.
Land of no fences, The

Shakespeare, W.
Pyramus and Thisbe

Shaler, E.
Loose

Sharp, H. S.
Germs

Sharpe, M.
Jimmy Jenkins' Hallowe'en
Land of play, The
Mother Goose's Christmas
School at Padding Lane

Sharpsteen, E. J.
His wife's first husband

"Whose husband are you?"
Will it come to this
Yes and no
Zoological

Simpson, Helen
Pan in Pimlico

Simpson, L.
By unanimous vote

Simpson, M.
Jolly health clown and his helpers, The

Singley, H.
Horatius at the bridge

Sissman, L.
On board the S. S. Health

Skerrett, J.
Mathematical nightmare, A

Skidmore, H. D.
Lassitude
Three-a-day

Skinner, A. M.
Christmas in many lands
Star in the East, The

Skinner, F.
Commencement dilemma, A
Pennies, nickels and dimes
Pie, pickle and ham

Skinner, R. D.
Really—Mr. Jenkins!

Sladen-Smith, F.
Crown of St. Felice, The
Edward about to marry
Invisible Duke, The
Man who wouldn't go to heaven,
The
Sacred cat, The
Saint's comedy, The
St. Simeon Stylites

Small, A. J.
'Ole in the road, The

Smedley, E. A.
Shall yes stay?

Smith, B. F.
Father and sons

Smith, Mrs. C. P.
Acid test, The
Grapes hang high, The
What would you do?

Smith, D. H.
Falling in love with plain geometry

Smith, Dorothy B.
Memorial day pageant, A

Smith, E. V.
'Lijah

Smith, Elizabeth W.
Day's work, The
Wives-in-law

Smith, Evelyn
Alchemist, The
Enchantment of Finn, The
Escape from Lochleven, The
Fool of Dunvegan, The
Goose-girl, The
Gudrun
Havelock the Dane
Kitchen knight, The
Marchioness, The
Shepherdess and the chimney-
sweeper, The
Siege of Ping, The
Town mouse and the country
mouse, The
Tragedy rehearsed, A
Tweedledum and tweedledee,
Visit to London, A

Smith, F. M. Bell, *see* **Bell-Smith,
F. M.**

Smith, G. J.
Forbidden fruit

Smith, Grace E.
Arrow maker's daughter

Smith, H. D.
Mother sets the stage

Smith, H. T.
Which is which?

Smith, J.
Out of the night
Pyentsa

Smith, J. W.
Quack doctor

Smith, L. R.
Real Santa Claus, The

Smith, L. J.
Cathedral clock, The

Smith, L.
Ramadan

Smith, M. S.
American grandfather, An
Good night
Hamburger King, The
Oft in the stilly night
Slow but sure
Wedding anniversary, The

Smith, Maude S.
Low-boy wins, The

Smith, N. A.
Christmas in the mouse-hole

Crowning of peace, The
Summer is calling

Smith, O. L.
Henpeck Holler gossip

Smith, P. G.
Yellow peril, The

Smith, S. T.
Uncle's will
Which is which?

Smith, V.
Simple soul, A

Smyth, R.
Jimmie's magic whistle

Sneddon, R.
Might-have-beens

Snell, N. S.
Pea-green cats

Snyder, H. H.
Reckoning, The

Snyder, R. L.
If

Sollenberger, J. K.
Marriage gown, The

Somple, *see* **Lloyd, Gladys**

Sompayrac, I.
Through the picture frame

Sorden, H. L.
Bag of fresh air dreams, The

Sorenson, G.
Adopted one, The
Golden Easter egg, The
Halloween porch party
Left-over boy, The
Little cousin, The
Meriwether fortune, The
Miss Bennett's house party
Mistake, The
Most beautiful Valentine, The
Mystery of the buried box, The
New teacher, The
Runaways, The
School clown, The
Spooky Halloween, The
Stupid Christmas, The

Soto, A. de
Executioner, The

Soule, G.
Profits & depression

Southgate, H.
Rusty door, The

Souvestre, E.
Mrs. Willis' will

Speare, F. L.
Bride and the burglar, The

Speirs, R.
Change of mind, A
Grave, The
Hogan's successor

Spence, E.
Fool's errand
Starter, The

Spence, M. C.
Blind

Spencer, E.
Christmas eve in the land of Nod
Christmas eve visitor, A
Christmas in America

Spencer, K.
Conn-eda

Spencer, W.
Carrying out a theory

Splane, H. B.
You tell 'em

Spofford, F. P.
Two quacks and a duck

Squires, E. L.
Come to my party
Criss cross ways
Did you ever?
Fern dust
Four in a box
Great grandmother's attic
Handy Andy Irons
Little Sun's birthday
Mice will play, The
Paper dolls
Pedlar man
Queen Jezebel
Who said pie?

Squires, Mrs. G. S.
Best hand, The
Greatest force, The
Shortest play in the world, The

Sramek, V.
Good appearance in school, A

Staadt, E.
Cabbages

Staats, P. G.
Good American, The

Stackhouse, P. J.
Babe of Bethlehem, The
Conversion of a dishonest tax-
collector, The
Disciple of the night, The
Facts are stubborn things
Joseph the dreamer
Joseph the interpreter of dreams
Joseph's dreams come true
Man of Kerioth, The
Queen who saved a nation from
death, The

Rich young ruler, The
Thomas the twin
Stafford, T. H.
Peace and comfort
Stahl, M. E.
La Carota
Stallard, Mrs. A.
Call, The
Feast, The
Gate of heaven, The
Hermit, The
Miracle, The
Stamflora, J. H.
Sam Weller visits his mother-in-
law
Stayton, M.
Mollie and the milliner
Stedman, M.
Mr. Santa Claus
Tonic
Steele, M. E.
Out of the book
Spring fantasy, A
Steele, Sidney, *see* **Kaser, A. L.**
Steele, W. D.
Giant's stair, The
Not smart
Ropes
Terrible woman, The
Steell, W.
Fifth commandment, The
Steiner, O.
Fortune teller, The
Ghost in the boarding school, The
Miss Nonchalance
Steinmetz, E. G.
At the fountain
Stenger, G.
Biter bites and the bitter bits,
The
Minuet, The
On the road to Bethlehem
This-a-way and that-a-way
Stephens, N. B.
Charivari
Stephenson, A.
Eternal question, The
Euclid was right
Pulling the show together
Sterling, F.
Lee, the Virginian
Modern Viking, A
Sterling, D.
Rhymes and reactions

Stevens, D.
Christmas Highwayman, A
Eliza gets kissed
Stevens, E. M.
Rocking chair row
Stevens, H. C. G.
Captain, The
Four's company
House on the hill, The
Murder most-polite
Off the lines
Release
Reprieved
Result, The
To meet the King!
Stevens, Henry B.
Early frost
Stevens, J. S.
Book of Job, The
Stevens, S. S.
Building a character
Fairy gifts
Stevens, T. W.
Duquesne Christmas mystery,
The
Friend Mary
Highways cross
Nursery-maid of heaven, The
Three wishes
Triumph of Punchinello, The
Stevenson, A. M.
School lunch room, The
Stevenson, Augusta
Beautiful song, The
Bernard Palissy, enameller
Big Claus and little Claus
Black pearl, The
Blind men and the elephant, The
Cat and the mouse, The
Cat that waited, The
Christopher Columbus
Clever cock, The
Clever kid, The
Crow and the fox, The
Daniel Boone
Don Quixota
Each in his own place
Emperor's test, The
Endless tale, The
Fairy and the cat, The
Fishing on dry land
Girl who trod on the loaf, The
Goblin and the huckster's jam,
The
Golden bucket, The
Hare and the hedgehog, The
Hare and the tortoise, The
Henry Hudson

Boy who hated trees, The
Christmas lesson, A
Commander in chief
Conversion of Saul, The
Crowning of Saul, The
Crowning of Solomon, The
Daniel in the lion's den
David and Goliath
Dog in the manger, The
Dove and the ant, The
Esther
Hans the shepherd boy
Hare and the tortoise, The
Hill, The
Imprisonment of Peter, The
Lesson in geography, A
Lion and the fox, The
Martyrdom of Stephen, The
Memorial day parade, A
Naaman the leper
Parable of the good Samaritan,
  The
Parable of the great supper, The
Parable of the prodigal son, The
Parable of the rich fool, The
Parable of the talents, The
Parable of the tares, The
Parable of the wicked servant,
  The
Paul and Silas at Philippi
Ruth
Shipwreck of Paul, The
Should we be more thankful than
  the pilgrims?
Training for the presidency
Wind and the sun, The

Whitson, A. L.
Christmas on a day coach
Gaining a member
Great decision, The

Wick, M. C.
Radio Christmas, A

Wiegand, C. v.
Emilia Viviani
Jasmine and the poet

Wiggin, K. D.
Fragments of a play

Wight, D.
Under the oak

Wilbur, E.
Godfather's Christmas
Marriage cake, The
Mistletoe and moonlight
Table set for himself, The
Wares never did so, The

Wilbur, H.
Christmas toy shop, The

Wilcox, C. G.
Blue and green mat of Abdul
  Hassan, The
Heart of Frances, The
Told in a Chinese garden

Wilcox, G.
Translated

Wilcox, P. V.
Radio for the family
Sketch for home mechanics

Wild, E. M.
Dish of scandal, A

Wilde, O.
Birthday of the Infanta, The
Salome

Wilde, P.
According to Darwin
Alias Santa Claus
Ashes of romance
Beautiful story, The
Con amore
Confessional
Costume de rigeur
Dawn
Duetto
Dyspeptic ogre
Enchanted Christmas tree, The
Ever upwards!
Facts, The
First client, The
Gadgets
Hush money
Inn of discontent, The
Kings in Nomania
Lady of dreams
Lost elevator, The
Lot's wife
Love is blind
Luck-piece, The
Meticulous customer, The
Mothers of men
Moving finger, The
National anthem, The
Noble lord, The
Nocturne
Out of the mouths of . . .
Past pluperfect, The
Phial, The
Playing with fire
Question of morality, A
Reverie
Robert Burns
Short cut, A
Standish pride
Stork, The
Thing, The
Toy shop, The
'Twas the night before
Unaccepted apology, The

Z

SUBJECT INDEX

ARIZONA

Cowpunchers

ARKANSAS

Bumblepuppy

ARMISTICE DAY

Crowning of Peace, The
Flags at war, The
New holiday, The
Plowshare or the sword, The
Spirit of the Red Cross, The
Tree of memory
Unseen host, The
See also WORLD WAR

ART AND ARTISTS

Animated art room, The
Bernard Palissy, enameller to His
  Majesty
Choosing a statue for Lincoln
  Park
Color demonstration
Color fairies
Color fantasy
Color play
Color play for grade children
Color wheel revue, The
Cup of tea, A
Does America discourage art?
Drama, The
Fanny Otcott
Fifteenth candle, The
Helping Mildred
Helpless Herberts
Implicable Aphrodite, The
In the art gallery
Jack and Jill and a friend
Johnny has a design dream
King's fool, The
Land of color, The
Laurel wreath, The
Making of an art scrap book, The
Mimi
Phryne
Portrait of Tiero, The
Potter's dream, The
Pottery
Purple at the window
Rainbow robe, The
Spirit of beauty, The
Tale of the five mystic colors, A
Through the picture frame
Towers
Varnishing day
When pictures come to life
Which is which?

ASTRONOMY

Good resolutions
Guki the moon boy

AUSTRIA

Festival of Bacchus, The
On the frontier
Tenor, The

AUTOMOBILE

Arrested for speeding
Finest flower of the age, The
Fliver family, The
Hightones buy a car, The
Hitting on all six
Judge and the speeder, The
Traffic cop, The
Wanted—a detour
What is truth? asked Pilate

AUTUMN, *see* SEASONS

AVIATION

Flyin'
Flying prince, The
In an aeroplane
In an airplane passenger station
Their appointed rounds
Youth must be served

BABY SHOW, *see* SOCIAL SATIRE

BALLADS

Barring of the door, The
Coming of Fair Annie, The
Duke of Gordon's daughter, The
Gohalt of Weirhawk
Heir of Linne, The
In the Good Greenwood
King Richard calls for ale
Little John and the Miller join
  Robin Hood's band
Robin Hood
Robin Hood in Sherwood
Shutting o' the door, The
Three princesses, The
Undaunted female, The
See also FOLK TALES

BANDITS, *see* CRIME

BEAUTY SHOP

Beauty secrets
Cherry special

Getting a permanent wave
On second thought
Permanent wave, The
Samson a la mode
Sun machine

BELGIUM

Interior

BENGAL

Chintamani

BIBLE

Abraham and Isaac
Abraham in Egypt
According to your faith
Adopted son, An
Ahaz casts away the heritage
Ambassador in bonds, An
Amos
Annunciation, The
As the twig is bent
At the beautiful gate
At the feet of the Apostles
At the gate beautiful
Babe in the bulrushes, The
Babe of Bethlehem, The
Bad bargain, A
Barabbas
Benjamin and the silver cup
Betrayal
Book of Job, The
Boy heroes of the Bible
Cain and Abel
Calvary
Captain's confession, A
Captive Israel
Captive maid, A
Children's king, The
City walls and open plains
Cleopas
Coat of many colors, The
Comeback, The
Conversion of a dishonest tax-
   collector, The
Conversion of Saul, The
Courage
Crowning of Saul, The
Crowning of Solomon, The
Daniel and the lions
Daniel in the lions' den
Daniel's loyalty
David and Goliath
David and Jonathan
David anointed King
David, the Shepherd boy

Delilah
Delivered from bondage
Delivered from prison
Delivered from the lion's mouth
Destiny
Diana of the Ephesians
Disciple of the night, The
Door, The
Down through the roof
East of Eden
Elijah and Elisha
Elisha
Esther
Facts are stubborn things
Faithful daughter, A
Father of nations, The
Feast of Belshazzar, The
Feast of faith, The
Fiery furnace, The
First day of the week, The
First gift, The
First martyr, The
Fish story, A
Fisherman, The
Flight into Egypt, The
For his name's sake
For thirty pieces of silver
Friend of Potiphar's wife, The
From palace to prairie
Gabbatha
Genesis
Giant story, A
Gift of Jehovah, The
Gift of self, The
Girl who knew how to be a friend,
   A
Golden calf, The
Good Samaritan, The
Handwriting on the wall
He came seeing
Healing of Naaman, The
Herald of the cross, A
Herod play, The
I am come
Imprisonment of Peter and John,
   The
In Herod's dungeon
In quest of a great treasure
In the desert
Interrupted coronation, An
Ishmael
Jacob's journey
James of Galilee
Jephthah's daughter
Jezebel
Joseph and his brethren
Joseph, the dreamer
Joseph, the dreamer of dreams
Joseph, the interpreter of dreams
Joseph's dreams come true

BIOGRAPHY

Calendar for poets' birthdays, A
Glimpses of great people
Little glimpses of great people

BIRDS

Air gun, The
Bird Strike, The
Birds' community sing, The
Birds' party, The
Blackbird pie
Wise owl's school, The

BLACKMAIL

Chee-chee
Hush money
Letters

BLAKE, WILLIAM

Mesengers, The

BOARDING HOUSE

Jonathan and the lovely lie
Ma's new boarders
Mrs. Greevy's boarders
Other side of the door, The
Riches

BOHEMIA

Witness, The

BOOKS & READING

Bargains in Cathay
Betty in bookland
Birthday party, The
Book folks' Christmas, The
Book play for high schools
Book review, The
Bookcase, The
Bookland
Bookland
Books in Sally's cupboard, The
Bringing up nine
British Museum's vacation, The
Broadcast from Bookland
Children's bookshelf, The
Christmas message, The
Dance of the books
Day dream, The
Do I hear twenty thousand?
Elsie in Bookland
Enchanted book-shelf, The
Exit Miss Lizzie Cox
Feast of adventure

Food for thought
Good book fairy, The
King of the bookcase
Kingdom of books, The
Land of books, The
Land of play, The
Library and the Joneses, The
Library for the first grade, A
Little pageant of story books, The
Magic windows
Mother Goose convention
Mother Library's tea party
On being a goop
On the shelf
One winter's night
Our library, a Dewey Decimal
   play
Party from Bookland, A
Pictures from Bookland
Play for good book week, A
Pollyanna's guest of honor
Primary book pageant, A
Story-book ball, The
Story Book pals
Story books before the judge, The
Story terrace
Stranger, The
Tea party in Bookland, A
Through the open book
Trip to Storyland, A
Uncle Bob chooses books

BORGIA, CAESAR

Hospitality

BOY SCOUT

Biter bites and the bitter bits,
   The
Boy who went, The
Honor of a scout, The
Sneakin's

BRADDOCK, GENERAL

Before Fort Duquesne

BRIDGE

Born nurse, A
Bridge as the ladies play it
Does bridge develop the mind?
If men played cards as women do
Late Mrs. Laite, The
Mr. Massy makes a fourth at
   bridge
Quiet game, A
Quiet rubber, A
Two tables of bridge

BROADCASTING, *see* RADIO

BRONTË, CHARLOTTE

At the Misses Brontë's establishlishment

BURGLAR

Aunt Sophy takes charge
Burglars
Burglars at Mrs. Day's, The
Deceivers
Grandma's Christmas guest
Hands up
Little cousin, The
Mrs. Bright's visitor
Nevertheless
Noël
Poet passes, A
Point of view, The
Prince Gabby
Rose-shaded lamp, The
Soul made clean, A
Whose money?
See also CRIME

BURKE, EDMUND

Counsel retained

BURMA

Inasmuch, a medical playlet
Mamagee and the robbers
Pyentsa

BURNEY, FANNY

Miss Burney at court
Silver lining, The

BURNS, ROBERT

Cutty stool, The
Scenes in the life of Robert Burns

BURROUGHS, JOHN

Gift of the fairies, The

BUSINESS

Avenue, The
Bargain day at Bloomstein's
Bargains
Beating the boss
Boots and shoes
Business à la Mode
Business in 2030 A. D.

Buying a tie
Change of heart, A
Columbine in business
Come here
Customer is always right, The
Dark days ahead
Efficiency test, The
Enter Dora—exit Dad
Escape
Forfeit, The
Fred joins the firm
Gadgets
Gaff
Georgie plays his hand
Gysers, Ltd.
Hat shoppe, The
He failed but succeeded
Home cured
Honeymoon specialist, The
Hopeless passion of Mr. Bunyon, The
House agent, The
Idyll of the shops, An
In a window
In the fire's shadow
In the hat shop
In the wall papers
It is so simple
Leap-year bride, A
Lenna looks down
Lonesome-like
Lost—a sale
Marketing
Master salesman, The
Mollie and the milliner
Mr. Richey changes his mind
Mrs. Wright gets in wrong
On the P.D.Q.
Paid to worry
Paris labels
Persecuted Dutchman
Pirtle drums it in
Potter Pancake Co., The
Sale by auction
Spirit of labor, The
Stanley takes the business
Tammy
Trap doors
Yes and no
You can't please everyone
You tell 'em

BYRON, LORD

Glorious martyr, A
Lord Byron

BYZANTINE

Byzantine afternoon, A
Their day

CALIFORNIA

Good vintage

CAMP FIRE GIRLS' see GAMES AND
SPORTS

CANADIAN

And they met again
Autumn blooming
Basket, The
Brothers in arms
Clever one, The
From their own place
Good Sainte Anne, The
Last cache, The
Low life
Man's world
Pierre
Turn of the road, The
Youth goes west

CARLYLE, THOMAS

Fire-lighter, The
Two passengers for Chelsea

CHARACTER BUILDING

Boaster, The
Boy and the echo, The
Boy and the nuts, The
Broken commandment, The
Building a character
Cotton roses
Courtesy play, A
Door of success, The
Enchanted dolls, The
Everyday courtesies
Fairy gifts
First sin, The
Flavor lasts, The
Giant and Jack, The
Giant temper, The
Grand evening, A
Great quest for character, A
Glutton, The
Hans the shepherd boy
Hill, The
Hilltop
I don't want to
Knight of the piney woods, A
Land o' the slowpokes, The
Lucy chooses
Magic word, The
Maidland Pt. II, the Land of desires
Merry Tyll

Modern knight—Theodore Roosevelt, A
Morality for the leisure class, A
Mr. February Thaw
One gift above another
Red-top
Secret, The
Silly goosegirls, The
Touchstone, The
Travelers, The
Treasure hunt, The
Twins' birthday party, The
Two sisters, The
Winter sunshine
Wish garden, The

CHARITABLE INSTITUTIONS

Christmas eve at the Poor farm
Come true
Duchess, The
Joint owners in Spain
See also SOCIOLOGY

CHATTERTON, THOMAS

Chatterton

CHAUCER, GEOFFREY

Canterbury pilgryms

CHEMISTRY

Arabian barber shop
Chemistry saves the day
Cinderella of the metals, The
Fraternity initiation, The
Janitor's life, A
Jest of Hahalaba, The
Night in alchemy, A
Second lie, The
Well, I declare!

CHILDREN'S BOOK WEEK,
see BOOKS & READING

CHINESE

Bit of brother, A
Blind man, The
Crinkum-Crankums
Dragon's glory
Drum dance, The
Fan Tan
Goosebery Mandarin, The
Joy lady, The
Kite, The
Lady in the sack, The
Lily Ling's first Christmas

Shepherd's pipe, The
Shepherd's play, The
Sled for Christmas, A
Snowbound for Christmas
Snowflakes and the fairies, The
Sonny Santa Claus
Spirit of Christmas, The
Spirit of Christmas via Santa
  Claus, The
Spirit of the Christ, The
Spreading Christmas cheer
Star, The
Star in the East, The
Station X-M-A-S
Story of old Bethlehem, A
Stranger child, The
Stupid Christmas, The
Surprise for Santa, A
Synthetic Santa
Table set for himself, The
Tale the fire told, The
Ten fingers of François, The
There is room
They that sit in darkness
Three cans of beans
Three little runaway threes
Three trees, The
Those Christmas gifts
To whom Christ came
Tommy's dream of Christmas
  night
Too much Christmas
Town that Santa forgot, The
Towneley play, The
Toy inspection
Toy shop, The
Toy shop mix-up, The
Toys' Christmas frolic
Transformation of Mary Lou,
  The
Traveling man, The
Trimming the Christmas tree
Troubadour's dream, A
Troublesome Christmas tree, A
True spirit of Christmas, The
'Twas the night before
Twelve o'clock one Christmas
  even
Twins' Christmas, The
Two Christmas boxes
Two sides of the door
Umbrian play, The
Uncle Caleb's quiet Christmas
Uncle Mel's Merry Christmas
Upon the waters
Van Dorn's Merry Christmas,
  The
Virgin's tree, The
Visit from Mr. and Mrs. Santa
  Claus, A

Visit from Santa Claus via radio,
  A
Visit to Santa, A
Visit to Toyland, A
Waif, The
Waking the Christmas spirit
Wandering child, The
Wandering Christmas cakes, The
Wanted—a Santa Claus
West o' the Alleghenies
When Betty Ann helped Santa
  Claus
When Santa came to the orphan-
  age
When the Christmas tree talked
Where lies the child
Whitethorn at Yule
Who said pie?
Why Johnnie changed his mind
Why Santa quit
Why the chimes rang
Wise gifts, The
Wise men seek Jesus, The
Wisemen, The
World's Christmas tree, The
Worship the Nativity
Ye who sit by the fire
See also BIBLE; RELIGIOUS; ST.
  FRANCIS

CIRCUS

After the reunion dinner
Bumbo the clown
Circus comes to town, The
Circus day
Dancing dolls
Fashion show, The
Flambo, the clown
It's all a matter of dress
Le jongleur de Dieu
Mademoiselle Diana
Mademoiselle Tania
Man with the iron jaw, The
Prize winner, The
Show must go on, The
Snake eater, The
Triumph of Punchinello, The
What's a fixer for?
When a clown laughs

CIVICS

City Council wakes up, The
Election day tea, An
First Thanksgiving, The
Secrets of long ago

CIVIL WAR, *see* U. S. CIVIL WAR

FIRE PREVENTION

Amateur fireman, The
Restraint of fire, The

FLAG DAY

Betsy Ross episode, A
Flag makers, The
Johnny on Colonial history
Making of a flag, The
Mollie teaches the code of the
    flag
Mystic numbers
Our country and its flag
Pageant of the flag, The
Prince of Ko-Am, The
Soul of the flag, The
Two flags, The
Washington and Betsy Ross
What our flag means to the chil-
    dren of other countries
What our flag stands for

FLAPPER, see SOCIAL SATIRE

FLORIDA HURRICANE

Hurricane

FLOWERS

Garden play, A
Kingdom of the Rose Queens, The
May Queen, The
Mistress Mary's garden
Mistress Spring's surprise party
Queen of the garden
Runaway posies
Save the wild flowers
Spring's flower garden

FOLK STORIES

Abu Achmet and the eggs
Aucassin and Nicolette
Beautiful song, The
Blind men and the elephant, The
Call, The
Cat that waited, The
Cinderella
Copper pot, The
Dickon goes to the fair
Endless tale, The
Golden bucket, The
He, on whom a sandal fell
House of brick, The
Immortals, The
King's good friend, The
Lark's nest, The
Lazy Kate

Man and the alligator, The
Nightingale
North Wind blowing, The
Pearl of dawn
Proud ring-finger, The
Sausage, The
Selfish woman, The
Slippers of Cinderella, The
Slippers that broke of themselves,
    The
Snow witch, The
Sparrows in the hat, The
Thor and his hammer
Three wishes, The
Two holes, The
Two Millers, The
Two questions, The
Wise men of Gotham, The
Wish-bird, The
Wooden bowl, The
Wooing, A
See also ARABIAN: BALLADS:
    DRAMATIZATIONS

FOURTH OF JULY

Glorious wish, The
National anthem, The
Reformed Fourth, The
Trial of the glorious Fourth, The

FRANCE

Conspirators, The
Executioner, The
Flight
For Russia
France
Green cuckatoo, The
Little king, The
Lord's prayer, The
Mimi
Minuet, A
Murder of Marat, The
Pierre Patelin
Red sunset
Three visitors, The
Toast that we can drink, A
Waif, The

FRANKLIN, BENJAMIN

Benjamin Franklin: journeyman
Franklin's forebodings
Journeyman, The
Poor Richard's dream
Poor Richard says

FRONTIER, see U. S. EXPANSION

Damon and Pythias
Daedelus and Icarus
Demos and Dionysus
Demeter and Triptolemus
Echo and Narcissus
Electra
Garden in Mitylene, A
Golden touch, The
Greek games and festivals
Hades and Persephone
Honest critic, An
Jason and the golden fleece
Labors of Heracles, The
Legend of the laurel, The
Lost Proserpine, The
Lycurgus the law maker
Marpessa
Midas
Nausicaa
Nausicaa and her maidens
Odysseus at Ogygia
Odysseus returns home
Orpheus and Eurydice
Pandora
Pericles and the builders of Athens
Persephone
Persians of Aeschylus, The
Phaethon and the sun chariot
Philemon and Baucis
Play of the luck of Troy, The
Pomona
Prometheus bound, The
Prometheus the friend of man
Pygmalion and Triptolemus
Pyramus and Thisbe
Quest of Perseus, The
Return of Eurylochus, The
Solon the legislator
Theseus
Theseus and the Minotaur
Torch of Hellas, The
Trial of the bow, The
Warrior's husband, The
Ulysses
When half-gods go
Wings of Daedalus, The

GYPSY

Visiting the gypsy camp
Water in a sieve

HALE, NATHAN

Nathan Hale

HALLOWEEN

Act foolish and be wise
At the stroke of twelve
Black cat entertains, The

Black rose of Halloween
Druid oak, The
Dwellers in darkness, The
Elfin knight of Hallowe'en
Five ghosts
Fortune telling
Ghost, The
Ghosts that walked on Hallowe'en
Giggle witch, The
Gingerbread house, The
Goblins, The
Going to the party
Hallowe'en
Hallowe'en adventure, A
Halloween guest
Hallowe'en hold-up, A
Hallowe'en in the garden
Halloween Merrymakers
Halloween on Baldy
Hallowe'en party, A
Hallowe'en porch party
Hallowe'en pumpkins
Hallowe'en surprise, A
Hallowe'en wish, The
Hansel and Gretel
Harvest blessings
Haunted cottage
Jimmy Jenkins' Hallowe'en
Lost firewood, The
Lucky Hallowe'en, A
Magic jack-o'-lantern, The
Mammy explains Hallowe'en
Mother Holloween's children
Pun'kin-headed servant, The
Sambo, Lil Sal and the pancake party
Schoolroom imps, The
Shades' Halloween Convention
Spooky Halloween, The
Travelling to a Hallowe'en party
Turning the tables
Two blind men and a donkey
Why Jack-o'-lantern keeps Hallowe'en
Wicked witch, The
Witches Halloween tea party

HAMILTON, ALEXANDER

Early shyness of an orator

HANCOCK, JOHN

John Hancock

HANDEL, GEORGE F.

Child Handel, The

Jubilee
Settin' up with Wilhelmina
When St. Nicholas comes

HOME ECONOMICS

Baking the cake
Contrast, The
Cupid and the cutlets
Ethel makes cocoa
Henri makes a sale
Home economics play
House beautiful, The
Importance of being clothed, The
Importance of being nice, The
Jones family, The
Kitchen convention, The
Lunch hour at the Greenwood
    cafeteria
Mother's day out
Mrs. Newly wed attends school
Party, The
Set-the-table lady, The
Smith family, The
Story of silk, The
Vite-em-in, the garden of health
Yes, we have no baking powder

HONESTY, *see* CHARACTER BUILDING

HOSPITAL

Bedside manners
Below par
Blind, The
Cup of life, The
Emergency case, An
Fixer, The
Foolin' 'em
Love at first sound
Ministering angel, The
Miracle, The
Not lost
Pyjamas

HOTELS

Carrying out a theory
Mrs. Markham on hotels
Mrs. Markham continues on ho-
    tels
Troubles of a hotel clerk

HUDSON VALLEY

Blood o' kings
Joe

HUNGARY

Bridegroom, The

Marshall
White cloud, The

IMMIGRATION, *see* AMERICANIZATION

INDIA

Cobra's head
Drums of Oude, The
Land of the outstretched hand
Tale from India, A
Tropics

INDIAN

Action!
And the tribes shall pass
Arrow maker's daughter
Butterfly girl and mirage boy
Carved woman
Christmas spirit of Swift Deer,
    The
Coming of summer, The
Earth-trapped
Falling Leaf
Golden eagle child, The
Hiawatha's childhood
Hiawatha's friends
Hiawatha's wedding feast
His voice is a whisper
How death came into the world
How peace was brought to the
    red man
How the turtles went to war
Indian boy's pet, An
Indians' Thanksgiving, The
Kills-with-her-man
Little scar-face
Living Solid Face
Lost child, The
Man who married the Thunder's
    daughter, The
Mirage
Mother Minnetonka
On Bayou La Batre
Pocahontas
Poor little Turkey maiden, The
Race of the ants, The
Rescue of Cynthia Ann, The
Sacajawea
Scalp, The
Sekala Ka'ajma
Turkey girl, The
Weeper, The
What do you say?
Where the trails cross
White Canoe, The

INDIAN TERRITORY

Reckless

MANUAL TRAINING

Change of heart, A
Fads and frills
Sketch for home mechanics

MARCH, *see* MONTHS

MARIONETTE

Candidate for Trepagny, The
Cataclysterium's medicine
Coq brothers, The
Every dog has his day
Junkdump Fair
Mirthful marionettes
Mr. Goodman and Mrs. Gracious
Petroushka
Fool, Tom
Scourge of Gulph, The

MARLOWE, CHRISTOPHER

Kit Marlow
Reckoning, The

MATHEMATICS

Dr. Arithmetic establishes a hospital
Euclid was right
Falling in love with plain geometry
Geometry humanized
If
Little journey to the land of mathematics, A
Mathematical nightmare, A
Mathesis
Near tragedy, A
New assistant, The
Oh, you mathematics
Old mathematics
Quarrel, The
Which, three R's or three R's

MAY DAY

Conspiracy of spring, The
Crowning the May Queen
Enchanted Maypole, The
Haunted circle, The
Magic May baskets
May treasure
May-basket magic
Maypole, The
Queen of May (Bates), The
Queen of May (Wagner), The
Saint George and the dragon
Sleeping beauty, The

Wedding of the flowers, The
When fairies come

MEDIAEVAL

Black death, The
Children's Crusade, The
Dagger of the Goth, The
Deus Vult: God wills it
I did but jest
Knights of the silver shield
Midsummer Eve
Rosamond
Sir Folly
Twelfth Night festivities
Witch's daughter, The

MEDICINE, *see* DOCTOR

MEMORIAL DAY

Boy in blue, The
Box from the attic, The
First Memorial day, The
Flower's sacrifice, The
Fourteenth veteran, The
Guarding angels, The
Hero, The
High heart, The
May pageant
Memorial day
Memorial day fantasy, A
Memorial day pageant, A
Memorial day parade, A
Mine eyes have seen the glory
Monument's message, The
Some there are who remember
Tiny play for Memorial day, A
Veteran's story, The

MERCIER, CARDINAL

Cardinal Mercier's hands

MEXICO

El Cristo
Sentence of death, The

MICHAELANGELO

Youth's highway

MICHIGAN

Tyranny of conscience, The

MILLS, JOHN STUART

Fire-lighters, The

Shipping mother east
Timely shower, A
Tree of the golden fruit, The
Where's your mother?

MOUNTAINEERS

"Ain't no use fer larnin'"
Dead expense
Door mats
Forfeit, The
Kidnapping Betty
Mountain laurel
Mountain wedding
Raising the devil
Salvage
Tie that binds, The
Waitin' fer sun-up

MOUNTAINEERS, *see also* KENTUCKY,
NO. CAROLINA, TENNESSEE

MOVIE

Chased lady, The
Evening's entertainment, An
Get in the Talkies
Immovable movie, The
Loves of Lionel, The
Malice in Blunderland
Mary Brice
Movieless movies
On the lot
Props
Publicity
Rural belle, A
Translated

MUSEUMS

Millennium morning
Theories and thumbs

MUSIC & MUSICIANS

Among old instruments
Artist, The
Brother musician
Casino gardens, The
Duetto
Evening in the studio
Flowers, music and sunbeams
Gilded wreath, The
Great snakes
If we only had "time"
Immortal beloved, The
Learning to memorize
Lost violin, The
Minuet, The
Muffins
Music fairy's story, The

Sally of the music store
Song in the heart, The
Violin-maker of Cremona, The
Willing performer, The
Words and music

MYSTERY

Back to your knitting
Blue lupines
Burglars, The
Confederates, The
Dais, The
Felton mystery, The
Great pearl mstery, The
Grill, The
Her husband's watch
Horror walks, The
Hunger
Hunt the tiger
Killing of Aaron Kale
Let it go at that
Mr. Jardyne
Mystery of the buried box, The
Now, Trixie
Orange colored necktie, The
Prince's secret, The
Shall we join the ladies?
Stroke of nine, The
These women! these women!
Thread of scarlet
Too much crime
Wedding rehearsal, The

NAPOLEON

Corsican Lieutenant
For the Empire
Josephine
Napoleon's barber

NATURE & NATURE STUDY

At the sign of the Bumblebee
Early frost
Enchanted summer
Flittermouse
Golden doom, The
Heart of oak
How mother nature awakens her
    children
How mother nature puts her chil-
    dren to bed
Hunting for spring
Loves of the elements, The
Moon and the moonstruck, The
Mother nature's picnic
Mythland of nature, The
Nature's thrifty workers
Pomona and Vertumnus

Fantasia
Flirtation, The
Halfway
Harlequin
Harlequinade in green and orange
Hearts to mend
Idyll
Maker of dreams
Matinate
Mourner, The
Pan or Pierrot
Pantaloon
Pierrette's heart
Pierrot before the seven doors
Pierrot—his play
Pierrot in hospital
Pierrot's mother
Pompons
Poor Columbine
Poor Maddalena
Rainbow gold
Rondo capriccioso
Runaway clowns
Sister of Pierrot, The
Spring dreams
Stars and groceries
Strings
Tables and chairs
Time will tell
Two plum puddings
Under the big tent
Valentines
While the mushrooms bubble
Wonder hat, The

PINOCCHIO

End of Pinocchio's dream, The
Forest of the blue fairy, The
Pinocchio runs away
Pinocchio turns donkey

PIRATE

Blackbeard
Gold altar, The
Late Captain Crow, The
Maripoza Bung
Mouse, The
Redbeard, the pirate
Under the skull and bones

POE, EDGAR ALLAN

Lost Lenore, The
Man of temperament, The

POLICE

Chinese slippers
Is peculiar

It isn't done
Killer, The
Light that jailed, The
Police matron, The

POLISH

Out of the river
Polonaise

POLITICAL

Bed of roses, A
Campaigner, The
Hero, The
Lady of destiny, The
'Lection
Mayor and the manicure, The
Mrs. Hamblett records her vote
Petticoat politics
Reticent convict, The
They who vote should read

POSTAL SERVICE

Catching the male
Resignation of Bill Snyder, The

POVERTY

Back of the yards
Bee, The
Brothers
Cash—$2,000
Christmas in the flop house
Half brothers
Helping hands, The
It's the poor that 'elps the poor
Joint owners in Spain
Nightshade
Other voice, The
Rats
Room with the black door, The
Saturday night
Servants of the people
Sleeping out
Sparks—an inbetween
Watch and the almond tart, The
Workhouse ward, The

PRE-HISTORIC

First mirror, The

PRISON & PRISONERS

Brighter Dartmoor
Guy upstairs, The
Jubilee
Law takes its course, The
Little stone house, The

Manhood
Men, women and goats
New hangman, The
Seven against one
Somebody
Sounding brass
Valiant, The

PROHIBITION

. . . And points west
Black suitcase, The
Can prohibition succeed?
Guts
Little brown jug
Should we obey prohibition laws?

PSYCHOLOGICAL

Black Oliver
Caleb Stone's death watch
Ever young
Giant's stair, The
Hanging and wiving
His sainted grandmother
Imagination
In May
Insomnia
Maurice's own idea
Midnight of Monsieur St. Jean,
  The
Monkey's paw, The
Moon of the Caribbees, The
Old boyhood
Outside this room
Phipps
Razor
Romantic interval, A
Seaweed
Singapore spider, The
Such a charming young man
Suppressed desires
Surprising bride, The
Theatre of the soul, The
Threshold, The
Undertones
Veil, The
Will, The
Winter's night
Yesterday

PUPPET

Goldilocks finds a new play-house
Jack and the beanstalk
King of the golden river, The
Manikin and Minikin
Mister punch
Pierre Patelin
Proserpina and the devil
Puppet

Rumplestiltskin
Tommy meets his excuses

RADIO

All jam
Art in the home
Atmospherics
Aunt Maria's wireless
Ben's box
Broadcast KDKA
By radio
Comedy of danger
Crystal set, The
Elopement, The
Face to face with the "mike"
A fire affair
The flapper and her friends
Getting Los Angeles
Hat trick
Hot air
Love or lucre
Mixed wave lengths
Murder will out
Mr. Gardener forges ahead
Please stand by
Rabbits, The
Radio
Radio for the family
Radio playlet, A
Radio widow, The
Seance, The
Switched
Taps
Station YYYY
Voice from the air, The
Wedding, The
What if they could?
While you wait
Will it come to this?
Wishing gate
Wonderful radio, The

RAILROAD

All aboard
At the junction
End of the trail, The
Nine-ten express, The
Sleeping car, The
Two little trunks

RED CROSS

Highway of brotherly love, The
In father world's garden
If the children of Europe could
  speak to us
Spirit of the Red Cross, The
Taking the picnic to the shut-in

RELIGIOUS

After twenty-five years
All for Christ
And he came to his father
And the sea shall give up its dead
Angel on the ship, The
Angel that troubled the waters, The
Angels of prayer
Angelus
Behold the man
Birth of God, The
Blocade
Blue gate, The
Bound or free
Boy bishop, The
Bread
Brooding calves
Burial of Alleluia, The
By the roadside
Childe Ronald to the dark tower came
Children of Eve, The
Christian slave, A
"Church"
Cloudbreak
Color line, The
Crown of St. Felice, The
Dame truth
Death in the tree
Devil's lane
Does the modern world need religion?
Dust of the road
Easter morning
Elijah
Summoning of Everyman, The
Fanatic, The
Five poor travellers
Gaining a member
Gate of Montsalvat, The
Glad tidings to all people
God's adopted son
Golden rule in courtship, The
Good Friday
"Greater love hath no man"
Grotesquerie
Half hour at the gate, A
Harbour
Hast thou considered my servant Job?
House thief, The
How the great guest came
Is religion necessary for progress?
Joanna the wife of Chuza
King's son, The
Lady Joanna, The
Laughing child, The

Lord's prayer, The
Lord's will, The
Lost coin, The
Lost saint, The
Madonna's picture, The
Melchizedek, Abraham and Isaac
Miracle of Saint Martin, The
Miracle of Saint Masha
Modern magi
Mozart and the gray steward
Nathaniel's quest
Nativity, The
New faith emerges, The
New God, The
Nine, The
Now the servant's name was Malchus
Nursery-maid of heaven, The
Old game, The
Other wise man, The
Our Lord of the ship
Outcasts
Overheard in Seville during the processions on Maundy Thursday
Pageant of the shearman & tailors, The
Peregrinus
Pharisees
Pilgrims of the way
Prodigal son, The
Return of Bob Gregory, The
Robert of Sicily
Saint Cyprian and the devil
St. Simeon Stylites
Saint's comedy, The
Science and God
Shepherd of Lattenden, The
Sight of the blind, The
Sisters' tragedy, The
"Speak to the earth and it shall teach thee"
Story of a story, The
Ten days later
Terrible meek, The
Thou faithful servant
Twilight of the moon
Unto such glory
Unto the least of these
Vespers
Wandering scholar, The
What men live by
Whither goest thou?
Wise and the foolish virgins, The
Young priest rebels, The
Youth prays

RELIGIOUS, *see also* BIBLE, CHRISTMAS, EASTER, MISSIONARY

RELIGIOUS EDUCATION

Architect, The
Call of the church, The
Evangels of the new day
For their sakes
Pentecost of youth, The

RENAISSANCE

Message and Jehanne, The
Square pegs
Torches

REVOLUTIONARY WAR, *see* U. S.

ROBIN HOOD, *see* BALLADS

ROME ANCIENT

Baths of Borcovicus, The
Caractacus and the Romans
Cornelia's jewels
Death of Nero, The
Justinian code, The
King Tarquin and the sibyl
Patria Potestas
Struggle between the Plebians
   and the Patricians in the Ro-
   man Senate, The
Teja
Trajan and the children of Rome

ROMNEY, GEORGE

Prince of court painters, The

ROOSEVELT, THEODORE

Matter of diplomacy, A
Modern knight, A
One country, one flag, one lan-
   guage
Rough Rider, The
Theodore Roosevelt
Theodore Roosevelt—a great sol-
   dier

ROUMANIA

Haiduc, The
Strong tower, The

RUBE

Cowology
Danger line, The
Needles
Time flies

RUSSIA

Ahasverus
Amicable settlement, An

Anniversary, The
At the fair
Babouscka
Boor, The
Boots
Broke
Conversation on the highway, A
Country woman, The
Diadem of snow, A
Duel about nothing, A
Evening in Sorrento, An
Flight of the herons, The
Fragment, A
Gamblers, The
Game of chess, The
Gloom
House with the twisty windows,
   The
Immortals, The
In holy Russia
In the terem
Lawsuit, A
Life on the Steppes
Love of one's neighbour
Marriage proposal, A
Official's morning, An
On the highway
Proposal, The
Servant's hall, The
Steed in the senate, A
Tatyana Riepin
Wedding, The
Where it is thin there it breaks
Yelenka the wise

SAFETY FIRST

Badge of honor, The
Bruin's Inn
Careful city plans for safety for
   all
Carelessness
Cracker conspiracy, The
Giant, The
How knowledge driveth away
   fear
Lake, The
Lost aster, The
Lost camping place, The
Other side of very bad luck, The
Partisans of precaution
Prevention goes marching on
Safety dialogue, A
Safety first (Corell)
Safety first (Ward)
Safety law court, The
Safety on the streets
Safety playlette, A
Safety Sam
Safety's victory

Sir safety scout
Uncle Armory's helpers

ST. CUTHBERT

Call, The
Feast, The
Gate of heaven, The
Hermit, The
Miracle, The

ST. FRANCIS

Blind eyes
Bride feast, The
Brief life
Brother Elias
Brother Juniper
Brother Sin
Brother Wolf
Builders, The
Chapter, The
Cure of souls
Fellow prisoners
Fools' errand, The
Last disciple, The
Lepers, The
Lovers' meeting
Order of release, The
Our Lady of Poverty
Revellers, The
St. Francis and the wolf
Saint Francis of Assisi
Seraphic vision, The
Sister Clare
Sister Death
Sister Gold

ST. PATRICK'S DAY

Aided by St. Patrick
Bogie men, The
Gifts of St. Patrick, The
Irish alibi, An
Little good people, The
Mrs. Pat and the law
Nora's elves
Saint and the fairies, The
St. Patrick's day in the land of
    the west
Seven kings of Atherry, The
Shamrock, The

SAINT VALENTINE'S DAY

Beau and Belle
Frank's valentine
Gift of the gods
Knight of the funny bone, The
Little George Washington's val-
    entine

Masque of old loves, A
Meeting of the hearts
Most beautiful valentine, The
Mysterious valentine, The
Path of roses
Real valentine
Saint Valentine
Saint Valentine entertains
"St. Valentine's eve"
Two valentines
Valentine hearts
Valentine scraps
Valentine shop, The

SAND, MADAME

Nocturne

SCHOOL

Attendance play
Back to school
Betty, behave!
Bobbed hair
Captive Princess
Christmas exiles
Day at Rawlings, A
Day before the test, The
Every student
Fair play
Getting by
Ghost in the boarding school, The
Good morning, teacher
Greek as she is taught
Heaven on Friday
How Bobby put it over
Injured, The
Mabel's aunt
Mistakes they left behind them,
    The
Morning in a superintendent's of-
    fice, A
Mother Goose school, The
New teacher, The
Oh! teacher
On the way to school
Out to win
Peter's night out
Project club, The
Rawlings Record Assembly
Return of spring, The
Ring leader
Scheming six, The
School clown, The
School days
School entertainment
School spirit
School-time
Summer is calling
Teacher, kin I go home?

They teach English
Trip with Mr. Brown, A
Turkish ambassador, The
Trouble at Satterlee's, The
Vacation days
Welcome, Miss McGregor
You may stay after school

SCHOOL, *see also* COLLEGE, EDUCATION,
GRADUATION

SCHUBERT, FRANZ

Scenes from the childhood of
Franz Schubert

SCIENCE, *see* NATURE

SCOTLAND

Ardvorlich's wife
Fool of Dunvegan, The
Grave, The
Gundy shop, The
Jon
Merlin's grave
Singing sands, The
Thomas the rhymer
Towie Castle

SEA & SAILORS

Aye, aye, sir!
Bound east for Cardiff
Brains
Breaking of the calm, The
Brink of silence, The
Call of the ninth wave, The
Course in piracy, A
In the zone
Just two men
Long voyage home, A
Lord Bateman
Love passage, A
Magic sea shell, The
Marriage gown, The
Men folk
Outside, The
Riders to the sea
Rusty door, The
Salt water
"Second best"
Shadowy waters, The
Ship comes in, The
Sintram of Skaggerak
Three wishes, The
Waning moon, The
When the ship goes down
Will-o'-the-wisp
Wondership, The
Yella

SEASONS

Autumn smiles
Advent of spring, The
Coming of spring, The
Happy summer time
King winter
Mother nature's carnival
Peter rabbit helps the children
Secret of happiness, The
Spring fantasy, A
Spring pageant for primary chil-
dren, A
Spring's awakening
Under the snow
When the beanstalk grew again

SERBIA

Stars, The

SERVANT PROBLEM

Hiring a servant
Jeremiad
References
Ruling class, The
Scraps

SEVIGNE, MADAME

Sal volatile

SHAKESPEARE

Highways cross
In Arden forest
Incorrigible
Portia pulls a pinch play
Pound of flesh, A
Shakespeare smiles
Shakespeare, the playmaker
Talisman, The

SHELLEY

Dream, The
Centaurs

SICILY

Atonement, The

SLUM

Dime lunch, The
Duke and the dices, The
Gentlemen of the road
Limping along
Man born to be hanged, The
My man
Outclassed

Something beautiful
Trash
Woman tamer, The

SLUM, *see also* POVERTY

SOCIAL SATIRE

Another moon
Baby show, The
Backing a winner
Cabaret drama, A
Cabbages
Carnival
Corinna
Crazy to reduce
Daily doesn't, The
Demands of society, The
Dish of scandal, A
Evening with the older set
Exit the Grand Duchess
Fool of a man, A
Five hours to go
Girl who slipped, The
Grown-up children
Happy journey to Trenton and
    Camden, The
In the flower shop
Jilted
Knock out, The
"L"
Lady of pain
Letters, The
Menu, The
Miss Bennett's house party
Noctes ambrosiae
None too good for Dodo
Party of the third part, Th
Precedence
Price of love, The
Rich man, poor man
Royal complex, A
Schnitzleresque
Sham
Sixth hat, The
Slump, The
Society notes
Some party
Spot cash
Those class distinctions
Traffic signals
Trap, The
Turn of a hair, The
Very social service
Waiting room, The
We are three
Why girls stay home
Wrong numbers
Yashmak !

SOCRATES

On self-government
Husband of Xanthippe, The
Xanthippe and Socrates

SPAIN

Bombito
Dance of the red, red rose, The
Devil comes to Alcaraz, The
Entremes of the cave of Sala-
    manca, The
Idyll
Lily among thorns, A
Olives, The
Street singer, The
Sunny morning, A
To die with a smile
Widow's eyes

SPELLING

A B C fairies, The
Rats !
Spelling match, The
Those tricky words
Wanted : an office boy

SPRING, *see* SEASONS

SUPERNATURAL

Dwellers in the darkness, The
Fourteenth guest, The
Into the everywhere
Poet's paradise, The
Rain
Weak spot, The
Well-remembered voice, A

SWEDEN

Poverty

SWIFT, JONATHAN

Swift and Stella

SWITZERLAND

Bronze bride, The
William Tell (Knowles)
William Tell (Stevenson)

TALKIES, *see* MOVIES

TENNESSEE

On Vengeance height

TENNYSON

Two passengers for Chelsea

TEXAS

Across the border
Austin, the capital
Battle of San Jacinto
Declaration of Independence
Ellis Bean
Fall of the Alamo
Fredonian rebellion
Goliad massacre
Lafitte
La Salle
Long's fort
On to San Antonio
Republic of Texas is no more, The
Saint Denis
San Jacinto ball
San Jose
Why not Texas?

THANKSGIVING DAY

Change of mind, A
Chief's Thanksgiving invitation, The
Come back, Mr. Turkey
Conscientious turkey, The
Day before, The
Everybody thankful
Fall day, A
Festival of the harvest moon
First Thanksgiving (Carter), The
First Thanksgiving (White), The
For what shall I be thankful?
Getting into step
Giving thanks today
Grandma Green's Thanksgiving
Grandmother's recollections of Thanksgiving
Great Thanksgivings in American history
Harvest Thanksgiving, The
How Thanksgiving came in November
In an old diary
In 1621
Indians Thanksgiving, The
It was a surprise
Jack smuggles in a guest
Kelly's friendship, The
Littlest pumpkins, The
Magic Thanksgiving pie, The
Mother Goose's Thanksgiving dream

Mrs. Brown's Thanksgiving turkey
Mysterious Thanksgiving guest
New-fangled Thanksgiving, A
Old gentleman Gay
Old man rabbit's Thanksgiving
Only good children, The
Patience's dream
Pilgrim ladies plan for the first Thanksgiving, The
Pilgrim thankfulness
Playing Pilgrim
Pumpkin pie, The
Pumpkin pie Peter
Plymouth's first Thanksgiving
Red shoes at Plymouth
Real Thanksgiving, A
Sailing of the Mayflower, The
She made a pumpkin pie
Should we be more thankful than the Pilgrims?
Sojourners, The
Tabby's Thanksgiving doll
Thankful at last
Thankful lives up to her name
Thanksgiving after-dinner playlet, A
Thanksgiving at usual
Thanksgiving day movie, A
Thanksgiving dinner, The
Thanksgiving in a cabin
Thanksgiving in the barnyard
Thanksgiving on Hickory Slope
Thanksgiving, past and present
Thanksgiving play, A
Thanksgiving pumpkin, The
Thanksgiving turkey, The
Thanksgiving with Mother Goose
Thanksgiving wonders
Tommy's Thanksgiving dinner
Three Thanksgivings, The
Turkey red
Tweedle-dum and Tweedle-dee
Uncle Sam's Thanksgiving
Unexpected guest, The
Uninvited guest, The
Verdict for the wishbone, A
Victory and Thanksgiving
What Thanksgiving 'means
When the turkeys turned the table
Wise turkey, The

THEATRE & THEATRE-FOLK

At the costumiers
Be a little cuckoo!
Budding star, A
Classical dancing school, The
Claude

Last rising, The
Maid, The
Marching men
Message, The
Nerves
Night watches
Official bondage
Old lady shows her medals, The
Out of the midst of hatred
Papers
Private Jones
Road of poplars, The
Skim milk
They just won't talk
Three wishes
Tommy-by-the-way
Treason
Two lamps, The
Unknown soldier, The
War brides

WORLD WAR, *see also* ARMISTICE DAY

WRITING

Conspiracy, The

Y. M. C. A. & Y. W. C. A.

Adventures of Ella Cinders, The
Deportation dialogue, A
Diamond pin, The
Here, there, and everywhere
Ragged edge, The
Within the four seas

YOUTH & AGE

All on a summer's day
Age-old dream, The
Baggage, The
Beautiful story, The
Case of Teresa, The
Crabbed youth and age
For the love of Pete
Ghost story, The
Hardhead, The
His come-uppance
His sainted grandmother
House on the hill, The
It's no use to argue
James and John
Mansions
Matter of choice, A
Mirror, The
Mother's old home
Nascuntur Poetae
New word, The
Old king's tale, The
On the razor edge
Pageant of sunshine, The
Peculiar old duffer, A
Old walnut
Perfect partnership, The
Puppeteer
Pretty farmer's daughter, The
Queer duck
Red Rowan
Release
So that's that
Tables turned
To meet the king!
Too much trouble
Vanishing Princess, The
Waiting for Dorothea

COLLECTIONS

Abel, Barbara. Finances behind the footlights. N. Y. Woman's Press, 1930.
The triangle Tess
Life is like that
The pain of it
Or what have you?
Much ado about ducats

Abercrombie, Lascelles. Interlude and poems. London. John Lane, n.d.
The new God: a miracle
Blind
The fool's adventure
An escape
Peregrinus

Alehin, A. F. The first sin and other one act plays. Boston. Expression Co., 1927.
The first sin
The boaster
The secret
The glutton

Alexander, Hartley. Manito masks. N. Y. Dutton, 1925.
How death came into the world
His-voice-is-a-whisper
Carved woman
The scalp
The man who married the Thunder's daughter
The weeper
Earth-trapped
Living solid face
Butterfly girl and mirage boy

Alexander, R. C. & Goslin, O. P., ed. Worship through drama. N. Y. Harper, 1930.

The Lord's prayer	Coppeé, François
The young Priest rebels	Alexander, R. C. & Goslin, O. P.
The new faith emerges	Alexander, R. C. & Goslin, O. P.
The other wise man	Alexander, R. C. & Goslin, O. P.
He came seeing	Hamlin, Mary P.
Robert of Sicily	Alexander, R. C. & Goslin, O. P.
The prodigal son	Alexander, R. C. & Goslin, O. P.
Abraham Lincoln (3 scenes)	Drinkwater, John
(Also services, pageants, etc.)	

Anderson, Lee. Ten one act plays. N. Y. Walter V. McKee, 1928.
The simple soul
"Man wants —"
The dawning
Bed for three
Give the audience a chance
Rondo
Such is love
Manhood
In the thousands of years to come
Arabesque

Andreas, Eulalie. Four one-act comedies. Hollywood, Cal. The Playworker's
Studio, 1924.
The woman of it
The lure of the stage
The divorce specialist
A modern David Garrick

Applegarth, Margaret T. More missionary plays. N. Y. Doran, 1923.
Empty stockings
Strictly private
Galatea takes a lease of life
The yes but-ers
Katy-did
Wait a minute
Jack the giant killer
The subscription clinic
Mrs. Jarley's wax-works
The child in the midst

Applegarth, Margaret T. Short missionary plays. N. Y. Doran, 1923.
Kimona
The latest Victor record
Just suppose
The girl who fell through the earth
Seven keys to Mr. Bald Pate
Hands up!
The gospel according to the telephone book
(Also two longer plays, and a pantomime)

Auditorium plays and stunts for high school. Franklin, Ohio. Eldridge
Entertainment House, 1930.

The lunch hour	
Save the surface and you save all	Wood, Evelyn
The first mirror	Wood, Evelyn
A visit from George Washington	Gilliland, C. H.
Redbeard the pirate	Shearouse, Lillian
The campus	Lyon, Clara O.
High lights in American history	Wesleyn College-Junior Class 1926
"The graduate"	Passmore, F. J.
At the first tee	Connell, Harriet
They went to the game	Crites, Lucile
Elmer and Elias	
(Also a longer play and several stunts)	

Bailey, Carolyn S., ed. Plays for the children's hour. Springfield, Mass.
Milton Bradley Co., 1931.

Mother Goose opens her door	Green, Clara S.
The land of play	Sharpe, Mary
Why Jack-o'-lantern keeps Hallowe'en	Bailey, Carolyn S.
Tabby's Thanksgiving doll	Rice, Rebecca
The home-coming	Howe, W. E. & Bailey, Carolyn S.
Three trees	Maynard, Gertrude
The Christmas card	D'Amico, Victor
The search for Santa Claus	Bailey, Carolyn S.
A Christmas party	Bailey, Carolyn S.
A Christmas dream	Hayes, Mildred A.
A pageant of time	Robeson, Anne G.
The rabbit who wanted wings	Bailey, Carolyn S.
All on the king's highway	Carpenter, Mary E.
Mothering day	Reynolds, Helen M.
The Maypole	Bailey, Carolyn S.
Runaway clowns	Creighton, Beatrice

Hans who made the Princess laugh   Carpenter, Mary E.
Baucis and Philemon   Carpenter, Mary E.
(Also two longer plays)

Balch, Norman. Six plays of business life. Franklin, Ohio. Eldridge Entertainment House, 1930.
Lost—a sale
Beating the boss
Fred joins the firm
The Potter Pancake Co.
Business in 2030 A. D.
In the fire's shadow

Banta, N. M. Autumn and winter festivals. Chicago. A. Flanagan Co., 1924.
Autumn smiles
A real Thanksgiving
(Also dialogues, drills, recitations, etc.)

Banta, N. M., ed. St. Nicholas Christmas book. Chicago. A. Flanagan Co., 1925.
Behind the scenes in Santa land   Holloway, Pearl
The book folks' Christmas   Gosselink, Sara E.
(Also recitations, dialogues and entertainments)

Barnes, Djuna. A night among horses. N. Y. Horace Liveright, 1929.
Three from the earth
To the dogs
The dove

Barr, Carolyn. Six plays for six grades. Philadelphia, Penn., 1930.
Bennie's dream
Santa Claus starts on his journey
Bricks
(Also three longer plays)

Barrie, J. M. The plays of J. M. Barrie. N. Y. Scribner, 1928.
Pantaloon
Half an hour
Seven women
Old friends
Rosalind
The will
The twelve-pound look
The new word
A well-remembered voice
Barbara's wedding
The old lady shows her medals
Shall we join the ladies?

Barrie, J. M. Shall we join the ladies? N. Y. Scribner, 1928.
Shall we join the ladies?
Half an hour
Seven women
Old friends

Barrnett, J. H. & others, comp. The green entertainment book. Chicago. A. Flanagan Co., 1930.
A cure for discontent   Norton, Mary
The Smith family   Funk, T. A.
The Jones family   Funk, T. A.
(Also dialogues, poems and entertainments)

Bates, Katharine L. Little Robin Stay-behind and other plays in verse for children. N. Y. Woman's Press, 1923.
Little Robin Stay-behind
The conscientious turkey

The bonbon tree
Good resolutions
Saint Valentine entertains
Under the snow
April Fool
The Queen of May
Roses
The reformed fourth
Prince Goldenrod
Mother Time's family

Bates, Katharine L. The pilgrim ship. N. Y. Woman's Press, 1926.
The blind boy of Bethlehem
Joanna the wife of Chuza
Pharisees

Beard, Patten. Acting plays for boys and girls. Chicago. Beckley-Cardy Co., 1927.
The butterfly
Little George Washington
When the beanstalk grew again
The Easter bonnet
We believe in fairies
The making of a flag
The Mother Goose school
The goblins
The children's bookshelf
The night before Christmas
The Christmas stocking
The three dwarf brothers

Beck, Warren. Imagination and four other one-act plays for boys and girls. Bost. Baker, 1925.
Imagination
The old sleuth,
Great Caesar
False pretense
The Estabrook nieces

Beck, Warren. Six Little Theatre plays. Boston. Baker, 1931.
The affairs of men
After all these years
Fine frenzy
The fixed canon
A heart too soon made glad
It's no use to argue

Benton, Rita. The Elf of Discontent and other plays. N. Y. Doran, 1927.
The Elf of Discontent
What men live by
The happy prince
Queen Cross-patch and the scullery wench
Ivan the fool
The liberty bell
Old gentleman Gay

Berman, Henry. Life demands! and other plays. N. Y. Brentano's, 1931.
Time's fool
Out of the dark
The law of compensation
The age of discretion
Vestiges

Best, Mrs. A. Starr & Patten, Cora M., ed. Dickon goes to the fair and other plays. N. Y. Doran, 1927.

Dickon goes to the fair   Alden, Alice W.
The merman's pipe   Commons, Mrs. J. R.
Midsummer night   Burt, Olive F. W.

Binyon, Laurence. Three short plays. London. Sidgwick & Jackson, 1930.
The Godstow nunnery
Love in the desert
Memnon

Bitney, Mayme. Pageants and plays for holidays. Dayton, Ohio. Paine Pub.
Co., 1926.
Boy who was kind
Friend Lincoln
Friendly valentines
Frank's valentine
Good George Washington
Washington at Valley Forge
Aided by St. Patrick
Georgie's piece
Bothersome books
Madame Summertime's guest
Honorable Madame
Halloween merrymakers
Halloween on Baldy
What Thanksgiving means
Thanksgiving in a cabin
Grandma Green's Thanksgiving
A new-fangled Thanksgiving
Just one Christmas
It isn't my dolly
Do your Christmas shopping early
Christmas troubles
Making Molly merry
(Also many pageants and one longer play)

Block, Etta., tr. One-act plays from the Yiddish. Second series. N. Y. Bloch
Pub. Co., 1929.
Bebele   Hirschbein, Perez
Lone worlds!   Hirschbein, Perez
After the funeral   Peretz, I. L.
Brothers   Raisen, Abraham
"Liars!"   Bimko, F.
Of an early morning   Peretz, I. L.
The sisters   Peretz, I. L.

Boggs, H. O. Children's comedies and comic recitations. Chicago. Beckley-
Cardy, 1929.
A lesson from an humble source
Abe Lincoln's kindness
Five prim little patriots
The quiz
Hero worshipers
Willie went and got lost
The right of boyhood
Only an only child
The six S's organize
The six S's hold a session
The six S's in action
The six S's admit Ferdie
Lemuel won't lie
The heroes of the haunted house
(Also dialogues and recitations)

Boggs, H. O. Comic plays and dialogues. Chicago. Beckley-Cardy, 1926.
A midnight excursion
Poor teacher
The kitchen convention
The singing teacher
Playing politics
A difference of opinion
Cheaters
The cripples
The new boy
The poets cornered
Bertha brings home the bacon
Gabriel's horn
(Also monologues and mock trials)

Boggs, H. O. Funny plays for happy days. Chicago. Beckley-Cardy, 1928.
George Washington and his hatchet
Salvation am free
Marie misses marriage
Teasing the teacher
The fools of April fool
Tom Taylor's troubles
The trouble-makers
A cat at school
(Also monologues, trials, and recitations)

Bosschère, Jean de. The closed door. tr. by F. S. Flint. N. Y. John Lane, 1917.
The offering of Plebs
The man of forty
The blackbird and the girl
(Also many poems)

Boston Theatre Guild Plays. Boston. Baker, 1924.

The three gifts	Converse, Florence
Desert smoke	Clarke, D. L.
An old Chester secret	Kemper, Sallie
Dorinda dares	Morris, Angela
Buying culture	Wood, C. Antoinette

Bottomley, Gordon. A parting and The return. N. Y. Macmillan, 1928.
A parting
The return

Bottomley, Gordon. Scenes and plays. N. Y. Macmillan, 1929.
A parting
The return
The sisters
The widow
Towie Castle
Merlin's grave
Ardvorlich's wife
The singing sands

Brandane, John. The treasure ship; Rory aforesaid; The happy war. London. Constable, 1928.
Rory aforesaid
The happy war
(Also The treasure ship,—a longer play)

Briggs, T. H., ed. Literature for the junior high school. Book 1. Chicago. Rand McNally, 1929.

And the tribes shall pass	Myall, Charles

(Also many examples of other types of literature)

Briggs, T. H. & others, ed. Literature for the junior high school. Book 3. Chicago. Rand McNally, 1929.

| The silver lining | Mackay, Constance D'A. |
| Spreading the news | Gregory, Lady |

(Also many examples of other types of literature)

Brighouse, Harold. Open air plays. N. Y. French. 1926.

Maypole morning
The Prince who was a piper
The rational Princess
The laughing mind
How the weather is made

British Drama League Library. Four one act plays. Oxford, England. Basil Blackwell, 1923.

Double demon	Herbert, A. P.
St. Simeon Stylites	Smith, F. S.
Thirty minutes in a street	Major, Beatrice
Pan in Pimlico	Simpson, Helen

British Drama League Library. Three one act plays. N. Y. French, 1925.

Persephone	Clarke, Amy K.
Cloudbreak	Roberts, A. O.
Wind o' the moors	Peach, L. du Garde

British Drama League Library of modern British drama. Oxford, England. Basil Blackwell, n.d.

Wind o' the moors	Peach, L. du Garde
Cloudbreak	Roberts, A. O.
Persephone	Clarke, Amy K.

Brody, Alter. Lamentations, four folk plays of the American Jew. N. Y. Coward-McCann, 1928.

Lowing in the night
Recess for memorials
Rapunzel
A house of mourning

Brown, Abbie F. The lantern and other plays for children. Boston. Houghton, Mifflin, 1928.

Rhoecus
The wishing moon
The little shadows

Bown, L. F. & Lecompt, Fay P., ed. Script. an anthology of literature produced by students of the College of William and Mary. Richmond, Va. Williams Printing Co., 1930.

| Mother sets the stage | Smith, Harriet D. |
| The lady older than time | Wertenbaker, G. P. |

Bryce, Catherine T. Bound or free, and The Wizard of words. Boston. Atlantic Monthly Press, 1922.

Bound or free
The wizard of words

Bufano, Remo. Pinocchio for the stage in four short plays. N. Y. Knopf, 1929.

Pinocchio runs away
The forest of the blue fairy
The end of Pinocchio's dream
Pinocchio turns donkey

Bugbee, Willis N. & Irish, Marie. Tip top Christmas book. Syracuse, N. Y. Willis N. Bugbee Co., 1927.

Aunty's Christmas basket
Christmas at Timothy Corners
The Christmas party

Jus' 'fore Christmas
Molly's merry Christmas
(Also dialogues, poems and entertainments)

Butler, Mildred A. Adapt. Literature dramatized for classroom use. N. Y.
  Harcourt, Brace, 1926.
  The mad tea-party
  The return of Rip Van Winkle
  The sword in the stone
  Little women
  The plan to set free Runaway Nigger Jim
  The Christmas spirit
  The death of Sohrab
  The marriage contract
  The knight and the banner
  In the enemy's camp
  The treasure hunt
  Roderick Dhu's proposal
  The trial of the bow
  The storming of Torquilstone
  At the Rainbow
  The birthday dance at the Red House
  Eppie's choice
  The pauper becomes a prince
  Beginning the tale of the Ancient Mariner

Cactus Club. Denver, Colorado. Separate plays.
  The Goldenrod Lode   Rogers, J. G.
  The magic hour   Rutherford, F. S.
  And the third day   Rogers, J. G.

Caldwell, Sybil & Hendrie, Ernest. Top dog and other sketches for
  Women's Institutes, Girl Guides, etc. London. French, 1926.
  Top dog
  Phoebe rebels
  Mr. John
  Next-of-kin

Cameron, Eleanor. Many-a-way for Christmas day. Boston. Baker, 1929.
  Santa's helpers
  Memories of Christmas
  (Also readings, acrostics, poems, and exercises)

Campbell, Wayne, ed. Amateur acting and play production. N. Y. Mac-
  millan, 1931.
  Raw men   Houston, Noel
  The turn of the road   Wilson, Alberta A.
  On second thought   Willis, Bess B.
  The promised land   Robinson, Horace
  The one thing needful   Wilson, Alberta A.

Canadian Authors Association. One act plays by Canadian authors.
  Montreal Branch, 1926.
  The blue pitcher   Morrow, T. M.
  The maid   Armour, Stuart
  Low life   Roche, Mazo de la
  All Hallows' Eve   Perrigard, Pauline B.
  For the Empire   Doane, Gregory
  Which?   Williams, Frances F.
  The traitor   Barnard, L. G.
  The hardhead   Rankin, Nancy
  The favours of my Lady Leone   Elliott, Margaret E.
  A dead woman bites not   Doane, Gregory
  The happiest place   Threlfall, ——

The dream	Brooks, Mary W.
Come true	Roche, Mazo de la
The midnight of Monsieur St. Jean	Barnard, L. G.
The King	Perrigard, Pauline B.
Voices	Brooks, Mary W.
The turn of the road	Church, Elizabeth J.
The death of Pierrot	Green, Harry
The newcomer	Armour, Stuart

Canadian plays from Hart House Theatre, ed. by Vincent Massey.
Vol. 1. Toronto, Canada. Macmillan Co. of Canada, 1926.

Brothers in arms	Denison, Merrill
The weather breeder	Denison, Merrill
Balm	Denison, Merrill
Pierre	Scott, D. C.
The point of view	Osborne, Marian
The second lie	MacKay, Isabel E.

Canfield, Curtis, ed. Plays of the Irish Renaissance, 1880–1930. N. Y.
Ives Washburn, 1929.

On Baile's strand	Yeats, W. B.
The only jealousy of Emer	Yeats, W. B.
Hyacinth Halvey	Gregory, Lady
The twisting of the rope	Hyde, Douglas
The dandy dolls	Fitzmaurice, George
Riders to the sea	Synge, J. M.
The singer	Pearse, Padraic
The big house	Robinson, Lennox
(Also longer plays)	

Cannan, Gilbert. Seven plays. London. Martin Secker, 1923.

Everybody's husband
The fat kine and the lean
In the park
Someone to whisper to
The same story
Pierrot in hospital
The polite art of conversation

Carolina Folk-plays. Second series. N. Y. Holt, 1924.

Trista	Lay, Elizabeth
The return of Buck Gavin	Wolfe, T. C.
Gaius and Gaius Jr.	Cobb, Lucy M.
Fixin's	Green, Erma & Green, Paul
The beaded buckle	Gray, Frances

Carolina Folk-plays. Third series. N. Y. Holt, 1928.

The Scuffletown outlaws	Cox, W. N.
Job's kinfolks	Bailey, Loretto C.
In Dixon's kitchen	Stout, Wilbur & Lay, Ellen
A shotgun splicin'	Coffin, Gertrude W.
Lighted candles	Bland, Margaret & Duls, Louisa
Quare medicine	Green, Paul

Carter, L. H. & Gall, Ellen M., ed. The banner anthology of one-act plays
by American authors. San Francisco, Cal. Banner Play Bureau, 1929.

The cracked teapot	Dobie, C. C.
Yat Pak	Bunje, E. T. H.
Aye, aye, sir!	Ellicott, J. M.
It's all a matter of dress	Hammond, Virginia M.
The grass grows red	Wright, E. A.
Pigs ears and purses	Melville, R. L.
Mistletoe and moonlight	Wilbur, Elene
Winter sunshine	Marshall, Laura

Tables turned   Dawson, Jessie
The Queen's shift   Ingersoll, J. H.
The path between   McCabe, Hazel G.
Fan Tan   Finn, John Jr.
Matrimony up-to-date   Tucker, C. D.
The golden eagle child   Lobner, Joyce E.
The immortals   Dobie, C. C.

Casey, Beatrice M. Good things for Halloween. Chicago. Denison, 1929.
Black rose of Halloween
Halloween guest
Haunted cottage
Shades' Halloween convention
Witches Halloween tea party
(Also dialogues, exercises, drills)

Casey, Beatrice M., ed. The popular Christmas book. Chicago. Denison, 1927.
Christmas exiles
Christmas dolls for sale
Christmas contributions
The transformation of Mary Lou
Noel's Christmas celebration
(Also dialogues, recitations, readings, and drills)

Catchy plays and recitations. Syracuse, N. Y. Willis N. Bugbee Co., 1929.
The awkward maid   Bugbee, W. N.
The Darky insurance agent   Bugbee, W. N.
The ladies' style show   Bugbee, W. N.
Look out for the constable   Bugbee, W. N.
Lucindy captures the minister   Bugbee, W. N.
Mary Jane and the Census man   Bugbee, W. N.
Pa's income tax   Bugbee, W. N.
Pat Hooligan's bet   Bugbee, W. N.
The project club   Bugbee, W. N.
Samantha changes her mind   Bugbee, W. N.
A change of heart   Walter, Nina W.
Keener's Christmas gifts   Vice, Fannie C.
The modern pirates   Irish, Marie
(Also longer plays, dialogues, and recitations)

Catchy plays and recitations. Number 2. Syracuse, N. Y. Willis N. Bugbee Co., 1930.
Bathing beauty contest   Kneas, J. C.
Codfish aristocracy   Bugbee, W. N.
The family in the upper flat   Bugbee, W. N.
Fat and happy   Minard, Maye C.
Lessons in love making   Irish, Marie
Now take it from me   Irish, Marie
That 'ere line fence   Irish, Marie
The troubles of Mose   Hamilton, H. W.
The Kelly's friendship Thanksgiv-   Minard, Maye C.
  ing dinner
The stronger force   Trout, Ethel W.
(Also recitations)

Cavanah, Frances. The knight of the funny bone and other plays for children. Boston. Baker, 1929.
The knight of the funny bone
The bunnie's Easter quiz
May treasure
The wishing hut

The glorious wish
The giggle witch
Feast of adventure
The dream dolls
Fairy dust
Whim-wham

Chapin, Katherine G. Outside of the world. N. Y. Duffield, 1930.
The lady of the inn
(Also many poems)

Charlton, Basil, & others. Green room rags. London. French, 1925.
"Wow wow!"
Concerning Coralie
Disgrace
The birthday gift
It is so simple
"Twinkle, twinkle, little star!"
The pact
The condemned cell
Mustard

Chekhov, Anton. The plays of Anton Chekhov. First Modern Library Ed. N. Y. The Modern Library, 1930.
The anniversary
On the high road
The wedding
(Also many longer plays)

Chesterton, Frances. Three plays for children. London. French, 1924.
The Children's Crusade
Sir Cleges
The Christmas gift

Christensen, Mayme. Christmas week in the primary grades. Chicago. Dramatic Pub. Co., 1930.
A sled for Christmas
The Christmas path
(Also drills, pantomimes, recitations)

Clark, Ada, & others. Little plays for Christmas. Chicago. Beckley-Cardy Co., 1928.

A Christmas joke	Clark, Ada
The twins' Christmas	Clark, Ada
Is Santa coming?	Kibbe, Margaret
A surprise for Santa	Kibbe, Margaret
Choosing a doll	Norton, Alice W.
The toy shop mix-up	Norton, Alice W.
The fairies and a Christmas tree	Norton, Alice W.
Christmas time at Santa's head-quarters	Norton, Alice W.
Christmas eve on the trolley car	Norton, Alice W.
The king's choice	Arnett, Anne W.
The fairies' Christmas party	Rice, Rebecca
The light in the window	Rice, Rebecca
The Christmas Eve Prince	Rice, Rebecca
Evelyn's Christmas lesson	Rice, Rebecca
(Also three longer plays)	

Clark, B. H. & Nicholson, Kenyon, ed. The American scene. N. Y. Appleton, 1930.

Greasy luck	Field. Rachel
Bound east for Cardiff	O'Neill, Eugene
Chuck	Mackaye, Percy
The quarry	Clark, J. A.

Blood o' kings	Dransfield, Jane
The last straw	Crocker, Bosworth
Money	Gold, Michael
No cause for complaint	Brooks, G. S.
Wanderlust	Halvey, Paul
The girl in the coffin	Dreiser, Theodore
Town	Baumer, Marie
The no 'count boy	Green, Paul
'Lijah	Smith, Edgar V.
The tie that binds	Cornelius, O. F.
Bumblepuppy	Rogers, J. W.
The medicine show	Walker, Stuart
The cow with wings	Levinger, Elma E.
The trysting place	Tarkington, Booth
The eldest	Ferber, Edna
The feast of the holy innocents	Ilsly, S. M.
The barbarians	Pride, L. B.
Bread	Eastman, Fred
Trifles	Glaspell, Susan
Minnie Field	Conkle, E. P.
The Cajun	Carver, Ada J.
Addio	Young, Stark
The resignation of Bill Snyder	Shaver, J. D.
Reckless	Riggs, Lynn
Across the border	Clements, Colin
The organ	Pendray, G. E.
Last day for grouse	Mack, Orin
The end of the trail	Culbertson, E. H.
Day's end	Pieratt, Alice
Good vintage	Totheroh, Dan

Clark, Sarah G., ed. Ready-made programs for every month. Dayton, Ohio
   Paine Pub. Co., 1928.
   Wake, Princess!
   What do you say?
   Nora's elves
   The unexpected guest
   Pollyanna's guest of honor
   The enchanted garden
   All in the lantern's glow
   (Also recitations, poems, and drills)

Clarke, Amy K. & others. Three one-act plays. London. French, 1925.

Persephone	Clarke, Amy K.
Cloudbreak	Roberts, A. O.
Wind o' the moors	Peach, L. du Garde

Clements, Colin C. Plays for Pagans. N. Y. Appleton, 1924.
   The Haiduc
   Harlequin
   Spring!
   Four who were blind
   Yesterday

Clements, Colin C., ed. Sea plays. Boston. Small, Maynard, 1923.

The ship comes in	Fuller, H. B.
The brink of silence	Galbraith, Esther E.
Just two men	Pillot, Eugene
The magic sea shell	Farrar, John
The outside	Glaspell, Susan
The rusty door	Southgate, Howard
"Second best"	Gaston, William

Sintram of Skagerrak   Cowan, Sada
Will-o'-the-wisp   Halman, Doris
The wondership   Cunningham, Leon

Cochran, Eve O. A half hour at the gate. Boston. Badger, 1930.
A half hour at the gate
The king's son
The home coming
The club paper

Coffman, G. R., ed. A book of modern plays. Chicago. Scott, Foresman, 1925.
Riders to the sea   Synge, J. M.
The workhouse ward   Gregory, Lady
Where the cross is made   O'Neill, Eugene
(Also many longer plays)

Cohen, Helen L. More one-act plays by modern authors. N. Y. Harcourt, Brace, 1927.
The night of "Mr. H."   Brighouse, Harold
The last of the Lowries   Green Paul
Hearts enduring   Erskine, John
Pearls   Totheroh, Dan
The dear departed   Houghton. Stanley
The poor house   Driscoll, Louise
The siege   Clements, Colin C.
The change-house   Brandane, John
The little father of the wilderness   Strong, Austin & Osbourne, Lloyd
The artist   Milne, A. A.
Good Theatre   Morley, Christopher
Carved woman   Alexander, H. B.
Where the cross is made   O'Neill, Eugene
A way out   Frost, Robert

Collins, Lillian F. The Little Theatre in school. N. Y. Dodd Mead, 1930.
The courtship of Miles Standish
The nightingale and the rose
The great bell of Peking
The magic fishbone

Columbia University—University Extension. Copy 1924. N. Y. Columbia University Press, 1924.
The cat comes back   Habberstad, Claude
Her country   Wyatt. Euphenia

Columbia University—University Extension. Copy 1925. N. Y. Appleton, 1925.
Bush queer   Habberstad, Claude
Our. John   MacDonald, Z. K.

Columbia University—University Extension. Copy 1926. N. Y. Appleton, 1926.
Nightshade   Giorloff, Ruth
White hands   Morrow, E. P.

Columbia University—University Extension. Copy 1927. N. Y. Appleton, 1927.
Close to the wind   Barnes, Eleanor A.
Yellow roses   Mathews. Alice L.

Conkle, E. P. Crick bottom plays. N. Y. French, 1928.
Minnie Field
Sparkin'
Warter-wucks
'Lection
Things is that-a-way

Connelly, J. M. Co. Publishers. Juvenile plays and readings. Hot Springs National Park, Arkansas, 1929.

Swat that fly!   Yates, Patty M.
When turkeys turned the tables   Cornish, Mary T.
(Also four monologues)

Conrad, Joseph. Laughing Ann; One day more. N. Y. Doubleday, Page, 1925.

One day more
(Also longer play)

Conway, Olive. Costume plays. London. French, 1926.

Becky Sharp
Mimi
Prudence corner
The King's waistcoat

Cooper, W. J. & Woolfolk, E. T. Four plays written and produced by Dramatic Club of Davidson College, N. C. Charlotte, N. C. The Queen City Printing Co., 1923.

A Christian slave   Russell, H. K.
I do   Woolfolk, E. T.
At the sign of the Sturgeon Head   Cooper, W. J.
Uncle Tommy's harem   Gallaway, W. F.

Corkery, Daniel. The yellow bittern and other plays. London. T. Fisher Unwin, 1920.

King and hermit
Clan Falvey
The yellow bittern

Cowan, Sada. Pomp and other plays. N. Y. Brentano's, 1926.

As I remember you
In the morgue
The ball and the chain
Pomp
Sintram of Skagerrak
The cat
Collaboration
The state forbids

Crawshay-Williams, Eliot. Five Grand Guignol plays. London. French, 1924.

E. & O. E.
Amends
Rounding the triangle
The nutcracker suite
Cupboard love

Crawshay-Williams, Eliot. More Grand Guignol plays. London. French, 1927.

The compleat lover
Grensal green
Teaching Teresa
A storm in a breakfast cup

Creagh-Henry, May. Four mystical plays. London. Society for the Promoting Christian Knowledge, 1924.

Outcasts
"Greater love hath no man"
The star
The gate of vision

Cross, Tom P. & others, ed. Good reading for high schools. American Writers. Boston. Ginn, 1931.

The neighbours   Gale, Zona
(Also many examples of other types of literature)

Cross, Tom P. & others, ed. Good reading for high schools. English Writers. Boston. Ginn, 1931.
The lost silk hat   Dunsany, Lord
(Also many examples of other types of literature)

Cross, Tom P. & others, ed. Good readings for high schools. II Achievement. Boston. Ginn, 1930.
The Grand Cham's diamond   Monkhouse, Alan
The ghost story   Tarkington, Booth
(Also many examples of other types of literature)

Crothers, Rachel. Six one-act plays. Boston. Baker, 1925.
The importance of being clothed
The importance of being nice
The importance of being married
The importance of being a woman
What they think
Peggy

Cuddy, Lucy & others. Mother Goose plays. Chicago. Rand McNally, 1925.
Jack and Jill
Little Miss Muffet
Six little mice and yellow pussy

Cummins, S. L. Plays for children. Book I. N. Y. Doran, 1923.
Bluebeard
Haroun el Rashid

Cummins, S. L. Plays for children. Book II. N. Y. Doran, 1923.
St. George and the dragon
The sleeping beauty

Cummins, S. L. Plays for children. Book III. N. Y. Doran, 1923.
Goldilocks and the three bears
Torquil MacFerron
Thomas Olifant
Tyranny

Curtis, Agnes. Clever plays for women. Syracuse, N. Y. Willis N. Bugbee Co., 1929.
Mrs. Ryan's boarders
Old lady Kendell
The Duchess
The mirror
Too much trouble
The trials of a dressmaker

Curtis, Agnes. Holiday plays for young people. Syracuse, N. Y. Willis N. Bugbee Co., 1929.
The Hallowe'en wish
The spirit of the tree
'Twas the night before Christmas
The Christmas stocking
The Easter lily
The boy without a flag
With charity toward all
Mine eyes have seen the glory
The Thanksgiving turkey
For what shall I be thankful?
The lost purse

Cuthrell, Faith B. Sign posts. Boston. Small Maynard, 1924.
A garden in Mitylene
(Also many poems)

Dall, Ian. Noah's wife. Oxford, England. Basil Blackwell, 1925.
The bargain
Noah's wife
Miching Malecho
One sunset
In the barnyard
Among old instruments

Dane, Essex. Shadows and lights. Boston. Baker, 1930.
Coming
Going
Cooled off!
My neighbor
Sweetheart

Darlington, Anne C. The Lady Joanna and two other plays. N. Y. Woman's Press, 1928.
The Lady Joanna
By the roadside
The nine

Darlington, Anne C. Yelenka the wise. N. Y. Woman's Press, 1926.
Yelenka the wise
At the fair
In the Terem
The stars
The strong tower
Polonaise
La Ronda
Tessa's tongue
The torch of Hellas

Dean, Alexander, ed. Seven to seventeen. N. Y. French, 1931.

Ring leader	Rogers, J. W.
Star dust	Gerstenberg, Alice
What's a fixer for?	Potter, H. C.
The 'nitiated	Conkle, E. P.
The palace of Knossos	McFadden, Elizabeth
The reunion	Ross, J. D.
The moon for a prince	Ruthenberg, Grace
The forks of the dilemma	Flowers, Priscilla
A woman of judgment	Pearson, L. M.
Toast and tea	Dean, Alexander
At the fountain	Bull, R. C. & Steinmetz, E. G. Jr.
The brand	Berkley-Boone, F. I.
Mrs. Magician's mistake	Dixon, Virginia
Breakfast	Cook, G. W.
The Thursday	Walker, Alice J.
Six	Schwartz, Theodore
The very sad unicorn	Cook, G. W. & Dixon, Virginia
The fatal quest	—————— (anon)
The rival peach-trees	Riley, Alice C. D.
Moon magic	Perkins, Eleanor E.
(Also a longer play)	

De Huff, Elsie. Five religious education plays. Franklin, Ohio. Eldridge Entertainment House, 1927.
When west meets east
Ten righteous
For their sake
The architect
(Also one longer play)

Denison, Merrill. The Unheroic North. Toronto, Canada. McClelland &
Stewart, 1923.
Brothers in arms
The weather breeder
From their own place

Denton, Clara J. Denton's best plays and dialogues. Chicago. Albert Whit-
man Co., 1925.
The revelation
The queer people
The burglars at Mrs. Day's
We few, we happy few
How the bag was mended
When father was left to himself
(Also a longer play, and several dialogues)

Denton, Eleanor. Sing-a-song-o'-sixpence. Oxford, England. Basil Black-
well, 1927.
Sing-a-song-o'-sixpence
The lion and the unicorn
Goosey-goosey-gander
Simple Simon
Old Mother Hubbard

Deseo, Lydia G. & Phipps, Hulda M., ed. Looking at life through drama.
N. Y. Abingdon Press, 1931.

The slave	Yates, Elizabeth
Bread	Eastman, Fred
X = O : A night of the Trojan War	Drinkwater, John

Detroit, Players of. The players book of one act plays. N. Y. Walter V.
McKee, 1928.

. . . and points west	Toms, R. M.
A glorious martyr	Pike, C. S.
Little brown jug	Weeks, A. L.
Mutiny	Anderson, Lee
A string of pearls	Pike, C. S.
Is peculiar	Anderson, Lee
Elsie	Weeks, A. L.
Fog	Neebe, J. H.
Their appointed rounds	Yerkes, R. G.
Murder will out	Winningham, C. C.
Vespers	Meadon, Joseph
Strategy	Anderson, Lee
Pearls before swine	Meadon, Joseph
Mary Brice	Murphy, T. F.
Guts	Neebe, J. H.
The pearl thief	Phelps, G. H. & Maxwell, I. P.
Cocktails	Weeks, A. L.

Dickinson, T. H., ed. Chief contemporary Dramatists. Third series. Boston.
Houghton, Mifflin, 1930.

Electra	Hofmansthal, Hugo von
A lily among thorns	Sierra, Gregorio & Sierra, Maria M.
The theatre of the soul	Yevreinov, Nikolai N.
(Also many longer plays)	

Dolan, Leonora K. Short plays and pageants for all occasions and grades.
Franklin, Ohio. Eldridge Entertainment House, 1930.
The cotton dresses
The circus comes to town
Everyday courtesies
The giant
Help us to live

The midshipman
The moods of spring
The Mother Goose convention
The mythland of nature
Nature's thrifty workers
Poor Richard says
The song of ripening grain
The soul of the flag
Spirits of the day
Story-book ball
The story of silk
Voices of June
The wedding of the flowers
A year of holidays

Donnelly, G. B. S. J. Pease porridge hot. St. Louis, Mo. The Queen's Work Press, 1928.
King Richard calls for ale
The flavor lasts
Spick and span
Under the big tent
Through the portals

Down, Oliphant. Three one-act plays. Boston. L. Phillips, 1923.
The dream-child
Bal Masqué
Tommy-by-the-way

Drama League—Longmans, Green & Co. Playwriting contest for 1928. Eleven short Bibical plays. N. Y. Longmans, Green, 1929.

Betrayal	Van Norman, Etta C.
Cleopas	Barton, Alice L.
The door	Crew, Helen C.
Elisha	Dunning, Luella M.
For his name's sake	Todd, Helen L.
The friend of Potiphar's wife	Rollins, Cecil A.
The gift of Jehovah	Pettey, Emma
Maundy Thursday	Doten, Edith K.
The third Shepherd play	Mansel, Ronald
The woman from Nod	Taylor, Edith F.
(Also one longer play)	

Dunsany, Lord. Alexander and three small plays. N. Y. Putnams, 1926.
The old king's tale
The evil kettle
The amusements of Khan Kharuda

Dunsany, Lord. Seven modern comedies. N. Y. Putnam, 1928.
Atalanta in Wimbledon
The raffle
The journey of the soul
In Holy Russia
His sainted grandmother
The hopeless passion of Mr. Bunyon
The jest of Hahalaba

Eastman, Fred., ed. Modern religious dramas. N. Y. Holt, 1928.

The neighbours	Gale, Zona
Confessional	Wilde, Percival
What men live by	Church, Virginia
The valiant	Hall, Holworthy & Middlemass, Robert
Bread	Eastman, Fred.
The deathless word	Tompkins, J. M. S.

El Christo	Larkin, Margaret
Dust of the road	Goodman, K. S.
The color line	MacNair, Irene T.
The golden rule in courtship	Cook, Corona R.
Modern magic	Brown, C. S.

Eaton, W. P., ed. Twelve one-act plays. N. Y. Longmans, Green, 1926.

The valiant	Hall, Holworthy & Middlemass, Robert
Romance of the Willow pattern	Van der Veer, Ethel B.
The grill	Johnston, G. W.
The master salesman	Upson, W. H.
Thank you, Doctor	Emery, Gilbert
Copy	Banning, Kendall
The trap	Gerstenberg, Alice
Good medicine	Arnold, Jack & Burke, Edwin
God winks	Burgess, Katharine S.
A woman of character	Brown, Estelle A.
Jazz and minuet	Giorloff, Ruth
The most foolish virgin	Gaskill, Helen G.

Edland, Elisabeth. The children's king and other plays for children. N. Y. Abingdon Press, 1928.

The children's king
Cotton roses
Red-top
Falling leaf
With the watermelon seeds

Edland, Elisabeth. Plum blossoms and other plays. N. Y. Abingdon Press, 1925.

Plum blossoms
The fool's story
The wise and the foolish virgins
The Madonna's picture
(Also a pageant)

Eldridge Entertainment House. Publishers. Church plays and entertainments for young people. Franklin, Ohio. Eldridge Entertainment House. 1924.

A missionary clinic	Fleming, Ethel
Gaining a member	Whitson, Alice L.
The great decision	Whitson, Alice L.
They who vote shall read	Utterbach, Edith G.
Entertaining Aunt Mina	Fleming, Ethel
The revivified lily	Palmer, Bell E.
Uncle Sam's Thanksgiving reception for the States	Hutchinson, Margaret L.

(Also longer plays, pageants, and entertainments)

Emerson College of Oratory. Vol. 1. The cathedral clock and other one act plays. Boston. Expression Co., 1927.

The cathedral clock	Smith, L. J.
The lover of Killcairne	Connor, J. E.
Luck o' Land	Dowling, Adele N.
The doormat	Lonergan, Grace E.
Gifts	Miller, Louise W.
Cold cream	Minchin, Nydia E.
Cured	Hurley, Margaret S.

Enloe, Mary A., ed. Year around primary programs. Chicago. A. Flanagan Co., 1928.

School-time
Hallowe'en

The real Santa Claus
St. Valentine's day with Mother Goose
Thor and his hammer
Two little trunks
How the fairies play
A Christmas journey
The three bears
(Also longer plays, poems, and exercises)

Ervine, St. John G. Four one-act plays. London. George Allen & Unwin, 1928.
The magnanimous lover
Progress
Ole George comes to tea
She was no lady

Esson, Louis. Dead timber and other plays. London. Hendersons, 1920.
Dead timber
The woman tamer
The drovers
The sacred place

Farjeon, Herbert. Happy New Year, and Your kind indulgence. London. French, 1929.
Happy New Year
Your kind indulgence

Farma, W. J., ed. Prose, poetry and drama for oral interpretation. N. Y. Harper, 1930.

A matter of choice	Farma, W. J.
Playgoers	Pinero, A. W.
The boor	Tchekoff, Anton

(Also many poems, and prose selections)

Farrar, John. The magic sea shell and other plays for children. N. Y. Doran, 1923.
The house gnomes
God Pan forgotten
The kingdom of the Rose Queen
The magic sea shell
Grandmother dozes
Birthdays come in February
Worship the nativity

Faxon, Grace B., ed. Many a way to closing day. Boston. Baker, 1926.

Elsie in Mother Goose Land	Cooke, Constance C.
In the days of Robin Hood	Cooke, Constance C.
The Princess and the pea	Cooke, Constance C.
School days	Allen, Alice E.
Broadcast from Bookland	Allen, Alice E.
Blackbird pie	Denby, Emily D.
Being a hero	Dickson, Margaret S.
Circus day	Dunlap, Henrietta F.
The Prince of Ko-Am	Dunlap, Henrietta F.
The set-the-table lady	Linsky, Fannie B.

(Also dialogues, longer plays, and recitations)

Faxon, Grace B., ed. Many a way for Memorial Day. Boston. Baker, 1926.

The flags at war	Dunlap, Henrietta F.
The box from the attic	Linsky, Fannie B.
The Rough Riders	Dunlap, Henrietta F.
A Memorial Day fantasy	Linsky, Fannie B.
The guarding angels	Dunlap, Henrietta F.

(Also dialogues, poems and entertainments)

Federal Council of Churches of Christ in America. Religious dramas. N. Y. Century, 1923.

Dust of the road	Goodman, K. S.
The pilgrim and the book	Mackaye, Percy
The friend of all men	Ferris, Anita
Larola	Willcox, Helen L.
A sinner beloved	Osgood, P. E.
The good Samaritan	Ferris, Anita

Federal Council of the Churches of Christ in America—Committee on Drama. Religious dramas. Vol. II. N. Y. Century, 1926.

The two thieves	Bates, Esther W.
The sword of Samuri	Mygatt, T. D.
Two sides of the door	Cropper, Margaret
Whither goest thou?	Currie, Carleton H.
At the gate beautiful	Mason, Harry S.
Barnabbas	Leamon, Dorothy
The shepherds	Goold, Marshall W.
(Also longer plays)	

Fernand, Weyl. Three gallant plays, tr. by Clarence Stratton. N. Y. William Edwin Rudge, 1929.
A Byzantine afternoon
The slipper of Aphrodite
(Also one longer play)

Field, Rachel. The cross-stitch heart and other plays. N. Y. Scribner, 1927.
The cross-stitch heart
Greasy luck
The nine days' Queen
The Londonderry air
At the junction
Bargains in Cathay

Field, Rachel. Patchwork plays. Garden City, N. Y. Doubleday, Doran, 1930.
Polly Patchwork
Little square-toes
Miss Ant, Miss Grasshopper, and Mr. Cricket
Chimney sweep's holiday
The sentimental scarecrow

Field, Rachel. Six plays. N. Y. Scribner, 1924.
Cinderella married
Three pills in a bottle
Columbine in business
The patchwork quilt
Wisdom teeth
Theories and thumbs

Finney, Stella B., ed. Plays old and new. N. Y. Allyn and Bacon. 1928.

Daniel Boone: patriot	Mackay, Constance D'A
The philosopher of Butterbriggens	Chapin, Harold
Robin Hood at Sherwood	Noyes, Alfred
Told in a Chinese garden	Wilcox, Constance
Spreading the news	Gregory, Lady
The farce of the worthy Master Pierre Patelin	————
Manikin and Minikin	Kreymborg, Alfred
Jephthah's daughter	Levinger, Elma E.
The golden doom	Dunsany, Lord

Firkins, O. W. Two passengers for Chelsea and other plays. N. Y. Longmans, Green, 1928.
Two passengers for Chelsea

The undying Prince
An odd entanglement
The unbidden guest
The reference
The emerald
The last meeting
The rim of the desert
The bloom on the grape
In the small hours
The looking-glass
The answer
Geoffrey's wife

Fish, Helen R. Drama and dramatics. N. Y. Macmillan, 1930.

A night at an inn	Dunsany, Lord
The weather breeder	Denison, Merrill
The proposal	Checkov, Anton
The twilight saint	Young, Stark
My lady's rose	Knoblock, Edward
The knave of hearts	Saunders, Louise

Fitzhugh, Carroll. Mon ami Pierrot and other plays. Boston. Houghton, Mifflin, 1928.
Mon ami Pierrot
Margaret in Naxos
The cough
May and December
The snake
The mountains of Bether

Flaurier, Noel. The last day of school in the primary grades. Dayton, Ohio. Paine Pub. Co., 1928.
Storybook frolics
Those tricky words
The voice from the air
The mistakes they left behind them
The truant leaves
The judge and the speeder
(Also dialogues, recitations, and drills)

Flaurier, Noel. The Thanksgiving treasure book. Dayton, Ohio. Paine Pub. Co., 1928.
A change of mind
The day before
In an old diary
Jack smuggles in a guest
Come back, Mr. Turkey
(Also recitations, pageants, songs, and drills)

Flaurier, Noel & others. Winning plays and dialogues. Chicago. Beckley-Cardy, 1930.

The last study	Roe, Orpha V.
Where are the flowers and the birds?	Roe, Orpha V.
Willie's success	Roe, Orpha V.
The Hollanders	Roe, Orpha V.
Their choice	Roe, Orpha V.
Hunting for spring	Roe, Orpha V.
Little girl confessions	Roe, Orpha V.
Fair play	Moroney, M. Josephine
Just as I please	Roe, Orpha V.
Rats!	Henderson, Gladys
The "mind your mother" club	Roe, Orpha V.

Friday afternoon	Roe, Orpha V.
Neighborly neighbors	Roe, Orpha V.
The wisest wish	Norton, Alice W.
A basket of beautiful things	Norton, Alice W.
The workers	Flaurier, Noel
A fall day	Flaurier, Noel
The street fair	Flaurier, Noel
The royal gift	Flaurier, Noel
The visit of the raindrops	Flaurier, Noel
The A. B. C. fairies	Henderson, Gladys
Lucy chooses	Henderson, Gladys

(Also a longer play and a pantomime)

Flavin, Martin. Brains and other one-act plays. N. Y. French, 1926.
Brains
The blind man
Casualties
An emergency case
A question of principle
Caleb Stone's death watch

Folmsbee, Beulah. Guki the moon boy and other plays. N. Y. Harcourt, Brace, 1928.
Guki the moon boy
Jacquenetta and the Queen's gown
The Princess and the crystal pipe
The King's cobbler
The gift of love

The 47 Workshop. Harvard Plays. Fourth series. N. Y. Brentano's, 1925.

The strongest man	Sullivan, Elizabeth H.
The slump	Day, F. L.
The mourner	Mahoney, James
Brotherhood	Wells, W. H.

Foster, Caroline H. W. Little comedies of to-day. Los Angeles, Cal. The Arroyo Press, 1906.
Not worth mentioning
A house party
A halt on the trail
A complete success
How they practiced their trio
A coup-de-main
A little company
This sordid world

Francis, Celia. Junior high varieties. Franklin, Ohio. Eldridge Entertainment House, 1930.
Who's who: George Washington
Interpretative reading
Baking the cake
Yeo ho! Yeo ho!
Ethel makes cocoa
An idyl of the new year
(Also short sketches)

Freeman, Carolyn R. & others, ed. The Kiddies' Christmas book. Syracuse, N. Y. Willis N. Bugbee Co., 1925.

The Christmas strike	Freeman, Carolyn R.
The wise gifts	Burt, Olive F. W.
Santa's gifts plus his surprise	Crites, Lucille

(Also many dialogues, drills, and recitations)

French, Samuel, Publisher. One-act plays for stage and study. First series. N. Y. French, 1924.

The man upstairs	Thomas, Augustus
The mayor and the manicure	Ade, George
The red owl	Gillette, William
The rector	Crothers, Rachel
A flower of Yeddo	Mapes, Victor
Deceivers	De Mille, W. C.
The girl	Peple, Edward
Peace manoeuvres	Davis, R. H.
Moonshine	Hopkins, Arthur
The robbery	Kummer, Clare
The dying wife	Taylor, Laurette
The little father of the wilderness	Strong, Austin & Osbourne, Lloyd
Such a charming young man	Akins, Zoe
Judge Lynch	Rogers, J. W., Jr.
The widow of Wasdale Head	Pinero, Sir Arthur
Dolly's little bills	Jones, H. A.
The man in the bowler hat	Milne, A. A.
Lonesome-like	Brighouse, Harold
Hanging and wiving	Manners, J. H.
'Op-o'-me-thumb	Fenn, Frederick & Pryce, Richard
Phipps	Houghton, Stanley
Spreading the news	Gregory, Lady
A minuet	Parker, L. N.
The ghost of Jerry Bundler	Jacobs, W. W. & Rock, Charles
Wealth and wisdom	Down, Oliphant

French, Samuel, Publisher. One-act plays for stage and study. Second series. N. Y. French, 1925.

The drums of Oude	Strong, Austin
Young America	Ballard, Fred & Franklin, Pearl
The prairie doll	Carpenter, E. C.
The passing of Chow-chow	Rice, E. L.
The Dickey bird	O'Higgins, Harvey & Ford, Harriet
Meet the Missus	Nicholson, Kenyon
The same old thing	Megrue, R. C.
Red carnations	Hughes, Glenn
Saved	Rogers, J. W., Jr.
The man who died at twelve o'clock	Green, Paul
A question of principle	Flavin, Martin
And there was light	Kennedy, C. O'B.
Among thieves	Gillette, William
The Corsican lieutenant	Housum, Robert
On the racecourse	Gregory, Lady
The black bottle	O'Brien, Seumas
The knife	Jones, H. A.
Claude	Ould, Hermon
The idealist	Down, Oliphant
At the telephone	Lorde, André de
The host	Molnar, Ferenc

French, Samuel, Publisher. One-act plays for stage and study. Third series. N. Y. French, 1927.

One of those things	Kelly, George
Dave	Gregory, Lady
Napoleon crossing the Rockies	Mackaye, Percy
Unto such glory	Green, Paul
Papers	Kummer, Clare
Cupid in Clapham	Baker, Elizabeth
The Londonderry air	Field, Rachel
The eligible Mr. Bangs	Housum, Robert
Knives from Syria	Riggs, Lynn

The kite	Hudson, Holland
The cobbler's den	O'Brien, Seumas
The betrayal	Colum, Padraic
Changing places	Ehrlich, Ida L.
The voice of the snake	Halman, Doris F.
The sundial	Pillot, Eugene
Duetto	Burgess, Katharine S
The weathervane elopes	Riley, Alice C. D.
Mary means what she says	Rogers, J. W.
Youth must be served	Ford, Harriet
When did they meet again?	Brighouse, Harold
Jane, Jean and John	Kreymborg, Alfred

French, Samuel, Publisher. One-act plays for stage and study. Fourth series. N. Y. French, 1928.

The snake eater	Nicholson, Kenyon
So's your old antique!	Kummer, Clare
Fortinbras in plain clothes	Brooks, G. S.
Three players, a fop and a duchess	Hughes, Babette
The witch's daughter	Brighouse, Harold
In-laws	Ford, Harriet
Reckless	Riggs, Lynn
Invitation	Basshe, Em Jo
A wedding	Kirkpatrick, John
The fourth Mrs. Phillips	Glick, Carl
Lenna looks down	Halman, Doris F.
A tune of a tune	Totheroh, Dan
Brother Bill	Kreymborg, Alfred
Cobweb kings	Davies, Mary C.
Things is that-a-way	Conkle, E. P.
The wily one	Monkhouse, Allan
The pipe in the fields	Murray, T. C.
Cured	Ehrlich, Ida L.
The miracle of Saint Martin	Dondo, Mathurin
Love in a French kitchen	Clements, Colin & Saunders, J. M.
Christmas eve	O'Brien, Seumas
Blue thunder	Green, Paul

French, Samuel, Publisher. One-act plays for stage and study. Fifth series. N. Y. French, 1929.

A diadem of snow	Rice, E. L.
The late Captain Crow	Armstrong, Louise V. V.
It's an ill wind	Baumer, Marie
The stoker	Brighouse, Harold
The wedding rehearsal	Farrar, John
No more Americans	Hughes, Babette
Art and Mrs. Palmer	Hughes, Glenn
The rescue of Cynthia Ann	Rogers, J. W.
Black Oliver	Guinan, John
Mrs. Adis	Kaye-Smith, Sheila & Hampden, John
The Widdy's mite	Totheroh, Dan
Angelus	Taylor, Helen L.
Limping along	Kreymborg, Alfred
Babouscka	Van der Veer, Ethel
Hot lemonade	Ryerson, Florence & Clements, Colin
Jumpin' the broom	Green, Clara M.
Maizie	Giorloff, Ruth
The haunted coal mine	Pride, L. B.
Words and music	Nicholson, Kenyon

The first dress suit   Medcraft, Russell
Tables and chairs   Davies, Mary C.

French, Samuel, Publisher. One-act plays for stage and study. Sixth series.
  N. Y. French, 1931.
The still alarm   Kaufman, G. S.
The snake charmer   Bennett, Arnold
The ghosts of Windsor Park   Brighouse, Harold
Speaking terms   Pertwee, Roland
Murder ! murder ! murder !   Hughes, Babette
Men, women and goats   Kennedy, C. O'B.
Colman and Guaire   Gregory, Lady
The willow plate   Ryerson, Florence & Clements,
                                          Colin
The woman who understood men   Kirkpatrick, John
Poetry and plaster   Medcraft, Russell
The bad penny   Field, Rachel
The lost Princess   Totheroh, Dan
The Chinese water wheel   Strachan, Edna H.
Traffic signals   Drummond, A. M.
Babbitt's boy   Hughes, Glenn
Josephine   Crocker, Bosworth
Saint Cyprian and the devil   Van der Veer, Ethel
The wolf at the door   Hanlon, D. E.
The pie and the tart   Jagendorf, M.
A change of mind   Speirs, Russell
The moving finger   Wilde, Percival

French, Samuel, Publisher. Play-bits fragments for concert folk. London.
  French, 1922.
A breakfast breeze   Macfarlane, W.
The old, old story   Holland, Harold
Hang it !   Sargent, H. C.
Gloom   Preston, E.
A. D. 2000   Preston, E.

French, Samuel, Publisher. Pulling the show together. London. French, 1928.
The eternal question   Stephenson, Ann & Macbeth, Allan
Euclid was right   Stephenson, Ann
The famous Bugle diamond mystery   Melville, Harold
A man of letters   Poultney, C. B.
Midnight murder   Aashdown, Arthur
Pulling the show together   Stephenson, Ann
Reprieved   Stevens, H. C. G.
The result   Stevens, H. C. G.
The unforgivable   Macbeth, Allan

French, Samuel, Publisher. Quite a cat, and other sketches for Woman's
  Institutes, Girl Guides, etc. London. French, 1927.
Quite a nice cat   Hendrie, Ernest & Caldwell, S.
Joint owners in Spain   Brown, Alice
Blood will tell   Kemper, Sallie
Sinking   Hendrie, Ernest & Caldwell, S.

French, Samuel, Publisher. Try one of these ! Revue sketches. London.
  French, 1927.
A telephone episode   Lane-Norcott, Maurice
At the Costumier's   Grace, Gerald
Swollen angels   Brown, Ivor
The tragedy of Jones   Lane-Norcott, Maurice
The house agent   Grace, Gerald
Four's company   Stevens, H. C. G.
After the reunion dinner   Lane-Norcott, Maurice

Murder most-polite   Stevens, H. C. G.
A matter of policy   Phillips, Gordon

Fyleman, Rose. Eight plays for children. N. Y. Doran, 1925.
Darby and Joan
The fairy riddle
Noughts and crosses
The weather clerk
The fairy and the doll
Cabbages and kings
In Arcady
Father Christmas

Gallup, G. H., ed. Best creative work in American high schools. Iowa City,
Ia. The National Honorary Society for high school journalists, 1927.
Trial   Williams, Peggy A.

Galsworthy, John. Plays. N. Y. Scribner, 1928.
The first and the last
The little man
Hall-marked
Defeat
The sun
Punch and go

Gardner, Flora C. & Gardner, Margaret. Up-to-date Christmas programs.
Lebannon, Ohio. March Bros., 1930.
All aboard for North Pole Land
The manger in Bethlehem
The first Christmas carol
Setting the world's Christmas table
The spirit of Christmas via Santa Claus
A visit from Santa Claus via radio
The wise men seek Jesus
(Also drills, dialogues, pantomimes, and recitations)

Gardner, Flora C. & Gardner, Margaret. Up-to-date community pro-
grams. Lebanon, Ohio. March Bros., 1930.
Friends indeed
Ha'nts
Socks and social engagements
The burglar
Photographing the family
Vite-em-in the garden of health
I'll tell you exactly what to do
Her social aspirations
Strange lands
The rehearsal
(Also dialogues, and entertainments)

Garnett, Louise A. Three to make ready. N. Y. Doran, 1923.
Hilltop
Muffins

Gates, Barrington. The Mulligatawny medallion. London. Ernest Benn,
1926.
The Mulligatawny medallion
The day's work
A small hour
The wonderful son
Time

Gerstenberg, Alice. Comedies all. N. Y. Longmans, Green, 1930.
The setback
Mere man

The menu
Facing fact
Upstage
Rhythm
The opera matinee
At the club
The puppeteer
Latchkeys

Gerstenberg, Alice. Four plays for four women. N. Y. Brentano's, 1924.
Mah-Jongg
Their husband
Ever young
Seaweed

Gibson, Emily M. English-class plays for new Americans. N. Y. Woman's Press, 1927.
The mother tongu
The common bond
The scrubwoman
Hot water
New worlds
The spirit of Lincoln
George Washington's birthday
Betsy Ross
Cornelia's jewels
Opening the gate

Gibson, Wilfred. Kestrel Edge and other plays. N. Y. Macmillan, 1924.
Gangrels
Red Rowan
Blackadder
Winter's Stob
Kestrel Edge

Githens, H. W. Dramatized stories from the Old Testament. Cincinnati, Ohio. The Standard Pub. Co., 1927.
A father of nations
Searching for a wife
A bad bargain
A long courtship
The coat of many colors
A prisoner promoted
Saved to serve
An adopted son
From palace to prairie
Delivered from bondage
The golden calf
A rash vow
A faithful daughter
A mother's gift
The shepherd king
A giant story
A wise king
A captive maid
A woman who dared
The fiery furnace
The handwriting on the wall
A persecuted prophet
A fish story

Githens, H. W. New Testament stories dramatized. Cincinnati, Ohio. The Standard Pub. Co., 1929.

808.82
C336t

The King's English	Bates, Herbert
The lost silk hat	Dunsany, Lord
The thrice promised bride	Hsuing, Cheng-Chin
The boor	Chekhov, Anton
The workhouse ward	Gregory, Lady
The unseen	Gerstenberg, Alice
Sham	Tompkins, F. G.
Confessional	Wilde, Percival
Dust of the road	Goodman, K. S.
Ile	O'Neill, Eugene
The God of quiet	Drinkwater, John
The white hawk	Kemp, Harry

Goodman, K. S. & Hecht, Ben. The wonder hat and other one-act plays. N. Y. Appleton, 1925.
The wonder hat
The two lamps
An idyll of the shops
The hand of Siva
The hero of Santa Maria

Granville, Edward. Tammy and four other plays. London. French, 1929.
Tammy
Leisure
Kalim's messenger
Seventeen fourteen
'Enery Brown

Green, Paul. The House of Connelly and other plays. N. Y. French, 1931.
Potter's field
Tread the green grass
(Also a longer play)

Green, Paul. In the valley and other Carolina plays. N. Y. French, 1928.
In the valley
Quare medicine
Supper for the dead
Saturday night
The man who died at twelve o'clock
Unto such glory
The no 'count boy
The man on the house
The picnic
In Aunt Mahaly's cabin
The goodbye

Green, Paul. Lonesome road. N. Y. McBride, 1926.
X In Abraham's bosom
White dresses
The hot iron
The prayer-meeting
The end of the row
Your fiery furnace

Green, Paul. The Lord's will and other Carolina plays. N. Y. French, 1928.
The Lord's will
Blackbeard
Old Wash Lucas
The no 'count boy
The old man of Edenton
The last of the Lowries

Gregory, Lady. Three last plays of Lady Gregory. N. Y. Putnam, 1929.
Dave

The would-be gentleman
(Also longer play)

Greenlaw, Edwin & others, ed. Literature and life. Book II. Special edition. Chicago. Scott Foresman, 1929.

The Beau of Bath   Mackay, Constance D'A.
Enter the hero   Helburn, Theresa
Sham   Tompkins, F. G.
(Also many examples of other types of literature)

Greenlaw, Edwin & Miles, Dudley, ed. Literature and life. Book III. Chicago. Scott Foresman, 1923.

Enter the hero   Helburn, Theresa
Sham   Tompkins, F. G.
(Also examples of other types of literature)

Greenlaw, Edwin & Miles, Dudley, ed. Literature and life. Book III. Special edition. Chicago. Scott Foresman, 1929.

Where but in America   Wolff, O. M.
Where the cross is made   O'Neill, Eugene
(Also examples of other types of literature)

Griffith, Mary M. Westward the course of empire. Austin, Texas. E. L. Steck Co., 1924.

La Salle
Saint Denis
San Jose (1721)
San Jose (1794)
Ellis Bean
Lafitte
Long's Fort
First three hundred
Fredonian rebellion
On to San Antonio
Declaration of Texas Independence
Fall of the Alamo
Goliad Massacre
The father of Texas is no more
San Jacinto ball
Austin, the capitol
The republic of Texas is no more

Haggard, Audrey. Little plays from Greek myths. N. Y. Dutton, 1929.

Pomona
Midas
Philemon and Baucis
Aurora and Tithonus

Haggerty, M. E. & Smith, Dora V., ed. Reading and literature. Book Three. Yonkers-on-Hudson, N. Y. World Book Co., 1928.

The silver lining   Mackay, Constance D'A.
What men live by   Tolstoi, Leo
Pyramus and Thisbe   Shakespeare, William
(Also many examples of other types of literature)

Hallock, Grace T., ed. Dramatized child health. N. Y. American Child Health Ass'n., 1925.

How Prince Joy was saved   Kunz, Edith
Green Rowan   Branch, Anna H.
The bag of fresh air dreams   Sorden, Hetty L.
The little vegetable men   Griffith, Eleanor G.
The magic oat field   Griffith, Eleanor G.
The house the children built   Griffith. Eleanor G.
(Also longer plays, and material for dramatization)

Hamilton, Dorothy T., ed. Primary Christmas programs. Chicago, A. Flanagan Co., 1928.

The real Santa Claus	Smith, Laura R.
The snowflakes and the fairies	Denton, C. J.
A Christmas stocking	Irish, Marie
(Also recitations, stories, readings, and drills)	

Hampden, John, ed. Nine modern plays. London, Thomas Nelson & Sons, 1926.

The Bishop's candlesticks	McKinnel, Norman
The philosopher of Butterbiggins	Chapin, Harold
The rehearsal	Baring, Maurice
The price of coal	Brighouse, Harold
Allison's lad	Dix, Beulah M.
The old bull	Gilbert, Bernard
The little man	Galsworthy, John
The poetasters of Ispahan	Bax, Clifford
Riders to the sea	Synge, J. M.

Hampden, John, ed. Ten modern plays. London, Thomas Nelson & Sons, 1928.

Thirty minutes in a street	Major, Beatrice
The house with the twisted windows	Pakington, Mary
Columbine	Arkell, Reginald
Moonshine	Hopkins, Arthur
The new wing at Elsmore	Hankin, St. John
Mrs. Adis	Kaye-Smith, Shiela & Hampden, John
Tickless time	Glaspell, Susan & Cook, G. C.
X-O: A night of the Trojan War	Drinkwater, John
Elizabeth refuses	Macnamara, Margaret
Brother Wolf	Housman, Laurence

Hanemann, H. W. As is; a book of miscellaneous revelations. N. Y. Harcourt, Brace, 1923.

Decorating the interior
O conscript fathers!
Three brass Bedouins
The florist's daughter
Anti-Pashto

Hanes, Ernest & McCoy, Martha J., ed. Readings in contemporary literature. N. Y. Macmillan, 1928.

A night at an inn	Dunsany, Lord
The Lord's prayer	Coppée, François
The maker of dreams	Down, Oliphant
Peggy	Williamson, Harold
The coming of fair Annie	Price, Graham
Dust of the road	Goodman, K. S.

Hartley, Roland E. & Power, Caroline M., ed. Short plays from great stories. N. Y. Macmillan, 1928.

The siege of Berlin	Daudet, Alphonse
The Sire of Maletroit's door	Stevenson, R. L.
The necklace	Maupassant, Guy de
Two of them	Barrie, J. M.
Wee Willie Winkie	Kipling, Rudyard
The ambitious guest	Hawthorne, Nathaniel
The shot	Pushkin, Alexander
Rip Van Winkle	Irving, Washington
Madame Delphine	Cable, G. W.
The substitute	Coppée, François
The outcast of Poker Flat	Harte, Bret

The purloined letter   Poe, E. A.
Mateo Falcone   Merimée, Prosper
A sisterly scheme   Bunner, H. C.
The young man with the cream   Stevenson, R. L.
  tarts
The three strangers   Hardy, Thomas
My double and how he undid me   Hale, E. E.
The rose of the Alhambra   Irving, Washington

Harvard Dramatic Club miracle plays, ed. by Donald Robinson.
    N. Y. French, 1928.
The pageant of the Shearmen and Tailors
The Towneley play
The Nativity : The Chantilly play
The Bened : Ktbeuren play
The Wisemen : The Spanish play
The Provençal play
The Hessian Christmas play
The Maastricht play
The Star : The Bilsen play
The Umbrian play

Harwood, H. M. Three one-act plays. London. Ernest Benn, 1926.
The mask
The confederates
Honour thy father

Hatfield, W. W. & Roberts, H. D., ed. The spirit of America in literature.
    N. Y. Century, 1931.
Ile   O'Neill, Eugene
The sleeping-car   Howells, W. D.
Sham   Tompkins, F. G.
Moonshine   Hopkins, Arthur
(Also examples of other types of literature)

Hazard, Lucy L., ed. In search of America. N. Y. Crowell, 1930.
The last of the Lowries   Green, Paul
(Also examples of other types of literature)

Herbert, A. P. & others. Double demon and other one-act plays. N. Y.
    Appleton, 1924.
Double demon   Herbert, A. P.
St. Simeon Stylites   Smith, Sladen
Thirty minutes in a street   Major, Beatrice
Pan in Pimlico   Simpson, Helen

Hervey, W. L., ed. Junior literature. Grade 7A. N. Y. Longmans, Green,
    1929.
The snow witch   Mackay, Constance D'A.
(Also examples of other types of literature)

Heywood, Delia A. & others, ed. The red entertainment book. Chicago.
    A. Flanagan Co., 1930.
The wonderful Mr. Venderhoof   Heywood, Delia A.
The good old times   Heywood, Delia A.
Mrs. Peabody's boarder   Heywood, Delia A.
Keeping up appearances   Heywood, Delia A.
Trials of a country editor   Heywood, Delia A.
Everystudent   Everett, Edith
(Also dialogues, entertainments, and charades)

Hobbs, Mabel & Miles, Helen. Six Bible plays. N. Y. Century, 1924.
Ruth and Naomi
Joseph and his brethren
Moses

Esther
The healing of Naaman
David and Jonathan

Hofer, Marie R., ed. Festivals and civic plays from Greek and Roman tales. Chicago. Beckley-Cardy, 1926.
Greek games and festivals
Jason and the golden fleece
Prometheus the friend of man
The labors of Heracles
The quest of Perseus
Theseus and the Minotaur
Atalanta's race
Arachne and Athene
Baucis and Philemon
Damon and Pythias
Pericles and the builders of Athens
Lycurgus the law maker
Solon the legislator
Socrates the philosopher
Pomona and Vertumnus
How Cincinnatus saved Rome
Cloelia the Roman girl scout
The choice of Coriolanus
Camillus and the schoolmaster
Trajan and the children of Rome
Cornelia the mother of the Gracchi
King Tarquin and the Sibyl
Patria Potestas
The Justinian code
Caractacus and the Romans

Holland, Norah M. When half-gods go and other poems. N. Y. Macmillan, 1924.
When half-gods go
The awakening of the lily
(Also many poems)

Holloway, Pearl. The paramount missionary book. Chicago. Meyer & Bro., 1926.
From small beginnings
Unto the least of these
The things that we can do
(Also many recitations, exercises, and pantomimes)

Housman, Laurence. Cornered poets. London. Jonathan Cape, 1929.
The fire-lighters
The messengers
Charles! Charles!
The Cutty-stool
Elegy of a country churchyard
Sal volatile
The mortuary

Housman, Laurence. Followers of St. Francis. Boston. Small, Maynard, n.d.
Cure of souls
Lovers meeting
The fool's errand
The last disciple

Housman, Laurence. Little plays of St. Francis. London. Sidgwick & Jackson, 1927.
The revellers
Fellow-prisoners

Brief life
Blind eyes
The bride feast
Our lady of poverty
The builders
Brother Wolf
Sister Claire
The lepers
Sister Gold
Brother Sun
The chapter
Brother Juniper
Brother Elias
The seraphic vision
Brother Sin
Sister Death

Hoxie, Evelyn. Hints and ha'nts for Hallowe'en. Franklin, Ohio. Eldridge
      Entertainment House, 1931.
Act foolish and be wise
Fortune telling
Travelling to a Hallowe'en party
(Also many dialogues, longer plays, and recitations)

Hoxie, Evelyn. Patriotic programs for patriotic days. Boston. Baker, 1926.
Johnny on Colonial history
Mollie teaches the code of the flag
History slightly mixed
(Also recitations, dialogues, readings, and pageants)

Hoxie, Evelyn. Seven snappy entertainments for adults. Boston. Baker,
      1926.
When Harold met his mother-in-law
Hildegard's elopement
(Also three longer plays, and an entertainment)

Hughes, Glenn. New plays for mummers. Seattle, Washington. University of
      Washington Book Store, 1926.
Manners and manors
Life on the steppes
Pretty little Plum-pit
Lucy the farmer's daughter
The vengeance of Hello-hello
The heart of old Kentucky
The killing of Aaron Kale
Nell of the golden west
Whittle
The suspicious drummer

Hughes, Glenn, ed. Short plays for modern players. N. Y. Appleton, 1931.

The ambush	Hughes, Rupert
Uncle Jimmy	Gale, Zona
The man with the iron jaw	Kennedy, C. O'B.
What never dies	Wilde, Percival
The calf that laid the golden eggs	Hughes, Babette
A small down payment	Savage, George
Under the oak	Wight, Douglas
Three cans of beans	Erskine, L. Y.
A duel for nothing	Ament, W. S.
Five minutes from the station	Carrington, Elaine S.
Gilt-edged	Peterson, Agnes E.
Really, my dear . . .	Morley, Christopher

Hughes, Richard. A rabbit and a leg. N. Y. Knopf, 1924.
The sister's tragedy
The man born to be hanged
A comedy of danger

Indiana Prize plays, 1922—23. Indianapolis, Indiana. Bobbs-Merrill, 1924.

The marriage gown	Sollenberger, Judith K.
Where do we go from here?	Bates, W. O.
Brothers	King, D. G.
Treason	Tull, M. C.
Two dollars please!	Stevenson. Margaretta
Nocturne	Earnest, H. L.

Inge, Benson & Chupét, Charles. The curtain rises. N. Y. Book Mart Pub. Co., 1926.
Ain't no use fer larnin'
The bronze bride
At the stake
Wolf of Zoty

Intercollegiate Literary Magazine Conference, ed. Young Pegasus. N. Y. Dial Press, 1926.
The red mill   Buell, Margaret A.
(Also many poems and examples of prose)

Irish, Marie. The grade school play book. Boston. Baker, 1929.
Excuse me
The food fairies
Grumps meet grouches
Midwinter's night's dream
Miss Miranda
Our friends the trees
Meeting of the hearts
So this is school
Uncle Ole's uncle
(Also longer plays, dialogues, pageants, and exercises)

Irish, Marie. Hallowe'en merrymakers. Syracuse, N. Y. Willis N. Bugbee Co., 1930.
Going to the party
A Hallowe'en hold-up
A lucky Hallowe'en
The Pun'kin-headed servant
(Also dialogues, longer plays, and poems)

Irish, Marie & others. Sunshine plays and dialogues. Syracuse, N. Y. Willis N. Bugbee Co., 1929.

Incentive	Irish, Marie
Aw, Gee	Irish, Marie
Just before midnight	Irish, Marie
Charles, the conqueror	Irish, Marie
Friendly advice	Irish, Marie
The awakening	Irish, Marie
Make your choice	Irish, Marie
What happened to Brown	Irish, Marie
A mended day	Irish, Marie
Two valentines	White, Kate A.
The mission of Midas	Baird, Mrs. Eva
Passing of the year	Leonard, E. J.

(Also longer plays)

Irish, Marie. Tip-top Thanksgiving book. Syracuse, N. Y. Willis N. Bugbee Co.. 1930.
Thanksgiving as usual

Getting into step
Victory and Thanksgiving
Everybody thankful
(Also dialogues, recitations, and pantomimes)

Isaacs, Edith J. R., ed. Plays of American life and fantasy. N. Y. Coward-McCann, 1929.

Moonshine	Hopkins, Arthur
The dreamy kid	ONeill, Eugene
Bumblepuppy	Rogers, John W., Jr.
Blocade	Dunbar, Oliva H.
The end of the trail	Cubbertson, E. H.
Charivari	Stephens, Nan B.
Kills-with-her-man	Alexander, Hartley
Brother Bill	Kreymborg, Alfred
Rapunzel	Brody, Alter
The no 'count boy	Green, Paul
Rose windows	Young, Stark
Spring sluicing	Ernst, Alice H.
Zombi	Scott, Natalie V.
The portrait of Tiero	Akins, Zoe
Trap doors	Kreymborg, Alfred
The Queen of Sheba	Young, Stark
The autocrat of the coffee-stall	Chapin, Harold
The gooseberry mandarin	Ruthenburg, Grace D.

Iwaska, Y. T. & Hughes, Glenn, tr. & ed. New plays from Japan. N. Y. Appleton, 1930.

Death	Arishima, Takeo
Burning her alive	Sudzuki, Senzabaro
(Also one longer play)	

Jacob, Fred. One-third of a bill. Toronto, Canada. The Macmillan Co., of Canada, 1925.

Autumn blooming
The clever one
And they met again
Man's world
The basket

Jagendorf, M. Fairyland and footlights. N. Y. Brentano's, 1925.

Ling Groog and his grouch
In King Lugdub's forest
Mee-Mee and But-Zee
The sad tale of the tarts of the terrible Queen of Hearts
Firefly night

Jagendorf, M., ed. Nine short plays written for young people to stage. N. Y. Macmillan, 1928.

The fairy ring	Andersen, Madge
Ding-a ling	Relonde, Maurice
The bean boy	Adair, Towle
Three of a different kind	Welff, Eric
Golden cornstalk goes home	Comfort, Florence C.
The clown of Doodle Doo	Barrows, Marjorie
The dowry of Columbine	Goes, Bertha
A tale of India	Moore, Florence
Merry Tyll	Jagendorf, M.

Jagendorf, M., ed. One-act plays for young folks. N. Y. Brentano's, 1924.

Which is witch?	Rostetter, Alice
The sing-a-song man	Comfort, Florence C.
The garden at the zoo	Farrar, John
Five ghosts	Wright, Rowe

Bumbo and Scrumbo and Blinko	Jagendorf, M.
The password	Crew, Helen C.
In the kitchen of the king	Lawler, Lillian B.
Mother Goose drops in	Shipley, Joseph
The sandman's brother	O'Donnell, T. C.
The heritage	Purdy, Nina
The east wind's revenge	Janney, Sam
Mr. Bunny's prize	Cavanah, Frances
Once in a hundred years	Jagendorf, M.

Jasspon, Ethel R. & Becker, Florence. Ritual and dramatized folkways. N. Y. Century, 1925.
The happy prince
The gate of the west
The three princesses
The king orders the drums to be beaten
Simple Simon
(Also rituals, ceremonies, pantomimes)

Jast, L. S. The lover and the dead woman, and five other plays in verse. London. George Routledge & Sons, 1923.
The lover and the dead woman
The Geisha's wedding
The loves of the elements
The call of the ninth wave
Venus and the shepherdess
Harbour

Jeans, Ronald. Bright intervals. London. French, 1927.
Catching the male
The customer is always right
The slow train to Wolverhampton
Missing links
Off the lines
Ring in the new
Gown and out
Shades of Shakespeare
Two's company

Jeans, Ronald. Charlot Revue sketches. London. French, 1925.
Great expectations
Lavender bags
The ministering angel
Mixed methods
Not lost
The old lady shows her muddles
On and off
On with the old
The parting

Jeans, Ronald. Odd Numbers. London. French, 1927.
Yours to hand
Duck and drake
Four to six-thirty
The one woman in the world
The price
Atmosphere
Grand Guignol
A gala night at Galashiels
The lady of the lake

Jeans, Ronald. "One dam' sketch after another." London. French, 1928.
The age of compromise
As others see us

Buying a tie
Community singing at home
Lost souls
The match-maker
A one-sided affair
The secrets of good health
The smart set

Jeans, Ronald. The review of revues. London. French, 1925.
Big fleas and little fleas
Caught in the act
Game to the end
Greek as she is taught
Intolerance
The rose
An X-ray dialogue
Yesterday, to-day, and to-morrow

Jeans, Ronald. Sundry sketches. London, French, 1924.
Coming events
Think before you speak
Incredible happenings
Peace and quiet
Home at last
No change
A bit of brother
The pulse of passion
A cabaret drama

John, Gwen. Plays. London. Duckworth & Co., 1916.
Outlaws
Corinna
Sealing the compact
Edge o' dark
The case of Teresa
In the rector's study

John, Gwen. Plays of innocence. London. Ernest Benn, 1925.
A tale that is told
On the road
Luck of war
A Peakland wakes

John o' London's Weekly. Competition for one act plays. Prize plays.
London. H. F. W. Deane & Sons, 1930.

The road of poplars	Sylvaine, Vernon
Chances	Lindsay, Walter (pseud)
An evening on Dartmoor	Munro, Noel

Johnson, Ella B. & others, ed. Christmas joy book. Syracuse, N. Y.
Willis N. Bugbee Co., 1930.

Santa's worries	Johnson, Ella B.
Spreading Christmas cheer	Johnson, Ella B.
Christmas with a bachelor	Johnson, Ella B.
Reuben springs a surprise	Bugbee, W. N.
Mrs. Santa Claus	Bugbee, W. N.

(Also dialogues, drills, pantomimes, recitations)

Johnson, Mamie T. Rural community plays. Lebanon, Ohio. March Bros.,
1925.
Cackle, cackle, cackle
Figures don't lie
John's gang
Show them the cup, Floyd

Solomon sings
(Also longer plays)

Johnson, Marie W., comp. Plays and pageants for the church school. Boston. The Beacon Press, 1929.

The star of Bethlehem	Letchworth, Ruth A.
Hope	Coyle, Clara V.
Speak to the earth and it shall teach you	Fenner, Marian W.

(Also longer plays and pageants)

Johnson, Philip. Four plays. London. Ernest Benn, 1929.

The cage
The lovely miracle
The good and the bad
(Also a longer play)

Johnson, Theodore, ed. The gingerbread house and eight other plays for children. Boston. Baker, 1928.

The gingerbread house	Richardson, Grace
King of the bookcase	Cavanah, Frances
When the moon learned to smile	Cavanah, Frances
October gave a party	Olson, Esther E.
The raggedy-girl's dream	Williams, Bertha
Puck in exile	Richardson, Grace
The dawn of freedom	Leighton, Etta V.
The ring of salt	Richardson, Grace
A summer day dream	Olson, Esther E.

Johnson, Theodore, ed. Miniature plays for stage and study. Boston. Baker, 1928.

Bargains	Kester, Katharine
Dispatch goes home	Mansur, F. L.
Early frost	Stevens. H. B.
The fifth commandment	Steell, Willis
The final refuge	Tomita, Kojiro
La Carota	Stahl, M. E.
For distinguished service	Knox, Florence C.
The lost saint	Hyde, Douglas
Love and lather	Kester, Katharine
The Singapore spider	Finnegan, Edward
The Greek vase	Baring, Maurice

Johnson, Theodore, ed. More plays in miniature. Boston. Baker, 1929.

His only way	Dane, Essex
Spring	Clements, C. C.
Famine and the ghost	Halman, Doris
Xanthippe and Socrates	Baring, Maurice
The other voice	Fairbanks, S. v K.
Secrets of the heart	Dobson, Austin
The drawback	Baring, Maurice
The marriage of Dotty	Thornton, Clare
Double dummy	Hunting, Ema S.
A vicious circle	Pain, Mrs. Barry
Yes and no	Bates, Arlo
Come here	Riddle, George
At the ferry	
Au revoir	Dobson, Austin
Just advertise	Cobb, Mrs. G. C.
The wooden leg	Dane, Essex

Johnson, Theodore, ed. Plays in miniature, Boston. Baker, n.d.

The baggage	Moore, Bertha
It sometimes happens	

Catherine Parr — Baring, Maurice
Wrong numbers — Dane, Essex
Square pegs — Bax, Clifford
At the sign of the cleft heart — Garrison, Theodora
Fleurette and Company — Dane, Essex
The umbrella duologue — Battiscombe, Dora E.
On the way home — Olson, Esther E.
Outwitted — Newton, H. L.
Confessions — Doyle, A. C.

Jones, J. E., ed. Scenes from Dickens. Toronto, Canada. McClelland & Stewart, 1923.

Bardell vs Pickwick — Bengough, J. W.
Wardle's Christmas party — Rostance, A. J.
Sam Weller's walentine — Jones, J. E.
Tony Weller's beneficence — Jones, J. E.
The trial of John Jasper for the murder of Edwin Drood — Dickens Fellowship Players
Mr. Bumble's proposal — Hatton, G. R. & Hatton, Mrs. G. R.
Sam Weller visits his mother-in-law — Stamfora, J. H.
Scenes from the old curiosity shop — Bell-Smith, F. M.
Something wrong somewhere — Lugsdin, L. J.
David at Aunt Betsy's — Rostance, Mrs. A.
The Cratchit's Christmas dinner — Bell-Smith, F. M.
(Also one longer play)

Kampmeier, Roland, ed. Contemporaries! current forms of composition from L. C. Woodman's Coe College Freshman English classes, 1927–28. Vinton, Iowa, Kruse Pub. Co., 1928.

Another moon — Coon, Ruth
Emy's end — Erickson, Edna
Just mere woman — Hutton, Marian
The tyranny of conscience — Kelley, Ronald
The kid — Moore, Ralph
The realm of Thanatos — Northey, Mary
Wind-swept hill — Petersen, Georgia
A summer morning in June — Vermazen, Ernest

Kaser, A. L. Talking acts for two. Chicago. Denison, 1927.

Cowology
The danger line
Hot stuff
Irish, too
Mine gracious
Oddervise and so on
On the P. D. Q.
Poor Izzy!
Skeletons and dynamite
Time flies
Trombonehead
Two against one less
Bab's boob
Cupid is speedy
Ee, fah, lahso, fahso
Jasper Henry Clay Applesauce
Marital mishaps
Needles
Palaver—that's all

Kaye-Smith, Sheila. Saints in Sussex. N. Y. Dutton, 1927.
The child born at the plough
The shepherd of Lattenden

Kelley, Owen. Stunt plays for your club night. N. Y. Town and Country
  Publishers, 1930.
  Nine and twenty candles
  Doctor!
  To meet the duke
  The scandal
  Mademoiselle Tania
  It happens every day
  A maiden in distress
  Bless our home
  A' la carte
  The interview
  His first case
  An evening of bridge
  The thirteenth trump
  The proposal
  The first May

Kelly, George. The flattering word and other one-act plays. Boston. Little,
  Brown, 1925.
  The flattering word
  Smarty's party
  The weak spot
  Poor Aubrey

Kemp, Harry. Bocaccio's untold tale and other one-act plays. N. Y. Bren-
  tano's, 1924.
  Bocaccio's untold tale
  The game called kiss
  The white hawk
  Solomon's song
  Judith
  Don Juan's Christmas eve
  Don Juan in a garden
  Calypso
  Their day
  The peril of the moon

Kennedy, C. R. A repertory of plays for a company of seven players and
  two short plays for smaller casts. Chicago. The University of Chicago
  Press, 1930.
  The terrible meek
  The necessary evil

Kimball, Rosamond. The wooing of Rebekah and other Bible plays. N. Y.
  Scribner, 1925.
  The wooing of Rebekah
  Jacob's journey
  The story of Joseph
  Moses in the bulrushes
  Ruth
  Samuel in the house of the Lord
  David and Jonathan
  Elijah and Elisha
  The nativity
  The prodigal
  The resurrection

Klein, Yetta & Schwarz, Florine. Plays for school children. Boston.
  Baker, 1930.
  If Lincoln were with us to-day
  The Lincoln Memorial, Washington, D. C.
  The monument's message

The pageant of the flag
Theodore Roosevelt
The land of books
A tea party in bookland
The spirit of beauty
The making of an art scrapbook
In father world's garden
If the children of Europe could speak to us
The highway of brotherly love
The spirit of the Red Cross
The spirit of independence
All America's children
The current event's plea
The march of the milestones on Fifth Avenue

Klein, Yetta & Schwarz, Florine. Our children's stage. Boston. Baker, 1928.
The greatest dreamer of the world
The gift of the fairies
Safety on the streets
In the land of clean children
The lonely little tree
The very first Arbor Day
The best food of all
Memorial Day
What our flag means to the children of other countries
A meeting of "The Young Citizens' League of America"
The unknown soldier
In the palace garden

Knickerboker, Edwin Van B., ed. Short plays. N. Y. Holt,. 1931.

The florist shop	Hawkridge, Winifred
The game of chess	Goodman, K. S.
Two crooks and a lady	Pillot, Eugene
Torches	Raisbeck, Kenneth
Poor Maddalene	Saunders, Louise
A wedding	Kirkpatrick, John
The valiant	Hall, Holworthy & Middlemass, Robert
Pyramus and Thisbe	Shakespeare, William
On vengeance height	Davis, Allan
The noble lord	Wilde, Percival
Allison's lad	Dix, Beulah M.
The stepmother	Bennett, Arnold
Where the cross is made	O'Neill, Eugene
Ulysses	Phillips, Stephan

Knickerbocker, Edwin Van B., ed. Twelve plays. N. Y. Holt, 1924.

Where but in America	Wolff, O. M.
The forfeit	Rogers, T. B.
Poor Maddalena	Saunders, Louise
Playing with fire	Wilde, Percival
The stepmother	Bennett, Arnold
On vengeance height	Davis, Allan
A marriage proposal	Tchekoff, Anton
A pipe of peace	Cameron, Margaret
Enter the hero	Helburn, Theresa
The pot boiler	Gerstenberg, Alice
Over the hills	Palmer, John
The game of chess	Goodman, K. S.

Koven, Joseph. The miracle of Saint Masha and other plays. N. Y. Lester
   L. Schick, 1924.
  In the desert
  By the beard of the prophet
  The miracle of Saint Masha
  God save the heir

Kreymborg, Alfred. Puppet plays. N. Y. French, 1926.
  When the willow nods
  Blue and green
  Manikin and Minikin
  Jack's house
  Lima beans
  People who die
  Pianissimo

Kreymborg, Alfred. Rocking chairs and other comedies. N. Y. French,
   1925.
  Rocking chairs
  Helpless Herberts
  Adverbs
  Trap doors
  Not too far from angels

Krohn, Josephine E. Old King Cole and other mediaeval plays. N. Y.
   Doran, 1925.
  Sing a song of sixpence
  (Also longer plays)

Kummer, F. A. Phryne. Philadelphia. Dorrance & Co., 1924.
  Phryne
  Finer clay
  The temptation

Ladies' Home Journal. One-act plays. Garden City, N. Y. Doubleday, Page,
   1925.

Evening dress indispensable	Pertwee, Ronald
Enter Dora—exit Dad	Tilden, Freeman
The lovliest thing	Pertwee, Roland
Bimbo, the pirate	Tarkington, Booth
The man in the bowler hat	Milne, A. A.

Lane, Bertha P. Lad and other story-plays for children to read or to act.
   N. Y. Woman's Press, 1926.
  Lad
  The fairy ring
  The three wishes
  The Christmas sheep
  Everychild's Christmas
  The star
  Pandora

Larrimer, Mary. Plays with a prologue. Boston. Badger, 1925.
  Sacrifice
  The gull of unrest
  Official bondage
  Mercurial youth
  Lies
  (Also poems, and impressions)

Law, F. H., ed. Modern plays, short and long. N. Y. Century, 1924.

Benjamin Franklin, Journeyman	Mackay, Constance D'A.
Just neighborly	Dean, Alexander
Masks	Corneau, Perry B.
What men live by	Tolstoi, Leo

Off Nags Head   Macmillan, Dougald
Bushido   Idzumo, Takeda

Lawton, V. B. Ballads for acting. London. Sheldon Press, 1927.
The Duke of Gordon's daughter
The heir of Linne
Lord Bateman
The undaunted female
The barring of the door

Lee, Mackenzie. For chaps and chits. London. French, 1930.
Everyman and Mr. Page
Perfumes
The fourth degree
The only thing to do
Illumination
Grace
Sweeties
The theatre ticket agency
The countersign
Seeing stars

Leonard, S. A. & Moffett, H. Y., ed. Junior literature. Book II. N. Y.
Macmillan, 1930.
The knave of hearts   Saunders, Louise
(Also many examples of other types of literature)

Levinger, Elma E. Jewish festivals in the religious school. Cincinnati,
Ohio. Union of American Hebrew Congregations, 1923.
How Succoth came to Chayim
The unlighted Menorah
A sick Purim
The silver cup
Ruth of Noab
(Also longer plays and pageants)

Levinger, Elma E. Through the school year. Boston. Baker, 1925.
At the gates of La Rabida
The plowshare or the sword
The sailing of the Mayflower
The birthday of a prince
A present for Mr. Lincoln
The pilgrim
The planter of friends
Where's your mother?
The hero
The return of spring
The sad jester

Levy, S. J. Broken bridges. Brooklyn, N. Y. S. J. Levy, 1924.
Broken bridges
A successful dentist
A message from heaven
(Also a longer play, and several stories)

Lloyd, Gladys. The complete Christmas book. Lebanon, Ohio. March Bros.,
1923.
Good King Arthur
The children decide
(Also recitations, songs, dialogues, and pantomimes)

Lloyd, Gladys. Thanksgiving school programs. Franklin, Ohio. Eldridge En-
tertainment House, 1928.
Tweedle-dum and Tweedlee-dee
A verdict of the wishbone

Thanksgiving with Mother Goose
(Also recitations, exercises, and drills)

Locke, Alain, ed. Plays of negro life. N. Y. Harper, 1927.

The dreamy kid	O'Neill, Eugene
The rider of dreams	Torrence, Ridgley
Rackey	Culbertson, E. H.
The no 'count boy	Green, Paul
The flight of the natives	Richardson, Willis
White dresses	Green, Paul
In Abraham's bosom	Green, Paul
Sugar cane	Wilson, F. H.
Cruiter	Matheus, John
The starter	Spence, Eulalie
Judge Lynch	Rogers, J. W. Jr.
Granny Maumee	Torrence, Ridgley
The bird child	White, Lucy
Balo	Toomer, Jean
Plumes	Johnson, Douglas
The broken banjo	Richardson, Willis
The death dance	Duncan, Thelma
Emperor Jones	O'Neill, Eugene
The Danse Calinda	Torrence, Ridgley
Sahdji, and African Ballet	Bruce, Richard

Longmans, Green & Co. Publisher. Goin' home and other plays of the 1927 contest. N. Y. Longmans, Green, 1928.

Strings	Knight, Raymond
The machine age	Kelley, Estella
Spring sluicing	Ernst, Alice H.
Roads	Peterson, Agnes E.

Lord, Daniel A. S. J. Boyland and maidland. St. Louis, Mo. The Queen's Work Press, 1927.
Boyland Pt. I.
   The land of dreams
   The land of dreads
   The land of desires
Maidland Pt. II.
   The land of dreams
   The land of dreads
   The land of desires

Lord, Daniel A. S. J. Facts and fairy tales. St. Louis, Mo. The Queen's Work Press, 1930.
The giant and Jack
The giant temper
The discontented daughter
Angels of prayer
The silly goosegirls
God's adopted son

Lord, Daniel A. S. J. The magic gallery. St. Louis, Mo. The Queen's Work Press, 1927.
Just after the Civil War
The making of the flag
The secret, lovely garden
The pirates bold
Aboard the Santa Maria
Too fast for Pharoah
By radio

Lord, Daniel A. S. J. Six one-act plays. N. Y. Benziger Bros., 1925.
The road to Connaugh

Rainbow gold
The sight of the blind
Mistress Castlemaine's Christmas dinner
The flame leaps up
Sir Folly

Louisville, Ky., Girls high school drama class. Tested plays for high
    schools. Boston. Baker, 1928.
One gift above another
Do you believe in luck?
Whose money?
His best seller
Polly's hero

Lutkenhaus, Anna M. & Knox, Margaret, ed. New plays for school
    children. N. Y. Century, 1929.

America, the beautiful	Knox, M. & Lutkenhaus, A. M.
"Alice in Wonderland" trail scene	Carroll, Lewis
A modern Alice	Public School 15, Manhattan
Aunt Jane's story hour	Knox, Margaret
The future of America as our young folks see it	Knox, M. & Lutkenhaus, A. M.
What I would like to be	Wassung, Charlotte
Mother Goose's Thanksgiving dream	Fritz, Ethel L.
Education's progress	Lutkenhaus, Anna M.
Building a character	Stevens, Sophie S.
A great quest for character	Thomey, Elizabeth A.
Fairy gifts	Stevens, Sophie S.
Theodore Roosevelt—a great soldier	Lutkenhaus, A. M.
A modern knight—Theodore Roosevelt	Lutkenhaus, A. M.
Tommy's dream of Christmas night	Lutkenhaus, A. M.
What our flag stands for	Ryan, Helen P.
The meaning of America	Aitken, Irene M.
Our country and its flag	Aitken, Irene M.
(Also longer plays, and a ritual)	

Lyman, R. L. & Hill, H. C., ed. Literature and living. Book III. N. Y.
    Scribner, 1925.

The travelling man	Gregory, Lady
William Tell	Knowles, J. S.
(Also other types of literature)	

McCollum, Elsie M. Pieces and plays for all ages. Belmar, N. J. Edgar S.
    Werner & Co., 1929.
Somebody's boy
The tongue-twisters' tryst
Visiting the gypsy-camp
(Also many recitations, entertainments)

McGraw, H. W. & Parry, J. N., ed. Prose and poetry for the twelfth
    year. Syracuse, N. Y. L. W. Singer Co., 1930.

Circumstances alter cases	Giorloff, Ruth
The patchwork quilt	Field, Rachel L.
Post mortems	Divine, Charles
Trifles	Glaspell, Susan
Square pegs	Bax, Clifford
Moonshine	Hopkins, Arthur
The man who married a dumb wife	France, Anatole
On the shelf	Morley, Christopher
The grill	Johnston, G. W.
The beggar and the king	Parkhurst, Winthrop

Mackay, Constance D'Arcy. Youth's highway. N. Y. Holt, 1929.
Youth's highway
In the days of Piers Ploughman
A calendar of joyful saints
The pageant of sunshine and shadow
The first Noel

Mackaye, Percy. Kentucky mountain fantasies. N. Y. Longmans, Green. 1924.
Napoleon crossing the Rockies
The funeralizing of Crickneck
Timber

Mackaye, Percy. Kentucky mountain fantasies. N. Y. Longmans, Green. 1928.
Napoleon crossing the Rockies
The funeralizing of Crickneck
Timber

Mackaye, Percy. Yankee fantasies. New & rev. ed. N. Y. French, 1928.
Chuck
Gettysburg
The antick
The cat-boat
Sam Average

Mackendrick, Marda. Short plays for adult foreigners. Marda Mackendrick, 1928.
Right about-face
High prices and danger
How many Madame?
You can't please everyone
Freedom, or, the good sport
Helping hands
The gift box
An evening's entertainment
Christmas memories
Young glory
(Also longer plays)

McMullen, J. C. An evening of plays for men. Boston. Baker, 1930.
Nicked
Antoinette comes to town
Peculiar old duffer
The conjurer's stone

McPharlin, Paul. A repertory of Marionette plays. N. Y. Viking Press, 1929.
The scourge of the Gulph
School
Every dog has his day
The Coq brothers
Cataclysterium's medicine
Mr. Goodman and Mrs. Gracious
The candidate for Trepagny
Noël
Junkdump fair
Petroushka
The drum dance
(Also longer plays)
Yeats, J. B.
Fool, Tom
Dondo, Mathurin
Mourguet, Laurent
Duranty, L. E.
DeNeuville, Lemercier
Sand, Maurice
Bouchor, Maurice
Goethe, Johann W. von
Mitcoff, Elena Y.
Tsou Ku Chan Mien

Magnusson, Elva C. Three plays. Lancaster, Pa. Lancaster Press, 1928.
The hat shoppe

The week of weeks
A royal complex

Major, Clare T. Playing theatre. London. Oxford University Press, 1930.
Cinderella
Aladdin and his wonderful lamp
The Prince's secret
The maid of the Nile
Michio
Robin Hood

Major, Mabel & Smith Rebecca W., ed. The southwest in literature.
N. Y. Macmillan, 1929.

Judge Lynch	Rogers, J. W.

(Also other types of literature)

Manley, W. F., adapt. Bible dramas, radio plays adapted for church and
social gatherings. N. Y. Revell, 1928.
James of Galilee
Cain and Abel
Diana of the Ephesians
Sampson and Delilah
Saul of Tarsus
Ruth
The message from Sinai
Courage
Sacrifice
Ishmael
The mess of pottage
Judith

Manley, W. F., adapt. A second book of Bible dramas. N. Y. Revell, 1930.
The first gift
Judas Iscariot
The unconquered
The prodigal
The third soldier
Thou faithful soldier
The comeback
Naaman's cloak
Number one on the docket
The king dreams
Naboth's vineyard

Marks, Jeannette. The merry, merry cuckoo and other Welsh plays. N. Y.
Appleton, 1927.
The merry, merry cuckoo
The deacon's hat
Welsh honeymoon
A tress of hair
Love letters
Steppin' westward
Look to the end

Marriott, J. W., ed. One-act plays of to-day. Boston. Small, Maynard, 1924.

The boy comes home	Milne, A. A.
Followers	Brighouse, Harold
The stepmother	Bennett, Arnold
The maker of dreams	Down, Oliphant
The little man	Galsworthy, John
A night at an inn	Dunsany, Lord
Campbell of Kilmhor	Ferguson, J. A.
The Grand Cham's diamond	Monkhouse, Allan
Thread o' scarlet	Bell, J. J.

Becky Sharp	Conway, Olive
The Seraphic vision	Housman, Laurence

Marriott, J. W., ed. One-act plays of to-day. Second ser. Boston. Small, Maynard, 1926.

Waterloo	Doyle, A. C.
It's the poor that 'elps the poor	Chapin, Harold
A marriage has been arranged	Sutro, Alfred
Lonesome-like	Brighouse, Harold
The rising of the moon	Gregory, Lady
The king's waistcoat	Conway, Olive
The dear departed	Houghton, Stanley
'Op-o'-me-thumb	Fenn, Frederick & Pryce, Richard
The monkey's paw	Jacobs, W. W.
Night watches	Monkhouse, Allan
The child in Flanders	Hamilton, Cicely

Marriott, J. W., ed. One-act plays of to-day. Third ser. London. Harrap & Co., 1927.

The dumb and the blind	Chapin, Harold
How the weather is made	Brighouse, Harold
The golden doom	Dunsany, Lord
Rory aforesaid	Brandane, John
The master of the house	Houghton, Stanley
Friends	Farjeon, Herbert
Mini	Conway, Olive
The Bishop's candlesticks	McKinnell, Norman
Between the soup and the savoury	Jennings, Gertrude
Master wayfarer	Terry, J. E. H.
The pot of broth	Yeats, W. B.
A king's hard bargain	Drury, W. P.

Marsh, Florence A. Plays for young people. Adapt. Boston. Allyn & Bacon, 1931.
Rip Van Winkle
The Boston Tea Party
(Also longer plays)

Masefield, John. A poem and two plays. London. Heinemann, 1919.
The locked chest
The Sweeps of ninety-eight

Masefield, John. Prose plays. N. Y. Macmillan, 1925.
The Campden wonder
Mrs. Harrison
The Sweeps of ninety-eight
The locked chest

Masefield, John. Verse plays. N. Y. Macmillan, 1925.
Good Friday
(Also three longer plays)

Merrill, John & Fleming, Martha. Play-making and plays. N. Y. Macmillan, 1930.
Harvest feast
The Pine-tree shillings
The box of Pandora
The departure
(Also material on playmaking and longer plays)

Millay, Edna St. Vincent. (Nancy Boyd, pseud.) Distressing dialogues. N. Y. Harper, 1924.
The implacable Aphrodite
The same boat
No bigger than a man's hand

Powder, rouge and lipstick
For winter, for summer
Two souls with but a single thought
Tea for the muse
Rolls and salt
Breakfast in bed
(Also poems, and prose sketches)

Millay, Edna St. Vincent. Three plays. N. Y. Harper, 1926.
Aria da Capo
Two slatterns and a king
(Also a longer play)

Miller, H. A., ed. Adventures in prose and poetry. N. Y. Harcourt, Brace, 1929.

Confessional — Wilde, Percival
The lost silk hat — Dunsany, Lord
(Also examples of other types of literature)

Milne, A. A. First plays. N. Y. Knopf, 1930.
Wurzel-Flummery
The boy comes home
The red feather
(Also two longer plays)

Milne, A. A. Four plays. London. Chatto & Windus, 1926.
Portrait of a gentleman in slippers
(Also three longer plays)

Minchin, Nydia E. The jester's purse and other plays for boys and girls. N. Y. Harcourt, Brace, 1926.

The jester's purse — Minchin, Nydia E.
The coming of summer — Driscoll, Gertrude & Peterson, Clara B.
The birthday cake — Minchin, Nydia E.

Mitchison, Naomi. Nix-nought-nothing; four plays for children. London. Jonathan Cape, 1928.
My ain sel
Nix-nought-nothing
Hobyah! Hobyah!
Elfen hill

Molnár, Ferenc. The plays of Ferenc Molnár. N. Y. Macy-Masius, The Vanguard Press, 1929.
The white cloud
A prologue to King Lear
Marshall
The violet
Still life
The witch

Moore, F. F. Kitty Clive and other plays in one act. London. A. & C. Black, 1929.
Kitty Clive
The Jessamy bride
A poor actress
The sword of Damocles

Morley, Christopher. Off the deep end. Garden City, N. Y. Doubleday, Doran, 1928.
Really, my dear . . .
Wagon-lits
The birth of God
Three friends

Morley, Christopher. One act plays. Garden City, N. Y. Doubleday, Page, 1924.
East of Eden
Walt
On the shelf
Bedroom suite
Rehearsal
Thursday evening

Morrette, Edgar. Six one act plays. Boston. Badger, 1924.
The short cut
A scherzo in two flats
The waif
In the swath
The woman's verdict
The nine-ten express

Morse, Katharine D. Goldtree and silvertree. N. Y. Macmillan, 1925.
The pudding pan
Kit Cat and Cross-patch
The golden goose
The proud Princess
Goldtree and silvertree
The wise men of Gotham

Moses, M. J., ed. Another treasury of plays for children. Boston. Little, Brown, 1926.
The slippers of Cinderella   Robertson, W. G.
The evil kettle   Dunsany, Lord
The birthday of the Infanta   Wilde, Oscar
The king with the iron heart   Young, Stark

Moses, M. J., ed. Representative British dramas Victorian and modern. Boston. Little, Brown, 1918.
The gods of the mountains   Dunsany, Lord
Riders to the sea   Synge, J. M.
The workhouse ward   Gregory, Lady
Cathleen ni Houlihan   Yeats, W. B.

Moses, M. J., ed. Representative British dramas Victorian and modern. New rev. ed. Boston. Little, Brown, 1931.
Cathleen Ni Houlihan   Yeats, W. B.
The workhouse ward   Gregory, Lady
Riders to the sea   Synge, J. M.

Nichols, Adelaide. The haunted circle and other outdoor plays. N. Y. Dutton, 1924.
The haunted circle
The gardener's cap
The devil's field
The shepherd's pipe

Nicholson, Kenyon, ed. The Appleton book of short plays. N. Y. Appleton, 1926.
The managers   Lincoln, J. C.
Finders-keepers   Kelly, George
Apartments to let   Nugent, Elliott & Lindsay, Howard
One egg   Hughes, Babette
The end of the trail   Culbertson, E. H.
George Washington at the Delaware   Mackaye, Percy
Society notes   West, Duffy
Social balance   Fayder, Samuel
The wedding dress   Hoffman, Phoebe
When the clock strikes   Parish, John

Pierrot's mother   Hughes, Glenn
The ghost story   Tarkington, Booth

Nicholson, Kenyon, ed. The Appleton book of short plays. Second ser. N. Y.
    Appleton, 1927.
The eldest   Ferber, Edna
Post mortems   Divine, Charles
Samson a la mode   Carb, David
The warrior's husband   Thompson, J. F.
Ambush   Whitehouse, Henry
The melancholy dame   Cohen, O. R.
A cup of tea   Ryerson, Florence
Gas, air and earl   Bloch, Bertram
Appearances   Taylor, Rex
'Twas ever thus   Erlich, Ida L.
Prince Gabby   Murfin, Jane
Delilah   Emery, Gilbert

Nicholson, Kenyon. Garden varieties. N. Y. Appleton, 1924.
White elephant
The bug man
Confession
The anonymous letter
The Casino gardens
The marriage of little Eve
So this is Paris green

Nicholson, Kenyon, ed. Hollywood plays. N. Y. French, 1930.
Ace is trumped   Stinson, H. H.
A simple soul   Smith, Vernon
On the razor edge   Hughes, Rupert
Private Jones   Schayer, E. R.
A pound of flesh   Geraghty, T. J.
The cup of life   Marion, Frances
A bird in hand   Heath, E. P.
To die with a smile   Blackmore, Madeline
Miss Baxter   Fulton, Maude
Twelve before three   Ahearn, T. J.
Semper Fidelis   Cohen, A. A.
Troupers   Ingersoll, P. G.

Nicholson, Kenyon, ed. Revues. N. Y. Appleton, 1926.
Amateur night   Buck, Gene
Fair enough   Connell, Richard
Seeing New York   Gribble, Harry W.
The yellow peril   Smith, P. G.
Etiquette   Halvey, Paul
Loose   Shaler, Eleanor & Macauley, Thurs-
                                      ton
The return   Clark, H. W.
Our American language   Marks, Maurice
Don't believe everything you hear! Levis, Marjorie R.
The daily doesn't   Knox, Charles
It isn't what you say but how you
    say it!   Block, Bertram
Green Chartreuse   Heywood, C. D.
Back to the woodshed   Keenan, Thomas
Business is business   Carroll, Earl

Niemeier, Minnie A. New plays for every day the schools celebrate. N. Y.
    Noble & Noble, 1928.
The joys of the New Year
Choosing a statue for Lincoln Park

George Washington at the helm of state
The veteran's story
News of the adoption of the Constitution
A visit from Mr. and Mrs. Santa Claus
One country, one flag, one language

Niemeier, Minnie A. New plays for every day the schools celebrate. Enlarged ed. N. Y. Noble & Noble, 1929.
The joys of New Year
Choosing a statue for Lincoln Park
Washington at the helm of state
St. Patrick's day in the land of the west
A message of Easter
Jack-in-the-pulpit is preaching today
The veteran's story
The adoption of the Constitution
A visit from Mr. and Mrs. Santa Claus
One country, one flag, one language
A calendar for poets' birthdays
The quarrel of the seasons

Oakden, E. C. & Sturt, Mary. Adapt. Pattern plays. London. Thomas Nelson & Sons, 1926.
The play of the Pied Piper
The play of the travelling musicians
The play of Pastorella
The play of the luck of Troy
The play of Mediaeval magic
The play of thrice is too much

Olcott, Virginia. Household plays for young people. N. Y. Dodd, Mead, 1928.
The rainbow robe
A cart-load of kettles
Magic cargoes

Olcott, Virginia. Industrial plays. N. Y. Dodd, Mead, 1927.
The jewel boy of Florence
T'ien Jung and the eight immortals
The alphabet tree
The fire of icicles

Olcott, Virginia. International plays for young people. N. Y. Dodd, Mead, 1925.
The wings of Daedalus
The little invisible guest
Lady White and Lady Yellow

Olcott, Virginia. World friendship plays for young people. N. Y. Dodd, Mead, 1929.
Singing pipes
The little Yashmak
Father-of-a-hump and old cobbler shoes
In the path of the children
Kind enemy
The golden bracelet
Athene's secret
The makers of the world

Oliver, Margaret S. Tea & little rice cakes. Boston. Badger, 1926.
Tea & rice cakes
The king's son
He, on whom the sandal fell
The lost child

Hallie in high
Shadow and substance

Oller, Marie & Dawley, Eloise K. Adapt. Little plays from Greek myths.
N. Y. Century, 1928.
Pandora
Baucis and Philemon
Echo and Narcissus
Arachne and the spider
Asclepius
Alcestis
Marpessa
Phaethon and the sun chariot
Pyramus and Thisbe
Pygmalion and Galatea
Demeter and Triptolemus
Hades and Persephone
Orpheus and Eurydice
Cupid and Psyche
The golden touch
Daedalus and Icarus
Theseus
The apple of discord
Achilles in Scyros
Achilles' quarrel with Agamemnon
Achilles sulks in his tent
Circe
Odysseus at Ogygia
Nausicaa
Odysseus returns home

Oneal, Billie, ed. Prize-winning one act plays. Book I. Dallas, Texas. Southwest Press, 1930.

Tombs	Strong, Mable R.
The inspiration	Oneal, Billie
The pedlar	Lanham, F. G.
'Limination	Newett, J. H.
Crude and unrefined	Bowen, Margaret E.

O'Neill, Eugene. The great god Brown, The fountain, The moon of the
Caribbees and other plays N. Y. Boni & Liveright, 1926.
X The moon of the Caribbees
X Bound east for Cardiff
X A long voyage home
X In the zone
X Ile
X Where the cross is made
X The rope
(Also two longer plays)

O'Ryan, Francis & O'Ryan, Anna W. Adapt. Plays from American his-
tory adapted for elementary grades by Myrtle G. Gee. N. Y. Hinds,
Hayden & Eldridge, 1925.
A historical coincidence
Roger Sherman at his last and at his best
Franklin's forebodings
First public appearance of a noted character
Early shyness of an orator
The hiding of the charter
A precarious situation in Boston history
The capture of Major Andre

Greene and Morgan on the Yadkin
Lincoln as a young clerk

Osgood, P. E., ed. Old-time church drama. Adapted. N. Y. Harper, 1928.
The burial of the Allelnia
The boy bishop
The quem quaeritis
Malchizedek, Abraham and Isaac
The annunciation
The nativity
The shepherd's play
The meeting of the three kings
The summoning of Everyman
Elijah
Judas Maccabaeus
The Herod play
The adoration of the three kings

Osgood, P. E. Pulpit dramas. N. Y. Harper, 1929.
Destiny
Under authority
In Herod's dungeon
Outcast
Lazarus tells of his death
Judas of Kerioth drives a bargain
Gabbatha
Naked evil
Without a city wall
The first day of the week

Osgood, P. E. The sinner beloved and other religious plays. N. Y. Harper, 1928.
The sinner beloved
Shepherds all?
The gift of self
As it was in the beginning
City walls and open plains
The story of a story
(Also pageants, monologues, and dialogues)

Ould, Hermon. Adapt. New Plays from old stories. London, Oxford University Press, 1924.
Peter the Pied Piper
The Princess in the sleeping wood
Rip Van Winkle

Ould, Hermon. Plays of pioneers. London. French, 1925.
Joan the maid
The discovery
The pathfinder

Ould, Hermon. Three comedies. London. French, 1925.
Episode
Claude
Thy father and thy mother

Ouless, E. U. Seven Shrovetide plays. London. Deane & Sons, 1930.
The children of Eve
Dame truth
The wandering scholar
The old game
The horse thief
Five poor travellers
Death in the tree

Overton, Grace S. Dramatic activities for young people. N. Y. Century, 1927.
The living Christ
Youth's prophetic vision
The eternal quest
The age-old dream

Painton, Edith F. A. U. and others, ed. The blue entertainment book. Chicago. A. Flanagan Co. 1930.

Waiting for the 2.40 train	Baxter, J. A.
Hiring a servant	Baxter, J. A.
Trials of a canvasser	Baxter, J. A.
The new scholar	Baxter, J. A.
Grandma Shaw's visit	Baxter, J. A.
His sweet bouquet	Baxter, J. A.
The baby show	Baxter, J. A.
The spelling match	Baxter, J. A.
(Also longer plays and pageants)	

Painton, Edith F. A. U. The commencement manual. Chicago. Denison, 1915.
Non Palma sine Labore
Climb, though the rocks be rugged
Under sealed orders
The victor's tournament

Parsons, Margaret G. In the children's play-house. Boston. Baker, 1923.
The prophecy
The trial of the glorious Fourth
The Christmas message
The Easter lily
The Thanksgiving dinner dance
The birthday cake
The Thanksgiving pumpkin

Parsons, Margaret G. Ten stirring Bible Plays. Franklin, Ohio. Eldridge Entertainment House, 1927.
The babe in the bulrushes
The little prophet, Samuel
David, the shepherd boy
Joseph, the dreamer of dreams
Benjamin and the silver cup
Ruth
Daniel and the lions
The widow's cruse
Boy heroes of the Bible
(Also a shadow picture)

Peach, L. du Garde. Broadcast sketches. London. French, 1927.
All jam
Switched
The seance
The rabbits
Love or lucre
Hat trick
A fire affair
Taps
The wedding
While you wait

Pearson, P. M., comp. The humorous speaker. N. Y. Noble & Noble, 1925.

A scene from Shanghraun	Boncicault, Dion
Ringing the changes	Moore, Bertha

Poor dear mamma   Kipling, Rudyard
(Also scenes from longer plays, poetry, prose)

Peattie, Elia W. The wander weed and seven other little theatre plays. Chicago. Charles H. Sergel & Co., 1923.
The wanderweed
The great delusion
Family reunion
Sunrise
Pity
Spring cleaning
When the silver bell tree blooms
Job's tears

Pence, Raymond W., ed. Dramas by present-day writers. N. Y. Scribner 1927.

The slave with two faces	Davies, Mary C.
Cophetua	Drinkwater, John
A night at an inn	Dunsany, Lord
Trifles	Glaspell, Susan
Spreading the news	Gregory, Lady
A love passage	Jacobs, W. W.
The goal	Jones, H. A.
Counsel retained	Mackay, Constance D'A.
Thursday evening	Morley, Christopher
'Ile'	O'Neill, Eugene
A marriage has been arranged	Sutro, Alfred
Confessional	Wilde, Percival

Pertwee, Guy & Pertwee, Ernest. Adapt. Scenes from Dickens. London. Routledge, n.d.
David Copperfield and his aunt
The Micawbers dine with David
Jingle's wooing of the spinster aunt
Bob Sawyer's supper party
Bardwell v. Pickwick
Sam Weller and the Bath footman
Mrs. Nickleby and the gentleman next door
Mr. Jones Chuzzlewit proposes marriage
The falling out of Mrs. Gamp and Mrs. Prig
Dick Swiveller and the Marchioness
Mrs. Corney's tea party for two
Oliver Twist in Fagin's den
Bob Cratchit's Christmas dinner
Bella Wilfer's return
The Holly-tree inn

Philippine Islands, Bureau of Education, Department of Public Instruction. Philippine prose and poetry. Manila, Bur. of Printing, 1927.
The ghost   Romulo, Carlos P.
(Also many poems and prose selections)

Phillips, Le Roy & Johnson, Theodore, ed. Baker's anthology of one-act plays. Boston. Baker, 1925.

Tea	Carson, W. G. B.
Little red shoes	Brighouse, Harold
Tie game	Thanhouser, L. F.
On the park bench	Dane, Essex
Jon	Savage, Dorothy O.
Rory aforesaid	Brandane, John
The bitter end	Taylor, Rica B.
Evarannie	Vachell, Horace A.
Not quite such a goose	Gale, Elizabeth

Insomnia	Rubenstein, H. F.
"Thirst"	Bell, J. J.

812.08 **Phillips, Le Roy & Johnson, Theodore, ed.** Types of modern dramatic
Ph   composition. N. Y. Ginn, 1927.

The Kelly kid	Norris, Kathleen & Totheroh, Dan
The dweller in the darkness	Berkeley, Reginald
Wanderlust	Nicholson, Kenyon
Grandma pulls the string	Delano, Edith B. & Carb, David
Cabbages and kings	Fyleman, Rose
A fool of a man	Finnegan, Edward
Dawn	Wilde, Percival
Bethlehem	Housman, Laurence
Maurice's own idea	Malleson, Miles
The crumbs that fall	Hubbard, Philip
'Lijah'	Smith, E. V.
Meredew's right hand	Gibbs, A. H.
Trifles	Glaspell, Susan
Peggy	Crothers, Rachel
Uncle Jimmy	Gale, Zona
The closet	Halman, Doris F.
The killer	Cowles, Albert
The lean years	Reely, Mary K.
Pierrot before the seven doors	Cantillon, Arthur
Daggers and diamonds	Moseley, Katharine P.

Pirandello, Luigi. The one-act plays of. N. Y. Dutton, 1928.
 The imbecile
 By judgment of Court
 Our Lord of the ship
 The doctor's duty
 Chee-Chee
 The man with the flower in his mouth
 At the gate
 The vise
 The house with the column
 Sicilian limes
 The jar

Playground and Recreation Ass'n of America. Community drama. N. Y.
    Century, 1926.
 Pageant of play
 A masque of old loves.

Pohl, F. J. When things were new. Brooklyn, N. Y. F. J. Pohl, 1925.
 Laugh and grow wise
 Love and grow wise
 Live and grow wise
 Gold of the sun god
 Gas
 The new god
 The embarrassing baby
 Cobra's head
 (Also one longer play)

Pollock, John. Twelve one-acters. London. The Cayme Press, 1926.
 Rosamond
 The invention of Dr. Metzler
 Mademoiselle Diana
 The love of Mrs. Pleasance
 On the frontier
 Lolotte
 Conchita

A king in England
For Russia
In the forest of the night
The luck king
The dream of a winter evening

Preston, Effa E., comp. The Christmas gayety book. Dayton, Ohio. Paine
Pub. Co., 1924.
Santa's surprise
Why Johnnie changed his mind
Christmas Eve in a shoe
Rosetta runs away
The joke on Santa Claus
(Also dialogues, recitations, and pantomimes)

Preston, Effa E. Ten clever plays for children. Franklin, Ohio. Eldridge En-
tertainment House, 1927.
Carrie, the courteous cook
How spring came to Fern Dale
White Owl's feather
Safety Sam
Tardy Town
The dream-maker
Old friends are best
Curing the invalid
The last day of school
In polite society

Price, Olive M. American history in masque and wig. Boston. Baker, 1931.
The Mayflower compact
Towne Hall
Cavalier
The rose of Ann Rutledge
A matter of diplomacy
The god of the mountains
The flight

Price, Olive M. Short plays from American History and literature. Vol. I.
N. Y. French, 1925.
Hiawatha
Little Lady Dresden
Memories

Price, Olive M. Short plays from American history and literature. Vol. II.
N. Y. French, 1928.
Red dusk
West o' the Alleghenies

Pride, L. B. The shadow of the mine and other plays of the coal fields. N. Y.
French, 1928.
The shadow of the mine
Foursquare
The barbarians
On the way home
The devils
Fortune's hired man
Aftermath

Priestley, J. B. & others. The second omnibus book. London. Heinemann,
1930.
Catherine Parr   Baring, Maurice
The rehearsal   Baring, Maurice
King Alfred and the neat-herd   Baring, Maurice
(Also many novels, stories, poems)

Raine, J. W. Bible dramatics. N. Y. Century, 1927.
The king forgets
The selling of Joseph
Naboth's vineyard
The lost son
Ahaz casts away the heritage
The stone rolled away
Joshua's decision
Saul's awakening
The witch of Endor
The babe of Bethlehem
Delivered from the lion's mouth
Daniel's loyalty

Rawlings Junior high school (Cleveland, Ohio). One winter's night
and other plays for assembly programs. Cleveland, Ohio. Rawlings Junior
high school, 1928.
A courtesy play
The party
One winter's night
A patriotic assembly
Great Thanksgivings in American history
The Student Council play
Rawlings Record Assembly
A day at Rawlings

Reely, Mary K. Three one-act plays. Boston. Baker, 1924.
Daily bread
A window to the south
The lean years

Reighard, Catherine F. Plays for people and puppets. N. Y. Dutton, 1928.
Jack and the beanstalk
King of the Golden River
Rumpelstiltskin
Pierre Patelin

Reznikoff, Charles. Nine plays. N. Y. Charles Reznikoff, 1927.
Uriel Acosta
Abram in Egypt
Chatterton
Meriwether Lewis
Captive Israel
The black death
Coral
Rashi
Genesis

Rich, Mabel I., ed. Classified types of literature. N. Y. Century, 1926.

Post-scripts	Augier, Emile
The rising of the moon	Gregory, Lady
A marriage proposal	Tchekoff, Anton
Tatters	Burton, Richard
The little shepherdess	Rivoire, Andre
Just neighborly	Dean, Alexander
The widdy's might	Totheroh, Dan
Hyacinths	Hanna, Tacie M.
The curtain	Flanagan, Hallie F.
The war woman	Lovell, Caroline C.
(Also other types of literature)	

Richardson, Willis, ed. Plays and pageants from the life of the negro.
Washington, D. C. The Associated Publishers, 1930.
Sacrifice   Duncan, Thelma M.

Ti Yette   Matheus, John
Graven images   Miller, May
Riding the goat   Miller, May
The black horseman   Richardson, Willis
The king's dilemma   Richardson, Willis
The house of sham   Richardson, Willis
Ethiopia at the bar of justice   McCoo, E. J.
(Also pageants, and a longer play)

Ridge, W. P. London please; four Cockney plays. London. French, 1925.
Some showers
Early closing
Damages for breach
Happy returns

Riley, Alice C. D. The mandarin coat and five other one-act plays for Little
     Theatres. N. Y. Brentano's, 1925.
The mandarin coat
The sponge
Their anniversary
Radio
The black suitcase
Skim-milk

Ring, Barbara. Three plays under three flags. Boston. Baker, 1928.
A bit o' Dimocrasy
Monsieur Tytgat
Are all men like that?

Robins, Gertrude. Makeshifts & realities. Fourth ed. London. Werner
     Laurie, n.d.
Makeshifts
Realities

Roche, Mazo de la. Low life and other plays. Boston. Little, Brown, 1929.
Low life
Come true
The return of the emigrant

Rohrbough, Katherine F., ed. Successful stunts. Garden City, N. Y.
     Doubleday, Doran, 1929.
Woman's way   Rice, A. L.
The wasted tip   Beach, Nancy
The boss of the king   Rice, A. L.
The obedient Princess   Penland, Anna
(Also many short dialogues, and stunts)

Ross, J. M., ed. Adventures in literature. Book 7. N. Y. Harcourt, Brace,
     1927.
The three wishes   Mackay, Constance D'A.
The snow witch   Mackay, Constance D'A.
(Also other types of literature)

Ross, J. M., ed. Adventures in literature. Grade 7B. N. Y. Harcourt, Brace,
     1928.
The snow witch   Mackay, Constance D'A.
(Also many examples of stories, and poems)

Ross, J. M. & Schweikert, H. C., ed. Adventures in literature. Book 9.
     N. Y. Harcourt, Brace, 1928.
Not quite such a goose   Gale, Elizabeth
The brink of silence   Galbraith, Esther E.
(Also other types of literature)

Rubinstein, H. F. What's wrong with the theatre? N. Y. Stokes, n.d.
The theatre
A specimen

Repertory
Arms and the drama
Grand Guignol

Russell, Mary M. Dramatized Bible stories for young folks. N. Y. Doran, 1921.
A mother's faith
In quest of a great treasure
A woman who dared
The outcome of a secret
Easter morn
Easter morning
A search for a wife
The value of preparation
The secret of success
A neighbor and his work
A girl who knew how to be a friend
A Thanksgiving service
The first Christmas

Ryerson, Florence & Clements, Colin. All on a summer's day and six other short plays. N. Y. French, 1928.
All on a summer's day
On the lot
Men folk
Storm
Letters
A romantic interval
Love is like that

Sand, Maurice. Plays for marionettes. Trans. from French. N. Y. French, 1931.
The rose-queen of Viremollet
The flageolet
The spirit rappers
(Also longer plays)

Sanford, A. P. & Schauffler, R. H., ed. Armistice day. N. Y. Dodd, Mead, 1927.

The unseen host	Wilde, Percival
They just won't talk	Reely, Mary K.
The crowning of peace	Smith, Nora A.
(Also projects, programs, poems, and stories)	

Sanford, A. P., ed. George Washington plays. N. Y. Dodd, Mead, 1931.

Young Washington at Mt. Vernon	Mackaye, Percy
Before Fort Duquesne	Harnwell, Anna J.
She who will not when she may	Harnwell, Anna J.
The prophecy	Parsons, Margaret G.
Little George Washington's valentine	Beard, Patten
The choice	Emerson, Jerry
Brandywine	Holbrook, Marion
Mount Vernon	Holbrook, Marion
The general goes home	Barton, Lucy
George Washington, midshipman	Thompson, Alta E.
At the sign of the Boar's Head	Sutton, Vida R.
Captain Washington	Garvey, Olive W.
Nathan Hale (act three)	Fitch, Clyde
General George Washington	Corneau, Maude S.
The baby's fortune	Beagle, Maude S.
The young general	Beagle, Maude S.
Washington the lover	Beagle, Maude S.

Valley Forge	Beagle, Maude S.
Tea and gingerbread	Beagle, Maude S.
Washington as president	Beagle, Maude S.
A wedding at Mount Vernon	Beagle, Maude S.
George Washington (the spirit of Americanization)	Marschall, Phyllis

Sanford, A. P. & Schauffler, R. H., ed. Little plays for little people. N. Y. Dodd, Mead, 1929.

Abe's first fish	Walker, Alice J.
Abraham Lincoln, the boy	Kimball, Rosamond
Marching home!	Barrows, Marjorie
Children of the Civil War	Rice, Wallace
The underground railroad	Rice, Wallace
Path of roses	Veer, Ethel van der
The seven kings of Atherry	Gosser, L. G.
When fairies come	Thorp, Josephine
The enchanted Maypole	Holbrook, Marion
The making of the flag	Kimball. Rosamond
Little lost aster	Olcott, Virginia
Bruin's inn	Townsend, Anne
David and the good health elves	Downes, Maynard
Pirate Percy and the slovenly goops	Calver, H. N.
The wicked witch	Ryerson, Florence & Clements, Colin
Story terrace	Atchinson, Frances E.
Elsie in bookland	Parsons, Margaret
Magic windows	Barrows, Marjorie
The new holiday	Parsons, Margaret
The birthday gift	Ruthenberg, Grace D.
The virgin's tree	Kennedy, Anna R.
The little fir tree	Rowell, Adelaide
The toy shop	Wilde, Percival
The littlest shepherd	Ryerson, Florence & Clements, Colin

Sanford, A. P. & Schauffler, R. H., ed. The magic of books, an anthology for Book Week. N. Y. Dodd, Mead, 1929.

The book revue	Beagle, Maude S.
Bringing up nine	Reely. Mary K.
The enchanted book-shelf	Thorp, Josephine

(Also many stories, projects, and programs)

Sanford, A. P., ed. Outdoor plays for boys and girls. N. Y. Dodd, Mead, 1930.

Pan's secret	Barrows, Marjorie
The wistful witch	Barrows, Marjorie
The little general	Holbrook, Marion
Backwoods	Holbrook, Marion
Captain Lincoln's way	Woodman, Rea
For his country	Woodman, Rea
The wise owl's school	Merrill, Marie G.
The magic basket	————————
Chief Black Hawk	Wells, C. F.
Here we come!	Henderson, Ruth E.
The enchanted garden	————————
The lake	Barton, Lucy
Gohalt of Weirhawk	Lyon, E. S.
This-a-way and that-a-way	Stenger, Georgia
The pirate's life is the life for me	Lyon, E. S.
Little John and the miller join Robin Hood's band	Corneau, P. B.

Schauffler, R. H. & Sanford, A. P., ed. Plays for our American holidays.
Vol. II. N. Y. Dodd, Mead, 1928.

Baby New Year	Arkwright, Ruth
When the horns blow	Veer, Ethel van der
Twelfth Night festivals	Knox, Ethel L.
The treasure chest	Thorp, Josephine
The conspiracy of spring	Edgar, Mary S.
The noble lord	Wilde, Percival
The sleeping beauty	Cummins, S. L.
Festival of the harvest moon	Wilson, Sue A.
The three Thanksgivings	Vilas, Faith V. V.
Sojourners	Meaker, Isabelle J. & Harnwell, Anna J.

Schauffler, R. H. & Sanford, A. P., ed. Plays for our American holidays.
Vol. III. N. Y. Dodd, Mead, 1928.

Abraham Lincoln, rail-splitter	Mackay, Constance D'A.
The day that Lincoln died	Warren, Prescott & Hutchins, Will
George Washington at the Delaware	Mackaye, Percy
God winks	Burgess, Katharine S.
George Washington's wedding	Archer, William
Washington and Betsy Ross	Mackaye, Percy
The boy in blue	Price, Olive M.
The high heart	Rowell, Adelaide C.
The knife	Harnwell, Anna J. & Meaker, Isabelle J.
Tree of memory	Moses, Grace C.
The message	Gribble, H. W.

Schauffler, R. H. & Sanford, A. P., ed. Plays for our American holidays.
Vol. IV. N. Y. Dodd, Mead, 1928.

Shipping mother east	Veer, Ethel van der
The mothers they forgot	Parsons, Margaret
Mothers of men	Wilde, Percival
At the Mule: a fragment	Lewis, D. B. W.
St. Francis and the wolf	Branch, Anna H.
Daily bread	Reely, Mary K.
Fixins	Green, Erme & Green, Paul
The evil kettle	Dunsany, Lord
The jewels of Isabella	Sanford, A. P.
The house the children built	Griffith, Eleanor G.
Clean up!	Russell, Floyd K.
Nelagony, or good water	Pemberton, Anemone
Brother musicians	Sanford, A. P.
The birthday party	Sanford, A. P.
On the shelf	Morley, Christopher
Taking the picnic to the shut-in	American Junior Red Cross
What becomes of it	Jordan, Ethel B.
A close call	Muse, G. A.

Schofield, Stephen, ed. The marble god and other one-act plays. N. Y.
Brentano's, 1927.

The marble god	Schofield, Stephen
The house with the twisty windows	Pakington, Mary
The net	Nesbitt, C. M.
Incorrigible	Talbot, A. J.

Scholastic Publishing Co. Publishers. Saplings. Third ser. Pittsburgh, Pa.
Scholastic Pub. Co., 1928.

The clown and the undertaker	Preis, A. C.
Discordia descends	Shmutzer, Johanna
(Also poems and stories)	

Schweikert, H. C. & others, ed. Adventures in English literature. N. Y. Harcourt, Brace, 1930.

The trysting place	Tarkington, Booth
Where the cross is made	O'Neill, Eugene

(Also other types of literature)

Schweikert, H. C. & others, ed. Adventures in English literature. N. Y. Harcourt, Brace, 1931.

Riders to the sea	Synge, J. M.

(Also examples of other types of literature)

Scudder, Antoinette. The maple's bride and other one-act plays. Boston. Badger, 1930.

The maple's bride
Thomas the Rhymer
The poppet
The never ending wrong
Flight
Prince Pentaur

Seiler, Conrad. The husband of Xanthippe and other short plays. Boston. Baker, 1929.

The husband of Xanthippe
In a window
Matrimony
Box seats
Eyes
The lady in the sack

Seiler, Conrad. Suicide and other one-act comedies. N. Y. French, 1926.

Suicide
Time will tell
Poets all
Crime
An eye for an eye
Fantasia

Sexton, Ethelyn, comp. Mistletoe and holly. Franklin, Ohio. Eldridge Entertainment House, 1927.

When Betty Ann helped Santa Claus
When the Christmas tree talked
Santa gets the blues
Santa Claus in the White House
Introducing Scrooge
(Also readings, dialogues, and drills)

Shay, Frank, ed. The Appleton book of Christmas plays. N. Y. Appleton, 1929.

Dust of the road	Goodman, K. S.
The littlest shepherd	Ryerson, Florence & Clements, Colin
Christmas eve	O'Brien, Seumas
A Christmas tale	Harper, Harold
A modern Viking	Sterling, Fred
A boy on the meadow	Veer, Ethel van der
Exile	Doyle, A. C.
The enchanted Christmas tree	Wilde, Percival
The Duquesne Christmas mystery	Stevens, T. W.
A Christmas carol	Dickens, Charles
The seven gifts	Walker, Stuart

Shay, Frank, ed. The Appleton book of holiday plays. N. Y. Appleton, 1930.

The pie and the tart	Dondo, Mathurin
Lee the Virginian	Sterling, Fred

The child of the frontier	Levinger, Elma E.
Young Washington at Mt. Vernon	Mackaye, Percy
Two blind men and a donkey	Dondo, Mathurin
Washington and Betsy Ross	Mackaye, Percy
Some there are who remember	Shay, Frank
For God and for Spain	Willson, Dixie
Two plum puddings	Clements, Colin
Columbine Madonna	Hughes, Glenn

Shay, Frank, ed. Fifty more contemporary one-act plays. N. Y. Appleton, 1928.

Liars	Aleichem, Sholem
Marthe	Armstrong, Moel
Faithful admirer	Baker, Elizabeth
A morality play for the leisure class	Balderston, J. L.
Winter's night	Boyce, Neith
Death says it isn't so	Broun, Heywood
Orlando Furioso	Bufano, Remo
The Duchess says her prayers	Canfield, Mary C.
Across the border	Clements, Colin
Mountain laurel	Cooksey, Curtis
A lady and the law	Cronyn, G. W.
The weather breeder	Denison, Merrill
Whose money?	Dickson, Lee & Hickson, L. M.
Winners all	Ehrlich, Ida L.
Two passengers for Chelsea	Firkins, O. W.
The home for the friendly	Frank, Florence K.
Bumbo the clown	Gibson, Lawrence
The vanishing princess	Golden, John
The death of Nero	Gorman, Herbert
Quare medicine	Green, Paul
Juliet and Romeo	Gribble, H. W.
Jack and Jill and a friend	Hamilton, Cicely
The demands of society	Hartleben, O. E.
Creeds	Healey, Frances
The unruly member	Heath, Crosby
A leap-year bride	Hickson, Leslie M.
Pottery	Hudson, Holland
The liar and the unicorn	Hughes, Babette
The Eve in Evelyn	Hughes, Glenn
A comedy of danger	Hughes, Richard
Blue blood	Johnson, Georgia D.
Don Juan's Christmas eve	Kemp, Harry
The threshold	McCauley, Clarice V.
The avenue	Merrill, Fenimore
The razor	Nakamura, Kichizo
The marriage of little Eve	Nicholson, Kenyon
The bird catcher	O'Brien, Seumas
The moon of the Caribbees	O'Neill, Eugene
Wind o' the moors	Peach, L. du Garde
Escape	Pratt, Theodore
Brothers	Reisin, Abraham
The chip woman's fortune	Richardson, Willis
The veil	Rodenbach, Georges
Bumblepuppy	Rogers, J. W. Jr.
The third angle	Ryerson, Florence
Moral courage	Salten, Felix
The giant's stair	Steele, W. D.
The dance below	Strode, Hudson & Hornthal, Larry

A Budapest salesman should not   Szenes, Bela
    read French illustrated magazines
The letters   Tompkins, F. G.

Shay, Frank, ed. Plays for strolling mummers. N. Y. Appleton. 1926.
Dancing dolls   Goodman, K. S.
Inside stuff   Pratt, Theodore
Great moments   Moore, Raymond
The flirtation   Forrester, Frank
All on a summer's day   Clements, Colin
My tailor   Capus, Alfred
A course in piracy   Russell, Phillips
Creatures of impulse   Gilbert, W. S.

Shay, Frank, ed. Twenty contemporary one-act plays (American). Cincin-
    nati, Ohio. Stewart Kidd Co., 1922.
Mirage   Baird, G. M. P.
Napoleon's barber   Caeser, Arthur
Goat alley   Culbertson, E. H.
Sweet and twenty   Dell, Floyd
Tickless time   Cook, G. C. & Glaspell, Susan
The hero of Santa Maria   Hecht, Ben & Goodman, K. S.
All gummed up   Gribble, H. W.
Thompson's luck   Grover, H. G.
Fata Deorum   Guske, C. W.
Pearl of dawn   Hudson, Holland
Finders—keepers   Kelley, George
Solomon's song   Kemp, Harry
Matinata   Langner, Lawrence
The conflict   McCauley, Clarice V.
Two slatterns and a king   Millay, Edna St. V.
Thursday evening   Morley, Christopher
The dreamy kid   O'Neill, Eugene
Forbidden fruit   Smith, G. J.
Jezebel   Stockbridge, Dorothy
Sir David wears a crown   Walker, Stuart

Shay, Frank, ed. Twenty-five short plays. International. N. Y. Appleton,
    1925.
The accomplice   Marshall, Abigail
The festival of Bacchus   Schnitzler, Arthur
Interior   Maeterlinck, Maurice
Chintamani   Ghose, G. C.
The witness   Vrchlicky, Jaroslav
Pyentsa   Smith, J. tr.
Brothers in arms   Denison, Merrill
The thrice promised bride   Cheng-Chin Hsiung
When love dies   Ramos, J. A.
Eyes that cannot see   Gnudtzmann, Albert
Pan in Pimlico   Simpson, Helen
Pierre Patelin   Jagendorf, M. ad.
Jubilee   Heijermans, Herman
The bridegroom   Biro, Lajos
The marriage   Hyde, Douglas
A snowy night   Bracco, Roberto
The cherry blossom river   Clements, Colin ad.
The sentence of death   Issasi, Teresa F. de
In confidence   Prydz, Alvilde
On the highway   Checkhov, Anton
The street singer   Echegaray, Jose
Poverty   Alin, Hans
The disenchanted   Izzet, Melyh

Joe   Dransfield, Jane
The Shunamite   Yehoash

Sheridan, Don. Impromptu entertainments. Chicago. Dramatic Pub. Co., 1930.
Face to face with the mike
I do! I do! I do!
Get in the talkies
You may stay after school
Troubles of an editor
(Also pantomimes)

Simpson, Harold. Airy nothings. London. French, 1927.
Will it come to this?
Cook
Zoological
The anti-marriage club
Yes and no
Where there's a will there's a way
Between the devil and the deep she
The marriage morning
Shall we join the gentlemen?
Phonetics
The lady with a load of hay fever
Number thirteen

Simpson, Harold. Harold Simpson's revue sketches. London. French, 1924.
The gentle-man
Rat poison
A titled triangle
A quiet rubber
A safe bet
"Whose husband are you?"
Two flats and one key
Having it out

Simpson, Harold. The "Nine o'clock revue" book. London. French, 1924.
References
Proverbs
A square triangle
The play's the thing
A budding star
Grave v. Gay
Backing a winner
One touch of nature
(Also a dialogue)

Simpson, Harold. Nine to eleven. London. French, 1927.
The punter's friend
Cook gets her notice
Dot and go two
Noreen
John citizen's dream
Lipstick
Cyrano de Bermondsey
Comparisons are odious
The best policy

Simpson, Harold. Oh—by the way! London. French, 1926.
Cleansing the stage
The miracle
Honeymoon hall
All the world's a links
Tea for three

The ermine cloak
Blood will tell
Lucky Jim
On the journey

Simpson, Harold. Straws on the wind. London. French, 1925.
Honour among thieves
Which taken at the flood
Simultaneous sketches
The finishing touch
A reversed triangle
Kitty on the keys
What it may come to
A telephone tragedy
Virtue its own reward

Sisters of Mercy—Mount Mercy Academy. Chrysalid. Grand Rapids.
Michigan, 1927.
Fairy facts   McDonald, Lucille

Skinner, Ada M., ed. Christmas stories and plays. Chicago. Rand, McNally,
1925.
Christmas in many lands   Skinner, Ada M.
The star in the east   Skinner, Ada M.
On Christmas eve   Mackay, Constance D'A.
(Also stories)

Smith, Evelyn, ed. Form-room plays. Intermediate book. N. Y. Dutton, 1926.
The goose-girl
The town mouse and the city mouse
The shepherdess and the chimney-sweeper
Tweedledum and tweedledee
A visit to London
The fool of Dunvegan
Havelok the Dane
The enchantment of Finn
Gudrun
The siege of Ping
The kitchen knight
The marchioness
The escape from Lochleven

Smith, Evelyn, ed. Form-room plays. Senior book. N. Y. Dutton, 1921.
A tragedy rehearsed
The alchemist
(Also five longer plays and a masque)

Smith, Milton M., ed. Short plays of various types. N. Y. Merrill Co., 1924.
The dark of the dawn   Dix, Beulah M.
The maker of dreams   Down, Oliphant
A night at an inn   Dunsany, Lord
The brink of silence   Galbraith. Esther E.
The rising of the moon   Gregory, Lady
The silver lining   Mackay, Constance D'A.
The turtle dove   Oliver, Margaret S.
The romancers   Rostand, Edmund
Pyramus and Thisbe   Shakespeare, William
A comedie Royall   Sutherland, Evelyn G.
The falcon   Tennyson, Alfred, Lord
Where but in America   Wolfe, O. M.

Smith, W. P., ed. Prose and verse for speaking and reading. N. Y. Harcourt,
Brace, 1930.
The beau of Bath   Mackay, Constance D'A.
A lesson in dramatics   Sutherland, Edna G.

The trial of Thomas Doughty   Parker, L. N.
When something turned up   Halliday, Andrew

Sorenson, Grace. Juvenile comedies. Chicago. Denison, 1926.
The adopted one
The golden Easter egg
The Halloween porch party
The left-over boy
The little cousin
The Meriwether fortune
Miss Bennett's house party
The mistake
The most beautiful Valentine
The mystery of the buried box
The new teacher
The runaways
The school clown
The spooky Hallowe'en
The stupid Christmas

South High School. Minneapolis, Minn. Glints in the sand. 1924.
The flamingo feather   Lounberg, Katherine

Squires, Edith L. Ten little plays for little tots. Boston. Baker, 1930.
Come to my party
Criss cross ways
Great grandmother's attic
Handy Andy Irons
Did you ever?
Little Sun's birthday
Fern dust
Paper dolls
Pedlar man
The mice will play

Stackhouse, Perry J. Bible dramas in the pulpit. Philadelphia, Pa. The
Judson Press, 1926.
Joseph, the dreamer
Joseph, the intrepreter of dreams
Joseph's dreams come true
A queen who saved a nation from death
The babe of Bethlehem
The disciple of the night
The conversion of a dishonest tax-collector
Facts are stubborn things
The rich young ruler
The man of Kerioth
Thomas, the twin

Stallard, Mrs. Arthur. Small plays of St. Cuthbert. London. Society for
Promoting Christian Knowledge, 1930.
The miracle
The call
The feast
The hermit
The gate of heaven

Steele, W. D. The terrible woman and other one act plays. N. Y. Appleton,
1925.
Ropes
Not smart
The giant's stair
The terrible woman

Stevens, H. C. G. "To meet the king!" and three other plays. London. Deane & Sons, 1930.
"To meet the king!"
Release
The house on the hill
The captain

Stevens, T. W. The nursery-maid of heaven and other plays. N. Y. Appleton, 1926.
The nursery-maid of heaven
Three wishes
Highways cross
The triumph of Punchinello
Friend Mary
The Duquesne Christmas mystery

Stevenson, Augusta. Children's classics in dramatic form. Book I. New ed. Boston. Houghton, Mifflin, 1928.
The two holes
The little fish
The hare and the tortoise
How a prince was saved
A piece of cheese
In bad company
The sick deer
The golden bucket
The sparrows in the hat
The house of brick
The cat that waited
The honest woodman
The tracks to the den
The moon's silver cloak
The clever cock
The king's good friend
An Indian boy's pet
The fairy and the cat
The lark's nest
The beautiful song
The mill that ground hot porridge
The torn dresses
The Christmas pitcher
The return of spring
The twelve dancing Princesses

Stevenson, Augusta. Children's classics in dramatic form. Book II. New ed. Boston. Houghton, Mifflin, 1928.
The clever kid
The wolf and the horse
The wise crow
The wolf and the lamb
The selfish woman.
The blind men and the elephant
The stag and the fawn
The shepherd-boy who called wolf
The wish-bird
Lazy Kate
The proud ring-finger
The two millers
The vain jackdaw
The little jackal and the camel
The endless tale
The hole in the dike

The pot of gold
The hare and the hedgehog
Fishing on dry land
The wise men of Gotham
The two questions
Pocahontas and Captain Smith
Pocahontas saves Jamestown
Little Scarface

Stevenson, Augusta. Children's classics in dramatic form. Book III. New
  ed. Boston. Houghton, Mifflin, 1930.
The travellers and the hatchet
The old man and his grandson
The crow and the fox
The miller, his son, and their donkey
Each in his own place
What the goodman does is always right
The cat and the mouse
The girl who trod on the loaf
The ugly duckling
The red shoes
The story of Ali Cogia
The wild swans
Big Claus and little Claus
The man and the alligator
The song in the heart
The emperor's test
Christopher Columbus

Stevenson, Augusta. Children's classics in dramatic form. Book IV. New
  ed. Boston. Houghton, Mifflin, 1928.
The pen and the inkstand
The goblin and the huckster's jam
The honest critic
The white canoe
William Tell
Peter the Great's school
The sandlewood box
Bernard Palessy, enameller to his majesty
The keys to Calais
Persephone
Henry Hudson
Lafayette's toast
Daniel Boone
How they saved the fort
The spy
Don Quixote

Stevenson, Augusta. Children's classics in dramatic form. Book V. New ed.
  Boston. Houghton, Mifflin, 1928.
The black pearl
(Also ten long plays)

Stone, Mary I. Plays from Bible stories. Kansas City, Mo. Burton Pub. Co.,
  1927.
According to your faith
David anointed King
Esther
Living pictures
Naaman, the Syrian leper
Nicodemus, a ruler of Jews
Onesimus, the runaway slave

Stephen, the first Christian martyr
The angel's song

Stopes, Marie C. & Sakurai, Joji. Plays of old Japan the 'Nō.' London. The Eclipse Press, 1927.
The maiden's tomb
Kagekiyo
Tamura
The Sumida River

Strindberg, August. Easter and other plays. London. Jonathan Cape, 1929.
The ghost sonata
A dream play
(Also longer plays)

Strong, Austin. The drums of Oude and other one-act plays. N. Y. Appleton, 1926.
The drums of Oude
The little father of the wilderness

Strutton, Rebecca & others. Best primary plays. Chicago. Beckley-Cardy, 1930.

The S'prise party	Johnson, M. C.
A double surprise	Johnson, M. C.
William and the sandman	Corell, Mildred & Liccione, Irma
A Hallowe'en nutting party	Corell, Mildred & Liccione, Irma
Thanksgiving in the barnyard	Corell, Mildred & Liccione, Irma
Animated toys	Corell, Mildred & Liccione, Irma
The snow-man	Corell, Mildred & Liccione, Irma
The conscience elf	Corell, Mildred & Liccione, Irma
The March wind	Corell, Mildred & Liccione, Irma
Spare the trees!	Corell, Mildred & Liccione, Irma
Safety first	Corell, Mildred & Liccione, Irma
Dr. Bluejay's patient	Corell, Mildred & Liccione, Irma
Spirits of autumn	Strutton, Rebecca
Spirits of winter	Strutton, Rebecca
Spirits of spring	Strutton, Rebecca
Spirits of summer	Strutton, Rebecca
The week family	Strutton, Rebecca
The first rehearsal	Strutton, Rebecca
A visit to fairyland	Strutton, Rebecca
The queen of Roseland	Strutton, Rebecca
The doll shop	Strutton, Rebecca
Wild flowers	Strutton, Rebecca
A fall day	Flaurier, Noel
The workers	Flaurier, Noel
In Jack-o'-lantern row	Flaurier, Noel
The visit of the raindrops	Flaurier, Noel
The tale the fire told	Flaurier, Noel

Swinton, Phyllis McNeal. Plays for classroom and auditorium. Paterson, N. J. The Call Printing & Pub. Co., 1929.
Columbus, the courageous
Pilgrim Thankfulness
Spreading Christmas cheer
Andy sees Lincoln
Washington's life story
Old Ironsides

Taylert, Gertrude E. & Rodney, Martina B. Three splendid plays for junior high. Franklin, Ohio. Eldridge Entertainment House, 1927.
The flag makers
The song in the heart
(Also one longer play)

Taylor, Katharine & Greene, H. C. The shady hill play book. N. Y. Macmillan, 1928.
The prophets
The shepherds
Sigurd the Volsung
Deus Vult : God wills it
Roland
Our Lady's tumbler
The miracle of Theophile
Aucassin and Nicolette

Taylor, Rica B. Four Jewish sketches. London. French, 1927.
Benny proposes !
The boomerang !
Damages—two hundred !
Paul robs Peter !

Taylor, Sara V., ed. Word-hoard. Omaha, Nebraska. Douglas Printing Co., 1931.

Ramadan	Smith, Lloyd
Conn-eda	Spencer, Kathleen
(Also many poems and essays)	

Thomas, C. S., ed. The Atlantic book of junior plays. Boston. The Atlantic Monthly Press, 1924.

What men live by	Tolstoi, Leo
Nerves	Farrar, John
The violin-maker of Cremona	Coppée, François
The dyspeptic orge	Wilde, Percival
The fifteenth candle	Field, Rachel L.
A marriage proposal	Tchekoff, Anton
Jephthah's daughter	Levinger, Elma E.
A minuet	Parker, Louis N.
The play of Saint George	Crum, J. M. C.
The birthday of the Infanta	Wilde, Oscar
The Christmas guest	Mackay, Constance D'A.

Thompson, Edward & Thompson, Theodosia. Three Eastern plays. London. George Allen & Unwin, 1927.
Easter morning
The queen of ruin
The clouded mirror

Thornton, E. W., ed. More Christian Endeavor playlets. Cincinnati, Ohio. The Standard Pub. Co., 1929.

Why pray for others?	Moore, Daisy M.
How can nations practice the golden rule?	Moore, Daisy M.
Faith and what it does	Browne, Mabel M.
Peter a great evangelist	Browne, Mabel M.
Successful evangelism in mission fields	Browne, Mabel M.
Some good summer reading	Baird, Eva R.
Marks of a good citizen	Averill, Esther C.
(Also dialogues, and playlets)	

Thorpe, Clarence D. & Walter, Erich A., ed. University readings. N. Y. Harper, 1931.

The valiant	Hall, H. & Middlemass, R.
Ile	O'Neill, Eugene
A way out	Frost, Robert
(Also examples of other types of literature)	

Titheradge, Dion. Behind the curtain. London. French, 1926.
Zara the great

No jazz to-night
For England
Garrick revised
Relativity
The very devil
The permanent wave
The violin
Gooseberries in Piccadilly

Titheradge, Dion. From the prompt corner. London. French, 1925.
The cure
The difference
The eighth wonder
The green-eyed monster
Domestic bliss
Waiting
A dog's life
The stoic
Props

Titheradge, Dion. Out of the box. London. French, 1925.
The indicator
Essential to the action
The new Portia
The company will recite
A sense of humour
The unwritten law
Tea-shop tattle
Sleeping out
The "altogether"

Titheradge, Dion. Ups and downs from Revue. London. French, 1926.
But is it art?
A social inconvenience
The lion tamer!
Adventure!
Us Browns
Delaying tactics
Saved
Telephone tattle!
Tickets please!

Totheroh, Dan. One-act plays for everyone. N. Y. French, 1931.
The stolen Prince
The lost Princess
Good vintage
In the darkness
The breaking of the calm
Pearls
The great dark
While the mushrooms bubble
The widdy's mite
A tune for a tune
Mirthful marionettes

Tucker, S. M., ed. Twelve one-act plays for study and production. Boston. Ginn, 1929.

The trysting place	Tarkington, Booth
A night at an inn	Dunsany, Lord
Thursday evening	Morley, Christopher
Confessional	Wilde, Percival
The hundredth trick	Dix, Beulah M.
The Aulis difficulty	Baring, Maurice

A minuet	Parker, L. N.
Where the cross is made	O'Neill, Eugene
The workhouse ward	Gregory, Lady
Moonshine	Hopkins, Arthur
Back of the yards	Goodman, K. S.
The Grand Cham's diamond	Monkhouse, Allan

Turgenev, Ivan S. The plays of Ivan S. Turgenev, tr. from the Russian by M. S. Mandell. N. Y. Macmillan, 1924.
Carelessness
Broke
Where it is thin, there it breaks
An amicable settlement
The country woman
A conversation on the highway
An evening in Sorrento

Turner, J. H. Rescued from Revue. London. French, 1924.
When love flies in at the back door
The honours list
The fur coat
Perverted history
The house next door
Arnold
The wickedest woman
Boots and shoes
Sisters under the skin
———— Two health plays. Boston. Baker, 1930.

Speaking of exercise	Whitbeck, Ruth
Just a family affair	Faulds, Ruth E.

University of Michigan plays ed. by Kenneth Thorpe Rowe. Ann Arbor, Michigan. George Wahr, 1929.

Outside this room	Ackerman, Dorothy L.
Passion's progress	Askren, R. L.
My man	McCarthy, J. F.
The joiners	Hinkley, A. M.
Puppet	Adles, Helen E.

University of Michigan plays. Book II. Ann Arbor, Michigan, 1930.

Lassitude	Skidmore, H. D.
The day's work	Smith, Elizabeth W.
Three-a-day	Skidmore, H. D.
"Many happy returns!"	Wetzel, Robert
Wives-in-law	Smith, Elizabeth W.
They too	Askren, R. L.

University of Utah plays, ed. by B. R. Lewis. Boston. Baker, 1928.

The exchange	Thurston, Althea
And the devil laughs	Thurston, Althea
The grey switch	Keener, Sara
The boomer	Stoker, Edwin
Sara	Wooley, Olive F.
The turkey girl	Williams, Sara M.
A man of temperament	Cook, J. D.

University of Washington plays, ed. by Glenn Hughes. Second ser. Seattle, Washington. University of Washington Press, 1924.

Last day for grouse	Mack, Orrin
The gate	O'Connor, Matthew
Peg O'Nell's night	Radford, Z. F.
The black scarab	Plechner, Babette
A surprise for Helen	Crouch, C. W.
Pompoms	Strobach, Nettina L.

University of Washington plays, ed. by Glenn Hughes. Third ser.
N. Y. French, 1927.

Great minds	Kimball, W. A.
Aladdin's wife	Hughes, Babette
A soul made clean	George, Dorothy T.
The executioner	Soto, Alex de
Grotesquerie	Urquhart, Irene
Below par	Akins, Marian

Van Derveer, Lettie C. Short plays for just us fellows. Franklin, Ohio.
Eldridge Entertainment House, 1930.
You tell 'er
Sneakin's
The non-stop flight
Taxi
Boy wanted
A troublesome Christmas tree
Christmas scouts
The Christmas "good turn"
(Also a longer play)

Wade, Leila A. Plays from Browning. Boston. Cornhill Pub. Co., 1923.
My last Duchess
Porphyria's lover
(Also two longer plays)

Webber, J. P. & Webster, H. H., ed. Short plays for junior and senior
high schools. Boston. Houghton, Mifflin, 1925.

The Prince of Stamboul	Dunsany, Lord
The toy shop	Wilde, Percival
The stolen prince	Totheroh, Dan
The end of the rainbow	Webber, J. P.
The Princess on the road	Greene, Kathleen C.
"Good-night Babette!"	Dobson, Austin
To dust returning	Branch, Anna H.
The traveling man	Gregory, Lady
The shutting o' the door	Dickson, W. G.
The Wraggle-taggle gypsies	The Perse School
Pyramus and Thisbe	Shakespeare, William
Miss Burney at court	Frank, Maude M.
John Silver off duty	Stevenson, R. L.
The little boy out of the wood	Greene, Kathleen C.
The legend of Saint Dorothy	King, Georgana G.
In the good green wood	Cooke, Marjorie B.
The lion's whelp	Leighton, G. R.
Benjamin Franklin, journeyman	Mackay, Constance D'A.
The Boston Tea Party	Mackay, Constance D'A.
The little king	Bynner, Witner

Webber, J. P. & Webster, H. H., ed. Typical plays for young people.
Boston. Houghton, Mifflin, 1929.

The rehearsal	Baring, Maurice
A mistake at the manor	Frank, Maude M.
The prince of court painters	Mackay, Constance D'A.
Frances and Francis	Webber, J. P.
Augustus in search of a father	Chapin, Harold
Pharoah's daughter	Kotzebue, August von
The thrice promised bride	Houing, Cheng-Chin
The copper pot	Healey, Frances

White, Kate. Tested project plays for the grade school. Boston. Baker, 1929.
Dr. Arithmetic establishes a hospital
The quarrel

Mrs. Newlywed attends school
Henri makes a sale
A change of heart
The escape of the germs
Frank goes on a diet
Through the open book
Reading wins his case
Hiring a new teacher
The City Council wakes up
The first Thanksgiving
An election day tea
Better speech wins
The conspiracy
Wanted: an office boy
Around the world
The professor makes a mistake
On the way to school
The day before the test

Whiting, Margaret A., ed. Plays and pageants for children. Vol. I. Boston. Educational Pub. Co., 1925.
Mother Goose and her friends
The wise turkey
Fire spirits
Three foolish bears
A primary book pageant
Peter Pan
Christmas in many lands
Old man rabbit's Thanksgiving
Christmas eve in Santa's workshop
A Christmas play
The flower of cheer
Being like Washington
The fairy cakes
Spring's awakening
Enchanted summer
The gifts of autumn
Harvest blessings
Hansel and Gretel
Among the stars
The princess and the pea
The service the fairies did
(Also longer plays and pageants)

Whitney, Mary E., ed. Bible plays and how to produce them. N. Y. Revell Co., 1927.
Abraham and Isaac
The crowning of Saul
David and Goliath
The crowning of Solomon
Naaman the leper
Esther
Daniel in the lion's den
Ruth
The parable of the tares
The parable of the wicked servant
The parable of the great supper
The parable of the talents
The parable of the good Samaritan
The parable of the rich fool
The parable of the prodigal son

The imprisonment of Peter and John
The martyrdom of Stephen
The conversion of Saul
Paul and Silas at Philippi
The shipwreck of Paul

Whitney, Mary E. Some little plays and how to act them. Chicago. Beckley-
Cardy, 1927.
The boy and the echo
The hill
The boy and the nuts
The dog and the manger
The ant and the grasshopper
The dove and the ant
The hare and the tortoise
The lion and the fox
The wind and the sun
Hans the shepherd boy
Training for the presidency
Commander-in-chief
A Memorial day parade
The boy who hated trees
Should we be more thankful than the Puritans?
A Christmas lesson
A lesson in geography

Wilde, Percival. The inn of discontent and other fantastic plays. Boston.
Little, Brown, 1924.
The inn of discontent
Lady of dreams
The lucky-piece
Ashes of romance
Nocturne

Wilde, Percival. A question of morality and other plays. Boston. Little,
Brown, 1922.
A question of morality
Confessional
The villain in the piece
According to Darwin
The beautiful story

Wilde, Percival. Ten plays for Little Theatres. Boston. Little, Brown, 1931.
Gadgets
Standish pride
The thing
The lost elevator
Lot's wife
What never dies
A short cut
Vignette
Out of the mouths of . .
(Also a longer play)

Wilde, Percival. Three-minute plays. N. Y. Greenberg, 1927.
Robert Burns
Ever upwards!
The meticulous customer
Yashmak!
The phial
The first client
'Twas the night before
The stork

The national anthem
Duetto
Movieless movies
Hush money
Love is blind
Out of the mouths of
The past pluperfect
Costume de rigeur
Con amore
The unacceptable apology
The facts
Vignette

Wilder, Thornton. The angel that troubled the waters and other plays. N. Y. Coward-McCann, 1928.
Nascuntur Poetae
Proserpina and the devil
Fanny Otcott
Brother fire
The penny that beauty spent
The angel on the ship
The message and Jehanne
Childe Ronald to the dark tower came
Centaurs
Leviathan
And the sea shall give up its dead
Now the servant's name was Malchus
Mozart and the gray steward
Hast thou considered my servant Job?
The flight into Egypt
The angel that troubled the waters

Wilder, Thornton. The long Christmas dinner and other plays in one act. N. Y. Coward-McCann, 1931.
The long Christmas dinner
Queens of France
Pullman car Hiawatha
Love, and how to cure it
Such things only happen in books
The happy journey to Trenton and Camden

Williams, E. H. Three fairy plays. London. French, 1925.
The Emperor's new clothes
Beauty and the beast
The wooden bowl

Willis, Richard. Six playlets. N. Y. Richard Willis, 1928.
The old grouch
The show must go on
The confession
The little old gent
Cowards
Too much crime

Woods, Marjorie. Why we celebrate, holiday plays for young people. N. Y. French, 1927.
A New Year's gift
The birthday ball
The Druid oak
The Christmas angel

Wordsworth, Elizabeth. Poems and plays. London. Oxford University Press, 1930.

The apple of discord
(Also many poems and a longer play)

Yale one-act plays. N. Y. French, 1930.

The mistress	Gnesin, Maurice
Hans Bulow's last puppet	Ruthenburg, Grace D.
Immersion	Humphrey, Maude
Yella	McGuire, Harry
Minnie Field	Conkle, E. P.
"L"	Atlas, L. L.

Yale Playcraftsmen plays. Boston. Baker, 1924.

The end of the rope	Thanhouser, L. F.
Trash	Thanhouser, L. F.
The man without a head	Thanhouser, L. F.
The biddie sweeps out	Thanhouser, L. F.

Yates, Elizabeth H. Small plays for small casts. Philadelphia. Penn Pub.
Co., 1926.
The blind
Coral beads
The laughing child
"Spot cash"
A rich young lady
Millennium morning
The slave

Yeats, W. B. Later poems. N. Y. Macmillan, 1924.
The sad shepherd
Phases of the moon
(Also many poems)

Yeats, W. B. Plays and controversies. N. Y. Macmillan, 1924.
Land of heart's desire
At the Hawk's well
The only jealousy of Emer
Dreaming of the bones
Calvary

Yeats, W. B. Plays in prose and verse. N. Y. Macmillan, 1924.
Cathleen ni Houlihan
The pot of broth
The hour-glass
The king's threshold
On Baile's strand
The shadowy waters
Deirdre
The green helmet
The player queen

Young, Stark. Sweet times and the Blue policeman. N. Y. Holt, 1925.
The blue policeman
Sweet times
All eyes
Wild manners
The naughty duck
The blessed bird
The laughing doors
The magic sea
The glove of gold
The shepherd's dream
The king with the iron heart
The prince of the moon
The flower tree